The Anthropology of the State

Blackwell Readers in Anthropology

As anthropology moves beyond the limits of so-called area studies, there is an increasing need for texts that do the work of synthesizing the literature while challenging more traditional or subdisciplinary approaches to anthropology. This is the object of this exciting new series, *Blackwell Readers in Anthropology*.

Each volume in the series offers seminal readings on a chosen theme and provides the finest, most thought-provoking recent works in the given thematic area. Many of these volumes bring together for the first time a body of literature on a certain topic. The series thus both presents definitive collections and investigates the very ways in which anthropological inquiry has evolved and is evolving.

The Anthropology of the State

A Reader

Edited by

Aradhana Sharma and Akhil Gupta

Blackwell Publishing

BLACKWELL PUBLISHING
350 Main Street, Malden, MA 02148-5020, USA
9600 Garsington Road, Oxford OX4 2DQ, UK
550 Swanston Street, Carlton, Victoria 3053, Australia

First published 2006 by Blackwell Publishing Ltd

1   2006

Library of Congress Cataloging-in-Publication Data

The anthropology of the state: a reader/edited by Aradhana Sharma and Akhil Gupta.
  p. cm. – (Blackwell readers in anthropology; 9)
Includes bibliographical references and index.
ISBN-13: 978-1-4051-1467-7 (hardcover : alk. paper)
ISBN-10: 1-4051-1467-3 (hardcover : alk. paper)
ISBN-13: 978-1-4051-1468-4 (pbk.: alk. paper)
ISBN-10: 1-4051-1468-1 (pbk.: alk. paper) 1. Political anthropology. 2. State, The. 3. National state. 4. Sovereignty. 5. World politics. I. Sharma, Aradhana. II. Gupta, Akhil, 1959– III. Series.

GN492.A54 2006
306.2—dc22

                                                             2005013799

A catalogue record for this title is available from the British Library.

Set in 10/12 Sabon
by SPI Publisher Services, Pondicherry, India

The publisher's policy is to use permanent paper from mills that operate a sustainable forestry policy, and which has been manufactured from pulp processed using acid-free and elementary chlorine-free practices. Furthermore, the publisher ensures that the text paper and cover board used have met acceptable environmental accreditation standards.

For further information on
Blackwell Publishing, visit our website:
www.blackwellpublishing.com

Dedication by Aradhana Sharma
For Vijay Dhawan

Dedication by Akhil Gupta
For two generations whose courage and can-do spirit is
inspiring and infectious
My father, Jwala P. Gupta and my daughter,
Deeya Shivani Gupta

Contents

Acknowledgments

This book is a result of the collaborative work of several individuals. Donald Moore and K. Sivaramakrishnan gave us helpful suggestions as we conceptualized this book. Anonymous reviewers guided the project through their detailed feedback on the introduction and the proposed contents. Lalaie Ameeriar and Aaron David Shaw provided Akhil Gupta with crucial research assistance. Purnima Mankekar read our introduction and contributed greatly to its substance and style. Akhil Gupta would also like to thank the South Asia Center at the University of Hawaii at Manoa for inviting him to present an earlier version of the introduction there. We are grateful to colleagues at Hawaii for their valuable comments. Jane Huber and Emily Martin at Blackwell are an inspiring editorial team. Not only did they make this project possible, but they provided invaluable input and support for the project right through to its final stages. We would not have been able to write this book without the support, encouragement, and critical engagement of all these colleagues, and we are grateful to each one of them. The mistakes are, of course, solely ours.

The editor and publisher gratefully acknowledge the permission granted to reproduce the copyright material in this book:

1   Max Weber, "Bureaucracy," pp. 956–1005 from G. Roth and C. Wittich, *Economy and Society: An Outline of Interpretive Sociology*, trans. E. Fischoff, H. Gerth, A. M. Henderson, F. Kolegar, C. Wright Mills, T. Parsons, M. Rheinstein, G. Roth, E. Shils, and C. Wittich. New York: Bedminster Press, 1968.

2   Antonio Gramsci, "State and Civil Society," pp. 228–70 from *Selections from the Prison Notebooks of Antonio Gramsci*, ed. and trans. Q. Hoare and G. Nowell Smith. New York and London: International Publishers and Lawrence & Wishart, 1971.

3   Louis Althusser, "Ideology and Ideological State Apparatuses (Notes towards an Investigation)," pp. 127–86 from *Lenin and Philosophy and Other Essays*, trans. B. Brewster. New York and London: Monthly Review Press, 1971. Copyright © 1971 by Monthly Review Press. Reprinted by permission of Monthly Review Foundation.

4   Philip Abrams, "Notes on the Difficulty of Studying the State," pp. 58–89 from *Journal of Historical Sociology*, 1(1), March 1988 (1977). Reprinted by permission of Blackwell Publishing.

5   Michel Foucault, "Governmentality," pp. 87–104 from G. Burchell, C. Gordon, and P. Miller (eds.), *The Foucault Effect: Studies in Governmentality.* Hemel Hempstead and Chicago: Harvester Wheatsheaf and University of Chicago Press, 1991. Reprinted by permission of The University of Chicago Press.

6   Nikolas Rose, "Governing 'Advanced' Liberal Democracies," pp. 37–64 from A. Barry, T. Osborne, and N. Rose (eds.), *Foucault and Political Reason: Liberalism, Neo-Liberalism and Rationalities of Government.* Chicago and London: University of Chicago Press and UCL Press, 1996. Reprinted by permission of The University of Chicago Press.

7   Timothy Mitchell, "Society, Economy, and the State Effect," pp. 76–97 from G. Steinmetz (ed.), *State/Culture: State-Formation after the Cultural Turn.* Ithaca, NY and London: Cornell University Press, 1999. Used by permission of the publisher.

8   Wendy Brown, "Finding the Man in the State," pp. 166–96 from Wendy Brown, *States of Injury: Power and Freedom in Late Modernity.* Princeton, NJ: Princeton University Press, 1995. © 1995 Princeton University Press. Reprinted by permission of Princeton University Press.

9   Akhil Gupta, "Blurred Boundaries: The Discourse of Corruption, the Culture of Politics, and the Imagined State," pp. 375–402 from *American Ethnologist*, 22(2), 1995. © 1995 American Anthropological Association. All rights reserved. Used by permission.

10 James C. Scott, "Cities, People, and Language," pp. 53–83, 369–76 from James C. Scott, *Seeing Like a State: How Certain Schemes to Improve the Human Condition Have Failed.* New Haven, CT and London: Yale University Press, 1998. Reprinted by permission of the publisher, Yale University Press.

11 James Ferguson, "The Anti-Politics Machine," pp. 251–77, 302–13 from *The Anti-Politics Machine: "Development," Depoliticization, and Bureaucratic Power in Lesotho.* Minneapolis: University of Minnesota Press, 1994.

12 Catherine Lutz, "Making War at Home in the United States: Militarization and the Current Crisis," pp. 723–35 from *American Anthropologist*, 104(3), 2002. © 2002, American Anthropologist Association. All rights reserved. Used by permission.

13 Susan Bibler Coutin, "Cultural Logics of Belonging and Movement: Transnationalism, Naturalization, and US Immigration Politics," pp. 508–26 from *American Ethnologist*, 30(4), 2003. © 2003, American Anthropological Association. All rights reserved. Used by permission.

14 Anannya Bhattacharjee, "The Public/Private Mirage: Mapping Homes and Undomesticating Violence Work in the South Asian Immigrant Community," pp. 308–29, 396–8 from M. J. Alexander and C. T. Mohanty, *Feminist Genealogies, Colonial Legacies, Democratic Futures.* New York and London: Routledge, 1997.

15 Stuart Hall, "Popular Culture and the State," pp. 22–49 from T. Bennett, C. Mercer, and J. Woollacott (eds.), *Popular Culture and Social Relations.* Milton Keynes and Philadelphia: Open University Press, 1986.

16 Achille Mbembe, "The Banality of Power and the Aesthetics of Vulgarity in the Postcolony," trans. J. Roitman, pp. 1–30 from *Public Culture*, 4(2), Spring 1992. All rights reserved. Used by permission of the publisher.

Every effort has been made to trace copyright holders and to obtain their permission for the use of copyright material. The publisher apologizes for any errors or omissions in the above list and would be grateful if notified of any corrections that should be incorporated in future reprints or editions of this book.

Organization of the Book

This reader introduces, in a focused and historical manner, both classic theoretical works and new ethnographic studies of the state in diverse geographical settings. Our approach is one of doing a "history of the present," that is, of understanding contemporary states by tracing linkages backwards to the birth of modern, or capitalist, or colonial eras. Although not all the contributions to this volume are by anthropologists, they have been chosen to highlight anthropological approaches to the institutions, spaces, ideas, and practices that comprise the domain we call "the state."

The reader consists of two parts: (1) theoretical genealogies; and (2) ethnographic mappings. Part I, "Theoretical Genealogies," revisits "classic" as well as more contemporary theorizations of "the state." The texts included in the second part of the book – "Ethnographic Mappings" – engage with and build on the ideas and frameworks laid out in the first part, and stress the interplay between theory, ethnography, and critique.

Part II of the reader is subdivided into four sections: "Bureaucracy and Governmentality"; "Planning and Development"; "Violence, Law, and Citizenship"; and "Popular Culture". The selections in each section track the representational strategies and work practices of specific state institutions, such as development institutions, the military, and welfare bureaucracies. These articles examine the operation and proliferation of different mechanisms of rule. They highlight the effects of various technologies of power in multiple social and institutional arenas, and draw attention to the often-contested nature of these processes. While the selections included in this reader do not pretend to exhaustively cover the field of the "anthropology of the state," they do construct a critical genealogy of this subject. Our goal is to map key past and contemporary moments as well as future directions for the anthropological study of the state. These texts also engage, from different theoretical standpoints, two of the most important questions relating to the study of the state – questions of culture and transnationalism.

Introduction: Rethinking Theories of the State in an Age of Globalization

Introduction

It is close to midnight on a warm and muggy monsoon evening in the middle of August 2003. Gupta navigates the potholed streets leading from South Delhi to Gurgaon, crossing a border checkpoint along the way. Once in Gurgaon, Gupta heads off from the main street and pulls up in front of a building that looks like a large house. This is the hottest new development in the landscape of post-reform urban India: a call center. The owner, just barely old enough to be out of high school, proudly gives Gupta a tour of the building.

The ground floor consists of executive offices and other facilities. The next level is "the floor," the space where hundreds of college-age men and women are sitting on low booths arranged in an open-plan office. The space is brightly lit, and it is fairly throbbing with energy. One can feel the adrenalin pumping in this large room; there is a "buzz" that one associates with a newsroom on deadline or a project team whose product is due the following morning. The owner explains that they deliberately do not mute sounds because the high energy level prevents the operators from feeling drowsy through their shifts, which last all or most of the night.

Gupta is encouraged by the floor manager to listen in to one of the conversations. A young man is persuading a customer to refinance his mortgage in an accent that is a mix of Midwestern American and Haryanvi Hindi. The script that he is supposed to use flashes across the screen in front of him but he does not need to look at it. It is clear that he has already committed the script to memory. The floor manager, a woman in her early thirties, a veteran of the industry, goes around checking how many calls each of the operators have managed in the last few minutes. She tells a new employee that she expects her to complete a certain number of calls before taking a break.

As a symbol of economic globalization, call centers have come to occupy a central place in debates on the "outsourcing" of jobs from the North. Corporations, and increasingly state bureaucracies in the North, are farming out customer service and processing-related jobs to the South as part of their cost-cutting measures. Countries like India, with a significant English-speaking population and comparatively low labor costs, are prime destinations for job outsourcing. It is not only national governments in the South that are soliciting these contracts as part of their liberalization efforts. City and state governments are also independently seeking out outsourced businesses, like call centers, as an important entrepreneurial-based development strategy.

Call centers differ from each other in terms of size, function, ownership, and client profile. There are numerous small, family-owned enterprises like the one Gupta visited; however, the ones that get the most media attention are the huge call centers operated by enterprises like GE Capital, which employed more than 2000 people in Gurgaon in 2002 (Online Asia Times, August 7, 2002; http:/ www.atimes.com/atimes/South_Asia/DH07Df01.html). Apart from being family owned, the call center Gupta visited was an "independent" one that served multiple clients rather than what is called a "captive" center operated by the Indian subsidiary of a large transnational corporation. Not all independents are family owned or small enterprises; many are large corporations in their own right or subsidiaries of giant software companies like Wipro. The "captive" centers are set up to provide services to the employees and customers of only one corporation. From "captive" centers, it is a short step to the criticism that the entire industry represents a new form of indenture in the global division of labor, the "cyber-coolie" (Bidwai 2003: 32).[1]

Centers are distinguished by the type of work that they do, which is classified according to its position in the value chain. The lowest-level work is that of data entry, telemarketing, and transcription. The floor manager of the small call center that Gupta visited was aware that there was not much of a future in cold-calling, which is what they were doing for most of their clients. She emphasized the importance of moving up the value chain to doing more sophisticated tasks, such as customer service and support. Not only were the margins higher in such tasks, but also cold-calling was getting increasingly hazardous because the center was responsible for any fines due to the "DNC." A company that solicits business from a person registered on the "Do Not Call" list can be fined up to $11,000 for a single mistake, enough to wipe out the profits from an entire contract.

Higher up the value chain are jobs that include credit-card processing, and customer interaction, such as responding to calls made to corporate help numbers, low-end IT support such as that of resetting passwords for employees of large corporations, helping customers with problems on their mortgage payments, and so on. Finally, the top level of the value chain consists of highly specialized work, like software development and testing done by IT professionals, image interpretation conducted by radiologists, corporate earnings and tax-related work done by accountants, and legal research conducted by lawyers for corporate offices in the USA and the UK.

Although not all jobs that are outsourced go from the North to the South, the geographical distribution of outsourced jobs is uneven and hierarchical in that (a) some regions in the North serve primarily, though not exclusively, as "senders" of outsourced jobs and others in the South as primarily "receivers" of this work, and (b) the kind of work sent to "receiving" regions depends on the skill and technology levels that the work requires, the prevailing political climate, the economic policy context, and so on.[2] While transnational corporations are key players in the circuit of outsourcing, national and regional states (both in those regions where outsourced jobs originate and those in which these jobs end up) are also important actors.

Let us first turn to those states that serve primarily as destinations of outsourced jobs, and to India in particular. What do outsourcing and call centers have to do with the Indian state, especially the post-liberalization state? The usual answer to this question is that the state provides the larger macroeconomic framework and the critical infrastructure for outsourcing to be successful. The costs of this infrastructure are social but corporations who use the infrastructure at highly subsidized rates privately appropriate its benefits. However, most cheerleaders of the technology revolution in India summarily dismiss this argument. Typical of such positions is the one articulated by Thomas Friedman: "In some ways, the whole tech sector in Bangalore could be called India's 'Golden Enclave' – disconnected from the country's bad governance, as companies create their own walled enclaves, with their own electricity, bus service, telecommunications and security, and disconnected from the countryside, where many Indians still live in abject poverty" (2004: B7). Here we have a familiar narrative of the bracing impact of a progressive global capitalism succeeding *despite* states that fail to deliver basic infrastructure. Thus, Friedman finds that Bangalore's airport is like "a seedy bus station with airplanes" (2004). Anyone who has navigated the potholes outside the gleaming call-center buildings, giant air-conditioned malls, and world-class luxury apartment buildings in Gurgaon would have to agree with this narrative of the "relative autonomy" of capitalist enclaves from the provisioning of infrastructure by the local state.

But there are other benefits that the Indian state provides that enable outsourcing to succeed, most notably that the export of IT services is tax-exempt, and that the technology that such centers require can be imported without paying duty. The most important service, however, is the training given to graduates of state institutions of higher education that creates a large pool of technically adept English-speaking workers available for hire. Although many news stories about the growth of call centers mention this pool of labor, almost none of the reports, especially in the foreign press, comment on the fact that this is the remarkable result of a conscious Nehruvian import-substituting, socialist, autarchic model of development. Both the Bharatiya Janata Party-led Indian government and the press had launched broad critiques of the Nehruvian model, but in embracing the "technical excellence" of India's graduates, failed to consider that the current situation is the direct result of at least two generations of state-sponsored investment in scientific and technical education. These workers are not, for the most part, graduates of private universities; their university educations are obtained almost free of change in public institutions, probably the cheapest education of such a high quality to be found anywhere in the world. The success of the call centers hinges on the availability of this labor force, which can supply labor power of superior quality at a tenth of the price that would be paid in the USA or the UK. Of course, the 300,000 (DiCarlo 2003) college graduates hired by call centers in the last two years benefit the Indian state by helping to increase the tax base and boosting domestic spending and, thus, tax collection. More importantly, these companies absorb the most *politically* problematic sector of the workforce, the educated unemployed.

The flight of jobs from the North to the South also implicates Northern states, in which the bulk of outsourced work originates, in multiple ways. While outsourcing of customer-service and data-processing jobs has been a key corporate strategy for some time, it is increasingly also being deployed by state bureaucracies who are under pressure to downsize government and decrease costs. Thus, we find airline ticket stubs being processed in Barbados (Freeman 2002), while New York City's parking tickets are processed in Ghana (Worth 2002). Some US states, such as Wisconsin and New Jersey, have farmed out their welfare-processing functions and other governmental contracts to businesses in the global South.

Both corporate and government outsourcing have come under increasingly severe scrutiny and criticism in the North. In the USA, for example, outsourcing emerged as a key issue in the 2004 presidential elections. One of the most important fears fueling the backlash against outsourcing is that high-end white-collar workers in the North are now in danger of being displaced by cheaper labor in the South (and especially in the Indian subcontinent). Some of those who cheered the "efficiency" of global competition in hastening the decline of the heavily unionized smokestack industries in the North have now become economic nationalists, as they find themselves in danger of being displaced by the very same capitalist forces. The emergent transnational economic order is not only reshaping the global labor map, but also transforming the relationship between citizenship, national identity, and the state.

Outsourcing is seen as both a sign of state "openness," modernity, and good macroeconomic liberalization by the defenders of transnational capitalism, *and* as a charged symbol of decreasing state sovereignty and control by economic nationalists. Concerns about national sovereignty are evident in calls made by various interest groups to the US government to put a stop to the outsourcing of corporate-sector jobs. They are also evidenced by the strong backlash against the contracting of work by government departments to firms that lie outside the territorial boundaries of the US nation-state. For instance, state legislator Shirley Turner of New Jersey introduced a bill in the state senate banning the outsourcing of government contracts to non-nationals. The bill was passed unanimously.[3] Similarly, in Wisconsin state senator Judy Robson has argued against state contracts to call centers in India. When unemployed residents of Wisconsin call with questions about their Quest card (which replaced food stamps), they talk to someone in India, not Wisconsin. In the context of increased unemployment within the state, Senator Robson contends that it is a "cruel irony that unemployed cardholders find themselves speaking with a person using a fake American name and a fake American accent who is employed through the state of Wisconsin contract. Many of my unemployed constituents would jump at the chance to have a customer service job with a company that has a state contract" (2004: 1). Ms. Robson has drafted a bill called the "American Jobs Act" that seeks to ensure that all state services and contracts must be performed within the United States (Robson 2004).[4]

The striking irony in these discussions about outsourcing is that even as the US national government demands that other nation-states open up their borders to unrestricted trade, capital, and technology and media flows, state governments within the USA are arguing for shutting down their borders to prevent the outflow of jobs. What is at stake in these debates is not simply a concern for rising unemployment within the North. Questions of state sovereignty, the territoriality of the state, and who can "legitimately" do government work loom equally large. The idea is that state jobs are deserved by, and reserved for, "real" citizens (who do not simulate American-ness through "fake" accents or names). In this way, the rhetoric of legislation against the flight of jobs abroad seamlessly weaves together national belonging, citizenship, culture, race, state work, and state control. It articulates a fear of the loss of sovereignty to globalization, which in turn presumes a certain understanding of the state and of the state's role in governing a territory and the resources and population within that territory.

In this Introduction, we attempt to make anthropological sense of "the state" and the nature of rule in a (neo)liberalizing, transnational world. The organization is as follows. We begin by introducing the problematic. Next we consider what might be involved in an anthropological approach to studying the state by focusing on two aspects for analytical clarity: (a) everyday practices, and (b) representations of the state. We argue that, when combined, these two approaches yield something disciplinarily distinctive in the study of the state. Finally, we tackle the problem of theorizing the state in a transnational frame (see also Trouillot 2003) reflecting, in particular, on its relation to global governmentality.

The Problematic

The title of this Introduction could be parsed such that we first deal with "Rethinking Theories of the State" and then with "Rethinking Theories of the State in an Age of Globalization." Our argument here is that new insights into the state could be obtained by thinking about states as cultural artifacts while simultaneously framing them within transnational dynamics. This complex theoretical task requires (1) examining how cultural and representational frames articulate with structural and functional approaches to studying states, and what they reveal about the deeply cultural nature of states (see Steinmetz 1999); and (2) shifting the focus from a national to a transnational frame, thus highlighting the translocality of the state (Gupta 1995, Chapter 9 in this volume). How can an anthropological approach further our understandings of the state as a multilayered, contradictory, translocal ensemble of institutions, practices, and people in a globalized context? We are especially concerned about the frequent reductionism encountered in public discourse, and sometimes even in scholarly work, in which the equation "more globalization = less nation-state sovereignty = weaker states" appears with some regularity.

Transnational phenomena such as outsourcing make us reconsider how the reorganization of the forces of global capitalism or the regime of accumulation (from Fordism to post-Fordism) has impacted and altered the role of the *national* state (Jessop 1999; Trouillot 2003). In many popular, official, and expert discourses, the national state is seen as compromised by globalization because globalization challenges the two key concepts that lie at the heart of the idea of a *national* state – territoriality and sovereignty. The territorial inviolability of nation-states is being contested by border-transgressing circulations of people, images, money, and goods, and the demands of separatist ethnic movements.[5] Such phenomena are rendering national borders porous and states' control over territories tenuous. State sovereignty is also increasingly challenged by the rise of quasi-"state-like" institutions, like the World Trade Organization (WTO), that operate and regulate the conduct of states, economies, and people at a supranational level. Whether seen from the standpoint of those who profess alarm over the weakening of states, or from the perspective of those neoliberal gurus who advocate the retreat of states in the name of small and more efficient government, the current regime of transnational governance has emerged as a key theoretical, policy, and activist concern. Resistance to different aspects of globalization is itself organized in ways that challenge and go beyond nation-states. Margaret Keck and Kathryn Sikkink (1998) use the term "transnational networks" to describe loose transborder affiliations of activist groups organized around specific "local" issues like the environment and violence against women (which nevertheless have translocal appeal and organizational potential). These networks transcend the boundaries of nation-states even though they are composed of groups that are located within them. They work by bringing transnational pressure to bear upon individual nation-states and on international institutions such as the WTO.

The nature and role of the state and of sovereignty in a globalized world are hotly debated issues. Whether they argue for a retreat of the state (Ohmae 1990, 1995; Strange 1996), an altered role of the state (Higgott et al. 2000) and of state regulation of the economy (Stiglitz 2002), or market-led regulation and democratization that deprivilege the state (Friedman 1999), scholars who study the globalization–state–economy nexus tend to assume a relatively cohesive *national* state (Jessop 1999) and an inevitable analytical link between state and nation. Thus one key issue becomes the extent to which the *national* state can and should regulate an increasingly globally articulated post-Fordist economy. As we have seen above, this is the critical area of debate in the controversy on outsourcing. Critics of globalization also frequently use the nation as the privileged space within which to pitch their claims. For example, organizations and politicians in the USA that have taken an ultra-nationalist stance against the export of jobs across US borders contend that transnational processes threaten both state sovereignty and the hegemony of the nation-state. The state here is inevitably conceived as a national state and a national economy is seen as the natural object of intervention by this state (Jessop 1999; Mitchell 1999; Steinmetz 1999; Trouillot 2003). While there is some debate about the need for state intervention and about the ability of states to regulate national economies, it is taken for granted that state sovereignty *should* be territorially based.

Transnational processes have clearly reshaped the presumed association between nation-states, sovereignty, and territoriality. Saskia Sassen uses the term "unbundling of sovereignty" to indicate the altered relationship between the territory of a nation-state and sovereignty in a situation where political power and regulatory mechanisms are being reorganized at a transnational level (1998: 92; see also Sassen 1996). Sovereignty, in other words, can no longer be seen as the sole purview or "right" of the modern state but is, instead, partially disentangled from the nation-state and mapped onto supranational and nongovernmental organizations. As Sassen contends, however, just because some of the regulatory mechanisms that used to be managed by states are now shifting to non-state, supranational actors, it would be wrong to assume that national laws and conventional forms of regulation based in nation-states are now irrelevant. Transnational economic processes and political reorganization may have altered the nature of and the presumed link between sovereignty and territoriality; however, that does not necessarily imply that the nation-state, as a conceptual framework and a material reality, is passé. The hyphen that connects the two parts of this composite entity, as scholars like Ruggie (1993), Appadurai (1990; 1993a), and Gupta (1998)[6] contend, is simultaneously contested and reified by the processes of globalization.

How has the relationship between the state and the nation been theorized in the existing literature? First, the concept of the nation-state has so thoroughly conjoined the state with the nation that it is almost impossible to think of one without the other (see also Aretxaga 2003; Trouillot 2003). In fact, the terms "the state," "the nation," and "the nation-state" are often used interchangeably in scholarly discourse. Theories of the state always have implicit in them theories of nationalism; similarly, theories of nationalism assume some theory of the state in that nationalism is often seen as a state project (Anderson 1983; Borneman 1993, 1998; Corrigan and Sayer 1985; Steinmetz 1999). Second, while theories of nationalism wrestle with questions of cultural difference, theories of the state are largely silent on these questions. States are seen as being devoid of culture. Why is that the case? Does the recognition that nationalism is both an *affect* and *affective* make it easier to think of its cultural moorings, unlike the state, which is primarily conceptualized in institutional terms (Stoler 2004)? Third, theories of the state assume the frame of the nation-state and a world of nation-states. Here the reification of the state is easy to see – "it" is the legitimate representative of the nation and acts on behalf of the nation. But the shifts in the global order from "inter-nationalism," which depended on nation-states, to "trans-nationalism," which has a more troubled relationship with bounded and natural(ized) nation-states, and the emergence of "state-like" regimes of supranational regulation (consisting of bodies such as the WTO and the European Union) are forcing us to rethink *national* states (Jessop 1999).[7] What would the state look like in a trans-national frame where nation-states are not the only legitimate actors?

What Can Anthropology Contribute to the Study of the State?

The study of the state has particularly, though not exclusively, interested political scientists.[8] Timothy Mitchell (1991b; 1999, Chapter 7 in this volume) identifies two main approaches that postwar American political science has taken in this regard: the systems approach and the statist approach. Systems theorists (for instance see Easton 1953, 1957; Almond et al. 1955; Almond and Coleman 1960) highlighted the difficulties in delineating clear boundaries of "the state" and argued for abandoning the study of states in favor of the broader idea of a "political system."[9] The changed political context of the 1960s revived an interest in the state and many theorists argued for bringing the state back into scholarly focus (Evans et al. 1985; see also Krasner 1978; Skocpol 1979). However, in their attempt to counter Marxist functionalism that saw the state as the instrument of capitalist class interests, these state-centered theorists, as Mitchell (1999) and Steinmetz (1999) contend, resurrected "the state" as a discrete social fact. In state-centric theories, "the state" is viewed as a clearly bounded institution that is distinct from society, and is often portrayed as a unitary and autonomous actor that possesses the supreme authority to regulate populations within its territory. Scholars like Abrams (1988, Chapter 4 in this volume), Corrigan and Sayer (1985), Jessop (1982, 1990), Joseph and Nugent (1994), Mitchell (1991b, 1999), Radcliffe-Brown (1940), and Trouillot (2003) have critically interrogated the assumption that "the state" is an *a priori* conceptual or empirical object. Following these scholars we do not take the state as a given – a distinct, fixed and unitary entity that defines the terrain in which other institutions function. Rather, we seek to bring together the ideological and material aspects of state construction, and understand how "the state" comes into being, how "it" is differentiated from other institutional forms, and what effects this construction has on the operation and diffusion of power throughout society.

Mitchell (1991b; 1999, Chapter 7 in this volume) has argued that the appearance of the state as a discrete and relatively autonomous social institution is itself a reification that is constituted through everyday social practices. How the line separating the state from civil society comes to be drawn, he claims, becomes an exercise in power and social control.[10] Indeed, the discipline of political science, along with other social sciences, in analyzing and describing the phenomenon of the state, has participated in discursively constructing "the state" as a distinct entity with particular functions (Abrams 1988, Chapter 4 in this volume). Disciplinary practices help shape both everyday understandings of what "the state" is and what "it" does as well as influence the practices of state agents. Nikolas Rose (1996, Chapter 6 in this volume; 1999) suggests that social science disciplines and "experts" themselves constitute a crucial part of the apparatus of rule – they become instruments through which strategies for governing populations and communities, and fashioning proper selves, are deployed and legitimized. Further, these theoretical conceptualizations shape activist practices vis-à-vis the state. Anannya Bhattacharjee (1997, Chapter 14 in this volume) shows how feminist conceptions of the public and private realms have impacted feminist praxis in relation to the state in problematic ways. She uses the issues of domestic labor and domestic violence in immigrant South Asian communities in the USA to illustrate the potential pitfalls of hegemonic Western feminist notions of public and private spheres and their practices against the state (see also Brown 1995, Chapter 8 in this volume; MacKinnon 1989).

Once we see that the boundary between the state and civil society is itself an effect of power, then we can begin to conceptualize "the state" *within* (and not automatically distinct from) other institutional forms through which social relations are lived, such as the family, civil society, and the economy. Such an analysis of state formation does not simply assume that the state stands at the apex of society and is the central locus of power. Instead, the problem becomes one of figuring out how "the state" *comes to assume* its vertical position as the supreme authority that manages all other institutional forms that social relations take (Ferguson and Gupta 2002), and that functions as the super-coordinator of the governance of social and individual conduct by these other institutions (Hansen and Stepputat 2001).

In addition, analyzing the process of state formation impels us to reconsider the mechanics of rule and workings of power through such apparently mundane state activities as the collection of taxes, the distribution of subsidized food to the poor, or the issuance of passports. Following these everyday tracks of rule, process, and surplus extraction allows us to study the operation of power in a disaggregated manner and to de-emphasize the state as the ultimate seat of power (Foucault 1979; Foucault 1991, Chapter 5 in this volume; Steinmetz 1999). It enables us to examine the dispersed institutional and social networks through which rule is coordinated and consolidated, and the roles that "non-state" institutions, communities, and individuals play in mundane processes of governance (see also Trouillot 2003) – processes which Foucault termed the "*etatisation* of society" (Foucault 1991:103; emphasis in original) and that Nikolas Rose has called the "de-statization of government" (1996:56).

Anthropology offers an especially useful lens with which to examine state formation (Corrigan and Sayer 1985; Joseph and Nugent 1994) and understand how the "state" and its boundaries are culturally constructed.[11] Anthropology's focus on particular branches and levels of state institutions enables a disaggregated view of "the state" that shows the multilayered, pluri-centered, and fluid nature of this ensemble that congeals different contradictions (Hall 1986, Chapter 15 in this volume). The anthropological project attempts to understand the conditions in which the state successfully represents itself as coherent and singular (Gupta 1995, Chapter 9 in this volume).

Second, anthropology brings to the foreground the role of cultural difference in forming and informing states. Steinmetz (1999) has argued that while culture has not been entirely ignored in historical and comparative analyses of states, it has generally not been accorded a central or even crucial place in processes of state formation.[12] According to Steinmetz, both (neo) Marxist and (neo) Weberian accounts tend to see culture as produced by the state, but do not see states as effects of cultural processes. In Weber's developmentalist conception of the state, culture did not matter where the bureaucratic rationality of *modern* states was concerned (Weber 1968, Chapter 1 in this volume). Steinmetz contends that neo-Weberian accounts of the state (Evans et al. 1985) also neglect culture – they view culture as lying firmly on the "society" side of the state–society divide. When culture is included in such analyses, Steinmetz argues, it is often essentialized as a system of elite or expert ideas (1999: 17–18).[13]

Structural and functional conceptions of the state view it as a set of institutions that perform specific functions related to governance and security, as in Weber's famous dictum about the state possessing a monopoly over violence in a given territory. The classification of regimes and states into various categories, such as "bureaucratic authoritarian" or "liberal democratic," for instance, not only takes the meanings of terms like "authoritarian" and "democratic" to be self-evident, but is also premised on a certain set of core assumptions about the nature and function of states.[14] Such a comparative analysis of states rests on the assumption that the units being compared to each other – states – are *essentially* similar. If cultural difference matters to such forms of analyses, then it is only as a variable and often not a very important variable (Steinmetz 1999). For if cultural difference truly mattered, then states that are institutionally similar would "be" and mean very different things. For example, a liberal democratic state and a totalitarian state might actually look alike at the level of everyday practices of state bureaucracies. Instead of presuming that similarly classified states share a "natural" likeness and affinity, an anthropological lens forces us to critically interrogate the assumption that cultural difference is epiphenomenal to the functional and structural characteristics of states.

Many comparative and classificatory analyses of states, such as those that rank states as "weak" or "strong," effectively strip the unit of analysis – the state – from its cultural moorings. When a state does not have a fully developed set of functional elements or if such elements are completely absent, that nation-state is classified as having a "transitioning" or "weak" state or a "stateless" society (see Weber, 1968, Chapter 1 in this volume).[15] In addition, such exercises take for granted that "fully developed" and "ideal" states are Western liberal democratic ones. Western states are thus often employed as the norm against which other states are judged; the criteria for a "strong" state are almost always those that apply to a specific subset of Western nation-states.

An anthropological perspective allows us to pay careful attention to the cultural constitution of the state – that is, how people perceive the state, how their understandings are shaped by their particular locations and intimate and embodied encounters with state processes and officials, and how the state manifests itself in their lives.[16] Analyzing these cultural processes through which "the state" is instantiated and experienced also enables us to see that the illusion of cohesion and unitariness created by states is always contested and fragile, and is the result of hegemonic processes that should not be taken for granted.

The Cultural Constitution of States I: Everyday Practices

Anthropological analyses of the state, then, begin with the counter-intuitive notion that states that are structurally similar may nonetheless be profoundly different from each other in terms of the meanings they have for their populations. Cultural struggles determine what a state means to its people, how it is instantiated in their daily lives, and where its boundaries are drawn. These cultural struggles are waged in the sphere of representation but also in the domain of the everyday practices of state agencies. In emphasizing the "cultural constitution" of states, therefore, we are primarily interested in these two interrelated aspects of states.

The sphere of everyday practices is the primary arena in which people learn something about the state. Whether it is the practice of standing in line to obtain monthly rations or to mail a letter, getting a statement notarized or answering the questions of an official surveyor, paying taxes or getting audited, applying for a passport or attending a court hearing, the state as an institution is substantiated in people's lives through the apparently *banal* practices of bureaucracies. What the state means to people such as government officials situated inside a bureaucracy, as well as to those outside, such as the clients of government programs and other citizens, is profoundly shaped through the *routine* and *repetitive* procedures of bureaucracies.

At one level this proceduralism is so thoroughly commonplace and ordinary as to be uninteresting. It is therefore not surprising, as scholars such as James Ferguson (1994) have pointed out, that bureaucratic proceduralism is considered "apolitical" (see Weber 1968, Chapter 1 in this volume), consisting as it does of the technical work of the state.[17] At another level, however, it is these putatively technical and unremarkable practices that render tenable the political tasks of state formation, governance, and the exertion of power. An example is provided by James C. Scott's (1998; Chapter 10 in this volume) work on the techniques of urban planning. Practices like mapping and surveying, Scott demonstrates, work as important parts of the apparatus of legibility and control – they mold what states see, how they govern, and how the population, in turn, perceives states.[18]

Mundane bureaucratic procedures thus provide important clues to understanding the micropolitics of state work, how state authority and government operate in people's daily lives, and how the state comes to be imagined, encountered, and reimagined by the population. For example, the Indian state is often characterized as one in which "rule-following" behavior is the bureaucratic norm. Violating rules to accomplish necessary tasks can incur severe negative penalties. Nonetheless, one sees high levels of corruption and actions, regularly taken, which contravene existing rules (see Gupta, Chapter 9 in this volume). What one finds in a case such as this is that an excessive devotion to proceduralism itself either creates the possibility of actions that exploit mutually contradictory rules of procedure, or forces bureaucrats and their clients to skirt the rules. When conflicts arise within the bureaucracy, rules are often used to bring errant subordinates into line.

An ethnographic example from lower-level state bureaucracies in Uttar Pradesh (UP), India can help to clarify this point. The Integrated Child Development Services or ICDS is a nation-wide government development program targeting young children and women. It was launched in Mandi subdistrict of UP (where Gupta conducted his ethnography) in 1985, with the goal of providing a set of services that consisted of supplementary nutrition for pregnant women and young children, and education, immunizations, and preventive medicine for poor and lower-caste children.[19]

Gupta observed that all officials had to routinely maintain a detailed travel log which contained separate entries on where those individuals were going, what time they left the office, whom they went to meet and for what purpose, when they were expected back, and when they actually returned. This travel log had to be filled out before they left the office. The register could be double-checked with the logbook and mileage on the official jeep, which also had to be filled out every time the jeep was driven for official work.

On one occasion, Asha Agarwal, head of the ICDS Program in Mandi district, showed Gupta her travel log, where some lines had been scribbled in between the regularly spaced register-entries. She told him that her supervisor had reprimanded her for making up visits and falsifying her travel record.[20] She said that sometimes she just forgot to make an entry in the register. She pointed out that the particular day for which her supervisor had upbraided her was the day she had gone to meet the District Magistrate (the highest-ranking official in the entire administrative area). This was certainly not a meeting that she could have made up, given the importance and position of the official involved. Nonetheless, her supervisor suspected that she was cheating because she did not follow the *procedure* of making an entry in her travel log. The fact that she had a crucial substantive meeting with the district's head official held less importance for him than observing the correct bureaucratic rule.

The outcome of a circumvention of the rules might very well be desirable since the rules themselves are often arcane colonial accretions, but any effort to make things work at the expense of following the rules inevitably brings forth accusations of corruption. Since charges of corruption are closely tied to questions of legitimacy (a corrupt government is widely seen as an illegitimate one), and since state legitimacy itself depends on what states mean to their citizens, the routine practices of bureaucracies become intimately linked to cultural contestation and construction.

Official procedures are not devised or directed by anyone in particular. They are authorless strategies through which power is exercised and inequalities instituted (Ferguson 1994). Looking at everyday practices therefore allows us to disentangle intentionality from the operation of power. Examining everyday state practices also allows us to understand how state institutions are both recognized and reproduced – sometimes silently, without drawing attention to themselves, and at other times through asserting their presence and power – through the daily work of bureaucracies.

The *structure* of bureaucratic authority depends on the repetitive re-enactment of everyday practices. These iterative practices are performative (Butler 1990) in that rather than being an outward reflection of a coherent and bounded state "core" they actually constitute that very core. It is *through* these re-enactments that the coherence and continuity of state institutions is constituted and sometimes destabilized. Using the model of performativity to understand bureaucratic practices and political spectacles (Taylor 1997) is useful in another sense as well. Performances assume an interface between actors and spectators; performances both constitute and are constituted by an audience. The repetitive performance of state procedures, for a variety of audiences located at different levels (such as rural peasants, local and national bureaucrats, activists, international development or human rights experts, and officials of other nation-states), shapes audiences' ideas about the translocal nature of the state and their relationship to "it."

Proceduralism, the banal repetition of everyday actions, and the mundane realities of following precedent, reproduce "the state" as an institution across time and space. But do such actions do more than just (re)produce the conditions that allow for the continuity of an institution? We argue that they do much more. It is through such mundane activities that the primacy of the state is reproduced, and its superiority over other social institutions established. And it is through the daily routines of proceduralism and precedent setting that social inequalities, such as those of class and gender, are produced and maintained.

One simple example may make this clear. The Indian state places a high value on writing for its everyday procedures. Whether it is an application or a complaint, unless it is submitted in writing, it has little value, as it is not "actionable." Given the high levels of rural illiteracy, especially given the gendered inequalities of rural schooling, the state's emphasis on the written word immediately places poor, uneducated people, and particularly low-caste, non-literate women, in a position of disadvantage. Many state-implemented development and empowerment programs are purportedly intended to reduce economic and social inequality; yet it is ironic that the very procedures of state institutions perpetuate, rather than reduce, those inequalities. Upper-class and higher-caste men are often better situated to take advantage of state programs than poorer and lower-caste women.

The premium placed on writing and proper procedure in official circles forces grassroots women's development and empowerment programs, which attempt to challenge and alter social inequalities, to train their staff and clients in constructing proper paper trails. Aradhana Sharma studied one such women's empowerment program initiated by the Government of India, called the *Mahila Samakhya* (henceforth "MS") program, in the eastern part of the Indian state of Uttar Pradesh (UP). MS seeks to empower low-caste poor rural women, through collective consciousness-raising and mobilization, to challenge caste, class, and gender oppression, engender social change, and develop themselves and their communities. The power of writing was brought home to Sharma when some MS program participants claimed that "empowered" women were those who knew how to "wield the pen." Wielding the pen implied having the knowledge required to negotiate the world of the powerful: men, officials, and people with salaried jobs. These women, the majority of whom were non-literate, understood that their struggles for social change depended on their access to basic literacy skills, to knowledge of state procedures (which themselves required reading and writing skills), and to sympathetic and supportive officials. Demands for development, for example, which are a crucial component of social change efforts, almost always reference the state. The postcolonial Indian state has positioned itself as the harbinger of national development, and its legitimacy is crucially tied to its development efforts (see Chatterjee 1993, 1998; Gupta 1998; Ludden 1992). MS participants were aware of the centrality of the state to their transformatory mobilizations. They knew that if they were to expect any action on development goals by local bureaucrats, they must forward their concerns in writing and keep officially stamped copies of all correspondence.

Whenever any demand for village development, such as digging a well, constructing a road, or building subsidized housing, arose in MS villages where Sharma did her fieldwork, MS staff members assisted program participants in writing formal applications addressed to local development bureaucrats like Block Development Officers (BDOs).[21] They made two copies of all applications. The staff members either read the contents of the applications out loud, or, alternatively, MS participants asked some schoolgoing child in the village to read the applications so as to make sure that their concerns were correctly represented in written form. Program participants then submitted the applications at the local Block Office, the lowest tier in the state's developmental bureaucracy, ensuring that the receiving official stamped them with "received" and signed both copies of the application. They kept one copy of the signed and stamped application for their records. While following the proper procedure and documenting their interactions with officials through paper trails did not necessarily ensure that their requests were met, it enabled MS women to voice a "legitimate" critique of local bureaucrats' inaction, when and if they had to take up the issue with higher-level bureaucrats. Demands made on paper made possible a certain degree of accountability.

The reproduction of the state as an institution through bureaucratic practices, however, is not as smooth and inevitable a process as it sometimes appears. People may, to various degrees, be suspicious or critical of the premium placed on the written word by state officials, and resist the hierarchicalism and proceduralism inherent in bureaucratic practices. The possibility of subversion always looms large. Routine activities of recording, like the census, give us a sense of how much people avoid being literally written into state registers (see Scott 1998, Chapter 10 in this volume; Appadurai 1993b; Cohn 1987). During one such rural appraisal drive undertaken by the MS program in the village of Banipur in eastern UP, which Sharma observed, some residents simply refused to participate while others participated in the hope of deriving some material benefit. MS workers arrived in Banipur in the usual blue program jeep, which had government license plates, and introduced MS as a Government of India program. Banipur's residents thus viewed the census exercise as an official encounter. Some of them simply walked away from the MS staff – they did not want to be recorded in "official" registers. One female resident said to the surveyors, "You will write our names for the purpose of your job and leave. Meanwhile we will continue to live our lives of drudgery." Not only did she refuse to divulge her name unless she was given money in exchange for providing personal information but in a parodic reversal of authority, asked for the names of the surveyors in return for revealing hers. Other residents agreed to be surveyed, but used this encounter to criticize the general lack of government-provided development facilities in the village and to ask for help. Many residents who participated in the survey asked to be placed in the "below poverty line" category in the hope of receiving the government assistance earmarked for the poorest, and thus sought material benefits and social capital in exchange for being counted.

Such incidents demonstrate two key things. First, they show the extent to which representations, symbols, practices, and materiality are interlinked. Jeeps with official license plates, and development workers with census forms and a particular tone of voice are markers of power and status. Rural residents read such markers in specific ways. They associate these symbols with statist authority (which is critiqued but also taken seriously); this authority, however, comes with moral responsibility for poverty alleviation and development. The Banipur incident clearly illustrates how state representations are connected with both the fabric of power inequalities and with material need. Second, such incidents demonstrate how those outside state institutions contest the *reproduction* of social inequalities contained within such apparently innocuous state procedures such as that of data collection.

These subversions, however, are not limited to those at the receiving end of state practices. Bureaucrats may not carry out the orders of their superiors in a proper manner or they may adhere to the letter but not to the spirit of policy directives, thereby disrupting the smooth functioning of the state system. As James Ferguson's work on Lesotho demonstrates, the intentions and goals of high-ranking officials (as, for instance, in the context of state-initiated development programs) may either never be realized during the implementation of these programs or may work out in unintended ways with unlikely consequences. Also, officials at lower levels of state bureaucracies may not support programs initiated by others higher up in the hierarchy, and might even actively try to sabotage the execution and goals of initiatives planned from above. This was apparent in the everyday workings of the MS program. Even though MS is a *state-initiated* program, it did not receive unequivocal support within the governmental system.

MS is a program of the New Delhi-based central government. While many senior administrators in the central government clearly supported the program, some stated that MS did not receive full government backing at national level because it was a program with a relatively small budget. MS's low budget is a direct consequence of the fact that it does not disburse material benefits to its participants. This put MS at a disadvantage in a political context in which the status, capital, and power of state officials are linked to their ability to distribute benefits. The program also faced a potentially more dangerous constraint in that many officials, across various levels of the bureaucracy, were suspicious of a program that overtly attempted to "empower" its women beneficiaries and to challenge intertwined social and state hierarchies. MS staff members often recounted the ignorance or active hostility they encountered from officials, especially at the lower (block and district) levels of the bureaucracy. While some local bureaucrats did not think that a low-budget women's empowerment program was worthy of their attention, others openly expressed their suspicions about a program that had women's empowerment as its explicit goal. "What does 'empowerment' mean?" they asked. Some went further and asked MS workers if they intended to break up families by empowering women.

Paying attention to everyday bureaucratic practices thus brings to light the sources and nature of interbureaucratic conflicts, which may help explain impediments to the proper implementation of development programs. It also illustrates the vexed and discordant processes through which the state (and its attendant inequalities) is reproduced. Intra-institutional conflict is considered dysfunctional in the ideal-type Weberian bureaucracy – it poses obstacles to the smooth functioning and reproduction of the institution. Yet we argue that far from being symbols of the improper development of states, these conflicts, "corruptions," and inconsistencies are *central* to institutional organization and the reproduction of states.

Finally, the routine practices of state bureaucracies help establish limits of the state to produce what Timothy Mitchell (Chapter 7, this volume) calls the "effect of the state." The line between state and non-state realms is partly drawn by bureaucrats' everyday work practices and encounters with others. For example, Sharma (forthcoming) shows how everyday discussions between officials and development activists about the structure and workings of development programs, meetings between local bureaucrats and NGO workers, and interactions between NGO workers and participants of development programs help (re)draw the line between state and non-state realms, and constitute what the state is and what it does. Drawing upon the structure and functioning of the MS program as a "GONGO" (Government Organized Non-Governmental Organization), and the discussions about MS's hybrid form that took place between government and non-governmental representatives, Sharma ethnographically elaborates the processes by which the state is discursively produced as an entity that is distinct from and sits above the non-state realm. MS's hybrid "GONGO" form attempts to fuse together the positive aspects of governmental and non-governmental development strategies (for example, combining the "reach" of the state with the "bottom-up" or grassroots approach of NGOs). Yet, even as this hybrid structure tries to transcend the boundary between state and non-state arenas, it simultaneously rests on the assumption that the state and non-state realms exist in "pure," mutually exclusive forms.

The boundary between state and non-state realms is thus drawn through the contested cultural practices of bureaucracies, and people's encounters with, and negotiations of, these practices. Everyday statist encounters not only shape people's imagination of what the state is and how it is demarcated, but also enable people to devise strategies of resistance to this imagined state. Those who are the subjects or targets of state programs, and thus "outside" bureaucracies, learn to use the very same techniques that lower-level state agents use to sabotage official mandates and orders. They learn about paper pushing, leaving paper trails, and adopting official mannerisms. They use these practices in their everyday interactions with officials to gain institutional access or to subvert official scrutiny; they also use them when interacting with non-officials in order to establish their authority over others.

Official practices, therefore, are not only redeployed as strategies of resistance (and thus always dangerously mired within the logic of bureaucratic power), but they are also not limited to "the state." Practices of bureaucratic hierarchicalism and proceduralism spread from state institutions into "non-state" realms, as the earlier example of MS participants following proper application procedures for demanding development facilities demonstrated. Similarly, MS program workers routinely used bureaucratic techniques to subvert governmental authority and get their work done (Sharma forthcoming). As employees of a *government-initiated* program, MS staff members were not allowed to participate in anti-government mobilizations. Yet many actually did so by taking time off work, putting "official" leave applications on file, and participating in anti-government protests as regular citizens or as NGO workers. MS's dual identity, as both a governmental and non-governmental program, gave staff members room to maneuver around governmental dictates. Some MS workers told Sharma that they kept two program letterheads on file. The first, a letterhead that represents MS as an NGO, was used when writing non-confrontational, support-seeking letters (for instance, to other grassroots organizations). Staff members used a second program identification, with its official "Ministry of Human Resource Development" letterhead, when they wanted to put pressure on someone. As one MS employee explained, "We ... stamp our seal on these letters ... [and] write them exactly like government letters are written." Hence, in order to appear "official," MS employees used appropriate letterheads, seals, signatures, and tone of voice. They deployed the state's disciplinary procedures to get things accomplished and to deter possible repression from officials. This dispersal of the techniques of regulation and government throughout society also illustrates the governmentalization of society (Foucault 1991).

In sum, then, bureaucratic practices are a crucial mechanism through which the shifting effect of the state is produced and reproduced. There is, however, nothing straightforward or obvious about the production and reproduction of the state effect. Everyday practices are also important because they are signifying practices, and this brings us into the complex relationship of such practices with the sphere of the circulation of representations of the state.

The Cultural Constitution of States II: Representations

Representations comprise another key modality through which states are culturally constituted, and through which state power is enacted. People learn about particular state agencies and officers at local and national levels through newspapers (Gupta 1995, Chapter 9 in this volume); they read government reports about topics such as population control, as Anagnost (1995) demonstrates in her work on China; they discuss their experiences of particular bureaucracies and officials in different forums; they watch election-related propaganda on television or listen to speeches by elected officials at public rallies; they observe military parades, activities, and violence (Lutz 2002, Chapter 12 in this volume; Taylor 1997); and they participate in other ceremonial rituals staged by state officials, for example, to inaugurate a dam (Tennekoon 1988), initiate a village housing scheme (Brow 1996), or to celebrate national independence. It is in the realm of representation that explicit discourse of the state is produced. Public cultural representations and performance of statehood crucially shape people's perceptions about the nature of the state.

Employees of various bureaucratic institutions also come to understand the entity they work for as well as their place in it through the representational sphere. For instance, banal techniques of representation such as official letterheads, seals, memos, photographs of official buildings, special uniforms, spatial arrangements of offices, monitoring and surveillance visits by senior officials, cars with government license plates and official motorcades, personnel files and procedures for promotion, and organizational charts, play a key role in presenting "the state" and its organizational hierarchy to its functionaries. The public circulation and dissemination of such images of "the state" and of state leaders and their actions enable people at different levels of the bureaucracy, as well as those outside these institutions, to imagine what the state is, what it is supposed to do, where its boundaries lie, and what their place is in relation to state institutions.

How does one study the "represented" state? Textual analysis is one key method, which might entail analyzing statistical reports[22] and examining other kinds of public cultural narratives which have come into focus since the "cultural turn" (Steinmetz 1999) but still remain understudied. Here we are thinking of public cultural texts such as newspapers, radio, television, and cinematic representations of the state, and reports and leaflets produced by government and nongovernment agencies.[23] Analyses of how states are represented intertextually, that is, across different media (for example, television and print media) and in documents produced by diverse agencies (for example, country reports published by the World Bank or national plans produced by governments), and the circulation

of representations transnationally, nationally, and regionally become very important. Such analyses permit us to tease out shifts, overlaps, and disjunctures in the
(re)production of the state in a spatial frame that transcends the nation. Besides
examining the production and circulation of discourses about the state, ethnographies of the state also involve analyzing how messages about the state are
interpreted and mobilized by people according to their particular contexts and
social locations.

It is also through these kinds of specific and "localized" images and experiences
that the state is discursively imagined as something greater than simply its local
manifestations. Public cultural discourses about corrupt state officials and a
generally corrupt state system, as Akhil Gupta (Chapter 9, this volume) illustrates, allow people to connect up the disparate levels of the state and imagine it
as a "translocal" entity. Representational techniques such as organizational
charts, official seals, and photographs of state leaders help suture the various
levels of bureaucracy into an apparently neat, organized, distinct, and coherent
whole, and define state functionaries' relation to this larger system. By lending to
the state a veneer of consistency, systematicity, centralized control, and whole-
ness, and by thus eliding the messiness, contradictions, and tensions that states
congeal, statist representations play a crucial role in entrenching the borders and
vertical authority of the state and in shaping resistance to the state.

We want to make two further points of clarification here. First, although we
have made an analytical distinction between everyday bureaucratic practices and
statist representations, these are, in effect, deeply co-implicated and mutually
constitutive. How people experience bureaucratic practices is shaped by representations of the state; in turn, how people read representations is mediated by
their daily encounters with bureaucratic practices. This dialectic operates not
only for citizens but for bureaucrats as well. What needs to be analyzed here is
how contradictory *representations* of the state are interpreted and operationalized in the everyday practices of bureaucrats. Furthermore, we need to understand how these practices fit within the "institutional culture" of the state while
simultaneously reshaping both the institution and its representations.

The dialectic between practices and representations also opens up the possibility of *dissonance* between ideas of the state gleaned from representations and
those arising from encounters with particular officials. Such discords and differences can lead to a rearticulation of peoples' relationship to the state. The
sometimes conflicting effects of the state produced by the complex dialectic
between practices and representations rupture the hegemony and singularity of
the state, and highlight the contradictions that it congeals.

The second point we wish to make is that focusing on practices and representations of the state allows us to see their central role in the perpetration of
exploitation and inequality. It enables us to examine the *mechanisms* by which
the extraction and redistribution of surplus, and the reproduction of the relations
of production, are accomplished and legitimated. Delineating precisely how
ruling class ideologies are mobilized, how they become state ideology, and how
they reproduce inequalities, even if never in a straightforward or unchallenged

manner, presents a vexing theoretical problem (see Althusser 1971, Chapter 3 in this volume; Gramsci 1971, Chapter 2 in this volume). Analyses of ideological entrenchment and shifts in different institutional and social sites, through every-day statist practices and representations, are important because they suggest how and where struggles against marginalization and exploitation can be waged.

We earlier illustrated how everyday statist proceduralism, and the reliance on literacy and written documents in particular, encode and reinforce class, caste, and gender privilege. Similarly, ethnographically examining encounters among state officials, and between bureaucrats, politicians, and their constituents reveals how the state is made "real" in people's lives through the self-representational practices of those in power. We might, for instance, look at how government, GONGO, and even NGO employees present themselves as agents of the state, or as bearers of a special status by virtue of their association with the state, and how they also present their particular institution and position within and outside the bureaucratic hierarchy. What tone, language, and manner of dress do they adopt in different contexts, and how is that linked with power and authority? Or, for example, how do seating arrangements at meetings between officials and non-officials reflect and reinforce hierarchy? *How* official and non-official groups of people interact among themselves and with each other might illustrate the con-crete ways in which the distinction between state and non-state arenas and social hierarchies are mobilized in everyday state practices, what kinds of social capital and power are associated with this work, and how this official status intersects with and feeds upon existing, contextually specific social hierarchies. Such ana-lyses would reveal how ideologies of gender and class difference are ensconced in and operationalized through different institutional mechanisms (including but not limited to "conventional" state apparatuses), how these ideologies shift over time, how they reconstitute difference, and how they can be challenged and altered.

What we have outlined above are some of the key reasons why states need to be seen as cultural artifacts and effects, and the role that anthropology has played and can continue to play in this endeavor.[24] We now move on to elaborating the second main axis of our argument – seeing states through the prism of transna-tionalism – and make a case for taking a transnational approach to the study of states.

States in a Transnational Frame

To see the role that transnational discourses play in constructing states, consider the example of how statistical reports published by United Nations (UN) agen-cies, such as the Human Development Report, and the World Bank represent Third World states by ranking them in a decreasing order of development. James Ferguson (1994), for instance, demonstrates how the World Bank produces Lesotho as a Least Developed Country, or an LDC, which then connotes a certain set of characteristics, needs, and interventions (see also Mitchell 1991a). Transnational development discourse also positions states as primary agents for national development and as the chief institutions for the implementation of policy. Economic development interventions, through such instruments as Structural Adjustment Programs, take place through negotiations between transnational development organizations and government officials. Representatives of non-governmental organizations or NGOs are rarely included in these negotiations. The image of the classic "developmentalist" Third World state can thus itself be viewed as a partial effect of transnational development discourse. Such a location has material consequences for how governments and officials understand the mandate for national development and how they, in turn, represent it to their citizens.

For instance, the scramble by officials and elected leaders around the world to appear democratic, reorganize institutions in civil society, streamline state agencies, and represent their governments as improved and more efficient, must be read in the context of the global circulation of neoliberal discourses of good governance, the strengthening of civil society, privatization, and the rollback of welfare programs (see Barry et al. 1996; Ferguson and Gupta 2002; Paley 2002; Rose 1996, Chapter 6 in this volume). While the particular shape that this reorganization takes varies across postcolonial and postsocialist contexts, as do its social and cultural effects, neoliberalism or "advanced liberalism" (Rose 1996, Chapter 6 in this volume) *is* critically reshaping the representations and contours of "the state," and the forms and modalities of government and rule. Analyzing these shifts sheds light on the nature of the political rationality that underwrites neoliberalism.

For example, the neoliberal focus on smaller government, as Nikolas Rose (1996, Chapter 6 in this volume) argues, illustrates the market logic that guides it and the new forms of rule that secure it. Leaner government does not translate into less regulation or weaker states – in fact, it ends up proliferating the sites for regulation and domination by creating "autonomous" entities of government that are not part of the formal state apparatus and are guided by the enterprise logic (Burchell 1996; see also Barry, et al. 1996). This government-at-a-distance involves social institutions such as non-governmental organizations, schools, communities, and even individuals that are removed from a centralized state apparatus and are made responsible for activities that were heretofore carried out by state agencies.

The currently popular discourses of "participation," "empowerment," and "democratization" take this line of thinking to its logical conclusion (see Chatterjee 2004; Cruikshank 1999; Leve 2001; Paley 2001; Sharma forthcoming). The deployment of these terms as strategies of governance rests on tutoring people to build their capacities and become self-dependent, responsible citizens who can take care of their own welfare and govern themselves. This provides yet another example of the neoliberal "unloading" of public services onto empowered and "responsibilized" selves and communities who, as Julia Paley (2002) suggests, are thereby made complicit in the contemporary workings of power and governance.

Current usage of empowerment, democracy, civil society, and good governance discourses points to a reconfigured global apparatus of rule – neoliberalism – that reflects the post-Fordist regime of global capitalism (Jessop 1999). One way to comprehend the underlying logic of neoliberalism is through observing changes in how it is publicly represented. Does neoliberalism necessarily include a key transformation in how the nature, boundary, and role of the state are represented? If so, then one of the important tasks at hand is to critically interrogate the politics of the ostensibly "shrinking" boundaries of the state that have accompanied the emergence of flexible capitalism and quasi-autonomous "state-like" institutions at supra- and sub-national levels. One could argue, for instance, that the state in the neoliberal moment is contracting in two ways. First, the transnational organization of global capitalism is forcing a different regime of regulation of national economies by their respective states. Some forms of regulation, like tariffs on trade, are being weakened and governed by transnational organizations such as the WTO; other forms of regulation, such as immigration and increasingly aggressive forms of policing, are being strengthened.

Second, states are increasingly unable to perform their redistributive role: the resources they are able to extract and distribute are becoming smaller. In the case of postcolonial "Third World" states, liberalization policies and transnational governance mechanisms like Structural Adjustment Programs and austerity meas-ures have played a significant role in the shrinking of these resources. In such a context, the "privatization" of the state entails a dispersal of the state's govern-ance and redistributive functions to non-state and charitable organizations. While this farming out may well signal a "degovernmentalization of the state" (Barry et al. 1996: 11) or a "de-statization of government" (Rose 1996: 56), it also represents an increased governmentalization of society (Foucault 1991).

Jessop (1999) argues that the state in the post-Fordist, neoliberal context is a qualitatively new state form and we need to shift our frame of analysis from *government* to *governance*. He contends that while the Keynesian Welfare Na-tional State (KWNS) of the Euro-American type may well be eroding, by becom-ing denationalized, destatized, and internationalized, not all national state forms are necessarily retreating. How does one make sense of the transformation of welfare states in different parts of the postcolonial world, which may never have had the resources of Keynesian welfare state? Clearly the imperatives, processes, and implications of the "rollback" of postcolonial welfare states will be quite different from those of the Keynesian welfare states in the North. The micro-politics of these seismic shifts, and their implications for the cultural construction of the state and the reorganization of authority, need to be delineated through careful ethnographic and historical analyses.

The key advantage that the frame of transnationalism brings to the study of states is that it forces us to rethink the triad "state–territory–people" and the presumed symmetry of its constituent parts. For example, the Weberian notion of the state defines it as: (1) exercising monopoly over violence in a given territory; (2) securing the territorial border and sovereignty; and (3) governing a particular population in a specific territory. The state here is theorized as a unitary actor who regulates the territory of the nation-state and the people who inhabit that territory.

Whether states in fact monopolize the use of violence over a particular territory and are able to secure their territorial sovereignty is open to debate (see also Aretxaga 2003). Counterexamples are not hard to find. The US occupation of Iraq is an obvious case, but so are UN peacekeeping missions that organize forces from various national militaries to keep "order" in politically sensitive areas or those nation-states torn apart by civil war. But could globally organized terrorist networks be included as troubling this straightforward definition of the state as well? After all, the idea that the state is responsible for maintaining security within its sovereign borders is profoundly brought into doubt by each of these examples.

The ability of states to secure their sovereignty and defend the sanctity of their borders is also challenged by border crossings of various sorts, and by transnational regimes that regulate not just states but, also, individual citizens within those states. The European Union (EU) would be a good example of one such transnational regime.

Another example is offered by the organization and operation of the transnational human rights regime which looks into violations of human rights across the globe and tries states, state leaders, and even those citizens whom particular nation-states may refuse to indict. Here is a massive machinery of surveillance and regulation, which is organized at a transnational level. It consists of activists, judges, tribunals, covenants, human rights organizations, truth commissions, witnesses and testimonials, and courts. These institutions, organizations, and individuals together operate on a plane that is of a different order than that of nation-states, that troubles states' claims to sovereign control over their territories and citizens, and that also challenges state monopoly over the exertion of violence within their sovereign territories. The human rights regime deploys national and international means to bring to light human rights abuses by states, but it also goes beyond the frame of the nation-state and the international system of states in that its moral authority works through a transnational network of people, practices, institutions, and rules (Keck and Sikkink 1998; see also Sassen 1996; Sikkink 1993).

Human rights activists work with both transnational mechanisms of enforcement as well as with national legislative measures. For instance, US-based human rights organizations have not only lobbied international organizations like the UN to put pressure on "errant" states, but have often lobbied Congress to consider the human rights ratings of nations while making foreign policy and trade decisions. A poor human rights record can result in a demotion of a state's favorability as a trade partner. Human rights abuses have been particularly relevant in the geopolitical and economic negotiations between the USA and China. Human rights organizations have repeatedly invoked Tibet, or Chinese prison labor, to influence US trade relationships and foreign policy with China. The use of the language of human rights as an instrument by both "state" and "non-state" actors to regulate the behavior of other nation-states illustrates how justice-based and often anti-state resistance strategies can also be appropriated as strategies of domination. It also problematizes our received notions of territoriality, state sovereignty, and the legitimate use of state violence in the context of transnational networks of governance. Moreover, it raises the thorny issue of human rights themselves functioning as a disciplinary instrument that spreads governmental power transnationally and can potentially strengthen the hegemony of Northern states (Grewal 1998). In the current post-Cold War transnational neoliberal order, human rights instruments are an increasingly powerful means available to the marginalized for articulating their concerns and needs as rights. Yet, as Grewal has pointed out, we need to be careful about celebrating the current incarnation of the human rights regime as *the* solution to global inequalities – it may not be less dangerous as a form of global governance or less dependent on US hegemony than previous versions that relied solely upon international organizations like the UN (Grewal 1998:509; see also Kothari 1995; Kothari and Sethi 1991). The employment of both national and international instruments by loose transnational networks of human rights activists, NGOs, lawyers, commissions, and so on both rests on and reinforces geopolitical inequalities between nation-states even as it provides a powerful means of challenging other inequalities.

Using the transnational perspective on the state allows us to disentangle the governance of a space or territory from the governance of a people. We can then ask whether different states, in the current neoliberal context, are able to equally control and regulate both territory and people. Even a cursory look at the transnational development regime, for example, shows how complicated this picture about states has become. We are witnessing how international development agencies like the International Monetary Fund (IMF) and the World Bank are, in effect, dictating policies to Third World nation-states. Even when these policies are not directly imposed, policy making in the Third World is overdetermined by the neoliberal context of structural adjustment, austerity measures, controlled social-sector or "welfare" spending, and market-based distributive mechanisms. How does this transnational context impinge upon and redefine the ability of states to govern what is happening within their territorial borders? The development regime also includes transnational NGOs and foundations, such as CARE, Oxfam, Save the Children and the Ford Foundation, all of which bring models of development and resources directly to specific populations without necessarily going through national governments. We need to account for their "regulatory" work and think about how transnational development discourse mitigates and reshapes the presumed ability of states to manage their own national populations and take care of their needs (Bornstein 2003).

Analytically separating the question of the governance of space and territory from the governance of populations allows us not only to move beyond the framework of the nation-state within which the study of the state has so often been confined, but also to broaden the discussion from "the state" to "governance" more generally. This is precisely where Foucault's notion of governmentality (Foucault, Chapter 5 in this volume) is very useful. Often explained as the direction of conduct toward specific ends, which has as its objects both individuals and populations and which combines techniques of domination and discipline with technologies of self-government (Barry et al. 1996; Burchell et al. 1991; Dean 1999; Rose 1996 and Chapter 6 in this volume; see also Merry 2001), governmentality enables us to unhinge rule from the "body" of the state by enlarging the space of governance. Instead of assuming that states are the supreme "holders" of power and deploy that power exclusively to dominate and rule, governmentality offers a lens to understand how power is exercised in society through varied social relations, institutions, and "bodies" that do not automatically fit under the rubric of "the state." It enables us to see how rule is secured, sometimes in tenuous ways, through a variety of not necessarily coordinated methods and by a web of institutional and social arrangements that transcend our received understandings of the state. It helps us to move beyond conventional functionalist definitions of the state (what the state does) and to think through the dispersal of these functions across different social institutions and individuals. The state, in this frame, is but one node (although at times a "coordinating" node) in a horizontal network of institutions and individuals through which power is exercised, and not *the* vertically highest institution in which power inheres.

Despite appearing to explode the space in which to examine rule and governance, the concept of governmentality has itself often been caught in the framework of the nation-state (see Ferguson and Gupta 2002). Foucault grounded his analysis of governmentality in a world of *European nation-states*. This world, which saw the emergence of a new rationality of government grounded in the care of the population (its welfare, wealth, and security), was also one in which these European states were extensively involved in colonial conquest and rule. Yet Foucault does not invoke colonialism when delineating the logic and modalities of governmentality (see Scott 1999; Stoler 1995). When Foucault talked about the "care of the national population," he meant only the metropolitan population of the colonial powers whose welfare and wealth emerged as key concerns of their governments. It is clear that "welfare" was not the operative term where the colonized were concerned. But the questions that need to be asked are (a) whether this shift toward governmentality delineated by Foucault in the European context was *predicated* upon a very different modality of power in the colonies; and (b) what are the processes and effects of neoliberal governmentalization in the post-colonial world (Appadurai 2002; Chatterjee 2004; Das and Poole 2004; Ferguson 1994; Gupta 2001; Hansen and Stepputat 2001; Paley 2001; Sharma forthcoming) and in post-socialist contexts (Burawoy and Verdery 1999; Hemment 1999; Verdery 1996b; Yurchak 2002).

We thus need to think about how the analytics of government can be widened to make sense of the neoliberal world. We are living in a moment when states are doing less and less in terms of the care and welfare of their national populations.[25] We need to analytically rethink "the state" in a context where (a) the national space is transnationally defined, and (b) many functions traditionally tied with "it" are being carried out by non-governmental organizations which do not necessarily operate within a national structure.

One way to approach these processes of transnational governance is to examine migration, to ask why people move, who moves, from where, and to where. Human migrations are not only articulated to the needs of global capitalism, they are also transforming how we think about the nation, citizenship (or belonging, more broadly), and the state (Alexander 1997; Bhattacharjee 1997, Chapter 14 in this volume; Coutin 2003, Chapter 13 in this volume; Malkki 1995; Ong 1999). Diasporic movements point to how the space of the nation, or "home," and the affective ties that bind this imagined community are expanding across the boundaries of the nation-state (Basch et al. 1994; Glick Schiller et al. 1992). For this reason, citizenship too is being imagined, practiced, and regulated transnationally and flexibly (Balibar 2003; Coutin 2003, Chapter 13 in this volume; Ong 1999). Citizenship is unevenly experienced and spatialized – both transnationally and nationally.[26] People inhabiting different circuits of the global capitalist economy are subjected to different regimes of rights and citizenship (Ong 1999; Paley 2002).

The Indian state's policies vis-à-vis its diaspora, especially since the early 1990s, provide an interesting illustration of how transnational neoliberal political economic processes are impacting nation-states, nationalism, national policy-making, and citizenship. From instituting the category "Non-Resident Indian" or NRI, to setting up the "People of Indian Origin" or PIO cards that enables NRIs to own property and have easy access to investment opportunities in India, to recently approving dual citizenship,[27] the Indian government has enacted a series of measures aimed at diasporic subjects who are seen as potential economic saviors of the liberalizing Indian nation-state. In fact, these measures, along with particular investment opportunities created for diasporic subjects, went a long way toward boosting India's sagging foreign currency reserves and bringing India out of its fiscal crisis of the early 1990s, when it nearly defaulted on its debt commitments to multilateral lending agencies (Mankekar 1999). Similarly, as Susan Coutin (2003, Chapter 13 in this volume) argues, "sending states" like El Salvador view first world citizenship regimes and diasporic subjects' negotiations with these regimes as important parts of their *national* foreign policy and economic agendas.

These examples demonstrate how the nation and citizenship are being transected by global processes. We are living in a world where citizenship is transnationally administered and exercised – not only is the conduct of nationals of certain states regulated by transnational entities (in the EU, for example), but also national elections – that classic signifier of democratic citizenship and sovereign nationhood – are held under the aegis of international bodies and secured by foreign militaries in places like Iraq and the former Yugoslavia (Verdery 1998). Moreover, states in our current transnational context are not simply governing territories or the "national" populations that live within their territories, but are indeed claiming and managing populations that no longer live, or have never lived, in their territories. As the space of the nation is defined and transformed through the trans-nation, so is the shape and scope of the state, and of governance.

Our second example of the reconfiguration of space and institutions of governance refers back to transnational NGOs which are in the "business" of caring for populations – that is, of providing food, education, and health-related or legal resources to groups in many different parts of the world. They are expressly not tied to any national population. Instead, these NGOs link up communities across the globe not through affective "national" ties but through other "characteristics" such as poverty, or human rights abuses, and attempt to address the resource needs of these constructed communities. How can we account for the govern-

mental roles and modalities of such institutions whose spatial reach and populations served might be quite different from that of states? What does the presence
of these institutions do to the legitimacy that states derive from the care of their
national populations? And finally, what are the implications of the existence and
work of such organizations for the relationship between state and nation on the
one hand, and state and governance on the other?

Conclusion

In this Introduction we proposed that the conditions for studying the state have
shifted, and that this requires new ways of thinking about the state. We argued
that anthropological analyses of the state, in the current age of globalization, need
to seriously contend with questions of culture and transnationalism.

The first analytic move entailed in reconceptualizing states consists of seeing
them as culturally embedded and discursively constructed ensembles. Instead of
viewing states as preconstituted institutions that perform given functions, we
argued that they are produced through everyday practices and encounters and
through public cultural representations and performances. How states are portrayed and imagined by people located in different social positions affects both
scholarly and activist engagements with the state.

Focusing on everyday practices and representations as modes through which the
state comes into being has important methodological implications – it opens up
a vast terrain of sites and texts through which states can be anthropologically
examined (see also Trouillot 2003). The articles included in this volume represent
the diversity of ways in which such an examination can proceed. Thinking about
how states are culturally constituted, how they are substantiated in people's lives,
and about the sociopolitical and everyday consequences of these constructions,
involves moving beyond macro-level institutional analyses of "the state" to looking
at social and bureaucratic practices and encounters and at public cultural texts. It
requires conducting institutional ethnographies of specific state bureaucracies,
inquiring into the micropolitics and daily practices of such institutions, and seeking
to understand their relation to the public (elite or subaltern) that they serve. This
might include, for example, following the tracks of bureaucrats in their roles as
state officials and as multiply positioned citizens; attending official meetings;
observing interactions between bureaucrats and citizens on the one hand, and
those between bureaucrats and international agency officials on the other; sitting
in on and participating in everyday public conversations about state work, corruption scandals, and specific officials; attending state rituals, ceremonies, and spectacles, such as parades, political rallies, and development project inaugurations;
and following print and visual media representations of state agencies and officials.
This kind of work will reveal how the boundary between the state and non-state
realms is drawn, how the state is reproduced and challenged as a vertically encom-
passing entity (Ferguson and Gupta 2002), and how power inequalities are shaped
and reinforced through statist practices, interactions, and representations.

It is not, however, enough to examine "the state" as a cultural artifact in and of itself. Rather, the current regime of globalization necessitates that we unhinge the study of the state from the frame of the nation-state. We have argued that a cultural analysis of the state must now be put into a transnational frame. What would the state look like, and what would it mean, in a world where the meaning and function of the nation-state has significantly altered? How do mechanisms of rule operate not simply *within* the borders of nation-states but at a scale and in a space that is of a different order? The reorganization of capital on a global scale has had important repercussions for the regulatory functions of nation-states, both because of new electronics technologies and the speed of transactions, and because the global coordination of markets and suppliers has forced a significant reduction of transaction costs in the movement of goods and commodities across the boundaries of nation-states. The current regime of neoliberal governmentality, which is spreading governmental methods across different contexts and proliferating state-like bodies that operate transnationally, is reconfiguring conventional and territorial notions of the state, of state power, and of rule. The task for contemporary anthropology, therefore, is to examine exactly what these transformations look like and entail in particular locations, and how they complicate and enhance our understandings of the workings of rule, power, and the nation-state. Indeed, if we are in the midst of a post-national order, as some contend, can we also imagine this moment of transnational governmentality holds the possibility of a post-statist order?

Overlaying the culture and transnational frames when analyzing states brings up one final issue: if we say that the state is culturally constituted, but culture itself is globalized, then what does transnational governmentality mean in cultural terms? Put differently, how can we think of the culture of transnational governmentality? Governmentality, like the state, has been generally approached as a universal idea whose structural and functional specification means that it is not located anywhere. However, different forms and techniques of governmentality have their own cultural moorings. How conduct is conducted, towards what ends, what care means, how "welfare" is perceived, and how a national population or community is defined are *cultural* questions that need to be interrogated.

Let us invoke the global development regime one final time, as a key example and modality of transnational governmentality, to sketch some of the issues surrounding the "culture of governmentality." Development programs for the care of specifically defined populations such as "the poor," "the disempowered," or "the underdeveloped" are implemented all over the world. Despite employing a sophisticated understanding of "local" needs and the contexts in which they operate, such programs continue to be based on a set of universalized norms and hegemonic meanings of poverty, disempowerment, and tradition (see Escobar 1995; Esteva 1992; Ferguson 1994). Even though poverty may manifest itself differently in different places, and poor people in these places may have different perceptions of their situations and needs, development discourse expounds and circulates a dominant understanding of poverty (it is essentially defined by a common set of indicators the world over, by "the lack of ...") and a general model for addressing it. Similarly, healthcare programs define the "problem" of health in a particular way, and encode hegemonic interpretations of what counts as "health," what is defined as an unhealthy body, and how the "problem" of ill health needs to addressed through "traditional" (read "culturally appropriate") means. Even programs that attempt to account for cultural difference deploy this universalist logic. Stacy Pigg (1997) shows, for example, that programs directed at training "Traditional Medical Practitioners" or TMPs, while mindful of culturally variant ideas and practices of healthcare, are premised on the universal assumption that TMPs exist in all societies and they can be productively annexed to address local health concerns in a locally sensitive manner.

While these development programs may be based on dominant (Northern) meanings and techniques, how people in different places interpret these meanings, and how they experience these practices, are overdetermined by a variety of factors. The experiences and understandings of the "target population" as they encounter these programs, and the meaning they make of them, are also shaped by their sedimented histories and memories, their place and time. Deeply layered understandings of development, health, or "welfare," in any one place may lead to quite divergent interactions, meaning making, and consequences. In a similar vein, globalized representations of the state in the present neoliberal context put a particular spin on how the state should be. The currently hegemonic images of good and lean government, and the "enterprise model" (Burchell 1996) of the state (that is, firm-like in its organization and behavior, following "best practices"), certainly affect both bureaucrats' and citizens' imaginations of the state. Yet how exactly these globalized representations meet sedimented ideas and expectations, and what specific affects they produce, are contingent on time, place, and historical memory.

The cultural outcomes of these complex interactions are not predetermined. We cannot know beforehand whether the localization of transnational neoliberal discourses will produce stable effects in reproducing hegemonic understandings of the state or not, or how it will transform the forms and institutions of governance. All one can say is that there might be some pressure or some general direction in which one might expect transnational governance to proceed. But we cannot predict the outcomes of these processes beforehand; they need to be ethnographically investigated. Analyses of such encounters and the effects they produce will also allow us to see shifts in their effects over time and across contexts.

NOTES

1   An article by Praful Bidwai coining this term provoked a vigorous discussion on the BBC News webpage (http://newsvote.bbc.co.uk/mpapps/pagetoo ... ws.bbc.co. uk/2/ hi/south_asia/3292619.stm). The responses ranged from people who agreed with Bidwai that call centers represented low-end jobs without a future to those who argued that such jobs were better than no employment, and that no one could find

fault with an industry that created 150,000 new jobs in five years where none would have existed for the army of educated unemployed.

2   It should be clear that we are using "North" and "South" not as geographical terms, but as geopolitical ones.

3   See http://www.cwanj.org/news.asp?id=531; accessed 5/7/04.

4   An exception is made for services that are not available in the USA.

5   Ironically, while separatist movements such as those in the Balkans and in Kashmir challenge the territorial sanctity of nation-states and highlight their deeply historical and at times arbitrary construction, they also rely upon the idiom of the nation-state to further their claims (see Hall 1997). While some ethnic movements for sovereign statehood are successful in reorganizing existing nation-states, they also end up reinforcing the naturalized linkages between nation-state, territory, sovereignty, and culture (for a discussion on the changing relationship between people, place, and culture in the context of globalization, see Gupta and Ferguson 1997). These movements raise the issues of *who* has legitimate control over *which* territory; they reorganize the map of the nation through contested and reconstructed definitions of ethnic/cultural/national belonging; however, they do so within the ideological frame of the nation-state, not outside it.

6   For a discussion on the historical (and often contentious) relation between national and state sovereignty, territoriality, and the nation-state, see also Charles Tilly (1975), R. B. J. Walker (1993), R. B. J. Walker and Saul H. Mendlovitz (1990), and Michael Shapiro (1991).

7   Bob Jessop (1999) connects up the (re)organization of the state with the (re)organization of the capitalist regime of accumulation. He argues that the current neoliberal post-Fordist regime has not only seen the decline of the Keynesian Welfare National State (KWNS), which was crucial to the functioning of Atlantic Fordism, but is also seeing the emergence of a qualitatively new state form that is denationalized, destatized, and internationalized.

8   For a discussion of the Marxist/neo-Marxist, and Weberian/neo-Weberian approaches to the study of the state, and how these approaches engage the issue of culture, see Steinmetz 1999.

9   The systems approach, as Mitchell shows, faced the problem of dealing with an object of study – "the political system" – that was too broad and imprecise. Moreover, it theorized the "political" and the "social" as distinct orders of reality. Thus, in working around the difficulties of precisely defining the state and reifying "it," the systems approach ended up reifying "the political" as a separate and identifiable realm.

10 Other scholars have also problematized the rigid conceptual and on-the-ground separation of state and civil society. See Borneman 1998, Chatterjee 1993, Gupta (1995, Chapter 9 in this volume), Navaro-Yashin 2002, and Trouillot 2003.

11 Making the claim that the state is culturally constructed means paying attention to the dynamic, processual, contested, and contextual notions of culture itself. Both everyday and theoretical imaginings of the state are culturally informed, context-specific, and historical. Therefore, we would expect that anthropological theories of state formation, which have been inspired by a common set of ideas about culture and statehood, take a different cast in various regions of the world. Why is it, for instance, that studies of state formation in Latin America are heavily influenced by dependency theories (see Roseberry 1989), whereas in South Asia the Subaltern Studies school (Guha and Spivak 1988) has crucially shaped scholarship on the cultural politics and discursive nature of states (Cohn 1996)? We thank an anonymous reviewer for pointing this out. While we do not develop this argument here, it might be interesting

to explore how theories about the culture of states travel and how they are synthesized in different cultural-historical settings.

12 The exceptions to classic Marxist conceptualizations of the relationship between the state and culture are Althusser (1971) and Gramsci (1971). Gramsci shifted Marxist perspectives on the state by recognizing that in advanced capitalist societies, the nature of revolutionary struggle needed to be altered from the classic conception of a "war of maneuver" to a tactical "war of position" fought largely in the realm of culture. Althusser's work builds on Gramsci's insights by highlighting the crucial role played by ideology and ideological state apparatuses in reproducing relations of production (thus also expanding the sphere of the state).

13 Such ideas could be tremendously important to how states function but reduce the role of "culture" to that of "ideas" (Steinmetz 1999: 18).

14 Julia Paley (2002) discusses the taken-for-grantedness of the meaning of the term "democracy" in typologies of regimes and states as well as in analyses that judge the success or failure of former socialist and military regimes that are "transitioning" to democracy (see also Creed 1998, Greenhouse et al. 2002, Hann 2002, and Verdery 1996a). Rather than assuming an *a priori* definition of democracy, contemporary anthropology's key contribution has been to analyze the discursive nature of democracy in different contexts (for instance, how it is given meaning, what shapes it takes, and what are its effects on power relations).

15 See Bayart (1993) for a critique of the notion of stateless societies.

16 There is now a substantial body of work that makes the case for why culture should matter to theories of the state. In addition to the scholars included in this volume, others such as Alexander 1997, Aretxaga 2000, Bayart 1993, Bourdieu 1999, Brubaker 1992, Clarke 2004, Coronil 1997, Corrigan and Sayer 1985, Darian-Smith and Fitzpatrick 1999, Das and Poole 2004, Enloe 2000, Eyal 2003, Gal and Kligman 2000, Geertz 1980, Hansen and Stepputat 2001, Herzfeld 1992, Jean-Klein 2000, Joseph and Nugent 1994, Kapferer 1988, Mann 1986, Mukerji 1997, Navaro-Yashin 2002, Nelson 1999, Nugent 1997, Steinmetz 1993, Stoler 2004, Taussig 1997, and Verdery 1996a have contributed a great deal to our understanding of the cultural nature of states.

17 For further analysis of the deeply political and cultural nature of bureaucracy, see also Brown, Chapter 8, this volume; Ferguson 1984; Herzfeld 1992; Rose 1996.

18 Similarly, Bernard Cohn (1987) and Arjun Appadurai (1993b) have shown how the census worked as a key technology of rule in colonial India, through which the colonized were rendered legible and manageable, and through which they came to construct and negotiate their social identities and relations with each other and with the state.

19 The national program was launched in 1975. The ICDS program in any one block (a block is an administrative unit consisting of approximately 100 villages) was considered a "project," and each project received funding independently. In Mandi subdistrict (*tehsil*), there were two ICDS programs.

20 The reason why an official might be interested in making up additional trips was to collect a travel allowance that was administered to defray the costs of travel.

21 A Block Development Officer is a government official who oversees the development activities of a block of approximately 100 villages.

22 Statistics are one of the main ways in which people study the actions of states, and states attempt to catalog their activities exhaustively through statistics. For an analysis of the historical role played by statistics in the consolidation of rule and the exercise of biopower, see Ian Hacking (1982, 1991).

23 Examples of ethnographic studies that delve into public cultural representations of the state include Anagnost 1995 and 1997, Gupta 1995 (Chapter 9, this volume), Mbembe 1992 (Chapter 16, this volume), Navaro-Yashin 2002, and Taylor 1997.

24 Michel-Rolph Trouillot (2003) contends that anthropologists are ideally situated to study states "from below" (2003:95). Since the state has no institutional fixity but is an effect of practices and representations, and since state effects do not obtain solely in governmental or national sites, Trouillot argues for studying state effects in multiple locations in which governmental practices are enacted. He particularly emphasizes the need for examining state effects through the subjects and identities they produce.

25 This begs the question if, and to what extent, "Third World" states were ever able to adequately address the needs of their most marginalized populations, and the dangerous implications of the current neoliberal moment for survival of these groups and their relationships to processes of governance (see Sunder Rajan 2003).

26 The literature on disjunctions between legal equality of generically constituted citizens and the substantive inequalities experienced by citizens-constituted-through-difference (race, ethnicity, gender, sexuality, immigrant status, and class) in different national contexts is vast. In addition to the Bhattacharjee (1997) and Coutin (2003) articles included as Chapters 14 and 13 in this volume, see also Alexander 1997, Berlant 1993, Collier et al. 1995, Gal and Kligman 2000, Gilroy 1987, Holston and Caldeira 1998, Humphrey 2002, Maurer 1997, Povinelli 1998, and Verdery 1998.

27 In early 2004, the ruling Bharatiya Janata Party put forward a proposal granting dual citizenship for nationals of certain "First World" states. In January 2005, the Congress party-dominated central government expanded the eligibility criteria somewhat, approving dual citizenship for Indians who had migrated after 1950. The fact that "First World" and oil-rich nations account for a major proportion of post-1950 Indian emigration means that dual citizenship is effectively targeted to nationals of wealthy countries (who have resources to invest in their "home" country).

REFERENCES

Abrams, Philip
   1988 Notes on the Difficulty of Studying the State. Journal of Historical Sociology 1(1):58–89.
Alexander, M. Jacqui
   1997 Erotic Autonomy as a Politics of Decolonization: An Anatomy of Feminist and State Practice in the Bahamas Tourist Economy. In Feminist Genealogies, Colonial Legacies, Democratic Futures. M. J. Alexander and C. T. Mohanty, eds. Pp. 63–100. New York: Routledge.
Almond, Gabriel A., Taylor Cole, and Roy C. Macridis
   1955 A Suggested Research Strategy in Western European Government and Politics. American Political Science Review 49:1042–1044.
Almond, Gabriel A., and James Coleman
   1960 The Politics of the Developing Areas. Princeton, NJ: Princeton University Press.
Althusser, Louis
   1971 Ideology and Ideological State Apparatuses (Notes Towards an Investigation). In Lenin and Philosophy and Other Essays. Pp. 127–186. New York: Monthly Review Press.

Anagnost, Ann
1995 A Surfeit of Bodies: Population and the Rationality of the State in Post-Mao China. In Conceiving the New World Order: The Global Politics of Reproduction. F. Ginsburg and R. Rapp, eds. Pp. 22–41. Berkeley: University of California Press.
1997 National Past-Times: Narrative, Representation, and Power in Modern China. Durham, NC: Duke University Press.

Anderson, Benedict
1983 Imagined Communities: Reflections on the Origins and Spread of Nationalism. London: Verso.

Appadurai, Arjun
1990 Disjuncture and Difference in the Global Political Economy. Public Culture 2(2):1–24.
1993a Patriotism and Its Futures. Public Culture 5(3):411–429.
1993b Number in the Colonial Imagination. In Orientalism and the Postcolonial Predicament. C. Breckenridge and P. van der Veer, eds. Pp. 314–339. Philadelphia: University of Pennsylvania Press.
2002 Deep Democracy: Urban Governmentality and the Horizon of Politics. Public Culture 14(1):21–47.

Aretxaga, Begona
2000 Playing Terrorist: Ghastly Plots and the Ghostly State. Journal of Spanish Cultural Studies 1(1):43–58.
2003 Maddening States. Annual Review of Anthropology 32:393–410.

Balibar, Etienne
2003 We, the People of Europe? Reflections on Transnational Citizenship (Translation/Transnation). J. Swenson, trans. Princeton, NJ: Princeton University Press.

Barry, Andrew, Thomas Osborne, and Nikolas Rose
1996 Introduction. In Foucault and Political Reason: Liberalism, Neo-Liberalism, and Rationalities of Government. A. Barry, T. Osborne, and N. Rose, eds. Pp. 1–18. Chicago: University of Chicago Press.

Basch, Linda, Nina Glick Schiller, and Cristina Szanton Blanc, eds.
1994 Nations Unbound: Transnational Projects, Postcolonial Predicaments, and Deterritorialized Nation-States. Langhorne, PA: Gordon and Breach.

Bayart, Jean-François
1993 The State in Africa: The Politics of the Belly. New York: Longman.

Berlant, Lauren
1993 The Theory of Infantine Citizenship. Public Culture 5:395–410.

Bhattacharjee, Anannya
1997 The Public/Private Mirage: Mapping Homes and Undomesticating Violence Work in the South Asian Immigrant Community. In Feminist Genealogies, Colonial Legacies, Democratic Futures. J. M. Alexander and C. T. Mohanty, eds. Pp. 308–329. New York: Routledge.

Bidwai, Praful
2003 The Rise of the Cyber-Coolies. New Statesman, November 10: 32–33.

Borneman, John
1993 Uniting the German Nation: Law, Narrative and Historicity. American Ethnologist 20(2):288–311.
1998 Subversions of International Order: Studies in Political Anthropology of Culture. Albany: State University of New York Press.

Bornstein, Erica
2003 The Spirit of Development: Protestant NGOs, Morality, and Economics in Zimbabwe. New York: Routledge.

Bourdieu, Pierre
  1999 Rethinking the State: Genesis and Structure of the Bureaucratic Field. *In* State/
      Culture: State Formation after the Cultural Turn. G. Steinmetz, ed. Loic Wacquant
      and Samar Farage, trans. Pp. 53–75. Ithaca, NY: Cornell University Press.
Brow, James
  1996 Demons and Development: The Struggle for Community in a Sri Lankan Village.
      Tucson: University of Arizona Press.
Brown, Wendy
  1995 Finding the Man in the State. *In* States of Inquiry: Power and Freedom in Late
      Modernity. Pp. 166–196. Princeton, NJ: Princeton University Press.
Brubaker, Rogers
  1992 Citizenship and Nationhood in France and Germany. Cambridge, MA: Harvard
      University Press.
Burawoy, Michael, and Katherine Verdery, eds.
  1999 Uncertain Transition: Ethnographies of Change in the Postsocialist World. New
      York: Rowman and Littlefield.
Burchell, Graham
  1996 Liberal Government and the Techniques of the Self. *In* Foucault and Political
      Reason: Liberalism, Neo-liberalism and Rationalities of Government. A. Barry, T.
      Osborne, and N. Rose, eds. Pp. 19–36. Chicago: University of Chicago Press.
Burchell, Graham, Colin Gordon, and Peter Miller, eds.
  1991 The Foucault Effect: Studies in Governmentality (with Two Lectures by and an
      Interview with Michel Foucault). Chicago: University of Chicago Press.
Butler, Judith
  1990 Gender Trouble: Feminism and the Subversion of Identity. New York: Routledge.
Chatterjee, Partha
  1993 The Nation and Its Fragments: Colonial and Postcolonial Histories. Princeton,
      NJ: Princeton University Press.
  1998 Development Planning and the Indian State. *In* State and Politics in India. P.
      Chatterjee, ed. Pp. 271–297. Delhi: Oxford University Press.
  2004 The Politics of the Governed: Reflections on Popular Politics in Most of the
      World. New York: Columbia University Press.
Clarke, John
  2004 Changing Welfare, Changing States: New Directions in Social Policy. Thousand
      Oaks, CA: Sage.
Cohn, Bernard S.
  1987 The Census, Social Structure and Objectification in South Asia. *In* An Anthropologist
      Among the Historians and Other Essays. Pp. 224–254. Delhi: Oxford University Press.
  1996 Colonialism and Its Forms of Knowledge: The British in India. Princeton, NJ:
      Princeton University Press.
  1997 The Magical State: Nature, Money, and Modernity in Venezuela. Chicago:
      University of Chicago Press.
Collier, Jane F., Bill Maurer, and Liliana Suarez-Navaz
  1995 Sanctioned Identities: Legal Constructions of Modern Personhood. Identities
      2(1–2):1–27.
Coronil, Fernando
  1997 The Magical State: Nature, Money, and Modernity in Venezuela. Chicago:
      University of Chicago Press.
Corrigan, Philip, and Derek Sayer
  1985 The Great Arch: English State Formation as Cultural Revolution. Oxford: Basil
      Blackwell.

Coutin, Susan Bibler
  2003   Cultural Logics of Belonging and Movement: Transnationalism, Naturalization, and U.S. Immigration Politics. American Ethnologist 30(4):508–526.
Creed, Gerald
  1998   Domesticating Revolution: From Socialist Reform to Ambivalent Transition in a Bulgarian Village. University Park, PA: Pennsylvania State University Press.
Cruikshank, Barbara
  1999   The Will to Empower: Democratic Citizens and Other Subjects. Ithaca, NY: Cornell University Press.
Darian-Smith, Eve, and Peter Fitzpatrick
  1999   Laws of the Postcolonial. Ann Arbor: University of Michigan Press.
Das, Veena, and Deborah Poole, eds.
  2004   Anthropology in the Margins of the State. School of American Research Seminar Series. Santa Fe, NM: School of American Research Press.
Dean, Mitchell
  1999   Governmentality: Power and Rule in Modern Society. London: Sage.
DiCarlo, Lisa
  2003   Face of the Year. Electronic document. http://www.forbes.com/2003/12/19/cx_ld_1219faceoftheyear.html.
Easton, David
  1953   The Political System: An Inquiry into the State of Political Science. New York: Knopf.
  1957   An Approach to the Analysis of Political Systems. World Politics 9:383–400.
Enloe, Cynthia
  2000   Maneuvers: The International Politics of Militarizing Women's Lives. Berkeley: University of California Press.
Escobar, Arturo
  1995   Encountering Development: The Making and Unmaking of the Third World. Princeton, NJ: Princeton University Press.
Esteva, Gustavo
  1992   Development. In The Development Dictionary: A Guide to Knowledge as Power. W. Sachs, ed. Pp. 6–25. Atlantic Highlands, New Jersey: Zed Books.
Evans, Peter B., Dietrich Rueschemeyer, and Theda Skocpol, eds.
  1985   Bringing the State Back In. Cambridge: Cambridge University Press.
Eyal, Gil
  2003   The Origins of Postcommunist Elites: From Prague Spring to the Breakup of Czechoslovakia. Minneapolis: University of Minnesota Press.
Ferguson, James
  1994   The Anti-Politics Machine: "Development," Depoliticization, and Bureaucratic Power in Lesotho. Minneapolis: University of Minnesota Press.
Ferguson, James, and Akhil Gupta
  2002   Spatializing States: Toward an Ethnography of Neoliberal Governmentality. American Ethnologist 29(4):981–1002.
Ferguson, Kathy E.
  1984   The Feminist Case Against Bureaucracy. Philadelphia, PA: Temple University Press.
Foucault, Michel
  1979   Discipline and Punish: The Birth of a Prison. New York: Random House.
  1991   Governmentality. In The Foucault Effect: Studies in Governmentality. G. Burchell, C. Gordon, and P. Miller, eds. Pp. 87–104. London: Harvester/Wheatsheaf.

Freeman, Carla
    2002   Designing Women: Corporate Discipline and Barbados's Off-shore Pink-collar
           Sector. *In* The Anthropology of Globalization: A Reader. J. X. Inda and R. Rosaldo Jr.,
           eds. Pp. 83–99. Malden, MA: Blackwell.
Friedman, Thomas L.
    1999   The Lexus and the Olive Tree. New York: Farrar, Straus and Giroux.
    2004   Will India Seize the Moment? The Seattle Post-Intelligencer, March 24: B7.
Gal, Susan, and Gail Kligman
    2000   The Politics of Gender after Socialism. Princeton, NJ: Princeton University Press.
Geertz, Clifford
    1980   Negara: The Theatre State In Nineteenth-Century Bali. Princeton, NJ: Princeton
           University Press.
Gilroy, Paul
    1987   There Ain't No Black in the Union Jack: The Cultural Politics of Race and
           Nation. London: Hutchinson.
Glick Schiller, Nina, Linda Basch, and Cristina Blanc-Szanton, eds.
    1992   Towards a Transnational Perspective on Migration: Race, Class, Ethnicity, and
           Nationalism Reconsidered. New York: New York Academy of Sciences.
Gramsci, Antonio
    1971   Selections from the Prison Notebooks. Q. Hoare and G. N. Smith trans. New
           York: International Publishers.
Greenhouse, Carol, Elizabeth Mertz, and Kay B. Warren, eds.
    2002   Ethnography in Unstable Places: Everyday Lives in Contexts of Dramatic Polit-
           ical Change. Durham, NC: Duke University Press.
Grewal, Inderpal
    1998   On the New Global Feminism and the Family of Nations: Dilemmas of Trans-
           national Feminist Practice. *In* Talking Visions: Multicultural Feminism in a Trans-
           national Age. E. Shohat, ed. Pp. 501–530. Cambridge, MA: MIT Press.
Guha, Ranajit, and Gayatri Chakravorty Spivak
    1988   Selected Subaltern Studies. Delhi: Oxford University Press.
Gupta, Akhil
    1995   Blurred Boundaries: The Discourse of Corruption, the Culture of Politics, and
           the Imagined State. American Ethnologist 22(2):375–402.
    1998   Postcolonial Developments: Agriculture in the Making of Modern India. Dur-
           ham, NC: Duke University Press.
    2001   Governing Population: The Integrated Child Development Services Program
           in India. *In* States of Imagination: Ethnographic Explorations of the Postcolonial State.
           T. B. Hansen and F. Stepputat, eds. Pp. 65–96. Durham, NC: Duke University Press.
Gupta, Akhil, and James Ferguson
    1997   Beyond "Culture": Space, Identity, and the Politics of Difference. *In* Culture,
           Power, Place: Explorations in Critical Anthropology. A. Gupta and J. Ferguson, eds.
           Pp. 33–51. Durham, NC: Duke University Press.
Hacking, Ian
    1982   Biopower and the Avalanche of Printed Numbers. Humanities in Society 5
           (3 & 4): 279–295.
    1991   How Should We Do the History of Statistics? *In* The Foucault Effect: Studies in
           Governmentality. G. Burchell, C. Gordon, and P. Miller, eds. Pp. 181–196. Chicago:
           University of Chicago Press.
Hall, Stuart
    1986   Popular Culture and the State. *In* Popular Culture and Social Relations. T. Bennett,
           C. Mercer, and J. Woollacott, eds. Pp. 22–49. Milton Keynes: Open University Press.

1997   The Local and the Global: Globalization and Ethnicity. *In* Culture, Globalization and the World System: Contemporary Conditions for the Representation of Identity. A. King, ed. Pp. 19–39. Minneapolis: University of Minnesota Press.

Hann, Chris M., ed.
2002   Postsocialism: Ideals, Ideologies and Practices in Eurasia. New York: Routledge.

Hansen, Thomas Blom, and Finn Stepputat, eds.
2001   States of Imagination: Ethnographic Explorations of the Postcolonial State. Durham, NC: Duke University Press.

Hemment, Julie
1999   Gendered Violence in Crisis: Russian NGOs Help Themselves to Liberal Feminist Discourse. Anthropology of Eastern Europe Review 17(1):35–58.

Herzfeld, Michael
1992   The Social Production of Indifference: Exploring the Symbolic Roots of Western Bureaucracy. Chicago: University of Chicago Press.

Higgott, Richard A., Geoffrey R. D. Underhill, and Andreas Bieler, eds.
2000   Non-State Actors and Authority in the Global System. London: Routledge.

Holston, James and Teresa P. R. Caldeira
1998   Democracy, Law, and Violence: Disjunctions of Brazilian Citizenship. *In* Fault Lines of Democracy in Post-Transition Latin America. F. Aguero and J. Stark, eds. Pp. 263–296. Miami, FL: North-South Center.

Humphrey, Caroline
2002   The Unmaking of Soviet Life: Everyday Economies After Socialism. Ithaca, NY: Cornell University Press.

Jean-Klein, Iris
2000   Mothercraft, Statecraft, and Subjectivity in the Palestinian Intifada. American Ethnologist 29(1):100–127.

Jessop, Bob
1982   The Capitalist State: Marxist Theories and Methods. New York: New York University Press.
1990   Anti-Marxist Reinstatement and Post-Marxist Deconstruction. *In* State Theory: Putting States in Their Place. Pp. 278–306. University Park: Pennsylvania State University Press.
1999   Narrating the Future of the National Economy and the National State: Remarks on Remapping Regulation and Reinventing Governance. *In* State/Culture: State Formation After the Cultural Turn. G. Steinmetz, ed. Pp. 378–405. Ithaca, NY: Cornell University Press.

Joseph, Gilbert M., and Daniel Nugent, eds.
1994   Everyday Forms of State Formation: Revolution and the Negotiation of Rule in Rural Mexico. Durham, NC: Duke University Press.

Kapferer, Bruce
1988   Legends of People, Myths of State: Violence, Intolerance and Political Culture in Sri Lanka and Australia. Washington, DC: Smithsonian Institution Press.

Keck, Margaret E., and Kathryn Sikkink
1998   Activists Beyond Borders: Advocacy Networks in International Politics. Ithaca, NY: Cornell University Press.

Kothari, Rajni
1995   Globalization and "New World Order": What Future for the United Nations? Economic and Political Weekly of India:2513–2517.

Kothari, Smitu, and Harsh Sethi, eds.
1991   Rethinking Human Rights. Delhi: Lokayan.

Krasner, Stephen D.
   1978   Defending the National Interest: Raw Materials Investments and U.S. Foreign
          Policy. Princeton, NJ: Princeton University Press.
Leve, Lauren
   2001   Between Jesse Helms and Ram Bahadur: Women, "Participation," and "Empower-
          ment" in Nepal. PoLAR: Political and Legal Anthropology Review 24(1):108–128.
Ludden, David
   1992   India's Development Regime. In Colonialism and Culture. N. B. Dirks, ed.
          Pp. 247–287. Ann Arbor: University of Michigan Press.
Lutz, Catherine
   2002   Making War at Home in the United States: Militarization and the Current Crisis.
          American Anthropologist 104(3):723–735.
MacKinnon, Catharine A.
   1989   Toward a Feminist Theory of the State. Cambridge, MA: Harvard University
          Press.
Malkki, Liisa
   1995   Purity and Exile: Violence, Memory, and National Cosmology among Hutu
          Refugees in Tanzania. Chicago: University of Chicago Press.
Mankekar, Purnima
   1999   Brides Who Travel: Gender, Transnationalism, and Nationalism in Hindi Films.
          Positions 7(3):731–761.
Mann, Michael
   1986   The Sources of Social Power. New York: Cambridge University Press.
Maurer, Bill
   1997   Recharting the Caribbean: Land, Law, and Citizenship in the British Virgin
          Islands. Ann Arbor: University of Michigan Press.
Mbembe, Achille
   1992   The Banality of Power and the Aesthetics of Vulgarity in the Postcolony. Public
          Culture 4(2): 1–30.
Merry, Sally E.
   2001   Spatial Governmentality and the New Urban Social Order: Controlling Gender
          Violence through Law. American Anthropologist 103(1):16–29.
Mitchell, Timothy
   1991a   America's Egypt: Discourse of the Development Industry. Middle East Report
          21(2):18–36.
   1991b   The Limits of the State: Beyond Statist Approaches and Their Critics. American
          Political Science Review 85(1):77–96.
   1999   Society, Economy, and the State Effect. In State/Culture: State Formation after
          the Cultural Turn. G. Steinmetz, ed. Pp. 76–97. Ithaca, NY: Cornell University Press.
Mukerji, Chandra
   1997   Territorial Ambitions and the Gardens of Versailles. New York: Cambridge
          University Press.
Navaro-Yashin, Yael
   2002   Faces Of The State: Secularism and Public Life in Turkey. Princeton, NJ: Prince-
          ton University Press.
Nelson, Diane
   1999   A Finger in the Wound: Body Politics in Quincentennial Guatemala. Berkeley:
          University of California Press.
Nugent, David
   1997   Modernity at the Edge of Empire: State, Individual, and Nation in the Northern
          Peruvian Andes, 1885–1935. Stanford, CA: Stanford University Press.

Ohmae, Kenichi
    1990   The Borderless World: Power and Strategy in the Interlinked Economy. London: Collins.
    1995   The End of the Nation State: The Rise of Regional Economies. New York: Free Press.
Ong, Aihwa
    1999   Flexible Citizenship: The Cultural Logics of Transnationality. Durham, NC: Duke University Press.
Paley, Julia
    2001   Marketing Democracy: Power and Social Movements in Post-Dictatorship Chile. Berkeley: University of California Press.
    2002   Toward an Anthropology of Democracy. Annual Review of Anthropology 31:469–496.
Pigg, Stacy Leigh
    1997   Found in Most Traditional Societies: Traditional Medical Practitioners between Culture and Development. In International Development and the Social Sciences: Essays on the History and Politics of Knowledge. F. Cooper and R. Packard, eds. Pp. 259–290. Berkeley: University of California Press.
Povinelli, Elizabeth A.
    1998   The State of Shame: Australian Multiculturalism and the Crisis of Indigenous Citizenship. Critical Inquiry 24:575–610.
Radcliffe-Brown, A. R.
    1940   Preface. In African Political Systems. M. Fortes and E. E. Evans-Pritchard, eds. P. xxi. London: International Institute of African Languages and Cultures/Oxford University Press.
Robson, Judy
    2004   Indiafare Electronic document. http://www.fightingbob.com/article.cfm?article ID=158, January 3. Last accessed May 7, 2004.
Rose, Nikolas
    1996   Governing "Advanced" Liberal Democracies. In Foucault and Political Reason: Liberalism, Neo-liberalism and Rationalities of Government. A. Barry, T. Osborne, and N. Rose, eds. Pp. 37–64. Chicago: University of Chicago Press.
    1999   Governing the Soul: The Shaping of the Private Self. London: Free Association Books.
Roseberry, William
    1989   Anthropologies and Histories: Essays in Political Culture, History, and Political Economy. New Brunswick, NJ: Rutgers University Press.
Ruggie, John Gerard
    1993   Territoriality and Beyond: Problematizing Modernity in International Relations. International Organization 47(1):139–174.
Sassen, Saskia
    1996   Losing Control: Sovereignty in an Age of Globalization. New York: Columbia University Press.
    1998   Globalization and Its Discontents. New York: New Press.
Scott, David
    1999   Colonial Governmentality. In Refashioning Futures: Criticism After Postcoloniality. Pp. 23–52. Princeton Studies in Culture/Power/History. Princeton, NJ: Princeton University Press.
Scott, James C.
    1998   Seeing Like a State: How Certain Schemes to Improve the Human Condition Have Failed. New Haven, CT: Yale University Press.

Shapiro, Michael
  1991   Sovereignty and Exchange in the Orders of Modernity. Alternatives 16(4):447–
     477.
Sharma, Aradhana
  forthcoming   Cross-breeding Institutions, Breeding Struggle: Women's "Empowerment,"
     Neoliberal Governmentality, and State (Re)Formation in India Cultural Anthropology.
Sikkink, Kathryn
  1993   Human Rights, Principled Issue-Networks, and Sovereignty in Latin America.
     International Organization 47(3):411–441.
Skocpol, Theda
  1979   States and Social Revolutions: A Comparative Analysis of France, Russia, and
     China. Cambridge: Cambridge University Press.
Steinmetz, George
  1993   Regulating the Social: The Welfare State and Local Politics in Imperial Germany.
     Princeton, NJ: Princeton University Press.
Steinmetz, George, ed.
  1999   State/Culture: State-Formation After the Cultural Turn. Ithaca, NY: Cornell
     University Press.
Stiglitz, Joseph E.
  2002   Globalization and Its Discontents. New York: W.W. Norton.
Stoler, Ann L.
  1995   Race and the Education of Desire: Foucault's History of Sexuality and the
     Colonial Order of Things. Durham, NC: Duke University Press.
  2004   Affective States. In A Companion to the Anthropology of Politics. D. Nugent and
     J. Vincent, eds. Pp. 4–20. Malden, MA: Blackwell.
Strange, Susan
  1996   The Retreat of the State. Cambridge: Cambridge University Press.
Sunder Rajan, Rajeswari
  2003   The Scandal of the State: Women, Law, and Citizenship in Postcolonial India.
     Durham, NC: Duke University Press.
Taussig, Michael T.
  1997   The Magic of the State. New York: Routledge.
Taylor, Diana
  1997   Disappearing Acts: Spectacles of Gender and Nationalism in Argentina's "Dirty
     War". Durham, NC: Duke University Press.
Tennekoon, Serena N.
  1988   Rituals of Development: The Accelerated Mahavali Development Program in Sri
     Lanka. American Ethnologist 15(2):294–310.
Tilly, Charles
  1975   The Formation of National States in Western Europe. Princeton, NJ: Princeton
     University Press.
Trouillot, Michel-Rolph
  2003   The Anthropology of the State in the Age of Globalization: Close Encounters of
     the Deceptive Kind. In Global Transformations: Anthropology and the Modern
     World. Pp. 79–96. New York: Palgrave Macmillan.
Verdery, Katherine
  1996a   What Was Socialism, And What Comes Next? Princeton, NJ: Princeton Uni-
     versity Press.
  1996b   Faith, Hope and Caritas in the Land of the Pyramids, Romania, 1990–1994. In
     What Was Socialism, And What Comes Next. Pp. 168–203. Princeton, NJ: Princeton
     University Press.

1998   Transnationalism, Nationalism, Citizenship, and Property: Eastern Europe Since 1989. American Ethnologist 25(2):291–306.

Walker, R. B. J.
1993   Inside/Outside: International Relations as Political Theory. Cambridge: Cambridge University Press.

Walker, R. B. J., and Saul H. Mendlovitz
1990   Interrogating State Sovereignty. *In* Contending Sovereignties: Redefining Political Community. R. B. J. Walker and S. H. Mendlovitz, eds. Boulder, Co: Lynne Rienner.

Weber, Max
1968   Bureaucracy. *In* Economy and Society: An Outline of Interpretive Sociology. G. Roth and C. Wittich, eds. Pp. 956–1005, Vol. 2. New York: Bedminster Press.

Worth, Robert F.
2002   In New York Tickets, Ghana Sees Orderly City. New York Times, July 22: A1-B2. New York.

Yurchak, Alexei
2002   Entrepreneurial Governmentality in Post-Socialist Russia: A Cultural Investigation of Business Practices. *In* The New Entrepreneurs of Europe and Asia. V. Bonnell and T. Gold, eds. Armonk, NY: M. E. Sharpe.

Part I
Theoretical Genealogies

Introduction

The articles in this part examine Western states, societies, and governance at different historical moments, and take us from sixteenth-century Europe to the present neo-liberal context. Although their authors represent different theoretical standpoints, they all interrogate the nature of the state and grapple with questions of power and rule.

All the authors in this section interrogate the boundary between states and societies and compel us to consider rule more broadly. They force us to think of the state not simply as a set of government agencies and functions that are clearly marked off from society at large. Indeed, they delineate how social relations in institutions such as schools, churches, and families, which are normally thought to lie on the "society" side of the state–society dichotomy, are annexed to the project of domination and governance.

Antonio Gramsci and Louis Althusser creatively extend the classic Marxist conception of the state in new directions. Rather than forwarding an instrumental vision of the state as a tool of the capitalist class, Gramsci and Althusser expand the theorization of the state by giving a central role to culture. They demonstrate the critical function of civil society in both consolidating and challenging the rule of dominant classes. Gramsci discusses the ethical-cultural state, highlighting its role in forming and transforming individuals and groups, and in educating consent to a particular regime of domination. At times Gramsci seems to argue that the state is the entire apparatus (including civil society or "private" institutions and procedures) that dominant classes must mobilize in their attempts to consolidate their hegemony. Althusser builds on Gramsci's theorization of culture in his examination of the role of ideology and ideological state apparatuses. Althusser argues that social structures, such as the media, schools, church, family, and political parties, are connected to the state. He illustrates the central role that such institutions, which he terms Ideological State Apparatuses or ISAs (because they work primarily through ideology and not repression), play in the *reproduction* of the relations of production. These ISAs are also key sites for struggles against hegemonic ideologies. Like Gramsci, Althusser both underscores the importance of cultural struggles to class politics and expands the conventional arena of the state.

In his classic account of bureaucracy, Max Weber too questions the boundaries of the state by discussing bureaucratization as a social phenomenon that is not limited to the state. In Weber's view, bureaucracy is a dehumanized system of impersonal, rationalized procedures and rules. Weber argues that capitalist modernity entails a bureaucratic rationalization of all aspects of social life. The extension of bureaucratic organization and procedures throughout society becomes a crucial and specifically "modern" way to legitimize domination and rule, to quell protest, and to inhibit social change. The routine operation of bureaucracies creates and maintains the socioeconomic order, social hierarchies, and the private–public distinction.

Philip Abrams extends and critically interrogates Marxist and Weberian notions of the state by posing anew the question, "What is the state?" He warns against reifying the state as an ontological and material object. The state is neither a thing, nor a political reality that stands behind the state system (government agencies and political practices) and the state idea. He proposes that we seriously examine the *idea* of the state, which has been so influential, but that we suspend *belief* in the real existence of the state as a backstage political reality. Abrams describes the state idea variously as an ideological project that legitimates subjection, a claim to domination, a mask that hides the institutionalization of political power in the state system, a unifying misrepresentation of the actual disunity and incoherence of the workings of political power and government practices, and an exercise in moral regulation. These descriptors, which highlight ideological, moral, and regulatory dimensions, clearly hark back to Gramsci. If the state is an exercise that legitimizes patently illegitimate domination, Abrams continues, then the study of the state should involve examining precisely how this legitimation proceeds and how it is consolidated; in other words, analyzing how politically organized social subjection is carried out. Abrams emphasizes the importance of looking at coercive state institutions like prisons and the military in ensuring legitimation. He stresses political practices and the processes that legitimize domination in opposition to those who reify the state as an invisible structure that shapes existing institutions. Such a focus on political practices and legitimation exercises exceeds an exclusive concern with the institutional state system.

The project of examining the spread of practices and processes of governance to different social realms beyond state agencies is carried forward by Michel Foucault and Nikolas Rose, who also disentangle strategies of rule from state institutions and relocate them elsewhere. For these scholars the state is but one modality of government, and not the only source and seat of power. They discuss the forms, institutions, and mechanisms of rule specific to pre-modern or monarchical systems of power, and to liberal, welfare, and neoliberal nation-states. They also delineate the concomitant shifts in the nature and form of the state.

Using the concept of governmentality, Foucault explains the transition from (repressive) sovereign power, which was concerned solely with control over territory, to a form of power and rule that is centrally concerned with the welfare of the population. The care and security of the aggregate population, in other words, becomes the object of government intervention. Rose focuses on the current "post-welfare" period of advanced liberalism or neoliberalism. This era, dominated by the market mentality and its related discourse of small government, efficiency, and competition, has refocused attention on newly reconstituted individuals who exercise free choice in pursuing their own well-being and advancement. Mechanisms of governance have now shifted to these individuals and the communities to which they belong. Who needs a big, centralized state or "big government" to reproduce unequal power relations when the same outcome can be achieved by mechanisms of power and systems of rule that produce self-governing, self-empowering, self-fulfilling individuals and communities?

The second main conversation that most of these authors engage in, which we want to briefly highlight here, concerns knowledge, disciplines, and professional expertise, and their connections with power and rule. Weber provides the example of bureaucrats and the production of specialized, official knowledge; Abrams delineates the role played by political sociologists and Marxists in the reification of the state that has important implications for political struggles; Foucault and Rose mention the role played by political economists, statisticians, sociologists, and hygienists in the working of governmentality; Althusser highlights the role of teachers in his discussion of schools; and Gramsci talks of the "educative" state. In order to govern, one needs to know the object to be regulated, and trained experts are the bearers of this knowledge. The authority and social rank of experts rests on varied factors, including disciplinary training, claim to exclusive knowledge, special examinations, or even political sanction. Governance and expert knowledge are integrally enmeshed. Rule relies on a network of knowledges and experts to both construct the object of governmental intervention in such a way as to make it manageable, and to legitimize the exercise of authority.

SUGGESTED READINGS

Barry, Andrew, Thomas Osborne, and Nikolas Rose, eds.
    1996   Foucault and Political Reason: Liberalism, Neo-Liberalism, and Rationalities of Government. Chicago: University of Chicago Press.
Bourdieu, Pierre
    1999   Rethinking the State: Genesis and Structure of the Bureaucratic Field. *In* State/Culture: State Formation after the Cultural Turn. G. Steinmetz, ed. Loïc Wacquant and Samar Farage, trans. Pp. 53–75. Ithaca, NY: Cornell University Press.
Burchell, Graham, Colin Gordon, and Peter Miller, eds.
    1991   The Foucault Effect: Studies in Governmentality (with Two Lectures by and an Interview with Michel Foucault). Chicago: University of Chicago Press.

Carnoy, Martin
    1984   The State and Political Society. Princeton, NJ: Princeton University Press.
Corrigan, Philip, and Derek Sayer
    1985   The Great Arch: English State Formation as Cultural Revolution. Oxford: Basil Blackwell.
Dean, Mitchell
    1999   Governmentality: Power and Rule in Modern Society. London: Sage.
Donzelot, Jacques
    1980   The Policing of Families. R. Hurley, trans. New York: Pantheon Books.
Engels, Frederick
    1959   Ludwig Feuerbach and the End of Classical German Philosophy. *In* Marx and Engels: Basic Writings on Politics and Philosophy. L. Feuer, ed. New York: Doubleday.
    1972   The Origin of the Family, Private Property and the State. E. B. Leacock, ed. New York: International Publishers.
Evans, Peter B., Dietrich Rueschemeyer, and Theda Skocpol, eds.
    1985   Bringing the State Back In. Cambridge: Cambridge University Press.
Foucault, Michel
    1979   Discipline and Punish: The Birth of the Prison. New York: Random House.
    1980   Power/Knowledge: Selected Interviews and Other Writings 1972–1977. C. Gordon, ed. New York: Pantheon Books.
Held, David
    1989   Political Theory and the Modern State. Stanford, CA: Stanford University Press.
Jessop, Bob
    1982   The Capitalist State: Marxist Theories and Methods. New York: New York University Press.
Lenin, V. I.
    1943   State and Revolution. New York: International Publishers.
Lloyd, David, and Paul Thomas
    1998   Culture and the State. New York: Routledge.
Marx, Karl
    1963   The Eighteenth Brumaire of Louis Bonaparte. New York: International Publishers.
Miliband, Ralph
    1969   The State in Capitalist Society. New York: Basic Books.
Nettl, J. P.
    1968   The State as a Conceptual Variable. World Politics 20:559–92.
Poulantzas, Nikos
    1973   Political Power and Social Classes. London: New Left Books.
    1978   State, Power, Socialism. London: Verso.
Radcliffe-Brown, A. R.
    1940   Preface. *In* African Political Systems. M. Fortes and E. E. Evans-Pritchard, eds. P. xxi. London: International Institute of African Languages and Cultures/Oxford University Press.
Taussig, Michael T.
    1992   Maleficium: State Fetishism. *In* The Nervous System. Pp. 111–140. New York: Routledge.
Trouillot, Michel-Rolph
    2003   The Anthropology of the State in the Age of Globalization: Close Encounters of the Deceptive Kind. *In* Global Transformations: Anthropology and the Modern World. Pp. 79–96. New York: Palgrave Macmillan.

1

Bureaucracy

Max Weber

Characteristics of Modern Bureaucracy

Modern officialdom functions in the following manner:

I. There is the principle of official *jurisdictional areas*, which are generally ordered by rules, that is, by laws or administrative regulations. This means:

(1) The regular activities required for the purposes of the bureaucratically governed structure are assigned as official duties.

(2) The authority to give the commands required for the discharge of these duties is distributed in a stable way and is strictly delimited by rules concerning the coercive means, physical, sacerdotal, or otherwise, which may be placed at the disposal of officials.

(3) Methodical provision is made for the regular and continuous fulfillment of these duties and for the exercise of the corresponding rights; only persons who qualify under general rules are employed.

In the sphere of the state these three elements constitute a bureaucratic *agency*, in the sphere of the private economy they constitute a bureaucratic *enterprise*. Bureaucracy, thus understood, is fully developed in political and ecclesiastical communities only in the modern state, and in the private economy only in the most advanced institutions of capitalism. . . .

II. The principles of *office hierarchy* and of channels of appeal (*Instanzenzug*) stipulate a clearly established system of super- and subordination in which there is a supervision of the lower offices by the higher ones. Such a system offers the governed the possibility of appealing, in a precisely regulated manner, the decision of a lower office to the corresponding superior authority. With the full development of the bureaucratic type, the office hierarchy is *monocratically* organized. The principle of hierarchical office authority is found in all bureaucratic structures: in state and ecclesiastical structures as well as in large party organizations and private en-

From G. Roth and C. Wittich, *Economy and Society: An Outline of Interpretive Sociology*, trans. E. Fischoff, H. Gerth, A. M. Henderson, F. Kolegar, C. Wright Mills, T. Parsons, M. Rheinstein, G. Roth, E. Shils, and C. Wittich, pp. 956–1005. New York: Bedminster Press, 1968.

terprises. It does not matter for the character of bureaucracy whether its authority is called "private" or "public."

When the principle of jurisdictional "competency" is fully carried through, hierarchical subordination – at least in public office – does not mean that the "higher" authority is authorized simply to take over the business of the "lower." Indeed, the opposite is the rule; once an office has been set up, a new incumbent will always be appointed if a vacancy occurs.

III. The management of the modern office is based upon written documents (the "files"), which are preserved in their original or draft form, and upon a staff of subaltern officials and scribes of all sorts. The body of officials working in an agency along with the respective apparatus of material implements and the files makes up a *bureau* (in private enterprises often called the "counting house," *Kontor*).

In principle, the modern organization of the civil service separates the bureau from the private domicile of the official and, in general, segregates official activity from the sphere of private life. Public monies and equipment are divorced from the private property of the official. This condition is everywhere the product of a long development. Nowadays, it is found in public as well as in private enterprises; in the latter, the principle extends even to the entrepreneur at the top. In principle, the *Kontor* (office) is separated from the household, business from private correspondence, and business assets from private wealth. The more consistently the modern type of business management has been carried through, the more are these separations the case. . . .

It is the peculiarity of the modern entrepreneur that he conducts himself as the "first official" of his enterprise, in the very same way in which the ruler of a specifically modern bureaucratic state [Frederick II of Prussia] spoke of himself as "the first servant" of the state. The idea that the bureau activities of the state are intrinsically different in character from the management of private offices is a continental European notion and, by way of contrast, is totally foreign to the American way.

IV. Office management, at least all specialized office management – and such management is distinctly modern – usually presupposes thorough training in a field of specialization. This, too, holds increasingly for the modern executive and employee of a private enterprise, just as it does for the state officials.

V. When the office is fully developed, official activity demands the *full working capacity* of the official, irrespective of the fact that the length of his obligatory working hours in the bureau may be limited. In the normal case, this too is only the product of a long development, in the public as well as in the private office. Formerly the normal state of affairs was the reverse: Official business was discharged as a secondary activity.

VI. The management of the office follows *general rules*, which are more or less stable, more or less exhaustive, and which can be learned. Knowledge of these rules represents a special technical expertise which the officials possess. It involves jurisprudence, administrative or business management.

The reduction of modern office management to rules is deeply embedded in its very nature. The theory of modern public administration, for instance, assumes that the authority to order certain matters by decree – which has been legally granted to an agency – does not entitle the agency to regulate the matter by individual commands given for each case, but only to regulate the matter abstractly. This stands in extreme contrast to the regulation of all relationships through individual privileges and bestowals of favor, which, as we shall see, is absolutely dominant in patrimonialism, at least in so far as such relationships are not fixed by sacred tradition.

The Position of the Official Within and Outside of Bureaucracy

All this results in the following for the internal and external position of the official:

Office Holding As A Vocation

That the office is a "vocation" (*Beruf*) finds expression, first, in the requirement of a prescribed course of training, which demands the entire working capacity for a long period of time, and in generally prescribed special examinations as prerequisites of employment. Furthermore, it finds expression in that the position of the official is in the nature of a "duty" (*Pflicht*). This determines the character of his relations in the following manner: Legally and actually, office holding is not considered ownership of a source of income, to be exploited for rents or emoluments in exchange for the rendering of certain services, as was normally the case during the Middle Ages and frequently up to the threshold of recent times, nor is office holding considered a common exchange of services, as in the case of free employment contracts. Rather, entrance into an office, including one in the private economy, is considered an acceptance of a specific duty of fealty to the purpose of the office (*Amtstreue*) in return for the grant of a secure existence. It is decisive for the modern loyalty to an office that, in the pure type, it does not establish a relationship to a *person*, like the vassal's or disciple's faith under feudal or patrimonial authority, but rather is devoted to *impersonal* and *functional* purposes. These purposes, of course, frequently gain an ideological halo from cultural values, such as state, church, community, party or enterprise, which appear as a surrogate for a this-worldly or other-worldly personal master and which are embodied by a given group.

The political official – at least in the fully developed modern state – is not considered the personal servant of a ruler. Likewise, the bishop, the priest and the preacher are in fact no longer, as in early Christian times, carriers of a purely personal charisma, which offers other-worldly sacred values under the personal mandate of a master, and in principle responsible only to him, to everybody who appears worthy of them and asks

for them. In spite of the partial survival of the old theory, they have become officials in the service of a functional purpose, a purpose which in the present-day "church" appears at once impersonalized and ideologically sanctified.

The Social Position of the Official

Social Esteem and Status Convention

Whether he is in a private office or a public bureau, the modern official, too, always strives for and usually attains a distinctly elevated *social esteem* vis-à-vis the governed. His social position is protected by prescription about rank order and, for the political official, by special prohibitions of the criminal code against "insults to the office" and "contempt" of state and church authorities.

The social position of the official is normally highest where, as in old civilized countries, the following conditions prevail: a strong demand for administration by trained experts; a strong and stable social differentiation, where the official predominantly comes from socially and economically privileged strata because of the social distribution of power or the costliness of the required training and of status conventions. The possession of educational certificates or patents – discussed below – is usually linked with qualification for office; naturally, this enhances the "status element" in the social position of the official. Sometimes the status factor is explicitly acknowledged; for example, in the prescription that the acceptance of an aspirant to an office career depends upon the consent ("election") by the members of the official body. This is the case in the officer corps of the German army. Similar phenomena, which promote a guild-like closure of officialdom, are typically found in the patrimonial and, particularly, in prebendal officialdom of the past. The desire to resurrect such policies in changed forms is by no means infrequent among modern bureaucrats. . . .

Usually the social esteem of the officials is especially low where the demand for expert administration and the hold of status conventions are weak. This is often the case in new settlements by virtue of the great economic opportunities and the great instability of their social stratification: witness the United States.

Appointment Versus Election: Consequences for Expertise

Typically, the bureaucratic official is appointed by a superior authority. An official elected by the governed is no longer a purely bureaucratic figure. Of course, a formal election may hide an appointment – in politics especially by party bosses....

In all circumstances, the designation of officials by means of an election modifies the rigidity of hierarchical subordination. In principle, an official who is elected has an autonomous position vis-à-vis his superiors, for he does not derive his position "from above" but "from below," or at least not from a superior authority of the official hierarchy but from powerful party men ("bosses"), who also determine his further career. The career of the elected official is not primarily dependent upon his chief in the administration. The official who is not elected, but appointed by a master, normally functions, from a technical point of view, more accurately because it is more likely that purely functional points of consideration and qualities will determine his selection and career. As laymen, the governed can evalute the expert qualifications of a candidate for office only in terms of experience, and hence only after his service. Moreover, if political parties are involved in any sort of selection of officials by election, they quite naturally tend to give decisive weight not to technical competence but to the services a follower renders to the party boss....

Where the demand for administration by trained experts is considerable, and the party faithful have to take into account an intellectually developed, educated, and free "public opinion," the use of unqualified officials redounds upon the party in power at the next election. Naturally, this is more likely to happen when the officials are appointed by the

chief. The demand for a trained administration now exists in the United States, but wherever, as in the large cities, immigrant votes are "corralled," there is, of course, no effective public opinion. Therefore, popular election not only of the administrative chief but also of his subordinate officials usually endangers, at least in very large administrative bodies which are difficult to supervise, the expert qualification of the officials as well as the precise functioning of the bureaucratic mechanism, besides weakening the dependence of the officials upon the hierarchy. The superior qualification and integrity of Federal judges appointed by the president, as over and against elected judges, in the United States is well known, although both types of officials are selected primarily in terms of party considerations. The great changes in American metropolitan administrations demanded by reformers have been effected essentially by elected mayors working with an apparatus of officials who were appointed by them. These reforms have thus come about in a "caesarist" fashion. Viewed technically, as an organized form of domination, the efficiency of "caesarism," which often grows out of democracy, rests in general upon the position of the "caesar" as a free trustee of the masses (of the army or of the citizenry), who is unfettered by tradition. The "caesar" is thus the unrestrained master of a body of highly qualified military officers and officials whom he selects freely and personally without regard to tradition or to any other impediments. Such "rule of the personal genius," however, stands in conflict with the formally "democratic" principle of a generally elected officialdom.

Tenure and the inverse relationship between judicial independence and social prestige

Normally, the position of the official is held for life, at least in public bureaucracies; and this is increasingly the case for all similar structures. As a factual rule, *tenure for life* is presupposed even where notice can be given or periodic reappointment occurs. In a private enterprise, the fact of such tenure normally differentiates the official from the worker. Such legal or actual life-tenure, however, is not viewed as a proprietary right of the official to the possession of office as was the case in many structures of authority of the past. Wherever legal guarantees against discretionary dismissal or transfer are developed...they merely serve the purpose of guaranteeing a strictly impersonal discharge of specific office duties.

Within the bureaucracy, therefore, the measure of "independence" legally guaranteed in this manner by tenure is not always a source of increased status for the official whose position is thus secured. Indeed, often the reverse holds, especially in communities with an old culture and a high degree of differentiation. For the subordination under the arbitrary rule of the master also guarantees the maintenance of the conventional seigneurial style of living for the official, and it does this the better, the stricter it is. Therefore the conventional esteem for the official may rise precisely because of the absence of such legal guarantees.... In Germany, the military officer or the administrative official can be removed from office at any time, or at least far more readily than the "independent" judge, who never pays with loss of his office for even the grossest offense against the "code of honor" or against the conventions of the *salon*. For this very reason the judge is, if other things are equal, considered less socially acceptable by "high society" than are officers and administrative officials whose greater dependence on the master is a better guarantee for the conformity of their life style with status conventions. Of course, the average official strives for a civil-service law which in addition to materially securing his old age would also provide increased guarantees against his arbitrary removal from office. This striving, however, has its limits. A very strong development of the "right to the office" naturally makes it more difficult to staff offices with an eye to technical efficiency and decreases the career opportunities of ambitious candidates. This, as well as the preference of officials to be dependent upon their equals rather than upon

the socially inferior governed strata, makes for the fact that officialdom on the whole does not "suffer" much under its dependency from the "higher-up." ...

Rank as the basis of regular salary

The official as a rule receives a *monetary* compensation in the form of a *salary*, normally fixed, and the old age security provided by a pension. The salary is not measured like a wage in terms of work done, but according to "status," that is, according to the kind of function (the "rank") and, possibly, according to the length of service. The relatively great security of the official's income, as well as the rewards of social esteem, make the office a sought-after position, especially in countries which no longer provide opportunities for colonial profits. In such countries, this situation permits relatively low salaries for officials.

Fixed career lines and status rigidity

The official is set for a "career" within the hierarchical order of the public service. He expects to move from the lower, less important and less well paid, to the higher positions. The average official naturally desires a mechanical fixing of the conditions of promotion: if not of the offices, at least of the salary levels. He wants these conditions fixed in terms of "seniority," or possibly according to grades achieved in a system of examinations. Here and there, such grades actually form a *character indelebilis* of the official and have lifelong effects on his career. To this is joined the desire to reinforce the right to office and to increase status group closure and economic security. All of this makes for a tendency to consider the offices as "prebends" of those qualified by educational certificates. The necessity of weighing general personal and intellectual qualifications without concern for the often subaltern character of such patents of specialized education, has brought it about that the highest political offices, especially the "ministerial" positions, are as a rule filled without reference to such certificates.

Monetary and Financial Presuppositions of Bureaucracy

The development of the *money economy* is a presupposition of a modern bureaucracy insofar as the compensation of officials today takes the form of money salaries. The money economy is of very great importance for the whole bearing of bureaucracy, yet by itself it is by no means decisive for the existence of bureaucracy.

Historical examples of relatively clearly developed and quantitatively large bureaucracies are: (a) Egypt, during the period of the New Kingdom, although with strong patrimonial elements; (b) the later Roman Principate, and especially the Diocletian monarchy and the Byzantine polity which developed out of it; these, too, contained strong feudal and patrimonial admixtures; (c) the Roman Catholic Church, increasingly so since the end of the thirteenth century; (d) China, from the time of Shi Hwangti until the present, but with strong patrimonial and prebendal elements; (e) in ever purer forms, the modern European states and, increasingly, all public bodies since the time of princely absolutism; (f) the large modern capitalist enterprise, proportional to its size and complexity.

To a very great extent or predominantly, cases (a) to (d) rested upon compensation of the officials in kind. They nevertheless displayed many of the traits and effects characteristic of bureaucracy. The historical model of all later bureaucracies – the New Kingdom in Egypt – is at the same time one of the most grandiose examples of an organized natural economy. This coincidence of bureaucracy and natural economy is understandable only in view of the quite unique conditions that existed in Egypt, for the reservations – they are quite considerable – which one must make in classifying these structures as bureaucracies are based precisely on the prevalence of a natural economy. A certain measure of a developed money economy is the normal precondition at least for the unchanged

survival, if not for the establishment, of pure bureaucratic administrations.

According to historical experience, without a money economy the bureaucratic structure can hardly avoid undergoing substantial internal changes, or indeed transformation into another structure. The allocation of fixed income in kind from the magazines of the lord or from his current intake...easily means a first step toward appropriation of the sources of taxation by the official and their exploitation as private property. Income in kind has protected the official against the often sharp fluctuations in the purchasing power of money. But whenever the lord's power subsides, payments in kind, which are based on taxes in kind, tend to become irregular. In this case, the official will have direct recourse to the tributaries of his bailiwick, whether or not he is authorized. The idea of protecting the official against such oscillations by mortgaging or transferring the levies and therewith the power to tax, or by transferring the use of profitable lands of the lord to the official, is close at hand, and every central authority which is not tightly organized is tempted to take this course, either voluntarily or because the officials compel it to do so. The official may satisfy himself with the use of these resources up to the level of his salary claim and then hand over the surplus. But this solution contains strong temptations and therefore usually yields results unsatisfactory to the lord. Hence the alternative process involves fixing the official's monetary obligations...: the official hands over a stipulated amount and retains the surplus.

[...]

Office purchase, prebendal and feudal administration

The purely economic conception of the office as a private source of income for the official can also lead to the direct purchase of offices. This occurs when the lord finds himself in a position in which he requires not only a current income but money capital – for instance, for warfare or for debt payments. The purchase of office as a regular institution has existed especially in modern states – in the Papal State as well as in France and England, in the cases of sinecures as well as of more important offices (for example, officers' commissions) well into the nineteenth century. In individual cases, the economic meaning of such a purchase of office can be altered so that the purchasing sum is partly or wholly in the nature of bail deposited to assure faithful service, but this has not been the rule.

Every sort of assignment of usufructs, tributes and services claimed by the lord to the official for personal exploitation always means an abandonment of typical bureaucratic organization. The official in such positions has a property right to his office. This is the case to a still higher degree when official duty and compensation are interrelated in such a way that the official does not transfer to the lord any of the yields gained from the objects left to him, but handles these objects for his private ends and in turn renders to the lord services of a personal or a military, political, or ecclesiastical character.

We shall speak of *prebends* and of a *prebendal* organization of offices in all cases of life-long assignment to officials of rent payments deriving from material goods, or of the essentially *economic* usufruct of land or other sources of rent, in compensation for the fulfillment of real or fictitious duties of office, for the economic support of which the goods in question have been *permanently* allocated by the lord.

The transition [from such prebendal organization of office] to salaried officialdom is quite fluid. . . .

When not only economic but also lordly [political] rights are bestowed [upon the official] to exercise on his own, and when this is associated with the stipulation of *personal* services to the lord to be rendered in return, a further step away from salaried bureaucracy has been taken. The nature of the prerogatives conferred can vary; for instance, in the case of a political official they may tend

more toward seigneurial or more toward office authority. In both instances, but most definitely in the latter case, the specific nature of bureaucratic organization is completely destroyed and we enter into the realm of feudal organization of domination.

All assignments of services and usufructs in kind as endowments for officials tend to loosen the bureaucratic mechanism, and especially to weaken hierarchic subordination, which is most strictly developed in the discipline of modern officialdom. A precision similar to that of the contractually employed official of the modern Occident can only be attained – under very energetic leadership – where the subjection of the officials to the lord is also personally absolute, i.e., where slaves or employees treated like slaves are used for administration.

[. . .]

Summary

Even though the full development of a money economy is thus not an indispensable precondition for bureaucratization, bureaucracy as a permanent structure is knit to the one presupposition of the availability of continuous revenues to maintain it. Where such income cannot be derived from private profits, as it is in the bureaucratic organization of modern enterprises, or from land rents, as in the manor, a stable system of *taxation* is the precondition for the permanent existence of bureaucratic administration. For well-known general reasons only a fully developed money economy offers a secure basis for such a taxation system. Hence the degree of administrative bureaucratization has in urban communities with fully developed money economies not infrequently been relatively greater than in the contemporaneous and much larger territorial states. As soon, however, as these states have been able to develop orderly systems of taxation, bureaucracy has there developed far more comprehensively than in the city states where, whenever their size remained confined to moderate limits, the tendency for a plutocratic and collegial administration by notables has corresponded most adequately to the requirements. For the basis of bureaucratization has always been a certain development of administrative tasks, both quantitative and qualitative.

[. . .]

Qualitative Changes of Administrative Tasks: The Impact of Cultural, Economic and Technological Developments

Bureaucratization is stimulated more strongly, however, by intensive and qualitative expansion of the administrative tasks than by their extensive and quantitative increase. But the direction bureaucratization takes, and the reasons that occasion it, can vary widely. In Egypt, the oldest country of bureaucratic state administration, it was the technical necessity of a public regulation of the water economy for the whole country and from the top which created the apparatus of scribes and officials; very early it found its second realm of operation in the extraordinary, militarily organized construction activities. In most cases, as mentioned before, the bureaucratic tendency has been promoted by needs arising from the creation of standing armies, determined by power politics, and from the related development of public finances. But in the modern state, the increasing demands for administration also rest on the increasing complexity of civilization.

Great power expansions, especially overseas, have, of course, been managed by states ruled by notables (Rome, England, Venice). Yet the "intensity" of the administration, that is, the assumption of as many tasks as possible by the state apparatus for continuous management and discharge in its own establishment was only slightly developed in the great states ruled by notables, especially in Rome and England, by comparison with the bureaucratic polities; this will become evident in the appropriate context. To be sure, the *structure* of state power has influenced culture very strongly both in England and in Rome. But it has done so to a very small extent in the form of management and control by the state. This holds from justice to education. The growing demands on culture, in turn, are determined, though to a varying extent, by the growing wealth of the most influential strata in the state. To this extent increasing bureaucratization is a function of the increasing possession of consumption goods, and of an increasingly sophisticated technique of fashioning external life – a technique which corresponds to the opportunities provided by such wealth. This reacts upon the standard of living and makes for an increasing subjective indispensability of public, interlocal, and thus bureaucratic, provision for the most varied wants which previously were either unknown or were satisfied locally or by the private economy.

Among purely political factors, the increasing demand of a society accustomed to absolute pacification for order and protection ("police") in all fields exerts an especially persevering influence in the direction of bureaucratization. A direct road leads from mere modifications of the blood feud, sacerdotally or by means of arbitration, to the present position of the policeman as the "representative of God on earth." The former means still placed the guarantees for the individual's rights and security squarely upon the members of his sib who were obligated to assist him with oath and vengeance. Other factors operating in the direction of bureaucratization are the manifold tasks of social welfare policies which are either saddled upon the modern state by interest groups or which the state usurps for reasons of power or for ideological motives. Of course, these tasks are to a large extent economically determined.

Among essentially technical factors, the specifically modern means of communication enter the picture as pacemakers of bureaucratization. In part, public roads and waterways, railroads, the telegraph, etc., can only be administered publicly; in part, such administration is technically expedient. In this respect, the contemporary means of communication frequently play a role similar to that of the canals of Mesopotamia and the regulation of the Nile in the ancient Orient. A certain degree of development of the means of communication in turn is one of the most important prerequisites for the possibility of bureaucratic administration, though it alone is not decisive. Certainly in Egypt bureaucratic centralization could, against the backdrop of an almost purely "natural" economy, never have reached the degree of perfection which it did without the natural route of the Nile. In order to promote bureaucratic centralization in modern Persia, the telegraph officials were officially commissioned with reporting to the Shah, over the heads of the local authorities, all occurrences in the provinces; in addition, everyone received the right to remonstrate directly by telegraph. The modern Occidental state can be administered the way it actually is only because the state controls the telegraph network and has the mails and railroads at its disposal. (These means of communication, in turn, are intimately connected with the development of an inter-local traffic of mass goods, which therefore is one of the causal factors in the formation of the modern state. As we have already seen, this does not hold unconditionally for the past.)

The Technical Superiority of Bureaucratic Organization over Administration by Notables

The decisive reason for the advance of bureaucratic organization has always been its purely *technical* superiority over any other form of organization. The fully developed bureaucratic apparatus compares with other organizations exactly as does the machine with the non-mechanical modes of production. Precision, speed, unambiguity, knowledge of the files, continuity, discretion, unity, strict subordination, reduction of friction and of material and personal costs – these are raised to the optimum point in the strictly bureaucratic administration, and especially in its monocratic

form. As compared with all collegiate, honorific, and avocational forms of administration, trained bureaucracy is superior on all these points. And as far as complicated tasks are concerned, paid bureaucratic work is not only more precise but, in the last analysis, it is often cheaper than even formally unremunerated honorific service.

Honorific arrangements make administrative work a subsidiary activity: an avocation and, for this reason alone, honorific service normally functions more slowly. Being less bound to schemata and more formless, it is less precise and less unified than bureaucratic administration, also because it is less dependent upon superiors. Because the establishment and exploitation of the apparatus of subordinate officials and clerical services are almost unavoidably less economical, honorific service is less continuous than bureaucratic and frequently quite expensive. This is especially the case if one thinks not only of the money costs to the public treasury – costs which bureaucratic administration, in comparison with administration by notables, usually increases – but also of the frequent economic losses of the governed caused by delays and lack of precision. Permanent administration by notables is normally feasible only where official business can be satisfactorily transacted as an avocation. With the qualitative increase of tasks the administration has to face, administration by notables reaches its limits. ... Work organized by collegiate bodies, on the other hand, causes friction and delay and requires compromises between colliding interests and views. The administration, therefore, runs less precisely and is more independent of superiors; hence, it is less unified and slower. ...

Today, it is primarily the capitalist market economy which demands that the official business of public administration be discharged precisely, unambiguously, continuously, and with as much speed as possible. Normally, the very large modern capitalist enterprises are themselves unequalled models of strict bureaucratic organization. Business management throughout rests on increasing precision, steadiness, and, above all, speed of operations. This, in turn, is determined by the peculiar nature of the modern means of communication, including, among other things, the news service of the press. The extraordinary increase in the speed by which public announcements, as well as economic and political facts, are transmitted exerts a steady and sharp pressure in the direction of speeding up the tempo of administrative reaction towards various situations. The optimum of such reaction time is normally attained only by a strictly bureaucratic organization. (The fact that the bureaucratic apparatus also can, and indeed does, create certain definite impediments for the discharge of business in a manner best adapted to the individuality of each case does not belong in the present context.)

Bureaucratization offers above all the optimum possibility for carrying through the principle of specializing administrative functions according to purely objective considerations. Individual performances are allocated to functionaries who have specialized training and who by constant practice increase their expertise. "Objective" discharge of business primarily means a discharge of business according to *calculable rules* and "without regard for persons."

"Without regard for persons," however, is also the watchword of the market and, in general, of all pursuits of naked economic interests. Consistent bureaucratic domination means the leveling of "status honor." Hence, if the principle of the free market is not at the same time restricted, it means the universal domination of the "class situation." That this consequence of bureaucratic domination has not set in everywhere proportional to the extent of bureaucratization is due to the differences between possible principles by which polities may supply their requirements. However, the second element mentioned, calculable rules, is the most important one for modern bureaucracy. The peculiarity of modern culture, and specifically of its technical and economic basis, demands this very "calculability" of results. When fully developed, bureaucracy also stands, in a specific sense, under the principle of *sine ira ac studio*. Bureaucracy develops the more perfectly, the more it is "dehumanized," the more completely it succeeds in eliminating from official business love, hatred, and all purely personal, irrational, and emotional elements which escape calculation. This is appraised as its special virtue by capitalism.

The more complicated and specialized modern culture becomes, the more its external supporting apparatus demands the personally detached and strictly objective *expert*, in lieu of the lord of older social structures who was moved by personal sympathy and favor, by grace and gratitude. Bureaucracy offers the attitudes demanded by the external apparatus of modern culture in the most favorable combination. In particular, only bureaucracy has established the foundation for the administration of a rational law conceptually systematized on the basis of "statutes."[. . .]

Bureaucratic objectivity, raison d'etat and popular will

It is perfectly true that "matter-of-factness" and "expertness" are not necessarily identical with the rule of general and abstract norms. Indeed, this does not even hold in the case of the modern administration of justice. The idea of a "law without gaps" is, of course, under vigorous attack. The conception of the modern judge as an automaton into which legal documents and fees are stuffed at the top in order that it may spill forth the verdict at the bottom along with the reasons, read mechanically from codified paragraphs – this conception is angrily rejected, perhaps because a certain approximation to this type would precisely be implied by a consistent bureaucratization of justice. Thus even in the field of law-finding there are areas in which the bureaucratic judge is directly held to "individualizing" procedures by the legislator.

For the field of administrative activity proper, that is, for all state activities that fall outside the field of law creation and court procedure, one has become accustomed to claims for the freedom and the paramountcy of individual circumstances. General norms are held to play primarily a negative role, as barriers to the official's positive and "creative" activity which should never be regulated. The bearing of this thesis may be disregarded here. Decisive is that this "freely" creative administration (and possibly judicature) would not constitute a realm of *free*, arbitrary action and discretion, of *personally* motivated favor and valuation, such as we shall find to be the case among prebureaucratic forms. The rule and the rational pursuit of "objective" purposes, as well as devotion to these, would always constitute the norm of conduct. Precisely those views which most strongly glorify the "creative" discretion of the official accept, as the ultimate and highest lodestar for his behavior in public administration, the specifically modern and strictly "objective" idea of *raison d'état*. Of course, the sure instincts of the bureaucracy for the conditions of maintaining its *own* power in the home state (and through it, in opposition to other states) are inseparably fused with this canonization of the abstract and "objective" idea of "reasons of state." Most of the time, only the power interests of the bureaucracy give a concretely exploitable content to this by no means unambiguous ideal; in dubious cases, it is always these interests which tip the balance. . . . The only decisive point for us is that in principle a system of rationally debatable "reasons" stands behind every act of bureaucratic administration, namely, either subsumption under norms, or a weighing of ends and means.

In this context, too, the attitude of all "democratic" currents, in the sense of currents that would minimize "domination," is necessarily ambiguous. "Equality before the law" and the demand for legal guarantees against arbitrariness demand a formal and rational "objectivity" of administration, as opposed to the personal discretion flowing from the "grace" of the old patrimonial domination. If, however, an "ethos" – not to speak of other impulses – takes hold of the masses on some individual question, its postulates of *substantive* justice, oriented toward

some concrete instance and person, will unavoidably collide with the formalism and the rule-bound and cool "matter-of-factness" of bureaucratic administration. Emotions must in that case reject what reason demands.

The propertyless masses especially are not served by the formal "equality before the law" and the "calculable" adjudication and administration demanded by bourgeois interests. Naturally, in their eyes justice and administration should serve to equalize their economic and social life-opportunities in the face of the propertied classes. Justice and administration can fulfill this function only if they assume a character that is informal because "ethical" with respect to substantive content (*Kadi*-justice). Not only any sort of "popular justice" – which usually does not ask for reasons and norms – but also any intensive influence on the administration by so-called "public opinion" – that is, concerted action born of irrational "sentiments" and usually staged or directed by party bosses or the press – thwarts the rational course of justice. . . .

The Concentration of the Means of Administration

The bureaucratic structure goes hand in hand with the concentration of the material means of management in the hands of the master. This concentration occurs, for instance, in a well-known and typical fashion in the development of big capitalist enterprises, which find their essential characteristics in this process. A corresponding process occurs in public organizations.

The bureaucratization of the army by the state and by private capitalism

. . . War in our time is a war of machines, and this makes centralized provisioning technically necessary, just as the dominance of the machine in industry promotes the concentration of the means of production and management. In the main, however, the bureaucratic armies of the past, equipped and provisioned by the lord, came into being when social and economic development had diminished, absolutely or relatively, the stratum of citizens who were economically able to equip themselves, so that their number was no longer sufficient for putting the required armies in the field.... Only the bureaucratic army structure allows for the development of the professional standing armies which are necessary for the constant pacification of large territories as well as for warfare against distant enemies, especially enemies overseas. Further, military discipline and technical military training can normally be fully developed, at least to its modern high level, only in the bureaucratic army. [...]

[...]

The concentration of resources in other spheres, including the university

In this same way as with army organizations, the bureaucratization of administration in other spheres goes hand in hand with the concentration of resources....

In the field of scientific research and instruction, the bureaucratization of the inevitable research institutes of the universities is also a function of the increasing demand for material means of operation.... Through the concentration of such means in the hands of the privileged head of the institute the mass of researchers and instructors are separated from their "means of production," in the same way as the workers are separated from theirs by the capitalist enterprises.

The Leveling of Social Differences

In spite of its indubitable technical superiority, bureaucracy has everywhere been a relatively late development. A number of obstacles have contributed to this, and only under certain social and political conditions have they definitely receded into the background.

Administrative democratization

Bureaucratic organization has usually come into power on the basis of a leveling of economic and social differences. This leveling has been at least relative, and has concerned the significance of social and economic differences for the assumption of administrative functions.

Bureaucracy inevitably accompanies modern *mass democracy*, in contrast to the democratic self-government of small homogeneous units. This results from its characteristic principle: the abstract regularity of the exercise of authority, which is a result of the demand for "equality before the law" in the personal and functional sense – hence, of the horror of "privilege," and the principled rejection of doing business "from case to case." Such regularity also follows from the social preconditions of its origin. Any non-bureaucratic administration of a large social structure rests in some way upon the fact that existing social, material, or honorific preferences and ranks are connected with administrative functions and duties. This usually means that an economic or a social exploitation of position, which every sort of administrative activity provides to its bearers, is the compensation for the assumption of administrative functions.

Bureaucratization and democratization within the administration of the state therefore signify an increase of the cash expenditures of the public treasury, in spite of the fact that bureaucratic administration is usually more "economical" in character than other forms.... Mass democracy which makes a clean sweep of the feudal, patrimonial, and – at least in intent – the plutocratic privileges in administration unavoidably has to put paid professional labor in place of the historically inherited "avocational" administration by notables.

Mass parties and the bureaucratic consequences of democratization

This applies not only to the state. For it is no accident that in their own organizations the democratic mass parties have completely broken with traditional rule by notables based upon personal relationships and personal esteem. Such personal structures still persist among many old conservative as well as old liberal parties, but democratic mass parties are bureaucratically organized under the leadership of party officials, professional party and trade union secretaries, etc. . . . Every advance of simple election techniques based on numbers alone as, for instance, the system of proportional representation, means a strict and inter-local bureaucratic organization of the parties and therewith an increasing domination of party bureaucracy and discipline, as well as the elimination of the local circles of notables – at least this holds for large states.

The progress of bureaucratization within the state administration itself is a phenomenon paralleling the development of democracy, as is quite obvious in France, North America, and now in England. Of course, one must always remember that the term "democratization" can be misleading. The *demos* itself, in the sense of a shapeless mass, never "governs" larger associations, but rather is governed. What changes is only the way in which the executive leaders are selected and the measure of influence which the *demos*, or better, which social circles from its midst are able to exert upon the content and the direction of administrative activities by means of "public opinion." "Democratization," in the sense here intended, does not necessarily mean an increasingly active share of the subjects in government. This may be a result of democratization, but it is not necessarily the case.

We must expressly recall at this point that the political concept of democracy, deduced from the "equal rights" of the governed, includes these further postulates: (1) prevention of the development of a closed status group of officials in the interest of a universal accessi-

bility of office, and (2) minimization of the authority of officialdom in the interest of expanding the sphere of influence of "public opinion" as far as practicable. Hence, wherever possible, political democracy strives to shorten the term of office through election and recall, and to be relieved from a limitation to candidates with special expert qualifications. Thereby democracy inevitably comes into conflict with the bureaucratic tendencies which have been produced by its very fight against the notables. The loose term "democratization" cannot be used here, in so far as it is understood to mean the minimization of the civil servants' power in favor of the greatest possible "direct" rule of the *demos*, which in practice means the respective party leaders of the *demos*. The decisive aspect here – indeed it is rather exclusively so – is the *leveling of the governed* in face of the governing and bureaucratically articulated group, which in its turn may occupy a quite autocratic position, both in fact and in form.

[. . .]

Economic and political motives behind passive democratization

It is obvious that almost always economic conditions of some sort play their part in such "democratizing" developments. Very frequently we find at the base of the development an economically determined origin of new classes, whether plutocratic, petty-bourgeois, or proletarian in character. Such classes may call on the aid of, or they may call to life or recall to life, a political power of legitimate or of caesarist stamp in order to attain economic or social advantages through its political assistance. On the other hand, there are equally possible – and historically documented – cases in which the initiative came "from on high" and was of a purely political nature, drawing advantages from political constellations, especially in foreign affairs. Here such leadership exploited economic and social antagonisms as well as class interests merely as a means for its own purposes, throwing the antagonistic classes out of their almost always unstable equilibrium and calling their latent interest conflicts into battle. It seems hardly possible to give a general statement of this.

[. . .]

The advance of the bureaucratic structure rests upon "technical" superiority. In consequence – as always in the area of "techniques" – we find that the advance proceeded most slowly wherever older structural forms were in their own way technically highly developed and functionally particularly well adapted to the requirements at hand. This was the case, for instance, in the administration of notables in England, and hence England was the slowest of all countries to succumb to bureaucratization or, indeed, is still only partly in the process of doing so. . . .

The Objective and Subjective Bases of Bureaucratic Perpetuity

Once fully established, bureaucracy is among those social structures which are the hardest to destroy. Bureaucracy is *the* means of transforming social action into rationally organizing action. Therefore, as an instrument of rationally organizing authority relations, bureaucracy was and is a power instrument of the first order for one who controls the bureaucratic apparatus. Under otherwise equal conditions, rationally organized and directed action (*Gesellschaftshandeln*) is superior to every kind of collective behavior (*Massenhandeln*) and also social action (*Gemeinschaftshandeln*) opposing it. "Where administration has been completely bureaucratized, the resulting system of domination is practically indestructible."

The individual bureaucrat cannot squirm out of the apparatus into which he has been harnessed. In contrast to the "notable" performing administrative tasks as a honorific duty or as a subsidiary occupation (avocation), the professional bureaucrat is chained to his activity in his entire economic and ideological existence. In the great majority of cases he is only a small cog in a ceaselessly moving mechanism which prescribes to him an essentially fixed route of march. The official is entrusted with specialized tasks, and normally the mechanism cannot be put into motion or arrested by him, but only from the very top. The individual bureaucrat is, above all, forged to the common interest of all the functionaries in the perpetuation of the apparatus and the persistence of its rationally organized domination.

The ruled, for their part, cannot dispense with or replace the bureaucratic apparatus once it exists, for it rests upon expert training, a functional specialization of work, and an attitude set on habitual virtuosity in the mastery of single yet methodically integrated functions. If the apparatus stops working, or if its work is interrupted by force, chaos results, which it is difficult to master by improvised replacements from among the governed. This holds for public administration as well as for private economic management. Increasingly the material fate of the masses depends upon the continuous and correct functioning of the ever more bureaucratic organizations of private capitalism, and the idea of eliminating them becomes more and more utopian.

Increasingly, all order in public and private organizations is dependent on the system of files and the discipline of officialdom, that means, its habit of painstaking obedience within its wonted sphere of action. The latter is the more decisive element, however important in practice the files are. The naive idea of Bakuninism of destroying the basis of "acquired rights" together with "domination" by destroying the public documents overlooks that the settled orientation of *man* for observing the accustomed rules and regulations will survive independently of the documents. Every reorganization of defeated or scattered army units, as well as every restoration of an administrative order destroyed by revolts, panics, or other catastrophes, is effected by an appeal to this conditioned orientation, bred both in the officials and in the subjects, of obedient adjustment to such [social and political] orders. If the appeal is successful it brings, as it were, the disturbed mechanism to "snap into gear" again.

The objective indispensability of the once-existing apparatus, in connection with its peculiarly "impersonal" character, means that the mechanism – in contrast to the feudal order based upon personal loyalty – is easily made to work for anybody who knows how to gain control over it. A rationally ordered officialdom continues to function smoothly after the enemy has occupied the territory; he merely needs to change the top officials. It continues to operate because it is to the vital interest of everyone concerned, including above all the enemy. After Bismarck had, during the long course of his years in power, brought his ministerial colleagues into unconditional bureaucratic dependence by eliminating all independent statesmen, he saw to his surprise that upon his resignation they continued to administer their offices unconcernedly and undismayedly, as if it had not been the ingenious lord and very creator of these tools who had left, but merely some individual figure in the bureaucratic machine which had been exchanged for some other figure. . . .

Such an apparatus makes "revolution," in the sense of the forceful creation of entirely new formations of authority, more and more impossible – technically, because of its control over the modern means of communication (telegraph etc.), and also because of its increasingly rationalized inner structure. The place of "revolutions" is under this process taken by *coups d'état*, as again France demonstrates in the classical manner since all successful transformations there have been of this nature.

[. . .]

The Power Position of the Bureaucracy

The political irrelevance of functional indispensability

The democratization of society in its totality, and in the *modern* sense of the term, whether actual or perhaps merely formal, is an especially favorable basis of bureaucratization, but by no means the only possible one. After all, bureaucracy has merely the [limited] striving to level those powers that stand in its way in those concrete areas that, in the individual case, it seeks to occupy. We must remember the fact which we have encountered several times and which we shall have to discuss repeatedly: that "democracy" as such is opposed to the "rule" of bureaucracy, in spite and perhaps because of its unavoidable yet unintended promotion of bureaucratization. Under certain conditions, democracy creates palpable breaks in the bureaucratic pattern and impediments to bureaucratic organization. Hence, one must in every individual historical case analyze in which of the special directions bureaucratization has there developed.

For this reason, it must also remain an open question whether the *power* of bureaucracy is increasing in the modern states in which it is spreading. The fact that bureaucratic organization is technically the most highly developed power instrument in the hands of its controller does not determine the weight that bureaucracy as such is capable of procuring for its own opinions in a particular social structure. The ever-increasing "indispensability" of the officialdom, swollen to the millions, is no more decisive on this point than is the economic indispensability of the proletarians for the strength of the social and political power position of that class (a view which some representatives of the proletarian movement hold.[1] If "indispensability" were decisive, the equally "indispensable" slaves ought to have held this position of power in any economy where slave labor prevailed and consequently freemen, as is the rule, shunned work as degrading. Whether the power of bureaucracy as such increases cannot be decided *a priori* from such reasons. . . . In general, only the following can be said here:

The power position of a fully developed bureaucracy is always great, under normal conditions overtowering. The political "master" always finds himself, vis-à-vis the trained official, in the position of a dilettante facing the expert. This holds whether the "master," whom the bureaucracy serves, is the "people" equipped with the weapons of legislative initiative, referendum, and the right to remove officials; or a parliament elected on a more aristocratic or more democratic basis and equipped with the right or the *de facto* power to vote a lack of confidence; or an aristocratic collegiate body, legally or actually based on self-recruitment; or a popularly elected president or an "absolute" or "constitutional" hereditary monarch.

Administrative secrecy

This superiority of the professional insider every bureaucracy seeks further to increase through the means of *keeping secret* its knowledge and intentions. Bureaucratic administration always tends to exclude the public, to hide its knowledge and action from criticism as well as it can.... This tendency toward secrecy is in certain administrative fields a consequence of their objective nature: namely, wherever power interests of the given structure of domination *toward the outside* are at stake, whether this be the case of economic competitors of a private enterprise or that of potentially hostile foreign polities in the public field. If it is to be successful, the management of diplomacy can be publicly supervised only to a very limited extent. The military administration must insist on the concealment of its most important measures with the increasing significance of purely technical aspects.... Every fighting posture of a social structure toward the outside tends in itself to have the effect of buttressing the position of the group in power.

However, the pure power interests of bureaucracy exert their effects far beyond these areas of functionally motivated secrecy. The concept of the "office secret" is the specific invention of bureaucracy, and few things it defends so fanatically as this attitude which, outside of the specific areas mentioned, cannot be justified with purely functional arguments. In facing a parliament, the bureaucracy fights, out of a sure power instinct, every one of that institution's attempts to gain through its own means (as, e.g., through the so-called "right of parliamentary investigation")[2] expert knowledge from the interested parties. Bureaucracy naturally prefers a poorly informed, and hence powerless, parliament – at least insofar as this ignorance is compatible with the bureaucracy's own interests.

The ruler's dependence on the bureaucracy

The absolute monarch, too, is powerless in face of the superior knowledge of the bureaucratic expert – in a certain sense more so than any other political head. All the irate decrees of Frederick the Great concerning the "abolition of serfdom" were derailed in the course of their realization because the official mechanism simply ignored them as the occasional ideas of a dilettante. A constitutional king, whenever he is in agreement with a socially important part of the governed, very frequently exerts a greater influence upon the course of administration than does the absolute monarch since he can control the experts better because of the at least relatively public character of criticism, whereas the absolute monarch is dependent for information solely upon the bureaucracy....

The concentration of the power of the central bureaucracy in a single pair of hands is inevitable with every transition to constitutional government. Officialdom is placed under a monocratic head, the prime minister, through whose hands everything has to go before it gets to the monarch. This puts the latter to a large extent under the tutelage of the chief of the bureaucracy.... Under the rule of expert knowledge, the influence of the monarch can attain steadiness only through continuous communication with the bureaucratic chiefs which is methodically planned and directed by the central head of the bureaucracy. At the same time, constitutionalism binds the bureaucracy and the ruler into a community of interests against the power-seeking of the party chiefs in the parliamentary bodies. But *against* the bureaucracy the ruler remains powerless for this very reason, unless he finds support in parliament.... the power position of a monarch is on the whole far stronger vis-à-vis bureaucratic officials than it was in any feudal or in a "stereotyped" patrimonial state. This is because of the constant presence of aspirants for promotion with whom the monarch can easily replace inconvenient and independent officials. Other circumstances being equal, only economically independent officials, that is, officials who belong to the propertied strata, can permit themselves to risk the loss of their offices. Today as always, the recruitment of officials from among propertyless strata increases the power of the rulers. Only officials who belong to a socially influential stratum which the monarch believes to have to take into account as support of his person, like the so-called *Kanalrebellen* in Prussia, can permanently and completely paralyze the substance of his will.[3]

Only the expert knowledge of private economic interest groups in the field of "business" is superior to the expert knowledge of the bureaucracy. This is so because the exact knowledge of facts in their field is of direct significance for economic survival. Errors in official statistics do not have direct economic consequences for the responsible official, but miscalculations in a capitalist enterprise are paid for by losses, perhaps by its existence. Moreover, the "secret," as a means of power, is more safely hidden in the books of an enterprise than it is in the files of public authorities. For this reason alone authorities are held within narrow boundaries when they seek to influence economic life in the capitalist epoch, and very frequently their measures take an unforeseen and unintended course or are made illusory by the superior expert knowledge of the interested groups.

Excursus *on Collegiate Bodies and Interest Groups*

Since the specialized knowledge of the expert became more and more the foundation for the power of the officeholder, an early concern of the ruler was how to exploit the special knowledge of experts without having to abdicate in their favor. With the qualitative extension of administrative tasks and therewith the indispensability of expert knowledge, it typically happens that the lord no longer is satisfied by occasional consultation with proven confidants or even with an assembly of such men called together intermittently and in difficult situations. He begins to surround himself with *collegiate* bodies which deliberate and resolve in continuous session....

The position of such collegiate bodies naturally varies according to whether they themselves become the highest administrative authority, or whether a central and monocratic authority, or several such authorities, stand at their side. In addition, a great deal depends upon their procedure. When the type is fully developed, such bodies meet – either actually or as a fiction – with the lord in the chair, and all important matters are resolved, after elucidation by the formal position papers of the responsible experts and the reasoned *vota* of other members, by a decision which the lord will sanction or reject by an edict. This kind of collegiate body thus is the typical form in which the ruler, who increasingly turns into a "dilettante," at the same time exploits expert knowledge and – what frequently remains unnoticed – seeks to fend off the threatening dominance of the experts. He keeps one expert in check by others, and by such cumbersome procedures seeks personally to gain a comprehensive picture as well as the certainty that nobody prompts him into arbitrary decisions....

By the collegiate principle the ruler furthermore tries to fashion a sort of synthesis of *specialized experts* into a collective unit. His success in doing this cannot be ascertained in general. The phenomenon itself, however, is common to very different forms of state, from the patrimonial and feudal to the early bureaucratic, and it is especially typical for early princely absolutism. The collegiate principle has proved itself to be one of the strongest educative means for "matter-of-factness" in administration. It also made it possible to counsel with socially influential private persons and thus to combine in some measure the authority of notables and the practical knowledge of private enterprisers with the specialized expertness of professional bureaucrats. The collegiate bodies were one of the first institutions to allow the development of the modern concept of "public authorities," in the sense of enduring structures independent of the person.

As long as an expert knowledge of administrative affairs was the exclusive product of a long *empirical* practice, and administrative norms were not regulations but elements of tradition, the council of *elders* – often with priests, "elder statesmen," and notables participating – was the adequate form for collegiate authorities, which in the beginning merely gave counsel to the ruler. But since such bodies, in contrast to the changing rulers, were perennial formations, they often usurped actual power. The Roman Senate and the Venetian Council, as well as the Athenian Areopagus until its downfall and replacement by the rule of the *demagogos*, acted in this manner. We must, of course, sharply distinguish such authorities from the corporate bodies under discussion here.

In spite of manifold transitions, collegiate bodies, as a type, emerge on the basis of the rational specialization of functions and the rule of expert knowledge. On the other hand, they must be distinguished from advisory bodies selected from among private and *interested* circles, which are frequently found in the modern state and whose nucleus is not formed of officials or of former officials. These collegiate bodies must also be distinguished sociologically from the collegiate supervisory "board of directors" (*Aufsichtsrat*) found in the bureaucratic structures of

the modern private economy (joint stock corporation)....

With great regularity the bureaucratic collegiate principle was transferred from the central authority to the most varied lower authorities. Within locally closed, and especially within urban units, collegiate administration is the original form of the rule of notables.... Originally it worked through elected, later on, usually, or at least in part, through co-opted councilors, colleges of magistrates, *decuriones* and *scabini*. Such bodies are a normal element of organized "self-government," that is, the management of administrative affairs by local interest groups under the control of the bureaucratic authorities of the state. The above-mentioned examples of the Venetian Council and even more so of the Roman Senate represent transfers of the rule of notables, normally rooted in local political associations, to great overseas empires. In the bureaucratic state, collegiate administration disappears again once progress in the means of communication and the increasing technical demands upon the administration necessitate quick and unambiguous decisions and the other motives for full bureaucratization and monocracy,... push themselves dominantly to the fore. Collegiate administration disappears when, from the point of view of the ruler's interests, a strictly unified administrative leadership appears to be more important than thoroughness in the preparation of administrative decisions. This is the case as soon as parliamentary institutions develop and – usually at the same time – as criticism from the outside and publicity increase.

Under these modern conditions the thoroughly rationalized system of specialized ministers and [territorial] prefects, as in France, offers significant opportunities for pushing the old forms everywhere into the background, probably supplemented by the interest groups, normally in the form of advisory bodies recruited from among the economically and socially most influential strata....

This latter development, which seeks to put the concrete experience of the interest groups into the service of a rational administration by trained specialized officials, will certainly be important in the future and further increase the power of bureaucracy. . . .

Only with the bureaucratization of the state and of law in general can one see a definite possibility of a sharp conceptual separation of an "objective" legal order from the "subjective" rights of the individual which it guarantees, as well as that of the further distinction between "public" law, which regulates the relationships of the public agencies among each other and with the subjects, and "private" law which regulates the relationships of the governed individuals among themselves. These distinctions presuppose the conceptual separation of the "state," as an abstract bearer of sovereign prerogatives and the creator of legal norms, from all personal authority of individuals. These conceptual distinctions are necessarily remote from the nature of pre-bureaucratic, especially from patrimonial and feudal, structures of authority. They were first conceived and realized in urban communities; for as soon as their officeholders were appointed by periodic *elections*, the individual power-holder, even if he was in the highest position, was obviously no longer identical with the man who possessed authority "in his own right." Yet it was left to the complete depersonalization of administrative management by bureaucracy and the rational systematization of law to realize the separation of the public and the private sphere fully and in principle.

Bureaucracy and Education

Educational Specialization, Degree Hunting and Status Seeking

We cannot here analyze the far-reaching and general cultural effects that the advance of the rational bureaucratic structure of domination develops quite independently of the areas in which it takes hold. Naturally, bureaucracy promotes a "rationalist" way of life, but the concept of rationalism allows for widely differing contents. Quite generally, one can only say that the bureaucratization of all domination very strongly furthers the development of "rational matter-of-factness" and the personality type of the professional expert. This has far-reaching ramifications, but only one important element of the process can be briefly indicated here: its effect upon the nature of education and personal culture (*Erziehung und Bildung*).

Educational institutions on the European continent, especially the institutions of higher learning – the universities, as well as technical academies, business colleges, gymnasia, and other secondary schools – , are dominated and influenced by the need for the kind of "education" which is bred by the system of specialized examinations or tests of expertise (*Fachprüfungswesen*) increasingly indispensable for modern bureaucracies.

The "examination for expertise" in the modern sense was and is found also outside the strictly bureaucratic structures: today, for instance, in the so-called "free" professions of medicine and law, and in the guild-organized trades. Nor is it an indispensable accompaniment of bureaucratization: the French, English and American bureaucracies have for a long time done without such examinations either entirely or to a large extent, using in-service training and performance in the party organizations as a substitute.

"Democracy" takes an ambivalent attitude also towards the system of examinations for expertise, as it does towards all the phenomena of the bureaucratization which, nevertheless, it promotes. On the one hand, the system of examinations means, or at least appears to mean, selection of the qualified from all social strata in place of the rule by notables. But on the other, democracy fears that examinations and patents of education will create a privileged "caste," and for that reason opposes such a system.

Finally, the examination for expertise is found already in prebureaucratic or semibureaucratic epochs. Indeed, its earliest regular historical locus is in *prebendally* organized structures of domination. The expectation of prebends, first of church prebends – as in the

Islamic Orient and in the Occidental Middle Ages – and then, as was especially the case in China, also of secular prebends, is the typical prize for which people study and are examined. These examinations, however, have only in part the character of tests for specialized "expertise."

Only the modern development of full bureaucratization brings the system of rational examinations for expertise irresistibly to the fore. The American Civil-Service Reform movement gradually imports expert training and specialized examinations into the United States; the examination system also advances into all other countries from its main (European) breeding ground, Germany. The increasing bureaucratization of administration enhances the importance of the specialized examination in England. In China, the attempt to replace the old semi-patrimonial bureaucracy by a modern bureaucracy brought the expert examination; it took the place of the former and quite differently structured system of examinations. The bureaucratization of capitalism, with its demand for expertly trained technicians, clerks, etc., carries such examinations all over the world.

This development is, above all, greatly furthered by the social prestige of the "patent of education" acquired through such specialized examinations, the more so since this prestige can again be turned to economic advantage. The role played in former days by the "proof of ancestry," as prerequisite for equality of birth, access to noble prebends and endowments and, wherever the nobility retained social power, for the qualification to state offices, is nowadays taken by the patent of education. The elaboration of the diplomas from universities, business and engineering colleges, and the universal clamor for the creation of further educational certificates in all fields serve the formation of a privileged stratum in bureaus and in offices. Such certificates support their holders' claims for connubium with the notables (in business offices, too, they raise hope for preferment with the boss's daughter), claims to be admitted into the circles that adhere to "codes of honor,"

claims for a "status-appropriate" salary instead of a wage according to performance, claims for assured advancement and old-age insurance, and, above all, claims to the monopolization of socially and economically advantageous positions. If we hear from all sides demands for the introduction of regulated curricula culminating in specialized examinations, the reason behind this is, of course, not a suddenly awakened "thirst for education," but rather the desire to limit the supply of candidates for these positions and to monopolize them for the holders of educational patents. For such monopolization, the "examination" is today the universal instrument – hence its irresistible advance. As the curriculum required for the acquisition of the patent of education requires considerable expenses and a long period of gestation, this striving implies a repression of talent (of the "charisma") in favor of property, for the intellectual costs of the educational patent are always low and decrease, rather than increase, with increasing volume. The old requirement of a knightly style of life, the prerequisite for capacity to hold a fief, is nowadays in Germany replaced by the necessity of participating in its surviving remnants, the duelling fraternities of the universities which grant the patents of education; in the Anglo-Saxon countries, the athletic and social clubs fulfill the same function.

On the other hand, bureaucracy strives everywhere for the creation of a "right to the office" by the establishment of regular disciplinary procedures and by the elimination of the completely arbitrary disposition of the superior over the subordinate official. The bureaucracy seeks to secure the official's position, his orderly advancement, and his provision for old age. In this, it is supported by the "democratic" sentiment of the governed which demands that domination be minimized; those who hold this attitude believe themselves able to discern a weakening of authority itself in every weakening of the lord's arbitrary disposition over the officials. To this extent bureaucracy, both in business offices and in public service, promotes the rise of a specific status group, just as did the quite different officeholders of the past. We have already pointed out that these status characteristics are usually also exploited for, and by their nature contribute to, the technical usefulness of bureaucracy in fulfilling its specific tasks.

It is precisely against this unavoidable status character of bureaucracy that "democracy" reacts in its striving to put the election of officials for short terms in place of the appointment of officials and to substitute the recall of officials by referendum for a regulated disciplinary procedure, thus seeking to replace the arbitrary disposition of the hierarchically superordinate "master" by the equally arbitrary disposition of the governed or rather, of the party bosses dominating them.

Excursus on the "Cultivated man"

Social prestige based upon the advantage of schooling and education as such is by no means specific to bureaucracy. On the contrary. But educational prestige in other structures of domination rests upon substantially different foundations with respect to content. Expressed in slogans, the "cultivated man," rather than the "specialist," was the end sought by education and the basis of social esteem in the feudal, theocratic, and patrimonial structures of domination, in the English administration by notables, in the old Chinese patrimonial bureaucracy, as well as under the rule of demagogues in the Greek states during the so-called Democracy. The term "cultivated man" is used here in a completely value-neutral sense; it is understood to mean solely that a quality of life conduct which *was held to be* "cultivated" was the goal of education, rather than a specialized training in some expertise. Such education may have been aimed at a knightly or at an ascetic type, at a literary type (as in China) or at a gymnastic-humanist type (as in Hellas), or at a conventional "gentleman" type of the Anglo-Saxon variety. A personality "cultivated" in this sense formed the educational ideal stamped by the structure of dom-

ination and the conditions of membership in the ruling stratum of the society in question. The qualification of this ruling stratum rested upon the possession of a "plus" of such *cultural quality* (in the quite variable and value-neutral sense of the term as used here), rather than upon a "plus" of expert knowledge. Military, theological and legal expertise was, of course, intensely cultivated at the same time. But the point of gravity in the Hellenic, in the medieval, as well as in the Chinese educational curriculum was formed by elements entirely different from those which were "useful" in a technical sense.

Behind all the present discussions about the basic questions of the educational system there lurks decisively the struggle of the "specialist" type of man against the older type of the "cultivated man," a struggle conditioned by the irresistibly expanding bureaucratization of all public and private relations of authority and by the ever-increasing importance of experts and specialised knowledge. This struggle affects the most intimate aspects of personal culture.

Conclusion

During its advance, bureaucratic organization has had to overcome not only those essentially negative obstacles, several times previously mentioned, that stood in the way of the required leveling process. In addition, administrative structures based on different principles did and still do cross paths with bureaucratic organization. Some of these have already been mentioned in passing. Not all of the types existing in the real world can be discussed here – this would lead us much too far afield; we can analyze only some of the most important *structural principles* in much simplified schematic exposition. We shall proceed in the main, although not exclusively, by asking the following questions:

1. How far are these administrative structures in their developmental chances subject to economic, political or any other external

determinants, or to an "autonomous" logic inherent in their technical structure? 2. What, if any, are the economic effects which these administrative structures exert? In doing this, one must keep one's eye on the fluidity and the overlapping of all these organizational principles. Their "pure" types, after all, are to be considered merely border cases which are of special and indispensable analytical value, and bracket historical reality which almost always appears in mixed forms.

The bureaucratic structure is everywhere a late product of historical development. The further back we trace our steps, the more typical is the absence of bureaucracy and of officialdom in general. Since bureaucracy has a "rational" character, with rules, means-ends calculus, and matter-of-factness predominating, its rise and expansion has everywhere had "revolutionary" results, in a special sense still to be discussed, as had the advance of *rationalism* in general. The march of bureaucracy accordingly destroyed structures of domination which were not rational in this sense of the term. Hence we may ask: What were these structures?

NOTES AND REFERENCES

Unless otherwise indicated, all notes and emendations are by Roth and Wittich.

1   This is directed, among others, at Robert Michels, to whom Weber wrote in November 1906:

Indispensability in the economic process means nothing, absolutely nothing for the power position and power chances of a class. At a time when no "citizen" worked, the slaves were ten times, nay a thousand times as necessary as is the proletariat today. What does that matter? The medieval peasant, the Negro of the American South, they were all absolutely "indispensable."... The phrase contains a dangerous illusion.... Political democratization is the only thing which can perhaps be achieved in the foreseeable future, and that would be no mean achievement.... I cannot prevent you from believing in more, but I cannot force myself to do so.

   Quoted in Wolfgang Mommsen, *Max Weber und die deutsche Politik* 1890–1920 (Tübingen: Mohr, 1959), 97 and 121.

2   *Enquêterecht.* Weber assigned great significance to this right of parliamentary investigation, which the Reichstag was substantially lacking.

3   When in 1899 the German Reichstag discussed a bill for the construction of the Mittelland Kanal the conservative Junker party fought the project. Among the conservative members of the parliamentary party were a number of Junker officials who stood up to the Kaiser when he ordered them to vote for the bill. The disobedient officials were dubbed *Kanalrebellen* and temporarily suspended from office. Cf. Chancellor Bülow's *Denkwürdigkeiten* (Berlin: Ullstein 1930), vol. I, pp. 293ff.; H. Horn, "Der Kampf um die Mittelland-Kanal Vorlage aus dem Jahre 1899," in K. E. Born (ed.), *Moderne deutsche Wirtschaftsgeschichte* (Kiepenheuer & Witsch: Cologne 1966). (G/M)

2

State and Civil Society

Antonio Gramsci

The "Philosophy of the Epoch"

The discussion on force and consent [concerns] the debate about the "philosophy of the epoch", about the central theme in the lives of the various states in the post-war period. How to reconstruct the hegemonic apparatus of the ruling group, an apparatus which disintegrated as a result of the war, in every state throughout the world? Moreover, why did this apparatus disintegrate? Perhaps because a strong antagonistic[1] collective political will developed? If this were the case, the question would have been resolved in favour of such an antagonist. In reality, it disintegrated under the impact of purely mechanical causes, of various kinds: 1. because great masses, previously passive, entered into movement – but into a chaotic and disorganised movement, without leadership, i.e. without any precise collective political will;

2. because the middle classes, who during the war held positions of command and responsibility, when peace came were deprived of these and left unemployed – precisely after having learned how to command, etc.; 3. because the antagonistic forces proved to be incapable of organising this situation of disorder to their own advantage. The problem was to reconstruct a hegemonic apparatus for these formerly passive and apolitical elements. It was impossible to achieve this without the use of force – which could not be "legal" force, etc. Since the complex of social relations was different in each state, the political methods of using force and the ways in which legal and illegal forces were combined had to be equally diverse. The greater the mass of the apolitical, the greater the part played by illegal forces has to be. The greater the politically organised and educated forces, the more it is necessary to "cover" the legal State, etc. [1930–32]

From *Selections from the Prison Notebooks of Antonio Gramsci*, ed. and trans. Q. Hoare and G. Nowell Smith, pp. 228–70. New York and London: International Publishers and Lawrence & Wishart, 1971.

Political Struggle and Military War

In military war, when the strategic aim – destruction of the enemy's army and occupation of his territory – is achieved, peace comes. It should also be observed that for war to come to an end, it is enough that the strategic aim should simply be achieved potentially: it is enough in other words that there should be no doubt that an army is no longer able to fight, and that the victorious army "could" occupy the enemy's territory. Political struggle is enormously more complex: in a certain sense, it can be compared to colonial wars or to old wars of conquest – in which the victorious army occupies, or proposes to occupy, permanently all or a part of the conquered territory. Then the defeated army is disarmed and dispersed, but the struggle continues on the terrain of politics and of military "preparation".

Thus India's political struggle against the English (and to a certain extent that of Germany against France, or of Hungary against the Little Entente) knows three forms of war: war of movement, war of position, and underground warfare. Gandhi's passive resistance is a war of position, which at certain moments becomes a war of movement, and at others underground warfare. Boycotts are a form of war of position, strikes of war of movement, the secret preparation of weapons and combat troops belongs to underground warfare. A kind of commando tactics[2] is also to be found, but it can only be utilised with great circumspection. If the English believed that a great insurrectional movement was being prepared, destined to annihilate their present strategic superiority (which consists, in a certain sense, in their ability to manoeuvre through control of the internal lines of communication, and to concentrate their forces at the "sporadically" most dangerous spot) by mass suffocation – i.e. by compelling them to spread out their forces over a theatre of war which had simultaneously become generalised – then it would suit them to *provoke* a premature out-break of the Indian

fighting forces, in order to identify them and decapitate the general movement. Similarly it would suit France if the German Nationalist Right were to be involved in an adventurist *coup d'état*; for this would oblige the suspected illegal military organisation to show itself prematurely, and so permit an intervention which from the French point of view would be timely. It is thus evident that in these forms of mixed struggle – fundamentally of a military character, but mainly fought on the political plane (though in fact every political struggle always has a military substratum) – the use of commando squads requires an original tactical development, for which the experience of war can only provide a stimulus, and not a model.[...]

The relationship which existed in 1917–18 between the commando units and the army as a whole can lead, and has led, political leaders to draw up erroneous plans of campaign. They forget: 1. that the commandos are simple tactical units, and do indeed presuppose an army which is not very effective – but not one which is completely inert.... 2. that the phenomenon of commandos should not be considered as a sign of the general combativity of the mass of the troops, but, on the contrary, as a sign of their passivity and relative demoralisation. But in saying all this, the general criterion should be kept in mind that comparisons between military art and politics, if made, should always be taken *cum grano salis* [with a pinch of salt] ... In actual fact, in the case of the political militia there is neither any implacable penal sanction for whoever makes a mistake or does not obey an order exactly, nor do courts-martial exist – quite apart from the fact that the line-up of political forces is not even remotely comparable to the line-up of military forces.

In political struggle, there also exist other forms of warfare – apart from the war of movement and siege warfare or the war of position. True, i.e. modern, commandos belong to the war of position, in its 1914–18 form. The war of movement and siege warfare of the preceding periods also had their commandos, in a certain sense. The light and heavy cavalry, crack rifle corps,[3] etc. – and indeed mobile forces in general – partly functioned as commandos. Similarly the art of organising patrols contained the germ of modern commandos. This germ was contained in siege warfare more than in the war of movement: more extensive use of patrols, and particularly the art of organising sudden sorties and surprise attacks with picked men.

Another point to be kept in mind is that in political struggle one should not ape the methods of the ruling classes, or one will fall into easy ambushes. In the current struggles this phenomenon often occurs. A weakened State structure is like a flagging army; the commandos – i.e. the private armed organisations – enter the field, and they have two tasks: to make use of illegal means, while the State appears to remain within legality, and thus to reorganise the State itself. It is stupid to believe that when one is confronted by illegal private action one can counterpose to it another similar action – in other words, combat commando tactics by means of commando tactics. It means believing that the State remains perpetually inert, which is never the case – quite apart from all the other conditions which differ. The class factor leads to a fundamental difference: a class which has to work fixed hours every day cannot have permanent and specialised assault organisations – as can a class which has ample financial resources and all of whose members are not tied down by fixed work. At any hour of day or night, these by now professional organisations are able to strike decisive blows, and strike them unawares. Commando tactics cannot therefore have the same importance for some classes as for others. For certain classes a war of movement and manœuvre is necessary – because it is the form of war which belongs to them; and this, in the case of political struggle, may include a valuable and perhaps indispensable use of commando tactics. But to fix one's mind on the military model is the mark of a fool: politics, here too, must have priority over its military aspect, and only politics creates the possibility for manœuvre and movement.

From all that has been said it follows that in the phenomenon of military commandos, it is necessary to distinguish between the technical function of commandos as a special force linked to the modern war of position, and their politico-military function. As a special force commandos were used by all armies in the World War. But they have only had a politico-military function in those countries which are politically enfeebled and non-homogeneous, and which are therefore represented by a not very combative national army, and a bureaucratised General Staff, grown rusty in the service. [1929–30]

[...]

The truth is that one cannot choose the form of war one wants, unless from the start one has a crushing superiority over the enemy. It is well known what losses were caused by the stubborn refusal of the General Staffs to recognise that a war of position was "imposed" by the overall relation of the forces in conflict. A war of position is not, in reality, constituted simply by the actual trenches, but by the whole organisational and industrial system of the territory which lies to the rear of the army in the field. It is imposed notably by the rapid fire-power of cannons, machine-guns and rifles, by the armed strength which can be concentrated at a particular spot, as well as by the abundance of supplies which make possible the swift replacement of material lost after an enemy breakthrough or a retreat. A further factor is the great mass of men under arms; they are of very unequal calibre, and are precisely only able to operate as a mass force....Even those military experts whose minds are now fixed on the war of position, just as they were previously on that of manœuvre, naturally do not maintain that the latter should be considered as expunged from military science. They merely maintain that, in wars among the more industrially and socially advanced States, the war of manœuvre must be considered as reduced to more of a tactical than a strategic function; that it must be considered as occupying the same position as siege warfare used to occupy previously in relation to it.

The same reduction must take place in the art and science of politics, at least in the case of the most advanced States, where "civil society" has become a very complex structure and one which is resistant to the catastrophic "incursions" of the immediate economic element (crises, depressions, etc.). The superstructures of civil society are like the trench-systems of modern warfare. In war it would sometimes happen that a fierce artillery attack seemed to have destroyed the enemy's entire defensive system, whereas in fact it had only destroyed the outer perimeter; and at the moment of their advance and attack the the assailants would find themselves confronted by a line of defence which was still effective. The same thing happens in politics, during the great economic crises. A crisis cannot give the attacking forces the ability to organise with lightning speed in time and in space; still less can it endow them with fighting spirit. Similarly, the defenders are not demoralised, nor do they abandon their positions, even among the ruins, nor do they lose faith in their own strength or their own future. Of course, things do not remain exactly as they were; but it is certain that one will not find the element of speed, of accelerated time, of the definitive forward march...

The last occurrence of the kind in the history of politics was the events of 1917. They marked a decisive turning-point in the history of the art and science of politics. Hence it is a question of studying "in depth" which elements of civil society correspond to the defensive systems in a war of position....

The question of the meagre success achieved by new tendencies in the trade-union movement should be related to this series of problems.[4] One attempt to begin a revision of the current tactical methods was perhaps that outlined by L. Dav. Br. [Trotsky] at the fourth meeting, when he made a comparison between the Eastern and Western fronts.[5] The former had fallen at once, but unprecedented struggles had then ensued; in the case of the latter, the struggles would take place "beforehand". The question, therefore, was whether civil society resists before or after the attempt to seize power; where the latter takes place, etc....

It should be seen whether Bronstein's famous theory about the *permanent* character of the movement[6] is not the political reflection of the theory of war of manœuvre...– i.e. in the last analysis, a reflection of the general-economic-cultural-social conditions in a country in which the structures of national life are embryonic and loose, and incapable of becoming "trench or fortress". In this case one might say that Bronstein, apparently "Western", was in fact a cosmopolitan – i.e. superficially national and superficially Western or European. Ilitch [Lenin] on the other hand was profoundly national and profoundly European....

It seems to me that Ilitch understood that a change was necessary from the war of manœuvre applied victoriously in the East in 1917, to a war of position which was the only form possible in the West – where...armies could rapidly accumulate endless quantities of munitions, and where the social structures were of themselves still capable of becoming heavily-armed fortifications. This is what the formula of the "United Front" seems to me to mean....

Ilitch, however, did not have time to expand his formula – though it should be borne in mind that he could only have expanded it theoretically, whereas the fundamental task was a national one; that is to say it required a reconnaissance of the terrain and identification of the elements of trench and fortress represented by the elements of civil society, etc. In Russia the State was everything, civil society was primordial and gelatinous; in the West, there was a proper relation between State and civil society, and when the State trembled a sturdy structure of civil society was at once revealed. The State was only an outer ditch, behind which there stood a powerful system of fortresses and earthworks: more or less numerous from one State to the next, it goes without saying – but this precisely necessitated an accurate reconnaissance of each individual country.

[...]

The Transition from the War of Manœuvre (Frontal Attack) to the War of Position – in the Political Field As Well

This seems to me to be the most important question of political theory that the post-war period has posed, and the most difficult to solve correctly. It is related to the problems raised by Bronstein [Trotsky], who in one way or another can be considered the political theorist of frontal attack in a period in which it only leads to defeats. This transition in political science is only indirectly (mediately) related to that which took place in the military field, although certainly a relation exists and an essential one. The war of position demands enormous sacrifices by infinite masses of people. So an unprecedented concentration of hegemony is necessary, and hence a more "interventionist" government, which will take the offensive more openly against the oppositionists and organise permanently the "impossibility" of internal disintegration – with controls of every kind, political, administrative, etc., reinforcement of the hegemonic "positions" of the dominant group, etc. All this indicates that we have entered a culminating phase in the political-historical situation, since in politics the "war of position", once won, is decisive definitively. In politics, in other words, the war of manœuvre subsists so long as it is a question of winning positions which are not decisive, so that all the resources of the State's hegemony cannot be mobilised. But when, for one reason or another, these positions have lost their value and only the decisive positions are at stake, then one passes over to siege warfare; this is concentrated, difficult, and requires exceptional qualities of patience and inventiveness. In politics, the siege is a reciprocal one, despite all appearances, and the mere fact that the ruler has to muster all his resources demonstrates how seriously he takes his adversary. [1930–32]

"A resistance too long prolonged in a besieged camp is demoralising in itself. It implies suffering, fatigue, loss of rest, illness and the continual presence not of the acute danger which tempers but of the chronic danger which destroys." Karl Marx: Eastern Question. 14 September 1855.

Politics and Military Science

Tactic of great masses, and immediate tactic of small groups. Belongs to the discussion about war of position and war of movement, in so far as this is reflected in the psychology both of great leaders (strategists) and of their subordinates. It is also (if one can put it like that) the point of connection between strategy and tactics, both in politics and in military science. Individuals (even as components of vast masses) tend to conceive war instinctively as "partisan warfare" or "Garibaldine warfare" (which is a higher form of "partisan warfare"). In politics the error occurs as a result of an inaccurate understanding of what the State (in its integral meaning: dictatorship + hegemony) really is. In war a similar error occurs, transferred to the enemy camp (failure to understand not only one's own State but that of the enemy as well). In both cases, the error is related to individual particularism – of town or region; this leads to an underestimation of the adversary and his fighting organisation. [1930–32]

Problem of the "Collective Man" or of "Social Conformism"[7]

Educative and formative role of the State. Its aim is always that of creating new and higher types of civilisation; of adapting the "civilisation" and the morality of the broadest popular masses to the necessities of the continuous development of the economic apparatus of production; hence of evolving even physically new types of humanity. But how will each single individual succeed in incorporating himself into the collective man, and how will educative pressure be applied to single individuals so as to obtain their consent and their collaboration, turning necessity and coercion into "freedom"? Question of the "Law": this concept will have to be extended to include those activities which are at present classified as "legally neutral", and which belong to the domain of civil society; the latter operates without "sanctions" or compulsory "obligations", but nevertheless exerts a collective pressure and obtains objective results in the form of an evolution of customs, ways of thinking and acting, morality, etc.

Political concept of the so-called "Permanent Revolution", which emerged before 1848 as a scientifically evolved expression of the Jacobin experience from 1789 to Thermidor. The formula belongs to an historical period in which the great mass political parties and the great economic trade unions did not yet exist, and society was still, so to speak, in a state of fluidity from many points of view: greater backwardness of the countryside, and almost complete monopoly of political and State power by a few cities or even by a single one (Paris in the case of France); a relatively rudimentary State apparatus, and greater autonomy of civil society from State activity; a specific system of military forces and of national armed services; greater autonomy of the national economies from the economic relations of the world market, etc. In the period after 1870, with the colonial expansion of Europe, all these elements change: the internal and international organisational relations of the State become more complex and massive, and the Forty-Eightist formula of the "Permanent Revolution" is expanded and transcended in political science by the formula of "civil hegemony". The same thing happens in the art of politics as happens in military art: war of movement increasingly becomes war of position, and it can be said that a State will win a war in so far as it prepares for it minutely and technically in peacetime. The massive structures of the modern democracies, both as State organisations, and as complexes of associations in civil society, constitute for the art of politics as it were the "trenches" and the permanent fortifications of the front in the war of position: they render merely "partial" the element of movement which before used to be "the whole" of war, etc.

This question is posed for the modern States, but not for backward countries or for colonies, where forms which elsewhere have been superseded and have become anachronistic are still in vigour. The question of the value of ideologies must also be studied in a treatise of political science. [1933–34]

[...]

Hegemony (Civil Society) and Separation of Powers

The separation of powers,[8] together with all the discussion provoked by its realisation and the legal dogmas which its appearance brought into being, is a product of the struggle between civil society and political society in a specific historical period. This period is characterised by a certain unstable equilibrium between the classes, which is a result of the fact that certain categories of intellectuals (in the direct service of the State, especially the civil and military bureaucracy) are still too closely tied to the old dominant classes. In other words, there takes place within the society what Croce calls the "perpetual conflict between Church and State", in which the Church is taken as representing the totality of civil society (whereas in fact it is only an element of diminishing importance within it), and the State as representing every attempt to crystallise permanently a particular stage of development, a particular situation. In this sense, the Church itself may become State, and the conflict may occur between on the one hand secular (and secularising) civil society, and on the other State/Church (when the Church has become an integral part of the State, of political society monopolised by a specific privileged group, which absorbs the Church in order the better to preserve its monopoly with the support of that zone of "civil society" which the Church represents).

Essential importance of the separation of powers for political and economic liberalism; the entire liberal ideology, with its strengths and its weaknesses, can be encapsulated in the principle of the separation of powers, and the source of liberalism's weakness then becomes apparent; it is the bureaucracy – i.e the crystallisation of the leading personnel – which exercises coercive power, and at a certain point it becomes a caste. Hence the popular demand for making all posts elective – a demand which is extreme liberalism, and at the same time its dissolution (principle of the permanent Constituent Assembly, etc.; in Republics, the election at fixed intervals of the Head of State gives the illusion of satisfying this elementary popular demand).

Unity of the State in the differentiation of powers: Parliament more closely linked to civil society; the judiciary power, between government and Parliament, represents the continuity of the written law (even against the government). Naturally all three powers are also organs of political hegemony, but in different degrees: 1. Legislature; 2. Judiciary; 3. Executive. It is to be noted how lapses in the administration of justice make an especially disastrous impression on the public: the hegemonic apparatus is more sensitive in this sector, to which arbitrary actions on the part of the police and political administration may also be referred. [1930–32]

The Conception of Law

A conception of the Law which must be an essentially innovatory one is not to be found, integrally, in any pre-existing doctrine.... If every State tends to create and maintain a certain type of civilisation and of citizen (and hence of collective life and of individual relations), and to eliminate certain customs and attitudes and to disseminate others, then the Law will be its instrument for this purpose (together with the school system, and other institutions and activities). It must be developed so that it is suitable for such a purpose – so that it is maximally effective and productive of positive results.

The conception of law will have to be freed from every residue of transcendentalism and

from every absolute; in practice, from every moralistic fanaticism. However, it seems to me that one cannot start from the point of view that the State does not "punish" (if this term is reduced to its human significance), but only struggles against social "dangerousness". In reality, the State must be conceived of as an "educator", in as much as it tends precisely to create a new type or level of civilisation. Because one is acting essentially on economic forces, reorganising and developing the apparatus of economic production, creating a new structure, the conclusion must not be drawn that superstructural factors should be left to themselves, to develop spontaneously, to a haphazard and sporadic germination. The State, in this field, too, is an instrument of "rationalisation", of acceleration and of Taylorisation. It operates according to a plan, urges, incites, solicits, and "punishes"; for, once the conditions are created in which a certain way of life is "possible", then "criminal action or omission" must have a punitive sanction, with moral implications, and not merely be judged generically as "dangerous". The Law is the repressive and negative aspect of the entire positive, civilising activity undertaken by the State. The "prize-giving"[9] activities of individuals and groups, etc., must also be incorporated in the conception of the Law; praiseworthy and meritorious activity is rewarded, just as criminal actions are punished (and punished in original ways, bringing in "public opinion" as a form of sanction). [1933–34: 1st version 1931–32]

[...]

The State

In the new "juridical" tendencies represented by the *Nuovi Studi* of Volpicelli and Spirito, the confusion between the concept of class-State and the concept of regulated society[10] should be noted, as a critical point of departure....

As long as the class-State exists the regulated society cannot exist, other than metaphorically – i.e. only in the sense that the class-State too is a regulated society. The utopians, in as much as they expressed a critique of the society that existed in their day, very well understood that the class-State could not be the regulated society. So much is this true that in the types of society which the various utopias represented, economic equality was introduced as a necessary basis for the projected reform. Clearly in this the utopians were not utopians, but concrete political scientists and consistent critics. The utopian character of some of them was due to the fact that they believed that economic equality could be introduced by arbitrary laws, by an act of will, etc. But the idea that complete and perfect political equality cannot exist without economic equality...nevertheless remains correct ....

The confusion of class-State and regulated society is peculiar to the middle classes and petty intellectuals, who would be glad of any regularisation that would prevent sharp struggles and upheavals. It is a typically reactionary and regressive conception. [1930–32]

In my opinion, the most reasonable and concrete thing that can be said about the ethical State,[11] the cultural State, is this: every State is ethical in as much as one of its most important functions is to raise the great mass of the population to a particular cultural and moral level, a level (or type) which corresponds to the needs of the productive forces for development, and hence to the interests of the ruling classes. The school as a positive educative function, and the courts as a repressive and negative educative function, are the most important State activities in this sense: but, in reality, a multitude of other so-called private initiatives and activities tend to the same end – initiatives and activities which form the apparatus of the political and cultural hegemony of the ruling classes. Hegel's conception belongs to a period in which the spreading development of the bourgeoisie could seem limitless, so that its ethicity or universality could be asserted: all mankind will be bourgeois. But, in reality, only the social group that poses the end of the State and its own end as the target to be achieved can create an ethical State – i.e. one which tends to put an end to the internal divisions of the ruled, etc., and to create a technically and morally unitary social organism. [1931–32]

Hegel's doctrine of parties and associations as the "private" woof of the State. This derived historically from the political experiences of the French Revolution, and was to serve to give a more concrete character to constitutionalism. Government with the consent of the governed – but with this consent organised, and not generic and vague as it is expressed in the instant of elections. The State does have and request consent, but it also "educates" this consent, by means of the political and syndical associations; these, however, are private organisms, left to the private initiative of the ruling class. Hegel, in a certain sense, thus already transcended pure constitutionalism and theorised the parliamentary State with its party system. But his conception of association could not help still being vague and primitive, halfway between the political and the economic; it was in accordance with the historical experience of the time, which was very limited and offered only one perfected example of organisation—the "corporative" (a politics grafted directly on to the economy). Marx was not able to have historical experiences superior (or at least much superior) to those of Hegel; but, as a result of his journalistic and agitational activities, he had a sense for the masses. Marx's concept of organisation remains entangled amid the following elements: craft organisation; Jacobin clubs; secret conspiracies by small groups; journalistic organisation.

The French Revolution offered two prevalent types. There were the "clubs" – loose organisations of the "popular assembly" type, centralised around individual political figures. Each had its newspaper, by means of which it kept alive the attention and interest of a particular clientèle that had no fixed boundaries. This clientèle then upheld the theses of the paper in the club's meetings. Certainly, among those who frequented the clubs, there must have existed tight, select groupings of people who knew each other, who met separately and prepared the climate of the meetings, in order to support one tendency or another – depending on the circumstances and also on the concrete interests in play.

The secret conspiracies, which subsequently spread so widely in Italy prior to 1848, must have developed in France after Thermidor among the second-rank followers of Jacobinism: with great difficulty in the Napoleonic period on account of the vigilant control of the police; with greater facility from 1815 to 1830 under the Restoration, which was fairly liberal at the base and was free from certain preoccupations. In this period, from 1815 to 1830, the differentiation of the popular political camp was to occur. This already seemed considerable during the "glorious days" of 1830,[12] when the formations which had been crystallising during the preceding fifteen years now came to the surface. After 1830 and up to 1848, this process of differentiation became perfected....

The revolution which the bourgeois class has brought into the conception of law, and hence into the function of the State, consists especially in the will to conform (hence ethicity of the law and of the State). The previous ruling classes were essentially conservative in the sense that they did not tend to construct an organic passage from the other classes into their own, i.e. to enlarge their class sphere "technically" and ideologically: their conception was that of a closed caste. The bourgeois class poses itself as an organism in continuous movement, capable of absorbing the entire society, assimilating it to its own cultural and economic level. The entire function of the State has been transformed; the State has become an "educator", etc.

How this process comes to a halt, and the conception of the State as pure force is returned to, etc. The bourgois class is "saturated": it not only does not expand – it starts to disintegrate; it not only does not assimilate new elements, it loses part of itself (or at least its losses are enormously more numerous than its assimilations). A class claiming to be capable of assimilating the whole of society, and which was at the same time really able to express such a process, would perfect this conception of the State and of law, so as to conceive the end of the State and of law – rendered useless since they will have exhausted their function and will have been absorbed by civil society. [1931–32]

That the everyday concept of State is unilateral and leads to grotesque errors can be demonstrated with reference to Danièl Halévy's recent book *Décadence de la liberté*, of which I have read a review in *Nouvelles Littéraires*. For Halévy, "State" is the representative apparatus; and he discovers that the most important events of French history from 1870 until the present day have not been due to initiatives by political organisms deriving from universal suffrage, but to those either of private organisms (capitalist firms, General Staffs, etc.) or of great civil servants unknown to the country at large, etc. But what does that signify if not that by "State" should be understood not only the apparatus of government, but also the "private" apparatus of "hegemony" or civil society? It should be noted how from this critique of the State which does not intervene, which trails behind events, etc., there is born the dictatorial ideological current of the Right, with its reinforcement of the executive, etc.

[...]

In the (anyway superficial) polemic over the functions of the State (which here means the State as a politico-juridical organisation in the narrow sense), the expression "the State as *veilleur de nuit*" corresponds to the Italian expression "the State as policeman"[13] and means a State whose functions are limited to the safeguarding of public order and of respect for the laws. The fact is glossed over that in this form of régime (which anyway has never existed except on paper, as a limiting hypothesis) hegemony over its historical development belongs to private forces, to civil society – which is "State" too, indeed is the State itself.

It seems that the expression *veilleur de nuit*, which should have a more sarcastic ring than "the State as policeman", comes from Lassalle. Its opposite should be "ethical State" or "interventionist State" in general, but there are differences between the two expressions. The concept of ethical State is of philosophical and intellectual origin (belonging to the intellectuals: Hegel), and in fact could be brought into conjunction with the concept of State-*veilleur de nuit*; for it refers rather to the autonomous, educative and moral activity of the secular State, by contrast with the cosmopolitanism and the interference of the religious-ecclesiastical organisation as a mediaeval residue. The concept of interventionist State is of economic origin, and is connected on the one hand with tendencies supporting protection and economic nationalism, and on the other with the attempt to force a particular State personnel, of landowning and feudal origin, to take on the "protection" of the working classes against the excesses of capitalism (policy of Bismarck and of Disraeli).[14]

These diverse tendencies may combine in various ways, and in fact have so combined. Naturally liberals ("economists") are for the "State as *veilleur de nuit*", and would like the historical initiative to be left to civil society and to the various forces which spring up there – with the "State" as guardian of "fair play" and of the rules of the game. Intellectuals draw very significant distinctions as to when they are liberals and when they are interventionists (they may be liberals in the economic field and interventionists in the cultural field, etc.) The catholics would like the State to be interventionist one hundred per cent in their favour; failing that, or where they are in a minority, they call for a "neutral" State, so that it should not support their adversaries. [1935: 1st version 1930]

The following argument is worth reflecting upon: is the conception of the *gendarme*-nightwatchman State (leaving aside the polemical designation: *gendarme*, nightwatchman, etc.) not in fact the only conception of the State to transcend the purely "economic-corporate" stages?

We are still on the terrain of the identification of State and government – an identification which is precisely a representation of the economic-corporate form, in other words of the confusion between civil society and political society. For it should be remarked that the general notion of State includes elements which need to be referred back to the notion of civil society (in the sense that one might say that State = political society + civil society, in other words hegemony protected by the armour of coercion). In a doctrine of the State which conceives the latter as tendentially capable of withering away and of being subsumed into regulated society, the argument is a fundamental one. It is possible to imagine the coercive element of the State withering away by degrees, as ever-more conspicuous elements of regulated society (or ethical State or civil society) make their appearance.

The expressions "ethical State" or "civil society" would thus mean that this "image" of a State without a State was present to the greatest political and legal thinkers, in so far as they placed themselves on the terrain of pure science (pure utopia, since based on the premise that all men are really equal and hence equally rational and moral, i.e. capable of accepting the law spontaneously, freely, and not through coercion, as imposed by another class, as something external to consciousness).

... In the doctrine of the State as regulated society, one will have to pass from a phase in which "State" will be equal to "government", and "State" will be identified with "civil society", to a phase of the State as nightwatchman – i.e. of a coercive organisation which will safeguard the development of the continually proliferating elements of regulated society, and which will therefore progressively reduce its own authoritarian and forcible interventions. Nor can this conjure up the idea of a new "liberalism", even though the beginning of an era of organic liberty be imminent. [1930–32]

If it is true that no type of State can avoid passing through a phase of economic-corporate primitivism, it may be deduced that the content of the political hegemony of the new social group which has founded the new type of State must be predominantly of an economic order: what is involved is the reorganisation of the structure and the real relations between men on the one hand and the world of the economy or of production on the other. The superstructural elements will inevitably be few in number, and have a character of foresight and of struggle, but as yet few "planned" elements. Cultural policy will above all be negative, a critique of the past; it will be aimed at erasing from the memory and at destroying. The lines of construction will as yet be "broad lines", sketches, which might (and should) be changed at all times, so as to be consistent with the new structure as it is formed. This precisely did not happen in the period of the mediaeval communes; for culture, which remained a function of the Church, was precisely anti-economic in character (i.e. against the nascent capitalist economy); it was not directed towards giving hegemony to the new class, but rather to preventing the latter from acquiring it. Hence Humanism and the Renaissance were reactionary, because they signalled the defeat of the new class, the negation of the economic world which was proper to it, etc. [1931–32]

Another element to examine is that of the organic relations between the domestic and foreign policies of a State. Is it domestic policies which determine foreign policy, or vice versa? In this case too, it will be necessary to distinguish: between great powers, with relative international autonomy, and other powers; also, between different forms of government (a government like that of Napoleon III had two policies, apparently – reactionary internally, and liberal abroad).

Conditions in a State before and after a war. It is obvious that, in an alliance, what counts are the conditions in which a State finds itself at the moment of peace. Therefore it may happen that whoever has exercised hegemony during the war ends up by losing it as a result of the enfeeblement suffered in the course of the struggle, and is forced to see a "subordinate" who has been more skilful or "luckier" become hegemonic. This occurs in "world wars" when the geographic situation compels a State to throw all its resources into the crucible: it wins through its alliances, but victory finds it prostrate, etc. This is why in the concept of "great power" it is necessary to take many elements into account, and especially those which are "permanent" – i.e. especially "economic and financial potential" and population. [1931–32]

Organisation of National Societies

I have remarked elsewhere that in any given society nobody is disorganised and without party, provided that one takes organisation and party in a broad and not a formal sense. In this multiplicity of private associations (which are of two kinds: natural, and contractual or voluntary) one or more predominates relatively or absolutely – constituting the hegemonic apparatus of one social group over the rest of the population (or civil society): the basis for the State in the narrow sense of the governmental-coercive apparatus.

It always happens that individuals belong to more than one private association, and often to associations which are objectively in contradiction to one another. A totalitarian policy is aimed precisely: 1. at ensuring that the members of a particular party find in that party all the satisfactions that they formerly found in a multiplicity of organisations, i.e. at breaking all the threads that bind these members to extraneous cultural organisms; 2. at destroying all other organisations or at incorporating them into a system of which the party is the sole regulator. This occurs: 1. when the given party is the bearer of a new culture – then one has a progressive phase; 2. when the given party wishes to prevent another force, bearer of a new culture, from becoming itself "totalitarian" – then one has an objectively regressive and reactionary phase, even if that reaction (as invariably happens) does not avow itself, and seeks itself to appear as the bearer of a new culture.

[...]

Statolatry

Attitude of each particular social group towards its own State. The analysis would not be accurate if no account were taken of the two forms in which the State presents itself in the language and culture of specific epochs, i.e. as civil society and as political society. The term "statolatry" is applied to a particular attitude towards the "government by functionaries" or political society, which in everyday language is the form of State life to which the term of State is applied and which is commonly understood as the entire State. The assertion that the State can be identified with individuals (the individuals of a social group), as an element of active culture (i.e. as a movement to create a new civilisation, a new type of man and of citizen), must serve to determine the will to construct within the husk of political society a complex and well-articulated civil society, in which the individual can govern himself without his self-government thereby entering into conflict with political society – but rather becoming its normal continuation, its organic complement. For some social groups, which before their ascent to autonomous State life have not had a long independent period of cultural and moral development on their own (as was made possible in mediaeval society and under the absolute régimes by the juridical existence[15] of the privileged Estates or orders), a period of statolatry is necessary and indeed opportune. This "statolatry" is nothing other than the normal form of "State life", or at least of initiation to autonomous State life and to the creation of a "civil society" which it was not historically possible to create before the ascent to independent State life. However, this kind of "statolatry" must not be abandoned to itself, must not, especially, become theoretical fanaticism or be conceived of as "perpetual". It must be criticised, precisely in order to develop and produce new forms of State life, in which the initiative of individuals and groups will have a "State" character, even if it is not due to the "government of the functionaries" (make State life become "spontaneous"). [1931–32]

"Merits" of the Ruling Classes

In view of the fact that the identity State/class is not easy to understand, there is something strange about the way in which a government (State) is able to reflect back upon the class it represents, as a merit and a source of prestige, the fact that it has finally done what should have been done for fifty years and more – and which should therefore be a demerit and a source of shame.[16] One lets a man starve until he is fifty; when he is fifty, one finally notices him. In private life, such behaviour would warrant a good kicking. In the case of the State, it appears to be a "merit". Not merely that, but the fact that one "washes oneself" at the age of fifty appears to be a sign of superiority over other men of fifty who have always washed. One hears this kind of thing said about drainage schemes, public works, roads, etc., i.e. about a country's basic social equipment. The fact that a country provides itself with this equipment, with which others have provided themselves in their day, is loudly acclaimed and trumpeted forth, and the others are told: do as much, if you can. But the others cannot, because they have already done so in their day, and this is presented as a sign of their "impotence".

At all events, the fact that the State/government, conceived as an autonomous force, should reflect back its prestige upon the class upon which it is based, is of the greatest practical and theoretical importance, and deserves to be analysed fully if one wants a more realistic concept of the State itself. Moreover, this phenomenon is not something exceptional, or characteristic of one kind of State only. It can, it seems, be incorporated into the function of élites or vanguards, i.e. of parties, in relation to the class which they represent. This class, often, as an economic fact (which is what every class is essentially) might not enjoy any intellectual or moral prestige, i.e. might be incapable of establishing its hegemony, hence of founding a State. Hence the function of monarchies, even in the modern era; hence, too, in particular, the phenomenon (especially in England and in Germany) whereby the leading personnel of the bourgeois class organised into a State can be constituted by elements of the old feudal classes, who have been dispossessed of their traditional economic predominance (Junkers and Lords), but who have found new forms of economic power in industry and in the banks, and who have not fused with the bourgeoisie but have remained united to their traditional social group. [1933]

NOTES AND REFERENCES

1 I.e. antagonistic to the existing capitalist and bourgeois order.
2 "*Arditismo.*" During the First World War, the "*arditi*" were volunteer commando squads in the Italian army. The term was adopted by d'Annunzio for his nationalist volunteer "legions", and was also used by the "*arditi del popolo*", formed to combat the fascist squads in the summer of 1921. This latter organisation emerged outside the left parties, but the mass of its local leaders and members were communist or socialist. The PSI (who signed a "concilation pact" with the fascists at this time) condemned the organisation; they advocated a policy of non-resistance. The PCI also condemned the organisation, for sectarian reasons, preferring to concentrate on its own, purely communist, defence squads. Gramsci had written and published articles welcoming the organisation before the official condemnation, and even afterwards did so obliquely, by criticising the PSI's attitude. However, as his comments later in this note indicate, he did not feel that working-class "*arditi*" could in fact hope to stand up to the fascist squads, who enjoyed the connivance of the State. It was only *mass* as opposed to *volunteer* action which could provide a viable response.

3 "*Bersaglieri*" – an élite corps of the Italian army, founded by Lamarmora in 1836.
4 This is presumably a reference to the failure of communists in Italy between 1921 and 1926 to win more than a minority position within the trade-union movement, despite the betrayals of the CGL's reformist leaders.
5 The "fourth meeting" is the Fourth World Congress of the Comintern, at which Gramsci was present. Trotsky gave the report on NEP, in the course of which he said: "...it will hardly be possible to catch the European bourgeoisie by surprise as we caught the Russian bourgeoisie. The European bourgeoisie is more intelligent, and more farsighted; it is not wasting time. Everything that can be set on foot against us is being mobilised by it right now. The revolutionary proletariat will thus encounter on its road to power not only the combat vanguards of the counter-revolution but also its heaviest reserves. Only by smashing, breaking up and demoralising these enemy forces will the proletariat be able to seize state power. By way of compensation, after the proletarian overturn, the vanquished bourgeoisie will no longer dispose of powerful reserves from which it could draw forces for prolonging the civil war. In other words, after the conquest of power, the European proletariat will in all likelihood have far more elbow room for its creative work in economy and culture than we had in Russia on the day after the overturn. The more difficult and gruelling the struggle for state power, all the less possible will it be to challenge the proletariat's power after the victory." Trotsky, *The First Five Years of the Communist International*, Vol. II, pp. 221–2, Pioneer, New York 1953.
6 I.e. Trotsky's theory of Permanent Revolution.
7 See too IL nostro Marx, 1919–1920, pp. 150–1: "Tendency to conformism in the contemporary world, more widespread and deeper than in the past: the standardisation of thought and action assumes national or even continental

proportions. The economic basis of the 'collective man': big factories, Taylorisation, rationalisation, etc.... On social 'conformism', it should be stressed that the problem is not a new one, and that the alarm expressed by certain intellectuals is merely comic. Conformism has always existed: what is involved today is a struggle between 'two conformisms', i.e. a struggle for hegemony, a crisis of civil society. The old intellectual and moral leaders of society feel the ground slipping from under their feet; they perceive that their 'sermons' have become precisely mere 'sermons', i.e. external to reality, pure form without any content, shades without a spirit. This is the reason for their reactionary and conservative tendencies; for the particular form of civilisation, culture and morality which they represented is decomposing, and they loudly proclaim the death of all civilisation, all culture, all morality; they call for repressive measures by the State, and constitute resistance groups cut off from the real historical process, thus prolonging the crisis, since the eclipse of a way of living and thinking cannot take place without a crisis. The representatives of the new order in gestation, on the other hand, inspired by 'rationalistic' hatred for the old, propagate utopias and fanciful schemes. What is the point of reference for the new world in gestation? The world of production; work. The greatest utilitarianism must go to found any analysis of the moral and intellectual institutions to be created and of the principles to be propagated. Collective and individual life must be organised with a view to the maximum yield of the productive apparatus. The development of economic forces on new bases and the progressive installation of the new structure will heal the contradictions which cannot fail to exist, and, when they have created a new 'conformism' from below, will permit new possibilities for self-discipline, i.e. for freedom, including that of the individual."

8   The doctrine developed by Montesquieu in his *Esprit des Lois* – on the basis of

the contemporary bourgeois political system in England as he saw it – whereby executive, legislative and judiciary functions are exercised independently of each other. The principle inspired the American Constitution and others modelled on it.

9   " *Premiatrici*".

10 Spirito and Volpicelli were the principal theorists of the "corporate economy" in fascist Italy. They claimed that corporativism represented a "post-capitalist" economy, and that it had abolished the anarchy of liberal capitalism. Gramsci here refers to the confusion involved in the idea that a "regulated" society could co-exist with capitalism – the class-State. Elsewhere Gramsci uses "regulated society" to mean Communism. The concept is probably a reference to the concluding passage of "*Socialism: Utopian and Scientific*" where Engels discusses the withering away of the State. He writes: "With the seizing of the means of production by society, production of commodities is done away with, and, simultaneously, the mastery of the product over the producer. Anarchy in social production is replaced by *systematic, definite organisation*" (our italics). Spirito and Volpicelli claimed that the corporate economy had achieved order and harmony. Gramsci comments, in effect, that this will only be possible under Communism; until then, there will continue to be a class-State, and hence no "regulated" society....

11 The idea of the "ethical" State is associated with Croce. For the latter, the two moments of the State were the "ethical" and the "political" (or the "moral" and the "useful"); he saw these as being in perpetual dialectical contradiction – a conflict which he represented symbolically as that between Church and State. The term was also adopted by fascism, see e.g. Mussolini, in "*The Doctrine of Fascism*", 1932: "The fascist State has its own consciousness, its own will, and for that reason is called an 'ethical'

State. In 1929 ... I said 'For fascism the State is not the night-watchman ... it is a spiritual and moral fact ... it educates the citizens to civil virtue ... ', ," etc.

12 The three days in which the people of Paris rose and drove out Charles X.

13 *Veilleur de nuit* means "night-watchman"; see below. The Italian expression referred to is *"Stato-carabiniere"*.

14 Bismarck put through legislation providing for sickness and old-age pensions; Disraeli denounced certain of the worst excess of mid-Victorian capitalism in his novels, and his ministry (1874–80) limited the working day for women and children, passed the Combination Act of 1875 giving limited recognition to trade unions, and put through the Public Health Act and the Artisans' Dwelling Act in the same year, etc.

15 The Einaudi edition gives *esigenza* = "need", instead of Gramsci's original *esistenza* = "existence".

16 A clear reference to fascist propaganda extolling the régime's achievements in the field of public works, etc. In England in the 'thirties, approval for fascist Italy often took the form "at least Mussolini has got the trains to run on time", etc.

3

Ideology and Ideological State Apparatuses (Notes towards an Investigation)

Louis Althusser

On the Reproduction of the Conditions of Production[1]

... As Marx said, every child knows that a social formation which did not reproduce the conditions of production at the same time as it produced would not last a year.[2] The ultimate condition of production is therefore the reproduction of the conditions of production. This may be 'simple' (reproducing exactly the previous conditions of production) or 'on an extended scale' (expanding them). Let us ignore this last distinction for the moment.

What, then, is *the reproduction of the conditions of production?*

[...]

Let us try and examine the matter methodically.

To simplify my exposition, and assuming that every social formation arises from a dominant mode of production, I can say that the process of production sets to work the existing productive forces in and under definite relations of production.

It follows that, in order to exist, every social formation must reproduce the conditions of its production at the same time as it produces, and in order to be able to produce. It must therefore reproduce:

1. the productive forces,
2. the existing relations of production.

Reproduction of the means of production

Everyone (including the bourgeois economists whose work is national accounting, or the modern 'macro–economic' 'theoreticians') now recognizes, because Marx compellingly proved it in *Capital* Volume Two, that no production is possible which does not allow for the reproduction of the material conditions of production: the reproduction of the means of production.

The average economist, who is no different in this than the average capitalist, knows that each year it is essential to foresee what is

From *Lenin and Philosophy and Other Essays*, trans. B. Brewster, pp. 127–86. New York and London: Monthly Review Press, 1971. Copyright © 1971 by Monthly Review Press. Reprinted by permission of Monthly Review Foundation.

needed to replace what has been used up or worn out in production: raw material, fixed installations (buildings), instruments of production (machines), etc. I say the average economist = the average capitalist, for they both express the point of view of the firm, regarding it as sufficient simply to give a commentary on the terms of the firm's financial accounting practice.

But thanks to the genius of Quesnay who first posed this 'glaring' problem, and to the genius of Marx who resolved it, we know that the reproduction of the material conditions of production cannot be thought at the level of the firm, because it does not exist at that level in its real conditions. What happens at the level of the firm is an effect, which only gives an idea of the necessity of reproduction, but absolutely fails to allow its conditions and mechanisms to be thought.

A moment's reflection is enough to be convinced of this: Mr X, a capitalist who produces woollen yarn in his spinning-mill, has to 'reproduce' his raw material, his machines, etc. But *he* does not produce them for his own production – other capitalists do: an Australian sheep-farmer, Mr Y, a heavy engineer producing machine-tools, Mr Z, etc., etc. And Mr Y and Mr Z, in order to produce those products which are the condition of the reproduction of Mr X's conditions of production, also have to reproduce the conditions of their own production, and so on to infinity – the whole in proportions such that, on the national and even the world market, the demand for means of production (for reproduction) can be satisfied by the supply.

[...]

Reproduction of labour power

However, the reader will not have failed to note one thing. We have discussed the reproduction of the means of production – but not the reproduction of the productive forces. We have therefore ignored the reproduction of what distinguishes the productive forces

from the means of production, i.e. the reproduction of labour power.

From the observation of what takes place in the firm, in particular from the examination of the financial accounting practice which predicts amortization and investment, we have been able to obtain an approximate idea of the existence of the material process of reproduction, but we are now entering a domain in which the observation of what happens in the firm is, if not totally blind, at least almost entirely so, and for good reason: the reproduction of labour power takes place essentially outside the firm.

How is the reproduction of labour power ensured?

It is ensured by giving labour power the material means with which to reproduce itself: by wages. Wages feature in the accounting of each enterprise, but as 'wage capital',[3] not at all as a condition of the material reproduction of labour power.

However, that is in fact how it 'works', since wages represents only that part of the value produced by the expenditure of labour power which is indispensable for its reproduction: sc. indispensable to the reconstitution of the labour power of the wage-earner (the wherewithal to pay for housing, food and clothing, in short to enable the wage-earner to present himself again at the factory gate the next day – and every further day God grants him); and we should add: indispensable for raising and educating the children in whom the proletarian reproduces himself (in n models where n = 0, 1, 2, etc. ...) as labour power.

Remember that this quantity of value (wages) necessary for the reproduction of labour power is determined not by the needs of a 'biological' Guaranteed Minimum Wage (*Salaire Minimum Interprofessionnel Garanti*) alone, but by the needs of a historical minimum (Marx noted that English workers need beer while French proletarians need wine) – i.e. a historically variable minimum.

I should also like to point out that this minimum is doubly historical in that it is not defined by the historical needs of the working class 'recognized' by the capitalist class, but by the historical needs imposed by the proletarian class struggle (a double class struggle: against the lengthening of the working day and against the reduction of wages).

However, it is not enough to ensure for labour power the material conditions of its reproduction if it is to be reproduced as labour power. I have said that the available labour power must be 'competent', i.e. suitable to be set to work in the complex system of the process of production. The development of the productive forces and the type of unity historically constitutive of the productive forces at a given moment produce the result that the labour power has to be (diversely) skilled and therefore reproduced as such. Diversely: according to the requirements of the socio-technical division of labour, its different 'jobs' and 'posts'.

How is this reproduction of the (diversified) skills of labour power provided for in a capitalist regime? Here, unlike social formations characterized by slavery or serfdom, this reproduction of the skills of labour power tends (this is a tendential law) decreasingly to be provided for 'on the spot' (apprenticeship within production itself), but is achieved more and more outside production: by the capitalist education system, and by other instances and institutions.

What do children learn at school? They go varying distances in their studies, but at any rate they learn to read, to write and to add – i.e. a number of techniques, and a number of other things as well, including elements (which may be rudimentary or on the contrary thoroughgoing) of 'scientific' or 'literary culture', which are directly useful in the different jobs in production (one instruction for manual workers, another for technicians, a third for engineers, a final one for higher management, etc.). Thus they learn 'know-how'.

But besides these techniques and knowledges, and in learning them, children at school also learn the 'rules' of good behaviour, i.e. the attitude that should be observed by every agent in the division of labour,

according to the job he is 'destined' for: rules of morality, civic and professional conscience, which actually means rules of respect for the socio-technical division of labour and ultimately the rules of the order established by class domination. They also learn to 'speak proper French', to 'handle' the workers correctly, i.e. actually (for the future capitalists and their servants) to 'order them about' properly, i.e. (ideally) to 'speak to them' in the right way, etc.

To put this more scientifically, I shall say that the reproduction of labour power requires not only a reproduction of its skills, but also, at the same time, a reproduction of its submission to the rules of the established order, i.e. a reproduction of submission to the ruling ideology for the workers, and a reproduction of the ability to manipulate the ruling ideology correctly for the agents of exploitation and repression, so that they, too, will provide for the domination of the ruling class 'in words'.

In other words, the school (but also other State institutions like the Church, or other apparatuses like the Army) teaches 'know-how', but in forms which ensure *subjection to the ruling ideology* or the mastery of its 'practice'. All the agents of production, exploitation and repression, not to speak of the 'professionals of ideology' (Marx), must in one way or another be 'steeped' in this ideology in order to perform their tasks 'conscientiously' – the tasks of the exploited (the proletarians), of the exploiters (the capitalists), of the exploiters' auxiliaries (the managers), or of the high priests of the ruling ideology (its 'functionaries'), etc.

The reproduction of labour power thus reveals as its *sine qua non* not only the reproduction of its 'skills' but also the reproduction of its subjection to the ruling ideology or of the 'practice' of that ideology, with the proviso that it is not enough to say 'not only but also', for it is clear that *it is in the forms and under the forms of ideological subjection that provision is made for the reproduction of the skills of labour power.*

But this is to recognize the effective presence of a new reality: *ideology.*

Here I shall make two comments.

The first is to round off my analysis of reproduction.

I have just given a rapid survey of the forms of the reproduction of the productive forces, i.e. of the means of production on the one hand, and of labour power on the other.

But I have not yet approached the question of the *reproduction of the relations of production*. This is a *crucial question* for the Marxist theory of the mode of production.

[...]

The second comment is that in order to make this detour, I am obliged to re-raise my old question: what is a society?

Infrastructure and Superstructure

On a number of occasions[4] I have insisted on the revolutionary character of the Marxist conception of the 'social whole' insofar as it is distinct from the Hegelian 'totality'. I said (and this thesis only repeats famous propositions of historical materialism) that Marx conceived the structure of every society as constituted by 'levels' or 'instances' articulated by a specific determination: the *infrastructure*, or economic base (the 'unity' of the productive forces and the relations of production) and the *superstructure*, which itself contains two 'levels' or 'instances': the politico-legal (law and the State) and ideology (the different ideologies, religious, ethical, legal, political, etc.).

Besides its theoretico-didactic interest (it reveals the difference between Marx and Hegel), this representation has the following crucial theoretical advantage: it makes it possible to inscribe in the theoretical apparatus of its essential concepts what I have called their *respective indices of effectivity*. What does this mean?

It is easy to see that this representation of the structure of every society as an edifice containing a base (infrastructure) on which are erected the two 'floors' of the superstructure, is a metaphor, to be quite precise, a spatial metaphor: the metaphor of a topography (*topique*).[5] Like every metaphor, this metaphor suggests something, makes something visible. What? Precisely this: that the upper floors could not 'stay up' (in the air) alone, if they did not rest precisely on their base.

Thus the object of the metaphor of the edifice is to represent above all the 'determination in the last instance' by the economic base. The effect of this spatial metaphor is to endow the base with an index of effectivity known by the famous terms: the determination in the last instance of what happens in the upper 'floors' (of the superstructure) by what happens in the economic base.

Given this index of effectivity 'in the last instance', the 'floors' of the superstructure are clearly endowed with different indices of effectivity. What kind of indices?

It is possible to say that the floors of the superstructure are not determinant in the last instance, but that they are determined by the effectivity of the base; that if they are determinant in their own (as yet undefined) ways, this is true only insofar as they are determined by the base.

Their index of effectivity (or determination), as determined by the determination in the last instance of the base, is thought by the Marxist tradition in two ways: (1) there is a 'relative autonomy' of the superstructure with respect to the base; (2) there is a 'reciprocal action' of the superstructure on the base.

We can therefore say that the great theoretical advantage of the Marxist topography, i.e. of the spatial metaphor of the edifice (base and superstructure) is simultaneously that it reveals that questions of determination (or of index of effectivity) are crucial; that it reveals that it is the base which in the last instance determines the whole edifice; and that, as a consequence, it obliges us to pose the theoretical problem of the types of 'derivatory' effectivity peculiar to the superstructure, i.e. it obliges us to think what the Marxist tradition calls conjointly the relative autonomy of the superstructure and the reciprocal action of the superstructure on the base.

The greatest disadvantage of this representation of the structure of every society by the spatial metaphor of an edifice, is obviously the fact that it is metaphorical: i.e. it remains *descriptive*.

It now seems to me that it is possible and desirable to represent things differently. NB, I do not mean by this that I want to reject the classical metaphor, for that metaphor itself requires that we go beyond it. And I am not going beyond it in order to reject it as outworn. I simply want to attempt to think what it gives us in the form of a description.

I believe that it is possible and necessary to think what characterizes the essential of the existence and nature of the superstructure *on the basis of reproduction*. Once one takes the point of view of reproduction, many of the questions whose existence was indicated by the spatial metaphor of the edifice, but to which it could not give a conceptual answer, are immediately illuminated.

My basic thesis is that it is not possible to pose these questions (and therefore to answer them) *except from the point of view of reproduction*.

I shall give a short analysis of Law, the State and Ideology *from this point of view*. And I shall reveal what happens both from the point of view of practice and production on the one hand, and from that of reproduction on the other.

The State

The Marxist tradition is strict, here: in the *Communist Manifesto* and the *Eighteenth Brumaire* (and in all the later classical texts, above all in Marx's writings on the Paris Commune and Lenin's on *State and Revolution*), the State is explicitly conceived as a repressive apparatus. The State is a 'machine' of repression, which enables the ruling classes (in the nineteenth century the bourgeois class and the 'class' of big landowners) to ensure their domination over the working class, thus enabling the former to subject the latter to the process of surplus-value extortion (i.e. to capitalist exploitation).

The State is thus first of all what the Marxist classics have called *the State apparatus*. This term means: not only the specialized apparatus (in the narrow sense) whose existence and necessity I have recognized in relation to the requirements of legal practice, i.e. the police, the courts, the prisons; but also the army, which (the proletariat has paid for this experience with its blood) intervenes directly as a supplementary repressive force in the last instance, when the police and its specialized auxiliary corps are 'outrun by events'; and above this ensemble, the head of State, the government and the administration.

Presented in this form, the Marxist-Leninist 'theory' of the State has its finger on the essential point, and not for one moment can there be any question of rejecting the fact that this really is the essential point. The State apparatus, which defines the State as a force of repressive execution and intervention 'in the interests of the ruling classes' in the class struggle conducted by the bourgeoisie and its allies against the proletariat, is quite certainly the State, and quite certainly defines its basic 'function'.

[...]

When I say that the Marxist 'theory' of the State available to us is still partly 'descriptive', that means first and foremost that this descriptive 'theory' is without the shadow of a doubt precisely the beginning of the Marxist theory of the State, and that this beginning gives us the essential point, i.e. the decisive principle of every later development of the theory.

Indeed, I shall call the descriptive theory of the State correct, since it is perfectly possible to make the vast majority of the facts in the domain with which it is concerned correspond to the definition it gives of its object. Thus, the definition of the State as a class State, existing in the repressive State apparatus, casts a brilliant light on all the facts observable in the various orders of repression whatever their domains: from the massacres of June 1848 and of the Paris Commune, of

Bloody Sunday, May 1905 in Petrograd, of the Resistance, of Charonne, etc., to the mere (and relatively anodyne) interventions of a 'censorship' which has banned Diderot's *La Réligieuse* or a play by Gatti on Franco; it casts light on all the direct or indirect forms of exploitation and extermination of the masses of the people (imperialist wars); it casts light on that subtle everyday domination beneath which can be glimpsed, in the forms of political democracy, for example, what Lenin, following Marx, called the dictatorship of the bourgeoisie.

And yet the descriptive theory of the State represents a phase in the constitution of the theory which itself demands the 'supersession' of this phase. For it is clear that if the definition in question really does give us the means to identify and recognize the facts of oppression by relating them to the State, conceived as the repressive State apparatus, this 'interrelationship' gives rise to a very special kind of obviousness, about which I shall have something to say in a moment: 'Yes, that's how it is, that's really true!'[6] And the accumulation of facts within the definition of the State may multiply examples, but it does not really advance the definition of the State, i.e. the scientific theory of the State. Every descriptive theory thus runs the risk of 'blocking' the development of the theory, and yet that development is essential.

That is why I think that, in order to develop this descriptive theory into theory as such, i.e. in order to understand further the mechanisms of the State in its functioning, I think that it is indispensable to *add* something to the classical definition of the State as a State apparatus.

The essentials of the Marxist theory of the state

Let me first clarify one important point: the State (and its existence in its apparatus) has no meaning except as a function of *State power*. The whole of the political class struggle revolves around the State. By which I mean around the possession, i.e. the seizure and conservation of State power by a certain class or by an alliance between classes or class fractions. This first clarification obliges me to distinguish between State power (conservation of State power or seizure of State power), the objective of the political class struggle on the one hand, and the State apparatus on the other.

We know that the State apparatus may survive, as is proved by bourgeois 'revolutions' in nineteenth-century France (1830, 1848), by *coups d'état* (2 December, May 1958), by collapses of the State (the fall of the Empire in 1870, of the Third Republic in 1940), or by the political rise of the petty bourgeoisie (1890–95 in France), etc., without the State apparatus being affected or modified: it may survive political events which affect the possession of State power.

Even after a social revolution like that of 1917, a large part of the State apparatus survived after the seizure of State power by the alliance of the proletariat and the small peasantry: Lenin repeated the fact again and again.

It is possible to describe the distinction between State power and State apparatus as part of the 'Marxist theory' of the State, explicitly present since Marx's *Eighteenth Brumaire* and *Class Struggles in France*.

To summarize the 'Marxist theory of the State' on this point, it can be said that the Marxist classics have always claimed that (1) the State is the repressive State apparatus, (2) State power and State apparatus must be distinguished, (3) the objective of the class struggle concerns State power, and in consequence the use of the State apparatus by the classes (or alliance of classes or of fractions of classes) holding State power as a function of their class objectives, and (4) the proletariat must seize State power in order to destroy the existing bourgeois State apparatus and, in a first phase, replace it with a quite different, proletarian, State apparatus, then in later phases set in motion a radical process, that of the destruction of the State (the end of State power, the end of every State apparatus).

In this perspective, therefore, what I would propose to add to the 'Marxist theory' of the State is already there in so many words. But it seems to me that even with this supplement, this theory is still in part descriptive, although it does now contain complex and differential elements whose functioning and action cannot be understood without recourse to further supplementary theoretical development.

The state ideological apparatuses

Thus, what has to be added to the 'Marxist theory' of the State is something else.

Here we must advance cautiously in a terrain which, in fact, the Marxist classics entered long before us, but without having systematized in theoretical form the decisive advances implied by their experiences and procedures. Their experiences and procedures were indeed restricted in the main to the terrain of political practice.

In fact, i.e. in their political practice, the Marxist classics treated the State as a more complex reality than the definition of it given in the 'Marxist theory of the State', even when it has been supplemented as I have just suggested. They recognized this complexity in their practice, but they did not express it in a corresponding theory.[7]

I should like to attempt a very schematic outline of this corresponding theory. To that end, I propose the following thesis.

In order to advance the theory of the State it is indispensable to take into account not only the distinction between *State power* and *State apparatus*, but also another reality which is clearly on the side of the (repressive) State apparatus, but must not be confused with it. I shall call this reality by its concept: *the ideological State apparatuses*.

What are the ideological State apparatuses (ISAs)?

They must not be confused with the (repressive) State apparatus. Remember that in Marxist theory, the State Apparatus (SA) contains: the Government, the Administration, the Army, the Police, the Courts, the Prisons,

etc., which constitute what I shall in future call the Repressive State Apparatus. Repressive suggests that the State Apparatus in question 'functions by violence' – at least ultimately (since repression, e.g. administrative repression, may take non-physical forms).

I shall call Ideological State Apparatuses a certain number of realities which present themselves to the immediate observer in the form of distinct and specialized institutions. I propose an empirical list of these which will obviously have to be examined in detail, tested, corrected and reorganized. With all the reservations implied by this requirement, we can for the moment regard the following institutions as Ideological State Apparatuses (the order in which I have listed them has no particular significance):

– the religious ISA (the system of the different Churches),

– the educational ISA (the system of the different public and private 'Schools'),

– the family ISA,[8]

– the legal ISA,[9]

– the political ISA (the political system, including the different Parties),

– the trade-union ISA,

– the communications ISA (press, radio and television, etc.),

– the cultural ISA (Literature, the Arts, sports, etc.).

I have said that the ISAs must not be confused with the (Repressive) State Apparatus. What constitutes the difference?

As a first moment, it is clear that while there is *one* (Repressive) State Apparatus, there is a *plurality* of Ideological State Apparatuses. Even presupposing that it exists, the unity that constitutes this plurality of ISAs as a body is not immediately visible.

As a second moment, it is clear that whereas the – unified – (Repressive) State Apparatus belongs entirely to the *public* domain, much the larger part of the Ideological State Apparatuses (in their apparent dispersion) are part, on the contrary, of the *private* domain. Churches, Parties, Trade Unions, families, some schools, most newspapers, cultural ventures, etc., etc., are private.

We can ignore the first observation for the moment. But someone is bound to question the second, asking me by what right I regard as Ideological *State* Apparatuses, institutions which for the most part do not possess public status, but are quite simply *private* institutions. As a conscious Marxist, Gramsci already forestalled this objection in one sentence. The distinction between the public and the private is a distinction internal to bourgeois law, and valid in the (subordinate) domains in which bourgeois law exercises its 'authority'. The domain of the State escapes it because the latter is 'above the law': the State, which is the State *of* the ruling class, is neither public nor private; on the contrary, it is the precondition for any distinction between public and private. The same thing can be said from the starting-point of our State Ideological Apparatuses. It is unimportant whether the institutions in which they are realized are 'public' or 'private'. What matters is how they function. Private institutions can perfectly well 'function' as Ideological State Apparatuses. A reasonably thorough analysis of any one of the ISAs proves it.

But now for what is essential. What distinguishes the ISAs from the (Repressive) State Apparatus is the following basic difference: the Repressive State Apparatus functions 'by violence', whereas the Ideological State Apparatuses *function 'by ideology'*.

I can clarify matters by correcting this distinction. I shall say rather that every State Apparatus, whether Repressive or Ideological, 'functions' both by violence and by ideology, but with one very important distinction which makes it imperative not to confuse the Ideological State Apparatuses with the (Repressive) State Apparatus.

This is the fact that the (Repressive) State Apparatus functions massively and predominantly *by repression* (including physical repression), while functioning secondarily by ideology. (There is no such thing as a purely repressive apparatus.) For example, the Army and the Police also function by ideology both to

ensure their own cohesion and reproduction, and in the 'values' they propound externally.

In the same way, but inversely, it is essential to say that for their part the Ideological State Apparatuses function massively and predominantly *by ideology*, but they also function secondarily by repression, even if ultimately, but only ultimately, this is very attenuated and concealed, even symbolic. (There is no such thing as a purely ideological apparatus.) Thus Schools and Churches use suitable methods of punishment, expulsion, selection, etc., to 'discipline' not only their shepherds, but also their flocks. The same is true of the Family.... The same is true of the cultural IS Apparatus (censorship, among other things), etc.

Is it necessary to add that this determination of the double 'functioning' (predominantly, secondarily) by repression and by ideology, according to whether it is a matter of the (Repressive) State Apparatus or the Ideological State Apparatuses, makes it clear that very subtle explicit or tacit combinations may be woven from the interplay of the (Repressive) State Apparatus and the Ideological State Apparatuses? Everyday life provides us with innumerable examples of this, but they must be studied in detail if we are to go further than this mere observation.

Nevertheless, this remark leads us towards an understanding of what constitutes the unity of the apparently disparate body of the ISAs. If the ISAs "function" massively and predominantly by ideology, what unifies their diversity is precisely this functioning, insofar as the ideology by which they function is always in fact unified, despite its diversity and its contradictions, *beneath the ruling ideology*, which is the ideology of "the ruling class". Given the fact that the "ruling class" in principle holds State power (openly or more often by means of alliances between classes or class fractions), and therefore has at its disposal the (Repressive) State Apparatus, we can accept the fact that this same ruling class is active in the Ideological State Apparatuses insofar as it is ultimately the ruling ideology which is realized in the Ideological State Apparatuses, precisely in its contradictions.

Of course, it is a quite different thing to act by laws and decrees in the (Repressive) State Apparatus and to "act" through the intermediary of the ruling ideology in the Ideological State Apparatuses. We must go into the details of this difference – but it cannot mask the reality of a profound identity. To my knowledge, *no class can hold State power over a long period without at the same time exercising its hegemony over and in the State Ideological Apparatuses*. I only need one example and proof of this: Lenin's anguished concern to revolutionize the educational Ideological State Apparatus (among others), simply to make it possible for the Soviet proletariat, who had seized State power, to secure the future of the dictatorship of the proletariat and the transition to socialism.[10]

This last comment puts us in a position to understand that the Ideological State Apparatuses may be not only the *stake,* but also the *site* of class struggle, and often of bitter forms of class struggle. The class (or class alliance) in power cannot lay down the law in the ISAs as easily as it can in the (repressive) State apparatus, not only because the former ruling classes are able to retain strong positions there for a long time, but also because the resistance of the exploited classes is able to find means and occasions to express itself there, either by the utilization of their contradictions, or by conquering combat positions in them in struggle.[11]

Let me run through my comments.

If the thesis I have proposed is well-founded, it leads me back to the classical Marxist theory of the State, while making it more precise in one point. I argue that it is necessary to distinguish between State power (and its possession by . . .) on the one hand, and the State Apparatus on the other. But I add that the State Apparatus contains two bodies: the body of institutions which represent the Repressive State Apparatus on the one hand, and the body of institutions which represent the body of Ideological State Apparatuses on the other.

But if this is the case, the following question is bound to be asked, even in the very summary state of my suggestions: what exactly is the extent of the role of the Ideological State Apparatuses? What is their importance based on? In other words: to what does the 'function' of these Ideological State Apparatuses, which do not function by repression but by ideology, correspond?

On the Reproduction of the Relations of Production

I can now answer the central question which I have left in suspense for many long pages: *how is the reproduction of the relations of production secured?*

In the topographical language (Infrastructure, Super-structure), I can say: for the most part,[12] it is secured by the legal-political and ideological superstructure.

But as I have argued that it is essential to go beyond this still descriptive language, I shall say: for the most part,[12] it is secured by the exercise of State power in the State Apparatuses, on the one hand the (Repressive) State Apparatuses, on the other the Ideological State Apparatuses.

What I have just said must also be taken into account, and it can be assembled in the form of the following three features:

1. All the State Apparatuses function both by repression and by ideology, with the difference that the (Repressive) State Apparatus functions massively and predominantly by repression, whereas the Ideological State Apparatuses function massively and predominantly by ideology.

2. Whereas the (Repressive) State Apparatus constitutes an organized whole whose different parts are centralized beneath a commanding unity, that of the politics of class struggle applied by the political representatives of the ruling classes in possession of State power, the Ideological State Apparatuses are multiple, distinct, 'relatively autonomous' and capable of providing an objective field to contradictions which express, in forms which may be limited or extreme, the effects

of the clashes between the capitalist class struggle and the proletarian class struggle, as well as their subordinate forms.

3. Whereas the unity of the (Repressive) State Apparatus is secured by its unified and centralized organization under the leadership of the representatives of the classes in power executing the politics of the class struggle of the classes in power, the unity of the different Ideological State Apparatuses is secured, usually in contradictory forms, by the ruling ideology, the ideology of the ruling class.

Taking these features into account, it is possible to represent the reproduction of the relations of production[13] in the following way, according to a kind of 'division of labour'.

The role of the repressive State apparatus, insofar as it is a repressive apparatus, consists essentially in securing by force (physical or otherwise) the political conditions of the reproduction of relations of production which are in the last resort *relations of exploitation*. Not only does the State apparatus contribute generously to its own reproduction (the capitalist State contains political dynasties, military dynasties, etc.), but also and above all, the State apparatus secures by repression (from the most brutal physical force, via mere administrative commands and interdictions, to open and tacit censorship) the political conditions for the action of the Ideological State Apparatuses.

In fact, it is the latter which largely secure the reproduction specifically of the relations of production, behind a 'shield' provided by the repressive State apparatus. It is here that the role of the ruling ideology is heavily concentrated, the ideology of the ruling class, which holds State power. It is the intermediation of the ruling ideology that ensures a (sometimes teeth-gritting) 'harmony' between the repressive State apparatus and the Ideological State Apparatuses, and between the different State Ideological Apparatuses.

We are thus led to envisage the following hypothesis, as a function precisely of the diversity of ideological State Apparatuses in

their single, because shared, role of the reproduction of the relations of production.

Indeed we have listed a relatively large number of ideological State apparatuses in contemporary capitalist social formations: the educational apparatus, the religious apparatus, the family apparatus, the political apparatus, the trade-union apparatus, the communications apparatus, the 'cultural' apparatus, etc.

But in the social formations of that mode of production characterized by 'serfdom' (usually called the feudal mode of production), we observe that although there is a single repressive State apparatus which, since the earliest known Ancient States, let alone the Absolute Monarchies, has been formally very similar to the one we know today, the number of Ideological State Apparatuses is smaller and their individual types are different. For example, we observe that during the Middle Ages, the Church (the religious ideological State apparatus) accumulated a number of functions which have today devolved on to several distinct ideological State apparatuses, new ones in relation to the past I am invoking, in particular educational and cultural functions. Alongside the Church there was the family Ideological State Apparatus, which played a considerable part, incommensurable with its role in capitalist social formations. Despite appearances, the Church and the Family were not the only Ideological State Apparatuses. There was also a political Ideological State Apparatus (the Estates General, the *Parlement*, the different political factions and Leagues, the ancestors of the modern political parties, and the whole political system of the free Communes and then of the *Villes*). There was also a powerful 'proto-trade-union' Ideological State Apparatus, if I may venture such an anachronistic term (the powerful merchants' and bankers' guilds and the journeymen's associations, etc.). Publishing and Communications, even, saw an indisputable development, as did the theatre; initially both were integral parts of the Church, then they became more and more independent of it.

In the pre-capitalist historical period which I have examined extremely broadly, it is absolutely clear that *there was one dominant Ideological State Apparatus, the Church,* which concentrated within it not only religious functions, but also educational ones, and a large proportion of the functions of communications and 'culture'. It is no accident that all ideological struggle, from the sixteenth to the eighteenth century, starting with the first shocks of the Reformation, was *concentrated* in an anti-clerical and anti-religious struggle; rather this is a function precisely of the dominant position of the religious ideological State apparatus.

The foremost objective and achievement of the French Revolution was not just to transfer State power from the feudal aristocracy to the merchant-capitalist bourgeoisie, to break part of the former repressive State apparatus and replace it with a new one (e.g., the national popular Army)– but also to attack the number-one Ideological State Apparatus: the Church. Hence the civil constitution of the clergy, the confiscation of ecclesiastical wealth, and the creation of new ideological State apparatuses to replace the religious ideological State apparatus in its dominant role.

Naturally, these things did not happen automatically: witness the Concordat, the Restoration and the long class struggle between the landed aristocracy and the industrial bourgeoisie throughout the nineteenth century for the establishment of bourgeois hegemony over the functions formerly fulfilled by the Church: above all by the Schools. It can be said that the bourgeoisie relied on the new political, parliamentary-democratic, ideological State apparatus, installed in the earliest years of the Revolution, then restored after long and violent struggles, for a few months in 1848 and for decades after the fall of the Second Empire, in order to conduct its struggle against the Church and wrest its ideological functions away from it, in other words, to ensure not only its own political hegemony, but also the ideological hegemony indispensable to the reproduction of capitalist relations of production.

That is why I believe that I am justified in advancing the following Thesis, however precarious it is. I believe that the ideological State apparatus which has been installed in the *dominant* position in mature capitalist social formations as a result of a violent political and ideological class struggle against the old dominant ideological State apparatus, is the *educational ideological apparatus.*

This thesis may seem paradoxical, given that for everyone, i.e. in the ideological representation that the bourgeoisie has tried to give itself and the classes it exploits, it really seems that the dominant ideological State apparatus in capitalist social formations is not the Schools, but the political ideological State apparatus, i.e. the regime of parliamentary democracy combining universal suffrage and party struggle.

However, history, even recent history, shows that the bourgeoisie has been and still is able to accommodate itself to political ideological State apparatuses other than parliamentary democracy: the First and Second Empires, Constitutional Monarchy (Louis XVIII and Charles X), Parliamentary Monarchy (Louis-Philippe), Presidential Democracy (de Gaulle), to mention only France. . . .

Hence I believe I have good reasons for thinking that behind the scenes of its political Ideological State Apparatus, which occupies the front of the stage, what the bourgeoisie has installed as its number-one, i.e. as its dominant ideological State apparatus, is the educational apparatus, which has in fact replaced in its functions the previously dominant ideological State apparatus, the Church. One might even add: the School–Family couple has replaced the Church–Family couple.

Why is the educational apparatus in fact the dominant ideological State apparatus in capitalist social formations, and how does it function?

For the moment it must suffice to say:

1. All ideological State apparatuses, whatever they are, contribute to the same result: the reproduction of the relations of production, i.e. of capitalist relations of exploitation.

2. Each of them contributes towards this single result in the way proper to it. The political apparatus by subjecting individuals to the political State ideology, the 'indirect' (parliamentary) or 'direct' (plebiscitary or fascist) 'democratic' ideology. The communications apparatus by cramming every 'citizen' with daily doses of nationalism, chauvinism, liberalism, moralism, etc, by means of the press, the radio and television. The same goes for the cultural apparatus (the role of sport in chauvinism is of the first importance), etc. The religious apparatus by recalling in sermons and the other great ceremonies of Birth, Marriage and Death, that man is only ashes, unless he loves his neighbour to the extent of turning the other cheek to whoever strikes first. The family apparatus ... but there is no need to go on.

3. This concert is dominated by a single score, occasionally disturbed by contradictions (those of the remnants of former ruling classes, those of the proletarians and their organizations): the score of the Ideology of the current ruling class which integrates into its music the great themes of the Humanism of the Great Forefathers, who produced the Greek Miracle even before Christianity, and afterwards the Glory of Rome, the Eternal City, and the themes of Interest, particular and general, etc. nationalism, moralism and economism.

4. Nevertheless, in this concert, one ideological State apparatus certainly has the dominant role, although hardly anyone lends an ear to its music: it is so silent! This is the School.

It takes children from every class at infant-school age, and then for years, the years in which the child is most 'vulnerable', squeezed between the family State apparatus and the educational State apparatus, it drums into them, whether it uses new or old methods, a certain amount of 'know-how' wrapped in the ruling ideology (French, arithmetic, natural history, the sciences, literature) or simply the ruling ideology in its pure state (ethics, civic instruction, philosophy). Somewhere around

the age of sixteen, a huge mass of children are ejected 'into production': these are the workers or small peasants. Another portion of scholastically adapted youth carries on: and, for better or worse, it goes somewhat further, until it falls by the wayside and fills the posts of small and middle technicians, white-collar workers, small and middle executives, petty bourgeois of all kinds. A last portion reaches the summit, either to fall into intellectual semi-employment, or to provide, as well as the 'intellectuals of the collective labourer', the agents of exploitation (capitalists, managers), the agents of repression (soldiers, policemen, politicians, administrators, etc.) and the professional ideologists (priests of all sorts, most of whom are convinced 'laymen').

Each mass ejected *en route* is practically provided with the ideology which suits the role it has to fulfil in class society: the role of the exploited (with a 'highly-developed' 'professional', 'ethical', 'civic', 'national' and a-political consciousness); the role of the agent of exploitation (ability to give the workers orders and speak to them: 'human relations'), of the agent of repression (ability to give orders and enforce obedience 'without discussion', or ability to manipulate the demagogy of a political leader's rhetoric), or of the professional ideologist (ability to treat consciousnesses with the respect, i.e. with the contempt, blackmail, and demagogy they deserve, adapted to the accents of Morality, of Virtue, of 'Transcendence', of the Nation, of France's World Role, etc.).

Of course, many of these contrasting Virtues (modesty, resignation, submissiveness on the one hand, cynicism, contempt, arrogance, confidence, self-importance, even smooth talk and cunning on the other) are also taught in the Family, in the Church, in the Army, in Good Books, in films and even in the football stadium. But no other ideological State apparatus has the obligatory (and not least, free) audience of the totality of the children in the capitalist social formation, eight hours a day for five or six days out of seven.

But it is by an apprenticeship in a variety of know-how wrapped up in the massive inculcation of the ideology of the ruling class that the *relations of production* in a capitalist social formation, i.e. the relations of exploited to exploiters and exploiters to exploited, are largely reproduced. The mechanisms which produce this vital result for the capitalist regime are naturally covered up and concealed by a universally reigning ideology of the School, universally reigning because it is one of the essential forms of the ruling bourgeois ideology: an ideology which represents the School as a neutral environment purged of ideology (because it is…lay), where teachers respectful of the 'conscience' and 'freedom' of the children who are entrusted to them (in complete confidence) by their 'parents' (who are free, too, i.e. the owners of their children) open up for them the path to the freedom, morality and responsibility of adults by their own example, by knowledge, literature and their 'liberating' virtues.

I ask the pardon of those teachers who, in dreadful conditions, attempt to turn the few weapons they can find in the history and learning they 'teach' against the ideology, the system and the practices in which they are trapped. They are a kind of hero. But they are rare and how many (the majority) do not even begin to suspect the 'work' the system (which is bigger than they are and crushes them) forces them to do, or worse, put all their heart and ingenuity into performing it with the most advanced awareness (the famous new methods!). So little do they suspect it that their own devotion contributes to the maintenance and nourishment of this ideological representation of the School, which makes the School today as 'natural', indispensable-useful and even beneficial for our contemporaries as the Church was 'natural', indispensable and generous for our ancestors a few centuries ago.

In fact, the Church has been replaced today *in its role as the dominant Ideological State Apparatus* by the School. It is coupled with the Family just as the Church was once coupled with the Family. We can now claim that the unprecedentedly deep crisis which is now shaking the education system of so many States across the globe, often in conjunction with a crisis (already proclaimed in the *Communist Manifesto*) shaking the family system, takes on a political meaning, given that the School (and the School–Family couple) constitutes the dominant Ideological State Apparatus, the Apparatus playing a determinant part in the reproduction of the relations of production of a mode of production threatened in its existence by the world class struggle.

On Ideology

When I put forward the concept of an Ideological State Apparatus, when I said that the ISAs 'function by ideology', I invoked a reality which needs a little discussion: ideology.

It is well known that the expression 'ideology' was invented by Cabanis, Destutt de Tracy and their friends, who assigned to it as an object the (genetic) theory of ideas. When Marx took up the term fifty years later, he gave it a quite different meaning, even in his Early Works. Here, ideology is the system of the ideas and representations which dominate the mind of a man or a social group. The ideologico-political struggle conducted by Marx as early as his articles in the *Rheinische Zeitung* inevitably and quickly brought him face to face with this reality and forced him to take his earliest intuitions further.

However, here we come upon a rather astonishing paradox. Everything seems to lead Marx to formulate a theory of ideology. In fact, *The German Ideology* does offer us, after the *1844 Manuscripts*, an explicit theory of ideology, but…it is not Marxist (we shall see why in a moment). As for *Capital*, although it does contain many hints towards a theory of ideologies (most visibly, the ideology of the vulgar economists), it does not contain that theory itself, which depends for the most part on a theory of ideology in general.

I should like to venture a first and very schematic outline of such a theory. The theses I am about to put forward are certainly not off the cuff, but they cannot be sustained and tested, i.e. confirmed or rejected, except by much thorough study and analysis.

Ideology has no history

One word first of all to expound the reason in principle which seems to me to found, or at least to justify, the project of a theory of ideology *in general,* and not a theory of particular ideolog*ies,* which, whatever their form (religious, ethical, legal, political), always express *class positions.*

It is quite obvious that it is necessary to proceed towards a theory of ideolog*ies* in the two respects I have just suggested. It will then be clear that a theory of ideolog*ies* depends in the last resort on the history of social formations, and thus of the modes of production combined in social formations, and of the class struggles which develop in them. In this sense it is clear that there can be no question of a theory of ideolog*ies in general,* since ideolog*ies* (defined in the double respect suggested above: regional and class) have a history, whose determination in the last instance is clearly situated outside ideologies alone, although it involves them.

On the contrary, if I am able to put forward the project of a theory of ideology *in general,* and if this theory really is one of the elements on which theories of ideolog*ies* depend, that entails an apparently paradoxical proposition which I shall express in the following terms: *ideology has no history.*

As we know, this formulation appears in so many words in a passage from *The German Ideology.* Marx utters it with respect to metaphysics, which, he says, has no more history than ethics (meaning also the other forms of ideology).

In *The German Ideology,* this formulation appears in a plainly positivist context. Ideology is conceived as a pure illusion, a pure dream, i.e. as nothingness. All its reality is external to it. Ideology is thus thought as an imaginary construction whose status is exactly like the theoretical status of the

dream among writers before Freud. For these writers, the dream was the purely imaginary, i.e. null, result of 'day's residues', presented in an arbitrary arrangement and order, sometimes even 'inverted', in other words, in 'disorder'. For them, the dream was the imaginary, it was empty, null and arbitrarily 'stuck together' (*bricolé*), once the eyes had closed, from the residues of the only full and positive reality, the reality of the day. This is exactly the status of philosophy and ideology (since in this book philosophy is ideology *par excellence*) in *The German Ideology.*

Ideology, then, is for Marx an imaginary assemblage (*bricolage*), a pure dream, empty and vain, constituted by the 'day's residues' from the only full and positive reality, that of the concrete history of concrete material individuals materially producing their existence. It is on this basis that ideology has no history in *The German Ideology,* since its history is outside it, where the only existing history is, the history of concrete individuals, etc. In *The German Ideology,* the thesis that ideology has no history is therefore a purely negative thesis, since it means both:

1. ideology is nothing insofar as it is a pure dream (manufactured by who knows what power: if not by the alienation of the division of labour, but that, too, is a *negative* determination);
2. ideology has no history, which emphatically does not mean that there is no history in it (on the contrary, for it is merely the pale, empty and inverted reflection of real history) but that it has no history *of its own.*

Now, while the thesis I wish to defend formally speaking adopts the terms of *The German Ideology* ('ideology has no history'), it is radically different from the positivist and historicist thesis of *The German Ideology.*

For on the one hand, I think it is possible to hold that ideolog*ies have a history of their own* (although it is determined in the last instance by the class struggle); and on the other, I think it is possible to hold that ideology *in general has no history*, not in a negative sense (its history is external to it), but in an absolutely positive sense.

This sense is a positive one if it is true that the peculiarity of ideology is that it is endowed with a structure and a functioning such as to make it a non-historical reality, i.e. an *omni-historical* reality, in the sense in which that structure and functioning are immutable, present in the same form throughout what we can call history, in the sense in which the *Communist Manifesto* defines history as the history of class struggles, i.e. the history of class societies.

To give a theoretical reference-point here, I might say that, to return to our example of the dream, in its Freudian conception this time, our proposition: ideology has no history, can and must (and in a way which has absolutely nothing arbitrary about it, but, quite the reverse, is theoretically necessary, for there is an organic link between the two propositions) be related directly to Freud's proposition that the *unconscious is eternal*, i.e. that it has no history.

If eternal means, not transcendent to all (temporal) history, but omnipresent, transhistorical and therefore immutable in form throughout the extent of history, I shall adopt Freud's expression word for word, and write *ideology is eternal*, exactly like the unconscious. And I add that I find this comparison theoretically justified by the fact that the eternity of the unconscious is not unrelated to the eternity of ideology in general.

That is why I believe I am justified, hypothetically at least, in proposing a theory of ideology *in general*, in the sense that Freud presented a theory of the unconscious *in general*.

To simplify the phrase, it is convenient, taking into account what has been said about ideologies, to use the plain term ideology to designate ideology in general, which I have just said has no history, or, what comes to the same thing, is eternal, i.e. omnipresent in its immutable form throughout history (= the history of social formations containing social classes). For the moment I shall restrict myself to 'class societies' and their history.

Ideology is a 'representation' of the imaginary relationship of individuals to their real conditions of existence

In order to approach my central thesis on the structure and functioning of ideology, I shall first present two theses, one negative, the other positive. The first concerns the object which is 'represented' in the imaginary form of ideology, the second concerns the materiality of ideology.

THESIS I: Ideology represents the imaginary relationship of individuals to their real conditions of existence.

We commonly call religious ideology, ethical ideology, legal ideology, political ideology, etc., so many 'world outlooks'. Of course, assuming that we do not live one of these ideologies as the truth (e.g. 'believe' in God, Duty, Justice, etc....), we admit that the ideology we are discussing from a critical point of view, examining it as the ethnologist examines the myths of a 'primitive society', that these 'world outlooks' are largely imaginary, i.e. do not 'correspond to reality'.

However, while admitting that they do not correspond to reality, i.e. that they constitute an illusion, we admit that they do make allusion to reality, and that they need only be 'interpreted' to discover the reality of the world behind their imaginary representation of that world (ideology = *illusion/allusion*)....

The essential point is that on condition that we interpret the imaginary transposition (and inversion) of ideology we arrive at the conclusion that in ideology 'men represent their real conditions of existence to themselves in an imaginary form'.

Unfortunately, this interpretation leaves one small problem unsettled: why do men 'need' this imaginary transposition of their real conditions of existence in order to 'represent to themselves' their real conditions of existence?

The first answer (that of the eighteenth century) proposes a simple solution: Priests or Despots are responsible. They 'forged' the Beautiful Lies so that, in the belief that they were obeying God, men would in fact obey the Priests and Despots, who are usually in alliance in their imposture, the Priests acting in the interests of the Despots or *vice versa*, according to the political positions of the 'theoreticians' concerned. There is therefore a cause for the imaginary transposition of the real conditions of existence: that cause is the existence of a small number of cynical men who base their domination and exploitation of the 'people' on a falsified representation of the world which they have imagined in order to enslave other minds by dominating their imaginations.

The second answer (that of Feuerbach, taken over word for word by Marx in his Early Works) is more 'profound', i.e. just as false. It, too, seeks and finds a cause for the imaginary transposition and distortion of men's real conditions of existence, in short, for the alienation in the imaginary of the representation of men's conditions of existence. This cause is no longer Priests or Despots, nor their active imagination and the passive imagination of their victims. This cause is the material alienation which reigns in the conditions of existence of men themselves. This is how, in *The Jewish Question* and elsewhere, Marx defends the Feuerbachian idea that men make themselves an alienated (= imaginary) representation of their conditions of existence because these conditions of existence are themselves alienating (in the *1844 Manuscripts*: because these conditions are dominated by the essence of alienated society – '*alienated labour*').

All these interpretations thus take literally the thesis which they presuppose, and on which they depend, i.e. that what is reflected in the imaginary representation of the world found in an ideology is the conditions of existence of men, i.e. their real world.

Now I can return to a thesis which I have already advanced: it is not their real conditions of existence, their real world, that 'men' 'represent to themselves' in ideology, but above all it is their relation to those conditions of existence which is represented to them there. It is this relation which is at the centre of every ideological, i.e. imaginary,

representation of the real world. It is this relation that contains the 'cause' which has to explain the imaginary distortion of the ideological representation of the real world. Or rather, to leave aside the language of causality it is necessary to advance the thesis that it is the *imaginary nature of this relation* which underlies all the imaginary distortion that we can observe (if we do not live in its truth) in all ideology.

To speak in a Marxist language, if it is true that the representation of the real conditions of existence of the individuals occupying the posts of agents of production, exploitation, repression, ideologization and scientific practice, does in the last analysis arise from the relations of production, and from relations deriving from the relations of production, we can say the following: all ideology represents in its necessarily imaginary distortion not the existing relations of production (and the other relations that derive from them), but above all the (imaginary) relationship of individuals to the relations of production and the relations that derive from them. What is represented in ideology is therefore not the system of the real relations which govern the existence of individuals, but the imaginary relation of those individuals to the real relations in which they live.

If this is the case, the question of the 'cause' of the imaginary distortion of the real relations in ideology disappears and must be replaced by a different question: why is the representation given to individuals of their (individual) relation to the social relations which govern their conditions of existence and their collective and individual life necessarily an imaginary relation? And what is the nature of this imaginariness? Posed in this way, the question explodes the solution by a 'clique',[14] by a group of individuals (Priests or Despots) who are the authors of the great ideological mystification, just as it explodes the solution by the alienated character of the real world. We shall see why later in my exposition. For the moment I shall go no further.

THESIS II: Ideology has a material existence.

I have already touched on this thesis by saying that the 'ideas' or 'representations', etc., which seem to make up ideology do not have an ideal (*idéale* or *idéelle*) or spiritual existence, but a material existence. I even suggested that the ideal (*idéale*, *idéelle*) and spiritual existence of 'ideas' arises exclusively in an ideology of the 'idea' and of ideology, and let me add, in an ideology of what seems to have 'founded' this conception since the emergence of the sciences, i.e. what the practicians of the sciences represent to themselves in their spontaneous ideology as 'ideas', true or false. Of course, presented in affirmative form, this thesis is unproven. I simply ask that the reader be favourably disposed towards it, say, in the name of materialism. A long series of arguments would be necessary to prove it.

This hypothetical thesis of the not spiritual but material existence of 'ideas' or other 'representations' is indeed necessary if we are to advance in our analysis of the nature of ideology. . . .

While discussing the ideological State apparatuses and their practices, I said that each of them was the realization of an ideology (the unity of these different regional ideologies – religious, ethical, legal, political, aesthetic, etc. – being assured by their subjection to the ruling ideology). I now return to this thesis: an ideology always exists in an apparatus, and its practice, or practices. This existence is material.

Of course, the material existence of the ideology in an apparatus and its practices does not have the same modality as the material existence of a paving-stone or a rifle. But, at the risk of being taken for a Neo-Aristotelian (NB Marx had a very high regard for Aristotle), I shall say that 'matter is discussed in many senses', or rather that it exists in different modalities, all rooted in the last instance in 'physical' matter.

Having said this, let me move straight on and see what happens to the 'individuals' who live in ideology, i.e. in a determinate (religious, ethical, etc.) representation of the world whose imaginary distortion depends on their imaginary relation to their condi-

tions of existence, in other words, in the last instance, to the relations of production and to class relations (ideology = an imaginary relation to real relations). I shall say that this imaginary relation is itself endowed with a material existence.

Now I observe the following.

An individual believes in God, or Duty, or Justice, etc. This belief derives (for everyone, i.e. for all those who live in an ideological representation of ideology, which reduces ideology to ideas endowed by definition with a spiritual existence) from the ideas of the individual concerned, i.e. from him as a subject with a consciousness which contains the ideas of his belief. In this way, i.e. by means of the absolutely ideological 'conceptual' device (*dispositif*) thus set up (a subject endowed with a consciousness in which he freely forms or freely recognizes ideas in which he believes), the (material) attitude of the subject concerned naturally follows.

The individual in question behaves in such and such a way, adopts such and such a practical attitude, and, what is more, participates in certain regular practices which are those of the ideological apparatus on which 'depend' the ideas which he has in all consciousness freely chosen as a subject. If he believes in God, he goes to Church to attend Mass, kneels, prays, confesses, does penance (once it was material in the ordinary sense of the term) and naturally repents and so on. If he believes in Duty, he will have the corresponding attitudes, inscribed in ritual practices 'according to the correct principles'. If he believes in Justice, he will submit unconditionally to the rules of the Law, and may even protest when they are violated, sign petitions, take part in a demonstration, etc.

Throughout this schema we observe that the ideological representation of ideology is itself forced to recognize that every 'subject' endowed with a 'consciousness' and believing in the 'ideas' that his 'consciousness' inspires in him and freely accepts, must 'act according to his ideas', must therefore inscribe his own ideas as a free subject in the actions of his material practice. If he does not do so, 'that is wicked'.

Indeed, if he does not do what he ought to do as a function of what he believes, it is because he does something else, which, still as a function of the same idealist scheme, implies that he has other ideas in his head as well as those he proclaims, and that he acts according to these other ideas, as a man who is either 'inconsistent' ('no one is willingly evil') or cynical, or perverse.

In every case, the ideology of ideology thus recognizes, despite its imaginary distortion, that the 'ideas' of a human subject exist in his actions, or ought to exist in his actions, and if that is not the case, it lends him other ideas corresponding to the actions (however perverse) that he does perform. This ideology talks of actions: I shall talk of actions inserted into *practices. And* I shall point out that these practices are governed by the *rituals* in which these practices are inscribed, within the *material existence of an ideological apparatus,* be it only a small part of that apparatus: a small mass in a small church, a funeral, a minor match at a sports' club, a school day, a political party meeting, etc.

[...]

I shall therefore say that, where only a single subject (such and such an individual) is concerned, the existence of the ideas of his belief is material in that *his ideas are his material actions inserted into material practices governed by material rituals which are themselves defined by the material ideological apparatus from which derive the ideas of that subject.* Naturally, the four inscriptions of the adjective 'material' in my proposition must be affected by different modalities: the materialities of a displacement for going to mass, of kneeling down, of the gesture of the sign of the cross, or of the *mea culpa,* of a sentence, of a prayer, of an act of contrition, of a penitence, of a gaze, of a hand-shake, of an external verbal discourse or an 'internal' verbal discourse (consciousness), are not one and the same materiality. I shall leave on one side the problem of a theory of the differences between the modalities of materiality.

It remains that in this inverted presentation of things, we are not dealing with an 'inver-

sion' at all, since it is clear that certain notions have purely and simply disappeared from our presentation, whereas others on the contrary survive, and new terms appear.

Disappeared: the term *ideas.*

Survive: the terms *subject, consciousness, belief, actions.*

Appear: the terms *practices, rituals, ideological apparatus.*

[...]

Ideas have disappeared as such (insofar as they are endowed with an ideal or spiritual existence), to the precise extent that it has emerged that their existence is inscribed in the actions of practices governed by rituals defined in the last instance by an ideological apparatus. It therefore appears that the subject acts insofar as he is acted by the following system (set out in the order of its real determination): ideology existing in a material ideological apparatus, prescribing material practices governed by a material ritual, which practices exist in the material actions of a subject acting in all consciousness according to his belief.

But this very presentation reveals that we have retained the following notions: subject, consciousness, belief, actions. From this series I shall immediately extract the decisive central term on which everything else depends: the notion of the *subject.*

And I shall immediately set down two conjoint theses:

1. there is no practice except by and in an ideology;

2. there is no ideology except by the subject and for subjects.

I can now come to my central thesis.

Ideology interpellates individuals as subjects

This thesis is simply a matter of making my last proposition explicit: there is no ideology except by the subject and for subjects. Meaning, there is no ideology except for concrete subjects, and this destination for ideology is only made possible by the subject: meaning, *by the category of the subject* and its functioning.

By this I mean that, even if it only appears under this name (the subject) with the rise of bourgeois ideology, above all with the rise of legal ideology,[15] the category of the subject (which may function under other names: e.g., as the soul in Plato, as God, etc.) is the constitutive category of all ideology, whatever its determination (regional or class) and whatever its historical date – since ideology has no history.

I say: the category of the subject is constitutive of all ideology, but at the same time and immediately I add that *the category of the subject is only constitutive of all ideology insofar as all ideology has the function (which defines it) of 'constituting' concrete individuals as subjects.* In the interaction of this double constitution exists the functioning of all ideology, ideology being nothing but its functioning in the material forms of existence of that functioning.

In order to grasp what follows, it is essential to realize that both he who is writing these lines and the reader who reads them are themselves subjects, and therefore ideological subjects (a tautological proposition), i.e. that the author and the reader of these lines both live 'spontaneously' or 'naturally' in ideology in the sense in which I have said that 'man is an ideological animal by nature'.

That the author, insofar as he writes the lines of a discourse which claims to be scientific, is completely absent as a 'subject' from 'his' scientific discourse (for all scientific discourse is by definition a subject-less discourse, there is no 'Subject of science' except in an ideology of science) is a different question which I shall leave on one side for the moment.

As St Paul admirably put it, it is in the 'Logos', meaning in ideology, that we 'live, move and have our being'. It follows that, for you and for me, the category of the subject is a primary 'obviousness' (obviousnesses are always primary): it is clear that you and I are subjects (free, ethical, etc....). Like all

obviousnesses, including those that make a word 'name a thing' or 'have a meaning' (therefore including the obviousness of the 'transparency' of language), the 'obviousness' that you and I are subjects... is an ideological effect, the elementary ideological effect.[16] It is indeed a peculiarity of ideology that it imposes (without appearing to do so, since these are 'obviousnesses') obviousnesses as obviousnesses, which we cannot *fail to recognize* and before which we have the inevitable and natural reaction of crying out (aloud or in the 'still, small voice of conscience'): 'That's obvious! That's right! That's true!'

At work in this reaction is the ideological *recognition* function which is one of the two functions of ideology as such (its inverse being the function of *misrecognition* – *méconnaissance*).

To take a highly 'concrete' example, we all have friends who, when they knock on our door and we ask, through the door, the question 'Who's there?', answer (since 'it's obvious') 'It's me'. And we recognize that 'it is him', or 'her'. We open the door, and 'it's true, it really was she who was there'. To take another example, when we recognize somebody of our (previous) acquaintance ((*re*)-*connaissance*) in the street, we show him that we have recognized him (and have recognized that he has recognized us) by saying to him 'Hello, my friend', and shaking his hand (a material ritual practice of ideological recognition in everyday life – in France, at least; elsewhere, there are other rituals).

In this preliminary remark and these concrete illustrations, I only wish to point out that you and I are *always already* subjects, and as such constantly practice the rituals of ideological recognition, which guarantee for us that we are indeed concrete, individual, distinguishable and (naturally) irreplaceable subjects. The writing I am currently executing and the reading you are currently[17] performing are also in this respect rituals of ideological recognition, including the 'obviousness' with which the 'truth' or 'error' of my reflections may impose itself on you.

But to recognize that we are subjects and that we function in the practical rituals of the most elementary everyday life (the handshake, the fact of calling you by your name, the fact of knowing, even if I do not know what it is, that you 'have' a name of your own, which means that you are recognized as a unique subject, etc.) – this recognition only gives us the 'consciousness' of our incessant (eternal) practice of ideological recognition – its consciousness, i.e. its *recognition* – but in no sense does it give us the (scientific) *knowledge* of the mechanism of this recognition. Now it is this knowledge that we have to reach, if you will, while speaking in ideology, and from within ideology we have to outline a discourse which tries to break with ideology, in order to dare to be the beginning of a scientific (i.e. subjectless) discourse on ideology.

Thus in order to represent why the category of the 'subject' is constitutive of ideology, which only exists by constituting concrete subjects as subjects, I shall employ a special mode of exposition: 'concrete' enough to be recognized, but abstract enough to be thinkable and thought, giving rise to a knowledge.

As a first formulation I shall say: *all ideology hails or interpellates concrete individuals as concrete subjects*, by the functioning of the category of the subject.

This is a proposition which entails that we distinguish for the moment between concrete individuals on the one hand and concrete subjects on the other, although at this level concrete subjects only exist insofar as they are supported by a concrete individual.

I shall then suggest that ideology 'acts' or 'functions' in such a way that it 'recruits' subjects among the individuals (it recruits them all), or 'transforms' the individuals into subjects (it transforms them all) by that very precise operation which I have called *interpellation* or hailing, and which can be imagined along the lines of the most commonplace everyday police (or other) hailing: 'Hey, you there!'[18]

Assuming that the theoretical scene I have imagined takes place in the street, the hailed individual will turn round. By this mere one-hundred-and-eighty-degree physical conversion, he becomes a *subject*. Why? Because he has recognized that the hail was 'really' addressed to him, and that 'it was *really him* who was hailed' (and not someone else). Experience shows that the practical telecommunication of hailings is such that they hardly ever miss their man: verbal call or whistle, the one hailed always recognizes that it is really him who is being hailed. And yet it is a strange phenomenon, and one which cannot be explained solely by 'guilt feelings', despite the large numbers who 'have something on their consciences'.

Naturally for the convenience and clarity of my little theoretical theatre I have had to present things in the form of a sequence, with a before and an after, and thus in the form of a temporal succession. There are individuals walking along. Somewhere (usually behind them) the hail rings out: 'Hey, you there!' One individual (nine times out of ten it is the right one) turns round, believing/suspecting/ knowing that it is for him, i.e. recognizing that 'it really is he' who is meant by the hailing. But in reality these things happen without any succession. The existence of ideology and the hailing or interpellation of individuals as subjects are one and the same thing.

I might add: what thus seems to take place outside ideology (to be precise, in the street), in reality takes place in ideology. What really takes place in ideology seems therefore to take place outside it. That is why those who are in ideology believe themselves by definition outside ideology: one of the effects of ideology is the practical *denegation* of the ideological character of ideology by ideology: ideology never says, 'I am ideological'. It is necessary to be outside ideology, i.e. in scientific knowledge, to be able to say: I am in ideology (a quite exceptional case) or (the general case): I was in ideology. As is well known, the accusation of being in ideology only applies to others, never to oneself (unless one is really a Spinozist or a Marxist, which, in this matter, is to be exactly the same thing).

Which amounts to saying that ideology *has no outside* (for itself), but at the same time *that it is nothing but outside* (for science and reality).

[...]

Thus ideology hails or interpellates individuals as subjects. As ideology is eternal, I must now suppress the temporal form in which I have presented the functioning of ideology, and say: ideology has always-already interpellated individuals as subjects, which amounts to making it clear that individuals are always-already interpellated by ideology as subjects, which necessarily leads us to one last proposition: *individuals are always-already subjects*. Hence individuals are 'abstract' with respect to the subjects which they always-already are. This proposition might seem paradoxical.

That an individual is always-already a subject, even before he is born, is nevertheless the plain reality, accessible to everyone and not a paradox at all. Freud shows that individuals are always 'abstract' with respect to the subjects they always-already are, simply by noting the ideological ritual that surrounds the expectation of a 'birth', that 'happy event'. Everyone knows how much and in what way an unborn child is expected. Which amounts to saying, very prosaically, if we agree to drop the 'sentiments', i.e. the forms of family ideology (paternal/maternal/conjugal/fraternal) in which the unborn child is expected: it is certain in advance that it will bear its Father's Name, and will therefore have an identity and be irreplaceable. Before its birth, the child is therefore always-already a subject, appointed as a subject in and by the specific familial ideological configuration in which it is 'expected' once it has been conceived. I hardly need add that this familial ideological configuration is, in its uniqueness, highly structured, and that it is in this implacable and more or less 'pathological' (presupposing that any meaning can be assigned to that term) structure that the former subject-to-be will have to 'find' 'its' place, i.e. 'become' the sexual subject (boy or girl) which it already is in advance. It is clear that this ideological

constraint and pre-appointment, and all the rituals of rearing and then education in the family, have some relationship with what Freud studied in the forms of the pre-genital and genital 'stages' of sexuality, i.e. in the 'grip' of what Freud registered by its effects as being the unconscious. But let us leave this point, too, on one side.

Let me go one step further. What I shall now turn my attention to is the way the 'actors' in this *mise en scène* of interpellation, and their respective roles, are reflected in the very structure of all ideology.

An example: the Christian religious ideology

As the formal structure of all ideology is always the same, I shall restrict my analysis to a single example, one accessible to everyone, that of religious ideology, with the proviso that the same demonstration can be produced for ethical, legal, political, aesthetic ideology, etc.

Let us therefore consider the Christian religious ideology. I shall use a rhetorical figure and 'make it speak', i.e. collect into a fictional discourse what it 'says' not only in its two Testaments, its Theologians, Sermons, but also in its practices, its rituals, its ceremonies and its sacraments. The Christian religious ideology says something like this:

It says: I address myself to you, a human individual called Peter (every individual is called by his name, in the passive sense, it is never he who provides his own name), in order to tell you that God exists and that you are answerable to Him. It adds: God addresses himself to you through my voice (Scripture having collected the Word of God, Tradition having transmitted it, Papal Infallibility fixing it for ever on 'nice' points). It says: this is who you are: you are Peter! This is your origin, you were created by God for all eternity, although you were born in the 1920th year of Our Lord! This is your place in the world! This is what you must do! By these means, if you observe the 'law of love' you will be saved, you, Peter, and will become part of the Glorious Body of Christ! Etc....

Now this is quite a familiar and banal discourse, but at the same time quite a surprising one.

Surprising because if we consider that religious ideology is indeed addressed to individuals,[19] in order to 'transform them into subjects', by interpellating the individual, Peter, in order to make him a subject, free to obey or disobey the appeal, i.e. God's commandments; if it calls these individuals by their names, thus recognizing that they are always-already interpellated as subjects with a personal identity . . . ; if it interpellates them in such a way that the subject responds: 'Yes, it really is me!' if it obtains from them the recognition that they really do occupy the place it designates for them as theirs in the world, a fixed residence: 'It really is me, I am here, a worker, a boss or a soldier!' in this vale of tears; if it obtains from them the recognition of a destination (eternal life or damnation) according to the respect or contempt they show to 'God's Commandments', Law become Love; – if everything does happen in this way (in the practices of the well-known rituals of baptism, confirmation, communion, confession and extreme unction, etc. . . .), we should note that all this 'procedure' to set up Christian religious subjects is dominated by a strange phenomenon: the fact that there can only be such a multitude of possible religious subjects on the absolute condition that there is a Unique, Absolute, Other Subject, i.e. God.

It is convenient to designate this new and remarkable Subject by writing Subject with a capital S to distinguish it from ordinary subjects, with a small s.

It then emerges that the interpellation of individuals as subjects presupposes the 'existence' of a Unique and central Other Subject, in whose Name the religious ideology interpellates all individuals as subjects. All this is clearly[20] written in what is rightly called the Scriptures. 'And it came to pass at that time that God the Lord (Yahweh) spoke to Moses in the cloud. And the Lord cried to Moses, "Moses!" And Moses replied "It is (really) I! I am Moses thy servant, speak and I shall lis-

ten!" And the Lord spoke to Moses and said to him, "I am that I am" '.

God thus defines himself as the Subject par excellence, he who is through himself and for himself ('I am that I am'), and he who interpellates his subject, the individual subjected to him by his very interpellation, i.e. the individual named Moses. And Moses, interpellated-called by his Name, having recognized that it 'really' was he who was called by God, recognizes that he is a subject, a subject of God, a subject subjected to God, a subject through the Subject and subjected to the Subject. The proof: he obeys him, and makes his people obey God's Commandments.

God is thus the Subject, and Moses and the innumerable subjects of God's people, the Subject's interlocutors-interpellates: his mirrors, his reflections. Were not men made in the image of God? As all theological reflection proves, whereas He 'could' perfectly well have done without men, God needs them, the Subject needs the subjects, just as men need God, the subjects need the Subject. Better: God needs men, the great Subject needs subjects, even in the terrible inversion of his image in them (when the subjects wallow in debauchery, i.e. sin).

Better: God duplicates himself and sends his Son to the Earth, as a mere subject 'forsaken' by him (the long complaint of the Garden of Olives which ends in the Crucifixion), subject but Subject, man but God, to do what prepares the way for the final Redemption, the Resurrection of Christ. God thus needs to 'make himself' a man, the Subject needs to become a subject, as if to show empirically, visibly to the eye, tangibly to the hands (see St Thomas) of the subjects, that, if they are subjects, subjected to the Subject, that is solely in order that finally, on Judgement Day, they will re-enter the Lord's Bosom, like Christ, i.e. re-enter the Subject.[21]

Let us decipher into theoretical language this wonderful necessity for the duplication of the Subject into subjects and of the Subject itself into a subject-Subject.

We observe that the structure of all ideology, interpellating individuals as subjects in the name of a Unique and Absolute Subject is *speculary*, i.e. a mirror-structure, and *doubly* speculary: this mirror duplication is constitutive of ideology and ensures its functioning. Which means that all ideology is *centred*, that the Absolute Subject occupies the unique place of the Centre, and interpellates around it the infinity of individuals into subjects in a double mirror-connexion such that it *subjects* the subjects to the Subject, while giving them in the Subject in which each subject can contemplate its own image (present and future) the *guarantee* that this really concerns them and Him, and that since everything takes place in the Family (the Holy Family: the Family is in essence Holy), 'God will *recognize* his own in it', i.e. those who have recognized God, and have recognized themselves in Him, will be saved.

Let me summarize what we have discovered about ideology in general.

The duplicate mirror-structure of ideology ensures simultaneously:

1. the interpellation of 'individuals' as subjects;
2. their subjection to the Subject;
3. the mutual recognition of subjects and Subject, the subjects' recognition of each other, and finally the subject's recognition of himself;[22]
4. the absolute guarantee that everything really is so, and that on condition that the subjects recognize what they are and behave accordingly, everything will be all right: Amen – 'So be it'.

Result: caught in this quadruple system of interpellation as subjects, of subjection to the Subject, of universal recognition and of absolute guarantee, the subjects 'work', they 'work by themselves' in the vast majority of cases, with the exception of the 'bad subjects' who on occasion provoke the intervention of one of the detachments of the (repressive) State apparatus. But the vast majority of (good) subjects work all right 'all by themselves', i.e. by ideology (whose concrete forms are realized in the Ideological State Apparatuses). They are inserted into practices governed by the rituals of the ISAs. They 'recognize' the existing state of affairs (*das Bestehende*), that 'it really is true that it is so and not otherwise', and that they must be obedient to God, to their conscience, to the priest, to de Gaulle, to the boss, to the engineer, that thou shalt 'love thy neighbour as thyself', etc. Their concrete, material behaviour is simply the inscription in life of the admirable words of the prayer: '*Amen – So be it*'.

Yes, the subjects 'work by themselves'. The whole mystery of this effect lies in the first two moments of the quadruple system I have just discussed, or, if you prefer, in the ambiguity of the term *subject*. In the ordinary use of the term, subject in fact means: (1) a free subjectivity, a centre of initiatives, author of and responsible for its actions; (2) a subjected being, who submits to a higher authority, and is therefore stripped of all freedom except that of freely accepting his submission. This last note gives us the meaning of this ambiguity, which is merely a reflection of the effect which produces it: the individual *is interpellated as a (free) subject in order that he shall submit freely to the commandments of the Subject, i.e. in order that he shall (freely) accept his subjection*, i.e. in order that he shall make the gestures and actions of his subjection 'all by himself'. *There are no subjects except by and for their subjection*. That is why they 'work all by themselves'.

'*So be it!*...' This phrase which registers the effect to be obtained proves that it is not 'naturally' so ('naturally': outside the prayer, i.e. outside the ideological intervention). This phrase proves that it *has* to be so if things are to be what they must be, and let us let the words slip: if the reproduction of the relations of production is to be assured, even in the processes of production and circulation, every day, in the 'consciousness', i.e. in the attitudes of the individual-subjects occupying the posts which the socio-technical division of labour assigns to them in production, exploitation, repression, ideologization, scientific practice, etc. Indeed, what is really in question in this mechanism of the mirror recognition of the Subject and of the individuals interpellated as subjects, and of the guarantee given by the Subject to the subjects if they freely accept their subjection to the Subject's 'commandments'? The reality in question in this mechanism, the reality which is necessarily *ignored (méconnue)* in the very forms of recognition (ideology = misrecognition/ignorance) is indeed, in the last resort, the reproduction of the relations of production and of the relations deriving from them.

January–April 1969

P.S. If these few schematic theses allow me to illuminate certain aspects of the functioning of the Superstructure and its mode of intervention in the Infrastructure, they are obviously *abstract* and necessarily leave several important problems unanswered, which should be mentioned:

1. The problem of the *total process* of the realization of the reproduction of the relations of production.

As an element of this process, the ISAs *contribute* to this reproduction. But the point of view of their contribution alone is still an abstract one.

It is only within the processes of production and circulation that this reproduction is *realized*. It is realized by the mechanisms of those processes, in which the training of the workers is 'completed', their posts assigned them, etc. It is in the internal mechanisms of these processes that the effect of the different ideologies is felt (above all the effect of legal-ethical ideology).

But this point of view is still an abstract one. For in a class society the relations of production are relations of exploitation, and therefore relations between antagonistic classes. The reproduction of the relations of production, the ultimate aim of the ruling class, cannot therefore be a merely technical operation training and distributing individuals for the different posts in the 'technical division' of labour. In fact there is no 'technical division' of labour except in the ideology of the ruling class: every 'technical'

division, every 'technical' organization of labour is the form and mask of a *social* (= class) division and organization of labour. The reproduction of the relations of production can therefore only be a class undertaking. It is realized through a class struggle which counterposes the ruling class and the exploited class.

The *total process* of the realization of the reproduction of the relations of production is therefore still abstract, insofar as it has not adopted the point of view of this class struggle. To adopt the point of view of reproduction is therefore, in the last instance, to adopt the point of view of the class struggle.

2. The problem of the class nature of the ideologies existing in a social formation.

The 'mechanism' of ideology *in general* is one thing. We have seen that it can be reduced to a few principles expressed in a few words (as 'poor' as those which, according to Marx, define production *in general*, or in Freud, define *the* unconscious *in general*). If there is any truth in it, this mechanism must be *abstract* with respect to every real ideological formation.

I have suggested that the ideologies were *realized* in institutions, in their rituals and their practices, in the ISAs. We have seen that on this basis they contribute to that form of class struggle, vital for the ruling class, the reproduction of the relations of production. But the point of view itself, however real, is still an abstract one.

In fact, the State and its Apparatuses only have meaning from the point of view of the class struggle, as an apparatus of class struggle ensuring class oppression and guaranteeing the conditions of exploitation and its reproduction. But there is no class struggle without antagonistic classes. Whoever says class struggle of the ruling class says resistance, revolt and class struggle of the ruled class.

That is why the ISAs are not the realization of ideology *in general*, nor even the conflict-free realization of the ideology of the ruling class. The ideology of the ruling class does not become the ruling ideology by the grace of God, nor even by virtue of the seizure of State power alone. It is by the installation of the ISAs in which this ideology is realized and realizes itself that it becomes the ruling ideology. But this installation is not achieved all by itself; on the contrary, it is the stake in a very bitter and continuous class struggle: first against the former ruling classes and their positions in the old and new ISAs, then against the exploited class.

But this point of view of the class struggle in the ISAs is still an abstract one. In fact, the class struggle in the ISAs is indeed an aspect of the class struggle, sometimes an important and symptomatic one: e.g. the anti-religious struggle in the eighteenth century, or the 'crisis' of the educational ISA in every capitalist country today. But the class struggles in the ISAs is only one aspect of a class struggle which goes beyond the ISAs. The ideology that a class in power makes the ruling ideology in its ISAs is indeed 'realized' in those ISAs, but it goes beyond them, for it comes from elsewhere. Similarly, the ideology that a ruled class manages to defend in and against such ISAs goes beyond them, for it comes from elsewhere.

It is only from the point of view of the classes, i.e. of the class struggle, that it is possible to explain the ideologies existing in a social formation. Not only is it from this starting-point that it is possible to explain the realization of the ruling ideology in the ISAs and of the forms of class struggle for which the ISAs are the seat and the stake. But it is also and above all from this starting-point that it is possible to understand the provenance of the ideologies which are realized in the ISAs and confront one another there. For if it is true that the ISAs represent the *form* in which the ideology of the ruling class must *necessarily* be realized, and the form in which the ideology of the ruled class must *necessarily* be measured and confronted, ideologies are not 'born' in the ISAs but from the social classes *at grips in the class struggle: from their conditions of existence, their practices*, their experience of the struggle, etc.

April 1970

NOTES AND REFERENCES

1 This text is made up of two extracts from an ongoing study. The sub-title 'Notes towards an Investigation' is the author's own. The ideas expounded should not be regarded as more than the introduction to a discussion.

2 Marx to Kugelmann, 11 July 1868, *Selected Correspondence*, Moscow, 1955, p. 209.

3 Marx gave it its scientific concept: *variable capital*.

4 In *For Marx* and *Reading Capital*, 1965 (English editions 1969 and 1970, respectively).

5 *Topography* from the Greek *topos*: A topography represents in a definite space the respective *sites* occupied by several realities: thus the economic is *at the bottom* (the base), the superstructure *above it*.

6 See p. 98 below, *On Ideology*.

7 To my knowledge, Gramsci is the only one who went any distance in the road I am taking. He had the 'remarkable' idea that the State could not be reduced to the (Repressive) State Apparatus, but included, as he put it, a certain number of institutions from '*civil society*': the Church, the Schools, the trade unions, etc. Unfortunately, Gramsci did not systematize his institutions, which remained in the state of acute but fragmentary notes (cf. Gramsci, *Selections from the Prison Notebooks*, International Publishers, 1971, pp. 12, 259, 260–3; see also the letter to Tatiana Schucht, 7 September 1931, in *Lettre del Carcere*, Einaudi, 1968, p. 479.

8 The family obviously has other 'functions' than that of an ISA. It intervenes in the reproduction of labour power. In different modes of production it is the unit of production and/or the unit of consumption.

9 The 'Law' belongs both to the (Repressive) State Apparatus and to the system of the ISAs.

10 In a pathetic text written in 1937, Krupskaya relates the history of Lenin's

desperate efforts and what she regards as his failure.

11 What I have said in these few brief words about the class struggle in the ISAs is obviously far from exhausting the question of the class struggle.

To approach this question, two principles must be borne in mind:

The first principle was formulated by Marx in the Preface to *A Contribution to the Critique of Political Economy*: "In considering such transformations [a social revolution] a distinction should always be made between the material transformation of the economic conditions of production, which can be determined with the precision of natural science, and the legal, political, religious, aesthetic or philosophic – in short, ideological forms in which men become conscious of this conflict and fight it out." The class struggle is thus expressed and exercised in ideological forms, thus also in the ideological forms of the ISAs. But the class struggle *extends far beyond* these forms, and it is because it extends beyond them that the struggle of the exploited classes may also be exercised in the forms of the ISAs, and thus turn the weapon of ideology against the classes in power.

This by virtue of the *second principle*: the class struggle extends beyond the ISAs because it is rooted elsewhere than in ideology, in the Infrastructure, in the relations of production, which are relations of exploitation and constitute the base for class relations.

12 For the most part. For the relations of production are first reproduced by the materiality of the processes of production and circulation. But it should not be forgotten that ideological relations are immediately present in these same processes.

13 *For that part* of reproduction to which the Repressive State Apparatus and the Ideological State Apparatus *contribute*.

14 I use this very modern term deliberately. For even in Communist circles, unfortunately, it is a commonplace to 'explain' some political deviation (left or right opportunism) by the action of a 'clique'.

15 Which borrowed the legal category of 'subject in law' to make an ideological notion: man is by nature a subject.

16 Linguists and those who appeal to linguistics for various purposes often run up against difficulties which arise because they ignore the action of the ideological effects in all discourses – including even scientific discourses.

17 NB: this double 'currently' is one more proof of the fact that ideology is 'eternal', since these two 'currentlys' are separated by an indefinite interval; I am writing these lines on 6 April 1969, you may read them at any subsequent time.

18 Hailing as an everyday practice subject to a precise ritual takes a quite 'special' form in the policeman's practice of 'hailing' which concerns the hailing of 'suspects'.

19 Although we know that the individual is always already a subject, we go on using this term, convenient because of the contrasting effect it produces.

20 I am quoting in a combined way, not to the letter but 'in spirit and truth'.

21 The dogma of the Trinity is precisely the theory of the duplication of the Subject (the Father) into a subject (the Son) and of their mirror-connexion (the Holy Spirit).

22 Hegel is (unknowingly) an admirable 'theoretician' of ideology insofar as he is a 'theoretician' of Universal Recognition who unfortunately ends up in the ideology of Absolute Knowledge. Feuerbach is an astonishing 'theoretician' of the mirror connexion, who unfortunately ends up in the ideology of the Human Essence. To find the material with which to construct a theory of the guarantee, we must turn to Spinoza.

4

Notes on the Difficulty of Studying the State

Philip Abrams

'When the state itself is in danger', Lord Denning said in his judgment yesterday, 'our cherished freedoms may have to take second place, and even natural justice itself may have to suffer a setback'.

'The flaw in Lord Denning's argument is that it is the government who decide what the interests of the state should be and which invokes "national security" as the state chooses to define it', Ms Pat Hewitt, director of the National Council for Civil Liberties, said yesterday.

The Guardian, 18.2.77

When Jeremy Bentham set out to purge political discourse of the delusions and fantasies generated by the many 'alegorical contrivances' through which self-interest and sectional power are masked as independent moral entities, the notion of the state did not enjoy wide currency in English political or intellectual life. Had it done so he would surely have included it along with 'government' 'order' and 'the constitution' as one of those terms peculiarly apt to foster 'an atmosphere of

illusion' – a fallacy of confusion at best, an 'official malefactor's screen' at worst, giving spurious concreteness and reality to that which has a merely abstract and formal existence.[1] By 1919, however, the combined efforts of hegelians, marxists and politicians had wrought a change: 'nearly all political disputes and differences of opinion', Lenin could then observe, 'now turn upon the concept of the state' – and more particularly upon 'the question: what is the state?'[2] At least among sociologists his observation seems to be still very largely correct; fifty years of asking the question have not produced any very satisfactory or even widely agreed answers. At the same time the sort of invocation of the state as an ultimate point of reference for political practice voiced by Lord Denning, and the sort of objection to such invocations voiced by Ms Hewitt, have become steadily more commonplace. We have come to take the state for granted as an object of political practice and political analysis while remaining quite spectacularly unclear as to what the state is. We are variously urged to respect the state, or smash the state or study

From *Journal of Historical Sociology*, 1(1), March 1988 (1977), pp. 58–89. Reprinted by permission of Blackwell Publishing.

the state; but for want of clarity about the nature of the state such projects remain beset with difficulties. Perhaps a new Benthamite purge is opportune?

The Problem in General

Political sociology, according to W. G. Runciman, springs from the separation of the political – and more especially the state – from the social. It is constructed as an attempt to give a social account of the state with the latter envisaged as a concrete political agency or structure distinct from the social agencies and structures of the society in which it operates, acting on them and acted on by them. It is, we are told, this 'distinction . . . which makes possible a sociology of politics'.[3]

Marxism, sociology's only serious rival in the search for a contemporary theory of the state, builds, superficially at least, on a very similar distinction. Most varieties of marxism assume that adequate political analysis must, as Marx put it, proceed on the basis of 'the actual relation between the state and civil society, that is, their separation'.[4] Within that framework the crucial issue in marxist political analysis then becomes the question of the degree of actual independence enjoyed by the state in its relations with the principal formations of civil society, social classes. Even when marxist writers, such as Poulantzas, overtly reject this framework they do so only to substitute for the separation of state and civil society a problematic formulated as 'the specific autonomy of the political and the economic' within the capitalist mode of production. And the resulting problem about the nature and function of the state is to be resolved through analysis of the relations of the state to the field of class struggle by way of an unmasking of the autonomy of the former and the isolation of the latter. Here, too, the problematic envisages the state as in effect a distinct entity and the task is to determine the actual forms and modes of dependence or independence that relate it to the socio–economic.[5]

[. . .]

Marxist writers have attended to the analysis of the state more thoroughly and explicitly but, with the possible exception of the analysis of Bonapartism, not on the whole all that much more conclusively. The great debate on the relative autonomy of the state, which looked so promising when it was launched, ended with a sense that its problems had been exhausted rather than resolved. The main protagonists turned their attention to other issues. By 1974 Ralph Miliband was urging political sociologists 'from a marxist point of view' not to dissipate their energies in further studies of our speculations about the state but to embrace an alternative problematic couched in terms of wider and differently conceived processes and relationships of domination.[6] Meanwhile, Nicos Poulantzas moved from the opaque conclusions of his struggle to clarify a marxist theory of the state – 'the state has the particular function of constituting the factor of cohesion between the levels of a social formation' – not to attempt a more exact clear and empirically specific formulation of such ideas, but rather to the study of particular regimes and to the larger problem of the class structure of capitalism.[7] The only agreed results of the debate appeared to be a mutual recognition of a number of important features of the presumed relationship of state and society which could not, as yet anyway, be adequately demonstrated. Thus, the credibility of the notion of class domination is saved – but then it is of course *given* in all varieties of marxism – but the demonstration of such domination in the context of particular states remains unaccomplished. At this level the state once again succeeds in defying scrutiny.

It seems necessary to say, then, that the state, conceived of as a substantial entity separate from society has proved a remarkably elusive object of analysis. . . .

The Problem in Particular

The everyday life of politics suggests forcibly that the conception of the state offered in marxism and political sociology is – whatever the difficulties of operationalising it – well-founded. Commonsense impels us to the inference that there is a hidden reality in political life and that reality is the state. Either way, the search for the state and the presumption of its real, hidden existence are highly plausible ways of 'reading' the way the public aspects of politics are conducted. The naive research experience of sociologists who have attempted to study what they regard as the workings of the state or any of its presumed agencies is our most immediate store of commonsense in this respect. Anyone who has tried to negotiate a research contract with the Home Office or the Department of Health will be aware of the extreme jealousy with which such agencies instinctively protect information about themselves. The presumption, and its effective implementation, that the 'public sector' is in fact a private sector about which knowledge must not be made public is all too obviously the principal immediate obstacle to any serious study of the state. The implementation of the claim takes a variety of ingenious forms. One of the most familiar is the combination of bland public assurances that state agencies would welcome 'good' research into themselves, coupled with the apologetic but quite effective mutilation or vetoing of almost all actual research proposals on grounds of defective or inappropriate methodology or other 'technical' considerations. It is a nicely disabling technique of knowledge control to claim that it is the procedural defects of the proposed investigation rather than its object that justifies the refusal of access.... And if one approaches the more serious levels of the functioning of political, judicial and administrative institutions the control or denial of knowledge becomes at once simpler and more absolute of course: one encounters the world of official secrets.

[...]

In sum, the experience if not the findings of both academic and practical political research tends towards the conclusion that there is a hidden reality of politics, a backstage institutionalisation of political power behind the onstage agencies of government; that power effectively resists discovery; and that it may plausibly be identified as 'the state'. In other words it remains reasonable to assume that the state as a special separate and autonomous entity is really there and really powerful and that one aspect of its powerfulness is its ability to prevent the adequate study of the state. We seem to have evidence that the state itself is the source of the state's ability to defy our efforts to unmask it.

An Alternative

I want now to suggest that this whole involvement with the problem of the state may be in an important sense a fantasy. We have, I shall argue, been trapped ... by a reification which in itself seriously obstructs the effective study of a number of problems about political power which ought to concern us – even though the weight of post-Hegelian received ideas probably made the entrapment inevitable. The difficulty we have experienced in studying the state springs in part from the sheer powerfulness of political power.... But it is perhaps equally a consequence of the way we have presented that problem to ourselves.

In trying to reconstitute the issue I shall begin by suggesting that the difficulty of studying the state can be seen as in part a result of the nature of the state, but in an equally large part must be seen as a result of the predispositions of its students. In both respects the business of 'studying the state' seems to be shot through with highly Benthamite fallacies. And we might do better to abandon the project in those terms and study instead something which ... I will call politically organized subjection. In other words I am suggesting that the state, like *the* town and *the* family, is a spurious object of sociological concern and that we should now move beyond Hegel, Marx, Stein, Gumplowicz and Weber, on from the analysis of the state to a concern with the actualities of social subordination. If there is indeed a hidden reality of political power a first step towards discovering it might be a resolute refusal to accept the legitimating account of it that political theorists and political actors so invitingly and ubiquitously hold out to us – that is, the idea that it is 'the state'. My argument, in sum, is that we should take seriously the remark of Engels ... to the effect that, 'the state presents itself to us as the first ideological power over man'. Or the notion presented so forcibly in *The German Ideology* that the most important single characteristic of the state is that it constitutes the 'illusory common interest' of a society; the crucial word there being 'illusory'.[8]

Before developing that argument it will help to look a little more closely at the difficulties of marxism and political sociology in their contemporary intellectual dealings with the state.

The State of Political Sociology

Despite the constant assertion by political sociologists that their discipline is constituted as an attempt to give a social explanation of the state, the state is in practice hardly considered at all in the normal conduct of political sociology. What has happened instead is that the notion of the polity, or in Daniel Bell's most recent writing, 'the public household' has absorbed the notion of the state.[9] The sociological explanation of the state is replaced by the sociological reduction of the state – an observation made trenchantly by Sartori as long ago as 1968.[10] Nevertheless, this transformation is not entirely unprofitable. In advancing their case for making the polity the central concept of political sociology Parsons, Almond and Easton, the principal advocates of that project, had at least one strong card in their hand. This was of course the claim that the important thing to study was not structures but functions.[11] In effect they were going back on the proclaimed agenda of political sociology to the extent of arguing that the distinctiveness of the state, or the political was a matter of processes not of institutions; that the state was a practice not an apparatus. That claim still seems to me, as a principled revision of

the agenda, entirely sound. But if we go back to the models of the polity that functionalist writers offered us in the 1960s and then compare them with the empirical work that has actually been done by political sociologists in the last twenty years an odd discrepancy appears. Many of the formal accounts of the polity proposed in the pioneering days of political sociology took the form of input-output models.[12] In those models the commonsense functions of the state – the determining and implementing of goals, the enforcement of law, the legitimation of order, the expropriation and allocation of resources, the integration of conflict – were all characteristically assigned to the output side of the political process. There is of course an absurdly mechanistic quality about such models. Nevertheless, what must strike one about the body of work political sociologists have actually produced since their field was defined in this way is that almost all of it has been concerned with input functions not output functions. Even after its functional reconstitution the state has not really been studied.... What has been studied is political socialisation, political culture, pressure groups (interest-articulation), class and party (the aggregation of interests), social movements including the Michels' thesis about the oligarchic degeneration of social movements, riots, rebellion and revolution.[13] Overwhelmingly, attention has been paid to the grass-roots processes of the polity and not to the coordinating, power-deploying central functions. Why should this be?

A simple answer would be that political sociologists, like their colleagues in other fields are, in organising their research interests in this way – in studiously averting their eyes from the state and attending instead to its subjects – merely displaying the timorous and servile opportunism rightly and variously trounced by Andreski, Nicolaus, Gouldner, Schmid, and Horowitz but still it seems rampant in the normal determination and selection of social science research projects.[14] The temptations of the 'eyes down, palms up' mode of research organisation are compelling and reductive, not least for people who are themselves in positions of privilege which might not withstand much scrutiny from below.

Nevertheless, my own feeling is that venality is not the whole of the story... [T]he failure of political sociologists to attend to the state, even within their own problematic, must be explained in terms of their intellectual rather than their material proclivities. There is perhaps a strictly professional pathology of political sociology which defines the important and researchable problems of the discipline away from the state. The most obvious aspect of this pathology is methodological. The distinctive methods of political sociology, from public opinion polling onwards, are adapted to studying the attitudes and behaviour of large, accessible and compliant populations and are not adapted to studying relationships within small inaccessible and powerful networks. Conversely consider what happened to the efforts of American political sociologists to study even the modest power structures of local communities: the whole field was at once transformed into a swamp of virulent accusations of methodological ineptitude....[15] The notion that a sufficiently large accumulation of methodologically impure forays into the description of power... might add up to something convincing does not seem to have been considered.

Over and above the methodological prohibition, however, there is a more substantial theoretical obstacle within political sociology that serves to discourage attention to what political sociologists themselves claim is the central problem of their field.

Two main difficulties can be identified here. First, the functional translation of the notion of the state effected by Easton, Almond, Mitchell and others and generally accepted as a crucial defining strategy of political sociology has left political sociologists with a curiously nebulous, imprecise notion of just what or where their supposed principal explicandum is. A vague conception of the functions being performed – 'goal attainment', 'rule adjudication' and so forth – necessarily opens the door to a vague conception of the structures and processes involved in their performance. It is clear for example, to take the case of Almond and Coleman, that even under the conditions of high specificity of structure attributed to 'modern' polities no one-to-one relation between 'governmental' structures and the 'authoritative' functions is going to emerge. Thus, although 'the analytical distinction between society and polity' continues to be insisted on by these authors the structural identification of key phases of the polity, let alone their relation to society, defeats them.[16] Suzanne Keller is quite in line with the mood of her colleagues therefore when she abandons the concept of the state in favour of the more inclusive, and less committing, notions of 'a social centre, a core, a fulcrum', settling in the end for the idea of 'unification around a symbolic centre'.[17] The idea of the centre preserves the conception of state functions in principle but leaves all questions to do with the execution of such functions disastrously wide open. Moreover, it inhibits both empirical and conceptual analysis of the relevant processes by drastically reducing the specificity of the functions themselves. As indicated already the real tendency of political sociology is perhaps not to explain the state at all but to explain it away.

The second problem has to do with the persistence within political sociology of an initial interest in a particular type of substantive issue, the question of the entry into the arena of political action of previously quiescent subject populations. Within the broad intellectual framework of the field, the separation of state and society, this became the compelling practical problem for almost all of the pioneers whose work was taken as effectively defining what political sociologists did. There were many reasons for this concentration of interest, some radical, some conservative, but its overall consequence is clear. In practice political sociology became a body of work centred on such themes as 'the extension of citizenship to the lower classes', 'working class incorporation', 'conditions for stable democracy'. In almost all of this work the state, or some equivalently real, institutionalised nexus of central power was virtually taken for granted – either because it was thought of as historically given or because it was assumed to be a dependent variable vulnerable to the impact of the external social forces which were the immediate object of concern. Accordingly although a sense of the state was there the state was not treated effectively as part of the problem to be investigated....

Taken together, these theoretical and substantive inclinations of political sociology go a fair way to explain why its concern with the state has remained – for all its importance in principle – so rudimentary in practice. Insofar as it has been developed, moreover, it has been largely as an unexpected result of studies of the presumed 'input' functions and processes of the polity such as political socialisation and not a consequence of a direct assault on the central issue. That is to say, the best of the socialisation studies have found that sort of input to be rather strongly shaped by powerful downward actions and influences emanating from 'the centre'....

Of course, it is true that such studies discover the state in only a rather special aspect. What is perceived is a rather powerful agent of legitimation. Those sociologists attracted to a Weberian conception of politics, of whom Daniel Bell is perhaps the most interesting contemporary representative and for whom, in Bell's words 'the axial principle of the polity is legitimacy', will conclude that real progress is being made by research on political socialisation.[18] Those who envisage the state as an altogether more forcible agency of control and coordination will find such a conclusion bland and inadequate if not vacuous. But the question is, can sociologists of this second persuasion demonstrate that a state of the kind they believe in actually exists? What the socialisation studies have done ... is to establish the existence of a managed construction of belief about the state and to make clear the consequences and implications of that process for the binding of

subjects into their own subjection. Furthermore, they have shown that the binding process even if not effected by the state proceeds in terms of the creation of certain sorts of *perceptions* of the state.... The discovery that the *idea* of the state has a significant political reality even if the state itself remains largely undiscovered marks for political sociology a significant and rare meeting of empiricism and a possible theory of the political.

In other words the state emerges from these studies as an ideological thing. It can be understood as the device in terms of which subjection is legitimated; and as an ideological thing it can actually be shown to work like that. It presents politically institutionalised power to us in a form that is at once integrated and isolated and by satisfying both these conditions it creates for our sort of society an acceptable basis for acquiescence. It gives an account of political institutions in terms of cohesion, purpose, independence, common interest and morality without necessarily telling us anything about the actual nature, meaning or functions of political institutions. We are in the world of myth. At this point the implications for political sociology of my suggested alternative approach to the study of state perhaps become clear. One thing we can know about the state, if we wish, is that it is an ideological power. Is it anything more? Myth is of course a rendering of unobserved realities, but it is not necessarily a correct rendering. It is not just that myth makes the abstract concrete. There are senses in which it also makes the non-existent exist. From this point of view perhaps the most important single contribution to the study of the state made in recent years is a passing observation of Ralph Miliband's at the start of chapter 3 of *The State in Capitalist Society* to the effect that: 'There is one preliminary problem about the state which is very seldom considered, yet which requires attention if the discussion of its nature and role is to be properly focused. This is the fact that the "state" is not a thing, that it does not, as such, exist.'[19] In which case our efforts to study it as a thing can only be contributing to the persistence of an illusion. But this brings us to the point where it is necessary to consider the implications of my alternative approach to the study of the state for marxism.

The State of Marxist Theory

The most remarkable feature of recent marxist discussions of the state is the way authors have both perceived the non-entity of the state and failed to cling to the logic of that perception. There seem to be compelling reasons within marxism for both recognising that the state does not exist as a real entity, that it is at best an 'abstract-formal' object as Poulantzas puts it, and for nevertheless discussing the politics of capitalist societies as though the state was indeed a thing and did 'as such, exist'.[20] Of course, Marx, Engels and Lenin all lend their authority to this ambiguity, assuring us that the state is somehow at one and the same time an illusion and 'an organ superimposed on society' in a quite non-illusory way; both a mere mask for class power and 'an organised political force' in its own right.[21] Accordingly, instead of directing their attention to the manner and means by which the *idea* of the existence of the state has been constituted, communicated and imposed, they have come down more or less uneasily in favour of the view that the existence of the idea of the state does indicate the hidden existence of a substantial real structure of at least a state-like nature as well. There is an imperceptible but far-reaching slide from the principled recognition of the state as an abstract-formal object only to the treatment of it as a 'real-concrete' agent with will, power and activity of its own. Even Miliband, notably the least mystified of marxist analysts of the state, moves along that path to a point where we find that the state does, for example, 'interpose itself between the two sides of industry – not, however, as a neutral but as a partisan', and has a 'known and declared propensity to invoke its powers of coercion against one of the parties in the dispute rather than the other' . . . [22] But

the most complex and ambiguous version of this distinctive marxist ambiguity is of course that of Poulantzas.

Before attempting an account of Poulantzas' dealings with the state, however, it is worth considering why marxism generally should have proved so susceptible to this sort of ambiguity. I think it results from an unresolved tension between marxist theory and marxist practice. Marxist theory needs the state as an abstract-formal object in order to explain the integration of class societies. In this sense I can see little real discontinuity between the young Marx and the old or between Marx and marxists: all are hypnotised by the brilliant effect of standing Hegel the right way up, of discovering the state as the political concentration of class relationships. In particular the class relationships of capitalist societies are coordinated through a distinctive combination of coercive and ideological functions which are conveniently located as the functions of the state. Conversely, political institutions can then be analysed from the particular point of view of their performance of such functions within the general context of class domination. At the same time marxist practice needs the state as a real-concrete object, the immediate object of political struggle. Marxist political practice is above all a generation of political class struggle over and above economic struggle. To that extent it presumes the separateness of the economic and the political: separate political domination is to be met by separate political struggle. And one can easily see that to propose that the object of that struggle is merely an abstract-formal entity would have little agitational appeal. The seriousness and comprehensiveness of the struggle to conquer political power call for a serious view of the autonomous reality of political power. Paradoxically, they call for a suspension of disbelief about the concrete existence of the state. In effect to opt for political struggle thus becomes a matter of participating in the ideological construction of the state as a real entity.

Maintaining a balance between the theoretical and practical requirements of marxism thus becomes a rather intricate matter. It is achieved in *The German Ideology* but not often elsewhere: 'every class which is struggling for mastery, even when its domination...postulates the abolition of the old form of society in its entirety and of mastery itself, must first conquer for itself political power in order to represent its interest in turn as the general interest, a step to which in the first moment it is forced;...the practical struggle...makes practical intervention and control necessary through the illusory 'general interest' in the form of the state'.[23] More commonly, the requirement for a unity of theory and practice works itself out by the theoretical acceptance of the state as a genuine, extant, 'organised political force' acting in its own right; theory then becomes a matter of deciphering the relationship between the actions of that force and the field of class struggle. The ambiguity of many marxist accounts of the state may thus be understood not so much as a matter of doctrinal error but rather as expressing a conflation and confusion of theory and practice instead of a true unity.

Both Miliband and Poulantzas very nearly escape from this difficulty. But neither quite succeeds. Miliband, having recognised the non-entity of the state, substitutes a fairly familiar political scientists' alternative which he calls the 'state-system', a cluster of institutions of political and executive control and their key personnel, the 'state-elite': 'the government, the administration, the military and the police, the judicial branch, sub-central government and parliamentary assemblies'.[24] Plainly, these agencies and actors do exist in the naive empirical sense as concrete objects and it is perfectly possible, desirable and necessary to ask how they relate to one another – what *form* of state-system they comprise – and how they, as an ensemble, relate to other forces and elements in a society – what *type* of state is constituted by their existence. These are in effect just the questions that Miliband does pursue. The claim that, taken together, these agencies and actors 'make up the state', is a perfectly sound analytical proposition and serves to differentiate the state as an abstract object quite clearly from the political system as a whole. But there are other crucial questions about the nature and functions of that object in relation to which Miliband's approach is less helpful. The difficulty comes to the surface when at the end of *The State in Capitalist Society* Miliband tells us that 'the state' has been the 'main agent' that has 'helped to mitigate the form and content of class domination'.[25] The conclusion we might have expected, that political practice or class struggle has mitigated class domination by acting on and through politically institutionalised power or the state system is not forthcoming; instead the state reappropriates a unity and volition which at the outset the author had been at pains to deny.

Far from unmasking the state as an ideological power the more realistic notion of the state system serves if anything to make its ideological pretensions more credible. And thus a key task in the study of the state, the understanding and exposure of the way in which the state is constructed as an 'illusory general interest' remains both unattempted and if anything harder to attempt on the basis of this type of realism. A striking feature of the two long chapters in which the legitimation of capitalist society is discussed by Miliband is the virtual absence of the state from them. Not only does he see legitimation as occurring mainly outside the state system ('the engineering of consent in capitalist society is still largely an unofficial private enterprise'), through political parties, churches, voluntary associations, mass media and 'capitalism itself', but the legitimation of the state system itself *as the state* has no place in his account. If the construction of the state does indeed occur independently of the state to such a degree – the principal exception is naturally education – and can be attributed to agents with a quite immediate and concrete existence, perhaps other political processes, such as the mitigation of class domination, could also be explained in this more immediate and concrete manner. In any event it is odd that in a work written at the culmination of a period that had seen an ideological reconstruction of the state – as the 'welfare state' – as thorough as anything attempted since the 17th century that sort of link between domination and legitimation should have been ignored. Could it have anything to do with a failure to resolve the dilemma that marxism, knowing the state to be unreal 'for purposes of theory' needs it to be real 'for purposes of practice'?

Like Miliband, Poulantzas begins by proclaiming the unreality of the state. It is not for him a 'real, concrete singular' object, not something that exists 'in the strong sense of the term'.[26] Rather, it is an abstraction the conceptualisation of which is a 'condition of knowledge of real-concrete objects'.[27] My own view is rather that the conception of the state is a condition of ignorance, but more of that shortly. Consistently with this view of the problem he at once adopts a functional rather than a structural account of what the state is: by the state we are to understand the cohesive factor within the overall unity of a social formation. But actually, factor is an ambiguous word implying both function and agency. And functions are of course institutionalised. The slide begins. The function of cohesion is said to be located in what Poulantzas calls 'a place' – the place in which the contradictions of a social formation are condensed.[28] The particular point of studying the state is thus to elucidate the contradictions of a given system which are nowhere so discernible as in this particular site. And secondly, to apprehend just how the system in question is rendered cohesive despite its contradictions.

The idea of the state or the political as 'the factor of maintenance of a formation's unity' is in itself quite banal and conventional in non-marxist political science and therefore, apart from the way in which the definition directs attention to process rather than to structure in the first instance little special value can be claimed for this aspect of Poulantzas' analysis. The more specifically promising element has to be the claim that the maintenance of unity involves the creation of 'a place' within which contradictions are condensed – in other words the suggestion that an empirically accessible object of study is brought into being which, if studied aright will reveal to us the modalities of domination within given social systems. The question is, what sort of place is it – abstract-formal or real-concrete? A consistent functionalism would of course propose only the former. Poulantzas, however, appears to speak of the actual political-juridical structures of 'the state', of 'the political structures of the state', the institutionalised power of the state', 'the state as an organised political force' and so forth.[29] Suddenly we are in the presence of the real state again. And in this case the reappearance is quite explicitly linked to considerations of political practice: 'political practice is the practice of leadership of the class struggle in and for the state'.[30]

So function becomes place and place becomes agency and structure – the specific structures of the political. The crux of the analysis appears to be this: we are interested in the performance of a particular function, cohesion, and we postulate that that function is performed in a particular place, political structures, which we call the state: the empirical question to be answered concerns the relationship of the state to class struggles. What, then, is gained by introducing and insisting upon the state as meaning both the name of the place and the agent of the function? Does the naming not serve to make spuriously unproblematic things which are necessarily deeply problematic? I am not seeking to belittle what is in many ways a pioneering and important analysis of the political processes of class societies. But I think we do need to ask whether the centrality given to the state in that analysis is really a service to understanding. That there is a political function of cohesion effected repressively, economically and ideologically in class societies is plain enough and calls for elucidation. To identify it as 'the global role of the state' seems to me, by introducing a misplaced concreteness, to both over-simplify and over-mystify its nature.

The difficulty is compounded by the fact that Poulantzas clearly recognises that large parts of the process of cohesion, and of the condensation of contradictions, are not performed within commonsensically 'political' structures at all but are diffused ubiquitously through the social system in ways which make any simple equation of the state and political structures of the kind proposed by Miliband untenable if the functional conception of the state is to be seriously pursued.[31] The danger now is that the notion of the global functionality of the state will lead one into a forced recognition of the global structural existence of the state – a sense of its immanence in all structures perhaps. Certainly, the move is towards an abstract understanding of the state which is so structurally unspecific as to seem either to make the conception of the state redundant, or to substitute it for the conception of society. It seems that the key political functions cannot be definitively assigned to any particular personnel, apparatuses or institutions but rather 'float' with the tides of class power.[32]

And the same difficulty of location dogs the attempt to treat the problem from the structural side. Poulantzas adopts a familiar distinction between institutions and structures, a distinction in which institutions are already abstract-formal objects, normative systems rather than concrete agencies. Class power is exercised through specific institutions which are accordingly identified as power centres. But these institutions are not just vehicles of class power; they have functions and an existence more properly their own as well. At the same time a structure, an ideologically hidden organisation, is constituted out of their existence. This hidden structure of power centres appears to be what is meant by the state.[33] And the task of studying the state would thus seem to be primarily a matter of lifting the ideological mask so as to perceive the reality of state power – class power – in terms of which the structuring is achieved; and secondly, a matter of identifying the apparatuses – functions and personnel – in and through which state power is located and exercised. Neither task is unmanageable in principle; but the management of both presupposes a fairly determinate conception of state functions. And this, I have suggested, is what Poulantzas, for good reasons declines to adopt.

So functions refuse to adhere to structures, structures fail to engross functions. The particular functions of the state, economic, ideological and political, must be understood in terms of the state's global function of cohesion and unification. The global function, eludes structural location. Perhaps it would be simpler to dispense with the conception of the state as an intervening hidden structural reality altogether?[34] If one abandoned the hypothesis of the state would one then be in a better or a worse position to understand the relationship between political institutions and (class) domination?[35]

Before considering that possibility we should note the existence of a less drastic alternative. It would be possible to abandon the notion of the state as a hidden structure but retain it to mean simply the ensemble of institutionalised political power – much in the manner of Miliband. On page 92 of *Political Power and Social Classes* and at frequent intervals thereafter Poulantzas appears to favour this alternative. We are now offered the idea of institutionalised political power (that is, the state) as 'the cohesive factor in a determinate social formation and the nodal point of its transformations'. Here, too, we have a perfectly manageable basis for the study and understanding of the state. But unfortunately in the light of Poulantzas' correctly comprehensive sense of how cohesion is achieved – which is, of course, supported by Miliband's analysis of legitimation – the attribution of that function simply to institutionalised political power is plainly inadequate. Either the state is more than institutionalised political power or the state is not on its own the factor of cohesion.[36] We may therefore want to consider seriously the first possibility; the possibility of abandoning the study of the state.

The Withering Away of the State

In his Preface to *African Political Systems*, A R. Radcliffe-Brown proposed that the idea of the state should be eliminated from social analysis.[37] He found it a source of mystification and argued that the concepts of government and politics were all that was needed for an adequate conceptual grasp of the political. My suggestion is not as radical as that. I am proposing only that we should abandon the state as a material object of study whether concrete or abstract while continuing to take the *idea* of the state extremely seriously. The internal and external relations of political and governmental institutions (the state-system) can be studied effectively without postulating the reality of the state. So in particular can their involvements with economic interests in an overall complex of domination and subjection. But studies proceeding in that way invariably discover a third mode, dimension or region of domination – the ideological. And the particular function of the ideological is to mis-represent political and economic domination in ways that legitimate subjection. Here, at least in the context of capitalist societies, the *idea* of the state becomes a crucial object of study. In this context we might say that the state is the distinctive collective misrepresentation of capitalist societies. Like other collective (mis)representations it is a social fact – but not a fact in nature. Social facts should *not* be treated as things.

Since the 17th century the idea of the state has been a cardinal feature of the process of subjection. Political institutions, the 'state-system', are the real agencies out of which the idea of the state is constructed. The problem for political analysis is to see it as an essentially imaginative construction, however. Engels . . . came as near to understanding the issue in this way as anyone has done. As early as 1845 we find him arguing that the state is brought into being as an idea in order to present the outcome of the class struggle as the independent outcome of a classless legitimate will. Political institutions are turned into 'the state' so that a balance of class power – which is what Engels means by 'society' – may masquerade as unaffected by class. But . . . 'the consciousness of the interconnection' between the construction of the state as an independent entity and the actualities of class power 'becomes dulled and can be lost altogether'. More specifically, 'once the state has become an independent power vis-à-vis society, it produces forthwith a further ideology' – an ideology in which the reality of the state is taken for granted and the 'connection with economic facts gets lost for fair'.[38] My suggestion is that in seeking to dismantle that ideology it is not enough to try to rediscover the connection with economic facts *within* the general terms of the ideology as a whole, the acceptance of the reality of the state. Rather, we must make a ruthless assault on the whole set of claims in terms of which the being of the state is proposed.

The state, then, is not an object akin to the human ear. Nor is it even an object akin to human marriage. It is a third-order object, an ideological project. It is first and foremost an exercise in legitimation – and what is being legitimated is, we may assume, something which if seen directly and as itself would be illegitimate, an unacceptable domination. Why else all the legitimation-work? The state, in sum, is a bid to elicit support for or tolerance of the insupportable and intolerable by presenting them as something other than themselves, namely, legitimate, disinterested domination. The study of the state, seen thus, would begin with the cardinal activity involved in the serious presentation of the state: the legitimating of the illegitimate. The immediately present institutions of the 'state system' – and in particular their coercive functions – are the principal object of that task. The crux of the task is to over-accredit them as an integrated expression of common interest cleanly dissociated from all sectional interests and the structures – class, church, race and so forth – associated with them. The agencies in question, especially administrative and judicial and educational

agencies, are made into state agencies as part of some quite historically specific process of subjection; and made precisely as an alternative reading of and cover for that process....
Not to see the state as in the first instance an exercise in legitimation, in moral regulation, is ... surely to participate in the mystification which is the vital point of the construction of the state.

And in our sort of society at least mystification is the central mode of subjection. Armies and prisons are the back-up instruments of the burden of legitimacy. Of course what is legitimated is, insofar as it is legitimated, real power. Armies and prisons, the Special Patrol and the deportation orders as well as the whole process of fiscal exaction – which Bell shrewdly sees as 'the skeleton of the state stripped of all misleading ideologies' – are all forceful enough.[39] But it is their association with the idea of the state and the invocation of that idea that silences protest, excuses force and convinces almost all of us that the fate of the victims is just and necessary. Only when that association is broken do real hidden powers emerge. And when they do they are not the powers of the state but of armies of liberation or repression, foreign governments, guerilla movements, soviets, juntas, parties, classes. The state for its part never emerges except as a claim to domination – a claim which has become so plausible that it is hardly ever challenged. Appropriately enough the commonest source of challenge is not marxist theory or political sociology but the specific exigency created when individual revolutionaries find themselves on trial for subversion, sedition or treason. It is in documents like Fidel Castro's courtroom speech – and almost uniquely in such documents – that the pretensions of regimes to be states are unmasked.[40]

The state is, then, in every sense of the term a triumph of concealment. It conceals the real history and relations of subjection behind an a-historical mask of legitimating illusion; contrives to deny the existence of connections and conflicts which would if recognised be incompatible with the claimed autonomy

and integration of the state. The real official secret, however, is the secret of the non-existence of the state.

Deciphering Legitimacy

The form of misrepresentation achieved by the idea of the state in capitalist societies is incisively and thoroughly grasped by Poulantzas even though he fails to grasp the full extent to which it *is* a misrepresentation.[41] It seems to me that this combination of insight and failure of vision is directly attributable to his principled objection to historical analysis – and here we come to a serious practical question about the study of the state. He sees perfectly clearly what the idea of the state does socially but because history is not permissible in his scheme of analysis he can only explain how it is done by assuming that it is done by the state. The state has to exist for him to explain his own observations. Only a very careful investigation of the construction of the state as an ideological power could permit a recognition of the effects he observes in combination with a denial of the notion that they are effects of the state.

In capitalist societies the presentation of the state is uniquely pervasive, opaque and bemusing. Centrally it involves the segregation of economic relationships from political relationships, the obliteration within the field of political relationships of the relevance or propriety of class and the proclamation of the political as an autonomous sphere of social unification. Poulantzas perceives all this admirably and with a clarity not achieved in any previous text....[42]

His analysis of the 'effect of isolation' which is the special and pivotal mirage of the idea of the state in capitalist societies is wholly compelling. And yet, having come this far he cannot accept that the idea of the state is itself part of the mirage....[43]

His argument appears to involve both the claim that the state is an ideological fraud perpetrated in the course of imposing subjection and the belief that the state has a non-fraudulent existence as a vital structure of the capitalist mode of production.

I suggest that the former can be shown clearly to be the case and that the latter is an undemonstrable assertion making sense only within a closed theoretical system but having no independent warrant or validity....

What he really needs is two distinct objects of study: the state-system and the state-idea. We come, then, to a fundamental question. We may reasonably infer that the state as a special object of social analysis does not exist as a real entity. Can we agree with Radcliffe-Brown that it is also unnecessary as an abstract-formal entity – that it does nothing for us in the analysis of domination and subjection? Obviously my own conclusion is that we can. Indeed, that we must: the postulate of the state serves to my mind not only to protect us from the perception of our own ideological captivity but more immediately to obscure an otherwise perceptible feature of institutionalised political power, the state-system, in capitalist societies which would otherwise seize our attention and prove the source of a trenchant understanding of the sort of power politically institutionalised power is. I refer to the actual disunity of political power. It is this above all that the idea of the state conceals. The state is the unified symbol of an actual disunity. This is not just a disunity between the political and the economic but equally a profound disunity within the political. Political institutions, especially in the enlarged sense of Miliband's state-system, conspicuously fail to display a unity of practice – just as they constantly discover their inability to function as a more general factor of cohesion. Manifestly they are divided against one another, volatile and confused. What is constituted out of their collective practice is a series of ephemerally unified postures in relation to transient issues with no sustained consistency of purpose. Such enduring unity of practice as the ensemble of political institutions achieve is palpably imposed on them by 'external' economic, fiscal and military organisations and interests. In the United Kingdom for example, the only

unity that can actually be discerned behind the spurious unity of the idea of the state is the unity of commitment to the maintenance, at any price, of an essentially capitalist economy. This sort of disunity and imbalance is of course just what one would expect to find in an institutional field that is primarily a field of struggle. But it is just the centrality of struggle that the idea of the state – even for marxists – contrives to mask.

My suggestion, then, is that we should recognize the cogency of the *idea* of the state as an ideological power and treat that as a compelling object of analysis. But the very reasons that require us to do that also require us not to *believe* in the idea of the state, not to concede, even as an abstract formal-object, the existence of the state....

Towards a Recovery of History

The obvious escape from reification, the one rejected by Poulantzas and neglected by Miliband is historical. The only plausible alternative I can see to taking the state for granted is to understand it as historically constructed. Even so, the unmasking is not automatic as Anderson's analysis of Absolutism makes clear.[44] The argument of *Lineages of the Absolutist State* shows very clearly how a particular presentation of the state was constructed historically as a reconstitution of the political modalities of class power. Yet even this author is not able to shake off the notion of the state – indeed 'the State'. Every time he uses that word, others – regime, government, monarchy, absolutism – could be substituted for it and the only difference would be to replace an ambiguously concrete term with ones of which the implications are unambiguously either concrete or abstract. But it is not just a semantic matter. Anderson's treatment reveals two processes of political construction. The first is the centralisation and coordination of feudal domination...a shift from individualised to concerted coercive subjection of rural populations to noble domination through the

invention of new apparatuses of administration and law. Law provides the common
ground in which the first aspect of the construction of absolutism meets the second.
This was the *ideological* construction of the
'Absolutist State' as the panoply of doctrine
and legitimation under which the reorganisation of feudal domination proceeded and in
terms of which it was presented. The essential
elements of this ideological construction
were, Anderson argues, the adoption of
Roman law as a legitimating context for centralised administration and the formulation
in European political thought from Bodin to
Montesquieu of a general theory of sovereignty providing a still higher-level rationale
for the administrative reconstruction that
was taking place.[45] The idea of the state was
created and used for specific social purposes
in a specific historical setting – and that is
the only reality it had. Everything else
is more precise.

...For this particular historical context
Anderson does demonstrate just how the
idea of the state as a 'veil of illusion' is perpetrated in the course of an entirely concrete
institutional reconstruction of domination
and subjection. Even his own uncritical use
of the term 'the state' to indicate relations and
practices he persistently shows to be much
more precisely identifiable than that, although it weakens the impact of his argument, does not wholly undermine the
historical demonstration he achieves.

If that sort of radical unmasking of the
state is possible for absolutism, why not for
more recent political arrangements? Of
course there is a certain brutal candour and
transparency about absolutism which subsequent constructions have not reproduced.
'L'état, c'est moi' is hardly an attempt at legitimation at all; it so plainly means 'I and my
mercenaries rule – O.K.?' Yet on balance
I think it is not the devious cunning of more
recent political entrepreneurs that has de-
ceived us but rather our own willing or un-
witting participation in the idea of the reality
of the state. If we are to abandon the study of
the state as such and turn instead to the more

direct historical investigation of the political
practice of class (and other) relationships we
might hope to unmask, say, the Welfare State
as effectively as Anderson has unmasked the
Absolutist State. The state is at most a message of domination – an ideological artefact
attributing unity, morality and independence
to the disunited, a-moral and dependent
workings of the practice of government. In
this context the message is decidedly *not* the
medium – let alone the key to an understanding of the sources of its production, or even of
its own real meaning. The message – the
claimed reality of the state – is the ideological
device in terms of which the political institutionalisation of power is legitimated. It is of
some importance to understand how that legitimation is achieved. But it is much more
important to grasp the relationship between
political and non-political power – between
in Weber's terms class, status and party. There
is no reason to suppose that the concept, let
alone belief in the existence, of the state will
help us in that sort of enquiry.

In sum: the state is not the reality which
stands behind the mask of political practice.
It is itself the mask which prevents our seeing
political practice as it is. It is, one could almost say, the mind of a mindless world, the
purpose of purposeless conditions, the opium
of the citizen. There *is* a state-system in Miliband's sense; a palpable nexus of practice and
institutional structure centred in government
and more or less extensive, unified and dominant in any given society. And its sources,
structure and variations can be examined in
fairly straightforward empirical ways. There
is, too, a state-idea, projected, purveyed and
variously believed in in different societies at
different times. And its modes, effects and
variations are also susceptible to research.
The relationship of the state-system and the
state-idea to other forms of power should and
can be central concerns of political analysis.
We are only making difficulties for ourselves
in supposing that we have also to study the
state – an entity, agent, function or relation
over and above the state-system and the
state-idea. The state comes into being as a

structuration within political practice; it starts its life as an implicit construct; it is then reified – as the *res publica*, the public reification, no less – and acquires an overt symbolic identity progressively divorced from practice as an illusory account of practice. The ideological function is extended to a point where conservatives and radicals alike believe that their practice is not directed at each other but at the state; the world of illusion prevails. The task of the sociologist is to demystify; and in this context that means attending to the senses in which the state does not exist rather than to those in which it does.

NOTES AND REFERENCES

1   Jeremy Bentham, *The Handbook of Political Fallacies*, edited by H. A. Larrabee, Harper & Brothers, New York, 1962.
2   V. I. Lenin, 'The State', *Selected Works*, vol. II, New York, 1943, p.639.
3   W. G. Runciman, *Social Science and Political Theory*, Cambridge, 1963, p.32.
4   *Ibid.*, p.33, citing *Marx-Engels Gesamtausgabe*, I, p.492, 'Aus der Kritik der Hegelschen Staatsrecht'.
5   Cf., N. Poulantzas, *Political Power and Social Classes*, New Left Books, London, 1973, pp.130–7 and 150–3.
6   R. E. Dowse, *Report* of a Conference on Political Sociology sponsored by the Political Science Committee of SSRC, Social Science Research Council, London, 1974.
7   Poulantzas, *Political Power and Social Classes*, p.44; the question of the nature of the state is of course returned to at some length in two of this author's later works, *Fascism and Dictatorship*, New Left Books, 1974 and *Classes in Contemporary Capitalism*, New Left Books, 1975, but the problem of precisely identifying and locating the functions of the state is not advanced.
8   F. Engels, *Ludwig Feuerbach and the End of Classical German Philosophy* in (e.g.) L. Feuer (ed.) *Marx and Engels: Basic Writings on Politics and Philosophy*, Doubleday, New York, 1959, p.236; K. Marx and F. Engels, *The German Ideology*, Lawrence & Wishart, London, 1965, p.42 – although it must be admitted that the crucial statements of this view were marginal additions by Engels to the main text of the collaborative work; which possibly confirms a view I have long held that to have done himself full justice Engels should have collaborated with Durkheim rather than with Marx.
9   D. Bell, *The Cultural Contradictions of Capitalism*, Basic Books, New York, 1976.
10 G. Sartori, 'From Sociology of Politics to Political Sociology' in S. M. Lipset (ed.) *Politics and the Social Sciences*, Oxford University Press, 1969.
11 Cf., T. Parsons, 'Voting and the Equilibrium of the American Political System', in E. Burdick and A. Brodbeck (eds.) *American Voting Behaviour*, Free Press, 1959; D. Easton, *A Systems Analysis of Political Life*, John Wiley & Sons, New York, 1965; G. Almond and J. Coleman, *The Politics of the Developing Areas*, Princeton University Press, New Jersey, 1960; W. Mitchell, *The American Polity*, Free Press, 1966. The net perception of political process achieved by this school of analysis could perhaps be formalised in something like the following manner:

Political Systems
Social systems have common *functional problems*:

   adaptation
   integration
   pattern-maintenance
   goal-attainment

Functional problems are handled by *functional sub-systems*:

   economy
   household
   culture
   polity

Polities (political systems) perform common *functions*:

selection and specification of goals
allocation of costs and values
authorisation

The performance of these functions involves:

creation of a *political role-structure* within which binding decisions can be made

Political role-structure is generated through sets of *interchanges* between the polity and other social sub-systems:

Input: demands role output decision
  support structure/   implementations
  resources decision-   controls
    making

The *communications* involved in these interchanges generate also a *political culture*: political culture operates as a medium of feedback from output to new inputs, etc.

The social *processes* central to the operation of political systems may be further specified:

Input: political   Output: legitimation
  socialisation   promulgation
  recruitment   administra-
  articulation and   tion
  aggregation
  of interests.

All political systems have *structure*: but not common items of structure.

All political structure may be analysed in terms of common *organisational properties and levels*:

  levels: government – regime – community
  properties: external differentiation – internal
    differentiation and functional
    specificity of roles – visibility –
    formalisation – institutionalisation
    of competition for leadership roles –
    stratification of influence –
    balance of formal and informal
    structures.

The *style* of action of all political structure may be evaluated along four value-dimensions (pattern variables):

  ascription vs. achievement
  particularism vs. universalism
  effectivity vs. affective neutrality
  diffuseness vs. specificity

All real-world political structure is multifunctional; the style of all political performance is 'mixed'.

Plainly, such a conception has neither operational nor theoretical need for the concept of the state. The state has not been explained; but it has been explained away.

12 The best known of course is that suggested by David Easton, *op. cit.*

13 This pattern was already evident in the bibliographies of the field produced in the 1950s – for example, R. Bendix and S. M. Lipset, 'Political Sociology: an Essay and Bibliography', *Current Sociology*, 1957, p.vi. – and is no less so in the 1970s; consider the 'Further Reading' proposed by R. E. Dowse and J. Hughes, *Political Sociology*, John Wiley & Sons, New York, 1972.

14 S. Andreski, *Social Science as Sorcery*, Deutsch, London, 1972; M. Nicolaus, 'The Professional Organisation of Sociology; a View from Below', in R. Blackburn (ed.) *Ideology in Social Science*, Fontana, London, 1972; A. Gouldner, 'The Sociologist as Partisan', in *For Sociology*, Allen Lane, London, 1973; I. Horowitz, *Professing Sociology*, Allen Lane, London, 1972.

15 R. Dahl, *Who Governs?*, Yale University Press, New Haven, 1961; N. Polsby, *Community Power and Political Theory*, Yale University Press, New Haven, 1963, and 'Pluralism in the Study of Community Power', *The American Sociologist*, iv, 2, 1969, p.118; P. Bachrach and M. S. Baratz, *Power and Poverty*, Oxford University Press, 1970; S. Lukes, *Power: A Radical View*, Macmillan, London, 1974; P. Abell, 'The Many Faces of Power and Liberty', *Sociology*, xi, 3, 1977, p.3.

16 Almond and Coleman, *op. cit*: compare especially the promise of the Introduction with what is actually offered in the Conclusion.

17 Suzanne Keller, *Beyond the Ruling Class*, Random House, New York, 1963, p.34.

18 Daniel Bell, *The Cultural Contradictions of Capitalism*, Heinemann, London, 1976, especially pp.220–32.

19 R. Miliband, *The State in Capitalist Society*, Weidenfeld & Nicolson, London, 1969, p.49.

20 In a comment on an earlier version of this paper Dr P. R. D. Corrigan makes the point very forcefully, 'that the state is both illusory and there – indeed, its "thereness" is how the illusion is sustained' and again that the state is 'an illusion in the sense that its claim to be what it appeared to be is invalid; it is not illusory in the sense that it is not a logical error, a problem with our vision, or a conjuring trick that sustains it but precisely those powers and relations which its claim to be what it appears to be conceals'. It could also be said, however, that whether or not the state is really there marxist analysis has to treat it as really there in order to locate key phases of the integration of class power which otherwise remain elusive; this seems to be especially the case in Poulantzas, *Classes in Contemporary Capitalism* pp.155–8.

21 See the discussion of these dualities in the work of Marx, Engels and Lenin in S. W. Moore, *The Critique of Capitalist Democracy*, A. M. Kelley, New York, 1969.

22 R. Miliband, *op. cit.*, p.81.

23 *German Ideology*, part I, p.53.

24 R. Miliband, *op. cit.*, p.54.

25 *Ibid.*, p.266.

26 N. Poulantzas, *Political Power and Social Classes*, p. 12; 'It can be said that in the strong sense of the term, only *real, concrete, singular* objects exist. The final aim of the process of thought is knowledge of these objects: e.g. of France or England at a given moment of their development'. Quite apart from the epistemological shakiness of the distinction as illustrated by the example we are left with a situation in which all the tools of thought – mode of production, class, state and so forth – are in the strong sense agreed to be unreal and the task of thought is to use them without reifying them. My suggestion is that it is precisely when these tools are least useful that the danger of reification is greatest; in that sense 'mode of production' is an effective tool, 'the state' is not.

27 *Ibid.*, p.39.

28 *Ibid.*, pp.45, 47–51; and cf. *Classes in Contemporary Capitalism*, pp.158–9.

29 *Political Power and Social Classes*, pp.44, 93, 132.

30 *Ibid.*, p.43; Poulantzas is here citing the 'completely acceptable' words of J. Verret, *Théorie et Politique*, Paris, 1967, p.194. The problem for this sort of analysis is naturally especially evident in any consideration of political practice. For purposes of practice the state is treated as primarily a structure – and indeed the most obvious and delimited structure, political institutions ('the state as a specific level of structures in a social formation' p.43). For purposes of theory the state is primarily a set of functions – of cohesion, condensation of contradictions, isolation, and so forth. And the trouble is that the functions manifestly do not reside in the structures; the structures are simply not the 'place' where the functions are performed. So the state begins to be redefined as some more abstract, generalised, impalpable sort of structure.

31 Poulantzas makes this point against Miliband very effectively in the debate between the two authors originally published in the *New Left Review* and reprinted in R. Blackburn *op. cit.*, pp.238–63; see especially pp.251–2. Conversely, Miliband very effectively makes the point about the structural elusiveness of the state in Poulantzas' conception, see especially, p.256. Both criticisms are of course entirely well taken and appropriate.

32 This is especially evident in Poulantzas' discussions of the relationship between the state and the dominant class in capitalism; cf. *Political Power and Social Classes*, pp.296–307 and *Classes in Contemporary Capitalism* pp.156–62 where we are told, for example, that the state has a 'specific role' in 'elaborating the political strategy of monopoly capital' only to find that that role is

never in fact either specified or located by this author and indeed cannot be because as a matter of principle the state 'does not have its own power but... forms the contradictory locus of consideration for the balance of forces that divides even the dominant class itself'. For all its apparent precision the term 'the state' actually indicates chaos.

33 *Political Power and Social Classes*, pp.115–17; but once again any sense of concreteness, of a defined empirical referent for what one is talking about is quickly dissipated; 'the state', in the sense of political institutions is only one among a cluster of power centres, companies, cultural institutions and so forth being cited as others; yet it is via the *ensemble* of power centres that functions of the state are executed.

34 Alternatively one could in order to focus the mind on its abstract-formal character try to conceive of the state not as an agent, object or structure but as a relationship. This is indeed the solution favoured by Poulantzas in *Classes in Contemporary Capitalism* ('the state is not a thing but a relation', p.161). But unfortunately this formulation proves as unstable as all those that have gone before it; the relation turns out to be 'more exactly the condensation of the balance of forces' within the dominant class and between that class and others. Although this is in principle an empirical claim it is not in fact pursued as such. Meanwhile the relationship increasingly turns back to an agent. Although in any sort of common sense usage relationships would be said to have functions rather than ends Poulantzas seems driven to attribute independent volition to the relationship. Thus, the state 'takes responsibility for the interests of the hegemonic fraction, monopoly capital' (p.157); and again, it 'takes responsibility for the interests of monopoly capital as a whole' (p.158). Relationships, however do not act in this sense; marriage does not take responsibility for the interests of men in relation to women, though it

could well be said to function to that end. In practice Poulantzas does not 'avoid the false dilemma in which contemporary discussion of the state is trapped, between the state as a thing and the state as a subject' by regarding it as a relationship. His understanding of the dilemma is correct but the effort to treat the state consistently and exclusively as a relationship defeats him; instead of going on to ask what sort of relationship and between whom? he reverts to the sterile issue of the 'relative autonomy of the state... inscribed in its very structure'.

35 The point to be emphasised here is that domination is a crucially important problematic and that trying to deal with it by thinking about the state really seems to have proved extraordinarily unprofitable. I am not suggesting that if we think away the state we shall do away with domination – I would hate to be accused of that sort of Young Hegelianism. But it does begin to seem possible that the real relations of domination within the state-system and between it and other interests and institutions and groups might be seen more clearly were it not for the apparent problem of the state.

36 This was of course the nub of the debate between Miliband and Poulantzas referred to above; and it was their inability to agree on a locus for the factor of cohesion other than institutionalised political and governmental power (Miliband's state-system) which mainly explains the inconclusive and slightly demoralising way in which that debate ended.

37 A. R. Radcliffe-Brown, 'Preface', M. Fortes and E. E. Evans-Pritchard (eds.) *African Political Systems*, Oxford University Press, 1940.

38 F. Engels, *Ludwig Feuerbach and the End of Classical German Philosophy*, in (e.g.) L. Feuer, *op. cit.*, pp.236–7.

39 D. Bell, *op. cit.* p.220, quoting Rudolf Goldscheid.

40 M. Alexandre (ed.) *On Trial*, Lorrimer Publishing, London, 1968.

41 N. Poulantzas. *Political Power and Social Classes*, pp. 195–223.

42 *Ibid.*, p.133; but note that the state even here is an agent as well as a mystification; this author simply cannot escape from the veil of illusion created by the idea of the state even though he knows it to be a veil of illusion.

43 *Ibid.*, p. 134.

44 Perry Anderson, *Lineages of the Absolute State*, New Left Books, London, 1974.

45 *Ibid.*, pp.24–30, 424–6.

Editorial note: It is important to repeat that this paper was *written in 1977*, before the publication of Poulantzas's *State Power, Socialism* (London, New Left Books, 1978) Part 1 of which ('The institutional materiality of the state') could have led Philip Abrams to modify somewhat his commentary on Poulantzas. That this last work of Poulantzas draws from Foucault is another marker for an explainable absence in Abrams's text.

5

Governmentality

Michel Foucault

In a previous lecture on 'apparatuses of secur-ity', I tried to explain the emergence of a set of problems specific to the issue of population, and on closer inspection it turned out that we would also need to take into account the prob-lematic of government. In short, one needed to analyze the series: security, population, govern-ment. I would now like to try to begin making an inventory of this question of government.

Throughout the Middle Ages and classical antiquity, we find a multitude of treatises presented as 'advice to the prince', concern-ing his proper conduct, the exercise of power, the means of securing the acceptance and respect of his subjects, the love of God and obedience to him, the application of divine law to the cities of men, etc. But a more striking fact is that, from the middle of the sixteenth century to the end of the eighteenth, there develops and flourishes a notable series of political treatises that are no longer exactly 'advice to the prince', and not yet treatises of political science, but are instead presented as works on the 'art of government'. Govern-ment as a general problem seems to me to explode in the sixteenth century, posed by discussions of quite diverse questions. One has, for example, the question of the govern-ment of oneself, that ritualization of the problem of personal conduct which is charac-teristic of the sixteenth century Stoic revival. There is the problem too of the government of souls and lives, the entire theme of Catholic and Protestant pastoral doctrine. There is government of children and the great prob-lematic of pedagogy which emerges and de-velops during the sixteenth century. And, perhaps only as the last of these questions to be taken up, there is the government of the state by the prince. How to govern oneself, how to be governed, how to govern others, by whom the people will accept being governed, how to become the best possible governor – all these problems, in their multiplicity and intensity, seem to me to be characteristic of the sixteenth century, which lies, to put it schematically, at the crossroads of two processes: the one which, shattering the

From G. Burchell, C. Gordon, and P. Miller (eds.), *The Foucault Effect: Studies in Govern-mentality*, pp. 87–104. Hemel Hempstead and Chicago: Harvester Wheatsheaf and University of Chicago Press, 1991. Reprinted by permission of The University of Chicago Press.

structures of feudalism, leads to the establishment of the great territorial, administrative and colonial states; and that totally different movement which, with the Reformation and Counter-Reformation, raises the issue of how one must be spiritually ruled and led on this earth in order to achieve eternal salvation.

There is a double movement, then, of state centralization on the one hand and of dispersion and religious dissidence on the other: it is, I believe, at the intersection of these two tendencies that the problem comes to pose itself with this peculiar intensity, of how to be ruled, how strictly, by whom, to what end, by what methods, etc. There is a problematic of government in general.

Out of all this immense and monotonous literature on government which extends to the end of the eighteenth century, with the transformations which I will try to identify in a moment, I would like to underline some points that are worthy of notice because they relate to the actual definition of what is meant by the government of the state, of what we would today call the political form of government. The simplest way of doing this is to compare all of this literature with a single text which from the sixteenth to the eighteenth century never ceased to function as the object of explicit or implicit opposition and rejection, and relative to which the whole literature on government established its standpoint: Machiavelli's *The Prince*. It would be interesting to trace the relationship of this text to all those works that succeeded, criticized and rebutted it.

We must first of all remember that Machiavelli's *The Prince* was not immediately made an object of execration, but on the contrary was honoured by its immediate contemporaries and immediate successors, and also later at the end of the eighteenth century (or perhaps rather at the very beginning of the nineteenth century), at the very moment when all of this literature on the art of government was about to come to an end. *The Prince* re-emerges at the beginning of the nineteenth century, especially in Germany, where it is translated, prefaced and commented upon by writers such as Rehberg, Leo, Ranke and Kellerman, and also in Italy. It makes its appearance in a context which is worth analyzing, one which is partly Napoleonic, but also partly created by the Revolution and the problems of revolution in the United States, of how and under what conditions a ruler's sovereignty over the state can be maintained; but this is also the context in which there emerges, with Clausewitz, the problem (whose political importance was evident at the Congress of Vienna in 1815) of the relationship between politics and strategy, and the problem of relations of force and the calculation of these relations as a principle of intelligibility and rationalization in international relations; and lastly, in addition, it connects with the problem of Italian and German territorial unity, since Machiavelli had been one of those who tried to define the conditions under which Italian territorial unity could be restored.

This is the context in which Machiavelli re-emerges. But it is clear that, between the initial honour accorded him in the sixteenth century and his rediscovery at the start of the nineteenth, there was a whole 'affair' around his work, one which was complex and took various forms: some explicit praise of Machiavelli (Naudé, Machon), numerous frontal attacks (from Catholic sources: Ambrozio Politi, *Disputationes de Libris a Christiano detestandis*; and from Protestant sources: Innocent Gentillet, *Discours sur les moyens de bien gouverner contre Nicolas Machiavel*, 1576), and also a number of implicit critiques (G. de La Perrière, *Miroir politique*, 1567; Th. Elyott, *The Governor*, 1580; P. Paruta, *Della Perfezione della Vita politica*, 1579).

This whole debate should not be viewed solely in terms of its relation to Machiavelli's text and what were felt to be its scandalous or radically unacceptable aspects. It needs to be seen in terms of something which it was trying to define in its specificity, namely an art of government. Some authors rejected the idea of a new art of government centred on the state and reason of state, which they stigmatized with the name of Machiavellianism;

others rejected Machiavelli by showing that there existed an art of government which was both rational and legitimate, and of which Machiavelli's *The Prince* was only an imperfect approximation or caricature; finally, there were others who, in order to prove the legitimacy of a particular art of government, were willing to justify some at least of Machiavelli's writings (this was what Naudé did to the *Discourses* on Livy; Machon went so far as to attempt to show that nothing was more Machiavellian than the way in which, according to the Bible, God himself and his prophets had guided the Jewish people).

All these authors shared a common concern to distance themselves from a certain conception of the art of government which, once shorn of its theological foundations and religious justifications, took the sole interest of the prince as its object and principle of rationality. Let us leave aside the question of whether the interpretation of Machiavelli in these debates was accurate or not. The essential thing is that they attempted to articulate a kind of rationality which was intrinsic to the art of government, without subordinating it to the problematic of the prince and of his relationship to the principality of which he is lord and master.

The art of government is therefore defined in a manner differentiating it from a certain capacity of the prince, which some think they can find expounded in Machiavelli's writings, which others are unable to find; while others again will criticize this art of government as a new form of Machiavellianism.

This politics of *The Prince*, fictitious or otherwise, from which people sought to distance themselves, was characterized by one principle: for Machiavelli, it was alleged, the prince stood in a relation of singularity and externality, and thus of transcendence, to his principality. The prince acquires his principality by inheritance or conquest, but in any case he does not form part of it, he remains external to it. The link that binds him to his principality may have been established through violence, through family heritage or by treaty, with the complicity or the alliance of other princes; this makes no difference, the link in any event remains a purely synthetic one and there is no fundamental, essential, natural and juridical connection between the prince and his principality. As a corollary of this, given that this link is external, it will be fragile and continually under threat – from outside by the prince's enemies who seek to conquer or recapture his principality, and from within by subjects who have no *a priori* reason to accept his rule. Finally, this principle and its corollary lead to a conclusion, deduced as an imperative: that the objective of the exercise of power is to reinforce, strengthen and protect the principality, but with this last understood to mean not the objective ensemble of its subjects and the territory, but rather the prince's relation with what he owns, with the territory he has inherited or acquired, and with his subjects. This fragile link is what the art of governing or of being prince espoused by Machiavelli has as its object. As a consequence of this the mode of analysis of Machiavelli's text will be twofold: to identify dangers (where they come from, what they consist in, their severity: which are the greater, which the slighter), and, secondly, to develop the art of manipulating relations of force that will allow the prince to ensure the protection of his principality, understood as the link that binds him to his territory and his subjects.

Schematically, one can say that Machiavelli's *The Prince*, as profiled in all these implicitly or explicitly anti-Machiavellian treatises, is essentially a treatise about the prince's ability to keep his principality. And it is this *savoir-faire* that the anti-Machiavellian literature wants to replace by something else and new, namely the art of government. Having the ability to retain one's principality is not at all the same thing as possessing the art of governing. But what does this latter ability comprise? To get a view of this problem, which is still at a raw and early stage, let us consider one of the earliest texts of this great anti-Machiavellian literature: Guillaume de La Perrière's *Miroir Politique*.

This text, disappointingly thin in comparison with Machiavelli, prefigures a number of important ideas. First of all, what does La Perrière mean by 'to govern' and 'governor': what definition does he give of these terms? On page 24 of his text he writes: 'governor can signify monarch, emperor, king, prince, lord, magistrate, prelate, judge and the like'. Like La Perrière, others who write on the art of government constantly recall that one speaks also of 'governing' a household, souls, children, a province, a convent, a religious order, a family.

These points of simple vocabulary actually have important political implications: Machiavelli's prince, at least as these authors interpret him, is by definition unique in his principality and occupies a position of externality and transcendence. We have seen, however, that practices of government are, on the one hand, multifarious and concern many kinds of people: the head of a family, the superior of a convent, the teacher or tutor of a child or pupil; so that there are several forms of government among which the prince's relation to his state is only one particular mode; while, on the other hand, all these other kinds of government are internal to the state or society. It is within the state that the father will rule the family, the superior the convent, etc. Thus we find at once a plurality of forms of government and their immanence to the state: the multiplicity and immanence of these activities distinguishes them radically from the transcendent singularity of Machiavelli's prince.

To be sure, among all these forms of government which interweave within the state and society, there remains one special and precise form: there is the question of defining the particular form of governing which can be applied to the state as a whole. Thus, seeking to produce a typology of forms of the art of government, La Mothe Le Vayer, in a text from the following century (consisting of educational writings intended for the French Dauphin), says that there are three fundamental types of government, each of which relates to a particular science or discipline: the art of self-government, connected with morality; the art of properly governing a family, which belongs to economy; and finally the science of ruling the state, which concerns politics. In comparison with morality and economy, politics evidently has its own specific nature, which La Mothe Le Vayer states clearly. What matters, notwithstanding this typology, is that the art of government is always characterized by the essential continuity of one type with the other, and of a second type with a third.

This means that, whereas the doctrine of the prince and the juridical theory of sovereignty are constantly attempting to draw the line between the power of the prince and any other form of power, because its task is to explain and justify this essential discontinuity between them, in the art of government the task is to establish a continuity, in both an upwards and a downwards direction.

Upwards continuity means that a person who wishes to govern the state well must first learn how to govern himself, his goods and his patrimony, after which he will be successful in governing the state. This ascending line characterizes the pedagogies of the prince, which are an important issue at this time, as the example of La Mothe Le Vayer shows: he wrote for the Dauphin first a treatise of morality, then a book of economics and lastly a political treatise. It is the pedagogical formation of the prince, then, that will assure this upwards continuity. On the other hand, we also have a downwards continuity in the sense that, when a state is well run, the head of the family will know how to look after his family, his goods and his patrimony, which means that individuals will, in turn, behave as they should. This downwards line, which transmits to individual behavior and the running of the family the same principles as the good government of the state, is just at this time beginning to be called *police*. The prince's pedagogical formation ensures the upwards continuity of the forms of government, and police the downwards one. The central term of this continuity is the government of the family, termed *economy*.

The art of government, as becomes apparent in this literature, is essentially concerned with answering the question of how to introduce economy – that is to say, the correct manner of managing individuals, goods and wealth within the family (which a good father is expected to do in relation to his wife, children and servants) and of making the family fortunes prosper – how to introduce this meticulous attention of the father towards his family into the management of the state.

This, I believe, is the essential issue in the establishment of the art of government: introduction of economy into political practice. And if this is the case in the sixteenth century, it remains so in the eighteenth. In Rousseau's *Encyclopedia* article on 'Political economy' the problem is still posed in the same terms. What he says here, roughly, is that the word 'economy' can only properly be used to signify the wise government of the family for the common welfare of all, and this is its actual original use; the problem, writes Rousseau, is how to introduce it, *mutatis mutandis,* and with all the discontinuities that we will observe below, into the general running of the state. To govern a state will therefore mean to apply economy, to set up an economy at the level of the entire state, which means exercising towards its inhabitants, and the wealth and behaviour of each and all, a form of surveillance and control as attentive as that of the head of a family over his household and his goods.

An expression which was important in the eighteenth century captures this very well: Quesnay speaks of good government as 'economic government'. This latter notion becomes tautological, given that the art of government is just the art of exercising power in the form and according to the model of the economy. But the reason why Quesnay speaks of 'economic government' is that the word 'economy', for reasons that I will explain later, is in the process of acquiring a modern meaning, and it is at this moment becoming apparent that the very essence of government – that is, the art of exercising power in the form of economy –

is to have as its main objective that which we are today accustomed to call 'the economy'.

The word 'economy', which in the sixteenth century signified a form of government, comes in the eighteenth century to designate a level of reality, a field of intervention, through a series of complex processes that I regard as absolutely fundamental to our history.

The second point which I should like to discuss in Guillaume de La Perrière's book consists of the following statement: 'government is the right disposition of things, arranged so as to lead to a convenient end'.

I would like to link this sentence with another series of observations. Government is the right disposition of things. I would like to pause over this word 'things', because if we consider what characterizes the ensemble of objects of the prince's power in Machiavelli, we will see that for Machiavelli the object and, in a sense, the target of power are two things, on the one hand the territory, and on the other its inhabitants. In this respect, Machiavelli simply adapted to his particular aims a juridical principle which from the Middle Ages to the sixteenth century defined sovereignty in public law: sovereignty is not exercised on things, but above all on a territory and consequently on the subjects who inhabit it. In this sense we can say that the territory is the fundamental element both in Machiavellian principality and in juridical sovereignty as defined by the theoreticians and philosophers of right. Obviously enough, these territories can be fertile or not, the population dense or sparse, the inhabitants rich or poor, active or lazy, but all these elements are mere variables by comparison with territory itself, which is the very foundation of principality and sovereignty. On the contrary, in La Perrière's text, you will notice that the definition of government in no way refers to territory. One governs things. But what does this mean? I do not think this is a matter of opposing things to men, but rather of showing that what government has to do with is not territory but rather a sort of complex composed of men and things. The things with which in this sense government is to be concerned are in fact men, but men in their relations, their links, their imbrication with those other things which are wealth, resources, means of subsistence, the territory with its specific qualities, climate, irrigation, fertility, etc.; men in their relation to that other kind of things, customs, habits, ways of acting and thinking, etc.; lastly, men in their relation to that other kind of things, accidents and misfortunes such as famine, epidemics, death, etc. The fact that government concerns things understood in this way, this imbrication of men and things, is I believe readily confirmed by the metaphor which is inevitably invoked in these treatises on government, namely that of the ship. What does it mean to govern a ship? It means clearly to take charge of the sailors, but also of the boat and its cargo; to take care of a ship means also to reckon with winds, rocks and storms; and it consists in that activity of establishing a relation between the sailors who are to be taken care of and the ship which is to be taken care of, and the cargo which is to be brought safely to port, and all those eventualities like winds, rocks, storms and so on; this is what characterizes the government of a ship. The same goes for the running of a household. Governing a household, a family, does not essentially mean safeguarding the family property; what concerns it is the individuals that compose the family, their wealth and prosperity. It means to reckon with all the possible events that may intervene, such as births and deaths, and with all the things that can be done, such as possible alliances with other families; it is this general form of management that is characteristic of government; by comparison, the question of landed property for the family, and the question of the acquisition of sovereignty over a territory for a prince, are only relatively secondary matters. What counts essentially is this complex of men and things; property and territory are merely one of its variables.

This theme of the government of things as we find it in La Perrière can also be met with in the seventeenth and eighteenth centuries.

Frederick the Great has some notable pages on it in his *Anti-Machiavel*. He says, for instance, let us compare Holland with Russia: Russia may have the largest territory of any European state, but it is mostly made up of swamps, forests and deserts, and is inhabited by miserable groups of people totally destitute of activity and industry; if one takes Holland, on the other hand, with its tiny territory, again mostly marshland, we find that it nevertheless possesses such a population, such wealth, such commercial activity and such a fleet as to make it an important European state, something that Russia is only just beginning to become.

To govern, then, means to govern things. Let us consider once more the sentence I quoted earlier, where La Perrière says: 'government is the right disposition of things, arranged so as to lead to a convenient end'. Government, that is to say, has a finality of its own, and in this respect again I believe it can be clearly distinguished from sovereignty. I do not of course mean that sovereignty is presented in philosophical and juridical texts as a pure and simple right; no jurist or, *a fortiori*, theologian ever said that the legitimate sovereign is purely and simply entitled to exercise his power regardless of its ends. The sovereign must always, if he is to be a good sovereign, have as his aim, 'the common welfare and the salvation of all'. Take for instance a late seventeenth-century author. Pufendorf says: 'Sovereign authority is conferred upon them [the rulers] only in order to allow them to use it to attain or conserve what is of public utility'. The ruler may not have consideration for anything advantageous for himself, unless it also be so for the state. What does this common good or general salvation consist of, which the jurists talk about as being the end of sovereignty? If we look closely at the real content that jurists and theologians give to it, we can see that 'the common good' refers to a state of affairs where all the subjects without exception obey the laws, accomplish the tasks expected of them, practise the trade to which they are assigned, and respect the established order so far as this order conforms to the laws imposed by God on nature and men: in other words, 'the common good' means essentially obedience to the law, either that of their earthly sovereign or that of God, the absolute sovereign. In every case, what characterizes the end of sovereignty, this common and general good, is in sum nothing other than submission to sovereignty. This means that the end of sovereignty is circular: the end of sovereignty is the exercise of sovereignty. The good is obedience to the law, hence the good for sovereignty is that people should obey it. This is an essential circularity which, whatever its theoretical structure, moral justification or practical effects, comes very close to what Machiavelli said when he stated that the primary aim of the prince was to retain his principality. We always come back to this self-referring circularity of sovereignty or principality.

Now, with the new definition given by La Perrière, with his attempt at a definition of government, I believe we can see emerging a new kind of finality. Government is defined as a right manner of disposing things so as to lead not to the form of the common good, as the jurists' texts would have said, but to an end which is 'convenient' for each of the things that are to be governed. This implies a plurality of specific aims: for instance, government will have to ensure that the greatest possible quantity of wealth is produced, that the people are provided with sufficient means of subsistence, that the population is enabled to multiply, etc. There is a whole series of specific finalities, then, which become the objective of government as such. In order to achieve these various finalities, things must be disposed – and this term, *dispose,* is important because with sovereignty the instrument that allowed it to achieve its aim – that is to say, obedience to the laws – was the law itself; law and sovereignty were absolutely inseparable. On the contrary, with government it is a question not of imposing law on men, but of disposing things: that is to say, of employing tactics rather than laws, and even of using laws themselves as tactics – to arrange things in such a way that, through a

certain number of means, such and such ends may be achieved.

I believe we are at an important turning point here: whereas the end of sovereignty is internal to itself and possesses its own intrinsic instruments in the shape of its laws, the finality of government resides in the things it manages and in the pursuit of the perfection and intensification of the processes which it directs; and the instruments of government, instead of being laws, now come to be a range of multiform tactics. Within the perspective of government, law is not what is important: this is a frequent theme throughout the seventeenth century, and it is made explicit in the eighteenth-century texts of the Physiocrats which explain that it is not through law that the aims of government are to be reached.

Finally, a fourth remark, still concerning this text from La Perrière: he says that a good ruler must have patience, wisdom and diligence. What does he mean by patience? To explain it, he gives the example of the king of bees, the bumble-bee, who, he says, rules the bee-hive without needing a sting; through this example God has sought to show us in a mystical manner that the good governor does not have to have a sting – that is to say, a weapon of killing, a sword – in order to exercise his power; he must have patience rather than wrath, and it is not the right to kill, to employ force, that forms the essence of the figure of the governor. And what positive content accompanies this absence of sting? Wisdom and diligence. Wisdom, understood no longer in the traditional sense as knowledge of divine and human laws, of justice and equality, but rather as the knowledge of things, of the objectives that can and should be attained, and the disposition of things required to reach them; it is this knowledge that is to constitute the wisdom of the sovereign. As for his diligence, this is the principle that a governor should only govern in such a way that he thinks and acts as though he were in the service of those who are governed. And here, once again, La Perrière cites the example of the head of the family who rises first in the morning and goes to bed last, who concerns himself with everything in the household because he considers himself as being in its service. We can see at once how far this characterization of government differs from the idea of the prince as found in or attributed to Machiavelli. To be sure, this notion of governing, for all its novelty, is still very crude here.

This schematic presentation of the notion and theory of the art of government did not remain a purely abstract question in the sixteenth century, and it was not of concern only to political theoreticians. I think we can identify its connections with political reality. The theory of the art of government was linked, from the sixteenth century, to the whole development of the administrative apparatus of the territorial monarchies, the emergence of governmental apparatuses; it was also connected to a set of analyses and forms of knowledge which began to develop in the late sixteenth century and grew in importance during the seventeenth, and which were essentially to do with knowledge of the state, in all its different elements, dimensions and factors of power, questions which were termed precisely 'statistics', meaning the science of the state; finally, as a third vector of connections, I do not think one can fail to relate this search for an art of government to mercantilism and the Cameralists' science of police.

To put it very schematically, in the late sixteenth century and early seventeenth century, the art of government finds its first form of crystallization, organized around the theme of reason of state, understood not in the negative and pejorative sense we give to it today (as that which infringes on the principles of law, equity and humanity in the sole interests of the state), but in a full and positive sense: the state is governed according to rational principles which are intrinsic to it and which cannot be derived solely from natural or divine laws or the principles of wisdom and prudence; the state, like nature, has its own proper form of rationality, albeit of a different sort. Conversely, the art of government, instead of seeking to found itself in transcendental rules, a cosmological model

or a philosophico-moral ideal, must find the principles of its rationality in that which constitutes the specific reality of the state. In my subsequent lectures I will be examining the elements of this first form of state rationality. But we can say here that, right until the early eighteenth century, this form of 'reason of state' acted as a sort of obstacle to the development of the art of government.

This is for a number of reasons. Firstly, there are the strictly historical ones, the series of great crises of the seventeenth century: first the Thirty Years War with its ruin and devastation; then in the mid-century the peasant and urban rebellions; and finally the financial crisis, the crisis of revenues which affected all Western monarchies at the end of the century. The art of government could only spread and develop in subtlety in an age of expansion, free from the great military, political and economic tensions which afflicted the seventeenth century from beginning to end. Massive and elementary historical causes thus blocked the propagation of the art of government. I think also that the doctrine formulated during the sixteenth century was impeded in the seventeenth by a series of other factors which I might term, to use expressions which I do not much care for, mental and institutional structures. The pre-eminence of the problem of the exercise of sovereignty, both as a theoretical question and as a principle of political organization, was the fundamental factor here so long as sovereignty remained the central question. So long as the institutions of sovereignty were the basic political institutions and the exercise of power was conceived as an exercise of sovereignty, the art of government could not be developed in a specific and autonomous manner. I think we have a good example of this in mercantilism. Mercantilism might be described as the first sanctioned efforts to apply this art of government at the level of political practices and knowledge of the state; in this sense one can in fact say that mercantilism represents a first threshold of rationality in this art of government which La Perrière's text had defined in terms more moral than real. Mercantilism is the first rationalization of the exercise of power as a practice of government; for the first time with mercantilism we see the development of a *savoir* of state that can be used as a tactic of government. All this may be true, but mercantilism was blocked and arrested, I believe, precisely by the fact that it took as its essential objective the might of the sovereign; it sought a way not so much to increase the wealth of the country as to allow the ruler to accumulate wealth, build up his treasury and create the army with which he could carry out his policies. And the instruments mercantilism used were laws, decrees, regulations: that is to say, the traditional weapons of sovereignty. The objective was sovereign's might, the instruments those of sovereignty; mercantilism sought to reinsert the possibilities opened up by a consciously conceived art of government within a mental and institutional structure, that of sovereignty, which by its very nature stifled them.

Thus, throughout the seventeenth century up to the liquidation of the themes of mercantilism at the beginning of the eighteenth, the art of government remained in a certain sense immobilized. It was trapped within the inordinately vast, abstract, rigid framework of the problem and institution of sovereignty. This art of government tried, so to speak, to reconcile itself with the theory of sovereignty by attempting to derive the ruling principles of an art of government from a renewed version of the theory of sovereignty – and this is where those seventeenth-century jurists come into the picture who formalize or ritualize the theory of the contract. Contract theory enables the founding contract, the mutual pledge of ruler and subjects, to function as a sort of theoretical matrix for deriving the general principles of an art of government. But although contract theory, with its reflection on the relationship between ruler and subjects, played a very important role in theories of public law, in practice, as is evidenced by the case of Hobbes (even though what Hobbes was aiming to discover was the ruling principles of an art of government), it

remained at the stage of the formulation of general principles of public law.

On the one hand, there was this framework of sovereignty which was too large, too abstract and too rigid; and on the other, the theory of government suffered from its reliance on a model which was too thin, too weak and too insubstantial, that of the family: an economy of enrichment still based on a model of the family was unlikely to be able to respond adequately to the importance of territorial possessions and royal finance.

How then was the art of government able to outflank these obstacles? Here again a number of general processes played their part: the demographic expansion of the eighteenth century, connected with an increasing abundance of money, which in turn was linked to the expansion of agricultural production through a series of circular processes with which the historians are familiar. If this is the general picture, then we can say more precisely that the art of government found fresh outlets through the emergence of the problem of population; or let us say rather that there occurred a subtle process, which we must seek to reconstruct in its particulars, through which the science of government, the recentring of the theme of economy on a different plane from that of the family, and the problem of population are all interconnected.

It was through the development of the science of government that the notion of economy came to be recentred on to that different plane of reality which we characterize today as the 'economic', and it was also through this science that it became possible to identify problems specific to the population; but conversely we can say as well that it was thanks to the perception of the specific problems of the population, and thanks to the isolation of that area of reality that we call the economy, that the problem of government finally came to be thought, reflected and calculated outside of the juridical framework of sovereignty. And that 'statistics' which, in mercantilist tradition, only ever worked within and for the benefit of a monarchical administration that functioned according to the form of sovereignty, now becomes the major technical factor, or one of the major technical factors, of this new technology.

In what way did the problem of population make possible the derestriction of the art of government? The perspective of population, the reality accorded to specific phenomena of population, render possible the final elimination of the model of the family and the recentring of the notion of economy. Whereas statistics had previously worked within the administrative frame and thus in terms of the functioning of sovereignty, it now gradually reveals that population has its own regularities, its own rate of deaths and diseases, its cycles of scarcity, etc.; statistics shows also that the domain of population involves a range of intrinsic, aggregate effects, phenomena that are irreducible to those of the family, such as epidemics, endemic levels of mortality, ascending spirals of labour and wealth; lastly it shows that, through its shifts, customs, activities, etc., population has specific economic effects: statistics, by making it possible to quantify these specific phenomena of population, also shows that this specificity is irreducible to the dimension of the family. The latter now disappears as the model of government, except for a certain number of residual themes of a religious or moral nature. What, on the other hand, now emerges into prominence is the family considered as an element internal to population, and as a fundamental instrument in its government.

In other words, prior to the emergence of population, it was impossible to conceive the art of government except on the model of the family, in terms of economy conceived as the management of a family; from the moment when, on the contrary, population appears absolutely irreducible to the family, the latter becomes of secondary importance compared to population, as an element internal to population: no longer, that is to say, a model, but a segment. Nevertheless it remains a privileged segment, because whenever information is required concerning the population (sexual behaviour, demography, consumption, etc.), it has to be obtained through the family. But the family becomes an instrument rather than a model: the privileged instrument for the government of the population and not the chimerical model of good government. This shift from the level of the model to that of an instrument is, I believe, absolutely fundamental, and it is from the middle of the eighteenth century that the family appears in this dimension of instrumentality relative to the population, with the institution of campaigns to reduce mortality, and to promote marriages, vaccinations, etc. Thus, what makes it possible for the theme of population to unblock the field of the art of government is this elimination of the family as model.

In the second place, population comes to appear above all else as the ultimate end of government. In contrast to sovereignty, government has as its purpose not the act of government itself, but the welfare of the population, the improvement of its condition, the increase of its wealth, longevity, health, etc.; and the means that the government uses to attain these ends are themselves all in some sense immanent to the population; it is the population itself on which government will act either directly through large-scale campaigns, or indirectly through techniques that will make possible, without the full awareness of the people, the stimulation of birth rates, the directing of the flow of population into certain regions or activities, etc. The population now represents more the end of government than the power of the sovereign; the population is the subject of needs, of aspirations, but it is also the object in the hands of the government, aware, vis-à-vis the government, of what it wants, but ignorant of what is being done to it. Interest at the level of the consciousness of each individual who goes to make up the population, and interest considered as the interest of the population regardless of what the particular interests and aspirations may be of the individuals who compose it, this is the new target and the fundamental instrument of the government of population: the birth of a new art, or at any rate of a range of absolutely new tactics and techniques.

Lastly, population is the point around which is organized what in sixteenth-century texts came to be called the patience of the sovereign, in the sense that the population is the object that government must take into account in all its observations and *savoir*, in order to be able to govern effectively in a rational and conscious manner. The constitution of a *savoir* of government is absolutely inseparable from that of a knowledge of all the processes related to population in its larger sense: that is to say, what we now call the economy. I said in my last lecture that the constitution of political economy depended upon the emergence from among all the various elements of wealth of a new subject: population. The new science called political economy arises out of the perception of new networks of continuous and multiple relations between population, territory and wealth; and this is accompanied by the formation of a type of intervention characteristic of government, namely intervention in the field of economy and population. In other words, the transition which takes place in the eighteenth century from an art of government to a political science, from a regime dominated by structures of sovereignty to one ruled by techniques of government, turns on the theme of population and hence also on the birth of political economy.

This is not to say that sovereignty ceases to play a role from the moment when the art of government begins to become a political science; I would say that, on the contrary, the problem of sovereignty was never posed with greater force than at this time, because it no longer involved, as it did in the sixteenth and seventeenth centuries, an attempt to derive an art of government from a theory of sovereignty, but instead, given that such an art now existed and was spreading, involved an attempt to see what juridical and institutional form, what foundation in the law, could be given to the sovereignty that characterizes a state. It suffices to read in chronological succession two different texts by Rousseau. In his *Encyclopaedia* article on 'Political economy', we can see the way in which Rousseau sets up

the problem of the art of government by pointing out (and the text is very characteristic from this point of view) that the word 'oeconomy' essentially signifies the management of family property by the father, but that this model can no longer be accepted, even if it had been valid in the past; today we know, says Rousseau, that political economy is not the economy of the family, and even without making explicit reference to the Physiocrats, to statistics or to the general problem of the population, he sees quite clearly this turning point consisting in the fact that the economy of 'political economy' has a totally new sense which cannot be reduced to the old model of the family. He undertakes in this article the task of giving a new definition of the art of government. Later he writes *The Social Contract*, where he poses the problem of how it is possible, using concepts like nature, contract and general will, to provide a general principle of government which allows room both for a juridical principle of sovereignty and for the elements through which an art of government can be defined and characterized. Consequently, sovereignty is far from being eliminated by the emergence of a new art of government, even by one which has passed the threshold of political science; on the contrary, the problem of sovereignty is made more acute than ever.

As for discipline, this is not eliminated either; clearly its modes of organization, all the institutions within which it had developed in the seventeenth and eighteenth centuries – schools, manufactories, armies, etc. – all this can only be understood on the basis of the development of the great administrative monarchies, but nevertheless, discipline was never more important or more valorized than at the moment when it became important to manage a population; the managing of a population not only concerns the collective mass of phenomena, the level of its aggregate effects, it also implies the management of population in its depths and its details. The notion of a government of population renders all the more acute the problem of the foundation of sovereignty (consider Rousseau) and all the more acute equally the necessity for the development of discipline (consider all the history of the disciplines, which I have attempted to analyze elsewhere).

Accordingly, we need to see things not in terms of the replacement of a society of sovereignty by a disciplinary society and the subsequent replacement of a disciplinary society by a society of government; in reality one has a triangle, sovereignty–discipline–government, which has as its primary target the population and as its essential mechanism the apparatuses of security. In any case, I wanted to demonstrate the deep historical link between the movement that overturns the constants of sovereignty in consequence of the problem of choices of government, the movement that brings about the emergence of population as a datum, as a field of intervention and as an objective of governmental techniques, and the process which isolates the economy as a specific sector of reality, and political economy as the science and the technique of intervention of the government in that field of reality. Three movements: government, population, political economy, which constitute from the eighteenth century onwards a solid series, one which even today has assuredly not been dissolved.

In conclusion I would like to say that on second thoughts the more exact title I would like to have given to the course of lectures which I have begun this year is not the one I originally chose, 'Security, territory and population': what I would like to undertake is something which I would term a history of 'governmentality'. By this word I mean three things:

1. The ensemble formed by the institutions, procedures, analyses and reflections, the calculations and tactics that allow the exercise of this very specific albeit complex form of power, which has as its target population, as its principal form of knowledge political economy, and as its essential technical means apparatuses of security.

2. The tendency which, over a long period and throughout the West, has steadily led towards the pre-eminence over all other forms (sovereignty, discipline, etc.) of this type of power which may be termed government, resulting, on the one hand, in the formation of a whole series of specific governmental apparatuses, and, on the other, in the development of a whole complex of *savoirs*.

3. The process, or rather the result of the process, through which the state of justice of the Middle Ages, transformed into the administrative state during the fifteenth and sixteenth centuries, gradually becomes 'governmentalized'.

We all know the fascination which the love, or horror, of the state exercises today; we know how much attention is paid to the genesis of the state, its history, its advance, its power and abuses, etc. The excessive value attributed to the problem of the state is expressed, basically, in two ways: the one form, immediate, affective and tragic, is the lyricism of the *monstre froid* we see confronting us; but there is a second way of overvaluing the problem of the state, one which is paradoxical because apparently reductionist: it is the form of analysis that consists in reducing the state to a certain number of functions, such as the development of productive forces and the reproduction of relations of production, and yet this reductionist vision of the relative importance of the state's role nevertheless invariably renders it absolutely essential as a target needing to be attacked and a privileged position needing to be occupied. But the state, no more probably today than at any other time in its history, does not have this unity, this individuality, this rigorous functionality, nor, to speak frankly, this importance; maybe, after all, the state is no more than a composite reality and a mythicized abstraction, whose importance is a lot more limited than many of us think. Maybe what is really important for our modernity – that is, for our present – is not so much the *étatisation* of society, as the 'governmentalization' of the state.

We live in the era of a 'governmentality' first discovered in the eighteenth century.

This governmentalization of the state is a singularly paradoxical phenomenon, since if in fact the problems of governmentality and the techniques of government have become the only political issue, the only real space for political struggle and contestation, this is because the governmentalization of the state is at the same time what has permitted the state to survive, and it is possible to suppose that if the state is what it is today, this is so precisely thanks to this governmentality, which is at once internal and external to the state, since it is the tactics of government which make possible the continual definition and redefinition of what is within the competence of the state and what is not, the public versus the private, and so on; thus the state can only be understood in its survival and its limits on the basis of the general tactics of governmentality.

And maybe we could even, albeit in a very global, rough and inexact fashion, reconstruct in this manner the great forms and economies of power in the West. First of all, the state of justice, born in the feudal type of territorial regime which corresponds to a society of laws – either customs or written laws – involving a whole reciprocal play of obligation and litigation; second, the administrative state, born in the territoriality of national boundaries in the fifteenth and sixteenth centuries and corresponding to a society of regulation and discipline; and finally a governmental state, essentially defined no longer in terms of its territoriality, of its surface area, but in terms of the mass of its population with its volume and density, and indeed also with the territory over which it is distributed, although this figures here only as one among its component elements. This state of government which bears essentially on population and both refers itself to and makes use of the instrumentation of economic *savoir* could be seen as corresponding to a type of society controlled by apparatuses of security.

In the following lectures I will try to show how governmentality was born out of, on the one hand, the archaic model of Christian pastoral, and, on the other, a diplomatic-military technique, perfected on a European scale with the Treaty of Wesphalia; and that it could assume the dimensions it has only thanks to a series of specific instruments, whose formation is exactly contemporaneous with that of the art of government and which are known, in the old seventeenth- and eighteenth-century sense of the term, as *police*. The pastoral, the new diplomatic-military techniques and, lastly, police: these are the three elements that I believe made possible the production of this fundamental phenomenon in Western history, the governmentalization of the state.

6

Governing "Advanced" Liberal Democracies

Nikolas Rose

When feminists began to campaign under the slogan "the personal is the political", they drew attention to fundamental flaws in modern political reason.[1] Politics had become identified, on the one hand, with the party and the programme and, on the other, with the question of who possesses power in the State, rather than the dynamics of power relations within the encounters that make up the everyday experience of individuals. One of the virtues of the analyses carried out by Michel Foucault and his co-workers has been to further problematize the forms of political reason that constituted this orthodoxy, to demonstrate the debility of the language that has captivated political philosophy and sociology for over a century, with its constitutive oppositions of State/civil society, domination/emancipation, public/private and the like. In the name of public *and* private security, life has been accorded a "social" dimension through a hybrid array of devices for the management of insecurity. In the name of

national *and* individual prosperity, an "economic machine" has taken shape, which may have as its object an economy made up of enterprises competing in a market, but structures that domain through implanting modes of economic calculation, setting fiscal regimes and mandating techniques of financial regulation and accounting. In the name of public citizenship *and* private welfare, the family has been configured as a matrix for organizing domestic, conjugal and child-rearing arrangements and instrumentalizing wage labour and consumption. In the name of social *and* personal wellbeing, a complex apparatus of health and therapeutics has been assembled, concerned with the management of the individual and social body as a vital national resource, and the management of "problems of living", made up of techniques of advice and guidance, medics, clinics, guides and counsellors.

The strategies of regulation that have made up our modern experience of "power" are

From A. Barry, T. Osborne, and N. Rose (eds.), *Foucault and Political Reason: Liberalism, Neo-Liberalism and Rationalities of Government*, pp. 37–64. Chicago and London: University of Chicago Press and UCL Press, 1996. Reprinted by permission of The University of Chicago Press.

thus assembled into complexes that connect up forces and institutions deemed "political" with apparatuses that shape and manage individual and collective conduct in relation to norms and objectives but yet are constituted as "non-political". Each complex is an assemblage of diverse components – persons, forms of knowledge, technical procedures and modes of judgement and sanction – a machine for government only in the sense in which Foucault compared the French legal system to one of those machines constructed by Tinguely – more Heath Robinson than Audi, full of parts that come from elsewhere, strange couplings, chance relations, cogs and levers that don't work – and yet which "work" in the sense that they produce effects that have meaning and consequences for us (cited in Gordon 1980). The lines between public and private, compulsory and voluntary, law and norm operate as *internal* elements within each of these assemblages, as each links the regulation of public conduct with the subjective emotional and intellectual capacities and techniques of individuals, and the ethical regimes through which they govern their lives.

The term "politics" can no longer be utilized as if its meaning was self-evident; it must itself be the object of analysis. Indeed, at stake within our own unsettled political reason is the very meaning, legitimacy and limit of politics itself. The idea of the State was, and is, certainly one of the most powerful ways of seeking to codify, manage and articulate – or alternatively contest, overturn and rearticulate – the proliferation of practices of authoritative rule throughout our "modern" experience. But the dream or nightmare of a society programmed, colonized or dominated by "the cold monster" of the State is profoundly limiting as a way of rendering intelligible the way we are governed today. One needs to ask how, and in what ways, and to what extent the rationales, devices and authorities for the government of conduct in the multitude of bedrooms, factories, shopping malls, children's homes, kitchens, cinemas, operating theatres, classrooms and so forth

have become linked up to a "political" apparatus? How did the obligations of political authorities come to extend to the health, happiness and wellbeing of the population and those families and individuals who comprised it? How did different political forces seek to programme these new domains? To what extent were they successful in establishing centres of calculation and action such that events in distant places – hospitals, social security offices, workplaces, homes, schools – could be known and regulated by political decisions? What new authorities in the conduct of conduct – notably bureaucrats, managers and experts – were born or transformed in the process? And what, if anything, has been specific about attempts to govern in ways that term themselves liberal and democratic?

Three Propositions on Liberal Rule

What is liberalism if we consider it neither as a political philosophy nor as a type of society but from the perspective of governmentality? Let me put forward three hypotheses.

1. Nineteenth-century liberalism, if it is considered as a *rationality of rule* and not simply as a set of philosophical and normative reflections *upon* rule, produced a series of problems about the governability of individuals, families, markets and populations. These arose out of the insistence upon the necessary limits of political authority, notably in relation to economic and industrial life, public freedoms of debate and the expression of thought, religious practice, and familial authority. Expertise – authority arising out of a claim to knowledge, to neutrality and to efficacy – came to provide a number of solutions to this apparent opposition between the need to govern in the interests of morality and order, and the need to restrict government in the interests of liberty and economy. Liberal rule was thus rendered operable, not merely by the politico-philosophical pronouncement of the

sanctity of the opposition of public and private, politics and market, state and civil society, but through the capacity of various knowledgeable persons to render this formula operable. The philanthropist may be seen as one of the first of these personae, exercising a new form of moral and technical authority. But over the second half of the nineteenth century philanthropy was supplemented and displaced by the truths produced and disseminated by the positive sciences of economics, statistics, sociology, medicine, biology, psychiatry and psychology. One sees also the rise of the expert figures of the scientist, the engineer, the civil servant and the bureaucrat: new techniques for the ethical formation and capacitation of persons who would exercise authority and the deployment of a range of scientific and technical knowledges that allowed the possibility of exercising rule over time and space (Osborne 1994, Barry 1996).

2. Over the late nineteenth and early twentieth centuries this formula of government was perceived, from a variety of political, moral and philosophical perspectives, as failing to produce the necessary economic, social and ethical consequences. One sees the rise of a new formula for the exercise of rule, which one can call "social". The authority of expertise becomes inextricably linked to the formal political apparatus of rule, as rulers are urged to accept the obligation to tame and govern the undesirable consequences of industrial life, wage labour and urban existence in the name of society: social solidarity, social security, social peace, social prosperity. The theories, explanations, modalities of information and specialist techniques offered by experts were, through different struggles and strategies, connected into complex devices of rule that sought to re-establish the integration of individuals in a social form. This was not so much a process in which a central State extended its tentacles throughout society, but the invention of various "rules for rule" that sought to transform the State *into* a centre that *could* programme – shape, guide, channel, direct, control – events and persons distant from it. Persons and activities were to be governed *through society*, that is to say, through acting upon them in relation to a *social* norm, and constituting their experiences and evaluations in a *social* form. In the face of the threat of a socialism conceived as the swallowing up of society by the State, these formulae for a state of welfare sought to maintain a certain extra-political sphere at the same time as developing a proliferating set of techniques for acting upon it. The truth claims of expertise were highly significant here: through the powers of truth, distant events and persons could be governed "at arms length": political rule would not itself set out the norms of individual conduct, but would install and empower a variety of "professionals", investing them with authority to act as experts in the devices of social rule. And the subject of rule was reconceptualized: where the subject invented in the nineteenth century was subject to a kind of individualizing moral normativity, the subject of welfare was a subject of needs, attitudes and relationships, a subject who was to be embraced within, and governed through, a nexus of collective solidarities and dependencies.

3. The strategies of rule generated under this formula of "the state of welfare" have changed fundamentally [since the 1930s]. These changes have arisen, on the one hand, through an array of different critiques that problematized welfare from the point of view of its alleged failings and its deleterious consequences for public finances, individual rights and private morals. On the other hand, strategic mutations have been made possible through the proliferation of new devices for governing conduct that have their roots, in part at least, in the "success" of welfare in authorizing expertise in

relation to a range of social objectives, and in implanting in citizens the aspiration to pursue their own civility, well-being and advancement. In the multiple encounters between these two lines of force, a new formula of rule is taking shape, one that we can perhaps best term "advanced liberal". Advanced liberal rule depends upon expertise in a different way, and connects experts differently into the technologies of rule. It seeks to degovernmentalize the State and to de-statize practices of government, to detach the substantive authority of expertise from the apparatuses of political rule, relocating experts within a market governed by the rationalities of competition, accountability and consumer demand. It does not seek to govern through "society", but through the regulated choices of individual citizens, now construed as subjects of choices and aspirations to self-actualization and self-fulfilment. Individuals are to be governed through their freedom, but neither as isolated atoms of classical political economy, nor as citizens of society, but as members of heterogeneous communities of allegiance, as "community" emerges as a new way of conceptualizing and administering moral relations amongst persons.

Government

Colin Gordon has pointed out that Foucault utilized the concept of government in two senses (Gordon 1991, cf. Foucault 1981, Gordon 1986). First, to draw attention to a dimension of our experience – not itself specifically modern – constituted by all those ways of reflecting and acting that have aimed to shape, guide, manage or regulate the conduct of persons – not only other persons but also oneself – in the light of certain principles or goals. What made these forms of reflection *governmental*, rather than theoretical, philosophical or moral, is their wish to make themselves practical, to connect themselves up with various procedures and apparatuses that would seek to give them effect – whether these be the practice of diary writing in order to govern conscience, practices of child rearing in order to govern children, practices of security and subsistence in order to govern pauperism, or techniques of financial inscription and calculation in order to govern economic activity. No doubt throughout the ages humans have reflected upon the conduct of themselves and others, but such thought becomes governmental to the extent that it seeks to render itself technical, to insert itself into the world by "realizing" itself as a *practice*.

Foucault uses the term government in a second, and more circumscribed manner, one that helps us to repose our analyses of the problematics of rule as they have taken shape in the West over the last three centuries. By problematics of rule, I mean the ways in which those who would exercise rule have posed themselves the question of the reasons, justifications, means and ends of rule, and the problems, goals or ambitions that should animate it. Here the notion of government addresses itself specifically to the domain of the political, not as a domain of State or a set of institutions and actors but in terms of the varieties of political reason. Govern*mentality* both extends the concerns of rulers to the ordering of the multitudinous affairs of a territory and its population in order to ensure its wellbeing, and simultaneously establishes divisions between the proper spheres of action of different types of authority.

As *political rationality*, governmentalities are to be analyzed as practices for the "formulation and justification of idealized schemata for representing reality, analyzing it and rectifying it" – as a kind of intellectual machinery or apparatus for rendering reality thinkable in such a way that it is amenable to political programming (Rose & Miller 1992: 179, cf. Miller & Rose 1990). Despite the undoubted salience of all the petty deals and corruptions of political activity, political rationalities have a *moral* form, in so far as they concern such issues as the proper distribution of tasks between different authorities and the ideals or principles to which government should be addressed. Further, political rationalities have an *epistemological* character, in that they embody particular conceptions of the objects to be governed – nation, population, economy, society, community – and the subjects to be governed – citizens, subjects, individuals. And they deploy a certain *style of reasoning*: language here understood as itself a set of "intellectual techniques" for rendering reality thinkable and practicable, and constituting domains that are amenable – or not amenable – to reformatory intervention.

As an array of *technologies of government*, governmentality is to be analyzed in terms of the strategies, techniques and procedures through which different authorities seek to enact programmes of government in relation to the materials and forces to hand and the resistances and oppositions anticipated or encountered. Hence, this is not a matter of the implementation of idealized schema in the real by an act of will, but of the complex assemblage of diverse forces (legal, architectural, professional, administrative, financial, judgmental), techniques (notation, computation, calculation, examination, evaluation), devices (surveys and charts, systems of training, building forms) that promise to regulate decisions and actions of individuals, groups, organizations in relation to authoritative criteria (cf. Rose & Miller 1992: 183).

The technologies and devices that are assembled into the apparatus of a State have neither the unity nor the functionality often ascribed to them. The "power of the State" is a resultant, not a cause, an outcome of the composition and assembling of actors, flows, buildings, relations of authority into relatively durable associations mobilized, to a greater or lesser extent, towards the achievement of particular objectives by common means. This is not a matter of the domination of a "network" by "the State" but rather a matter of *translation*. The translation of political programmes articulated in rather general terms – national efficiency, democracy,

equality, enterprise – into ways of seeking to exercise authority over persons, places and activities in specific locales and practices. The translation of thought and action from a "centre of calculation" into a diversity of locales dispersed across a territory – translation in the sense of a movement from one place to another. Through a multitude of such mobile relays, relations are established between those who are spatially and temporally separated, and between events and decisions in spheres that none the less retain their formal autonomy. The composition of such networks is the condition of possibility for "action at a distance": it is only to the extent that such alignments of diverse forces can be established that calculated action upon conduct across space and time can occur at all (cf. Latour 1986). However, the strategies of government that I term "advanced liberal" explicitly seek to utilize and instrumentalize such possibilities: they are rationalities animated by the desire to "govern at a distance".

Liberalism

Eighteenth-century European science of police dreamed of a time in which a territory and its inhabitants would be transparent to knowledge – all was to be known, noted, enumerated and documented (Foucault 1989, 1991, cf. Pasquino 1991). The conduct of persons in all domains of life was to be specified and scrutinized in minute particulars, through detailed regulations of habitation, dress, manners and the like – warding off disorder through a fixed ordering of persons and activities (cf. Oestreich 1982). Liberalism, as a mentality of rule, abandons this megalomaniac and obsessive fantasy of a totally administered society. Government now confronts itself with realities – market, civil society, citizens – that have their own internal logics and densities, their own intrinsic mechanisms of self-regulation. As Graham Burchell has pointed out, liberalism thus repudiates *raison d'état* as a rationality of rule in which a sovereign exercises his totalizing will across a national space (Burchell 1991, and cf. Burchell 1986). Rulers are confronted, on the one hand, with subjects equipped with rights and interests that *should not* be interdicted by politics. On the other hand, rulers are faced with a realm of processes that they *cannot* govern by the exercise of sovereign will because they lack the requisite knowledge and capacities. The objects, instruments and tasks of rule must be reformulated with reference to these domains of market, civil society and citizenship, with the aim of ensuring that they function to the benefit of the nation as a whole.

The two, apparently illiberal, poles of "power over life" that Foucault identifies – the disciplines of the body and the bio-politics of the population – thus find their place within liberal mentalities of rule, as rule becomes dependent upon ways of rendering intelligible and practicable these vital conditions for the production and government of a polity of free citizens (Foucault 1977, 1979). Those mechanisms and devices operating according to a disciplinary logic, from the school to the prison, seek to produce the subjective conditions, the forms of self-mastery, self-regulation and self-control, necessary to govern a nation now made up of free and "civilized" citizens. At the same time, bio-political strategies – statistical enquiries, censuses, programmes for enhancement or curtailment of rates of reproduction or the minimization of illness and the promotion of health – seek to render intelligible the domains whose laws liberal government must know and respect: legitimate government will not be arbitrary government, but will be based upon intelligence concerning those whose wellbeing it is mandated to enhance (Foucault 1980). From this moment onwards, rule must be exercised in the light of a knowledge of that which is to be ruled – a child, a family, an economy, a community – a knowledge both of its general laws of functioning (supply and demand, social solidarity) of its particular state at any one time (rate of productivity, rate of suicide), and of the ways in which it can be shaped and guided in order to produce desirable objectives while at the same time respecting its autonomy.

We can draw out four significant features of liberalism from the perspective of government.

1. *A new relation between government and knowledge.* Although all formulae of government are dependent upon a knowledge of that which is to be governed, and indeed themselves constitute a certain form of knowledge of the arts of government, liberal strategies tie government to the positive knowledges of human conduct developed within the social and human sciences. The activity of government becomes connected up to all manner of facts (the avalanche of printed numbers and other information examined by Ian Hacking (1991)), theories (philosophies of progress, conceptualizations of epidemic disease...), diagrams (sanitary reform, child guidance...), techniques (double-entry book keeping, compulsory medical inspection of school children), knowledgeable persons who can speak "in the name of society" (sociologists, statisticians, epidemiologists, social workers). Knowledge here flows around a diversity of apparatuses for the production, circulation, accumulation, authorization and realization of truth: in the academy, in government bureaux, in reports of commissions, public enquiries and pressure groups; it is the "know-how" that promises to render docile the unruly domains over which government is to be exercised, to make government possible and to make government better.

2. *A novel specification of the subjects of rule as active in their own government.* Liberal mentalities of rule are characterized by the hopes that they invest in the subjects of government. The claim, in politics, law, morality and so forth, that subjects are individuals whose freedom, liberty and rights are to be respected by drawing certain limits to the legitimate

scope of political or legal regulation goes hand in hand with the emergence of a range of novel practices which seek to shape and regulate individuality in particular ways. Liberal strategies of government thus become dependent upon devices (schooling, the domesticated family, the lunatic asylum, the reformatory prison) that promise to create individuals who do not need to be governed by others, but will govern themselves, master themselves, care for themselves. And although the abstract subject of rights may be specified in universalistic form, novel technologies of rule throughout the nineteenth century produce new demands and possibilities for positive knowledges of particular subjects. This is the moment of the disciplines, which simultaneously specify subjects in terms of certain norms of civilization, and effect a division between the civilized member of society and those lacking the capacities to exercise their citizenship responsibly: the infanticidal woman or the monomaniacal regicide in the court of law, the delinquent boys and girls to be reformed in industrial or reformatory establishments, the prostitute or fallen women, the men and women thought mad. One sees the beginning of a painful and resisted migration of rights to truth over humans from theology or jurisprudence to the disciplines that owe their very conditions of disciplinization to these new technologies of government. From this time forth, liberal governmentalities will dream that the national objective for the good subject of rule will fuse with the voluntarily assumed obligations of free individuals to make the most of their own existence by conducting their life responsibly. At the same time, subjects themselves will have to make their decisions about their self-conduct surrounded by a web of vocabularies, injunctions, promises, dire warnings and threats of intervention, organized increasingly around a proliferation of norms and normativities.

3. *An intrinsic relation to the authority of expertise*. Liberal arts of rule from the middle of the nineteenth century sought to modulate events, decisions and actions in the economy, the family, the private firm, and the conduct of the individual person while maintaining and promoting their autonomy and self-responsibility. These modes of intervention did not answer to a single logic or form part of a coherent programme of "State intervention" (cf. Foucault 1980). Rather, largely through the proselytizing of independent reformers, a number of frictions and disturbances – epidemics and disease, theft and criminality, pauperism and indigence, insanity and imbecility, the breakdown of marital relations – were recorded as "social" problems that had consequences for national well-being and thus called for new forms of remedial authoritative attention. The relations that were brought into being between political authorities, legal measures and independent authorities differed according to whether one was seeking to regulate economic exchanges through contract, to mitigate the effects of factory labour upon health, to reduce the social dangers of epidemics through sanitary reform, to moralize the children of the labouring classes through industrial schools and so forth. In each case, experts, in demanding that economic, familial and social arrangements are governed according to their own programmes, attempt to mobilize political resources such as legislation, funding or organizational capacity for their own ends. Political forces seek to give effect to their strategies, not only through the utilization of laws, bureaucracies, funding regimes and authoritative State agencies and agents, but through utilizing and instrumentalizing forms of authority other than those of "the State" in order to govern – spatially and constitutionally – "at a distance". Authority is accorded to formally autonomous expert author-

ities and simultaneously the exercise of that autonomy is shaped through various forms of licensure, through professionalization and through bureaucratization. From this time forth, the domain of "politics" will be distinguished from other spheres of authoritative rule, yet inextricably bound to the authority of expertise.

4. *A continual questioning of the activity of rule.* Sociologies of our post-modern condition have stressed the "reflexivity" that they consider to be characteristic of our age (Giddens 1990, Lash & Urry 1994). But the "reflexivity" that imbues all attempts to exercise rule in our present is not distinctive to some terminal stage of modernity; it characterized liberal political rationalities from their inception. Liberalism confronts *itself* with the question "Why rule?" – a question that leads to the demand that a constant critical scrutiny be exercised over the activities of those who rule – by others and by authorities themselves. For if the objects of rule are governed by their own laws, "the laws of the natural", under what conditions can one legitimately subject them to "the laws of the political"? Further, liberalism confronts itself with the question "Who can rule?" Under what conditions is it possible for one to exercise authority over another, what founds the *legitimacy* of authority? This question of the authority of authority must be answered, not transcendentally or in relation to the charismatic *persona* of the leader, but through various technical means – of which democracy and expertise prove to be two rather durable solutions. Liberalism inaugurates a continual dissatisfaction with government, a perpetual questioning of whether the desired effects are being produced, of the mistakes of thought or policy that hamper the efficacy of government, a recurrent diagnosis of failure coupled with a recurrent demand to govern better.

Governing the State of Welfare

The real history of liberalism, over the late nineteenth and twentieth centuries, is bound up with a series of transformations in the problematics of rule. What Foucault refers to as the governmentalization of the State is here bound up with the emergence of a problem in which the governability of democracy – to use Jaques Donzelot's term – seems to raise a number of difficulties to which the "socialization of society" seemed to be the solution (Donzelot 1991, see also Rabinow 1989: Chs 4–6 and Ewald 1991). From a variety of perspectives it was argued that the projects of nineteenth-century liberalism had failed, and the philanthropic and disciplinary projects for avoiding demoralization and maintaining moral order in urban labouring classes were proving powerless in the face of the forces of social fragmentation and individualization of modern society, evidenced by rates of suicide, crime and social disaffection. Further, economic affairs – in particular the uncertainties of employment and the harsh conditions of factory work – had profound social consequences that had not been alleviated by the vestigial constraint of factory legislation and the like – they damaged health, produced danger through the irregularity of employment and encouraged the growth of militant labour. "Welfare" was one formula for recoding, along a number of different dimensions, the relations between the political field and the management of economic and social affairs, in which the authority of experts as those who can speak and enact truth about human beings in their individual and collective lives, was to be accorded a new role. Within this new formula of welfare, political authorities, through their utilization of the financial, technical and juridical possibilities of the State, were to become the guarantor of both the freedom of the individual and the freedom of the capitalist enterprise. The State was to take responsibility for generating an array of technologies of government that would "social-ize" both individual citizenship and economic life in the name of collective security. This was a formula of rule somewhere between classical liberalism and nascent socialism. Perhaps its most contested plane of action was the economic domain itself, where interventions would weaken the privacy of the market and the enterprise while retaining their formal autonomy. But the security of economy was also to be assured by acting upon the social milieux within which production and exchange occurred: by governing society itself (cf. Procacci 1989).

Social insurance and social work can exemplify two axes of this new formula of government – one inclusive and solidaristic, one individualizing and responsibilizing. Social insurance is an inclusive technology of government (O'Malley 1986, 1992, Rose 1993). It incarnates social solidarity in collectivizing the management of the individual and collective dangers posed by the economic riskiness of a capricious system of wage labour, and the corporeal riskiness of a body subject to sickness and injury, under the stewardship of a "social" State. And it enjoins solidarity in that the security of the individual across the vicissitudes of a life history is guaranteed by a mechanism that operates on the basis of what individuals and their families are thought to share by virtue of their common sociality. Social insurance thus establishes new connections and association between "public" norms and procedures and the fate of individuals in their "private" economic and personal conduct. It was only one of an assortment of ways in which, at the start of the twentieth century, the "privacy" of the private spheres of family and factory was attenuated. Together with other regulatory devices such as public housing schemes, health and safety legislation and laws on child-care, the autonomy of both economic and familial spaces was weakened, and new vectors of responsibility and obligation took shape between State and parent, child or employee.

Social work, correlatively, operates within a strategy in which security is to be secured by enjoining the responsibilities of citizenship upon individual incapable or aberrant members of society (Donzelot 1979, Rose 1985, Parton 1991). It acts on specific problematic *cases*, radiating out to them from locales of individualized judgement on particular conducts judged as pathological in relation to social norms. The juvenile court, the school, the child guidance clinic operate as centres of adjudication and co-ordination of these strategies, targeted not so much at the isolated individual citizen, but at individuals associated within the matrix of the family. The everyday activities of living, the hygienic care of household members, the previously trivial features of interactions between adults and children, were to be anatomized by experts, rendered calculable in terms of norms and deviations, judged in terms of their social costs and consequences and subject to regimes of education or reformation. The family, then, was to be instrumentalized as a *social machine* – both *made* social and utilized to *create* sociality – implanting the techniques of responsible citizenship under the tutelage of experts and in relation to a variety of sanctions and rewards. Complex assemblages would constitute the possibility of State departments, government offices and so forth acting as centres, by enabling their deliberations to be relayed into a whole variety of micro-locales within which the conduct of the citizen could be problematized and acted upon in terms of norms that calibrated personal normality in a way that was inextricably linked to its social consequences. The individual and the family were to be "simultaneously assigned their social duties, accorded their rights, assured of their natural capacities, and educated in the fact that they need to be educated by experts in order to responsibly assume their freedom" (Rose 1993: 13).

The political subject was thus to be reconceptualized as a citizen, with rights to social protection and social education in return for duties of social obligation and social responsibility, both refiguring and retaining the liberal character of "freedom" and "privacy" (Rose 1987). Security would be combined with responsibility in a way that was conducive both to democracy and to liberty. When counterposed to the moralistic, philanthropic and disciplinary projects of nineteenth-century liberalism, social government extends the boundaries of the sphere of politics through proliferating networks through which the state could seek to extend its rule over distant events, places and persons. Expertise acquires powerful capacities, not only in linking deliberations in one place with actions in another, but also in promising to align the self-governing capacities of subjects with the objectives of political authorities by means of persuasion, education and seduction rather than coercion. These new technologies of expert social government appear to depoliticize and technicize a whole swathe of questions by promising that technical calculations will overrule existing logics of contestation between opposing interests. Judgements and deliberations of experts as to rates of benefit or patterns of child-care are accorded capacities for action that were previously unthinkable. But in becoming so integral to the exercise of political authority, experts gain the capacity to generate "enclosures", relatively bounded locales or fields of judgement within which their authority is concentrated, intensified and rendered difficult to countermand.

Advanced Liberalism

The conditions that stripped the self-evidence away from social government were heterogeneous. In the immediate aftermath of the Second World War, at the very same time as some were learning the lesson that it was feasible for the whole of the productive and social organization of a nation to be governed, in some way or other, by a central State, a number of European intellectuals drew exactly the opposite conclusion. Most notable, perhaps, was Friedrich von Hayek's suggestion that the logics of the interventionist State, as they had been manifested in the wartime organization of social and economic life, were not only

inefficient and self-defeating, but set nations on the very path towards the total State that had been manifested in Nazi Germany and could be seen in Stalin's Soviet Union – they were subversive of the very freedoms, democracies and liberties they sought to enhance (Hayek 1944; cf. Gordon 1987, 1991, the following discussion draws on Rose 1994). The arguments set out in *The road to serfdom* (Hayek 1944) were to be elaborated in a series of subsequent texts: the principle of individual freedom was both the origin of our progress and the guarantor of future growth of civilization; although we must shed the hubristic illusion that we can, by decisions and calculations of authority, deliberately create "the future of mankind", we must also recognize that freedom itself is an artefact of civilization, that "the discipline of civilization . . . is at the same time the discipline of freedom" (Hayek 1979: 163).

Only some three decades later were such critiques of the social State to be assembled into a politically salient assault on the rationalities, programmes and technologies of welfare in Britain, Europe and the United States. An economic thesis articulated in different forms by Left and Right had a particular significance here – the argument that the increasing levels of taxation and public expenditure required to sustain social, health and welfare services, education and the like were damaging to the health of capitalism as they required penal rates of tax on private profit. This contradiction was formulated from the Left in terms of the "fiscal crisis of the state" and from the Right in terms of the contradiction between the growth of an "unproductive" welfare sector – that created no wealth – at the expense of the "productive" private sector in which all national wealth was actually produced (O'Connor 1972, Bacon & Eltis 1976). The very socialization of capitalist private enterprise and market relations that had been seen as its salvation in the face of the twin threats of socialism and moral and social disintegration now appeared to be antithetical to the very survival of a society based upon a capitalist economy.

This economic argument chimed with a range of other criticisms of social government: of the arrogance of government overreach; of the dangers of imminent government overload; the absurdity of politicians trying to second-guess the market by picking winners; claims that Keynesian demand management stimulated inflationary expectations and led to the debasement of the currency. Others claimed that measures intended to decrease poverty had actually increased inequality; that attempts to assist the disadvantaged had actually worsened their disadvantage; that controls on minimum wages hurt the worse paid because they destroy jobs. Further, welfare bureaucracies themselves, together with their associated specialisms of welfare and social expertise, came under attack from all parts of the political spectrum – from classical liberals and libertarians, from left-wing critics of the social control of deviance, from social democratic activists concerned about the lack of effectiveness of social government in alleviating inequality and disadvantage. It appeared that behind their impassioned demands for more funding for their services lay a covert strategy of empire-building and the advancement of sectional interests; that it was actually the middle classes, rather than the poor, who benefited both from the employment opportunities and from the services of the Welfare State; and that welfare services actually destroyed other forms of social support such as church, community and family; that they did not produce social responsibility and citizenship but dependency and a client mentality (Murray 1980, Adler & Asquith 1981, Friedman 1982, cf. for an earlier version Reich 1964 and for a discussion of all these "rhetorics of reaction" see Hirschman 1991).

Simultaneously, the empire of social expertise was itself fracturing into rivalry between different specialisms: experts on the child, the elderly, the disabled, the alcoholic, the drug abuser, the single mother, psychiatric nurses, community workers, occupational therapists and many more. Each of these "specialisms" sought to organize on professional lines, to

demand its own rights and field of discretion: the world of welfare fragmented through an ever-finer division of labour and through divergent conceptual and practical allegiances. Equally, clients of expertise came to understand and relate to themselves and their "welfare" in new ways. In a whole range of sectors, individuals came to reconceptualize themselves in terms of their own will to be healthy, to enjoy a maximized normality. Surrounded by images of health and happiness in the mass media and in the marketing strategies deployed in commodity advertising and consumption regimes, narrativizing their dissatisfactions in the potent language of rights, they organized themselves into their own associations, contesting the powers of expertise, protesting against relations that now appeared patronizing and demeaning of their autonomy, demanding increased resources for their particular conditions and claiming a say in the decisions that affected their lives. In the face of the simultaneous proliferation, fragmentation, contestation and de-legitimization of the place of experts in the devices of social government, a new formula for the relation between government, expertise and subjectivity would take shape.

A number of strategies were developed. Civil libertarians sought to surround experts with a paraphernalia of legal restraints, tribunals and rights that would modulate their decisions: these techniques were cumbersome, slow and expensive and merely redistributed social powers to new experts; in the UK they achieved only a limited foothold on reality (Reich 1964, Adler & Asquith 1981). Critics of the Left largely contented themselves with denouncing expert powers as covert social control by the state, with seeking to distinguish the use of knowledge from its abuse, or to separate emancipatory true knowledge from ideology that disguised and legitimated the exercise of power in "ideological State apparatuses". One radical politics of expertise, with its own version of the Maoist slogan "better Red than expert", sought to do away with all expertise (as in anti-psychiatry and some forms of feminism): the "counter-expertise" it generated rapidly professionalized itself, with its own organizations, pedagogies and so forth. Another left-wing politics of expertise operated under the rubric of "the generalization of competencies" as in certain movements for workers' co-operatives to replace hierarchically owned and managed workplaces (e.g. Cooley 1980). In the economic field, in Britain at least, this ran into difficulties not only from bosses but also from the traditional representatives of labour concerned about the erosion of their own powers and the co-optation of opposing interests into some new corporatism. An analogous fate lay in store for attempts to democratize expertise in other domains such as psychiatry and law.

It would be misleading to suggest that the neo-conservative political regimes that were elected in Britain and the United States in the late 1970s were underpinned by a coherent and elaborated political rationality that they then sought to implement, still less one that identified bureaucratic and professional power as a key problem. Initially, no doubt, these regimes merely sought to engage with a multitude of different problems of welfare, to reduce cost, to undercut the power of professional lobbies, etc. But gradually, these diverse skirmishes were rationalized within a relatively coherent mentality of government that came to be termed neo-liberalism. Neo-liberalism managed to re-activate the sceptical vigilance over political government basic to classical liberalism, by linking different elements of the "rhetoric of reaction" with a series of techniques – none of them in itself particularly new or remarkable – that could render these criticisms governmental. Indeed one thing that is perhaps paradoxical about neo-liberalism is that, despite posing itself as a critique of political government, it retains the programmatic *a priori*, the presupposition that the real is programmable by authorities: the objects of government are rendered thinkable in such a way that their difficulties appear amenable to diagnosis, prescription and cure (cf. Rose & Miller 1992: 183). Neo-liberalism does not abandon the "will to govern": it maintains the view

that failure of government to achieve its objectives is to be overcome by inventing new strategies of government that will succeed.

What is it "to govern in an advanced liberal way"? The breathless celebrations or condemnations of Thatcherism have proved to be overblown. But it is none the less possible to identify a more modest yet more durable transformation in rationalities and technologies of government. "Advanced liberal" strategies can be observed in national contexts from Finland to Australia, advocated by political regimes from left and right, and in relation to problem domains from crime control to health. They seek techniques of government that create a distance between the decisions of formal political institutions and other social actors, conceive of these actors in new ways as subjects of responsibility, autonomy and choice, and seek to act upon them through shaping and utilizing their freedom. Let me rapidly sketch out three characteristic shifts.

1. *A new relation between expertise and politics*. Welfare might be considered a "substantive" rationality of rule: expert conceptions of health, income levels, types of economic activity and the like, were to be more or less directly transcribed into the machinery and objectives of political government. Simultaneously, the very powers that the technologies of welfare accorded to experts enabled them to establish enclosures within which their authority could not be challenged, effectively insulating experts from external political attempts to govern them and their decisions and actions. In contrast, advanced liberal modes of rule have a certain "formal" character. The powers once accorded to positive knowledges of human conduct are to be transferred to the calculative regimes of accounting and financial management. And the enclosures of expertise are to be penetrated through a range of new techniques for exercising critical scrutiny over authority – budget disciplines,

accountancy and audit being three of the most salient. These certainly rely upon a claim to truth, but it is one that has a different character from that of the social and human sciences: these "grey sciences", these know-hows of enumeration, calculation, monitoring, evaluation, manage to be simultaneously modest and omniscient, limited yet apparently limitless in their application to problems as diverse as the appropriateness of a medical procedure and the viability of a university department.

Marketization, for example, seeks various forms of distance between the political and the expert machines: an apparent devolution of regulatory powers from "above" – planning and compulsion – to "below" – the decisions of consumers. In its ideal form, this imagines a "free market" where the relations between citizens and experts are not organized and regulated through compulsion but through acts of choice. It addresses the pluralization of expertise, not by seeking to adjudicate between the rival claims of different groups of experts, but by turning welfare agencies – social service departments, housing departments, health authorities – into "purchasers" who can choose to "buy" services from the range of options available. Whether it be in the "purchaser–provider" split in the health services, in "case management" techniques in social services, in the autonomization of schools from control by local educational authorities so that they may compete in a market for pupils, one sees a reconfiguration of the political salience of expertise, a new way of "responsibilizing" experts in relation to claims upon them other than those of their own criteria of truth and competence, their assembling into new relations of power.

Similarly, monetarization plays a key role in breaching welfare enclosures within the networks of social government. Transforming activities – operating on a patient, educating a student, providing a social work interview for a client – into cash terms establishes new relations of power. Making people write things down, prescribing what must be written down and how, is itself a kind of government of individual conduct, making it thinkable according to particular norms. Budgetary discipline transforms the activity of the budget holder, increasing choices at the same time as regulating them and providing new ways of ensuring the responsibility and fidelity of agents who remain formally autonomous. Not merely in the setting of the budget, but in the very "budgetization" of the activity, the terms of calculation and decision are displaced and new diagrams of force and freedom are assembled.

Within these new strategies of government, audit becomes one of the key mechanisms for responding to the plurality of expertise and the inherent controversy and undecidability of its truth claims. Michael Power has suggested that audit, in a range of different forms, has come to replace the trust that formulae of government once accorded to professional credentials (Power 1992, 1994). As Power points out, audit responds to "failure" and insecurity by the "remanagerialisation of risk". Risk is to be rendered manageable by new distantiated relations of control between political centres of decision and the "non-political" procedures, devices and apparatuses – such as schools, hospitals or firms – upon which the responsibility for health, wealth and happiness is to be devolved. In this process, the entities to be audited are transformed: they have to be "made auditable", producing a new grid of visibilities for the conduct of organizations and those who inhabit them. Audit may make heavy demands, but it travels well across space and time, is capable of being propagated in a multitude of locales, channelling and organizing activities and linking centres of calculation to sites of implementation according to new vectors. Despite the fact that its "epistemological profile" is, if anything, even lower than the knowledges that it displaces, and that there is nothing novel in the techniques of audit themselves, the mode of its operation – in terms of procedures rather than substantives, in terms of apparently stable and yet endlessly flexible criteria such as efficiency, appropriateness, effectiveness – renders it a versatile and highly transferable technology for governing at a distance.

2. *A new pluralization of "social" technologies.* Strategies of pluralization and autonomization, which characterize many contemporary programmes for reconfiguring social technologies from various parts of the political spectrum, embody a wish for a kind of "de-governmentalization of the State" and a "destatization of government" – a phenomenon that is linked to a mutation in the notion of "the social", that invention of the late nineteenth century that both sociology and welfare government constituted as their object and target. The relation between the responsible individual and their self-governing community comes to substitute for that between social citizen and their common society (cf. Rose 1996b). In the course of this mutation, one sees a detaching of the centre from the various regulatory technologies that, over the twentieth century, it sought to assemble into a single functioning network, and the adoption instead of a form of government through shaping the powers and wills of autonomous entities: enterprises, organizations, communities, professionals, individuals. This has entailed the implantation of particular modes of calculation into agents, the supplanting of certain norms, such as those of service and dedication, by others, such as those of competition, quality and customer demand. It has entailed the establishment of different networks of accountability and reconfigured flows of accountability and responsibility in fundamental ways.

Perhaps most significant has been the disassembling of a variety of governmental activities previously assembled within the political apparatus: the phenomenon referred to, in Britain, as the "quangoization" of the state. Quasi-autonomous non-governmental organizations have proliferated, taking on regulatory functions, such as the regulation of securities and investments in the financial sector, planning functions as in the rise of new entities for the government and regeneration of urban locales, educative functions as in the rise of organizations responsible for the provision of training to school leavers, responsibilities for the provision of previously "public" utilities such as water, gas, electricity, the "privatization" of the civil service, prisons and police. This has been linked to the invention and deployment of a raft of other measures for the government of these entities, measures whose emphasis upon the apparent objectivity and neutrality of numbers underpins a claim that they now operate according to an apolitical agenda (cf. Hood 1991). Contracts, targets, indicators, performance measures, monitoring and evaluation are used to govern their conduct while according them a certain autonomy of decisional power and responsibility for their actions. One sees the displacement of electoral mechanisms as the way of ensuring democratic control via the intermediary of local councils by novel techniques of accountability, such as representation of "partners" from different "communities" – business, local residents, voluntary organizations, local councils – on the boards. The reconfiguration of political power involved here cannot usefully be understood in terms of the opposition of State and market: shaped and programmed by political authorities, new mechanisms are utilized to link the calculations and actions of a heterogeneous array of organizations into political objectives, governing them "at a distance" through the instrumentalization of a regulated autonomy.

3. *A new specification of the subject of government.* The enhancement of the powers of the client as customer – consumer of health services, of education, of training, of transport – specifies the subjects of rule in a new way: as active individuals seeking to "enterprise themselves", to maximize their quality of life through acts of choice, according their life a meaning and value to the extent that it can be rationalized as the outcome of choices made or choices to be made (Rose 1992, 1996a). Political reason must now justify and organize itself by arguing over the arrangements that are adequate to the existence of persons as, in their essence, creatures of freedom, liberty and autonomy. Within this new regime of the actively responsible self, individuals are to fulfil their national obligations not through their relations of dependency and obligation to one another, but through seeking to *fulfil themselves* within a variety of micro-moral domains or "communities" – families, workplaces, schools, leisure associations, neighbourhoods. Hence the problem is to find means by which individuals may be made responsible through their individual choices for themselves and those to whom they owe allegiance, through the shaping of a lifestyle according to grammars of living that are widely disseminated, yet do not depend upon political calculations and strategies for their rationales or for their techniques (Rose 1996b).

It has become possible to actualize this notion of the actively responsible individual because of the development of new apparatuses that integrate subjects into a moral nexus of identifications and allegiances in the very processes in which they appear to act out their most personal choices. Contemporary political rationalities rely upon and utilize a range of technologies that install and support the civilizing project by shaping and governing the capacities, competencies and wills

of subjects, yet are outside the formal control of the "public powers". To such basic nation-forming devices as a common language, skills of literacy and transportation networks, our century has added the mass media of communication, with their pedagogies through documentary and soap opera; opinion polls and other devices that provide reciprocal links between authorities and subjects; the regulation of lifestyles through advertising, marketing and the world of goods; *and* the experts of subjectivity (Rose 1990). These technologies do not have their origin or principle of intelligibility in "the State", but none the less have made it possible to govern in an "advanced liberal" way. They have provided a plethora of indirect mechanisms that can translate the goals of political, social and economic authorities into the choices and commitments of individuals, locating them into actual or virtual networks of identification through which they may be governed.

The reconfiguring of the subject of government confers obligations and duties at the same time as it opens new spaces of decision and action. Each of the two dimensions of social government that I discussed earlier undergoes a mutation. Thus social insurance, as a principle of social solidarity, gives way to a kind of privatization of risk management. In this new prudentialism, insurance against the future possibilities of unemployment, ill health, old age and the like becomes a private obligation. Not merely in relation to previously socialized forms of risk management, but also in a whole range of other decisions, the citizen is enjoined to bring the future into the present, and is educated in the ways of calculating the future consequences of actions as diverse as those of diet to those of home security. The active citizen thus is to add to his or her obligations the need to adopt a calculative prudent personal relation to fate now conceived in terms of calculable dangers and avertable risks (O'Malley 1986, 1992). And social work, as a means of civilization under tutelage, gives way to the private counsellor, the self-help manual and the telephone helpline, as practices whereby each individual binds themselves to expert advice as a matter of their own freedom (Rose 1990). The regulation of conduct becomes a matter of each individual's desire to govern their own conduct freely in the service of the maximization of a version of their happiness and fulfilment that they take to be their own, but such lifestyle maximization entails a relation to authority in the very moment as it pronounces itself the outcome of free choice.

Here we can witness the "reversibility" of relations of authority – what starts off as a norm to be implanted into citizens can be repossessed as a demand which citizens can make of authorities. Individuals are to become "experts of themselves", to adopt an educated and knowledgeable relation of self-care in respect of their bodies, their minds, their forms of conduct and that of the members of their own families. Of course, this new configuration has its own complexities, its own logics of incorporation and exclusion. However, the "power effects" certainly do not answer to a simple logic of domination, and nor are they amenable to a "zero sum" conception of power. Consider, for example, the proliferation of the new psychological techniques and languages of empowerment in relation to those subjects now coded as "marginalized" or "excluded". It is true that neo-liberal political regimes enacted an array of measures to reduce benefits for those out of work, to discipline delinquents and lawbreakers and impose personal responsibility upon them, to dismantle the archipelago of institutions within which welfare government had isolated and managed their social problems. One would not wish to minimize the intensification of misery and impoverishment that these changed specifications

of the responsibilities of individuals for their own fate have brought about. It is difficult, for example, to contemplate the terminological change in which the unemployed person has come to be designated a "jobseeker" and the homeless person a "rough sleeper" without cynicism and repugnance. But these neo-liberal programmes that respond to the sufferer as if they were the author of their own misfortune share something with strategies articulated from other political perspectives. From a variety of directions, the disadvantaged individual has come to be seen as potentially and ideally an active agent in the fabrication of their own existence. Those "excluded" from the benefits of a life of choice and self-fulfilment are no longer merely the passive support of a set of social determinations: they are people whose self-responsibility and self-fulfilling aspirations have been deformed by the dependency culture, whose efforts at self-advancement have been frustrated for so long that they suffer from "learned helplessness", whose self-esteem has been destroyed. And, it thus follows, that they are to be assisted not through the ministrations of solicitous experts proffering support and benefit cheques, but through their engagement in a whole array of programmes for their ethical reconstruction as active citizens – training to equip them with the skills of self-promotion, counselling to restore their sense of self-worth and self-esteem, programmes of empowerment to enable them to assume their rightful place as the self-actualizing and demanding subjects of an "advanced" liberal democracy (cf. Cruikshank 1986).

This is not to suggest that the "making up" of the modern citizen as an active agent in his or her government is in some ways an "invention" of recent political regimes: the conditions for this shift in our "relation to ourselves" are complex, and have no single origin or cause (Rose 1995a, 1995b, cf. Hacking 1986). None the less, the ethical *a priori* of the active

citizenship in an active society, this respe-
cification of the ethics of personhood, is
perhaps the most fundamental, and most
generalizable, characteristic of these new
rationalities of government, and one that
justifies the assertion that what we are
seeing here is not merely the vicissitudes
of a single political ideology – that of neoliberal conservatism – but something with
a more general salience, which underpins
mentalities of government from all parts
of the political spectrum, and which justifies the designation of all these new attempts to "re-invent government" as
"advanced liberal".

The power of the governmentalities of
the Right over the past two decades lies in
the fact that it is the Right, rather than the
Left, that has managed to articulate a rationality of government consonant with
this new regime of the self, to develop
programmes that translate this ethic into
strategies for the regulation of precise
problems and difficulties such as those in
the housing market, or in relation to
health, and to invent the technical forms
that promise to give effect to it. It is the
Right, rather than the Left, that has made
the running in relation to a "politics of
human technologies", one that does not
merely question the relations of power between experts and their subjects but which
seeks to give this questioning a technological form. For all the Left critiques of
State and social control of the powers of
experts and the ills of professional and
bureaucratic discretion, it does not yet
seem to have been able to propose alternative models for regulating these citizen-
shaping devices that answer to the needs
of plurality. Is it possible for the Left to
provide an alternative rationality for articulating these plural technologies and
autonomizing ethics without losing the
gains that they represent, yet at the same
time providing security for those that they
expose? This would require the Left to
articulate an alternative ethics and pedagogy of subjectivity that is as compelling

as that inherent in the rationality of the
market and the "valorization" of choice.

Conclusions

The formulae of liberal government that
I have termed "advanced" are much more
significant than the brief flowering of neoliberal political rhetorics may indicate. Although strategies of welfare sought to govern
through society, "advanced" liberal strategies
of rule ask whether it is possible to govern
without governing *society*, that is to say, to
govern through the regulated and accountable choices of autonomous agents – citizens,
consumers, parents, employees, managers,
investors – and to govern through intensifying and acting upon their allegiance to particular "communities". As an autonomizing
and pluralizing formula of rule, it is dependent upon the proliferation of little regulatory instances across a territory and their
multiplication, at a "molecular" level,
through the interstices of our present experience. It is dependent, too, upon a particular
relation between political subjects and expertise, in which the injunctions of the experts
merge with our own projects for self-mastery
and the enhancement of our lives.

My aim in this chapter has not been to make
a judgement of these new programmes, strategies or relations, but rather to disturb those
political logics of Left and Right within which
judgement is easy, within which it appears easy
and self-evident to be "for" or "against" the
present. The "freedom" programmed by recent
reconfigurations of power and expertise is certainly no simple liberation of subjects from
their dreary confinement by the shackles of
political power into the sunny uplands of liberty and community. But neither is it merely an
ideological fiction or a rhetorical flourish.
I have tried to show that the freedom upon
which liberal strategies of government depend,
and which they instrumentalize in so many
diverse ways, is no "natural" property of political subjects, awaiting only the removal of constraints for it to flower forth in forms that will

ensure the maximization of economic and social wellbeing. The practices of modern freedom have been constructed out of an arduous, haphazard and contingent concatenation of problematizations, strategies of government and techniques of regulation. This is not to say that our freedom is a sham. It is to say that the agonistic relation between liberty and government is an intrinsic part of what we have come to know as freedom. And thus, I suggest, a key task for intellectual engagement with contemporary relations of power is the critical analysis of these practices of freedom.

NOTE

1 In this chapter I have drawn upon three earlier papers written with Peter Miller: Miller & Rose (1989, 1990), Rose & Miller (1992).

REFERENCES

Adler, M. & S. Asquith (eds) 1981. *Discretion and welfare*. London: Heinemann.

Bacon, R. & S. Eltis 1976. *Britain's economic problems: too few producers?* London: Macmillan.

Barry, A. 1986. Lines of communication and spaces of rule. See Barry et al. (1986), 123–42.

Burchell, G. 1986. Liberal government and techniques of the self. See Barry et al. (1986), 19–36.

Burchell, G. 1991. Peculiar interests: civil society and governing "the system of natural liberty". See Burchell et al. (1991), 119–50.

Burchell, G., C. Gordon, P. Miller (eds) 1991. *The Foucault effect: studies in governmentality*. Hemel Hempstead, England: Harvester Wheatsheaf.

Cooley, M. 1980. *Architect or bee: the human/technology relationship*. Slough, England: Langley Technical Services.

Cruikshank, B. 1986. Revolutions within self-government and self-esteem. See Barry et al. (1986), 231–52.

Donzelot, J. 1979. *The policing of families* [with a foreword by G. Deleuze]. London: Hutchinson.

Donzelot, J. 1991. The mobilization of society. See Burchell et al. (1991), 169–80.

Ewald, F. 1991. Insurance and risk. See Burchell et al. (1991), 197–210.

Foucault, M. 1977. *Discipline and punish: the birth of the prison*. London: Penguin.

Foucault, M. 1979. *The history of sexuality*, vol. I: *An introduction*. London: Penguin.

Foucault, M. 1980. The politics of health in the eighteenth century. In *Power/knowledge*, C. Gordon (ed.), 166–82. Brighton: Harvester.

Foucault, M. 1981. Omnes et singulatim: towards a criticism of "political reason". In *The Tanner Lectures on human values II*, S. McMurrin (ed.), 223–54. Salt Lake City: University of Utah Press.

Foucault, M. 1989. *Résumés des cours*. Collège de France, Paris.

Foucault, M. 1991. Governmentality. See Burchell et al. (1991), 87–104.

Friedman, M. 1982. *Capitalism and freedom*. Chicago: University of Chicago Press.

Giddens, A. 1990. *Consequences of modernity*. Cambridge: Polity.

Gordon, C. 1980. Afterword. In *Michel Foucault: Power/knowledge*, C. Gordon (ed.), 229–60. Brighton: Harvester.

Gordon, C. 1986. Question, ethos, event: Foucault on Kant and Enlightenment. *Economy and Society* 15(1), 71–87.

Gordon, C. 1987. The soul of the citizen: Max Weber and Michel Foucault on rationality and government. In *Max Weber, rationality and modernity*, S. Lash & S. Whimster (eds), 293–316. London: Allen & Unwin.

Gordon, C. 1991. Governmental rationality: an introduction. See Burchell et al. (1991), 1–52.

Hacking, I. 1986. Making up people. In *Reconstructing individualism*, T. C. Heller et al. (eds), 222–36. Palo Alto, California: Standford University Press.

Hacking, I. 1991. *The taming of chance*. Cambridge: Cambridge University Press.

Hayek, F. A. 1944. *The road to serfdom*. London: Routledge & Kegan Paul.

Hayek, F. A. 1979. *The constitution of liberty*. London: Routledge & Kegan Paul.

Hirschman, A. 1991. *The rhetoric of reaction*. Cambridge, Mass.: Belknap Harvard.

Hood, C. 1991. A public management for all seasons. *Public Administration* 69(1), 3–19.

Lash, S. & J. Urry 1994. *Economies of signs and spaces*. Cambridge: Polity.

Latour, B. 1986. The powers of association. In *Power, action and belief*, J. Law (ed.). London: Routledge & Kegan Paul.

Miller, P. & N. Rose 1989. Political rationalities and technologies of government. In *Texts, contexts, concepts*, S. Hanninen & K. Palonen (eds), 171–83. Helsinki: Finnish Political Science Association.

Miller, P. & N. Rose 1990. Governing economic life. *Economy and Society* 19(1), 1–31.

Murray, C. 1980. *Losing ground: American social policy 1950–1980*. New York: Basic Books.

O'Connor, J. 1972. *The fiscal crisis of the state*. New York: St. Martin's Press.

Oestreich, G. 1982. *Neostoicism and the modern state*. Cambridge: Cambridge University Press.

O'Malley, P. 1986. Risk and responsibility See Barry et al. (1986), 189–207.

O'Malley, P. 1992. Risk, power and crime prevention. *Economy and Society* 21(3), 283–99.

Osborne, T. 1994. Bureaucracy as a vocation: governmentality and administration in nineteenth century Britain. *Journal of Historical Sociology* 7(3), 289–313.

Parton, N. 1991. *Governing the family: child care, child protection and the State*. London: Macmillan.

Pasquino, P. 1991. "Theatrum Politicum": the genealogy of capital – police and the state of prosperity. See Burchell et al. (1991), 105–18.

Power, M. 1992. The audit society. Paper delivered to London History of the Present Research Network, 4 November 1992.

Power, M. 1994. *The audit society*. London: Demos.

Procacci, G. 1989. Sociology and its poor. *Politics and Society* 17, 163–87.

Rabinow, P. 1989. *French modern: norms and forms of the social environment*. Cambridge, Mass.: MIT Press.

Reich, C. 1964. Individual rights and social welfare. *Yale Law Journal* 74, 1245.

Rose, N. 1985. *The psychological complex: psychology, politics and society in England, 1869–1939*. London: Routledge & Kegan Paul.

Rose, N. 1987. Beyond the public/private division: law, power and the family. *Journal of Law and Society* 14(1), 61–76.

Rose, N. 1990. *Governing the soul: the shaping of the private self*. London: Routledge.

Rose, N. 1992. Governing the enterprising self. In *The values of the enterprise culture: the moral debate*, P. Heelas & P. Morris (eds), 141–64. London: Routledge.

Rose, N. 1993. *Towards a critical sociology of freedom*. Inaugural Lecture delivered on 5 May 1992 at Goldsmiths College, University of London: Goldsmiths College Occasional Paper.

Rose, N. 1994. Eriarvoisuus ja valta hyvinvointivaltion jalkeen (Finnish translation of Disadvantage and power "after the Welfare State"). *Janus* (Journal of the Finnish Society for Social Policy) 1, 44–68.

Rose, N. 1995a. Authority and the genealogy of subjectivity. In *De-traditionalization: authority and self in an age of cultural change*, P. Heelas, P. Morris, S. Lash (eds). Oxford: Basil Blackwell.

Rose, N. 1995b. Identity, genealogy, history. In *Questions of cultural identity*, S. Hall & P. du Gay (eds). London: Sage.

Rose, N. 1996a. *Inventing our selves: psychology, power and personhood*. Cambridge: Cambridge University Press.

Rose, N. 1996b. The death of the social? Refiguring the territory of government. *Economy and Society* 25(3), 327–56.

Rose, N. & P. Miller 1992. Political power beyond the state: problematics of government. *British Journal of Sociology* 43(2), 172–205.

Part II

Ethnographic Mappings

Section I

Bureaucracy and Governmentality

The three articles included here build on and interrogate the insights elaborated in Part I. These selections lay out important conceptual and methodological groundwork for ethnographically examining the state.

First, the authors move away from structural and functional analyses of the state that see "it" either as an autonomous actor or a set of conventional government institutions which serve the interests of particular classes and groups of people. Rather than viewing the state as a preconstituted structure, they see "it" as an effect of everyday practices, representational discourses, and multiple modalities of power. Mitchell shows how mundane governmental practices related to national frontiers such as border patrols, passport checks, and immigration laws help make abstract entities such as the state a very real presence in people's lives. Gupta uses the discourse on corruption in India – in everyday discussions as well as in public culture – to ethnographically demonstrate people's situated imaginations of the state. Brown argues that prerogative power – the legitimate power to use violence and make policies – actualizes the state in the interstate system, produces "it" as a masculinist entity, and has structuring effects on gender norms and hierarchies in society. These scholars demonstrate the difficulty in institutionally and procedurally delimiting the state. Rather than approach the state as a self-contained institutional reality, they focus on analyzing the nature, tactics, and effects of powers that operate through the entire social formation.

Second, the authors interrogate the autonomous, unified, and gender-neutral presentation of the state, emphasizing instead "its" incoherent, multilayered, contradictory, and masculinist nature. Both Mitchell and Gupta ask that we examine the conditions that enable apparently distinctive, autonomous, and cohesive constructions of the state. Gupta demonstrates that at local levels people experience the state as a fragmented and multi-leveled entity. But these localized encounters, which are shaped in a field of state-related discourses and practices that transcend the local level (national, regional, and transnational), also help people imagine the state as a translocal entity. Brown argues that the state is not a unitary actor with singular intentions. The state does not wield one kind of power. She breaks down the multiple dimensions of power – liberal, capitalist, prerogative, and bureaucratic – and delineates how these modalities are bound up with gender norms and privileges prevalent in society, and how they shape state practices and produce the state as a masculinist arena.

Third, and related to the previous two points, the authors problematize the boundary between "the state" and its "other" (society, civil society, economy, or community), and between the public and private realms. Mitchell demonstrates the ephemeral nature of this boundary and contends that instead of separating two intrinsic and freestanding entities this line is drawn internally in order to maintain social order. Gupta argues for historicizing and provincializing the distinction between state and civil society that is so often assumed to be universal and natural. A reflection of a particular conjuncture of European history, this distinction may not describe or capture postcolonial realities where the boundaries between the state and non-state realms are blurred. Brown grounds her feminist analysis of the "state–civil society" divide in the late capitalist US state, and illustrates the effects of this division on gender identities and relations. She argues that the Western liberal distinction between state and civil society or public and private spheres is a masculinist construction that reinforces gender hierarchies. Together, the authors in this section argue that everyday practices and representations simultaneously produce state and non-state entities and arenas. Gupta demonstrates how everyday practices and discourses of corruption trouble the ideal-type Weberian bureaucracy (wherein the lines between the public and private are clearly marked), and help people at once imagine the state (the good/benevolent state versus the bad/unaccountable state) and themselves as exploited and rights-bearing citizens. Brown illustrates how the gendered discourse of protection serves to construct both the masculinist state (as protector) and dependent/vulnerable female citizens. All three authors thus emphasize the social imbricatedness of the state and the socially constructed nature of the boundary between the state and the non-state realms, and demonstrate the power-laden effects of this construction.

In laying out important conceptual groundwork relating to the study of the state, these articles open up avenues and domains for ethnographically studying the state. Mitchell and Gupta demonstrate precisely why, when examining the discursive construction of the state, it is crucial to pay attention to everyday bureaucratic practices and to cultural texts like newspapers, where differentiated discourse about the state is generated and contested. The theoretical groundwork supplied by these articles also has crucial implications for activist practices relating to state agencies. At a basic level, how we imagine the state shapes our engagements with it. If, for example, oppositional practices reify "the state," how does that limit their effectiveness? At another level, if the boundaries of the state are not given, but culturally produced and historically shifting, then how does one resist "the state"? If, as Mitchell argues, the boundary delimiting the state is an internally drawn boundary, and if, as Gupta suggests, there is no outside to the state, then it is unproductive to think about activist practices through the binary of resistance versus cooperation. How, for instance, might one go about understanding the welfare-state-centered feminist practices that Brown discusses, and analyzing them in terms that do not fall into the dichotomy of radical versus reformist politics?

SUGGESTED READINGS

Abramovitz, Mimi
   1988   Regulating Women. Boston: South End Press.
Agrawal, Arun
   2001   State Formation in Community Spaces? Decentralization of Control over Forests in Kumaon Himalaya, India. Journal of Asian Studies 60(1):9–40.
Bayart, Jean-François
   1993   The State in Africa: The Politics of the Belly. New York: Longman.
Chatterjee, Partha
   1993   The Nation and Its Fragments: Colonial and Postcolonial Histories. Princeton, NJ: Princeton University Press.
   2004   The Politics of the Governed: Reflections on Popular Politics in Most of the World. New York: Columbia University Press.
Dean, Mitchell
   2001   "Demonic Societies": Liberalism, Biopolitics, and Sovereignty. In States of Imagination: Ethnographic Explorations of the Postcolonial State. T. B. Hansen and F. Stepputat, eds. Pp. 41–64. Durham, NC: Duke University Press.
Ferguson, Kathy E.
   1984   The Feminist Case Against Bureaucracy. Philadelphia, PA: Temple University Press.
Foucault, Michel
   1979   Discipline and Punish: The Birth of a Prison. New York: Random House.
Fraser, Nancy
   1989   Women, Welfare, and the Politics of Needs Interpretation. In Unruly Practices: Power, Discourse and Gender in Contemporary Social Theory. Pp. 144–160. Minneapolis: University of Minnesota Press.
Gal, Susan, and Gail Kligman
   2000   The Politics of Gender after Socialism. Princeton, NJ: Princeton University Press.
Gordon, Linda, ed.
   1990   Women, the State, and Welfare. Madison: University of Wisconsin Press.
Gupta, Akhil
   2001   Governing Population: The Integrated Child Development Services Program in India. In States of Imagination: Ethnographic Explorations of the Postcolonial State. T. B. Hansen and F. Stepputat, eds. Pp. 65–96. Durham, NC: Duke University Press.
Herzfeld, Michael
   1992   The Social Production of Indifference: Exploring the Symbolic Roots of Western Bureaucracy. Chicago: University of Chicago Press.

MacKinnon, Catharine A.
   1982   Feminism, Marxism, Method, and the State: An Agenda for Theory. Signs 7(3):
   515–544.
   1989   Toward a Feminist Theory of the State. Cambridge, MA: Harvard University
   Press.
Orloff, Ann Shola
   1999   Motherhood, Work, and Welfare in the United States, Britain, Canada, and
   Australia. *In* State/Culture: State-Formation after the Cultural Turn. G. Steinmetz,
   ed. Pp. 76–97. Ithaca, NY: Cornell University Press.

7

Society, Economy, and the State Effect

Timothy Mitchell

The state is an object of analysis that appears to exist simultaneously as material force and as ideological construct. It seems both real and illusory. This paradox presents a particular problem in any attempt to build a theory of the state. The network of institutional arrangement and political practice that forms the material substance of the state is diffuse and ambiguously defined at its edges, whereas the public imagery of the state as an ideological construct is more coherent. The scholarly analysis of the state is liable to reproduce in its own analytical tidiness this imaginary coherence and misrepresent the incoherence of state practice.

Drawing attention to this liability, Philip Abrams (1988) argues that we should distinguish between two objects of analysis, the state-system and the state-idea. The first refers to the state as a system of institutionalized practice, the second refers to the reification of this system that takes on "an overt symbolic identity progressively divorced from practice as an illusory account of practice." We should avoid mistaking the latter for the former, he suggests, by "attending to the senses in which the state does not exist rather than those in which it does" (82).

This seems a sensible suggestion. But if the coherence and definition of the state arise from the state-idea, then subtracting this from the state's existence as a system of power makes the limits of the system difficult to define. Foucault argues that the system of power extends well beyond the state: "One cannot confine oneself to analyzing the State apparatus alone if one wants to grasp the mechanisms of power in their detail and complexity...," he suggests. "In reality, power in its exercise goes much further, passes through much finer channels, and is much more ambiguous" (1980a: 72). If so, how does one define the state apparatus (as even Foucault still implies one should) and locate its limits? At what point does

From G. Steinmetz (ed.), *State/Culture: State-Formation after the Cultural Turn*, pp. 76–97. Ithaca, NY and London: Cornell University Press, 1999. Used by permission of the publisher.

power enter channels fine enough and its exercise become ambiguous enough that one recognizes the edge of this apparatus? Where is the exterior that enables one to identify it as an apparatus?

The answers cannot be found by trying to separate the material forms of the state from the ideological, or the real from the illusory. The state-idea and the state-system are better seen as two aspects of the same process. To be more precise, the phenomenon we name "the state" arises from techniques that enable mundane material practices to take on the appearance of an abstract, nonmaterial form. Any attempt to distinguish the abstract or ideal appearance of the state from its material reality, in taking for granted this distinction, will fail to understand it. The task of a theory of the state is not to clarify such distinctions but to historicize them.

In American social science of the postwar period, there have been two distinct responses to the difficulty of relating practice and ideology in the concept of the state. The first was to abandon *the state*, as a term too ideological and too narrow to be the basis for theoretical development, replacing it with the idea of *political system*. In rejecting the ideological, however, systems theorists found themselves with no way of defining the limits of the system. Their empiricism had promised precise definitions, but instead they were unable to draw any line distinguishing the political order from the wider society in which it functioned.

The second response, from the later 1970s, was to "bring the state back in" (Evans, Rueschemeyer, and Skocpol 1985). The new literature defined the state in a variety of ways, most of which took it to be not just distinguishable from society but autonomous from it. To reestablish the elusive line between the two, however, the literature made the state-society distinction correspond to a distinction between subjective and objective, or ideal and real. It did so by reducing the state to a subjective system of decision making, a narrow conception that failed to fit

even the evidence that the state theorists themselves present.

An alternative approach must begin with the assumption that we must take seriously the elusiveness of the boundary between state and society, not as a problem of conceptual precision but as a clue to the nature of the phenomenon. Rather than hoping we can find a definition that will fix the state-society boundary (as a preliminary to demonstrating how the object on one side of it influences or is autonomous from what lies on the other), we need to examine the political processes through which the uncertain yet powerful distinction between state and society is produced.

A theory of the contemporary state also must examine the parallel distinction constructed between state and economy. In the twentieth century, creating this opposition has become a perhaps more significant method of articulating the power of the state. Yet the boundary between state and economy represents a still more elusive distinction than that between state and society.

We must take such distinctions not as the boundary between two discrete entities but as a line drawn internally, within the network of institutional mechanisms through which a social and political order is maintained. The ability to have an internal distinction appear as though it were the external boundary between separate objects is the distinctive technique of the modern political order. One must examine the technique from a historical perspective (something most literature on the state fails to do), as the consequence of certain novel practices of the technical age. In particular, one can trace it to methods of organization, arrangement, and representation that operate within the social practices they govern, yet create the effect of an enduring structure apparently external to those practices. This approach to the state accounts for the salience of the phenomenon but avoids attributing to it the coherence, unity, and absolute autonomy that result from existing theoretical approaches.

Abandoning the State

When American social scientists eliminated the term *state* from their vocabulary in the 1950s, they claimed that the word suffered from two related weaknesses: its "ideological" use as a political myth, as a "symbol for unity," produced disagreement about exactly what it referred to (Easton 1953: 110–12); and even if agreement might be reached, these symbolic references of the term excluded significant aspects of the modern political process (106–15). These factors do not themselves account for the rejection of the concept of the state, however, for scholars had been disclosing its weaknesses and ambiguities for decades (Sabine 1934). What made the weaknesses suddenly significant was the changed postwar relationship between American political science and American political power. We can see this by rereading what was written at the time. Postwar comparative politics, according to a 1944 APSA report discussing the future "mission" of the discipline, would have to relinquish its narrow concern with the study of the state ("the descriptive analysis of foreign institutions") to become "a conscious instrument of social engineering" (Loewenstein 1944: 541). Scholars would use this intellectual machinery for "imparting our experience to other nations and . . . integrating scientifically their institutions into a universal pattern of government" (547). To achieve these ends, the discipline had to expand its geographical and theoretical territory and become what the report called "a 'total' science" (541). "We can no longer permit the existence of white spots on our map of the world," the report said, employing metaphors reflecting the imperial ambition of postwar American politics. "The frontier posts of comparative government must be moved boldly" (543), both to encompass the globe and, by expanding into the territory of other disciplines (anthropology, psychology, economics, and statistics), to open up each country to far more detailed methods of observation and

questioning and thereby "gain access to the true Gestalt of foreign political civilizations" (541).

Political science had to expand its boundaries to match the growth of postwar US power, whose ambitions it would offer to serve. Borrowing concepts and research methods from fields such as anthropology, political science planned not simply to shift its concern from state to society but to open up the workings of the political process to far closer inspection. The field was to become a discipline of detail, pushing its investigation into the meticulous examination of the activities of political groups, the behavior of social actors, even the motivations of individual psyches.

The opening of this new territory to scientific investigation seemed even more urgent by the 1950s, when postwar American optimism had turned into political uncertainty. It was what Easton (1953: 3) gravely called "our present social crisis" – the launching of the cold war and the accompanying domestic campaign against the Left – that made suddenly imperative the elimination of ambiguity from political vocabulary and the construction of general social-scientific laws broad enough to include all significant political phenomena and "pass beyond the experience . . . of any one culture" (319).

The *Suggested Research Strategy in Western European Government and Politics*, proposed in 1955 by the new Comparative Politics Committee of the Social Science Research Council chaired by Gabriel Almond, criticized once again the "too great an emphasis on the formal aspects of institutions and processes," but now spoke of the need for a change in terms of "urgent and practical considerations." In the major western European countries, the committee reported, "large bodies of opinion appear to be alienated from the West, politically apathetic, or actively recruited to Communism." The state was too narrow and formal a focus for research because "the basic problems of civic loyalty and political cohesion lie in large part outside of the formal government framework." Research was needed that would trace the degree of political cohesion and loyalty to the West beyond this formal framework "into the networks of social groupings, and the attitudes of the general population." Such close examination could confirm the committee's expectation that, in cases such as France, "there is at least the possibility of breaking the hold of the Communist party on a large part of its following" (Almond, Cole, and Macridis 1955: 1045).

Responding to the needs of the cold war, the discipline also expanded its geographical territory. In his foreword to *The Appeals of Communism*, Almond claimed that Communism had now begun to spread to non-Western areas, and warned that this was "so menacing a development that it is deserving of special attention" (Almond 1954: vii). These global concerns were the stimulus to the research undertaken in the late 1950s and subsequently published as *The Civic Culture*. The book's introduction addressed itself to the pressing need to export to the colonized areas of the world, now seeking their independence, the principles of the Anglo-American political process. To this end, it sought to codify not just the formal institutional rules of the state but the "subtler components" that formed its "social-psychological preconditions" – that combination of democratic spirit and proper deference toward authority that was celebrated as "the civic culture" (Almond and Verba 1963: 5).

The scientific tone of this literature offered the empiricism of political science an alternative to the concept of the state and its "ideological" (that is, Marxist) connotations. Yet abandoning the traditional focus on the institutions of state created a science whose new object, the political system, had no discernible limit. The ever-expanding empirical and theoretical knowledge that would have to be mastered by the future scientists of comparative politics, Almond warned in 1960, "staggers the imagination and lames the will." Despite the initial tendency "to blink and withdraw in pain," he wrote, there could be no hesitation in the effort to accumulate the

knowledge that will "enable us to take our place in the order of the sciences with the dignity which is reserved for those who follow a calling without limit or condition" (Almond and Coleman 1960: 64).

Advocates of the shift from the formal study of the state to the meticulous examination of political systems realized they were embarking on a scientific enterprise "without limit." They assumed, however, that the very notion of political system would somehow solve the question of limits, for, as Almond wrote, it implied the "existence of boundaries" – the points "where other systems end and the political system begins." The boundary required a "sharp definition," otherwise "we will find ourselves including in the political system churches, economies, schools, kinship and lineage groups, age-sets, and the like" (Almond and Coleman 1960: 5, 7–8; see also Easton 1957: 384). Yet this is precisely what happened. The edge of the system turned out to consist of not a sharp line but every conceivable form of collective expression of political demand, from "institutional" groups such as legislatures, churches, and armies, to "associated" groups such as labor or business organizations, "nonassociated" groups such as kinship or ethnic communities, and "anomic" groups such as spontaneous riots and demonstrations (Almond and Coleman 1960: 33).

In attempting to eliminate the ambiguity of a concept whose ideological functions prevented scientific precision, the systems approach substituted an object whose very boundary unfolded into a limitless and undetermined terrain.

The Return of the State

The attempt in the 1950s and 1960s to eliminate the concept of the state was unsuccessful. The notion of political system was too imprecise and unworkable to establish itself as an alternative. But there were several other reasons for the return of the state. First, by the late 1960s it was clear that US influence in the third world could not be built on the creation of "civic cultures." Modernization seemed to require the creation of powerful authoritarian states, as Huntington argued in 1968.

Second, from the late 1960s a more powerful critique of modernization theory was developed by neo-Marxist scholars in Latin America, the Middle East, and Europe. Samir Amin, Cardoso and Faletto, Gunder Frank, and others produced theories of capitalist development in which an important place was given to the nature and role of the third world state. As Paul Cammack (1989, 1990) suggests, this literature obliged US scholars to "return to the state" in an effort to reappropriate the concept by drawing on neo-Marxist scholarship and in most cases denying the significance of the underlying Marxian framework.

Third, in most countries of the West, the language of political debate continued to refer to the institutions of the state and to the role of the state in the economy and society. In 1968, J. P. Nettl pointed out that although the concept was out of fashion in the social sciences, it retained a popular currency that "no amount of conceptual restructuring can dissolve" (1968: 559). The state, he wrote, is "essentially a sociocultural phenomenon" that occurs due to the "cultural disposition" among a population to recognize what he called the state's "conceptual existence" (565–66). Notions of the state "become incorporated in the thinking and actions of individual citizens" (577), he argued, and the extent of this conceptual variable could be shown to correspond to important empirical differences between societies, such as differences in legal structure or party system (579–92).

Clearly, the importance of the state as a common ideological and cultural construct should be grounds not for dismissing the phenomenon but for taking it seriously. Yet Nettl's understanding of this construct as a subjective disposition that could be correlated with more objective phenomena remained thoroughly empiricist. A construct such as the state occurs not merely as a subjective belief, but as a representation

reproduced in visible everyday forms, such as the language of legal practice, the architecture of public buildings, the wearing of military uniforms, or the marking and policing of frontiers. The ideological forms of the state are an empirical phenomenon, as solid and discernible as a legal structure or a party system. Or rather, as I contend here, the distinction made between a conceptual realm and an empirical one needs to be placed in question if one is to understand the nature of a phenomenon such as the state.

Mainstream social science did not raise such questions. In fact the conceptual/empirical distinction provided the unexamined conceptual base on which to reintroduce the idea of the state. During the later 1970s, the state reemerged as a central analytic concern of American social science. "The lines between state and society have become blurred," warned Stephen Krasner in *Defending the National Interest* (1978: xi), one of the early contributions to this reemergence. "The basic analytic assumption" of the statist approach it advocated "is that there is a distinction between state and society" (5). The new literature presented this fundamental but problematic distinction, as in Nettl's article, in terms of an underlying distinction between a conceptual realm (the state) and an empirical realm (society). Such an approach appeared to overcome the problem the systems theorists complained about and reencountered, of how to discern the boundary between state and society: it was to be assimilated to the apparently obvious distinction between conceptual and empirical, between a subjective order and an objective one. As I have shown elsewhere, however, this depended on both an enormous narrowing of the phenomenon of the state and an uncritical acceptance of this distinction (Mitchell 1991).

State-centered approaches to political explanation presented the state as an autonomous entity whose actions were not reducible to or determined by forces in society. This approach required not so much a shift in focus, from society back to the state, but some way of reestablishing a clear boundary between the two. How were the porous edges where official practice mixes with the semi-official and the latter with the unofficial to be turned into lines of separation, so that the state could stand apart as a discrete, self-directing object? The popular Weberian definition of the state, as an organization that claims a monopoly within a fixed territory over the legitimate use of violence, is only a residual characterization. It does not explain how the actual contours of this amorphous organization are to be drawn.

The new theorists of the state did not fill in the organizational contours. They retreated to narrower definitions, which typically grasped the state as a system of decision making. The narrower focus locates the essence of the state not in the monopolistic organization of coercion, nor, for example, in the structures of a legal order, nor in the mechanisms by which social interests find political representation, nor in the arrangements that maintain a given relationship between the producers of capital and its owners, but in the formation and expression of authoritative intentions. Construed as a machinery of intentions – usually termed *rule making, decision making*, or *policymaking* – state becomes essentially a subjective realm of plans, programs, or ideas. This subjective construction maps the problematic state-society distinction on to the seemingly more obvious distinctions we make between the subjective and the objective, between the ideological and the material, or even between meaning and reality. The state appears to stand apart from society in the unproblematic way in which intentions or ideas are thought to stand apart from the external world to which they refer.

Elsewhere I have illustrated these problems in detail through a discussion of some of the leading contributions to the literature (Mitchell 1991). Even those who describe their approach as institutionalist, such as Theda Skocpol (1979, 1981), can demonstrate the alleged autonomy of the state only by appealing to a subjective interest or ideology of the ruler. When the account turns to wider institutional processes, the distinction between state and society fades away.

An Alternative Approach

The state-centered literature begins from the assumption that the state is a distinct entity, opposed to and set apart from a larger entity called society. Arguments are confined to assessing the degree of independence one object enjoys from the other. Yet in fact the line between the two is often uncertain. Like the systems theorists before them, the state theorists are unable to fix the elusive boundary between the political system or state and society. Cammack (1990, 1989) is surely correct to assert that the state theorists fail to refute the argument that modern states enjoy only a relative separation from the interests of dominant social classes and that their policies can be explained adequately only in relation to the structure of class relations. But then the questions remain: how is this relative separation of the state from society produced? And how is the effect created that the separation is an absolute one? These are questions that not even neo-Marxist theories of the state have addressed adequately.

To introduce an answer to these questions, I begin with a case discussed in Stephen Krasner's study of US government policy toward the corporate control of foreign raw materials: the relationship between the US government and the Arabian-American Oil Company (Aramco), the consortium of major US oil corporations that possessed exclusive rights to Saudi Arabian oil (Krasner 1978: 205–12). The case illustrates both the permeability of the state-society boundary and the political significance of maintaining it. After World War II, the Saudis demanded that their royalty payment from Aramco be increased from 12 percent to 50 percent of profits. Unwilling either to cut its profits or to raise the price of oil, Aramco arranged for the increase in royalty to be paid not by the company but in effect by US taxpayers. The

Department of State, anxious to subsidize the pro-American Saudi monarchy, helped arrange for Aramco to evade US tax law by treating the royalty as though it were a direct foreign tax, paid not from the company's profits but from the taxes it owed to the US Treasury (Anderson 1981: 179–497). This collusion between government and oil companies, obliging US citizens to contribute unknowingly to the treasury of a repressive Middle Eastern monarchy and to the bank balances of some of the world's largest and most profitable multinational corporations, does not offer much support for the image of a neat distinction between state and society.

Krasner copes with this complexity by arguing that the oil companies were "an institutional mechanism" used by central decision makers to achieve certain foreign policy goals, in this case the secret subsidizing of a conservative Arab regime. Policies that might be opposed by Congress or foreign allies could be pursued through such mechanisms "in part because private firms were outside of the formal political system" (1978: 212–13). This explanation offers only one side of the picture: the firms themselves also used the US government to further corporate goals, as the Aramco case illustrates and as several studies of the oil industry have demonstrated in detail (Anderson 1981; Blair 1976; Miller 1980).

Yet despite its failure to portray the complexity of such state-society relations, Krasner's explanation does inadvertently point to what is crucial about them. The Aramco case illustrates how the "institutional mechanisms" of a modern political order are never confined within the limits of what is called the state (or in this case, curiously enough, the "formal political system"). This is not to say simply that the state is something surrounded by parastatal or corporatist institutions, which buttress and extend its authority. It is to argue that the boundary of the state (or political system) never marks a real exterior. The line between state and society is not the perimeter of an intrinsic entity that can be thought of as a freestanding object or actor.

It is a line drawn internally, within the network of institutional mechanisms through which a certain social and political order is maintained. The point that the state's boundary never marks a real exterior suggests why it seems so often elusive and unstable. But this does not mean the line is illusory. On the contrary, as the Aramco case shows, producing and maintaining the distinction between state and society is itself a mechanism that generates resources of power. The fact that Aramco can be said to lie outside the "formal political system," thereby disguising its role in international politics, is essential to its strength as part of a larger political order.

One could explore many similar examples, such as the relationship between state and "private" institutions in the financial sector, in schooling and scientific research, or in health care and medical practice. In each case one could show that the state-society divide is not a simple border between two freestanding objects or domains, but a complex distinction internal to these realms of practice. Take the example of banking: the relations between major corporate banking groups, semipublic central banks or reserve systems, government treasuries, deposit insurance agencies and export-import banks (which subsidize up to 40 percent of exports of industrialized nations), and multinational bodies such as the World Bank (whose head is appointed by the president of the United States) represent interlocking networks of financial power and regulation. No simple line could divide this network into a private realm and a public one or into state and society or state and economy. At the same time, banks are set up and present themselves as private institutions clearly separate from the state. The appearance that state and society or economy are separate things is part of the way a given financial and economic order is maintained. This is equally true of the wider social and political order. The power to regulate and control is not simply a capacity stored within the state, from where it extends out into society. The apparent boundary of the state does not mark the limit of the processes of regulation. It is itself a product of those processes.

Another example is that of law. The legal system, a central component of the modern state when conceived in structural terms, consists of a complex system of rights, statutes, penalties, enforcement agencies, litigants, legal personnel, prisons, rehabilitation systems, psychiatrists, legal scholars, libraries, and law schools, in which the exact dividing line between the legal structure and the "society" it structures is once again very difficult to locate. In practice we tend to simplify the distinction by thinking of the law as an abstract code and society as the realm of its practical application. Yet this fails to correspond to the complexities of what actually occurs, where code and practice tend to be inseparable aspects of one another. The approach to the state advocated here does not imply an image of the state and private organizations as a single totalized structure of power. On the contrary, there are always conflicts between them, as there are between different government agencies, between corporate organizations, and within each of them. It means that we should not be misled into taking for granted the idea of the state as a coherent object clearly separate from "society" – any more than we should be misled by the vagueness and complexity of these phenomena into rejecting the concept of the state altogether.

Conceived in this way, the state is no longer to be taken as essentially an actor, with the coherence, agency, and autonomy this term presumes. The multiple arrangements that produce the apparent separateness of the state create effects of agency and partial autonomy, with concrete consequences. Yet such agency will always be contingent on the production of difference – those practices that create the apparent boundary between state and society. These arrangements may be so effective, however, as to make things appear the reverse of this. The state comes to seem an autonomous starting point, as an actor that intervenes in society. Statist approaches to political analysis take this reversal for reality.

What we need instead is an approach to the state that refuses to take for granted this dualism, yet accounts for why social and political reality appears in this binary form. It is not sufficient simply to criticize the abstract idealist appearance the state assumes in the state-centered literature. Gabriel Almond, for example, complains that the concept of the state employed in much of the new literature "seems to have metaphysical overtones" (1987: 476), and David Easton argues that the state is presented by one writer as an "undefinable essence, a 'ghost in the machine,' knowable only through its variable manifestations" (1981: 316). Such criticisms ignore the fact that this is how the state very often appears in practice. The task of a critique of the state is not just to reject such metaphysics, but to explain how it has been possible to produce this practical effect, so characteristic of the modern political order. What is it about modern society, as a particular form of social and economic order, that has made possible the apparent autonomy of the state as a free-standing entity? Why is this kind of apparatus, with its typical basis in an abstract system of law, its symbiotic relation with the sphere we call the economy, and its almost transcendental association with the "nation" as the fundamental political community, the distinctive political arrangement of the modern age? What particular practices and techniques have continually reproduced the ghost-like abstraction of the state, so that despite the effort to have the term "polished off a quarter of a century ago," as Easton (303) puts it, it has returned "to haunt us once again"?

The new theorists of the state ignore these historical questions. Even works that adopt a historical perspective, such as Skocpol's (1979) comparative study of revolutions, are unable to offer a historical explanation of the appearance of the modern state. Committed to an approach in which the state is an independent cause, Skocpol cannot explain the ability of the state to appear as an entity standing apart from society in terms of factors external to the state. The state must be an independent cause of events, even when those events, as in a case such as revolutionary France, involve the very birth of a modern, apparently autonomous state.

Discipline and Government

To illustrate the kind of explanation that might be possible, one can turn to Skocpol's account of the French state. She describes prerevolutionary France as a "statist" society, meaning a society in which the power and privileges of a landed nobility and the power of the central administration were inextricably bound together. We can now describe this situation another way, as a society in which those modern techniques that make the state appear to be a separate entity that somehow stands outside society had not yet been institutionalized. The revolutionary period represents the consolidation of such novel techniques. Skocpol characterizes the revolutionary transformation of the French state as principally a transformation in the army and the bureaucracy, both of which became permanent professional organizations whose staffs were for the first time set apart from other commercial and social activities and whose size and effectiveness were vastly extended. For Skocpol, such changes are to be understood as the consequence of an autonomous state, whose officials desired to embark on the expansion and consolidation of centralized power. We are therefore given little detail about the techniques on which such revolutionary transformations rested.

How was it now possible to assemble a permanent army of up to three-quarters of a million men, transform an entire economy into production for war, maintain authority and discipline on such a scale, and so "separate" this military machine from society that the traditional problem of desertion was overcome? By what parallel means were the corruptions and leakages of financial administration brought under control? What was the nature of the "mechanical efficiency and articulation," in a phrase quoted from J. F. Bosher (Skocpol 1979: 200), that in

every realm would now enable "the virtues of organization to offset the vices of individual men"? What kind of "articulation," in other words, could now seem to separate mechanically an "organization" from the "individual men" who composed it? Rather than attributing such transformations to policies of an autonomous state, it is more accurate to trace in these new techniques of organization and articulation the very possibility of appearing to set apart from society the free-standing apparatus of a state.

An exploration of such questions has to begin by acknowledging the enormous significance of those small-scale polymorphous methods of order that Foucault calls disciplines. The new bureaucratic and military strength of the French state was founded on powers generated from the meticulous organization of space, movement, sequence, and position. The new power of the army, for example, was based on such measures as the construction of barracks as sites of permanent confinement set apart from the social world, the introduction of daily inspection and drill, repetitive training in maneuvers broken down into precisely timed sequences and combinations, and the elaboration of complex hierarchies of command, spatial arrangement, and surveillance. With such techniques, an army could be made into what a contemporary military manual called an "artificial machine," and other armies now seemed like collections of "idle and inactive men" (Fuller 1955: vol. 2: 196).

Disciplinary power has two consequences for understanding the modern state – only the first of which is analyzed by Foucault. In the first place, one moves beyond the image of power as essentially a system of sovereign commands or policies backed by force. This approach is adopted by almost all recent theorists of the state. It conceives of state power in the form of a person (an individual or collective decision maker), whose decisions form a system of orders and prohibitions that direct and constrain social action. Power is thought of as an exterior constraint: its source is a sovereign authority above and outside society, and it operates by setting external limits to behavior, establishing negative prohibitions, and laying down channels of proper conduct.

Discipline, by contrast, works not from the outside but from within, not at the level of an entire society but at the level of detail, and not by constraining individuals and their actions but by producing them. As Foucault puts it, a negative exterior power gives way to an internal productive power. Disciplines work locally, entering social processes, breaking them down into separate functions, rearranging the parts, increasing their efficiency and precision, and reassembling them into more productive and powerful combinations. These methods produce the organized power of armies, schools, bureaucracies, factories, and other distinctive institutions of the technical age. They also produce, within such institutions, the modern individual, constructed as an isolated, disciplined, receptive, and industrious political subject. Power relations do not simply confront this individual as a set of external orders and prohibitions. His or her very individuality, formed within such institutions, is already the product of those relations.

The second consequence of modern political techniques is one that Foucault does not explain. Despite their localized and polyvalent nature, disciplinary powers are somehow consolidated into the territorially based, institutionally structured order of the modern state. Foucault does not dismiss the importance of this larger kind of structure; he simply does not believe that the understanding of power should begin there: "One must rather conduct an ascending analysis of power, starting, that is, from its infinitesimal mechanisms ... and then see how these mechanisms of power have been – and continue to be – invested, colonised, utilised, involuted, transformed, displaced, extended, etc., by ever more general mechanisms ..., [how they] came to be colonised and maintained by global mechanisms and the entire state system" (Foucault 1980b: 99–101). Yet Foucault does not explain how disciplinary

powers do come to be utilized, stabilized, and reproduced in state structures or other "generalized mechanisms."

An example of the relationship between infinitesimal and general mechanisms can be found in law, an issue already discussed above, where the micropowers of disciplinary normalization are structured into the larger apparatus of the legal code and the juridical system. In discussing this case, Foucault falls back on the notion that the general structure is an ideological screen (that of sovereignty and right) superimposed on the real power of discipline. "[O]nce it became necessary for disciplinary constraints to be exercised through mechanisms of domination and yet at the same time for their effective exercise of power to be disguised, a theory of sovereignty was required to make an appearance at the level of the legal apparatus, and to reemerge in its codes" (Foucault 1980b: 106). The organization of law at the general level "allowed a system of right to be superimposed upon the mechanisms of discipline in such a way as to conceal its actual procedures" (105). Foucault steps away again from the implication that the general level is related to the microlevel as a public realm of ideology opposed to the hidden realm of actual power, by recalling that disciplines, too, contain a public discourse. But his studies of disciplinary methods provide no alternative terms to conceive of the way in which local mechanisms of power are related to the larger structural forms, such as law, in which they become institutionalized and reproduced.

In subsequent lectures, Foucault did turn his attention to the large-scale methods of power and control characteristic of the modern state (Foucault 1991). He analyzed the emergence of these methods not in terms of the development of formal institutions, but in the emergence of a new object on which power relations could operate and of new techniques and tactics of power. He identified the new object as population and referred to the new techniques as the powers of "government." Foucault traces the emergence of the problem of population from the eighteenth century, associating it with in-creases in agricultural production, demo-graphic changes, and an increasing supply of money. Population, he argues, was an object now seen to have "its own regularities, its own rates of deaths and diseases, its cycles of scarcity, etc.," all susceptible to statistical measurement and political analysis (99). Such analysis produced a whole series of aggregate effects that were not reducible to those of the individual or the household. Politics came to be concerned with the proper management of a population in relation to resources, terri-tory, agriculture, and trade. Population re-placed the household as the principal object of politics. The household, or rather the fam-ily, was now considered an element internal to population, providing an instrument for obtaining information about and exercising power over the larger, aggregate object (99–100).

To describe this aggregate-level power, Fou-cault invokes a term that proliferated in the literature of the period, the word "govern-ment." For Foucault, the word refers not to the institutions of the state, but to the new tactics of management and methods of secur-ity that take population as their object. As with the term *discipline*, government refers to power in terms of its methods rather than its institutional forms. Government draws on the micropowers of discipline; in fact the de-velopment of disciplinary methods becomes more acute as they become applied to the problem of population. But government has its own tactics and rationality, expressed in the development of its own field of know-ledge, the emerging science of political econ-omy. Foucault also argues that the development of government and of political economy correspond not only to the emer-gence of population as a new datum and ob-ject of power, but also to the separation of the economy as its own sphere. "The word 'econ-omy,' which in the sixteenth century signified a form of government, comes in the eight-eenth century to designate a level of reality, a field of intervention" (Foucault 1991: 93). This argument is more problematic.

Conceived in terms of its methods and its object, rather than its institutional forms, government is a broader process than the relatively unified and functionalist entity sug-gested by the notion of the state. Government is a process "at once internal and external to the state, since it is the tactics of government which make possible the continual definition and redefinition of what is within the compe-tence of the state and what is not, the public versus the private, and so on" (Foucault 1991: 103). For this reason, Foucault sug-gests, the state probably does not have the unity, individuality, and rigorous functional-ity attributed to it. Indeed it may be "no more than a composite reality and a mythicized abstraction, whose importance is a lot more limited than many of us think" (103). One can agree with this sentiment, yet still not find in Foucault an answer to the question that is once again raised. If indeed modern govern-mental power exceeds the limits of the state, if the state lacks the unity and identity it always appears to have, how does this ap-pearance arise? How is the composite reality of the state composed? What tactics and methods in modern forms of power create and recreate this mythicized abstraction? One response to this question is to locate the answer in the phenomenon of the national project. In this view, the state acquires its unity at the level of ideology. Beyond the practical multiplicity of tactics, disciplines, and powers, the state articulates a national project that projects its unity onto society. But such an answer again falls back on the distinction between ideology and practice, instead of placing that distinction in question.

The Appearance of Structure

The relationship between methods of discip-line and government and their stabilization in such forms as the state, I argue, lies in the fact that at the same time as power relations be-come internal, in Foucault's terms, and by the same methods, they now take on the specific appearance of external "structures." The distinctiveness of the modern state, appearing as an apparatus that stands apart from the rest of the social world, is to be found in this novel structural effect. The effect is the counterpart of the production of modern individuality. For example, the new military methods of the late eighteenth century produced the disciplined individual soldier and, simultaneously, the novel effect of an armed unit as an "artificial machine." This military apparatus appeared somehow greater than the sum of its parts, as though it were a structure with an existence independent of the men who composed it. In comparison with other armies, which now looked like amorphous gatherings of "idle and inactive men," the new army seemed something two-dimensional. It appeared to consist on the one hand of individual soldiers and, on the other, of the "machine" they inhabited. Of course this apparatus has no independent existence. It is an effect produced by the organized partitioning of space, the regular distribution of bodies, exact timing, the coordination of movement, the combining of elements, and endless repetition, all of which are particular practices. There was nothing in the new power of the army except this distributing, arranging, and moving. But the order and precision of such processes created the effect of an apparatus apart from the men themselves, whose "structure" orders, contains, and controls them.

A similar two-dimensional effect can be seen at work in other institutions of modern government. The precise specification of space and function that characterize modern institutions, the coordination of these functions into hierarchical arrangements, the organization of supervision and surveillance, the marking out of time into schedules and programs, all contribute to constructing a world that appears to consist not of a complex of social practices but of a binary order: on the one hand individuals and their activities, on the other an inert "structure" that somehow stands apart from individuals, precedes them, and contains and gives a framework to their lives. Indeed the very notion of an institution, as an abstract framework separate from the particular practices it enframes, can be seen as the product of these techniques. Such techniques have given rise to the peculiar, apparently binary world we inhabit, where reality seems to take the two-dimensional form of individual versus apparatus, practice versus institution, social life and its structure – or society versus state (see Mitchell 1988, 1990). We must analyze the state as such a structural effect. That is to say, we should examine it not as an actual structure, but as the powerful, apparently metaphysical effect of practices that make such structures appear to exist. In fact, the nation state is arguably the paramount structural effect of the modern technical era. It includes within itself many of the particular institutions already discussed, such as armies, schools, and bureaucracies. Beyond these, the larger presence of the state in several ways takes the form of a framework that appears to stand apart from the social world and provide an external structure. One characteristic of modern governmentality, for example, is the frontier. By establishing a territorial boundary to enclose a population and exercising absolute control over movement across it, governmental powers define and help constitute a national entity. Setting up and policing a frontier involves a variety of fairly modern social practices – continuous barbed-wire fencing, passports, immigration laws, inspections, currency control, and so on. These mundane arrangements, most of them unknown two hundred or even one hundred years ago, help manufacture an almost transcendental entity, the nation-state. This entity comes to seem something much more than the sum of the everyday powers of government that constitute it, appearing as a structure containing and giving order and meaning to people's lives. An analogous example is the law. Once again, one could analyze how the mundane details of the legal process, all of which are particular social practices, are arranged to produce the effect that the law exists as a formal framework, superimposed above social practice. What we call the state, and think of as an intrinsic object existing apart from society, is the sum of these structural effects.

What is the relationship of this structural effect to the specifically capitalist nature of modernity? The state-centric theorists examined earlier argue that no particular relationship exists. To insist on the autonomy of the state, as they do, means that the programs it follows and the functions it serves should not be explained by reference even to the long-term requirements of the larger capitalist order, but primarily in terms of the independent ideas and interests of those who happen to hold high office. As we saw, however, the evidence they present fails to support this view and provides stronger support for neo-Marxist theories of the state, such as the work of Nicos Poulantzas. The state policies that Krasner describes in relation to the control of foreign raw materials or that Skocpol describes in her work on the New Deal (Skocpol 1981; see Mitchell 1991: 88–89) appear to serve the general requirements of capital. The relative separation of the state enables it to pursue the long-term interests of capital as a whole, sometimes working against the short-term interests of particular capitalists (see Cammack 1990). Yet, as Poulantzas himself recognized in his later work, this functionalist account cannot adequately explain the modern state. It does not account for the particular form taken by the modern state, as an aspect of the regulation of capitalist modernity. It does not explain how state power takes on the form of a seemingly external structure, or its association with an abstract system of law, or its apparent separation from, yet imbrication in, the sphere we call the economy. In other words, it does not tell us how the modern effect of the state is produced. There are two ways to approach this question of the relationship between capitalism and the state effect. One way is to explain the effect of the state as the consequence of capitalist production. The structural forms of the modern state could be explained by reference to certain distinctive features of the way in which the social relations of production are organized under capitalism (see Ollman

1992). This is the approach taken by Poulantzas in his later work, in which he responded to and was influenced by Foucault. Poulantzas (1978) argues that what Foucault (1977) describes as discipline – processes of individualization, the modern production of knowledge, and the reorganization of space and time – should be explained as aspects of the way capitalism organizes the relations of production. These same processes, he suggests, account for the form taken by the state. The discipline of factory production, for example, introduces the separation of mental labor from manual labor. The state embodies this same separation, representing a distinct mental order of expertise, scientific management, and administrative knowledge. Similarly, in Poulantzas's view, the serial, cellular organization of time and space in modern production processes is reproduced in the new geospatial power of the nation-state and the historical-spatial definition of national identity.

The other approach to the question of the state and capital is the one taken here. Rather than explain the form of the state as the consequence of the disciplinary regime of capitalist production, one can see both the factory regime and the power of the state as aspects of the modern reordering of space, time, and personhood and the production of the new effects of abstraction and subjectivity. It is customary to see the state as an apparatus of power and the factory as one of production. In fact, both are systems of disciplinary power and both are techniques of production. Both produce the effect of an abstraction that stands apart from material reality. In the case of political practice, as we have seen, this abstraction is the effect of the state – a nonmaterial totality that seems to exist apart from the material world of society. In the case of the organization of labor, the abstraction produced is that of capital. What distinguishes capitalist production, after all, is not just the disciplined organization of the labor process but the manufacture of an apparent abstraction – exchange value – that seems to exist apart from the mundane objects and processes from which it is created. The effect of capital is produced out of techniques of discipline, organization, and enframing analogous to those that produce the effect of the state.

Rather than deriving the forms of the state from the logic of capital accumulation and the organization of production relations, both capital and the state can been seen as aspects of a common process of abstraction. This approach to the question of the relation between the state and capital enables one, furthermore, to extend the critique of the concept of the state to include the parallel concept of the economy.

Inventing the Economy

Modern mass armies, bureaucracies, and education systems were creations largely of the late eighteenth and nineteenth centuries. Complex legal codes and institutions and the modern control of frontiers and population movement emerged mostly in the same period. The twentieth century was characterized by a further and different development: the emergence of the modern idea of the economy. Foucault, as we saw, placed the separation of the economy as its own sphere in the eighteenth and nineteenth centuries, as part of the emergence of the new techniques of government centered on the problem of population. This conflation of economy and population as political objects locates the emergence of the economy much earlier than it actually occurred. More important, it overlooks a critical shift that took place in the first half of the twentieth century, when the economy replaced population as the new object of the powers of government and the sciences of politics. This object played a central role in the articulation of the distinctive forms of the twentieth-century state as a set of bureaucratized science-based technologies of planning and social welfare. An adequate theory of the contemporary state must take into account not only the nineteenth-century developments described above but also the

new relationship that emerged between state and economy in the twentieth century. The contemporary structural effect of the state is inseparable from the relatively recent creation of "the economy."

The nineteenth-century tactics of power that Foucault describes as government took as their fundamental object, as was noted, the issue of population. Politics was concerned with the security and well-being of a population defined in relation to a given territory and resources, with the pattern of its growth or decline, with associated changes in agriculture and commerce, and with its health, its education, and above all its wealth. The political economy of Smith, Ricardo, and Malthus developed within this general problematic of population and its prosperity. The term *political economy* referred to the proper economy, or management, of the polity, a management whose purpose was to improve the wealth and security of the population. The term *economy* never carried, in the discourse of nineteenth-century political economy, its contemporary meaning referring to a distinct sphere of social reality – understood as the self-contained totality of relations of production, distribution, and consumption within a defined geospatial unit. Nor was there any other term denoting such a separate, self-contained sphere (Mitchell 1995).

Marx followed in the same tradition. "When we consider a given country politico-economically," he wrote, "we begin with its population, its distribution among classes, town, country, the coast, the different branches of production, export and import, annual production and consumption, commodity prices, etc." (1973: 100). He argued that this conventional approach was backward, for population presupposes capital, wage labor, and division into classes. Smith and Ricardo had developed a system that started from these simpler abstractions, but one-sidedly focusing on landed property and on exchange. A proper analysis, Marx argued, should start with capital and material production and then work back toward the totalities of bourgeois society, its concentration in the form of the state, the population, the colonies, and emigration (100–8). The concept of material production has subsequently been misinterpreted as meaning the same thing as the twentieth-century idea of the economy. But Marx had no greater conception of an economy as a separate social sphere than the political economists whom he criticized.

The economy was invented in the first half of the twentieth century, as part of the reconstruction of the effect of the state. The nineteenth-century understanding of the production and circulation of wealth and its relation to population growth, territorial expansion, and resources broke down during World War I and the decade of financial and political crises that followed. The abandoning of gold as the measure of the value of money, unprecedented levels of debt, unemployment and overproduction, rapid swings from economic boom to complete collapse, the ending of European territorial expansion and population growth, the beginning of the disintegration of empire, and the very fear of capitalism's collapse all created a need to reimagine the process of government and construct new objects and methods of political power. It is in this period that terms such as "economic system," "economic structure," and finally "the economy" came into political circulation.

Between the 1920s and the 1950s, "the economy" came to refer to the structure or totality of relations of production, circulation, and consumption within a given geographical space. The emergence of macroeconomics, as the new science of this object was called, coincided with developments in statistics that made it possible to imagine the enumeration of what came to be known as the gross national product of an economy and with the invention of econometrics, the attempt to represent the entire workings of an economy as a single mathematical model (Mitchell 1995). The isolating of production, circulation, and consumption as distinctively economic processes was nothing new. This had been done, within the problematic of population, by the classical political economists of the eighteenth and nineteenth centuries. What was new was the notion that the interrelation of these processes formed a space or object that was self-contained, subject to its own internal dynamics, and liable to "external" impulses or interventions that created reverberations throughout the self-contained object. Factors such as population, territory, and even other "economies" were now considered external to this object. But the most important thing imagined to stand outside the economy was the one considered most capable of affecting or altering it – the state.

The idea of an economy as a self-contained and internally dynamic totality, separate from other economies and subject to intervention, adjustment, and management by an externally situated state, could not have been imagined within the terms of nineteenth-century political economy. In the twentieth century, on the other hand, the contemporary concept of the state has become inseparable from the fundamental distinction that emerged between state and economy. In fact, much of the more recent theorizing about state and society is more accurately described as theorizing about the state in terms of its relation to the economy. Curiously, as the new distinction between state and economy emerged from the 1920s and 1930s onward, so-called economic processes and institutions became increasingly difficult to distinguish in practice from those of government or the state. With the collapse of the gold standard and the consolidation of central banks and reserve systems, money came to acquire its value as part of a "political" as much as an "economic" process. State bureaucracies gradually became the economy's largest employer, spender, borrower, and saver. The creation of quasipublic corporations such as port authorities; the nationalization of transport, communications, and other services; the state subsidy of agriculture and of military and other manufacturing; even the growth of publicly owned corporations in place of private firms, and especially (as the Aramco case illustrates) the transnational corporations, all blurred the distinction between private and public spheres or state and economy.

As with state and society, so with state and economy, one has to ask why the distinction between these two objects seems so obvious and is taken for granted so routinely, when on close examination their separation is difficult to discern. The answer has to address the same effects of structure already discussed in relation to state and society. One examines the practical arrangements that make the economy appear a concrete, material realm and the state an abstract, institutional structure standing apart from the economy's materiality. Besides the methods of structuring already discussed, two structural effects are especially important to create the distinction between state and economy. First, when twentieth-century political practice invented the economy, the boundaries of this object were understood to coincide with those of the nation-state. Although the new macroeconomics did not theorize the nation-state, it represented the economy in terms of aggregates (employment, savings, investment, production) and synthetic averages (interest rate, price level, real wage, and so on) whose geospatial referent was always the nation-state (Radice 1984: 121). So, without explicit theorization, the state came to stand as the geospatial structure that provided the economy with its external boundary and form. Second, the economy was constructed as an object of knowledge in the twentieth century through an extensive process of statistical representation. Almost all of this process was carried out as part of the new institutional practice of the state. So the relationship between state and economy appeared to take the form of the relation between representor and the object of representation. (Once again, this relationship to the state was not something analyzed by the new science of economics. In fact, economics came to be distinguished among the social sciences by two related features: It was the only major social science with no subdiscipline – "field economics" it could be called – dealing with issues of data

collection and questions of representation, and it was a discipline that became dependent on the state for almost all its data. The state thus appears to stand apart from the economy as a network of information, statistical knowledge, and imagery, opposed to the apparently real, material object to which this representational network refers. In practice, once again, this relationship is more complex, not least because the economy itself, in the course of the twentieth century, became more and more a hyperreal or representational object. Its elements came increasingly to consist of forms of finance, services, and so on that exist only as systems of representation; and the dynamics of the economy came to be determined increasingly by factors such as expectations, that are themselves issues of representation. Nevertheless, the appearance of the economy as a real object in opposition to its representation by the state provided a simple means of effecting the seeming separation between state and economy that remains so important to most contemporary theories of the state.

In conclusion, the argument for a different approach to the question of the state and its relationship to society and economy can be summarized in a list of five propositions:

1. We should abandon the idea of the state as a freestanding entity, whether an agent, instrument, organization, or structure, located apart from and opposed to another entity called economy or society.

2. We must nevertheless take seriously the distinction between state and society or state and economy. It is a defining characteristic of the modern political order. The state cannot be dismissed as an abstraction or ideological construct and passed over in favor of more real, material realities. In fact, we must place this distinction between conceptual and material, between abstract and real, in historical question if we are to grasp how the modern state has appeared.

3. For the same reason, the prevailing view of the state as essentially a phenomenon

of decision making or policy is inadequate. Its focus on one disembodied aspect of the state phenomenon assimilates the state-society and state-economy distinction to the same problematic opposition between conceptual and material.

4. We should address the state as an effect of mundane processes of spatial organization, temporal arrangement, functional specification, supervision and surveillance, and representation that create the appearance of a world fundamentally divided into state and society or state and economy. The essence of modern politics is not policies formed on one side of this division being applied to or shaped by the other, but the producing and reproducing of these lines of difference.

5. These processes create the effect of the state not only as an entity set apart from economy or society, but as a distinct dimension of structure, framework, codification, expertise, information, planning, and intentionality. The state appears as an abstraction in relation to the concreteness of the social, a sphere of representation in relation to the reality of the economic, and a subjective ideality in relation to the objectness of the material world. The distinctions between abstract and concrete, ideal and material, representation and reality, and subjective and objective, on which most political theorizing is built, are themselves partly constructed in those mundane social processes we recognize and name as the state.

REFERENCES

Abrams, Philip. 1988. "Notes on the Difficulty of Studying the State." *Journal of Historical Sociology* 1: 58–89.

Almond, Gabriel A. 1954. *The Appeals of Communism*. Princeton: Princeton University Press.

——— . 1987. "The Development of Political Development." In *Understanding Political Development*, edited by Myron Weiner and Samuel Huntington. Boston: Little, Brown.

Almond, Gabriel A., Taylor Cole, and Roy C. Macridis. 1955. "A Suggested Research Strategy in Western European Government and Politics." *American Political Science Review* 49: 1042–4.

Almond, Gabriel A., and James Coleman. 1960. *The Politics of the Developing Areas*. Princeton: Princeton University Press.

Almond, Gabriel A., and Sidney Verba. 1963. *The Civic Culture: Political Attitudes and Democracy in Five Nations*. Princeton: Princeton University Press.

Anderson, Irvine H. 1981. *Aramco, the United States, and Saudi Arabia: A Study of the Dynamics of Foreign Oil Policy*. Princeton: Princeton University Press.

Blair, John M. 1976. *The Control of Oil*. New York: Pantheon.

Cammack, Paul. 1989. "Bringing the State Back In? A Polemic." *British Journal of Political Science* 19, no. 2: 261–90.

——— . 1990. "Statism, Neo-Institutionalism, and Marxism." In *The Socialist Register 1990*. London: Merlin.

Easton, David. 1953. *The Political System: An Inquiry into the State of Political Science*. New York: Knopf.

——— . 1957. "An Approach to the Analysis of Political Systems." *World Politics* 9: 383–400.

——— . 1981. "The Political System Besieged by the State." *Political Theory* 9: 303–25.

Evans, Peter, Dietrich Rueschemeyer, and Theda Skocpol, eds. 1985. *Bringing the State Back In*. Cambridge: Cambridge University Press.

Foucault, Michel. 1977. *Discipline and Punish: The Birth of the Prison*. New York: Pantheon.

——— . 1980a. "Questions on Geography." In *Power/Knowledge*. New York: Pantheon.

——— . 1980b. "Two Lectures." In *Power/Knowledge*. New York: Pantheon.

——— . 1991. "Governmentality." In *The Foucault Effect: Studies in Governmentality*, edited by Graham Burchell, Colin Gordon, and Peter Miller, 87–104. Hemel Hempstead, Herts: Harvester Wheatsheaf.

Fuller, J. F. C. 1955. *The Decisive Battles of the Western World and Their Influences upon History,* 3 vols. London: Eyre and Spottiswoode.

Krasner, Stephen D. 1978. *Defending the National Interest: Raw Materials Investments and U.S. Foreign Policy.* Princeton: Princeton University Press.

Loewenstein, Karl. 1944. "Report on the Research Panel on Comparative Government." *American Political Science Review* 38: 540–8.

Marx, Karl. 1973. *Grundrisse: Foundations of the Critique of Political Economy.* Translated by Martin Nicolaus. Harmondsworth, Middlesex: Penguin Books.

Miller, Aaron David. 1980. *Search for Security: Saudi Arabian Oil and American Foreign Policy, 1939–1949.* Chapel Hill: University of North Carolina Press.

Mitchell, Timothy. 1988. *Colonising Egypt.* Cambridge: Cambridge University Press.

——. 1990. "Everyday Metaphors of Power." *Theory and Society* 19: 545–77.

——. 1991. "The Limits of the State: Beyond Statist Approaches and Their Critics." *American Political Science Review* 85, no. 1: 77–96.

——. 1995. "Origins and Limits of the Modern Idea of the Economy." Working Papers Series, no. 12. Advanced Study Center, University of Michigan.

Nettl, J. P. 1968. "The State as a Conceptual Variable." *World Politics* 20: 559–92.

Ollman, Bertell. 1992. "Going Beyond the State? A Comment." *American Political Science Review* 86, no. 4: 1014–17.

Poulantzas, Nicos. 1978. *State, Power, Socialism.* London: Verso.

Radice, Hugo. 1984. "The National Economy: A Keynesian Myth?" *Capital and Class* 22: 111–40.

Sabine, George. 1934. "The State." In *Encyclopedia of the Social Sciences.* New York: Macmillan.

Skocpol, Theda. 1979. *States and Social Revolutions: A Comparative Analysis of France, Russia and China.* Cambridge: Cambridge University Press.

——. 1981. "Political Response to Capitalist Crisis: Neo-Marxist Theories of the State and the Case of the New Deal." *Politics and Society* 10: 155–201.

8

Finding the Man in the State

Wendy Brown

Every man I meet wants to protect me. Can't figure out what from.

> – Mae West

State is the name of the coldest of all cold monsters.

> – Friederich Nietzsche, *Thus Spoke Zarathustra*

A maturing feminist epistemological intelligence and late modern reflections upon the socially constructed "self" combine to obstruct easy determinations about what, other than primary and secondary sex characteristics (themselves not immune to ambiguity and tractability), may be identified with confidence as female or male, feminine or masculine, woman or man. All such determinations, whether derived from feminist readings of history, biology, philosophy, anthropology, or psychoanalysis, have foundered on the shoals of fictional essentialism, false universals, and untenable unities. In addition to these theoretical interrogations,

political challenges to feminisms that are white, heterosexual, and middle class by women who are otherwise have made strikingly clear that "woman" is a dangerous and depoliticizing metonymy: no individual woman harbors the variety of modes of subjection, power, desire, danger, and resourcefulness experienced by women living inside particular skins, classes, epochs, or cultures. "All that is solid melts into air" – the sanguine "we" uttered in feminist theory and practice only two decades ago is gone for good.

Feminist theory rooted in female identity may be irreconcilable with the diverse and multiple vectors of power constructing and diversifying identity; however, feminist claims about masculine domination do not thereby disintegrate. The workings of power-producing subjects are recorded in different stories and require different tools of storytelling than the phenomenon of hegemonic or ubiquitous formations of power. Just as we can decipher the course(s) of capital even if we cannot deduce every important

From Wendy Brown, *States of Injury: Power and Freedom in Late Modernity*, pp. 166–96. Princeton, NJ: Princeton University Press, 1995. © 1995 Princeton University Press. Reprinted by permission of Princeton University Press.

feature of capitalist society from this course, so we can articulate some of the mechanisms of pervasive if unsystematic male domination even if we cannot deduce the precise identity of particular women and men from such articulation. Put differently, while gender *identities* may be diverse, fluid, and ultimately impossible to generalize, particular modes of gender *power* may be named and traced with some precision at a relatively general level. While these modes of power are themselves protean, porous, and culturally and historically specific, they are far more circumscribable than their particular agents, vehicles, and objects. It is in a similar vein that Foucault traces great variety in the effects of disciplinary power while grouping all these effects under the aegis of one kind of power.[1]

For purposes of developing a feminist critical theory of the contemporary liberal, capitalist, bureaucratic state, this means that the elements of the state identifiable as masculinist correspond not to some property contained within men but to the conventions of power and privilege *constitutive* of gender within an order of male dominance. Put another way, the masculinism of the state refers to those features of the state that signify, enact, sustain, and represent masculine power as a form of dominance. This dominance expresses itself as the power to describe and run the world *and* the power of access to women; it entails both a general claim to territory and claims to, about, and against specific "others." Bourgeois, white, heterosexual, colonial, monotheistic, and other forms of domination all contain these two moments – this is what distinguishes them from other kinds of power. The two moments are interwoven, of course, since control of vast portions of social territory – whether geographic or semiotic – carries with it techniques of marginalization and subordination. Thus, for example, dominant discourses render their others silent or freakish in speech by inscribing point-of-viewlessness in their terms of analysis and adjudications of value. The powerful are in this way discursively normalized, naturalized, while the dominated

appear as mutants, disabled. In this light, Aristotle's characterization of women as "deformed males" makes perfect sense.[2]

Amid late modern circumspection about grand theory, the absence of a comprehensive account of the masculinist powers of the state is an admittedly ambiguous lack.[3] However, two overlapping sets of political developments in the United States suggest the need for as full and complex a reading of the state powers that purvey and mediate male dominance as feminist theorists can achieve. First, the state figures prominently in a number of issues currently occupying and often dividing North American feminists, including campaigns for state regulation of pornography and reproductive technologies, contradictory agendas for reforms in labor, insurance, and parental leave legislation (the "difference-equality" debate in the public policy domain), and appeals to the state, at times cross-cut by appeals to the private sector, for pay equity, child support, and day care funding. Second, an unprecedented and growing number of women in the United States are today directly dependent upon the state for survival. Through the dramatic increase in impoverished "mother-headed households" produced by the socially fragmenting and dislocating forces of late-twentieth-century capitalism, and through the proliferation and vacillation in state policies addressing the effects of these forces, the state has acquired a historically unparalleled prominence – political and economic, social and cultural – in millions of women's lives.

State-centered feminist politics, and feminist debates about such politics, are hardly new. Nineteenth-century feminist appeals to the state included campaigns for suffrage, protective labor legislation, temperance, birth control, and marriage law reform. In the twentieth century, the list expanded to campaigns for equal opportunity, equal pay, equal rights, and comparable worth; reproductive rights and public day care; reform of rape, abuse, marriage, and harassment laws; and in the last decade, labor legislation concerned with maternity, as well as state regulation of pornography, surrogacy, and new reproductive technologies. In North American feminism's more militant recent past, argument about the appropriateness of turning to the state with such appeals frequently focused on the value of "reform politics" – a left skepticism – or on the appropriateness of state "intervention" in familial and sexual issues – a liberal nervousness. Less often raised is the question I want to pose centrally here: whether the state is a specifically problematic instrument or arena of *feminist* political change. If the institutions, practices, and discourses of the state are as inextricably, however differently, bound up with the prerogatives of manhood in a male dominant society as they are with capital and class in a capitalist society and with white supremacy in a racist society, what are the implications for feminist politics?

A subset of this question about feminist appeals to the state concerns the politics of protection and regulation, the inescapable politics of most state-centered social policy. While minimal levels of protection may be an essential prerequisite to freedom, freedom in the barest sense of participating in the conditions and choices shaping a life, let alone in a richer sense of shaping a common world with others, is also in profound tension with externally provided protection. Whether one is dealing with the state, the Mafia, parents, pimps, police, or husbands, the heavy price of institutionalized protection is always a measure of dependence and agreement to abide by the protector's rules. As Rousseau's elegant critique of "civil slavery" made so clear, institutionalized political protection necessarily entails surrendering individual and collective power to legislate and adjudicate for ourselves in exchange for external guarantees of physical security, including security in one's property.[4] Indeed, within liberalism, paternalism and institutionalized protection are interdependent parts of the heritage of social contract theory, as "natural liberty" is exchanged for the individual and collective security ostensibly guaranteed by the state.[5]

If those attached to the political value of freedom as self-legislation or direct democracy

thus have reason to be wary of the politics of protection, women have particular cause for greeting such politics with caution. Historically, the argument that women require protection by and from men has been critical in legitimating women's exclusion from some spheres of human endeavor and confinement within others. Operating simultaneously to link "femininity" to privileged races and classes, protection codes are also markers and vehicles of such divisions among women, distinguishing those women constructed as violable and hence protectable from other women who *are* their own violation, who are logically inviolable because marked *as* sexual availability without sexual agency.[6] Protection codes are thus key technologies in regulating privileged women as well as in intensifying the vulnerability and degradation of those on the unprotected side of the constructed divide between light and dark, wives and prostitutes, good girls and bad ones.[7] Finally, if the politics of protection are generically problematic for women and for feminism, still more so are the specific politics of sexual protection, such as those inherent in feminist antipornography legislation and criminalization of prostitution. Legally codifying and thereby ontologizing a cultural construction of male sexual rapaciousness and female powerlessness, such appeals for protection both desexualize and subordinate women in assigning responsibility to the state for women's fate as objects of sexist sexual construction. Moreover, if, as I will argue, state powers are no more gender neutral than they are neutral with regard to class and race, such appeals involve seeking protection *from* masculinist institutions *against* men, a move more in keeping with the politics of feudalism than freedom. Indeed, to be "protected" by the same power whose violation one fears perpetuates the very modality of dependence and powerlessness marking much of women's experience across widely diverse cultures and epochs.

As potentially deleterious but more subtle in operation than the politics of *protection* inherent in state-centered feminist reforms are the politics of *regulation* entailed by many such reforms. Foucault, and before him Weber and Marcuse, mapped in meticulous detail "the increasing organization of *everything* as the central issue of our time" and illuminated the evisceration of human depths and connection, as well as the violent structures of discipline and normalization achieved by this process.[8] Yet with few exceptions, feminist political thinkers and activists eschew this assessment, pursuing various political reforms without apparent concern for the intensification of regulation – the pervasively disciplining and dominating effects – attendant upon them. Comparable worth policy, for example, involves extraordinary levels of rationalization of labor and the workplace: the techniques and instruments of job measurement, classification, and job description required for its implementation make Taylorism look like child's play. Similarly, state-assisted child support guarantees, including but not only those utilizing wage attachments, invite extensive state surveillance of women's and men's daily lives, work activities, and sexual and parental practices, as well as rationalization of their relationships and expectations. Given a choice between rationalized, procedural unfreedom on one hand, and arbitrary deprivation, discrimination, and violence on the other, some, perhaps even most, women might opt to inhabit a bureaucratized order over a "state of nature" suffused with male dominance. So also would most of us choose wage work over slavery, but such choices offer nowhere a vital politics of freedom.

The second historical development calling for a feminist theory of the state – the dramatic increase in impoverished, woman-supported households over the last two decades – raises a related set of issues about dependence and autonomy, domination and freedom. The statistics are familiar: today, approximately one-fifth of all women are poor and two out of three poor adults are women; women literally replaced men on state poverty rolls over the last twenty years. The poverty rate for children under six is approximately 25 percent – and is closer to 50 percent for African American and Hispanic children. Nearly one-fifth of US families are officially "headed by women," but this fifth accounts for half of all poor families and harbors almost one-third of all children between three and thirteen.[9] Approximately half of poor "female-headed" households are on welfare; over 10 percent of all US families thus fit the profile of being headed by women, impoverished, and directly dependent on the state for survival.[10] These data do not capture the growing urban homeless population, male and female, whose poverty is neither registered nor attenuated by the state.

An appreciation of the gendered characteristics of the institutions now figuring so largely in the lives of millions of US poor women and children is surely critical to formulating intelligent feminist strategies for dealing with the state.[11] Indeed, quietly paralleling the controversial feminist advocacy of state regulation of pornography is an equally questionable but less hotly debated feminist insistence upon state solutions to female poverty. While Linda Gordon, Mimi Abramovitz, and a handful of other feminist welfare state critics do work to problematize this insistence, the dominant position in feminist political discourse is typified by Barbara Ehrenreich and Frances Fox Piven, who began arguing in the early 1980s that left and radical feminists must overcome their "categorical antipathy to the state."[12] In Ehrenreich and Piven's view, such indiscriminate (and implicitly unfounded) mistrust of authority and institutions obscures how potentially empowering for the women's movement is the considerable and growing involvement of women with the state – mostly as clients and workers but also as constituents and politicians. Largely on the basis of hypothetical alliances (between middle-class women in the welfare state infrastructure and their clients) and imagined possibilities for militant collective action (in the vein of welfare rights actions of the 1960s), Piven and Ehrenreich argue that the welfare state is not merely a necessary holding action for millions of women but constitutes the base for a progressive mass movement: "The emergence of women as active political subjects on a mass scale is due to the new consciousness and new capacities yielded women by their expanding relationships to state institutions."[13]

Ehrenreich and Piven are sanguine about precisely what I want to place in question, that US women's "expanding relationships to state institutions" unambiguously open and enrich the domain of feminist political possibilities. Do these expanding relationships produce only active *political* subjects, or do they also produce regulated, subordinated, and disciplined *state* subjects? Does the late-twentieth-century configuration of the welfare state help to emancipate women from compulsory motherhood or also help to administer it? Are state programs eroding or intensifying the isolation of women in reproductive work and the ghettoization of women in service work? Do female staff and clients of state bureaucracies – a critical population in Ehrenreich and Piven's vision of a militant worker-client coalition – transform the masculinism of bureaucracy or reiterate it, becoming servants disciplined and produced by it? Considering these questions in a more ecumenical register, in what ways might women's deepening involvement with the state entail exchanging dependence upon individual men for regulation by contemporary institutionalized processes of male domination? And how might the abstractness, the ostensible neutrality, and the lack of a body and face in the latter help to disguise these processes, inhibiting women's consciousness of their situation qua women, and thereby circumscribing the impetus for substantive feminist political change?

In the interest of addressing – developing more than answering – these questions, this essay offers a contour sketch of the specifically masculinist *powers* of the late modern US state. Although it does not build toward policy recommendations or a specific political program, it issues from and develops two political hunches: First, domination, dependence, discipline, and protection, the terms marking the itinerary of women's subordination in vastly different cultures and epochs, are also characteristic effects of state power and therefore cast state-centered feminist politics under extreme suspicion for possibly reiterating rather than reworking the condition and construction of women. Second, insofar as state power is, *inter alia*, a historical product and expression of male predominance in public life and male dominance generally, state power itself is surely and problematically gendered; as such, it gives a specifically masculinist spin to the generic problematic of the high tension and possible incompatibility between prospects for radical democracy and the growing, albeit diffused, powers of the state in the late twentieth century.

Discerning the socially masculine dimensions of the state requires coming to terms with the theoretical problematic of the state itself, specifically the paradox that what we call the state is at once an incoherent, multifaceted ensemble of power relations and a vehicle of massive domination. The contemporary US state is both modern and postmodern, highly concrete and an elaborate fiction, powerful and intangible, rigid and protean, potent and without boundaries, decentered and centralizing, without agency, yet capable of tremendous economic, political, and ecological effects. Despite the almost unavoidable tendency to speak of the state as an "it," the domain we call the state is not a thing, system, or subject, but a significantly unbounded terrain of powers and techniques, an ensemble of discourses, rules, and practices, cohabiting in limited, tension-ridden, often contradictory relation with one another.[14] The seemingly paradoxical dimension of a nonentity exercising this degree of power and control over a population may be best captured by Foucault's account in *The History of Sexuality*:

> *Power relations are both intentional and nonsubjective.* If in fact they are intelligible, this is not because they are the effect of another instance that "explains" them, but rather because they are imbued, through and through, with calculation: there is no power

that is exercised without a series of aims and objectives. But this does not mean that it results from the choice or decision of an individual subject; let us not look for the headquarters that presides over its rationality.... [T]he logic is perfectly clear, the aims decipherable, and yet it is often the case that no one is there to have invented them.[15]

Insofar as "the state" is not an entity or a unity, it does not harbor and deploy only one kind of political power; to start the story a bit earlier, political power does not come in only one variety. Any attempt to reduce or define power as such, and political thinkers from Machiavelli to Morgenthau to MacKinnon have regularly made such attempts, obscures that, for example, social workers, the Pentagon, and the police are not simply different faces of the state in an indigent woman's life but different *kinds* of power. Each works differently as power, produces different effects, engenders different kinds of possible resistance, and requires a different analytical frame; at the same time, each emerges and operates in specific historical, political, and economic relation with the others, and thus also demands an analysis that can nonreductively capture this relation.

In what follows, four distinct modalities of contemporary US state power are considered. These four are not exhaustive of the state's powers but each carries a feature of the state's masculinism and each has been articulated in traditional as well as feminist political thought. The *juridical-legislative* or *liberal* dimension of the state encompasses the state's formal, constitutional aspects. It is the dimension Marx, in his early writings, criticized as bourgeois, it is central to Catharine MacKinnon's and Carole Pateman's theorization of the state's masculinism, and it is the focus of the recently established field of feminist jurisprudence.[16] The *capitalist* dimension of the state includes provision of capitalism's moorings in private property rights as well as active involvement in capitalist production, distribution, consumption, and legitimation.[17] This dimension of the

state has been sketched by Marx in his later writings and exhaustively theorized by twentieth-century neo-Marxist scholars,[18] and a number of European and North American Marxist-feminists have analyzed aspects of masculine privilege inscribed in it.[19] The *prerogative* dimension of the state pertains to that which marks the state as a state: legitimate arbitrary power in policy making and legitimate monopolies of internal and external violence in the police and military. As the overt power-political dimension of the state, prerogative includes expressions of national purpose and national security as well as the whole range of legitimate arbitrary state action, from fiscal regulation to incarceration procedures. Machiavelli and Hobbes are prerogative power's classic theorists; the analyses of war and militarism undertaken by Judith Steihm, Carol Cohn, Jean Bethke Elshtain, Nancy Hartsock, and Cynthia Enloe, as well as by nonacademic cultural and eco-feminists, have opened the terrain of prerogative state power to feminist theoretical critique.[20] The *bureaucratic* dimension of the state, like the others, is expressed in tangible institutions as well as discourse: bureaucracy's hierarchicalism, proceduralism, and cult of expertise constitute one of several state "voices" and the organizational structure of state processes and activities. Classically theorized by Max Weber, cast in a narrower frame by Michel Foucault as the problematic of "disciplinary" power, this dimension of state power has been subjected to feminist critique by Kathy Ferguson.[21]

Before elaborating each of these dimensions of state power, three prefatory notes about male dominance and state power are in order. First, the argument I am here advancing is that all dimensions of state power, and not merely some overtly "patriarchal" aspects, figure in the gendering of the state. The state can be masculinist without intentionally or overtly pursuing the "interests" of men precisely because the multiple dimensions of socially constructed masculinity have historically shaped the multiple modes of power circulating through the domain called the state – this is what it means to talk about masculinist power rather than the power of men. On the other hand, while all state power is marked with gender, the same aspects of masculinism do not appear in each modality of state power. Thus, a feminist theory of the state requires simultaneously articulating, deconstructing, and relating the multiple strands of power composing both masculinity and the state. The fact that neither state power nor male dominance is unitary or systematic means that a feminist theory of the state will be less a linear argument than the mapping of an intricate grid of overlapping and conflicting strategies, technologies, and discourses of power.

A second significant feature of state and male domination and the quality of their interpenetration pertains to the homology in their characteristics – their similarly multiple, diverse, and unsystematic composition and dynamics. Apprehending and exploiting this homology entail recognizing that male dominance is not rooted, as domination by capital is, in a single mechanism that makes possible a large and complex system of social relations. What links together the diverse forms or "stages" of the economic order called capitalism – the liberal or competitive form, the monopoly or organized form, the postindustrial or disorganized form – is its linchpin of profit-oriented ownership and control of the means of production. Thus, however deeply and variously involved the state may be with capitalist accumulation and legitimation, the state's capitalist *basis* remains its guarantee of private ownership as private property rights. There is no parallel way in which the state is "male" because male dominance does not devolve upon a single or essential principle, which is why it is so hard to circumscribe and inappropriate to systematize.[22] In most cultures, male dominance includes the regularized production of men's access to women as unpaid servants, reproducers, sex, and cheap labor, as well as the production of men's monopolies of intellectual, political, cultural, and economic power. But the masculinity and hence the power of men is developed and expressed differently as fathers, as political rulers or members of a political brotherhood, as owners and controllers in the economy, as sexual subjects, as producers of particular kinds of knowledges and rationality, and as relative nonparticipants in reproductive work and other activities widely designated as women's purview. The diversity and diffuseness of masculinist power result in parallel diversity across women's experience inside the family and out, as mothers and prostitutes, scholars and secretaries, janitors and fashion models. These differences cannot be reduced to the intersection of gender with class, race, and sexuality; they pertain as well to the different effects of the multiple dimensions and domains of male power and female subordination.[23]

A related feature of the homology between masculinist and state power pertains to their ubiquitous quality. State and masculine domination both work through this ubiquitousness rather than through tight, coherent strategies. Neither has a single source or terrain of power; for both, the power producing and controlling its subjects is unsystematic, multi-dimensional, generally "unconscious," and without a center. Male power, like state power, is real but largely intangible except for the occasions when it is expressed as violence, physical coercion, or outright discrimination – all of which are important but not essential features of either kind of domination, especially in their late modern incarnations. The hegemonic effect of both modes of dominance lies in the combination of strategies and arenas in which power is exercised. Concretely, if men do not maintain some control over relations of reproduction, they cannot as easily control women's labor, and if they do not monopolize the norms and discourse of political life, they exercise much less effective sexual and economic control over women. But these strategies buttress and at times even contradict each other; they are not indissolubly linked to one another.[24] Women's subordination is the wide effect of all these modes of control, which is why no single feminist reform – in pay equity, reproductive rights, institutional access, child care arrangements, or sexual freedom – even theoretically topples the whole arrangement. The same is true of the state: its multiple dimensions make state power difficult to circumscribe and difficult to injure. There is no single thread that, when snapped, unravels the whole of state or masculine dominance.

One final prefatory note on discerning gender in the state: In the US context, as well as that of other historically colonial or slave-based political economies, state power is inevitably racialized as well as gendered and bourgeois. But the white supremacist nature of contemporary state power – the specific mores and mechanisms through which state power is systematically rather than incidentally racist – are only beginning to be theorized by scholars investigating the inscription of race and race supremacy in political power, and these speculations are not further developed here.[25] What can be argued with some certainty is that while the racialized, gendered, and class elements of state power are mutually constitutive as well as contradictory, the specific ways in which the state is racialized are distinctive, just as the gendered aspects of state power are analytically isolatable from those of class, even while they mingle with them historically and culturally. In other words, however these various modes of social, political, and economic domination intersect in the daily constitution and regulation of subjects, as modes of political power they require initially separate genealogical study. To do otherwise is to reiterate the totalizing, reductionistic moves of Marxist theories of power and society, in which analysis of one kind of social power, class, frames all modes of domination.

Let us now fill out the four modalities of masculinist state power sketched above.

1. The Liberal Dimension. Liberal ideology, legislation, and adjudication is predicated upon a division of the polity into the ostensibly autonomous spheres of family, civil society (economy), and state. In classical as well as much contemporary liberal discourse, the family is cast as the "natural" or divinely given – thus prepolitical and ahistorical – part of the human world. Civil society is also formulated as "natural" in the sense of arising out of "human nature," although the civility of civil society is acknowledged by liberal theorists to be politically "achieved" and it is also within civil society that the rights guaranteed by the (nonnatural) state are exercised. In the classic liberal account, the state is the one conventional and hence fully malleable part of this tripartite arrangement; it is constructed both to protect citizens from external danger and to guarantee the rights necessary for commodious commerce with one another.

The problem with this discourse for women has been rehearsed extensively by feminist political theorists such as Carole Pateman, Catharine MacKinnon, and Lorenne Clark. First, since the family is cast as natural and prepolitical, so also is woman, the primary worker within and crucial signifier of the family, constructed in these terms. In this discourse, women are "naturally" suited for the family, the reproductive work women do is "natural," and the family is a "natural" entity. Everywhere nature greets nature and the historical constructedness and plasticity of both women and the family is nowhere in sight. As the family is depoliticized, so is women's situation and women's work within it; recognized neither politically nor economically as labor, this work has a discursively shadowy, invisible character.[26] Second, since much of women's work and life transpires in the "private" or familial realm, women's involvement with the place where rights are conferred and exercised – civil society – is substantially limited by comparison with men. Thus, even when women acquire civil rights, they acquire something that is at best partially relevant to their daily lives and the main domain of their unfreedom. Third, historically the "private sphere" is not actually a realm of privacy for women to the extent that it is a place of unfettered access to a woman by her husband and children. "Privacy is everything women...have never been allowed to have; at the same time the private is everything women have been equated with and defined in terms of men's ability to have."[27] Insofar as it arises as a realm of privacy from other men for men, the private sphere may be the last place on earth women experience either privacy or safety – hence the feminist longing for a "room of one's own" within men's "haven in a heartless world." In classical formulations of liberalism, rights do not apply in this sphere; rather this realm is constructed as governed by norms of duty, love, and custom in addition to nature, and until quite recently it has been largely shielded from the reach of law. Indeed, the difficulties of establishing marital rape as rape, wife battering as battery, or child abuse as abuse derive, *inter alia*, from liberal resistance to recognizing personhood inside the household; in the liberal formulation, persons are rights-bearing individuals pursuing their interests in civil society.[28] Thus Tyrell in the eighteenth century, and Kant and Blackstone in the nineteenth, argued that it was reasonable for women to be politically represented by their husbands because "women have no civil personality" – they exist only as members of households, while personhood is achieved in civil society.[29] Within liberalism, the nonpersonhood of women, the extra-legal status of household relations, and the ontological association of both with nature are all mutually reinforcing.

According to the very origins myths of liberalism, men come out of the "state of nature" to procure rights for themselves *in* society; they do not establish the state to protect or empower individuals inside families.[30] The relevance of this for contemporary analysis lies in its revelation of the masculinism at the heart of the liberal formulation of political and civil subjects and rights: the liberal subject is a man who moves freely between family and civil society, bearing prerogative in the former and rights in the latter. This person is male rather than generic because his enjoyment of his civil rights is buttressed rather than limited by his relations in the private sphere, while the opposite is the case for women: within the standard sexual division of labor, women's access to civil society and its liberties is limited by household labor and responsibilities. Liberalism's discursive construction of the private sphere as neither a realm of work nor of power but of nature, comfort, and regeneration is inherently bound to a socially male position within it; it parallels the privileging of class entailed in bourgeois characterizations of civil society as a place of universal freedom and equality.

One problem with liberal state power for women, then, is that those recognized and granted rights by the state are walking freely about civil society, not contained in the family. Women doing primary labor and achieving primary identity inside the family are thus inherently constrained in their prospects for recognition as persons insofar as they lack the stuff of liberal personhood – legal, economic, or civil personality. They are derivative of their households and husbands, subsumed in identity to their maternal activity, and sequestered from the place where rights are exercised, wages are earned, and political power is wielded. Moreover, because the liberal state does not recognize the family as a political entity or reproduction as a social relation, women's situation as unpaid workers within the family is depoliticized. Finally, while women have now been granted roughly the same panoply of civil and political rights accorded men, these rights are of more limited use to women bound to the household and have different substantive meaning in women's lives. It is as gratuitous to dwell upon an impoverished single mother's freedom to pursue her own individual interests in society as it is to carry on about the property rights of the homeless.

This last point raises a final consideration about the liberal state's maleness, one suggested by the work of thinkers as different from each other as Luce Irigaray and Carol Gilligan.[31] The liberal subject – the abstract individual constituted and addressed by liberal political and legal codes – may be masculine not only because his primary domain of operations is civil society rather than the family, but because he is presumed to be morally if not ontologically oriented toward autonomy, autarky, and individual power. Gilligan's work suggests that social constructions of gender in this culture produce women who do not think or act like liberal subjects, that is, in terms of abstract rights and duties. For Gilligan, insofar as women develop much of their thinking and codes of action within and for the comparatively nonliberal domain of the family, relationships and needs rather than self-interest and rights provide the basis for female identity formation and decision-making processes. While Irigaray moves in the domain of philosophy and psychoanalysis rather than empirical social science, her insistence that "the subject is always masculine" is predicated upon a convergent account of the repudiation of dependency entailed in the psychic construction of the male subject.

By incorporating selected insights from these thinkers, I do not mean to suggest that there is something *essentially* masculine about the liberal subject or state. Supplementing either the theoretical or empirical accounts with historical, cultural, and political-economic components, one could plausibly argue that liberal discourse and practices are the basis for the social construction of bourgeois masculinity rather than the other way around. But causation is a poor analytical modality for appreciating the genealogical relationship between masculinity and liberalism, a relationship that is complexly interconstitutive. One effect of this genealogy is that the liberal state not only adjudicates for subjects whose primary activities transpire in civil society rather than the family, but does so in a discourse featuring and buttressing the interests of individualistic men against the *mandatory* relational situation of women in sequestered domains of caretaking. Similarly, not only does the liberal state grant men access to women in the private sphere by marking the private sphere as a natural and need-ordered realm largely beyond the state's purview, it requires that women enter civil

society on socially male terms. Recognition as liberal subjects requires that women abstract from their daily lives in the household and repudiate or transcend the social construction of femaleness consequent to this dailiness, requirements that in addition to being normatively problematic are – as every working woman knows – never fully realizable. Thus, not merely the structure and discourse but the ethos of the liberal state appears to be socially masculine: its discursive currencies are rights rather than needs, individuals rather than relations, autogenesis rather than interdependence, interests rather than shared circumstances.

2. The Capitalist Dimension. The masculinism of the capitalist dimension of the state, like that of the liberal dimension, is also moored in a public/private division, albeit one that moves along a somewhat different axis. In this division, men do paid "productive" work and keep women in exchange for women's unpaid work of reproducing the male laborers (housework), the species (child care), and caring for the elderly or infirm. The sexual division of labor historically developed by capitalism is one in which almost all women do unpaid reproductive work, almost all men do wage work, and the majority of women do both.

A large portion of the welfare state is rooted in capitalist development's erosion of the household aspect of this division of labor, in the collapse of the exchange between wage work in the economy and unpaid work in the family and the provision of household care for children, old, and disabled people that this exchange secured. But as feminist scholars of the welfare state Mimi Abramovitz, Nancy Fraser, and Linda Gordon make clear, the fact that the familial exchange process has broken down does not mean that capitalism and the capitalist state are no longer structured along gender lines.[32] First, these arrangements, on which the "family wage" and unequal pay systems were based, leave their legacy in women's sixty-four-cents-on-the-dollar earning capacity and ghettoization in low-paying jobs. Second, unpaid reproductive work continues, and continues being performed primarily by women, even though this work is increasingly (under)supported by the welfare state rather than by a male wage. Consequently, ever-larger numbers of working- and middle-class women are doing all of life's work – wage work, child care, domestic labor, sustenance and repair of community ties – within an economy that remains organizationally and normatively structured for male wage earning and privilege insofar as it assumes unpaid female labor, and especially child care, in the home.

In *Capital*, Marx speaks ironically of the double sense in which the worker within capitalism is "free": he is free to dispose of his own labor as a commodity and he is free from any other means of sustaining himself (i.e., property). Women, of course, do not bear the first kind of "freedom" when they are engaged in reproductive work – they cannot "freely" dispose of their labor as a commodity or "freely" compete in the labor market. This is one of the mechanisms by which capitalism is fundamentally rather than incidentally gendered. Indeed, as long as significant parts of domestic labor remain outside the wage economy and women bear primary responsibility for this work, women will be economically dependent on someone or something other than their own income-earning capacities when engaged in it.

The social transformation we are currently witnessing is one in which, on the one hand, for increasing numbers of women, this dependence is on the state rather than individual men; on the other hand, the state and economy, rather than individual men, are accorded the service work of women. While much work historically undertaken in the household is now available for purchase in the market, women follow this work out into the economy – the labor force of the service sector is overwhelmingly female.[33] Thus, as capitalism has irreversibly commodified most elements of the private sphere, the domain and character of "exchange" in the sexual division of labor has been trans-

ported from the private and individualized to the public and socialized. The twin consequences are that much of what used to be women's work in the home is now women's work in the economy and that the state and economy, rather than husbands, now sustain many women at minimal levels when they are bearing and caring for children.

In sum, the capitalist dimension of the state entails women's subordination on two levels. First, women supply unremunerated reproductive labor, and because it is both unremunerated and sequestered from wage work, most women are dependent upon men or the state for survival when they are engaged in it. Second, women serve as a reserve army of low-wage labor and are easily retained as such because of the reproductive work that interrupts their prospects for a more competitive status in the labor force.[34] The state's role in these arrangements lies in securing, through private property rights, capitalist relations of production in the first place; buttressing and mediating – through production subsidies, contracts, bailouts, and fiscal regulation – these relations of production; maintaining – through legal and political regulation of marriage, sexuality, contraception, and abortion – control of women's reproductive work; and perpetuating, through a gendered welfare and unemployment benefits system and the absence of quality public day care, the specifically capitalist sexual division of labor.[35]

3. The Prerogative Dimension. Prerogative power, the state's "legitimate" arbitrary aspect, is easily recognized in the domain of international state action. Here, as Hegel reminds us, "the Idea of the state is actualized" – the state expresses itself as a state and is recognized as such by other states.[36] For Locke, the occasional imperative of maximum efficiency and flexibility of state action in both the domestic and international arena justifies the cultivation and deployment of prerogative power.[37] Among political theory's canonical figures, however, it is neither Hegel nor Locke but Machiavelli who treats most extensively the dynamics and configurations of prerogative power – its heavily extralegal, adventurous, violent, and sexual characteristics. Machiavelli theorizes political power in a register in which violence, sexuality, and political purpose are thoroughly entwined, precisely the entwining that signals the presence of prerogative power.[38]

That an early-sixteenth-century Florentine could illuminate this feature of the late modern US state suggests that unlike liberal, capitalist, and bureaucratic modalities of state power, prerogative power is not specific to modernity. Indeed, for liberals, prerogative power is the liberal state's expressly nonliberal dimension. Classical liberal thought depicts princely prerogative as precisely what liberalism promises to diminish if not cancel: historically, monarchical power is dethroned, and mythically, the state of nature (in which everyone has unlimited prerogative power) is suppressed. In this regard, the emergence of liberalism is conventionally conceived as the advent of an epoch in which political organization bound to the privileges of the few is usurped by the needs of the many, in which *raison d'état* shifts from power to welfare, in which the night watchman replaces the prince. But there is another way of reading the origins of the liberal state, in which the arbitrary and concentrated powers of monarchy are not demolished. Rather, princely power is dissimulated and redeployed by liberalism as state prerogative that extends from war making to budget making. In this reading, the violence of the state of nature is not overcome but reorganized and resituated in, on the one hand, the state itself as the police and the military, and, on the other, the zone marked "private" where the state may not tread and where a good deal of women's subordination and violation is accomplished.

Max Weber's tale of origins about the state is quite suggestive for mapping the connections between the overt masculinism of international state action (the posturing, dominating, conquering motif in such action) and the internal values and structure of state-ruled societies. According to Weber, the state has a double set of origins. In one set, organized political institutions are prefigured in the formation of bands of marauding warriors, "men's leagues," who live off, without being integrated into, a particular territorial population and who randomly terrorize their own as well as neighboring populations. In the other, institutionalized political authority is prefigured in the earliest household formations, where male or "patrimonial" authority is rooted in a physical capacity to defend the household against the pillaging warrior leagues.[39]

The first set of origins, which features a combination of predatory sexuality, territoriality, violence, and brotherhood in warrior league activity, certainly adduces a familiar face of prerogative power – egregious in the ways of street gangs, rationalized and legitimized in most international state activity. In this vein, what Charles Tilly calls "war making and state making as organized crime" Ortega y Gasset conjures as the "sportive origins of the state," and Norman O. Brown anoints "the origins of politics in juvenile delinquency[:] . . . politics as gang rape." All posit, *contra* Marx, a gendered and sexual rather than economic underpinning to the political formations prefiguring states.[40] But if we add to this picture the second strain of Weber's origins story, that concerned with the foundations of male household authority, it becomes clear how contemporary prerogative power constructs and reinforces male dominance across the social order, and not only through overtly masculinist displays of power by the Pentagon or the police.

In Weber's account, while warrior leagues are initially consociated "beyond and above the everyday round of life," they are eventually "fitted into a territorial community," at which point a recognizable "political association is formed."[41] This association presumably retains many of the characteristics it had as a more mobile enterprise, especially its foundation in organized violence, which, for Weber, is *the* identifying characteristic of the state. During this transition, the social structure of the territorial population shifts from one of mother-children groups to father-headed households. The authority of the adult male, Weber suggests, derives not from his place in the division of labor but from his physical capacity to dominate and defend his household, a capacity significant only because of the omnipresent threat to household security posed by the warrior leagues.[42] Thus, male household authority would appear to be rooted in its provision of protection from institutionalized male violence. In other words, the patriarchal household and its legitimate structure of authority arise not merely as an economic unit but as a barrier between vulnerable individuals and the sometimes brutal demands or incursions of the state's prefigurative associations. This arrangement is codified and entrenched through asymmetrical legal privileges and an asymmetrical sexual division of labor: household patriarchs "protect" dependent and rightless women from the violence of male political organization. In this respect, the state is an insignia of the extent to which politics between men are always already the politics of exchanging, violating, protecting, and regulating women; the one constitutes the imperatives of the other.

Widely disparate Western political origins stories, from those of the Greek tragedians to Freud to modern social contract theorists, resonate with Weber's. In each, a single event or process heralds the disempowering and privatizing of women on the one hand and the emergence of formal political institutions on the other. According to these stories, the birth and consolidation of organized political power *entails* women's loss of power and public status. Moreover, once the women are conquered and the men are organized, the supreme political organ of society guarantees individual men access to individual women and protects each man's claim to his woman against infringement by other men. Thus, the basic narrative is always a version of Freud's contract among the brothers after they have killed the father: to prevent the situation that necessitated the patricide, they erect the state

and through it convenant to keep their hands off each other's women, thereby relaxing the tension that an absent father introduces into a brotherhood. From this perspective, the "private" sphere appears to be necessary for this deal to work: it is the place of access to women by men, a place outside the eyes or reach of law and other men, where every man is "king in his own castle." The threshold of the home is where the state's purview ends and individual man's begins. Not surprisingly, this threshold – what it marks, prohibits, and contains – is among the boundaries most actively contested and politicized by contemporary feminist jurisprudence concerned with marital rape, battery, property rights, reproductive rights, and other issues relevant to woman's achievement of personhood or "civil personality."

These stories articulate a basic political deal about women, a deal arranged by men and executed by the state, comprising two parts: one between men and the other between the state and each male citizen. In the first, the state guarantees each man exclusive rights to his woman; hence the familiar feminist charge that rape and adultery laws historically represent less a concern with violations of women's personhood than with individual men's propriety over the bodies of individual women. In the second, the state agrees not to interfere in a man's family (de facto, a woman's life) as long as he is presiding over it (de facto, her).[43]

According to Weber's version of these arrangements, the character of political power concerned with security, protection, or welfare is shaped by the ultimate "power purposes" of a political organization. This suggests that the gendered structure of liberalism is partly determined by the gendered character of prerogative power, in which women are cast as requiring protection from the world of male violence while the superior status of men is secured by their supposed ability to offer such protection. For Weber, the modern legacy of the warrior leagues lies in the state's telos of domination, realized through territorial monopoly of physical violence and resulting in a "legitimate authority" predicated upon this domination.

This reading of state origins also leads Weber to formulate politics and the state as appropriately concerned not with the well-being of the population but with what he terms the "prestige of domination."[44] The legitimacy of prerogative power is rooted in the state's pursuit of self-affirmation through displays of power and prestige, and not in protection or sustenance of human life.

The problem here is one most feminists can recite in their sleep. Historically, women have been culturally constructed and positioned as the creatures to whom this pursuit of power and glory for its own sake stand in contrast: women preserve life while men risk it; women tend the mundane and the necessary while men and the state pursue larger-than-life concerns; men seek immortality while women look after mundane affairs; men discount or threaten the realm of everyday life while women nurture and protect it. Simone de Beauvoir casts this not as an ideology or discourse of gender, but as indeed the factual history of gender's origin:

> The warrior put his life in jeopardy to elevate the prestige of the horde, the clan to which he belonged. And in this he proved dramatically that life is not the supreme value for man, but on the contrary that it should be made to serve ends more important than itself. The worst curse that was laid upon woman was that she should be excluded from these warlike forays. For it is not in giving life but in risking life that man is raised above the animal; that is why superiority has been accorded in humanity not to the sex that brings forth but to that which kills.[45]

The problem then, lies not in women's exclusion from the domain of prerogative state power but in its gendered character. The distinction between daily existence preserved by women and the male pursuit of power or prestige through organized violence simultaneously gives a predatory, rapacious, conquering ethos to prerogative power and disenfranchises women from this kind of power. Conventional constructions of masculine sexuality (as opposed to masculine rationality, interests, or privileges) are heavily featured in this domain because this dimension of state power is more immediately visceral and corporeal than, for example, bureaucratic or juridical power, both of which tend to organize and work on bodies without touching them so directly.

The masculinism of state prerogative power inheres in both its violent and its transcendent (i.e., above life) features, as well as in their relation: women are the "other" of both these moments of prerogative power as well as the conduit between them. Yet because prerogative power appears to its subjects as not just the power to violate but also the power to protect – quintessentially the power of the police – it is quite difficult to challenge from a feminist perspective. The prerogative of the state, whether expressed as the armed force of the police or as vacillating criteria for obtaining welfare benefits, is often all that stands between women and rape, women and starvation, women and dependence upon brutal mates – in short, women and unattenuated male prerogative.[46]

4. The Bureaucratic Dimension. Max Weber and Michel Foucault formulate bureaucratization and its normalizing, disciplining effects as *the* distinct and ubiquitous domination of our age.[47] Neither limits this mode of domination to the state; to the contrary, each regards the modern filtration of bureaucracy or disciplinary institutions across the social order as precisely what permits a decrease in the overt exercise of (prerogative) state power without a corresponding decline in political and social control.[48] Indeed, one of the most significant aspects of bureaucratization is its blurring of a clear line between state and civil society. Consider the proliferating social services bureaucracies, regulative bureaucracies, and military-(post)industrial complexes: the purview of each involves institutionalized penetration and fusion of formerly honored boundaries between the domain of political power, the household, and private enterprise.

In *The Feminist Case against Bureaucracy*, Kathy Ferguson employs the insights of Foucault and Weber to explore two different moments of masculinism in bureaucratic power. She argues first that bureaucratic power "feminizes" bureaucratic staff and clientele by rendering them dependent and submissive and by forcing them into strategies of impression managing that "protect them from the worst aspects of domination while simultaneously perpetuating that domination." Second, she insists that bureaucratic discourse is masculinist insofar as it bears what Carol Gilligan, Nancy Chodorow, Nancy Hartsock, and others identify as socially male values of abstract rationality, formal proceduralism, rights orientation, and hierarchy, while opposing or colonizing socially female values of substantive rationality, need-based decision making, relationality, and responsibility.[49] For Ferguson, the masculinism of bureaucratic discourse thus lies in a dual production: it creates *feminized* subjects while it excludes or colonizes *female* subjects.

Ferguson's distinction between "femininity" and "femaleness" is drawn from the complexity of women's experience as subordinates (the site of production of "femininity") *and* as caregivers (the site of production of "femaleness"). However, insofar as these are not separate sites of activity and women do not actually have these experiences separately, the distinction would appear to be rooted in a false essentializing of femaleness as caregiving.[50] Moreover, if bureaucracy's creation of subordinates *is* the process of feminization, then bureaucratic domination and male domination each lose their singularity; in assimilating them to each other, gender and bureaucracy both disappear as specifiable kinds of power. Domination in Ferguson's analysis thus begins to appear flatly generic, notwithstanding her effort to distill distinctly feminized modes of coping with subordination.

More persuasive than Ferguson's argument about bureaucracy's feminization of subjects is her account of the way the structures and values of bureaucracy – hierarchy, separation, abstract right, proceduralism – stand in relation to what she posits as women's socially constructed experience as caregivers. When measured by the norms of bureaucratic discourse, the values of a caregiving milieu appear immature or irrational: this is the political face of Gilligan's critique of the norms of Kohlberg's development psychology. Not only does bureaucratic discourse perpetuate the devaluation of practices oriented toward need and care, it carries the state's masculinism in agencies and agents dealing with women as caregivers insofar as it both judges its female clients in masculine terms and constructs them as feminized dependents.

Ferguson's critique of bureaucracy by no means exhausts the possible range of bureaucratic power's masculinist features. I have argued elsewhere that the instrumental rationality constituting both the foundation of bureaucratic order and the process of bureaucratic rationalization is grounded in the social valorization of maximized power through maximized technocratic control.[51] This particular expression of a will to power – domination through regimes of predictability, calculability, and control – appears to be socially masculine in the West insofar as the ultimate value is control, and the uncontrollable as well as that which is to be controlled – external nature or the body politic – are typically gendered female in these discourses. Finally, bureaucratic power quite obviously "serves" male dominant interests through its disciplinary function: state agencies of every variety create disciplined, obedient, rule-abiding subjects. This aspect of bureaucracy's involvement with masculine dominance does not require that bureaucratic power itself be masculinist, only that it be an effective instrument of domination and that the policies it executes are gendered, whether they be enacted through HUD, the IRS, or military regulations. In this mode, bureaucracy's regulatory and disciplining capacities enable and mask male dominant interests external to bureaucracy, much as Foucault casts the disciplinary organization of schools and hospitals as auxiliaries of a generalized aim of social control. The fact that bureaucracy as discipline is both an *end* and an *instrument*, and thereby operates *as power* as well as *in the service of other powers*, all the while presenting itself as extrinsic to or neutral with regard to power, makes it especially potent in shaping the lives of female clients of the state.

As the sites and registers of women's relationships to the state expand in late modernity, both the characteristics and the meaning of the state's maleness transmogrify. Ceasing to be primarily a domain of masculinist powers and an instrument of male privilege and hegemony, albeit maintaining these functions, the state increasingly takes over and transforms the project of male dominance. However, as it moves in this direction, the state's masculinism becomes more diffuse and subtle even as it becomes more potent and pervasive in women's lives. Indeed, while the state replaces the man for many women, its jurisprudential and legislative powers, its welfare apparatus, and even its police powers often appear as leading agents of sex equality or female protection. In this regard, the late modern state bears an eerie resemblance to the "new man" of pseudo-feminist infamy. Beneath a thin exterior of transformed/reformed gender identity and concern for women, the state bears all the familiar elements of male dominance. Through its police and military, the state monopolizes the institutionalized *physical* power of society. Through its welfare function, the state wields *economic* power over indigent women, arbitrarily sets the terms of their economic survival, and keeps them dangling and submissive by providing neither dependable, adequate income level nor quality public day care.[52] Through age-of-consent laws on contraception, regulation of abortion and other reproductive technologies, and stipulating that mothers be heterosexual and free of substance abuse, the state controls and regulates the *sexual* and *reproductive* construction and condition of women. Through its monopoly of political authority and discourse, the state mediates the *discursive, semiotic,* and *spatial* terms of women's political practices. Thus, while the state is neither hegemonic nor monolithic, it mediates or deploys almost all the powers shaping women's lives – physical, economic, sexual, reproductive, and political – powers wielded in previous epochs directly by men.

In short, in precise contrast to Foucault's argument about the declining importance of the state in the disciplinary age, *male* social power and the production of female subjects appears to be increasingly concentrated in the state. Yet like the so-called new man, the late modern state also represents itself as pervasively hamstrung, quasi-impotent, unable to come through on many of its commitments, because it is decentralizing (decentering) itself, because "it is no longer the solution to social problems," because it is "but one player on a global chessboard," or because it has forgone much of its power in order to become "kinder, gentler." The central paradox of the late modern state thus resembles a central paradox of late modern masculinity: its power and privilege operate increasingly through disavowal of potency, repudiation of responsibility, and diffusion of sites and operations of control.

We may now return to Piven and Ehrenreich's claim, rehearsed earlier, about the ostensibly radical potential inherent in women's growing involvement with the state. Such an argument depends upon a Marxist conviction about the inevitably radicalizing effects of collectivizing subjects previously isolated and dispersed in their oppression.[53] This conviction in turn presumes a transcendental subject, a subject who simply *moves* from isolated to collectivized conditions, as opposed to a subject who *is produced* or engendered by these respective conditions. In this regard, Piven and Ehrenreich's analysis is impervious to how the discursive and spatial disciplinary strategies of the late modern workplace and state affect workers or state clients. Just as microelectronics assembly plants in Third World Free Trade Zones do not simply employ women workers but produce them – their bodies, social relations, sexualities, life conditions, genders, psyches, consciousnesses[54] – the state does not simply handle clients or employ staff but produces state subjects, as bureaucratized, dependent, disciplined, and gendered. Put another way, capitalism's steady erosion of the liberal boundary between public and private, its late-twentieth-century disruption of the boundary between household and economy, and the politicization of heretofore private activities such as reproduction and sexuality achieved by these developments do not automatically generate political consciousness or struggles for freedom any more than the state's increasing entanglement with the economy automatically generates working-class consciousness or militance.[55] Again, this is because the state does not simply address private needs or issues but configures, administers, and produces them. While Piven speaks of women as "partly liberated from the overweening power of men by the 'breakdown' of the family,"[56] what is "liberated" from the private sphere may then be colonized and administered by one or more dimensions of masculinist state power. Indeed, the state may even assist in separating individuals and issues from the "private" sphere in order to effectively administer them. This is certainly one way of reading the workings of birth control legislation in the nineteenth century, and surrogacy legislation and "squeal laws" requiring parental notification in the late twentieth.[57] It is also an important caution to feminists evaluating current proposals by the Clinton administration to "end welfare as we know it," whose chief strategy appears to be workfare administered individually to women by "personal social workers." Here, not only intensified regulation of poor women at the individual level but greater levels of integration between invasive bureaucratic state power and the low-wage economy are the specters haunting the future of poor women's lives.

However important "the family" remains – particularly in its absence – in constructing the gendered unconscious, it is decreasingly the daily superintendent of masculine dominance in late modern life. Today, women's struggles for social, political, and economic freedom in the United States more often transpire in or near the domain of the state, whether these concern issues of poverty, welfare benefits and regulations, in vitro fertilization, abortion, day care, surrogacy, teenage reproductive rights, sexual freedom (including the rights and claims of sex workers), affirmative action, education, or employment. From what I have argued about the historical legacies and contemporary reworkings of masculinism in state powers, it is clear that there are dangers in surrendering control over the codification of these issues to the state, as well as in looking to the state as provider, equalizer, protector, or liberator. Yet like male dominance itself, masculinist state power, consequent to its multiple and unsystematic composition, is something feminists can both exploit and subvert, but only by deeply comprehending in order to strategically outmaneuver its contemporary masculinist ruses.

NOTES AND REFERENCES

1 *Discipline and Punish: The Birth of the Prison*, trans. A. Sheridan (New York: Random House, 1977).
2 "The female is as it were a deformed male; and the menstrual discharge is semen, though in an impure condition; i.e., it lacks one constituent, and one only, the principle of soul" (*Generation of Animals* 737a25).
3 A sampling of recent feminist literature on the state would include Kathy Ferguson, *The Feminist Case against Bureaucracy* (Philadelphia: Temple University Press, 1984); Catharine MacKinnon, "Feminism, Marxism, Method, and the State: Toward a Feminist Jurisprudence," *Signs* 8 (1983), pp. 635–58, *Feminism Unmodified: Discourses on Life and Law* (Cambridge: Harvard University Press, 1987), and *Toward a Feminist Theory of the State* (Cambridge: Harvard

University Press, 1989); Zillah Eisenstein, *Feminism and Sexual Equality* (New York: Monthly Review, 1984); Michèle Barrett, *Women's Oppression Today: Problems in Marxist Feminist Analysis* (London: New Left Books, 1980); Varda Burstyn, "Masculine Dominance and the State," *The Socialist Register*, ed. Ralph Miliband and John Saville (London: Merlin Press, 1983); Mary McIntosh, "The State and the Oppression of Women," in *Feminism and Materialism*, ed. Annette Kuhn and AnnMarie Wolpe (London: Routledge, 1978); Rosalind Petchesky, *Abortion and Women's Choice: The State, Sexuality, and Reproductive Freedom* (New York: Longman, 1984); Eileen Boris and Peter Bardaglio, "The Transformation of Patriarchy: The Historic Role of the State," in *Families, Politics and Public Policy: A Feminist Dialogue on Women and the State*, ed. Irene Diamond (New York: Longman, 1983); Carol Brown, "Mothers, Fathers, and Children: From Private to Public Patriarchy," in *Women and Revolution*, ed. Lydia Sargent (Boston: South End, 1980); Linda Nicholson, *Gender and History: The Limits of Social Theory in the Age of the Family* (New York: Columbia University Press, 1986); Eli Zaretsky, "The Place of the Family in the Origins of the Welfare State," in *Rethinking the Family: Some Feminist Questions*, ed. Barrie Thorne (New York: Longman, 1982); Rachel Harrison and Frank Mort, "Patriarchal Aspects of Nineteenth-Century State Formation," in *Capitalism, State Formation, and Marxist Theory: Historical Investigations*, ed. Phillip Corrigan (London: Quarttet Books, 1980); Nancy Fraser, *Unruly Practices: Power, Discourse, and Gender in Contemporary Social Theory* (Minneapolis: University of Minnesota Press, 1989), chaps. 7, 8; Mimi Abramovitz, *Regulating Women* (Boston: South End, 1988); Jennifer Dale and Peggy Foster, *Feminists and State Welfare* (London: Routledge, 1986); *Women, the State, and Welfare*, ed. Linda Gordon (Madison: University of Wisconsin Press, 1990); and *Playing the State: Australian Feminist Interventions*, ed. Sophie Watson (London: Verso, 1990).

4 See Rousseau's "Discourse on the Origin and Foundations of Inequality among Men," in *Jean-Jacques Rousseau: The First and Second Discourses*, ed. R. Masters (New York: St. Martin's, 1964), part 2, and *The Social Contract*, book 1, chap. 4.

5 The classic formulation of these arrangements are contained in Hobbes's *Leviathan* and Locke's *Second Treatise On Government*; the classic critic is Jean-Jacques Rousseau. For feminist commentary see Carole Pateman, *The Sexual Contract* (Stanford: Stanford University Press, 1988), and the essays in part 2 of *Feminist Challenges: Social and Political Theory*, ed. Carole Pateman and Elizabeth Grosz (Boston: Northeastern University Press, 1986).

6 See Hortense J. Spillers, "Interstices: A Small Drama of Words," in *Pleasure and Danger: Exploring Female Sexuality*, ed. Carol Vance (Boston: Routledge, 1984), for what remains one of the most complex explorations of this element in the construction of African American women.

7 See Jacqueline Dowd Hall, "The Mind That Burns in Each Body," in Vance, *Pleasure and Danger*; *Good Girls, Bad Girls: Feminists and Sex Trade Workers Face to Face*, ed. Laurie Bell (Toronto: Seal, 1987); and MacKinnon, *Feminism Unmodified*.

8 Herbert Dreyfus and Paul Rabinow, *Michel Foucault: Beyond Structuralism and Hermeneutics* (Chicago: University of Chicago Press, 1982), p. xxii. See also Sheldon Wolin, *Politics and Vision: Continuity and Innovation in Western Political Thought* (Boston: Little, Brown, 1960), chap. 10. Recently, several political economists and cultural theorists have argued that this tendency – a tendency specific to modernity and especially *organized* capitalism – is in decline, indeed that the hallmark of postmodernity is *disorganization*. See Scott Lash and

John Urry, *The End of Organized Capitalism* (Madison: University of Wisconsin, 1987), and Claus Offe, *Disorganized Capitalism* (Cambridge: MIT Press, 1985).

9 Ruth Sidel, *Women and Children Last: The Plight of Poor Women in Affluent America* (New York: Penguin, 1986), pp. 3, 16, 24; and Hilda Scott, *Working Your Way to the Bottom: The Feminization of Poverty* (London: Pandora, 1984), p. 19. Figures drawn from these volumes were updated with Census Bureau and Bureau of Labor Statistics data from the 1990s.

10 "Dependence" is, of course, the terminology chosen by neoconservatives to indict the growth of the welfare state for producing a "welfare-dependent" population, a formulation that can be criticized on a number of grounds. Empirically, a small fraction of those on the welfare rolls at any one time are "chronic," i.e., are on the welfare rolls for more than two years. According to Fred Block and John Noakes, "welfare dependent adults" comprise fewer than one in sixteen of all adults in poverty, including those with medical and emotional problems ("The Politics of the New-Style Workfare," *Socialist Review* 18, no. 3, [1988], p. 54). Moreover, as Ehrenreich and others have pointed out, the discourse of welfare "dependence" constructs welfare clients in the degrading idiom of addiction or the condescending idiom of childhood, and it also intends to contrast the supposedly independent condition of wage workers and the dependent straits of welfare clients. What, ask socialist feminist critics of this language, is so independent about the life of a woman bound to a low-paying job for survival? (See, for example, Barbara Ehrenreich, "The New Right Attack on Social Welfare," in *The Mean Season: The Attack on the Welfare State*, ed. Fred Block et al. [New York: Pantheon, 1987], pp. 187–8.) While I am in complete accord with this critique, it also begs a critical question: insofar as

the discourse of neoconservatives reflects rather than contests the discourse of the welfare state, how and in what ways does the state, through such discursive practices, *produce* dependent state subjects? If dependence on the state for survival is no "worse" – morally or economically – than dependence on the local MacDonald's franchise for survival, it is also not any less a site of production of women's lives and consciousnesses. Thus, critique of reactionary discourse *about* the welfare state opens rather than concludes a discussion of how the state constructs the women it processes.

11 See Wendy Brown, "Deregulating Women: The Trials of Freedom under a Thousand Points of Light," *sub/versions* 1 (1991), pp. 1–8.

12 Frances Fox Piven, "Ideology and the State: Women, Power, and the Welfare State," in Gordon, *Women, the State, and Welfare*, p. 250; and Barbara Ehrenreich and Frances Fox Piven, "Women and the Welfare State," in *Alternatives: Proposals for America from the Democratic Left*, ed. Irving Howe (New York: Pantheon, 1983).

13 Piven, "Ideology and the State," p. 251; see also pp. 258–9, and Ehrenreich and Piven, "Women and the Welfare State," p. 38.

14 Other feminist scholars concerned with the state have sought to grasp this feature of it. In Harrison and Mort's account, "the State should be seen not as a monolithic and unified 'subject,' but as a differentiated set of practices and institutions which at specific historical moments may stand in contradiction or opposition" ("Patriarchal Aspects of Nineteenth-Century State Formation," p. 82). According to Burstyn, "the term, 'state,' like the term 'mode of production'...is a generalization and abstraction. It sums up and schematises a system of relations, structures, institutions and forces which, in industrialized society, are vast, complex, differentiated and as an inevitable result, contradictory

at times as well" ("Masculine Dominance and the State," p. 46). While the emphasis upon "contradiction" in each of these descriptions is meant to mark something like what I am calling the incoherence of the state, it actually does the opposite. Contradiction, as it is employed in the Marxist tradition with which Harrison, Mort, and Burstyn identify, implies a coherent system containing a basic internal logic and set of conflicts. While I do not want to deny the presence of substantive internal conflicts in state power and processes – e.g., the state's simultaneous tendency toward bureaucratic rigidity and its need for flexibility, or its steadily increasing interventionism and its dependency upon neutrality for legitimacy – I am seeking to break with an understanding of state power as systematic or even adherent to a linear political logic.

15 *The History of Sexuality*, vol. 1, *An Introduction*, trans. R. Hurley (New York: Vintage, 1980), pp. 94–5, emphasis added.

16 MacKinnon, *Toward a Feminist Theory of the State*, and *Feminism Unmodified*; Pateman, *Sexual Contract*. Introductions to the prolific domain of feminist jurisprudence include Christina Brooks Whitman, "Feminist Jurisprudence," *Feminist Studies* 17 (1991), pp. 493–507; Christine Littleton, "In Search of a Feminist Jurisprudence," *Harvard Women's Law Journal* 10 (1987), pp. 1–7; Heather Ruth Wishik, "To Question Everything: The Inquiries of Feminist Jurisprudence," *Berkeley Women's Law Journal* 1 (1985), pp. 64–75; Ann Scales, "Towards a Feminist Jurisprudence," *Indiana Law Journal* 56 (1981), pp. 375–444, and "The Emergence of Feminist Jurisprudence," *Yale Law Journal* 95 (1986), pp. 1373–1403; Marie Ashe, "Mind's Opportunity: Birthing a Poststructuralist Feminist Jurisprudence," *Syracuse Law Review* 38 (1987), pp. 1129–73; and Ellen C. DuBois, Mary C. Dunlap, Carol J. Gilligan, Catharine A. MacKinnon and

Carrie J. Menkel-Meadow, "Feminist Discourse, Moral Values, and the Law – A Conversation," *Buffalo Law Review* 34, no. 1 (1985), pp. 11–87. Other sample literature in this genre includes Patricia Williams, *The Alchemy of Race and Rights* (Cambridge: Harvard University Press, 1991); *Feminist Legal Theory: Foundations*, ed. D. Kelly Weisberg (Philadelphia: Temple University Press, 1993); Mary Joe Frug, *Postmodern Legal Feminism* (New York: Routledge, 1992); Martha Minnow, *Making All the Difference: Inclusion, Exclusion, and American Law* (Ithaca: Cornell University Press, 1990); and *At the Boundaries of Law: Feminism and Legal Theory*, ed. Martha Fineman and Nancy Thomadsen (New York: Routledge, 1991).

17 The most succinct accounts of the state's involvement with "organized capitalism" are those of James O'Connor, *Fiscal Crisis of the State* (New York: St. Martin's, 1973), and *Accumulation Crisis* (London: Blackwell, 1986); Jurgen Habermas, *Legitimation Crisis*, trans. T. McCarthy (Boston: Beacon, 1975); and Claus Offe, *Contradictions of the Welfare State*, ed. J. Keane (Cambridge: MIT Press, 1984). On the postmodern state and postindustrial capitalism, see Lash and Urry, *End of Organized Capitalism*, and Offe, *Disorganized Capitalism*.

18 In addition to the works cited in the previous note, a short list of neo-Marxist accounts of the capitalist state would include Louis Althusser, *Lenin and Philosophy* (London: New Left Books, 1971); *State and Capital: A Marxist Debate* ed. John Holloway and Simon Picciotto (London: Arnold, 1978); Fred Block, "The Ruling Class Does Not Rule: Notes on the Marxist Theory of the State," *Socialist Revolution* 7 (1977), reprinted in *Revising State Theory: Essays in Politics and Postindustrialism* (Philadelphia: Temple University Press, 1987); Ralph Miliband, *The State in Capitalist Society* (New York: Basic Books, 1969); and Nicos Poulant-

zas, *Political Power and Social Classes,* trans. T. O'Hagen (London: New Left Books, 1973). Surveys and analyses of these debates can be found in Martin Carnoy, *The State and Political Theory* (Princeton: Princeton University Press, 1984); David Gold et al., "Recent Developments in Marxist Theories of the Capitalist State," *Monthly Review* 27, no. 5 (1975), pp. 29–43; no. 6 (1975), pp. 36–51; and Bob Jessop, "Recent Theories of the Capitalist State," *Cambridge Journal of Economics* 1, no. 4 (1977), pp. 553–73, and *The Capitalist State: Marxist Theories and Methods* (New York: New York University Press, 1982).

19 See Barrett, *Women's Oppression Today;* Burstyn, "Masculine Dominance and the State"; Eisenstein, *Feminism and Sexual Equality;* McIntosh, "State and the Oppression of Women"; and Zaretsky, "Place of the Family in the Origins of the Welfare State."

20 Judith Steihm, ed., *Women and Men's Wars* (Oxford: Pergamon, 1983), and *Women's Views of the Political Worlds of Men* (Dobbs Ferry, N. Y.: Transnational, 1984); Nancy Hartsock, *Money, Sex, and Power: Toward a Feminist Historical Materialism* (New York: Longman, 1983); Jean Bethke Elshtain, *Women and War* (New York: Basic Books, 1987); Cynthia Enloe, *Does Khaki Become You? The Militarization of Women's Lives* (Boston: South End, 1983); and *Radical America* 20, no. 1 (1986), an issue devoted to "Women and War."

21 *The Feminist Case against Bureaucracy.*

22 Many feminists have strained toward such systemization; none more fiercely, however, than Catharine MacKinnon. For more extended critique of this effort on MacKinnon's part, see my reviews of *Feminism Unmodified* in *Political Theory* 17 (1989), pp. 489–92, and of *Toward a Feminist Theory of the State* in *The Nation,* 8–15 January 1990, pp. 61–4.

23 This point may be sharpened by recalling the difficulties of analyzing gender relations utilizing unreconstructed tools of Marxism. Marx and Engels posit historical constructions of the family as a function of the sexual division of labor specified by a particular mode of production. But neither the sexual division of labor nor the more general structure of power within the family are simply produced by relations of production (as Engels implies without ever really establishing). Rather, it is politically procured privileges granted to men by men that make possible the sexual division of labor as such. Political power, buttressed and conditioned by but still distinguishable from economic power, confers privileges upon men that extend beyond the privileges conferred by the sexual division of labor in any particular epoch.

Political power may be used to secure privileges other than purely economic ones. Marx elided this because his focus was class, the economic moment of society and the place where political power most closely reiterates or simply mirrors economic power. Dominant economic interests must be very nearly directly served by a capitalist state, although this may include managing contradictions and dealing with legitimacy problems. But why is the dominant class male? And why, then, are women not all one class? It is the gap between these two phenomena – the pervasiveness of male dominance and the impossibility of persuasively formulating women as a class – that makes clear the extent to which political privilege is not so closely hinged to economic dominance in the case of men as in the case of the bourgeoisie.

24 Although drawn from outside the United States and focusing on different kinds of states than those I am analyzing here, two fascinating accounts of conflicting strands of male dominance negotiated through state policy and jurisprudence can be found in M. Jacqui Alexander, "Redrafting Morality: The Postcolonial State and the Sexual Offences Bill of Trinidad and Tobago," in

Third World Women and the Politics of Feminism, ed. Chandra Mohanty et al. (Bloomington: Indiana University Press, 1991), and in Zakia Pathak and Rajeswari Sunder Rajan, " 'Shahbano,' " in *Feminists Theorize the Political*, ed. Judith Butler and Joan W. Scott (New York: Routledge, 1992).

25 A sampling from this developing literature, particularly strong in Britain, would include *The Bounds of Race*, ed. Henry L. Gates, Jr., and Dominick LaCapra (Ithaca: Cornell University Press, 1990); Paul Gilroy, *There Ain't No Black in the Union Jack* (London: Hutchinson, 1987), and *The Black Atlantic: Modernity and Double Consciousness* (Cambridge: Harvard University Press, 1993); *Anatomy of Racism*, ed. David Goldberg (Minneapolis: University of Minnesota Press, 1990); Stuart Hall, *Race Articulation and Societies Structured in Dominance* (Paris: UNESCO, 1980); Manning Marable, *Race, Reform, and Rebellion: The Second Reconstruction in Black America, 1945–1982* (London: Macmillan, 1984); Martha Minnow, *Making All the Difference*; Michael Omi and Howard Winant, *Racial Formation in the United States: From the 1960s to the 1980s* (London: Routledge, 1986); Peter Scranton, *The State of the Police* (London: Pluto, 1985); Cornel West, *A Genealogy of Racism* (London: Routledge, 1990); Wahneema Lubiano, "Like Being Mugged By a Metaphor: The Worlding of Political Subjects," in *Multiculturalism?* ed. Avery Gordon and Christopher Newfield (Minneapolis: University of Minnesota Press, 1994); and Kimberle Crenshaw, "Demarginalizing the Intersection of Race and Sex: A Black Feminist Critique of Antidiscrimination Doctrine, Feminist Theory, and Antiracist Politics," *The University of Chicago Legal Forum* 139 (1989), pp. 139–52.

26 See Sheila Rowbotham, *Woman's Consciousness, Man's World* (Harmonds-worth, Middlesex: Penguin, 1973), chap. 4.

27 MacKinnon, "Feminism, Marxism, Method, and the State," p. 656.

28 The "right to privacy," tenuously established by the Supreme Court in *Griswold v. Connecticut*, generally deplored by conservatives and defensively clung to by liberals, perfectly expresses this difficulty with recognizing personhood in the household. In the sphere of the family, the Court recognizes household privacy in lieu of rights attendant upon civil persons. For critiques of the right to privacy along these lines, see Catharine MacKinnon, "The Male Ideology of Privacy: A Feminist Perspective on the Right to Abortion," *Radical America* 17, no. 4 (1983), pp. 23–35, and Wendy Brown, "Reproductive Freedom and the 'Right to Privacy': A Paradox for Feminists," in Diamond, *Families, Politics, and Public Policy*.

29 From Blackstone's *Commentaries on the Laws of England*: "By marriage, the husband and wife are one person in law; . . . the very being or legal existence of the woman is suspended" (cited in Carole Pateman, "Women and Consent," *Political Theory* 8 [1980], pp. 152, 155).

30 Hobbes, *Leviathan*, ed. C. B. MacPherson (Harmondsworth, Middlesex: Penguin, 1968), pp. 223–8; Locke, *Two Treatises of Government*, ed. P. Laslett (Cambridge: Cambridge University Press, 1960), pp. 361–77.

31 Carol Gilligan, *In a Different Voice* (Cambridge: Harvard University Press, 1982); Luce Irigaray, "The Subject Is Always Masculine," in *This Sex Which Is Not One*, trans. C. Porter (Ithaca: Cornell University Press, 1985). See also Nancy Hartsock's formulation of "abstract masculinity" in *Money, Sex, and Power*.

32 Abramovitz, *Regulating Women*; Gordon, introduction to *Women, the State and Welfare*; Fraser, "Struggle over Needs" and "Women, Welfare, and the

Politics of Need Interpretation," in *Unruly Practices*.

33 Sidel, *Women and Children Last*, pp. 61–2.

34 There is no better testimony to this than the "workfare" clauses of welfare enacted by the 1988 Family Support Act, stipulations that will do little to break "the cycle of poverty" or "the feminization of poverty" but will supply millions of cheap, docile female workers to the economy during a predicted shortfall of low-wage labor in the coming decade. Not ten years earlier, Reagan publicly named women in the workforce as a prime cause of high male unemployment rates. Reagan was not alone: very few politicians advocated workfare for female welfare clients in 1980.

35 See Barbara Nelson, "The Origins of the Two-Channel Welfare State: Workmen's Compensation and Mother's Aid," and Nancy Fraser, "Struggle Over Needs," in Gordon, *Women, the State, and Welfare*. See also Abramovitz, *Regulating Women*.

36 *Philosophy of Right*, trans. T. M. Knox (Oxford: Oxford University Press, 1957), p. 209.

37 *Two Treatises*, pp. 421–7. See also Sheldon Wolin, "Democracy and the Welfare State: The Political and Theoretical Connections between *Staatsräson* and *Wohlfahrtsstaatsräson*," in *The Presence of the Past: Essays on the State and the Constitution* (Baltimore: Johns Hopkins University Press, 1989).

38 In addition to Machiavelli's *oeuvre*, see Hanna Pitkin, *Fortune Is a Woman* (Berkeley: University of California Press, 1984); Wendy Brown, *Manhood and Politics: A Feminist Reading in Political Theory* (Totowa, NJ: Rowman and Littlefield, 1988); and Wolin, "Democracy and the Welfare State."

39 *Economy and Society*, ed. G. Roth and C. Wittich (Berkeley: University of California Press, 1978), pp. 357–9. Other theorists have suggested that these fraternal organizations reveal the extent to which what we call politics is rooted in "male juvenile delinquency" insofar as

the warriors raped and pillaged not out of necessity, as a Marxist reading would have it, but for sport, fun, and prestige. Underscoring the intensely homosocial nature of the leagues and the quintessential expression of their power in the abduction and gang rape of young women from neighboring tribes, these authors posit a gendered and sexual rather than economic underpinning to all political power and political formations. See Norman O. Brown, *Love's Body* (Wesleyan: Wesleyan University Press, 1959), and José Ortega y Gasset, "The Sportive Origin of the State," in *History as a System and Other Essays toward a Philosophy of History* (New York: Norton, 1961).

40 Charles Tilly, "War Making and State Making as Organized Crime," in *Bringing the State Back In*, ed. P. Evans et al. (Cambridge: Cambridge University Press, 1985); Ortega y Gasset, "The Sportive Origin of the State," pp. 26–32; Brown, *Love's Body*, p. 13.

41 *Economy and Society*, p. 906.

42 Ibid., p. 359.

43 In short, the state's purview begins where man's ends, and there lies the rub for millions of poor women today, since these arrangements contain only two possibilities for women who cannot singlehandedly provide for themselves and their families. Either the state guarantees the rights of the man in their lives or the state *is* the man in their lives. The state stays outside the household door unless there is no man presiding over the home; at that point, if the state assumes the provider role, it also assumes as much about its access rights to a woman's space as any man could ever display. The infamous AFDC "man in the house" rule was the concrete expression of this: Two men – the state and a woman's boy-friend or husband – could not be in the woman's home at the same time, but each was guaranteed access to her and her home in the absence of the other's claim.

44 *Economy and Society*, pp. 910–11; Arthur Mitzman, *The Iron Cage: An*

Historical Interpretation of Max Weber (New York: Knopf, 1970), p. 82.

45 *The Second Sex*, trans. H. M. Parshley (New York: Random House, 1952), p. 72.

46 For an unequivocal expression of the view that the state insulates women from more brutal victimization by sexism, see Frances Fox Piven and Richard A. Cloward, "The Contemporary Relief Debate," in Block et al., *The Mean Season*: "[J]ust as the availability of income supports helps people cope with the vagaries of the labor market, so does it reduce the helplessness of women and children in the face of the weakening of the traditional family" (p. 97).

47 *Economy and Society*, pp. 223, 987, 1393–4; and "Politics as a Vocation," in *From Max Weber*, ed. H. H. Gerth and C. W. Mills (New York: Oxford University Press, 1946), p. 82; Foucault, *Discipline and Punish*.

48 In Weber's understanding this is the triumph of rational legal authority, in Foucault's, it is the supplanting of sovereign or juridical power with disciplinary power.

49 *Feminist Case against Bureaucracy*, pp. 92, 158–69.

50 Ferguson certainly seeks to avoid such essentialism by identifying as a *political struggle* the "complex process of calling out that which is valuable in each gender and carefully disentangling it from that which is riddled with the effects of power" (*Feminist Case against Bureaucracy*, p. 170). However, in this formulation – which distinguishes what is "riddled with power" from what is not – and in her identification of "women's experience" as "*distorted* by oppression," there does seem to persist a notion of a female experience, if not subjectivity, that is unconstructed or undistorted by power and hence essential to a particular set of beings or activities.

51 *Manhood and Politics*, chap. 8.

52 Wolin, "Democracy and the Welfare State," pp. 160–3.

53 "The welfare state brings together millions of poor women who depend on welfare state programs. These constituencies are not . . . simply atomized and therefore helpless people. Rather the structure of the welfare state itself has helped to create new solidarities" (Piven, "Ideology and the State," p. 260).

54 On the production of a new culture of female workers in Free Trade Zones, see the excellent pamphlet by Annette Fuentes and Barbara Ehrenreich, *Women in the Global Factory* (Boston: South End, 1983).

55 In *Legitimation Crisis*, Habermas argued that the "recoupling" of the economic and political spheres effected by "advanced capitalism" would inherently repoliticize the economy and thereby intensify the state's legitimation problems (see pp. 46–8, 68–70). While this move from market capitalism (and its attendant ideology of inequality produced by natural forces) to state-administered and thereby politicized capitalism has certainly occurred, Habermas underestimated North Americans' tolerance for state-administered economic inequality.

56 "Ideology and the State," p. 259.

57 In the United States, nineteenth-century recognition of women in the household as separate legal personalities barely preceded state regulation of contraception, abortion, and female labor – state recognition of women as persons thus facilitated state regulation of women's sexuality and of reproductive and productive work (see Boris and Bardaglio, "The Transformation of Patriarchy," pp. 73–4). State recognition of women as persons becomes a means of control, for anything must be separated out from a mass, individuated, to be efficiently and effectively controlled. As Foucault reminds us, the key mechanisms of disciplinary power are precisely those of individuation and isolation. "Discipline is a political anatomy of detail[.] . . . disciplinary space tends to be divided into as many sections as there are bodies or elements to be distributed" (*Discipline and Punish*, pp. 139, 143).

9

Blurred Boundaries: The Discourse of Corruption, the Culture of Politics, and the Imagined State

Akhil Gupta

While doing fieldwork in a small village in North India (in 1984–85, and again in 1989) that I have named Alipur, I was struck by how frequently the theme of corruption cropped up in the everyday conversations of villagers. Most of the stories the men told each other in the evening, when the day's work was done and small groups had gathered at habitual places to shoot the breeze, had to do with corruption (*bhrashtaachaar*) and "the state."[1] Sometimes the discussion dealt with how someone had managed to outwit an official who wanted to collect a bribe; at other times with "the going price" to get an electrical connection for a new tubewell or to obtain a loan to buy a buffalo; at still other times with which official had been transferred or who was likely to be appointed to a certain position and who replaced, with who had willingly helped his caste members

or relatives without taking a bribe, and so on. Sections of the penal code were cited and discussed in great detail, the legality of certain actions to circumvent normal procedure were hotly debated, the pronouncements of district officials discussed at length. At times it seemed as if I had stumbled in on a specialized discussion with its own esoteric vocabulary, one to which, as a lay person and outsider, I was not privy.

What is striking about this situation, in retrospect, is the degree to which the state has become implicated in the minute texture of everyday life. Of course north Indian villages are not unique in this respect. It is precisely the unexceptionability of the phenomenon that makes the paucity of analysis on it so puzzling. Does the ubiquity of the state make it invisible? Or is the relative lack of attention to the state in ethnographic work due to a methodology that

From *American Ethnologist*, 22(2), 1995, pp. 375–402. © 1995 American Anthropological Association. All rights reserved. Used by permission.

privileges face-to-face contact and spatial proximity – what one may call a "physics of presence?"

In this article I attempt to do an ethnography of the state by examining the discourses of corruption in contemporary India. Studying the state ethnographically involves both the analysis of the *everyday practices* of local bureaucracies and the *discursive construction* of the state in public culture. Such an approach raises fundamental substantive and methodological questions. Substantively, it allows the state to be disaggregated by focusing on different bureaucracies without prejudging their unity or coherence. It also enables one to problematize the relationship between the translocality of "the state" and the necessarily localized offices, institutions, and practices in which it is instantiated. Methodologically, it raises concerns about how one applies ethnographic methods when the aim is to understand the workings of a translocal institution that is made visible in localized practices. What is the epistemological status of the object of analysis? What is the appropriate mode of gathering data, and what is the relevant scale of analysis?[2]

An ethnography of the state in a postcolonial context must also come to terms with the legacy of Western scholarship on the state. In this article I argue that the conventional distinction between state and civil society, on which such a large portion of the scholarship on the state is based, needs to be reexamined. Is it the "imperialism of categories" (Nandy 1990:69) that allows the particular cultural configuration of "state/civil society" arising from the specific historical experience of Europe to be naturalized and applied universally? Instead of taking this distinction as a point of departure, I use the analysis of the discourse of corruption to question its utility in the Indian context. The discourse of corruption turns out to be a key arena through which the state, citizens, and other organizations and aggregations come to be imagined. Instead of treating corruption as a dysfunctional aspect of state organizations, I see it as

a mechanism through which "the state" itself is discursively constituted.[3]

In addition to description and analysis, this article also has a programmatic aim: to mark some new trails along which future anthropological research on the state might profitably proceed. The goal is to map out some of the most important connections in a very large picture, thereby providing a set of propositions that can be developed, challenged, and refuted by others working on this topic. In so doing, this article seeks to add to a fast-growing body of creative work that is pointing the way to a richer analysis of "the state" (some examples are Abrams 1988; Anagnost 1994, 1995, n.d.; Ashforth 1990; Brow 1988; Cohn 1987a, 1987b; Handelman 1978, 1981; Herzfeld 1992a; Kasaba 1994; Mitchell 1989, 1991; Nugent 1994; Taussig 1992; Urla 1993; Yang 1989).

I should point out that much more needs to be done to lay the empirical basis for ethnographies of the state. Very little rich ethnographic evidence documents what lower-level officials actually do in the name of the state.[4] Research on the state, with its focus on large-scale structures, epochal events, major policies, and "important" people (Evans et al. 1985; Skocpol 1979), has failed to illuminate the quotidian practices (Bourdieu 1977) of bureaucrats that tell us about the effects of the state on the everyday lives of rural people. Surprisingly little research has been conducted in the small towns (in the Indian case, at the level of the subdistrict [*tehsil*]) where a large number of state officials, constituting the broad base of the bureaucratic pyramid, live and work – the village-level workers, land record keepers, elementary school teachers, agricultural extension agents, the staff of the civil hospital, and others. This is the site where the majority of people in a rural and agricultural country such as India come into contact with "the state," and this is where many of their images of the state are forged.

Although research into the practices of local state officials is necessary, it is not by itself sufficient to comprehend how the state comes to be constructed and represented. This necessitates some reflection on the limitations inherent in data collected in "the field." The discourse of corruption, for example, is mediated by local bureaucrats but cannot be understood entirely by staying within the geographically bounded arena of a subdistrict township. Although in this article I stress the role of public culture and transnational phenomena, I do not want to suggest that the face-to-face methods of traditional ethnography are irrelevant. But I do want to question the assumption regarding the natural superiority – the assertion of authenticity – implicit in the knowledge claims generated by the fact of "being there" (what one may call the "ontological imperative"). Such claims to truth gain their force precisely by clinging to bounded notions of "society" and "culture." Once cultures, societies, and nations are no longer seen to map unproblematically onto different spaces (Appadurai 1986; Gupta and Ferguson 1992; Hannerz 1986), one has to rethink the relationship between bodily presence and the generation of ethnographic data. The centrality of fieldwork as rite of passage, as adjudicator of the authenticity of "data," and as the ultimate ground for the judgment of interpretations rests on the rarely interrogated idea that one learns about cultural difference primarily through the phenomenological knowledge gained in "the field." This stress on the *experience* of being in spatial proximity to "the other," with its concomitant emphasis on sensory perception, is linked to an *empiricist* epistemology[5] that is unable to comprehend how the state is discursively constituted. It is for this reason that I have combined fieldwork with another practice employed by anthropologists, a practice whose importance is often downplayed in discussions of our collective methodological tool kit. This is the analysis of that widely distributed cultural text, the newspaper (for an early example, see Benedict 1946; an exemplary recent discussion can be found in Herzfeld 1992b).[6] I have looked at representations of the state and of "the public" in English-language and vernacular newspapers in India.

By focusing on the discursive construction of the state, I wish to draw attention to the powerful cultural practices by which the state is symbolically represented to its employees and to citizens of the nation.[7] These public cultural practices are enacted in a contested space that cannot be conceptualized as a closed domain circumscribed by national boundaries. Folk, regional, and national ideologies compete for hegemony with each other and with *transnational* flows of information, tastes, and styles embodied in commodities marketed by multinational capital.[8] Exploring the discursive construction of the state therefore necessarily requires attention to transnational processes in the interstate system (Calhoun 1989). The interstate system, in turn, is not a fixed order but is subject to transformations that arise from the actions of nation-states and from changes taking place in international political economy, in this period that has been variously designated "late capitalism" (Mandel 1975) or the era of "flexible accumulation" (Harvey 1989). For instance, the new liberalization policies being followed by the Congress government in India since the 1990 elections can only be understood in the context of a transnational discourse of "efficiency" being promoted by the International Monetary Fund (IMF) and the collapse of the former Soviet Union, one of India's most important strategic and economic partners. Similarly, intense discussions of corruption in India in 1989,[9] centering on a transaction in the international arms economy, bring home the complex intermingling of local discourses and international practices. What is the theoretical importance of these observations? Briefly, it is that any theory of the state needs to take into account its constitution through a complex set of *spatially* intersecting representations and practices. This is not to argue that every episode of grassroots interaction between villagers and state officials can be shown to have transparent transnational linkages; it is merely to note that such linkages have structuring effects that may overdetermine the contexts in which daily practices are carried out. Instead of attempting to search for the local-level or grassroots conception of the state as if it encapsulated its own reality and treating "the local" as an unproblematic and coherent spatial unit, we must pay attention to the "multiply mediated"[10] contexts through which the state comes to be constructed.

In developing my analysis I have drawn substantially on other ethnographers of South Asia who have paid attention to the state. In her analysis of the rituals of development performed at the inauguration of a large water project in Sri Lanka, Serena Tenekoon (1988) demonstrates that the symbolic distribution of water in all directions across the landscape of the country becomes a means by which the reach of the state is represented. In this case, the literal enactment of traversing the space of the nation comes to signify the ubiquity and translocality of the state. Conversely, James Brow (1988) shows how a government housing project in Sri Lanka makes the state concretely visible in the eyes of villagers. Here, the emphasis is on the possibilities of imagining the translocal that are enabled by the embodiment of the state through spatial markers such as houses.[11]

Since the ethnography of the state developed in this article focuses on the discourse of corruption, and since corruption lends itself rather easily to barely concealed stereotypes of the Third World,[12] it might be worthwhile to say something about how I proceed to develop a perspective on the state that is explicitly anti-orientalist. When notions of corrupt "underdeveloped" countries are combined with a developmentalist perspective, in which "state-society relations" in the Third World are seen as reflecting a prior position in the development of the "advanced" industrial nations, the temptation to compare "them" to "our own past" proves irresistible to many Western scholars.[13] Instead, one needs to ask how one can use the comparative study of Third World political formations to confront the "naturalness" of concepts that have arisen from the historical experience and cultural context of the West. Focusing on the discursive construction of

states and social groups allows one to see that the legacy of Western scholarship on the state has been to universalize a particular cultural construction of "state-society relations" in which specific notions of "statehood" and "civil society" are conjoined.[14] Instead of building on these notions, this article asks if one can demonstrate their provincialism in the face of incommensurable cultural and historical contexts.[15]

I begin with a series of vignettes that give a sense of the local level functioning of "the state" and the relationship that rural people have to state institutions. Everyday interactions with state bureaucracies are to my way of thinking the most important ingredient in constructions of "the state" forged by villagers and state officials. I then look at the broader field of representations of "the state" in public culture. Finally, I attempt to demonstrate how local level encounters with the state come together with representations in the mass media. This is followed by the conclusion, which systematically draws out the larger theoretical issues raised in the article.

Encountering "the State" at the Local Level

For the majority of Indian citizens, the most immediate context for encountering the state is provided by their relationships with government bureaucracies at the local level. In addition to being promulgated by the mass media, representations of the state are effected through the public practices of different government institutions and agents. In Mandi, the administrative center closest to Alipur, the offices of the various government bureaucracies themselves served as sites where important information about the state was exchanged and opinions about policies or officials forged. Typically, large numbers of people clustered in small groups on the grounds of the local courts, the district magistrate's office, the hospital, or the police station, animatedly discussing and debating the latest news. It was in places such as these, where villagers interacted with each other and with residents of the nearby towns, as much as in the mass media, that corruption was discussed and debated.

Therefore, looking closely at these settings allows us to obtain a sense of the texture of relations between state officials and clients at the local level. In this section I draw on three cases that together present a range of relationships between state officials and rural peoples. The first concerns a pair of state officials, occupying lowly but important rungs in the bureaucratic hierarchy, who successfully exploit the inexperience of two rural men. The second case concerns a lower-caste man's partially successful actions to protect himself from the threats of a powerful headman[16] who has allies in the bureaucracy by appealing to a higher official. The third example draws on a series of actions conducted by the powerful Bharatiya Kisan Union (literally, Indian Peasant Union), a grassroots farmers' movement that often strikes terror in the hearts of local state officials. Because they give a concrete shape and form to what would otherwise be an abstraction ("the state"), these everyday encounters provide one of the critical components through which the state comes to be constructed.

Small but prosperous, Mandi[17] houses the lowest ends of the enormous state and federal bureaucracy.[18] Most of the important officials of the district, including those whose offices are in Mandi, prefer to live in another, bigger town that serves as the district headquarters. Part of the reason is that rental accommodation is hard to come by in Mandi (as I discovered to my frustration); equally important, it enables them to stay in closer touch with their superior officers.

Sharmaji was a *patwari*, an official who keeps the land records of approximately five to six villages, or about five thousand plots, lying on the outskirts of Mandi. The patwari is responsible for registering land records, for physically measuring land areas to enter them in the records, and for evaluating the quality of land. The patwari also keeps a record of deaths in a family in the event of a dispute

among the heirs about property, or the need to divide it up at some point. There are a number of officials above the patwari whose main – if not sole – duty is to deal with land records. On average, the total comes to about two officials for each village. Astonishing as this kind of bureaucratic sprawl might appear, it must not be forgotten that land *is* the principal means of production in this setting.

Sharmaji lived in a small, inconspicuous house deep in the old part of town. Although I was confused at first, I eventually identified which turns in the narrow, winding lanes would lead me there. The lower part of the house consisted of two rooms and a small enclosed courtyard. One of those rooms had a large door that opened onto the street. This room functioned as Sharmaji's "office." That is where he was usually to be found, surrounded by clients, sycophants, and colleagues. Two men in particular were almost always by his side. One of them, Verma, himself a patwari of Sharmaji's natal village (and therefore a colleague) was clearly in an inferior position. He functioned as Sharmaji's alter ego, filling in his ledgers for him, sometimes acting as a front and sometimes as a mediator in complex negotiations over how much money it would take to "get a job done," and generally behaving as a confidant and consultant who helped Sharmaji identify the best strategy for circumventing the administrative and legal constraints on the transfer of land titles. The other person worked as a full-time Man Friday who did various odd jobs and chores for Sharmaji's "official" tasks as well as for his household.

Two of the side walls of the office were lined with benches; facing the entrance toward the inner part of the room was a raised platform, barely big enough for three people. It was here that Sharmaji sat and held court,[19] and it was here that he kept the land registers for the villages that he administered. All those who had business to conduct came to this "office." At any given time there were usually two or three different groups, interested in different transactions, assembled in the tiny room. Sharmaji conversed with all of them at the same time, often switching from one addressee to another in the middle of a single sentence. Everyone present joined in the discussion of matters pertaining to others. Sharmaji often punctuated his statements by turning to the others and rhetorically asking, "Have I said anything wrong?" or, "Is what I have said true or not?"

Most of the transactions conducted in this "office" were relatively straightforward: adding or deleting a name on a land title; dividing up a plot among brothers; settling a fight over disputed farmland. Since plots were separated from each other by small embankments made by farmers themselves and not by fences or other physical barriers, one established a claim to a piece of land by plowing it. Farmers with predatory intentions slowly started plowing just a few inches beyond their boundary each season so that in a short while they could effectively capture a few feet of their neighbors' territory. If a neighbor wanted to fight back and reclaim his land, he went to the patwari who settled the dispute by physically measuring the area with a tape measure. Of course, these things "cost money," but in most cases the "rates" were well-known and fixed.

But however open the process of giving bribes and however public the transaction, there was nevertheless a performative aspect that had to be mastered. I will illustrate this with a story of a botched bribe. One day, when I reached Sharmaji's house in the middle of the afternoon, two young men whose village fell in the jurisdiction of Verma were attempting to add a name to the title of their plot. They were sitting on the near left on one of the side benches. Both were probably in their late teens. Their rubber slippers and unkempt hair clearly marked them to be villagers, an impression reinforced by clothes that had obviously not been stitched by a tailor who normally catered to the "smart" set of town-dwelling young men. They appeared ill at ease and somewhat nervous in Sharmaji's room, an impression they tried hard to dispel by adopting an overconfident tone in their conversation.

Although I never did find out why they wanted to add a name to the land records, I was told that it was in connection with their efforts to obtain fertilizer on a loan for which the land was to serve as collateral. When I arrived on the scene, negotiations seemed to have broken down already: the men had decided that they were not going to rely on Verma's help in getting the paperwork through the various branches of the bureaucracy but would instead do it themselves.

Sharmaji and the others present (some of whom were farmers anxious to get their own work done) first convinced the young men that they would never be able to do it themselves. This was accomplished by aggressively telling them to go ahead and first try to get the job done on their own and that, if all else failed, they could always come back to Sharmaji. "If you don't succeed, I will always be willing to help you," he said. Thereupon one of the farmers present told the young men that Sharmaji was a very well-connected person. Without appearing to brag, Sharmaji himself said that when big farmers and important leaders needed to get their work done, it was to him that they came.

Perhaps because they had been previously unaware of his reputation, the nervous clients seemed to lose all their bravado. They soon started begging for help, saying "*Tau* [father's elder brother], you know what's best, why should we go running around when you are here?" Sharmaji then requested Verma to "help" the young men. "Help them get their work done," he kept urging, to which Verma would reply, "I never refused to help them." The two patwaris then went into an adjoining room, where they had a short whispered conference. Sharmaji reappeared and announced loudly that they would have to "pay for it." The young men immediately wanted to know how much would be required, to which Sharmaji responded, "You should ask him [Verma] that." Shortly thereafter, Verma made a perfectly timed reentrance. The young men repeated the question to him. He said, "Give as much as you like." When they asked the question again, he said, "It is not for me to say. Give whatever amount you want to give."

The two clients then whispered to each other. Finally, one of them broke the impasse by reaching into his shirt pocket and carefully taking out a few folded bills. He handed Rs. 10 to Verma.[20] Sharmaji responded by bursting into raucous laughter and Verma smiled. Sharmaji told him, "You were right," laughing all the while. Verma said to the young men, "I'll be happy to do your work even for Rs. 10, but first you'll need the signature of the headman of your village, that's the law." Sharmaji told them that they didn't know anything about the law, that it took more than Rs. 14 just for the cost of the application because in order to add a name to a plot, the application would have to be backdated by a few months. At the mention of the headman, the young men became dismayed. They explained that relations were not good between them and the headman and that they were in opposite camps. I sensed that Verma had known this all along.

Sharmaji then told the young men that they should have first found out "what it cost" to "get a name added to the register" these days. "Go and find out the cost of putting your name in the land register," he told them, "and then give Verma exactly half of that." He immediately turned to one of the farmers present and asked him how much he had paid ten years ago. The man said it had been something like Rs. 150. Then both Sharmaji and Verma got up abruptly and left for lunch.

The young men turned to the other people and asked them if they knew what the appropriate sum was. All of them gave figures ranging from Rs. 130–150 but said that their information was dated because that is how much it had cost ten or more years ago. The young men tried to put a good face on the bungled negotiation by suggesting that it would not be a big loss if they did not succeed in their efforts. If they did not get the loan, they would continue to farm as they usually did – that is, without fertilizer.

No one could tell them what the current figure was. Even Man Friday, who was still sitting there, refused to answer, saying it was not for him to intervene, and that it was all up to Sharmaji and Verma. The "practice" of bribe giving was not, as the young men learned, simply an economic transaction but a cultural practice that required a great degree of performative competence. When villagers complained about the corruption of state officials, therefore, they were not just voicing their exclusion from government services because these were costly, although that was no small factor. More importantly, they were expressing frustration because they lacked the cultural capital required to negotiate deftly for those services.[21]

The entire episode was skillfully managed by Sharmaji and Verma. Although they came away empty-handed from this particular round of negotiations, they knew that the young men would eventually be back and would then have to pay even more than the going rate to get the same job done. Sharmaji appeared in turns as the benefactor and the supplicant pleading with his colleague on behalf of the clients. Verma managed to appear to be willing to do the work. The act of giving the bribe became entirely a gesture of goodwill on the part of the customers rather than a conscious mechanism to grease the wheels. Interestingly, a great deal of importance was attached to not naming a sum.

In this case, state officials got the better of a couple of inexperienced clients. Petty officials, however, do not always have their way. In the implementation of development programs, for example, local officials often have to seek out beneficiaries in order to meet targets set by higher authorities. The beneficiaries of these programs can then employ the authority of the upper levels of the bureaucracy to exert some pressure on local officials.

Several houses have been constructed in Alipur under two government programs, the Indira Awaas Yojana and the Nirbal Varg Awaas Yojana (literally, the Indira Housing Program and the Weaker Sections Housing Program, respectively). Both programs are intended to benefit poor people who do not have a brick (*pucca*) house. The Indira Awaas Yojana was meant for landless *harijans* (untouchables), whereas the Nirbal Varg Awaas Yojana was for all those who owned less than one acre of land, lacked a brick house, and had an income below a specified limit.[22]

I was told that one of the "beneficiaries" was Sripal, so I spoke to him outside his new house. Sripal was a thin, small-boned man, not more than 25 years old, who lived in a cluster of low-caste (*jatav*) homes in the village. When I saw the brick one-room dwelling constructed next to his mother's house, I could not help remarking that it looked quite solid. But Sripal immediately dismissed that notion.

Sripal was selected for this program by the village headman, Sher Singh. When his name was approved, the village development worker[23] took him to the town, had his photograph taken, and then opened an account in his name in a bank. For the paperwork he was charged Rs. 200. After that he was given a slip (*parchi*) that entitled him to pick up predetermined quantities of building material from a store designated by the village development worker. The money required to get the material transported to the construction site came out of his own pocket. The village development worker asked him to pay an additional Rs. 500 to get the bricks. Sripal pleaded that he did not have any money. "Take Rs. 1,000 if you want from the cost of the material [from the portion of the house grant reserved for purchasing materials], but don't ask me to pay you anything."

Sripal claimed that this was exactly what the village development worker had done, providing him with material worth only Rs. 6,000 out of the Rs. 7,000 allocated to him.[24] Once again he had to fork out the transportation expense to have the bricks delivered from a kiln near the village. Sripal claimed that the bricks given to him were inferior yellow bricks (*peelay eenth*) that had been improperly baked. He also discovered that the cost of labor was supposed to be reimbursed to him. Although he had built the house himself because he was an expert mason, he never received the Rs. 300 allocated for labor costs in the program.

As if this were not enough, Sripal did not receive any material for a door and a window, so it was impossible to live in the new house. No official had come to inspect the work to see if there was anything missing. Sripal complained that those whose job it was to inspect the buildings just sat in their offices and approved the construction because they were the ones who had the authority to create the official record ("They are the ones who have pen and paper [*kaagaz-kalam unhee kay paas hai*]"). Sripal himself is illiterate.

Frustrated about his doorless house, he lodged complaints at the Block office and at the bank that lent him the money for construction. Meanwhile, Sher Singh, who had been employing Sripal as a daily laborer on his farm, became angry at Sripal for refusing to come to work one day. Sripal explained that he could not possibly have gone because his relatives had come over that day and that to leave them would have been construed as inhospitable. In any case, Sripal said, he could not do any heavy work because he had broken his arm some time ago.

When Sher Singh found out that Sripal had complained about him and the village development worker at the Block office, he threatened to beat him up so badly that he would never enter the village again. Fearing the worst, Sripal fled from the village and went to live with his in-laws. Despite the threat to his life, Sripal was not daunted in his efforts to seek justice. When he saw that his complaints elicited no response, he approached a lawyer to draft a letter to the District Magistrate, the highest administrative authority in the area. This strategy paid off in that a police contingent was sent to the village to investigate. When I asked Sripal to tell me what the letter said, he produced a copy of it for me. "What can I tell you?" he asked. "Read it yourself." The letter alleged that the village development worker had failed to supply the necessary material and that because the headman had threatened to beat him up he had been forced to flee the village.

After the police visit, Sher Singh made peace with Sripal. He even hired Sripal to construct a home for another person under the same program. In addition, Sher Singh stopped asking Sripal to come to labor on his farm. But the village development worker threatened Sripal with imprisonment unless he paid back Rs. 3,000 toward the cost of completing the house.[25] "One of my relatives is a jail warden [*thanedaar*]," he reportedly told Sripal. "If you don't pay up, I'll have you put away in jail." Sitting in front of the empty space that was to be the door to his house, Sripal told me that he was resigned to going to jail. "What difference does it make?" he asked. "Living like this is as good as being dead."

Even though he was ultimately unsuccessful in his appeals for justice, Sripal's case demonstrates that even members of the subaltern classes have a practical knowledge of the multiple levels of state authority. Faced with the depredations of the headman and village development worker, Sripal had appealed to the authority of a person three rungs higher in the bureaucratic hierarchy. Because the central and state governments are theoretically committed to protecting scheduled caste people such as Sripal, his complaint regarding the threat to his life was taken quite seriously. Sending the police to the village was a clear warning to Sher Singh that if he dared to harm Sripal physically, he would risk retaliation from the repressive arm of the state.

Before leaving this episode with Sripal, I want to address explicitly what it tells us about transnational linkages. Clearly, one cannot expect to find *visible* transnational dimensions to every grassroots encounter; that would require a kind of immediate determination that is empirically untrue and analytically indefensible. For example, IMF conditionalities do not directly explain this particular episode in the house-building program. But by forcing the Indian government to curtail domestic expenditure, the conditionalities do have budgetary implications for such programs. These influence which programs are funded, how they are implemented and at what levels, who is targeted, and for how many years such programs continue. Similarly, if one wants to understand why development programs such as building houses for the poor exist in the first place and why they are initiated and managed by the state, one must place them in the context of a regime of "development" that came into being in the postwar international order of decolonized nation-states (Escobar 1984, 1988; Ferguson 1990). What happens at the grassroots is thus complexly mediated, sometimes through multiple relays, sometimes more directly, by such linkages.[26]

Sripal's experience of pitting one organization of the state against others and of employing the multiple layers of state organizations to his advantage no doubt shaped his construction of the state. At the same time, he appeared defeated in the end by the procedures of a bureaucracy whose rules he could not comprehend. Sripal was among those beneficiaries of "development" assistance who regretted ever accepting help. He became deeply alienated by the very programs that the state employed to legitimate its rule. The implementation of development programs therefore forms a key arena where representations of the state are constituted and where its legitimacy is contested.

One can also find contrasting instances where local officials are on the receiving end of villagers' disaffection with state institutions. Some examples are provided by several actions of the Bharatiya Kisan Union (BKU). One of the most frequent complaints of farmers is that they have to pay bribes to officials of the Hydel Department to replace burned-out transformers. Each such transformer typically serves five to ten tubewells. A young farmer related a common incident to me. The transformer supplying electricity to his tubewell and those of 11 of his neighbors blew out. So they contributed Rs. 150 each (approximately $ 10 at exchange rates prevailing then) and took the money to the assistant engineer of the Hydel Department. They told him that their crops were dying for a lack of water and that they were in deep trouble. He reportedly said, "What can I do? We don't have the replacement equipment at the present time." So they gave him the Rs. 1,800 they had pooled and requested that the transformer be replaced as soon as possible. He took the money and promised them that the job would be done in a few days, as soon as the equipment was in. Being an "honest" man (that is, one true to his word), he had the transformer installed three days later.

When the same situation recurred shortly thereafter, the young man went to the Kisan Union people and requested that they help him get a new transformer. So about 50 of them climbed on tractors, went straight to the executive engineer's house and camped on his lawn (a common form of civil disobedience in India is to *gherao* [encircle and prevent movement of] a high official). They refused to move until a new transformer had been installed in the village. The executive engineer promised them that he "would send men at once." Sure enough, the linemen came the following day and replaced it.

Not all such incidents ended amicably. The quick response of these officials was due to the fact that the Kisan Union had already established itself as a powerful force in that particular area, as will be evident from a few examples. In one incident, a crowd walked off with six transformers from an electricity station in broad daylight (*Aaj* 1989f). The farmers no longer feared the police and revenue officials, on occasion "arresting" the officials, tying them to trees, and making them do "sit-ups." They refused to pay electricity dues (up to 60 percent of agricultural sector dues remain unpaid in a nearby district) and forced "corrupt" officials to return money allegedly taken as bribes. I also heard about an incident in an adjacent village where employees of the electricity board were caught stealing some copper wire from a transformer by irate villagers who proceeded to beat them up and "jail" them in a village house.

It should be clear from all the incidents described above that lower-level officials play a crucial role in citizens' encounters with "the state." Obviously, no singular characterization of the nature and content of the interaction of villagers and bureaucrats is possible. In contrast to Sharmaji and Verma, who manipulate their gullible clients, stand the officials who are manhandled by the peasant activists of the BKU. Similarly, just as local officials employ their familiarity with bureaucratic procedures to carry out or obstruct a transaction by maneuvering between different levels of the administrative hierarchy, so too do subaltern people such as Sripal demonstrate a practical competence in using the hierarchical nature of state institutions to their own ends. At the local level it becomes difficult to experience the state as an ontically coherent entity: what one confronts instead is much more discrete and fragmentary – land records officials, village development workers, the Electricity Board, headmen, the police, and the Block Development Office. Yet (and it is this seemingly contradictory fact that we must always keep in mind) it is precisely through the practices of such local institutions that a translocal institution such as the state comes to be imagined.

The local-level encounters with the state described in this section help us discern another significant point. Officials such as Sharmaji, who may very well constitute a majority of state employees occupying positions at the bottom of the bureaucratic pyramid, pose an interesting challenge to Western notions of the boundary between "state" and "society" in some obvious ways. The Western historical experience has been built on states that put people in locations distinct from their homes – in offices, cantonments, and courts – to mark their "rationalized" activity as office holders in a bureaucratic apparatus. People such as Sharmaji collapse this distinction not only between their roles as public servants and as private citizens at the site of their activity, but also in their styles of operation.[27] Almost all other similarly placed officials in different branches of the state operate in an analogous manner. One has a better chance of finding them at the roadside tea stalls and in their homes than in their offices. Whereas modernization theorists would invariably interpret this as further evidence of the failure of efficient institutions to take root in a Third World context, one might just as easily turn the question around and inquire into the theoretical adequacy (and judgmental character) of the concepts through which such actions are described. In other words, if officials like Sharmaji and the village development worker are seen as thoroughly blurring the boundaries between "state" and "civil society," it is perhaps because those categories are descriptively inadequate to the lived realities that they purport to represent.

Finally, it may be useful to draw out the implications of the ethnographic material presented in this section for what it tells us about corruption and the implementation of policy. First, the people described here – Sharmaji, the village development worker, the Electricity Board officials – are not unusual or exceptional in the manner in which they conduct their official duties, in their willingness to take bribes, for example, or in their conduct toward different classes of villagers. Second, despite the fact that lower-level officials' earnings from bribes are substantial, it is important to locate them in a larger "system" of corruption in which their superior officers are firmly implicated. In fact, Sharmaji's bosses depend on his considerable ability to maneuver land records for their own transactions, which are several orders of magnitude larger than his. His is a "volume business," theirs a "high margin" one. He helps them satisfy their clients and, in the process, buys protection and insurance for his own activities.

This latter aspect calls for elaboration. It is often claimed that even well-designed government programs fail in their implementation, and that the best of plans founder due to widespread corruption at the lower levels of the bureaucracy. If this is intended to explain why government programs fail, it is patently inaccurate (as well as being class-biased). For it is clear that lower-level officials are only one link in a chain of corrupt practices that extends to the apex of state organizations and reaches far beyond them to electoral politics (Wade 1982, 1984, 1985). Politicians raise funds through senior bureaucrats for electoral purposes, senior bureaucrats squeeze this money from their subordinates as well as directly from projects that they oversee, and subordinates follow suit. The difference is that whereas higher-level state officials raise large sums from the relatively few people who can afford to pay it to them, lower-level officials collect it in small figures and on a daily basis from a very large number of people. It is for this reason that corruption is so much more visible at the lower levels.

The "system" of corruption is of course not just a brute collection of practices whose most widespread execution occurs at the local level. It is also a discursive field that enables the phenomenon to be labeled, discussed, practiced, decried, and denounced. The next section is devoted to the analysis of the discourse of corruption, and especially to its historically and regionally situated character.

The Discourse of Corruption in Public Culture

Analyzing the discourse of corruption draws attention to the powerful cultural practices by which the state is symbolically represented to its employees and to citizens of the nation.[28] Representations of the state are constituted, contested, and transformed in public culture. Public culture is a zone of cultural debate conducted through the mass media, other mechanical modes of reproduction, and the visible practices of institutions such as the state (Appadurai 1990; Appadurai and Breckenridge 1988; Gilroy 1987; Gurevitch et al. 1982; Hall et al. 1980; Waites et al. 1982). It is "the site and stake" (Hall 1982) of struggles for cultural meaning. For this reason the analysis of reports in local and national newspapers tells us a great deal about the manner in which "the state" comes to be imagined.[29]

The importance of the media was brought home to me when, barely two months after Rajiv Gandhi was elected prime minister in late 1984, a higher-caste village elder whose son was a businessman with close connections to the Congress (I) told me, "Rajiv has failed." I was surprised to hear him say this and asked why he thought so. He replied, "Rajiv promised to eradicate corruption in his campaign but has it happened? He hasn't done anything about it." Although Rajiv Gandhi had not visited the area around Alipur during his campaign, this man was keenly aware of all of his campaign promises. Like many others in Alipur, he listened nightly to the BBC World Service news broadcast in Hindi as well as to the government-controlled national radio (*Akaashvaani*). He was well-informed on international events and would often ask me detailed questions regarding contemporary events in the United States or Iran.

Although radio and television obviously play a significant role as mass media, newspapers are perhaps the most important mechanism in public culture for the circulation of discourses on corruption.[30] In the study of translocal phenomena such as "the state," newspapers contribute to the raw material necessary for "thick" description. This should become evident by comparing newspaper reports – conceptualized as cultural texts and sociohistorical documents – to oral interviews. Since newspaper reports are invariably filed by locally resident correspondents, they constitute, as do oral interviews, a certain form of situated knowledge. Obviously, perceiving them as having a privileged relation to the truth of social life is naive; they have much to offer us, however, when seen as a major discursive form through which daily life is narrativized and collectivities imagined. Of course, the narratives presented in newspapers are sifted through a set of institutional filters, but their representations are not, for that reason alone, more deeply compromised. Treated with benign neglect by students of contemporary life, they mysteriously metamorphize into invaluable "field data" once

they have yellowed around the edges and fallen apart at the creases.[31] And yet it is not entirely clear by what alchemy time turns the "secondary" data of the anthropologist into the "primary" data of the historian.

Apart from theoretical reasons that may be adduced to support the analysis of newspaper reports, the importance of all vernacular newspapers, whether regional or national dailies, lies in the fact that they carry special sections devoted to local news.[32] These are distributed only in the region to which the news applies. Thus, if one picks up the same newspaper in two different cities in Uttar Pradesh, some of the pages inside will have entirely different contents. News about a particular area, therefore, can only be obtained by subscribing to newspapers within that area. In this restricted sense, newspaper reports about a particular area can only be obtained within "the field."[33]

The method of studying the state advanced in this article relates the discourse of corruption in the vernacular and English-language press to statements made by villagers and state officials. We will see that local discourses and practices concerning corruption were intimately linked with the reportage found in vernacular and national newspapers. This point will be demonstrated by first looking at a few examples from the national, English-language press and then mostly at vernacular newspapers.[34]

Corruption as an issue dominated two of the three national elections held in the 1980s. In its summary of the decade, the fortnightly news magazine *India Today* headlined the section on "The '80s: Politics" in the following manner: "The politics of communalism, corruption and separatism dominates an eventful decade" (Chawla 1990:18).[35] Rajiv Gandhi's election in November 1984 was fought largely on the slogans of the eradication of corruption and preserving the nation's integrity in the face of separatist threats from Sikhs. Precisely because he was initially dubbed "Mr. Clean," the subject of corruption later came to haunt him as his administration came under a cloud for allegedly accepting kickbacks from Bofors, a Swedish small-arms manufacturer. In fact, Bofors became the centerpiece of the opposition's successful effort to overthrow his regime. In the elections of 1989, in which a non-Congress government came to power for only the second time in 43 years of electoral politics, another Mr. Clean, V. P. Singh, emerged as the leader. He had earlier been unceremoniously booted out of Rajiv Gandhi's cabinet because, as defense minister, he had started an investigation into the "Bofors Affair." The effect of Bofors was electorally explosive precisely because it became a symbol of corruption at all levels of the state. For example, the conductor on the notoriously inefficient Uttar Pradesh State Roadways bus justified not returning change to me by saying, "If Rajiv Gandhi can take 64 crore in bribes, what is the harm in my taking 64 paisa on a ticket?"[36]

The discourse of corruption, however, went far beyond just setting the terms of electoral competition between political parties. It not only helped to define "the political" but also served to constitute "the public" that was perceived to be reacting to corruption. Since this was done largely through the mass media, we must pay careful attention to newspapers as cultural texts that give us important clues to the political culture of the period. In a series of major preelection surveys, the widely read metropolitan English daily, the *Times of India*, attempted to analyze the political impact of Bofors and set out to establish how the *electorate* viewed corruption. One of its articles begins by quoting a villager who remarked, "If one [political party, i.e., Congress] is a poisonous snake, the other [opposition party] is a cobra" (*Times of India* 1989:1). The article went on to say: "Whether the Congress is in power or the opposition makes no difference to the common man and woman who has to contend with proliferating corruption which affects every sphere of life.... Bofors doesn't brush against their lives. The pay-off for a ration card or a job does" (1989:1).

The article further elaborated the relationship between the "ordinary citizen" and the state with reference to the role of formal politics and politicians:

> In U.P., the majority felt that [increasing corruption] stemmed from the growing corruption in political circles. M. P. Verma, a backward class leader from Gonda pointed out that politicians today are driven by a one-point programme – to capture power at all costs. And the vast sums expended on elections are obtained by unfair means. "Without corruption there is no politics," said Aminchand Ajmera, a businessman from Bhopal. [*Times of India* 1989:1]

The theme of corruption was prominent in an article on a central government scheme to help the poor in *India Today*, which pointed out how the resources being allocated by the central government were being misused by the state government in Madhya Pradesh (1989).[37] In this example, formal politics was not reduced to competition among political *parties* and the bureaucratic apparatus (where payoffs for jobs are given) was not confused with the regime (where the benefits of Bofors presumably went). Instead, the discourse of corruption became a means by which a fairly complex picture of the state was symbolically constructed in public culture.

In addition, I examined the local editions of six Hindi newspapers with different political orientations most commonly read in the Mandi area: *Aaj, Dainik Jaagran, Amar Ujaala, Hindustan, Rashtriya Sahaara,* and *Jansatta*. There were significant differences between the English-language magazines and newspapers mentioned above, with their urban, educated, "middle-class" readership, and the vernacular press. The reason lay in the structural location of the national English-language dailies within the "core" regions – the urban centers of capital, high politics, administration, and education. The vernacular newspapers maintained a richer sense of the multilayered nature of the state because their reportage was necessarily focused on events in different localities, which corresponded to lower levels of the state hierarchy. They could not, however, simultaneously ignore events at the higher levels of state (region) and nation. By contrast, metropolitan newspapers focused almost exclusively on large-scale events, with local bureaucracies featuring chiefly in the letters of complaint written by citizens about city services. The vernacular press therefore particularly clearly delineated the multilayered and pluricentric nature of "the state."

The Hindi newspapers with limited regional circulations, read mostly by the residents of the many small towns and large villages dotting the countryside, in fact were, as opposed to the "national" Hindi dailies such as the *Navbharat Times*, much less prone to reify the state as a monolithic organization with a single chain of command. They made a practice of explicitly naming specific departments of the state bureaucracy. The vernacular press also seemed to pursue stories of corruption with greater zeal than its metropolitan counterpart.[38]

For example, the daily *Aaj* had headlines such as the following: "Police Busy Warming Own Pockets" (1989a),[39] "Plunder in T. B. Hospital" (1989e), and "Farmers Harassed by Land Consolidation Official" (1989d). In none of these reports was the state (*sarkaar*) invoked as a unitary entity. In all of them, specific departments were named, and very often specific people as well. They also documented in great detail exactly what these corrupt practices were. For example, the article on the tuberculosis hospital stated exactly how much money was "charged" for each step (Rs. 5 for a test, Rs. 10 for the doctor, Rs. 5 for the compounder, and so on) in a treatment that was supposed to be provided free of charge. The article on the land consolidation officer named him and stated how much money he demanded in bribes from specific farmers (also named). Similarly, the news story on the police reported that a specific precinct was extorting money from vehicle owners by threatening to issue bogus citations.

Two features of these reports were particularly striking. First, state officials higher up

the hierarchy were often depicted as completely unresponsive to complaints and even as complicit with the corrupt practices. "Despite several complaints by citizens to the head of the region, nothing has been done," was a familiar refrain in the reports. For instance, one short report stated that the dealer who had the contract to distribute subsidized rations of sugar and kerosene was selling them on the black market with political protection and the full knowledge of regional supervisors (*Aaj* 1989b). Similarly, another story, "To Get Telephone To Work, Feed Them Sweets" (*Aaj* 1989c), reported that corrupt employees of the telephone department told customers that they could go ahead and complain as much as they wanted, but, unless the telephone workers got their favorite sweetmeats,[40] the customers' telephones would not work.

The second noteworthy feature in regional newspaper accounts was their emphasis on, and construction of, *the public*. A common discursive practice was to talk of "the public" (*janata*) that was being openly exploited by the police, or "the citizens" (*naagarik*) who were harassed by blackmarketeering, or "the people" (*log*) whose clear accusation against the hospital was given voice in the paper, or "simple farmers" (*bholaay-bhaalaay kisaan*) who were ruthlessly exploited by the land consolidation officer. In all cases, the function of the press appeared to be that of creating a space in which the grievances of the masses could be aired and the common good (*janhit*) pursued.

The press was of course doing much more than simply airing preexisting grievances. The state constructed here was one that consisted of widely disparate institutions with little or no coordination among them, of multiple levels of authority, none of which were accountable to ordinary people, and employees (secure in the knowledge that they could not be fired) who treated citizens with contempt. At the same time, these reports also created subjects[41] who were represented as being exploited, powerless, and outraged. I foreground the newspapers' functions in order to draw attention to the rhetorical strategy deployed by the mass media to galvanize into action citizens who expect state institutions to be accountable to them.

Although I have sharply differentiated the English-language and vernacular press in their representations of "the state" and the construction of subjects, one must keep two caveats in mind at all times. First, if one looks at newspapers from different regions of Uttar Pradesh, and published in other languages (for example, Urdu), wide variations are to be found within the vernacular press.[42] Second, the mass media is not the only important source for the circulation of representations of "the state" in public culture. Police and administration officials repeatedly voice their frustration at their inability to counter "wild stories" and "rumors" that contest and contradict the official version of events. Police officials in an adjoining district are quoted in the *Times of India* as saying, "They go about spreading rumours and we can't fight them effectively. These rumours help gather crowds. And the agitated crowd then turns on the police, provoking a clash" (Mitra and Ahmed 1989:12). The "bush telegraph" [*sic*] spreads rumors quickly and convincingly (Mitra 1989).[43] Unlike other technologies of communication such as newspapers, radio, and television, rumor cannot be controlled by simply clamping down on the source of production (Coombe 1993). Rumor therefore becomes an especially effective vehicle to challenge official accounts, especially when agencies of the state transgress local standards of behavior.

By definition, corruption is a violation of norms and standards of conduct.[44] The other face of a discourse of corruption, therefore, is a discourse of accountability.[45] Herzfeld puts the emphasis in the right place when he says that "accountability is a socially produced, culturally saturated amalgam of ideas about person, presence, and polity...[whose] meaning is culturally specific...[and whose] management of personal or collective identity cannot break free of social experience" (1992a:47). Expectations of "right" behavior,

standards of accountability, and norms of conduct for state officials, in other words, come from social groups as well as from "the state."[46] Sometimes these standards and norms converge; more often, they do not. Thus, there are always divergent and conflicting assessments of whether a particular course of action is "corrupt." Subjects' deployment of discourses of corruption are necessarily mediated by their structural location (this point is developed further below). But state officials are also multiply positioned within different regimes of power: in consequence, they simultaneously employ, and are subject to, quite varying discourses of accountability. The manner in which these officials negotiate the tensions inherent in their location in their daily practices both helps to create certain representations of the state and powerfully shapes assessments of it, thereby affecting its legitimacy. In fact, struggles for legitimacy can be interpreted in terms of the effort to construct the state and "the public" symbolically in a particular manner.

Moreover, if one were to document the transformations in the discourse of corruption from colonial times to the present (a project beyond the scope of this article), it would be clear that the postcolonial state has itself generated new discourses of accountability. Actions tolerated or considered legitimate under colonial rule may be classified as "corrupt" by the rule-making apparatuses of the independent nation-state because an electoral democracy is deemed accountable to "the people." The sense of pervasive corruption in a country such as India might then itself be a consequence of the changes in the discourse of accountability promulgated by postcolonial nationalists. In addition, significant changes *during* the postcolonial period have arisen from the pressures of electoral politics (as evidenced by the Bofors controversy) and from peasant mobilization. In the Mandi region, the Kisan Union has been very successful in organizing peasants against the state by focusing on the issue of corruption among lower levels of the bureaucracy.

Although there are variations in the discourse of corruption *within* regions and *during* the postcolonial era, the end of colonialism constitutes a significant transition. One of the reasons for this is that nationalist as opposed to colonial regimes seek the kind of popular legitimacy that will enable them to act in the name of "the people." They thus place new responsibilities on state employees and vest new rights in subjects who are then constituted as citizens. The postcolonial state consciously sets out to create subject positions unknown during the colonial era: "citizenship" does not just mark inclusiveness in a territorial domain but indicates a set of rights theoretically invested in subjects who inhabit the nation.[47] One of the crucial ingredients of discourses of citizenship in a populist democracy such as India has been that state employees are considered accountable to "the people" of the country. The discourse of corruption, by marking those actions that constitute an infringement of such rights, thus acts to represent the rights of citizens to themselves.[48]

The role of the Kisan Union further highlights significant regional variations in the discourse of corruption. Western Uttar Pradesh, the region where Mandi is located, has been the center of very successful agrarian mobilizations led by the class of well-to-do peasants. This movement was first led by Chaudhary Charan Singh, a former prime minister who consistently mounted an attack on the "urban bias" of state policies. It is now been given a new direction by the Kisan Union led by Mahendar Singh Tikait.[49] The landowning castes in this region have become fairly prosperous as they have been the chief beneficiaries of the green revolution. But this newfound wealth has yet to be translated into bureaucratic power and cultural capital. In other words, given the central role that state institutions play in rural life, these groups seek to stabilize the conditions for the reproduction of their dominance. Because they perceive the state to be acting against their interests, they deploy the discourse of corruption to undermine the credibility of the state and to attack the manner in which government organizations operate.[50]

The discourse of corruption is central to our understanding of the relationship between the state and social groups precisely because it plays this dual role of enabling people to construct the state symbolically and to define themselves as citizens. For it is through such representations, and through the public practices of various government agencies, that the state comes to be marked and delineated from other organizations and institutions in social life. The state itself and whatever is construed to stand apart from it – community, polity, society, civil society (Kligman 1990), political society – are all culturally constructed in specific ideological fields. It is hence imperative that we constantly contextualize the construction of the state within particular historical and cultural conjunctures. I have employed the discourse of corruption as a means to demonstrate how the state comes to be imagined in one such historical and cultural context. The discourse of corruption here functions as a diagnostic of the state.

The Imagined State

Banwari, a scheduled caste resident of Ashanwad hamlet, 25 kms. from Jaipur said, "I haven't seen the vidhan sabha or the Lok Sabha.[51] The only part of the government I see is the police station four kms. from my house. And that is corrupt. The police demand bribes and don't register complaints of scheduled caste people like me." [*Times of India* 1989: 7]

So far, this article has dealt with the practices of local levels of the bureaucracy and the discourses of corruption in public culture, respectively. Together, they enable a certain construction of the state that meshes the imagined translocal institution with its localized embodiments. The government, in other words, is being constructed here in the imagination and everyday practices of ordinary people. Of course, this is exactly what "corporate culture" and nationalism do: they make possible and then naturalize the construction of such nonlocalizable institutions. It then becomes very important to understand the mechanisms, or modalities, that make it possible to imagine the state. What is the process whereby the "reality" of translocal entities comes to be experienced?

To answer this question, one must grasp the pivotal role of public culture, which represents one of the most important modalities for the discursive construction of "the state." Obviously, not everyone imagines the state in quite the same manner. So far, very little research has been done on the relationship between diversely located groups of people and their employment of the different media of representation and of varying resources of cultural capital in imagining "the state." For example, Ram Singh and his sons are relatively prosperous men from one of the lowest castes (*jatav*) in Alipur. They had recently acquired a television set as part of the dowry received in the marriage of one of the sons. Ram Singh told me, in a confession born of a mixture of pride and embarrassment, that since the television had arrived their farm work had suffered because, instead of irrigating the crop, they would all sit down and watch television. (Both the pumpsets used for irrigation and the television set were dependent on erratic and occasional supplies of electricity.) Television was a constant point of reference in Ram Singh's conversation.

I interviewed Ram Singh in the context of the impending elections (the elections took place in December 1989; the conversation dates from late July). He said:

The public is singing the praises of Rajiv [Gandhi].[52] He is paying really close attention to the needs of poor people [*Bahut gaur kar raha hain*]. Rajiv has been traveling extensively in the rural areas and personally finding out the problems faced by the poor. For this reason, I will definitely support the Congress (l).

We consider the government which supports us small people as if it were our mother and father [*Usi ko ham maa-baap key samaan maantey hain*]. If it weren't for the Congress, no one would pay any attention to the smaller castes [*chotee jaat*]. Not even god looks after us, only the Congress.

At this point, his son intervened:

The Congress is for all the poor, not just for the lower castes. It is exerting itself to the utmost, trying to draw people into [government] jobs [*Bahut jor laga rahen hain, naukri mein khichai kar rahen hain*].

Ram Singh returned to the discussion:

Although the government has many good schemes, the officials in the middle eat it all [*beech mey sab khaa jaate hain*]. The government is making full efforts to help the poor, but the officials don't allow any of the schemes to reach the poor.

"Doesn't the government knows that officials are corrupt?" I asked. "Why doesn't it do anything?" Ram Singh replied:

It does know a little bit but not everything. The reason is that the voice of the poor doesn't reach people at the top [*Garibon ki awaaz vahaan tak pahuchti nahin*]. If, for example, the government sets aside four lakhs for a scheme, only one lakh will actually reach us – the rest will be taken out in the middle.[53]

Ram Singh's position here displays some continuity with an older, hierarchical vision of the state.[54] Typically, in such views, the ruler appears as benevolent and charitable whereas the local official is seen as corrupt. While this may very well be the case, I think that one can adequately explain Ram Singh's outlook by examining contemporary practices rather than the sedimentation of beliefs.[55] One should look at practices of the state that reinforce this outlook. When a complaint of corruption is lodged against a local official, the investigation is always conducted by an official of a higher rank. Higher officials are thus seen as providing redressals for grievances and punishing local officials for corrupt behavior.

Ram Singh's case reminds us that all constructions of the state have to be situated with respect to the location of the speaker. Ram Singh's particular position helps us understand why he imagines the state as he does. He is an older, scheduled-caste man whose household now owns one of the five television sets in the village, a key symbol of upward mobility. Several of his sons are educated, and two of them have obtained relatively good government jobs as a consequence.[56] The scheduled castes of this area in general, and the jatavs in particular, have historically supported successive Congress regimes.

The first thing that impresses one about Ram Singh's interpretation of "the state" is how clearly he understands its composition as an entity with multiple layers and diverse locales and centers. Although the word for regime and state is the same in Hindi (sarkaar),[57] Ram Singh maintains a distinction between the regime and the bureaucracy. He sees the regime's good intentions toward the lower castes being frustrated by venal state officials. Clearly, Ram Singh has a sense that there are several layers of "government" above the one that he has always dealt with (the very top personified by then-Prime Minister Rajiv Gandhi), and that the different levels can exert opposing pulls on policy (specifically, those that affect a scheduled-caste person like him). Interestingly, Ram Singh reproduces an apologetics for the failure of policy (the formulation is all right, it is the implementors that are to blame) pervasively found in India's "middle classes," delivered by politicians belonging to the regime in power, and reproduced in the work of academics, higher bureaucrats, and sympathetic officials of international agencies.

The second striking fact about Ram Singh's testimony is that apart from his nuanced description of the state as a disaggregated and multilayered institution, his analysis closely parallels a discourse on the state that is disseminated by the mass media and is therefore translocal. Ram Singh's example demonstrates the importance of public culture in the discursive construction of the state: he talks knowledgeably about "the public's" perception of Rajiv and of Rajiv's itinerary. His son's perception of the Congress as being "for all the poor" clearly also owes a great deal to mass-mediated sources.

My suspicion that the close association with Rajiv Gandhi and the explanation about the corrupt middle levels of the state was influenced by the impact of television gained force when one of his sons explained:[58]

> We are illiterate people whose knowledge would be confined to the village. This way [i.e., by watching television], we learn a little bit about the outside world, about the different parts of India, about how other people live, we get a little more worldly [Kuch duniyaadaari seekh laayten hain].[59]

In the buildup to the elections, the government-controlled television network, Doordarshan, spent most of the nightly newscast following Rajiv Gandhi on his campaign tours. Obviously, it was not just the country that was being imagined on television through the representation of its different parts but also the national state through the image of "its" leader. Popular understandings of the state therefore are constituted in a discursive field where the mass media play a critical role. Ram Singh's words reveal the important part that national media play in "local" discourses on the state. Clearly, it is not possible to deduce Ram Singh's understanding of "the state" entirely from his personal interactions with the bureaucracy; conversely, it is apparent that he is not merely parroting the reports he obtains from television and newspapers.[60] Rather, what we see from this example is the articulation between (necessarily fractured) hegemonic discourses and the inevitably situated and interested interpretations of subaltern subjects. Ram Singh's everyday experiences lead him to believe that there *must* be government officials and agencies (whose presence, motives, and actions are represented to him through the mass media) interested in helping people like him. Only that could explain why his sons have succeeded in obtaining highly prized government jobs despite their neglect by local schoolteachers and their ill-treatment by local officials. Yet when he talks about "the public," and with a first-person familiarity about Rajiv's efforts on behalf of the poor, he is clearly drawing on a mass-mediated knowledge of *what* that upper-level of government comprises, who the agents responsible for its actions are, and what kinds of policies and programs they are promoting.[61]

There is obviously no Archimedean point from which to visualize "the state," only numerous situated knowledges (Haraway 1988). Bureaucrats, for example, imagine it through statistics (Hacking 1982), official reports, and tours, whereas citizens do so through newspaper stories, dealings with particular government agencies, the pronouncements of politicians, and so forth. Constructions of the state clearly vary according to the manner in which different actors are positioned. It is therefore important to situate a certain symbolic construction of the state with respect to the particular context in which it is realized. The importance of the mass media should not blind us to the differences that exist in the way that diversely situated people imagine the state.[62]

For instance, Ram Singh's position as a relatively well-to-do lower-caste person, whose family has benefited from rules regarding employment quotas for scheduled castes, explains his support for the higher echelons of government. At the same time, his interaction with local officials has taught him that they, like the powerful men in the villages, have little or no sympathy for lower-caste people like him. Therefore, he has a keen sense of the differences among different levels of the state. On the other hand, if he seems to share with the middle class a particular view

of the failure of government programs, it is the result of the convergence of what he has learned from his everyday encounters with the "state" with what he has discerned, as his son indicates, from the mass media. Congress rhetoric about being the party of the poor obviously resonates with Ram Singh's experience; that is why he calls the Congress government his guardians (*maa-baap*) and blames the officials in the middle for not following through with government programs. Ram Singh's view of the state thus is shaped both by his own encounters with local officials and by the translocal imagining of the state made possible by viewing television.

Conclusion

In this article I have focused on discourses of corruption in public culture and villagers' everyday encounters with local government institutions in order to work toward an ethnography of the state in contemporary India. Such a study raises a large number of complex conceptual and methodological problems, of which I have attempted to explore those that I consider central to any understanding of state institutions and practices.

The first problem has to do with the reification inherent in unitary descriptions of "the state."[63] When one analyzes the manner in which villagers and officials encounter the state, it becomes clear that it must be conceptualized in terms far more decentralized and disaggregated than has been the case so far. Rather than take the notion of "the state" as a point of departure, we should leave open the analytical question as to the conditions under which the state *does* operate as a cohesive and unitary whole.[64] All the ethnographic data presented in this article – the cases of Sharmaji, Sripal, Ram Singh, and the Kisan Union, and the reports from the vernacular press – point to a recognition of multiple agencies, organizations, levels, agendas, and centers that resists straightforward analytical closure.

The second major problem addressed in this article concerns the translocality of state institutions. I have argued that any analysis of the state requires us to conceptualize a space that is constituted by the intersection of local, regional, national, and transnational phenomena. Accordingly, I have stressed the role of public culture in the discursive construction of the state. Bringing the analysis of public culture together with the study of the everyday practices of lower levels of the bureaucracy helps us understand how the reality of translocal entities comes to be felt by villagers and officials.

The third important argument advanced in this article, also tied to the significance of public culture for an analysis of the state, has to do with the discursive construction of the state. Foregrounding the question of representation allows us to see the modalities by which the state comes to be imagined. The discourse of corruption and accountability together constitute one mechanism through which the Indian state came to be discursively constructed in public culture. It must be kept in mind that the discourse of corruption varies a great deal from one country to another, dependent as it is on particular historical trajectories and the specific grammars of public culture. Taking the international context of nation-states into account, however, brings their substantial similarities into sharp relief.[65] In order that a state may legitimately represent a nation in the international system of nation-states, it has to conform at least minimally to the requirements of a modern nation-state. The tension between legitimacy in the interstate system and autonomy and sovereignty is intensifying for nation-states with the continued movement toward an increasingly transnational public sphere. The accelerating circulation of cultural products – television and radio programs, news, films, videos, audio recordings, books, fashions – has been predicated on gigantic shifts in multinational capital. When this is tied to the reduction of trade barriers, the worldwide debt crisis (especially visible in Latin America, Africa, and Eastern Europe), offshore production, and the restructuring of markets (exemplified by the European Union), a

pattern of extensive crisscrossing emerges (Appadurai 1990). These complex cultural and ideological interconnections reveal that discourses of corruption (and hence of accountability) are *from the very beginning* articulated in a field formed by the intersection of many different transnational forces. In short, to understand how discourses of corruption symbolically construct "the state," we must inspect phenomena whose boundaries do not coincide with those of the nation-state. At the same time, however, these discourses do not operate homogeneously across the world. Rather, they articulate with distinctive historical trajectories to form unique hybridizations and creolizations in different settings (Gupta and Ferguson 1992).

The fourth significant point, which attends to the historical and cultural specificity of constructions of the state, has to do with vigilance toward the imperialism of the Western conceptual apparatus. Rather than begin with the notions of state and civil society that were forged on the anvil of European history, I focus on the modalities that enable the state (and, simultaneously, that which is not the state) to be discursively constructed. Looking at everyday practices, including practices of representation, and the representations of (state) practice in public culture helps us arrive at a historically specific and ideologically constructed understanding of "the state." Such an analysis simultaneously considers those other groupings and institutions that are imagined in the processes of contestation, negotiation, and collaboration with "the state." There is no reason to assume that there is, or should be, a unitary entity that stands apart from, and in opposition to, "the state," one that is mutually exclusive and jointly exhaustive of the social space. What I have tried to emphasize in this article is that the very same processes that enable one to construct the state also help one to imagine these other social groupings – citizens, communities (Chatterjee 1990), social groups (Bourdieu 1985), coalitions, classes, interest groups, civil society, polity, ethnic groups, subnational groups, political parties, trade unions, and farmers organizations. For the purposes of my argument, assembling these groups into some overarching relation was unnecessary. I therefore did not employ the notion of "civil society," which usually fills such a need, in this analysis of the discourses of corruption in India. Furthermore, it is not a concept indigenously invoked in the various processes of imagining identity that I have described here.[66]

The final question that this article addresses concerns political action and activism, concerns that should be included in the field of applied anthropology. In the context of the state, the collaboration/resistance dichotomy is unhelpful in thinking of strategies for political struggle. The reason is that such a gross bifurcation does not allow one to take advantage of the fact that the state is a formation that, as Stuart Hall puts it, "condenses" contradictions (Hall 1981, 1986a, 1986b). It also hides from view the fact that there is no position *strictly* outside or inside the state because what is being contested is the terrain of the ideological field. Any struggle against currently hegemonic configurations of power and domination involves a *cultural* struggle, what Gramsci has called the "war of position." What is at stake is nothing less than a transformation in the manner in which the state comes to be constructed. It is a struggle that problematizes the historical divide between those who choose to do political work "within" the state and those who work "outside" it, because the cultural construction of the state in public culture can result from, and affect, both in equal measure.

By pointing out that advocates of applied work and those who favor activist intervention may sometimes unintentionally share a common project of reifying "the state" and then locating themselves with respect to that totality (the one inside, the other outside), I neither intend to equate different modes of engagement nor to belittle the often politically sophisticated understandings that practitioners bring to their activities. All I wish to emphasize is that one's theory of "the state"

does greatly matter in formulating strategies for political action. Just as Gramsci's notion of hegemony led him to believe that 1917 may have been the last European example of vanguardism (what he called the "war of maneuver"), so my analysis of "the state" leads to the conclusion that we can attempt to exploit the contradictory processes that go into constituting "it." These contradictions not only address the divergent pulls exerted by the multiple agencies, departments, organizations, levels, and agendas of "the state" but also the contested terrain of public representation. If it is precisely in these practices of historical narrative and statistical abstraction, in equal parts thin fiction and brute fact, that the phenomenon of state fetishism emerges, we must remember how unstable and fragile this self-representation is and how it could *always* be *otherwise*. For example, I have shown how the discourse of corruption helps construct "the state"; yet at the same time it can potentially empower citizens by marking those activities that infringe on their rights.

One way to think about strategies of political action, about such dichotomies as applied/activist, inside/outside, policy analysis/class struggle, and developmentalism/revolution, is to draw an initial distinction between *entitlement* and *empowerment*.[67] The "machinery" of development, with its elaborate yet repetitive logic, focuses on the goal of delivering entitlements. As Jim Ferguson (1990) has argued, it does so in fact only to remove all discussion of empowerment from the discursive horizon (hence the title of his book, *The Anti-Politics Machine*). Yet the two are not mutually exclusive. And it is here that seizing on the fissures and ruptures, the contradictions in the policies, programs, institutions, and discourses of "the state" allows people to create possibilities for political action and activism.[68] I see critical reflection on the discourse of development as a point of departure for political action, not as a moment of arrival. Even as we begin to see that we need, as Arturo Escobar (1992) has felicitously put it, alternatives *to* development, and not development alternatives, we must learn not to scoff at a plebeian politics of opportunism, strategies that are alive to the conjunctural possibilities of the moment. Keynes served to remind economists and utopians that "*in the long run* we are all dead."[69] The poor, I might add, live only half as long.

NOTES

1   Instead of adopting the cumbersome technique of putting "the state" in quotation marks throughout the text, I will henceforth omit quotation marks except at points where I want to draw attention explicitly to the reified nature of the object denoted by that term.

2   Similar questions were raised earlier by Nader (1972:306–307).

3   Such an analysis has important implications for political action, as it suggests that the struggle for hegemony is built into the construction of the state. It rejects the reification of the state inherent both in vanguardist movements that seek to overthrow "it" and reformist movements that seek to work within "it."

4   Herzfeld remarks: "Thus anthropology, with its propensity to focus on the exotic and the remarkable, has largely ignored the practices of bureaucracy. . . . Yet this silence is, as Handelman has observed, a remarkable omission" (1992a:45). Handelman's work (1978, 1981) develops a call made by scholars such as Nader (1972) to "study up," and attempts to do for bureaucracies what ethnographers such as Rohlen (1974, 1983) have done for other institutions such as banks and schools.

5   It should be obvious that I am making a distinction between an empiricist epistemology and empirical methods. I am definitely *not* saying that empirical research needs to be abandoned.

6   The larger project has a significant oral historical and archival dimension as well as a wider sampling of the various media. See also Achille Mbembe's (1992) wonderful article for its suggestive use of newspaper reports.

7   See the articles by Mitchell (1989) and Taussig (1992) on this matter.

8   Handler's work (1985) very nicely demonstrates how these struggles work out in the case of objects that the regional government of Quebec wants to designate as the region's *patrimoine*.

9   The scandal, which came to be known as the Bofors Affair, allegedly involved a kickback in a gun ordered by the Indian government from a Swedish manufacturer. What gave the scandal such prominence is that it was widely believed that the kickback went to highly placed members of the government and the Congress party, perhaps even the prime minister. Naturally, the ruling party did not pursue the investigation with great enthusiasm, and no concrete proof was ever uncovered.

10 The phrase is Lata Mani's (1989).

11 Michael Woost's (1993) fine essay also addresses similar questions.

12 The term "Third World" encapsulates and homogenizes what are in fact diverse and heterogenous realities (Mohanty 1988). It implies further that "First" and "Third" worlds exist as separate and separable spaces (Ahmad 1987). I will thus capitalize it to highlight its problematic status. In a similar manner, "the West" is obviously not a homogenous and unified entity. I use it to refer to the effects of hegemonic representations of the West rather than its subjugated traditions. I therefore use the term simply to refer, not to a geographical space, but to a particular historical conjuncture of place, power, and knowledge.

13 A phenomenon that Johannes Fabian (1983) calls "allochronism."

14 This point has been made by Partha Chatterjee (1990) in response to Charles Taylor (1990); his recent book (1993) restates it and develops the argument further.

15 I am grateful to Dipesh Chakrabarty for first bringing this to my attention. See the excellent concluding chapter of his mono-

graph of the working class in Bengal (1989), in which he tackles this question head on.

16 The headman is an official elected by all the registered voters of a village. Political parties rarely participate in village elections in the sense that candidates do not represent national or regional parties when contesting these elections. Headmen are neither considered part of the administration nor the grassroots embodiment of political parties, although they may play important roles in representing the village to bureaucratic and party institutions.

17 Like all the other names in this article, this too is a pseudonym. In addition, owing to the sensitive nature of this material, the identities and occupations of all the people mentioned here have been altered beyond recognition.

18 Since the word "federal" is rarely used in India, I will refer to it by its Indian equivalent, that is, "central."

19 I use the term "hold court" because Sharmaji's mode of operation is reminiscent of an Indian *darbaar*, a royal court.

20 At the exchange rate prevailing at the time of the incident in 1989, $1 = Rs. 18, the client in effect handed Verma the equivalent of 56 cents. That figure is misleading, however, since it does not indicate purchasing power. Ten rupees would be enough to buy a hearty nonvegetarian lunch at a roadside restaurant for one person or one kilogram of high quality mangoes, but not enough for a pair of rubber slippers.

21 I find Judith Butler's (1990) concept of gender as performance very useful in thinking about this issue, particularly as it emphasizes that the agents involved are not following a cultural script governed by rule-following behavior. I am grateful to Don Moore for emphasizing this point to me.

22 This level was defined as Rs. 6,400 (approximately $215) per year for the 1992–93 fiscal year.

23 The village development worker is a functionary of the regional government who is responsible for the implementation of "development programs" in a small circle of villages, the number in the circle varying from three to a dozen depending on their populations. Like other government officials, the village development worker is subject to frequent transfers, at least once every three years.

24 Sripal claimed to know the exact amount by consulting "people who can read and write." The officials at the Block office told me, however, that a sum of Rs. 8,000 was allocated for such projects.

25 I later learned that Rs. 3,000 of the total cost is given as a loan that has to be paid back in 20 installments stretching across ten years.

26 To have explored the implications of the full chain of mediations for each ethnographic example would have taken the article far afield in too many different directions and made it lose its focus. This is a task that I propose to undertake in a full-length monograph. Here, I wanted to stress that we not forget that the detailed analysis of everyday life is overdetermined by transnational influences.

27 I would like to thank Joel Migdal for pointing this out to me.

28 The symbolic representation of the state is as yet largely unexplored territory, with a few notable exceptions. Bernard Cohn, for instance, has demonstrated how the Imperial Assemblage of 1877 enabled the British colonial state to represent its authority over India at the same time as it made "manifest and compelling the [colonial] sociology of India" (1987b:658). See also Nicholas Dirks's study of a small, independent state in precolonial and colonial South India (1987).

29 I have deliberately avoided use of the term "public sphere" in this article. As Habermas (1989[1962]) makes clear, the "public sphere" is the space where civil society emerges with the rise of bourgeois social formations. It is there

that critical, rational debate among bourgeois subjects could take place about a variety of topics, including the state, and it is there that checks on state power emerge through the force of literate public opinion (Peters 1993, 1995). Since the argument that follows raises doubts about the wholesale import of these categories to the particular context being analyzed, this notion of the "public sphere" is not particularly helpful. I should hasten to add that I am by no means implying that "the West" is unique in possessing a space for public debate and discussion. The notion of the public sphere, however, denotes a particular historical and cultural formation shaped by feudalism, kingly rule, the rise of capitalism, the importance of urban centers, and the dominant role of the church as an institution that is not replicated *in the same form* elsewhere in the world.

30   For those unfamiliar with the Indian context, it might be useful to point out that the reason why I am concentrating on newspapers is that whereas radio and television are strictly controlled by the government, the press is relatively autonomous and frequently critical of "the state." The only other important source of news in rural areas, transnational radio, remains limited in its coverage of India in that it remains focused on major stories and hence lacks the detail and specificity of newspaper accounts.

31   This is not to imply that anthropologists have not incorporated newspapers into their analysis in the past (see for example Benedict 1946). Herzfeld explains the marginal role of newspapers very clearly: "Journalism is treated as not authentically ethnographic, since it is both externally derived and rhetorically factual..... In consequence, the intrusion of media language into village discourse has largely been ignored" (1992b:94). Herzfeld makes a strong case for close scrutiny to newspapers even when the unit of analysis is "the village"; others

such as Benedict Anderson (1983) and Achille Mbembe (1992) have stressed the theoretical importance of newspapers in the construction of the nation and for the analysis of "the state," respectively.

32   This analysis of newspapers looks at connections between local and transnational *discourses* of corruption but not at the links between transnational *capital* and local newspapers. For example, although none of the locally distributed newspapers (English-language or vernacular) are even partially owned by transnational corporations, many of them depend on multinational wire service bureaus for international news. A detailed study would also have to account for the complex relationship between domestic and international capital accumulation. Further, the connection between the ownership and content of newspapers is an incredibly difficult one to establish and is quite beyond the scope of this article and the competence of the author. I wish to thank an anonymous reviewer for raising these stimulating questions.

33   Herzfeld has issued a warning that we would do well to heed: "We cannot usefully make any hard-and-fast distinctions between rural and urban, illiterate and learned (or at least journalistic), local and national. These terms – urbanity, literacy, the national interest, and their antonyms – appear *in* the villagers' discourse, and they are part *of* that discourse ... the larger discourses about Greece's place in the world both feed and draw nourishment from the opinions expressed in the tiniest village" (1992b:117). "Attacking 'the state' and 'bureaucracy' (often further reified as 'the system') is a tactic of social life, not an analytical strategy. Failure to recognize this is to essentialize essentialism. Ethnographically, it would lead us to ignore the multiplicity of sins covered by the monolithic stereotypes of 'the bureaucracy' and 'the state' " (1992a:45).

34 Although literacy rates are relatively low throughout the region, the impact of newspapers goes far beyond the literate population as news reports are orally transmitted across a wide range of groups. Political news on state-run television, *Doordarshan*, by contrast, is met with a high degree of skepticism, because everyone concerned knows that it is the mouthpiece of the government.

35 *India Today* is published in a number of Indian languages and has a large audience in small towns and villages. Corruption also figures prominently in the vernacular press, and in what follows I will compare the coverage there with magazines such as *India Today*.

36 At prevailing exchange rates, Rs. 64 crore = $36 million. Therefore, 64 paise was equal to 3.6 cents, less than the cost of a cup of tea.

37 The program in question is the Integrated Rural Development Programme.

38 This fact should dispel the myth that the discourse of corruption is to be found only among the urban middle class of "Westernized" Indians.

39 To warm one's pockets is a metaphor for taking a bribe. I have translated all the titles from the Hindi original.

40 The sweet in question is a regionally famous one – *pedaas*, from Mathura.

41 It would perhaps be more accurate to talk of "subject-positions" rather than "subjects" here.

42 In this article my analysis is limited to Hindi newspapers that publish local news of the Mandi region.

43 An excellent study of the importance of rumor in the countryside is to be found in Amin 1984. A fuller analysis would draw on the role of radio and television (both state-controlled) in all of this.

44 It is in this sense of violation of norms that the term is often extended to moral life quite removed from "the state," to mean debasement, dishonesty, immorality, vice, impurity, decay, and contamination. The literature on corruption has been bedeviled by the effort to find a set of culturally universal, invariable norms that would help decide if certain actions are to be classified as "corrupt." This foundational enterprise soon degenerated into ethnocentrism and dogma, leading to a prolonged period of intellectual inactivity. Of course, not all the contributions to the corruption literature fell into this ethnocentric trap; some quite explicitly set out to undermine the assumptions of modernization theory. The only reason I have chosen not to spend too much space here discussing the corruption literature is that it has very little to say about the chief concerns of my article, namely, the ethnographic analysis of the everyday functioning of the state and the discursive construction of the state in public culture. The only exception is to be found in the series of studies by Wade (1982, 1984, 1985), which ethnographically describe corruption through observation and interviews with state officials. A representative sample of the different viewpoints in the corruption literature can be obtained from Clarke 1983; Heidenheimer 1970; Huntington 1968; Leff 1964; Leys 1965; Monteiro 1970; Scott 1969, 1972; and Tilman 1968. For a recent monograph, see Klitgaard 1988.

45 I am grateful to Lata Mani for stressing this point to me.

46 For example, a highly placed official who fails to help a close relative or fellow villager obtain a government position is often roundly criticized by people for not fulfilling his obligations to his kinsmen and village brothers. On the other hand, the same people often roundly condemn any official of another caste or village who has done precisely that as being "corrupt" and as guilty of encouraging "nepotism."

47 The modernism of the postcolonial nation-state is exemplified by the concept of citizenship enshrined in the Indian constitution, a notion clearly rooted in Enlightenment ideas about the individual. My use of the term "citizens" might seem to hark back to a notion of "civil

society" that I argue against in the rest of
the article. What I am attempting to
stress here, however, is that in a postcolonial context the notion of citizenship
does not arise out of the bourgeois public sphere but out of the discourses and
practices of the modern nation-state.
Citizenship is therefore a hybridized
subject-position that has very different
resonances in a postcolonial context
than it does in places where it is inextricably blended with the emergence of
"civil society."

48 The discourse of accountability opened
up by the rhetoric of citizenship need not
become politically significant. Whether
it does or not has to do with the level of
organization of different groups that are
affected by it.

49 Interestingly enough, although the rhetoric of the Kisan Union predicates its opposition to the state in terms of the state's
anti-farmer policies, most of its grassroots
protests are organized around local instances of corruption. The behavior of
corrupt officials then becomes further evidence of the state's exploitation of farmers. Except at the very lowest levels, all
officials have jobs in which they are transferred frequently. Although the circle in
which they can be transferred varies by
rank, in a state as large as Uttar Pradesh,
what Anderson (1983) has termed "bureaucratic pilgrimages" usually cover quite
an extensive area. Officials cannot be
posted to their "home" village, block, tehsil, or district (depending on their circle of
responsibility).

50 If one were to analyze the discourse of
corruption in a region where dominant
landed groups and lower levels of the
state were more overtly complicit (as,
for example, in certain regions of
Bihar), one would probably find that it
attains a very different texture.

51 The Vidhan Sabha is the upper house of
Parliament and the Lok Sabha the lower
one.

52 At the time this interview took place,
Rajiv Gandhi was the prime minister of
India.

53 One lakh = 100,000. At the time of the
interview, Rs. 1 lakh were approximately equal to $6,000.

54 I am grateful to an anonymous reviewer
for raising this important question.

55 Other peasants who believe that lower,
but not upper, levels of government are
corrupt may not hold that belief for the
same reasons as Ram Singh.

56 All government positions have reservations or quotas for the scheduled castes –
a certain percentage of jobs at any given
rank are kept aside for people from the
lowest castes.

57 Sometimes the word *shaasan*, which is
closer to "administration," is also
employed.

58 I am by no means implying that the
viewing of television explains *why* Ram
Singh holds this opinion of the corrupt
middle levels of the state. He may very
well believe in it for other reasons as
well. Television, however, seems to
have influenced his views on this matter:
"we get a little more worldly."

59 His reference to "illiteracy" must not be
taken literally.

60 This point has been emphasized by
Herzfeld in his discussion of the Greek
village of Glendi and the provincial
town of Rethemnos: "There has never
been any serious doubt about the importance of the media in connecting villagers with larger national and
international events. Like the folklore
of earlier times, the media spawn an
extraordinarily homogenous as well as
pervasive set of political clichés. Much
less well-explored, however is *how* this
discourse is manipulated" (1992b:99;
emphasis in original). Talk of manipulation sometimes seems to make it appear
as if there is a "deep" intention working
toward particular goals; I prefer to think
of employability, the diverse ways in
which such discourse can be used in different circumstances.

61 It is not surprising that Ram Singh, like
other people, neither occupies a space of
pure oppositionality to dominant discourses and practices nor is simply

duped by them. Maddox (1990) suggests that scholars may have their own reasons for looking so hard for resistance. Forms of unambiguous resistance are rare indeed, as Foucault recognized (1980:109–145), and the simultaneity of co-optation and resistance baffles the familiar antinomies of analytical thought (Abu-Lughod 1990; Mankekar 1993). Indeed, the effort to show resistance even in overt gestures of deference requires the positing of hyperstrategic rational actors, an analytical strategy that is of dubious value.

62 It might be objected that this kind of statement involves an analytical circularity: constructions of the state are contextual and situated; yet any attempt to define context and situation involves the use of discourses that may themselves have been shaped by constructions of the state, among other things. Following Foucault and especially Haraway (1988), I want to argue that the search to escape the mutual determination of larger sociopolitical contexts and discursive positions is untenable. The analyst, too, is part of this discursive formation and cannot hope to arrive at a description of "situatedness" that stands above, beyond, or apart from the context being analyzed. This is precisely what "scientific" discourses seek to achieve – a universally verifiable description that is independent of observer and context. Haraway brilliantly undermines the claims of objectivity embodied in these discourses by showing that "the view from nowhere," or what she calls the "god-trick," masks a will-to-power that constitutes its own political project. She argues that all claims to objectivity are partial perspectives, context-dependent, and discursively embedded visions that are not for that reason unimportant or unredeemable. In other words, the recognition that the truths of scientific discourse are themselves located within specific webs of power-laden interconnections does not signal a slide toward "anything goes" randomness where all

positions are subjectively determined and hence irrefutable (see also Bernstein 1985). My effort to describe Ram Singh's position according to class, caste, gender, and age hierarchies flows out of a social scientific discourse and a sense of political engagement as a postcolonial subject in which inequality, poverty, and power are the central concerns. I doubt if an upper-caste villager would describe Ram Singh in this way; neither in all likelihood would a government official; nor would an official of the World Bank. While being a particular description, it is, I would argue, anything but an arbitrary one. I am grateful to an anonymous reviewer for forcing me to clarify this point.

63 Frustrated with the reification of the state and convinced that it was just a source of mystification, Radcliffe-Brown (1940:xxiii) argued that the state be eliminated from social analysis! One of the most thoughtful discussions on this topic is to be found in Abrams 1988.

64 Richard Fox's fine study of the colonial state in Punjab demonstrates the mutual construction of Sikh identities and "the state." He stresses that "the state" is "not a 'thing' but a 'happening'" (1985:156) and that it is riven by internal contradictions, incomplete consciousness of interests, incorrect implementation of projects aimed at furthering its interests, and conflict between individual officials and the organization (1985:157).

65 Anderson points to the similarity of nation-states by emphasizing the "modularity" of "the last wave" of nationalism (1983:104–28), and Chatterjee (1986) stresses the "derivative" character of Third World nationalisms.

66 I am not defending the naive possibility of "indigenous" theory, for it is not clear to me what such a concept could possibly mean in the era of postcolonialism and late capitalism. Instead, I am arguing that the use of concepts that originate in "the West" to understand the specificity of the Indian context enables

one to develop a critique of the analytical apparatus itself (Chakrabarty 1991). Jim Ferguson (personal communication, July 8, 1992) reminds me that even in the United States, the notion of "civil society" has very little purchase outside academic circles.

67 Amartya Sen's study of famines (1982) employs a theory of entitlements to explain who suffers in a famine and why. See also Appadurai 1984.

68 It should be clear that I am not suggesting that it is only here that possibilities for intervention exist.

69 The source is *A Tract on Monetary Reform* (Keynes 1971 [1923]).

REFERENCES

Aaj
  1989a Jayb Garmaanay May Juti Hai Police. (Police Busy Warming Own Pockets.) July 18.
  1989b Cheeni aur Mitti kay Tel ki Kaalabazaari. (Blackmarketeering in Sugar and Kerosene.) July 22.
  1989c Mathura ka Pedaa Khilaao to Telephone Bolnay Lagaingay. (To Get Telephone to Work, Feed Them Sweets.) July 22.
  1989d Chakbandi Adhikaari say Kisan Parayshaan. (Farmers Harassed by Land Consolidation Official.) July 22.
  1989e T. B. Aspataal may Loot Khasot. (Plunder in T. B. Hospital.) July 25.
  1989f Vidyut Station say Bheed Chay Transformer Uthaa lay Gayee. (Mob Carries away Six Transformers from Electricity Station.) August 11.
Abrams, Philip
  1988 Notes on the Difficulty of Studying the State. Journal of Historical Sociology 1(1):58–89.
Abu-Lughod, Lila
  1990 The Romance of Resistance: Tracing Transformations of Power through Bedouin Women. American Ethnologist 17:43–55.

Ahmad, Aijaz
  1987 Jameson's Rhetoric of Otherness and the "National Allegory." Social Text 17:3–25.
Amin, Shahid
  1984 Gandhi as Mahatma: Gorakhpur District, Eastern UP, 1921–1922. In Subaltern Studies III: Writings on South Asian History and Society. Ranajit Guha, ed. Pp. 1–61. Delhi: Oxford University Press.
Anagnost, Ann
  1994 The Politicized Body. In Body, Subject and Power in China. Angela Zito and Tani E. Barlow, eds. Pp. 131–156. Chicago: University of Chicago Press.
  1995 A Surfeit of Bodies: Population and the Rationality of the State in Post-Mao China. In Conceiving the New World Order: The Global Politics of Reproduction. Faye D. Ginsburg and Rayna Rapp, eds. Berkeley: University of California Press.
  n.d. National Past-Times: Writing, Narrative, and History in Modern China. Unpublished manuscript.
Anderson, Benedict
  1983 Imagined Communities: Reflections on the Origin and Spread of Nationalism. New York: Verso.
Appadurai, Arjun
  1984 How Moral Is South Asia's Economy? – A Review Article. Journal of Asian Studies 43(3):481–497.
  1986 Theory in Anthropology: Center and Periphery. Comparative Studies in Society and History 28(1):356–361.
  1990 Disjuncture and Difference in the Global Political Economy. Public Culture 2(2):1–24.
Appadurai, Arjun, and Carol A. Breckenridge
  1988 Why Public Culture? Public Culture 1(1):5–9.
Ashforth, Adam
  1990 The Politics of Official Discourse in Twentieth-Century South Africa. Oxford: Clarendon Press.
Benedict, Ruth
  1946 The Chrysanthemum and the Sword: Patterns of Japanese Culture. Boston: Houghton Mifflin.

Bernstein, Richard
  1985 Beyond Objectivism and Relativism: Science, Hermeneutics and Praxis. Philadelphia: University of Pennsylvania Press.
Bourdieu, Pierre
  1977 Outline of a Theory of Practice. Richard Nice, trans. Cambridge: Cambridge University Press.
  1985 The Social Space and the Genesis of Groups. Theory and Society 14(6):723–744.
Brow, James
  1988 In Pursuit of Hegemony: Representations of Authority and Justice in a Sri Lankan Village. American Ethnologist 15:311–327.
Butler, Judith
  1990 Gender Trouble, Feminist Theory, and Psychoanalytic Discourse. In Feminism/Postmodernism. Linda J. Nicholson, ed. Pp. 324–340. New York: Routledge.
Calhoun, Craig
  1989 Tiananmen, Television and the Public Sphere: Internationalization of Culture and the Beijing Spring of 1989. Public Culture 2(1):54–71.
Chakrabarty, Dipesh
  1989 Rethinking Working Class History. Princeton: Princeton University Press.
  1991 History as Critique and Critique(s) of History. Economic and Political Weekly 26(37):2162–2166.
Chatterjee, Partha
  1986 Nationalist Thought and the Colonial World: A Derivative Discourse? London: Zed Press.
  1990 A Response to Taylor's "Modes of Civil Society." Public Culture 3(1):119–132.
  1993 The Nation and Its Fragments: Colonial and Postcolonial Histories. Princeton: Princeton University Press.
Chawla, Prabhu
  1990 The '80s: Politics. Pp. 18–25, January 15, International Edition.
Clarke, Michael, ed.
  1983 Corruption: Causes, Consequences, and Control. London: Frances Pinter.

Cohn, Bernard S.
  1987a The Census, Social Structure and Objectification in South Asia. In An Anthropologist among the Historians and Other Essays. Pp. 224–254. Delhi: Oxford University Press.
  1987b Representing Authority in Victorian India. In An Anthropologist among the Historians and Other Essays. Pp. 632–682. Delhi: Oxford University Press.
Coombe, Rosemary J.
  1993 Tactics of Appropriation and the Politics of Recognition in Late Modern Democracies. Political Theory 21(3):411–433.
Dirks, Nicholas
  1987 The Hollow Crown: Ethnohistory of an Indian Kingdom. Cambridge: Cambridge University Press.
Escobar, Arturo
  1984 Discourse and Power in Development: Michel Foucault and the Relevance of His Work to the Third World. Alternatives 10:377–400.
  1988 Power and Visibility: Development and the Invention and Management of the Third World. Cultural Anthropology 3(4):428–443.
  1992 Imagining a Post-Development Era? Critical Thought, Development and Social Movements. Social Text 31/32:20–56.
Evans, Peter B., Dietrich Rueschemeyer, and Theda Skocpol, eds.
  1985 Bringing the State Back In. Cambridge: Cambridge University Press.
Fabian, Johannes
  1983 Time and the Other: How Anthropology Makes Its Object. New York: Columbia University Press.
Ferguson, James
  1990 The Anti-Politics Machine: "Development," Depoliticization, and Bureaucratic Power in Lesotho. Cambridge: Cambridge University Press.
Foucault, Michel
  1980 Power/Knowledge: Selected Interviews and Other Writings, 1972–1977. Colin Gordon, ed. New York: Pantheon Books.

Fox, Richard
 1985 Lions of the Punjab: Culture in the Making. Berkeley: University of California Press.
Gilroy, Paul
 1987 There Ain't No Black in the Union Jack. London: Hutchinson.
Gupta, Akhil, and James Ferguson
 1992 Beyond "Culture": Space, Identity, and the Politics of Difference. Cultural Anthropology 7(1):6–23.
Gurevitch, Michael, Tony Bennett, James Curran, and Janet Woollacott, eds.
 1982 Culture, Society and the Media. New York: Methuen.
Habermas, Jurgen
 1989[1962] The Structural Transformation of the Public Sphere: An Inquiry into a Category of Bourgeois Society. T. Burger and F. Lawrence, trans. Cambridge: MIT Press.
Hacking, Ian
 1982 Biopower and the Avalanche of Printed Numbers. Humanities in Society 5(3):279–295.
Hall, Stuart
 1981 Notes on Deconstructing "The Popular." In People's History and Socialist Theory. Raphael Samuel, ed. Pp. 227–240. London: Routledge.
 1982 Culture, the Media and the Ideological Effect. In Culture, Society and the Media. Michael Gurevitch, Tony Bennett, James Curran, and Janet Woollacott, eds. Pp. 315–348. New York: Methuen.
 1986a Gramsci's Relevance for the Study of Race and Ethnicity. Journal of Communication Inquiry 10(2):5–27.
 1986b Popular Culture and the State. In Popular Culture and Social Relations. Tony Bennett, Colin Mercer, and Janet Woollacott, eds. Pp. 22–49. Milton Keynes, England: Open University Press.
Hall, Stuart, Dorothy Hobson, Andrew Lowe, and Paul Willis, eds.
 1980 Culture, Media, Language. London: Hutchinson.
Handelman, Don
 1978 Introduction: A Recognition of Bureaucracy. In Bureaucracy and World-view: Studies in the Logic of Official Interpretation, by Don Handelman and Elliot Leyton. Pp. 1–14. St. Johns, Newfoundland: Institute of Social and Economic Research.
 1981 Introduction: The Idea of Bureaucratic Organization. Social Analysis 9:5–23.
Handler, Richard
 1985 On Having a Culture: Nationalism and the Preservation of Quebec's Patrimoine. In Objects and Others: Essays on Museums and Material Culture, George W. Stocking Jr., ed. History of Anthropology, 3. Pp. 192–217. Madison: University of Wisconsin Press.
Hannerz, Ulf
 1986 Theory in Anthropology: Small is Beautiful? Comparative Studies in Society and History 28(1):362–367.
Haraway, Donna
 1988 Situated Knowledges: The Science Question in Feminism and the Privilege of Partial Perspective. Feminist Studies 14(3):575–599.
Harvey, David
 1989 The Condition of Postmodernity: An Enquiry into the Origins of Cultural Change. New York: Blackwell.
Heidenheimer, Arnold J., ed.
 1970 Political Corruption. New York: Holt, Rinehart, and Winston.
Herzfeld, Michael
 1992a The Social Production of Indifference: Exploring the Symbolic Roots of Western Bureaucracy. New York: Berg.
 1992b History in the Making: National and International Politics in a Rural Cretan Community. In Europe Observed. João de Pina-Cabral and John Campbell, eds. Pp. 93–122. Houndsmills, England: MacMillan Press.
Huntington, Samuel P.
 1968 Political Order in Changing Societies. New Haven: Yale University Press.
India Today
 1989 A Methodical Fraud: IRDP Loans. Pp. 74–77, March 15.
Kasaba, Resat
 1994 A Time and a Place for the Non-State: Social Change in the Ottoman

Empire during the Long Nineteenth Century. *In* State Power and Social Forces: Domination and Transformation in the Third World. Joel Migdal, Atul Kohli, and Vivienne Shue, eds. Pp. 207–230. Cambridge: Cambridge University Press.

Keynes, John Maynard
1971 [1923] A Tract on Monetary Reform: The Collected Writings of John Maynard Keynes, 4. London: Macmillan.

Klitgaard, Robert
1988 Controlling Corruption. Berkeley: University of California Press.

Leff, Nathaniel H.
1964 Economic Development through Bureaucratic Corruption. American Behavioral Scientist 8(3):8–14.

Leys, Colin
1965 What Is the Problem about Corruption? Journal of Modern African Studies 3(2):215–230.

Maddox, Richard
1990 Bombs, Bikinis, and the Popes of Rock 'n' Roll: Reflections on Resistance, the Play of Subordinations, and Cultural Liberalism in Andalusia and Academia. Paper presented to the 87th annual meeting of the American Anthropological Association, Phoenix, AZ.

Mandel, Ernest
1975 Late Capitalism. Joris De Bres, trans. New York: Verso.

Mani, Lata
1989 Multiple Mediations: Feminist Scholarship in the Age of Multinational Reception. Inscriptions 5:1–23.

Mankekar, Purnima
1993 National Texts and Gendered Lives: An Ethnography of Television Viewers in a North Indian City. American Ethnologist 20:543–563.

Mbembe, Achille
1992 Provisional Notes on the Postcolony. Africa 62(1):3–37.

Mitchell, Timothy
1989 The Effect of the State. Department of Politics, New York University. Unpublished manuscript.

1991 The Limits of the State: Beyond Statist Approaches and their Critics. American Political Science Review 85(1):77–96.

Mitra, Chandran
1989 Tikait as Mini-Mahatma: Understanding the Rural Mind-Set. Times of India, August 9.

Mitra, Chandran, and Rashmee Z. Ahmed
1989 It's Naiyma's Niche, near the "Nahar." Times of India, August 8. Pp. 1, 12.

Mohanty, Chandra
1988 Under Western Eyes: Feminist Scholarship and Colonial Discourses. Feminist Review 30:61–88.

Monteiro, John B.
1970 The Dimensions of Corruption in India. *In* Political Corruption. Arnold J. Heidenheimer, ed. Pp. 220–228. New York: Holt, Rinehart and Winston.

Nader, Laura
1972 Up the Anthropologist – Perspectives Gained from Studying Up. *In* Reinventing Anthropology. Dell Hymes, ed. Pp. 284–311. New York: Pantheon Books.

Nandy, Ashis
1990 The Politics of Secularism and the Recovery of Religious Tolerance. *In* Mirrors of Violence: Communities, Riots and Survivors in South Asia. Veena Das, ed. Pp. 69–93. Delhi: Oxford University Press.

Nugent, David
1994 Building the State, Making the Nation: The Bases and Limits of State Centralization in "Modern" Peru. American Anthropologist 96(2):333–369.

Peters, John Durham
1993 Distrust of Representation: Habermas on the Public Sphere. Media Culture, and Society 15:541–571.

1995 Historical Tensions in the Concept of Public Opinion. *In* Public Opinion and the Communication of Consent. Theodore L. Glasser and Charles T. Salmon, eds. Pp. 3–32. New York: Guilford Press.

Radcliffe-Brown, A. R.
  1940 Preface. *In* African Political Systems. Meyer Fortes and E. E. Evans-Pritchard, eds. Pp. xi–xxiii. Oxford: Oxford University Press.
Rohlen, Tom
  1974 For Harmony and Strength: Japanese White-Collar Organization in Anthropological Perspective. Berkeley: University of California Press.
  1983 Japan's High Schools. Berkeley: University of California Press.
Scott, James C.
  1969 Corruption, Machine Politics, and Political Change. American Political Science Review 63(4):1142–1158.
  1972 Comparative Political Corruption. Englewood Cliffs, NJ: Prentice Hall.
Sen, Amartya
  1982 Poverty and Famines: An Essay on Entitlement and Deprivation. Oxford: Clarendon Press.
Skocpol, Theda
  1979 States and Social Revolutions: A Comparative Analysis of France, Russia, and China. Cambridge: Cambridge University Press.
Taussig, Michael
  1992 Maleficium: State Fetishism. *In* The Nervous System. Pp. 111–140. New York: Routledge.
Taylor, Charles
  1990 Modes of Civil Society. Public Culture 3(1):95–118.
Tenekoon, N. Serena
  1988 Rituals of Development: The Accelerated Mahavali Development Program in Sri Lanka. American Ethnologist 15:294–310.

Tilman, Robert O.
  1968 Emergence of Black-Market Bureaucracy: Administration, Development, and Corruption in New States. Public Administration Review 28(5):437–444.
Times of India
  1989 Bofors Is Not a Major Issue: Pre-Election Survey 4. August 13. Pp. 1, 7.
Urla, Jacqueline
  1993 Cultural Politics in an Age of Statistics: Numbers, Nations, and the Making of Basque Identity. American Ethnologist 20:818–843.
Wade, Robert
  1982 The System of Administrative and Political Corruption: Canal Irrigation in South India. Journal of Development Studies 18(3):287–328.
  1984 Irrigation Reform in Conditions of Populist Anarchy: An Indian Case. Journal of Development Economics 14(3):285–303.
  1985 The Market for Public Office: Why the Indian State is Not Better at Development. World Development 13(4):467–497.
Waites, Bernard, Tony Bennett, and Graham Martin, eds.
  1982 Popular Culture, Past and Present. London: Open University Press.
Woost, Michael D.
  1993 Nationalizing the Local Past in Sri Lanka: Histories of Nation and Development in a Sinhalese Village. American Ethnologist 20:502–521.
Yang, Mayfair Mei-hui
  1989 The Gift Economy and State Power in China. Comparative Studies in Society and History 31(1):25–54.

Section II

Planning and Development

The two articles in this section build on Foucauldian ideas about the state, power, panopticism, surveillance, and governmentality through an examination of the apparatus, practices, and effects of planning. Whether it concerns a city or the development of a nation, planning is a key governmental technique usually understood as a technical, apolitical, and expert intervention into socioeconomic realities and problems. To intervene effectively, planning relies on a thorough knowledge of "ground realities." Such knowledge invariably reduces complexity by techniques that seek to make the real legible through surveying, mapping, and classifying. The two articles in this section demonstrate that practices of planning do not just generate knowledge about different objects, they actually help produce the objects of intervention. Plans, in other words, do not simply describe an object or social reality, but actually shape this reality. Whether it is ethnic categories and surnames that people check off and report on census surveys, the "official" languages they are forced to learn, or the "underdeveloped" nation-state Lesotho that requires standardized development assistance, Scott and Ferguson illustrate how these realities are constructed through the discourse and practices of planning.

How the object of planning is constructed directly affects the kinds of interventions that are designed and the outcomes that can be expected from such interventions. After all, as Scott points out, the point of simplifying and making legible a certain socioeconomic reality is to manage and manipulate this reality toward achieving certain ends. This is clearly the case in city planning. Scott provides the example of nineteenth-century Paris where roads and residential buildings were laid out in a geometric and uniform pattern to maximize visibility and surveillance, and to thus reduce the likelihood of popular insurrection. The relationship between planners' intended goals for different interventions and the actual outcomes of plans, however, is not straightforward. Both Scott and Ferguson focus on how and why plans often fail in achieving their intended aims. People refuse to be rendered legible and enumerable through census surveys; and development programs aimed at boosting agricultural production end up producing no positive change. Even the most well-intentioned and well-thought-out interventions fail, Scott suggests, because they do not take into account social structures and local knowledges. Ferguson also describes this logic of failure, illustrating how complex interactions between plans and on-the-ground social structures and processes subvert the intended outcomes. But he takes failure a step further.

Ferguson seeks to comprehend what planned development interventions *succeed* in doing even when they fail in their stated goals. These unintended side effects of plans, or what Ferguson terms "instrument" effects, have a logic and coherence of their own, even when they do not correspond with the originally stated goals of the plans. In the case that Ferguson examines, the Thaba-Tseka project in Lesotho funded by the Canadian government, the key counter-intentional instrument-effects are the expansion and depoliticization of bureaucratic power. Bureaucratic power goes beyond "the state." Ferguson implies that its expansion implies a multiplication of knots of power throughout society and not just an increase in the power possessed by the state. Ferguson provides a powerful instance of the governmentalization of society through development at the same time that he also problematizes Foucault's Western-focused analysis of the increased role of the state in the efficient management of population and resources within its territory. In postcolonial contexts, like Lesotho, governmentalization has not necessarily meant an efficient and optimal state-centered management of population and resources.

Together, Scott and Ferguson open up the terrain for investigating the practices of legibility required by planning. They show that such techniques are employed not only by state bureaucracies, but also the market, and by parastatals and non-governmental institutions that function like the state. They examine the varied governmental effects of these practices in different post-colonial, post-conflict, and post-socialist societies.

SUGGESTED READINGS

Appadurai, Arjun
    1993   Number in the Colonial Imagination. *In* Orientalism and the Postcolonial Predicament. C. Breckenridge and P. van der Veer, eds. Pp. 314–339. Philadelphia: University of Pennsylvania Press.
    2002   Deep Democracy: Urban Governmentality and the Horizon of Politics. Public Culture 14(1):21–47.
Bornstein, Erica
    2003   The Spirit of Development: Protestant NGOs, Morality, and Economics in Zimbabwe. New York: Routledge.
Brow, James
    1996   Demons and Development: The Struggle for Community in a Sri Lankan Village. Tucson: University of Arizona Press.

Chatterjee, Partha
    1998   Development Planning and the Indian State. *In* State and Politics in India. Pp. 271–297. Delhi: Oxford University Press.
Cohn, Bernard S.
    1987   The Census, Social Structure and Objectification in South Asia. *In* An Anthropologist Among the Historians and Other Essays. Pp. 224–254. Delhi: Oxford University Press.
    1996   Colonialism and Its Forms of Knowledge: The British in India. Princeton, NJ: Princeton University Press.
Cruikshank, Barbara
    1999   The Will to Empower: Democratic Citizens and Other Subjects. Ithaca, NY: Cornell University Press.
Escobar, Arturo
    1995   Encountering Development: The Making and Unmaking of the Third World. Princeton, NJ: Princeton University Press.
Esteva, Gustavo
    1992   Development. *In* The Development Dictionary: A Guide to Knowledge as Power. W. Sachs, ed. Pp. 6–25. Atlantic Highlands, NJ: Zed Books.
Gupta, Akhil
    1998   Postcolonial Developments: Agriculture in the Making of Modern India. Durham, NC: Duke University Press.
Hacking, Ian
    1982   Biopower and the Avalanche of Printed Numbers. Humanities in Society 5 (3 & 4):279–295.
    1991   How Should We Do the History of Statistics *In* The Foucault Effect: Studies in Governmentality. G. Burchell, C. Gordon, and P. Miller, eds. pp. 181–196. Chicago: University of Chicago Press.
Leve, Lauren
    2001   Between Jesse Helms and Ram Bahadur: Women, "Participation," and "Empowerment" in Nepal. PoLAR: Political and Legal Anthropology Review 24(1):108–128.
Li, Tania Murray
    1999   Compromising Power: Development, Culture, and Rule in Indonesia. Cultural Anthropology 14(3):295–322.
Mitchell, Timothy
    1988   Colonising Egypt. Cambridge: Cambridge University Press.
    2002   Rule of Experts: Egypt, Techno Politics, Modernity. Berkeley: University of California Press.
Moore, Donald S.
    1999   The Crucible of Cultural Politics: Reworking "Development" in Zimbabwe's Eastern Highlands. American Ethnologist 26(3):654–689.
Paley, Julia
    2001   Marketing Democracy: Power and Social Movements in Post-Dictatorship Chile. Berkeley: University of California Press.
Pigg, Stacy Leigh
    1997   Found in Most Traditional Societies: Traditional Medical Practitioners between Culture and Development. *In* International Development and the Social Sciences: Essays on the History and Politics of Knowledge. F. Cooper and R. Packard, eds. pp. 259–290. Berkeley: University of California Press.

Sharma, Aradhana
> Forthcoming   Cross-breeding Institutions, Breeding Struggle: Women's "Empower-ment," Neoliberal Governmentality, and State Re(Formation) in India. Cultural Anthropology.

Sivaramakrishnan, K.
> 1999   Modern Forests: Statemaking and Environmental Change in Colonial Eastern India. Stanford, CA: Stanford University Press.

Tenekoon, Serena
> 1988   Rituals of Development: The Accelerated Mahavali Development Program of Sri Lanka. American Ethnologist 15(2):294–310.

Tsing, Anna L.
> 1993   In the Realm of the Diamond Queen: Marginality in an Out-of-the-Way Place. Princeton, NJ: Princeton University Press.

10

Cities, People, and Language

James C. Scott

And the Colleges of the Cartographers set up a Map of the Empire which had the size of the Empire itself and coincided with it point by point. . . . Succeeding generations understood that this Widespread Map was Useless, and not without Impiety they abandoned it to the Inclemencies of the Sun and the Winters.

> – Suarez Miranda, *Viajes de varones prudentes (1658)*

An aerial view of a town built during the Middle Ages or the oldest quarters (*medina*) of a Middle Eastern city that has not been greatly tampered with has a particular look. It is the look of disorder. Or, to put it more precisely, the town conforms to no overall abstract form. Streets, lanes, and passages intersect at varying angles with a density that resembles the intricate complexity of some organic processes. In the case of a medieval town, where defense needs required walls and perhaps moats, there may be traces of inner walls superseded by outer walls,

much like the growth rings of a tree. A representation of Bruges in about 1500 illustrates the pattern. What definition there is to the city is provided by the castle green, the marketplace, and the river and canals that were (until they silted up) the lifeblood of this textile-trading city.

The fact that the layout of the city, having developed without any overall design, lacks a consistent geometric logic does not mean that it was at all confusing to its inhabitants. One imagines that many of its cobbled streets were nothing more than surfaced footpaths traced by repeated use. For those who grew up in its various quarters, Bruges would have been perfectly familiar, perfectly legible. Its very alleys and lanes would have closely approximated the most common daily movements. For a stranger or trader arriving for the first time, however, the town was almost certainly confusing, simply because it lacked a repetitive, abstract logic that would allow a newcomer to orient herself. The cityscape of Bruges in 1500 could be said to privilege local

From James C. Scott, *Seeing Like a State: How Certain Schemes to Improve the Human Condition Have Failed*, pp. 53–83, 369–76. New Haven, CT and London: Yale University Press, 1998. Reprinted by permission of the publisher, Yale University Press.

knowledge over outside knowledge, including that of external political authorities.[1] It functioned spatially in much the same way a difficult or unintelligible dialect would function linguistically. As a semipermeable membrane, it facilitated communication within the city while remaining stubbornly unfamiliar to those who had not grown up speaking this special geographic dialect.

Historically, the relative illegibility to outsiders of some urban neighborhoods (or of their rural analogues, such as hills, marshes, and forests) has provided a vital margin of political safety from control by outside elites. A simple way of determining whether this margin exists is to ask if an outsider would have needed a local guide (a native tracker) in order to find her way successfully. If the answer is yes, then the community or terrain in question enjoys at least a small measure of insulation from outside intrusion. Coupled with patterns of local solidarity, this insulation has proven politically valuable in such disparate contexts as eighteenth- and early nineteenth-century urban riots over bread prices in Europe, the Front de Libération Nationale's tenacious resistance to the French in the Casbah of Algiers,[2] and the politics of the bazaar that helped to bring down the Shah of Iran. Illegibility, then, has been and remains a reliable resource for political autonomy.[3]

Stopping short of redesigning cities in order to make them more legible (a subject that we shall soon explore), state authorities endeavored to map complex, old cities in a way that would facilitate policing and control. Most of the major cities of France were thus the subject of careful military mapping (*reconnaissances militaires*), particularly after the Revolution. When urban revolts occurred, the authorities wanted to be able to move quickly to the precise locations that would enable them to contain or suppress the rebellions effectively.[4]

States and city planners have striven, as one might expect, to overcome this spatial unintelligibility and to make urban geography transparently legible from without. Their attitude toward what they regarded as the higgledy-piggledy profusion of unplanned cities was not unlike the attitude of foresters to the natural profusion of the unplanned forest. The origin of grids or geometrically regular settlements may lie in a straightforward military logic. A square, ordered, formulaic military camp on the order of the Roman *castra* has many advantages. Soldiers can easily learn the techniques of building it; the commander of the troops knows exactly in which disposition his subalterns and various troops lie; and any Roman messenger or officer who arrives at the camp will know where to find the officer he seeks.... Other things being equal, the city laid out according to a simple, repetitive logic will be easiest to administer and to police.

Whatever the political and administrative conveniences of a geometric cityscape, the Enlightenment fostered a strong aesthetic that looked with enthusiasm on straight lines and visible order. No one expressed the prejudice more clearly than Descartes: "These ancient cities that were once mere *straggling* villages and have become in the course of time great cities are commonly quite *poorly laid out* compared to those *well-ordered towns that an engineer lays out on a vacant plane* as it suits his fancy. And although, upon considering one-by-one the buildings in the former class of towns, one finds as much art or more than one finds in the latter class of towns, still, upon seeing how the buildings are arranged – *here a large one, there a small one* – and how *they make the streets crooked and uneven*, one will say that *it is chance more than the will of some men using their reason that has arranged them thus.*"[5]

Descartes's vision conjures up the urban equivalent of the scientific forest: streets laid out in straight lines intersecting at right angles, buildings of uniform design and size, the whole built according to a single, overarching plan.

The elective affinity between a strong state and a uniformly laid out city is obvious. Lewis Mumford, the historian of urban form, locates the modern European origin of this symbiosis in the open, legible baroque style of the Italian city-state....[6] [T]he baroque redesigning of medieval cities – with its grand edifices, vistas, squares, and attention to uniformity, proportion, and perspective – was intended to reflect the grandeur and awesome power of the prince. Aesthetic considerations frequently won out over the existing social structure and the mundane functioning of the city. "Long before the invention of bulldozers," Mumford adds, "the Italian military engineer developed, through his professional specialization in destruction, a bulldozing habit of mind: one that sought to clear the ground of encumbrances, so as to make a clear beginning on its own inflexible mathematical lines."[7]

The visual power of the baroque city was underwritten by scrupulous attention to the military security of the prince from internal as well as external enemies. Thus both Alberti and Palladio thought of main thoroughfares as military roads (*viae militaires*). Such roads had to be straight, and, in Palladio's view, "the ways will be more convenient if they are made everywhere equal: that is to say that there will be *no part in them where armies may not easily march*."[8]

There are, of course, many cities approximating Descartes's model. For obvious reasons, most have been planned from the ground up as new, often utopian cities.[9] Where they have not been built by imperial decrees, they have been designed by their founding fathers to accommodate more repetitive and uniform squares for future settlement.[10] A bird's-eye view of central Chicago in the late nineteenth century (William Penn's Philadelphia or New Haven would do equally well) serves as an example of the grid city.

From an administrator's vantage point, the ground plan of Chicago is nearly utopian. It offers a quick appreciation of the ensemble, since the entirety is made up of straight lines, right angles, and repetitions.[11] Even the rivers seem scarcely to interrupt the city's relentless symmetry. For an outsider – or a policeman – finding an address is a comparatively simple matter; no local guides are required. The knowledge of local citizens is not especially privileged vis-à-vis that of outsiders. If, as is the case in upper Manhattan, the cross streets are consecutively numbered and are intersected by longer avenues, also consecutively numbered, the plan acquires even greater transparency.[12] The aboveground order of a grid city facilitates its underground order in the layout of water pipes, storm drains, sewers, electric cables, natural gas lines, and subways – an order no less important to the administrators of a city. Delivering mail, collecting taxes, conducting a census, moving supplies and people in and out of the city, putting down a riot or insurrection, digging for pipes and sewer lines, finding a felon or conscript (providing he is at the address given), and planning public transportation, water supply, and trash removal are all made vastly simpler by the logic of the grid.

Three aspects of this geometric order in human settlement bear emphasis. The first is that the order in question is most evident, not at street level, but rather from above and from outside.... The symmetry is either grasped from a representation... or from the vantage point of a helicopter hovering far above the ground: in short, a God's-eye view, or the view of an absolute ruler. This spatial fact is perhaps inherent in the process of urban or architectural planning itself, a process that involves miniaturization and scale models upon which patron and planner gaze down, exactly as if they were in a helicopter.[13] There is, after all, no other way of visually imagining what a large-scale construction project will look like when it is completed except by a miniaturization of this kind. It follows, I believe, that such plans, which have the scale of toys, are judged for their sculptural properties and visual order, often from a perspective that no or very few human observers will ever replicate.

The miniaturization imaginatively achieved by scale models of cities or landscapes was practically achieved with the airplane. The mapping tradition of the bird's-eye view, evident in the map of Chicago, was no longer a mere convention. By virtue of its great distance, an aerial view resolved what might have seemed ground-level confusion into an apparently vaster order and symmetry. It would be hard to exaggerate the importance of the airplane for modernist thought and planning. . . .

A second point about an urban order easily legible from outside is that the grand plan of the ensemble has no necessary relationship to the order of life as it is experienced by its residents. Although certain state services may be more easily provided and distant addresses more easily located, these apparent advantages may be negated by such perceived disadvantages as the absence of a dense street life, the intrusion of hostile authorities, the loss of the spatial irregularities that foster coziness, gathering places for informal recreation, and neighborhood feeling. The formal order of a geometrically regular urban space is just that: formal order. Its visual regimentation has a ceremonial or ideological quality, much like the order of a parade or a barracks. The fact that such order works for municipal and state authorities in administering the city is no guarantee that it works for citizens. Provisionally, then, we must remain agnostic about the relation between formal spatial order and social experience.

The third notable aspect of homogeneous, geometrical, uniform property is its convenience as a standardized commodity for the market. Like Jefferson's scheme for surveying or the Torrens system for titling open land, the grid creates regular lots and blocks that are ideal for buying and selling. Precisely because they are abstract units detached from any ecological or topographical reality, they resemble a kind of currency which is endlessly amenable to aggregation and fragmentation. This feature of the grid plan suits equally the surveyor, the planner, and the real-estate speculator. Bureaucratic and commercial logic, in this instance, go hand in hand. . . .

The vast majority of Old World cities are, in fact, some historical amalgam of a Bruges and a Chicago. Although more than one pol-

itician, dictator, and city planner have devised plans for the total recasting of an existing city, these dreams came at such cost, both financial and political, that they have rarely left the drawing boards. Piecemeal planning, by contrast, is far more common. The central, older core of many cities remains somewhat like Bruges, whereas the newer outskirts are more likely to exhibit the marks of one or more plans. Sometimes, as in the sharp contrast between old Delhi and the imperial capital of New Delhi, the divergence is formalized.

Occasionally, authorities have taken draconian steps to retrofit an existing city. The redevelopment of Paris by the prefect of the Seine, Baron Haussmann, under Louis Napoleon was a grandiose public works program stretching from 1853 to 1869. Haussmann's vast scheme absorbed unprecedented amounts of public debt, uprooted tens of thousands of people, and could have been accomplished only by a single executive authority not directly accountable to the electorate.

The logic behind the reconstruction of Paris bears a resemblance to the logic behind the transformation of old-growth forests into scientific forests designed for unitary fiscal management. There was the same emphasis on simplification, legibility, straight lines, central management, and a synoptic grasp of the ensemble. As in the case of the forest, much of the plan was achieved. One chief difference, however, was that Haussmann's plan was devised less for fiscal reasons than for its impact on the conduct and sensibilities of Parisians. While the plan did create a far more legible fiscal space in the capital, this was a by-product of the desire to make the city more governable, prosperous, healthy, and architecturally imposing.[14] The second difference was, of course, that those uprooted by the urban planning of the Second Empire could, and did, strike back. As we shall see, the retrofitting of Paris foreshadows many of the paradoxes of authoritarian high-modernist planning that we will soon examine in greater detail.

The plan shows the new boulevards constructed to Haussmann's measure as well as the prerevolutionary inner boulevards, which were widened and straightened.[15] But the retrofit, seen merely as a new street map, greatly underestimates the transformation. For all the demolition and construction required, for all the new legibility added to the street plan, the new pattern bore strong traces of an accommodation with "old-growth" Paris. The outer boulevards, for example, follow the line of the older customs (*octroi*) wall of 1787. But Haussmann's scheme was far more than a traffic reform. The new legibility of the boulevards was accompanied by changes that revolutionized daily life: new aqueducts, a much more effective sewage system, new rail lines and terminals, centralized markets (Les Halles), gas lines and lighting, and new parks and public squares.[16] The new Paris created by Louis Napoleon became, by the turn of the century, a widely admired public works miracle and shrine for would-be planners from abroad.

At the center of Louis Napoleon's and Haussmann's plans for Paris lay the military security of the state. The redesigned city was, above all, to be made safe against popular insurrections.... Barricades had gone up nine times in the twenty-five years before 1851. Louis Napoleon and Haussmann had seen the revolutions of 1830 and 1848; more recently, the June Days and resistance to Louis Napoleon's coup represented the largest insurrection of the century. Louis Napoleon, as a returned exile, was well aware of how tenuous his hold on power might prove.

The geography of insurrection, however, was not evenly distributed across Paris. Resistance was concentrated in densely packed, working-class *quartiers*, which, like Bruges, had complex, illegible street plans.[17] The 1860 annexation of the "inner suburbs" (located between the customs wall and the outer fortifications and containing 240,000 residents) was explicitly designed to gain mastery over a *ceinture sauvage* that had thus far escaped police control. Haussmann described this area as a "dense belt of suburbs, given

over to twenty different administrations, built at random, covered by an inextricable network of narrow and tortuous public ways, alleys, and dead-ends, where a nomadic population without any real ties to the land [property] and without any effective surveillance, grows at a prodigious speed."[18] Within Paris itself, there were such revolutionary *foyers* as the Marais and especially the Faubourg Saint-Antoine, both of which had been determined centers of resistance to Louis Napoleon's coup d'état.

The military control of these insurrectionary spaces – spaces that had not yet been well mapped – was integral to Haussmann's plan.[19] A series of new avenues between the inner boulevards and the customs wall was designed to facilitate movement between the barracks on the outskirts of the city and the subversive districts. As Haussmann saw it, his new roads would ensure multiple, direct rail and road links between each district of the city and the military units responsible for order there.[20] Thus, for example, new boulevards in northeastern Paris allowed troops to rush from the Courbevoie barracks to the Bastille and then to subdue the turbulent Faubourg Saint-Antoine.[21] Many of the new rail lines and stations were located with similar strategic goals in mind. Where possible, insurrectionary quarters were demolished or broken up by new roads, public spaces, and commercial development....

The reconstruction of Paris was also a necessary public-health measure. And here the steps that the hygienists said would make Paris more healthful would at the same time make it more efficient economically and more secure militarily. Antiquated sewers and cesspools, the droppings of an estimated thirty-seven thousand horses (in 1850), and the unreliable water supply made Paris literally pestilential. The city had the highest death rate in France and was most susceptible to virulent epidemics of cholera; in 1831, the disease killed 18,400 people, including the prime minister. And it was in those districts of revolutionary resistance where, because of crowding and lack of sanitation, the rates of mortality were highest.[22] Haussmann's Paris was, for those who were not expelled, a far healthier city; the greater circulation of air and water and the exposure to sunlight reduced the risk of epidemics just as the improved circulation of goods and labor (healthier labor, at that) contributed to the city's economic well-being. A utilitarian logic of labor productivity and commercial success went hand in hand with strategic and public-health concerns.

[...]

As happens in many authoritarian modernizing schemes, the political tastes of the ruler occasionally trumped purely military and functional concerns. Rectilinear streets may have admirably assisted the mobilization of troops against insurgents, but they were also to be flanked by elegant facades and to terminate in imposing buildings that would impress visitors.[23] Uniform modern buildings along the new boulevards may have represented healthier dwellings, but they were often no more than facades. The zoning regulations were almost exclusively concerned with the visible surfaces of buildings, but behind the facades, builders could build crowded, airless tenements, and many of them did.[24]

The new Paris, as T. J. Clark has observed, was intensely visualized: "Part of Haussmann's purpose was to give modernity a shape, and he seemed at the time to have a measure of success in doing so; he built a set of forms in which the city appeared to be visible, even intelligible: Paris, to repeat the formula, was becoming a spectacle."[25]

Legibility, in this case, was achieved by a much more pronounced segregation of the population by class and function. Each fragment of Paris increasingly took on a distinctive character of dress, activity, and wealth – bourgeois shopping district, prosperous residential quarter, industrial suburb, artisan quarter, bohemian quarter. It was a more easily managed and administered city and a more "readable" city because of Haussmann's heroic simplifications.

As in most ambitious schemes of modern order, there was a kind of evil twin to Haussmann's spacious and imposing new capital. The hierarchy of urban space in which the rebuilt center of Paris occupied pride of place presupposed the displacement of the urban poor toward the periphery.[26] Nowhere was this more true than in Belleville, a popular working-class quarter to the northeast which grew into a town of sixty thousand people by 1856. Many of its residents had been disinherited by Haussmann's demolitions; some called it a community of outcasts. By the 1860s, it had become a suburban equivalent of what the Faubourg Saint-Antoine had been earlier – an illegible, insurrectionary *foyer*. "The problem was not that Belleville was not a community, but that it became the sort of community which the bourgeoisie feared, which the police could not penetrate, which the government could not regulate, where the popular classes, with all their unruly passions and political resentments, held the upper hand."[27] If, as many claim, the Commune of Paris in 1871 was partly an attempt to reconquer the city ("la reconquete de la Ville par la Ville")[28] by those exiled to the periphery by Haussmann, then Belleville was the geographical locus of that sentiment. The Communards, militarily on the defensive in late May 1871, retreated toward the northeast and Belleville, where, at the Belleville town hall, they made their last stand. Treated as a den of revolutionaries, Belleville was subjected to a brutal military occupation.

[...]

The Creation of Surnames

Some of the categories that we most take for granted and with which we now routinely apprehend the social world had their origin in state projects of standardization and legibility. Consider, for example, something as fundamental as permanent surnames.

A vignette from the popular film *Witness* illustrates how, when among strangers, we do rely on surnames as key navigational aids.[29] The detective in the film is attempting to locate a young Amish boy who may have witnessed a murder. Although the detective has a surname to go on, he is thwarted by several aspects of Amish traditionalism, including the antique German dialect spoken by the Amish. His first instinct is, of course, to reach for the telephone book – a list of proper names and addresses – but the Amish don't have telephones. Furthermore, he learns, the Amish have a very small number of last names. His quandary reminds us that the great variety of surnames and given names in the United States allows us to identify unambiguously a large number of individuals whom we may never have met. A world without such names is bewildering; indeed, the detective finds Amish society so opaque that he needs a native tracker to find his way.

Customary naming practices throughout much of the world are enormously rich. Among some peoples, it is not uncommon for individuals to have different names during different stages of life (infancy, childhood, adulthood) and in some cases after death; added to these are names used for joking, rituals, and mourning and names used for interactions with same-sex friends or with in-laws. Each name is specific to a certain phase of life, social setting, or interlocutor. A single individual will frequently be called by several different names, depending on the stage of life and the person addressing him or her. To the question "What is your name?" which has a more unambiguous answer in the contemporary West, the only plausible answer is "It depends."[30]

For the insider who grows up using these naming practices, they are both legible and clarifying. Each name and the contexts of its use convey important social knowledge. Like the network of alleys in Bruges, the assortment of local weights and measures, and the intricacies of customary land tenure, the complexity of naming has some direct and often quite practical relations to local purposes. For an outsider, however, this byzantine complexity of names is a formidable obstacle to understanding local society. Finding some-

one, let alone situating him or her in a kinship network or tracing the inheritance of property, becomes a major undertaking. If, in addition, the population in question has reason to conceal its identity and its activities from external authority, the camouflage value of such naming practices is considerable.

The invention of permanent, inherited patronyms was, after the administrative simplification of nature (for example, the forest) and space (for example, land tenure), the last step in establishing the necessary preconditions of modern statecraft. In almost every case it was a state project, designed to allow officials to identify, unambiguously, the majority of its citizens. When successful, it went far to create a legible people.[31] Tax and tithe rolls, property rolls, conscription lists, censuses, and property deeds recognized in law were inconceivable without some means of fixing an individual's identity and linking him or her to a kin group. Campaigns to assign permanent patronyms have typically taken place, as one might expect, in the context of a state's exertions to put its fiscal system on a sounder and more lucrative footing. Fearing, with good reason, that an effort to enumerate and register them could be a prelude to some new tax burden or conscription, local officials and the population at large often resisted such campaigns.

[...]

Until at least the fourteenth century, the great majority of Europeans did not have permanent patronymics.[32] An individual's name was typically his given name, which might well suffice for local identification. If something more were required, a second designation could be added, indicating his occupation (in the English case, smith, baker), his geographical location (hill, edgewood), his father's given name, or a personal characteristic (short, strong). These secondary designations were not permanent surnames; they did not survive their bearers, unless by chance, say, a baker's son went into the same trade and was called by the same second designation.

[...]

A connection between state building and the invention of permanent patronyms exists for fourteenth- and fifteenth-century England. In England only wealthy aristocratic families tended to have fixed surnames. In the English case such names referred typically to families' places of origin in Normandy (for example, Baumont, Percy, Disney) or to the places in England that they held in fief from William the Conqueror (for example, Gerard de Sussex). For the rest of the male population, the standard practice of linking only father and son by way of identification prevailed.[33] Thus, William Robertson's male son might be called Thomas Williamson (son of William), while Thomas's son, in turn, might be called Henry Thompson (Thomas's son). Note that the grandson's name, by itself, bore no evidence of his grandfather's identity, complicating the tracing of descent through names alone. A great many northern European surnames, though now permanent, still bear...particles that echo their antique purpose of designating who a man's father was (Fitz-, O'-, -sen, -son, -s, Mac-, -vich).[34] At the time of their establishment, last names often had a kind of local logic to them: John who owned a mill became John Miller; John who made cart wheels became John Wheelwright; John who was physically small became John Short. As their male descendants, whatever their occupations or stature, retained the patronyms, the names later assumed an arbitrary cast.

The development of the personal surname (literally, a name added to another name, and not to be confused with a permanent patronym) went hand in hand with the development of written, official documents such as tithe records, manorial dues rolls, marriage registers, censuses, tax records, and land records.[35] They were necessary to the successful conduct of any administrative exercise involving large numbers of people who had to be individually identified and who were not known personally by the authorities. Imagine the dilemma of a tithe or capitation-tax collector faced with a male population, 90 percent of whom bore just six Christian names (John, William, Thomas, Robert, Richard, and Henry). Some second designation was absolutely essential for the records, and, if the subject suggested none, it was invented for him by the recording clerk. These second designations and the rolls of names that they generated were to the legibility of the population what uniform measurement and the cadastral map were to the legibility of real property. While the subject might normally prefer the safety of anonymity, once he was forced to pay the tax, it was then in his interest to be accurately identified in order to avoid paying the same tax twice. Many of these fourteenth-century surnames were clearly nothing more than administrative fictions designed to make a population fiscally legible. Many of the subjects whose "surnames" appear in the documents were probably unaware of what had been written down, and, for the great majority, the surnames had no social existence whatever outside the document.[36] Only on very rare occasions does one encounter an entry, such as "William Carter, tailor," that implies that we may be dealing with a permanent patronym.

The increasing intensity of interaction with the state and statelike structures (large manors, the church) exactly parallels the development of permanent, heritable patronyms. Thus, when Edward I clarified the system of landholding, establishing primogeniture and hereditary copyhold tenure for manorial land, he provided a powerful incentive for the adoption of permanent patronyms. Taking one's father's surname became, for the eldest son at least, part of a claim to the property on the father's death.[37] Now that property claims were subject to state validation, surnames that had once been mere bureaucratic fantasies took on a social reality of their own. One imagines that for a long time English subjects had in effect two names – their local name and an "official," fixed patronym. As the frequency of interaction with impersonal administrative structures increased, the official name came to prevail in all but a man's intimate circle.

Those subjects living at a greater distance, both socially and geographically, from the organs of state power, as did the Tuscans, acquired permanent patronyms much later. The upper classes and those living in the south of England thus acquired permanent surnames before the lower classes and those living in the north did. The Scottish and Welsh acquired them even later.[38]

State naming practices, like state mapping practices, were inevitably associated with taxes (labor, military service, grain, revenue) and hence aroused popular resistance. The great English peasant rising of 1381 (often called the Wat Tyler Rebellion) is attributed to an unprecedented decade of registrations and assessments of poll taxes.[39] For English...peasants, a census of all adult males could not but appear ominous, if not ruinous.

The imposition of permanent surnames on colonial populations offers us a chance to observe a process, telescoped into a decade or less, that in the West might have taken several generations. Many of the same state objectives animate both the European and the colonial exercises, but in the colonial case, the state is at once more bureaucratized and less tolerant of popular resistance. The very brusqueness of colonial naming casts the purposes and paradoxes of the process in sharp relief.

Nowhere is this better illustrated than in the Philippines under the Spanish.[40] Filipinos were instructed by the decree of November 21, 1849, to take on permanent Hispanic surnames. The author of the decree was Governor (and Lieutenant General) Narciso Claveria y Zaldua, a meticulous administrator as determined to rationalize names as he had been determined to rationalize existing law, provincial boundaries, and the calendar.[41] He had observed, as his decree states, that Filipinos generally lacked individual surnames, which might "distinguish them by families," and that their practice of adopting baptismal names drawn from a small group of saints' names resulted in great "confusion." The remedy was the *catalogo*, a compendium not only of personal names but also of nouns and adjectives drawn from flora, fauna, minerals, geography, and the arts and intended to be used by the authorities in assigning permanent, inherited surnames. Each local official was to be given a supply of surnames sufficient for his jurisdiction, "taking care that the distribution be made by letters [of the alphabet]."[42] In practice, each town was given a number of pages from the alphabetized catalogo, producing whole towns with surnames beginning with the same letter. In situations where there has been little in-migration in the past 150 years, the traces of this administrative exercise are still perfectly visible across the landscape: "For example, in the Bikol region, the entire alphabet is laid out like a garland over the provinces of Albay, Sorsogon, and Catanduanes which in 1849 belonged to the single jurisdiction of Albay. Beginning with *A* at the provincial capital, the letters *B* and *C* mark the towns along the coast beyond Tabaco to Tiwi. We return and trace along the coast of Sorsogon the letters *E* to *L*; then starting down the Iraya Valley at Daraga with *M*, we stop with *S* to Polangui and Libon, and finish the alphabet with a quick tour around the island of Catanduanes."[43]

The confusion for which the decree is the antidote is largely that of the administrator and the tax collector. Universal last names, they believe, will facilitate the administration of justice, finance, and public order as well as make it simpler for prospective marriage partners to calculate their degree of consanguinity.[44] For a utilitarian state builder of Claveria's temper, however, the ultimate goal was a complete and legible list of subjects and taxpayers. This is abundantly clear from the short preamble to the decree: "In view of the extreme usefulness and practicality of this measure, the time has come to issue a directive for the formation of a civil register [formerly a clerical function], which may not only fulfill and ensure the said objectives, but may also serve as a basis for the statistics of the country, guarantee the collection of taxes, the regular performance of personal services, and the receipt of payment for exemptions. It likewise provides exact information of the movement of the population, thus avoiding unauthorized migrations, hiding taxpayers, and other abuses."[45]

Drawing on the accurate lists of citizens throughout the colony, Claveria envisioned each local official constructing a table of eight columns specifying tribute obligations, communal labor obligations, first name, surname, age, marital status, occupation, and exemptions. A ninth column, for updating the register, would record alterations in status and would be submitted for inspection every month. Because of their accuracy and uniformity, these registers would allow the state to compile the precise statistics in Manila that would make for fiscal efficiency. The daunting cost of assigning surnames to the entire population and building a complete and discriminating list of taxpayers was justified by forecasting that the list, while it might cost as much as twenty thousand pesos to create, would yield one hundred thousand or two hundred thousand pesos in continuing annual revenue.

What if the Filipinos chose to ignore their new last names? This possibility had already crossed Claveria's mind, and he took steps to make sure that the names would stick. Schoolteachers were ordered to forbid their students to address or even know one another by any name except the officially inscribed family name. Those teachers who did not apply the rule with enthusiasm were to be punished. More efficacious perhaps, given the minuscule school enrollment, was the proviso that forbade priests and military and civil officials from accepting any document, application, petition, or deed that did not use the official surnames. All documents using other names would be null and void.

Actual practice, as one might expect, fell considerably short of Claveria's administrative utopia of legible and regimented taxpayers. The continued existence of such non-Spanish surnames as Magsaysay or Macapagal suggests that part of the population was never mustered for this exercise. Local officials submitted incomplete returns

or none at all. And there was another serious problem, one that Claveria had foreseen but inadequately provided for. The new registers rarely recorded, as they were supposed to, the previous names used by the registrants. This meant that it became exceptionally difficult for officials to trace back property and taxpaying to the period before the transformation of names. The state had in effect blinded its own hindsight by the very success of its new scheme.

With surnames, as with forests, land tenure, and legible cities, actual practice never achieved anything like the simplified and uniform perfection to which its designers had aspired. As late as 1872, an attempt at taking a census proved a complete fiasco, and it was not tried again until just before the revolution of 1896. Nevertheless, by the twentieth century, the vast majority of Filipinos bore the surnames that Claveria had dreamed up for them. The increasing weight of the state in people's lives and the state's capacity to insist on its rules and its terms ensured that.

Universal last names are a fairly recent historical phenomenon. Tracking property ownership and inheritance, collecting taxes, maintaining court records, performing police work, conscripting soldiers, and controlling epidemics were all made immeasurably easier by the clarity of full names and, increasingly, fixed addresses. While the utilitarian state was committed to a complete inventory of its population, liberal ideas of citizenship, which implied voting rights and conscription, also contributed greatly to the standardization of naming practices. The legislative imposition of permanent surnames is particularly clear in the case of Western European Jews who had no tradition of last names. A Napoleonic decree . . . in 1808 mandated last names.[46] Austrian legislation of 1787, as part of the emancipation process, required Jews to choose last names or, if they refused, to have fixed last names chosen for them. In Prussia the emancipation of the Jews was contingent upon the adoption of surnames.[47] Many of the immigrants to the United States, Jews and non-Jews alike, had no permanent surnames when they set sail. Very few, however, made it through the initial paperwork without an official last name that their descendants carry still.

The process of creating fixed last names continues in much of the Third World and on the "tribal frontiers" of more developed countries.[48] Today, of course, there are now many other state-impelled standard designations that have vastly improved the capacity of the state to identify an individual. The creation of birth and death certificates, more specific addresses (that is, more specific than something like "John-on-the-hill"), identity cards, passports, social security numbers, photographs, fingerprints, and, most recently, DNA profiles have superseded the rather crude instrument of the permanent surname. But the surname was a first and crucial step toward making individual citizens officially legible, and along with the photograph, it is still the first fact on documents of identity.

The Directive for a Standard, Official Language

The great cultural barrier imposed by a separate language is perhaps the most effective guarantee that a social world, easily accessible to insiders, will remain opaque to outsiders.[49] Just as the stranger or state official might need a local guide to find his way around sixteenth-century Bruges, he would need a local interpreter in order to understand and be understood in an unfamiliar linguistic environment. A distinct language, however, is a far more powerful basis for autonomy than a complex residential pattern. It is also the bearer of a distinctive history, a cultural sensibility, a literature, a mythology, a musical past.[50] In this respect, a unique language represents a formidable obstacle to state knowledge, let alone colonization, control, manipulation, instruction, or propaganda.

Of all state simplifications, then, the imposition of a single, official language may be the most powerful, and it is the precondition of many other simplifications. This process should probably be viewed, as Eugen Weber suggests in the case of France, as one of domestic colonization in which various foreign provinces (such as Brittany and Occitanie) are linguistically subdued and culturally incorporated.[51] In the first efforts made to insist on the use of French, it is clear that the state's objective was the legibility of local practice. Officials insisted that every legal document – whether a will, document of sale, loan instrument, contract, annuity, or property deed – be drawn up in French. As long as these documents remained in local vernaculars, they were daunting to an official sent from Paris and virtually impossible to bring into conformity with central schemes of legal and administrative standardization. The campaign of linguistic centralization was assured of some success since it went hand in hand with an expansion of state power. By the late nineteenth century, dealing with the state was unavoidable for all but a small minority of the population. Petitions, court cases, school documents, applications, and correspondence with officials were all of necessity written in French. One can hardly imagine a more effective formula for immediately devaluing local knowledge and privileging all those who had mastered the official linguistic code. It was a gigantic shift in power. Those at the periphery who lacked competence in French were rendered mute and marginal. They were now in need of a local guide to the new state culture, which appeared in the form of lawyers, *notaires*, schoolteachers, clerks, and soldiers.[52]

A cultural project, as one might suspect, lurked behind the linguistic centralization. French was seen as the bearer of a national civilization; the purpose of imposing it was not merely to have provincials digest the Code Napoleon but also to bring them Voltaire, Racine, Parisian newspapers, and a national education.... Where the command of Latin had once defined participation in a wider culture for a small elite, the command of standard French now defined full participation in French culture. The implicit logic of the move was to define a hierarchy of cultures, relegating local languages and their regional cultures to, at best, a quaint provincialism. At the apex of this implicit pyramid was Paris and its institutions: ministries, schools, academies (including the guardian of the language, l'Académie Française). The relative success of this cultural project hinged on both coercion and inducements.... Standard (Parisian) French and Paris were not only focal points of power; they were also magnets. The growth of markets, physical mobility, new careers, political patronage, public service, and a national educational system all meant that facility in French and connections to Paris were the paths of social advancement and material success. It was a state simplification that promised to reward those who complied with its logic and to penalize those who ignored it.

The Centralization of Traffic Patterns

The linguistic centralization impelled by the imposition of Parisian French as the official standard was replicated in a centralization of traffic. Just as the new dispensation in language made Paris the hub of communication, so the new road and rail systems increasingly favored movement to and from Paris over interregional or local traffic. State policy resembled, in computer parlance, a "hardwiring" pattern that made the provinces far more accessible, far more legible, to central authorities than even the absolutist kings had imagined.

Let us contrast, in an overly schematic way, a relatively uncentralized network of communication, on one hand, with a relatively centralized network, on the other. If mapped, the uncentralized pattern would be the physical image of the actual movements of goods and people along routes *not* created by administrative fiat. Such movements would not be random; they would reflect both the ease of travel along valleys, by watercourses, and around defiles and also the location of important resources and ritual sites. Weber captures

the wealth of human activities that animate these movements across the landscape: "They served professional pursuits, like the special trails followed by glassmakers, carriers or sellers of salt, potters, or those that led to forges, mines, quarries, and hemp fields, or those along which flax, hemp, linen, and yarn were taken to market. There were pilgrimage routes and procession trails."[53]

If we can imagine, for the sake of argument, a place where physical resources are evenly distributed and there are no great physical barriers to movement (such as mountains or swamps), then a map of paths in use might form a network resembling a dense concentration of capillaries. The tracings would, of course, never be entirely random. Market towns based on location and resources would constitute small hubs, as would religious shrines, quarries, mines, and other important sites.[54] In the French case as well, the network of roads would have long reflected the centralizing ambitions of local lords and the nation's monarchs. The point of this illustrative idealization, however, is to depict a landscape of communication routes that is only lightly marked by state centralization....

Beginning with Colbert, the state-building modernizers of France were bent on superimposing on this pattern a carefully planned grid of administrative centralization.[55] Their scheme, never entirely realized, was to align highways, canals, and ultimately rail lines to radiate out from Paris like the spokes of a wheel.... The layout was designed "to serve the government and the cities and lacking a network of supporting thoroughfares had little to do with popular habit or need. Administrative highways, a historian of the center called them, [were] made for troops to march on and for tax revenues to reach the treasury."[56]

[...]

As a centralizing aesthetic, the plan defied the canons of commercial logic or cost-effectiveness. The first phase of the grid, the line from Paris east to Strasbourg and the frontier, ran straight through the plateau of Brie rather than following the centers of population along the Marne. By refusing to conform to the topography in its quest of geometric perfection, the railway line was ruinously expensive compared to English or German railroads. The army had also adopted the Ponts et Chaussées logic, believing that direct rail lines to the borders would be militarily advantageous. They were proven tragically wrong in the Franco-Prussian War of 1870–71.[57]

This retrofitting of traffic patterns had enormous consequences, most of which were intended: linking provincial France and provincial French citizens to Paris and to the state and facilitating the deployment of troops from the capital to put down civil unrest in any department in the nation. It was aimed at achieving, for the military control of the nation, what Haussmann had achieved in the capital itself. It thus empowered Paris and the state at the expense of the provinces, greatly affected the economics of location, expedited central fiscal and military control, and severed or weakened lateral cultural and economic ties by favoring hierarchical links. At a stroke, it marginalized outlying areas in the way that official French had marginalized local dialects.

Conclusion

Officials of the modern state are, of necessity, at least one step – and often several steps – removed from the society they are charged with governing. They assess the life of their society by a series of typifications that are always some distance from the full reality these abstractions are meant to capture. Thus the foresters' charts and tables, despite their synoptic power to distill many individual facts into a larger pattern, do not quite capture (nor are they meant to) the real forest in its full diversity. Thus the cadastral survey and the title deed are a rough, often misleading representation of actual, existing rights to land use and disposal. The functionary of any large organization "sees" the human activity that is of interest to him largely through the simplified approximations of documents and statistics: tax proceeds, lists of taxpayers, land records, average incomes, unemployment numbers, mortality rates, trade and productivity figures, the total number of cases of cholera in a certain district.

These typifications are indispensable to statecraft. State simplifications such as maps, censuses, cadastral lists, and standard units of measurement represent techniques for grasping a large and complex reality; in order for officials to be able to comprehend aspects of the ensemble, that complex reality must be reduced to schematic categories. The only way to accomplish this is to reduce an infinite array of detail to a set of categories that will facilitate summary descriptions, comparisons, and aggregation. The invention, elaboration, and deployment of these abstractions represent, as Charles Tilly has shown, an enormous leap in state capacity – a move from tribute and indirect rule to taxation and direct rule. Indirect rule required only a minimal state apparatus but rested on local elites and communities who had an interest in withholding resources and knowledge from the center. Direct rule sparked widespread resistance and necessitated negotiations that often limited the center's power, but for the first time, it allowed state officials direct knowledge of and access to a previously opaque society.

Such is the power of the most advanced techniques of direct rule, that it discovers new social truths as well as merely summarizing known facts. The Center for Disease Control in Atlanta is a striking case in point. Its network of sample hospitals allowed it to first "discover" – in the epidemiological sense – such hitherto unknown diseases as toxic shock syndrome, Legionnaires' disease, and AIDS. Stylized facts of this kind are a powerful form of state knowledge, making it possible for officials to intervene early in epidemics, to understand economic trends that greatly affect public welfare, to gauge whether their policies are having the desired effect, and to make policy with many of the crucial facts at hand.[58] These facts permit discriminating interventions, some of which are literally lifesaving.

The techniques devised to enhance the legibility of a society to its rulers have become vastly more sophisticated, but the political motives driving them have changed little. Appropriation, control, and manipulation (in the nonpejorative sense) remain the most prominent. If we imagine a state that has no reliable means of enumerating and locating its population, gauging its wealth, and mapping its land, resources, and settlements, we are imagining a state whose interventions in that society are necessarily crude. A society that is relatively opaque to the state is thereby insulated from some forms of finely tuned state interventions, both welcomed (universal vaccinations) and resented (personal income taxes). The interventions it does experience will typically be mediated by local trackers who know the society from inside and who are likely to interpose their own particular interests. Without this mediation – and often with it – state action is likely to be inept, greatly overshooting or undershooting its objective.

An illegible society, then, is a hindrance to any effective intervention by the state, whether the purpose of that intervention is plunder or public welfare. As long as the state's interest is largely confined to grabbing a few tons of grain and rounding up a few conscripts, the state's ignorance may not be fatal. When, however, the state's objective requires changing the daily habits (hygiene or health practices) or work performance (quality labor or machine maintenance) of its citizens, such ignorance can well be disabling. A thoroughly legible society eliminates local monopolies of information and creates a kind of national transparency through the uniformity of codes, identities, statistics, regulations, and measures. At the same time it is likely to create new positional advantages for those at the apex who have the knowledge and access to easily decipher the new state-created format.

The discriminating interventions that a legible society makes possible can, of course, be deadly as well. A sobering instance is wordlessly recalled by a map produced by the City Office of Statistics of Amsterdam, then under Nazi occupation, in May 1941.[59] Along with lists of residents, the map was the synoptic representation that guided the rounding up of the city's Jewish population, sixty-five thousand of whom were eventually deported.

The map is titled "The Distribution of Jews in the Municipality." Each dot represents ten Jews, a scheme that makes the heavily Jewish districts readily apparent. The map was compiled from information obtained not only through the order for people of Jewish extraction to register themselves but also through the population registry ("exceptionally comprehensive in the Netherlands")[60] and the business registry. If one reflects briefly on the kind of detailed information on names, addresses, and ethnic backgrounds (determined perhaps by names in the population registry or by declaration) and the cartographic exactitude required to produce this statistical representation, the contribution of legibility to state capacity is evident. The Nazi authorities, of course, supplied the murderous purpose behind the exercise, but the legibility provided by the Dutch authorities supplied the means to its efficient implementation.[61] That legibility, I should emphasize, merely amplifies the capacity of the state for discriminating interventions – a capacity that in principle could as easily have been deployed to feed the Jews as to deport them.

Legibility implies a viewer whose place is central and whose vision is synoptic. State simplifications of the kind we have examined are designed to provide authorities with a schematic view of their society, a view not afforded to those without authority. Rather like US highway patrolmen wearing mirrored sunglasses, the authorities enjoy a quasi-monopolistic picture of selected aspects of the whole society. This privileged vantage point is typical of all institutional settings where command and control of complex human activities is paramount. The monastery, the barracks, the factory floor, and the administrative bureaucracy (private or public) exercise many statelike functions and often mimic its information structure as well.

State simplifications can be considered part of an ongoing "project of legibility," a project that is never fully realized. The data from which such simplifications arise are, to varying degrees, riddled with inaccuracies, omissions, faulty aggregations, fraud, negligence, political distortion, and so on. A project of legibility is immanent in any statecraft that aims at manipulating society, but it is undermined by intrastate rivalries, technical obstacles, and, above all, the resistance of its subjects.

State simplifications have at least five characteristics that deserve emphasis. Most obviously, state simplifications are observations of only those aspects of social life that are of official interest. They are *interested*, utilitarian facts. Second, they are also nearly always written (verbal or numerical) *documentary* facts. Third, they are typically *static* facts.[62] Fourth, most stylized state facts are also *aggregate* facts. Aggregate facts may be impersonal (the density of transportation networks) or simply a collection of facts about individuals (employment rates, literacy rates, residence patterns). Finally, for most purposes, state officials need to group citizens in ways that permit them to make a collective assessment. Facts that can be aggregated and presented as averages or distributions must therefore be *standardized* facts. However unique the actual circumstances of the various individuals who make up the aggregate, it is their sameness or, more precisely, their differences along a standardized scale or continuum that are of interest.

The process by which standardized facts susceptible to aggregation are manufactured seems to require at least three steps. The first, indispensable step is the creation of common units of measurement or coding. Size classes of trees, freehold tenure, the metric system for measuring landed property or the volume of grain, uniform naming practices, sections of prairie land, and urban lots of standard sizes are among the units created for this purpose. In the next step, each item or instance falling within a category is counted and classified according to the new unit of assessment. A particular tree reappears as an instance of a certain size class of tree; a par-

ticular plot of agricultural land reappears as coordinates in a cadastral map; a particular job reappears as an instance of a category of employment; a particular person reappears bearing a name according to the new formula. Each fact must be recuperated and brought back on stage, as it were, dressed in a new uniform of official weave – as part of "a series in a total classificatory grid."[63] Only in such garb can these facts play a role in the culmination of the process: the creation of wholly new facts by aggregation, following the logic of the new units. One arrives, finally, at synoptic facts that are useful to officials: so many thousands of trees in a given size class, so many thousands of men between the ages of eighteen and thirty-five, so many farms in a given size class, so many students whose surnames begin with the letter *A*, so many people with tuberculosis. Combining several metrics of aggregation, one arrives at quite subtle, complex, heretofore unknown truths, including, for example, the distribution of tubercular patients by income and urban location.

To call such elaborate artifacts of knowledge "state simplifications" risks being misleading. They are anything but simpleminded, and they are often wielded with great sophistication by officials. Rather, the term "simplification" is meant in two quite specific senses. First, the knowledge that an official needs must give him or her a synoptic view of the ensemble; it must be cast in terms that are replicable across many cases. In this respect, such facts must lose their particularity and reappear in schematic or simplified form as a member of a class of facts.[64] Second, in a meaning closely related to the first, the grouping of synoptic facts necessarily entails collapsing or ignoring distinctions that might otherwise be relevant.

Take, for example, simplifications about employment. The working lives of many people are exceptionally complex and may change from day to day. For the purposes of official statistics, however, being "gainfully employed" is a stylized fact; one is or is not gainfully employed. Also, available characterizations of many rather exotic working lives are sharply restricted by the categories used in the aggregate statistics.[65] Those who gather and interpret such aggregate data understand that there is a certain fictional and arbitrary quality to their categories and that they hide a wealth of problematic variation. Once set, however, these thin categories operate unavoidably as if all similarly classified cases were in fact homogeneous and uniform.... There is, as Theodore Porter notes in his study of mechanical objectivity, a "strong incentive to prefer precise and standardizable measures to highly accurate ones," since accuracy is meaningless if the identical procedure cannot reliably be performed elsewhere.[66]

To this point, I have been making a rather straightforward, even banal point about the simplification, abstraction, and standardization that are necessary for state officials' observations of the circumstances of some or all of the population. But I want to make a further claim, one analogous to that made for scientific forestry: the modern state, through its officials, attempts with varying success to create a terrain and a population with precisely those standardized characteristics that will be easiest to monitor, count, assess, and manage. The utopian, immanent, and continually frustrated goal of the modern state is to reduce the chaotic, disorderly, constantly changing social reality beneath it to something more closely resembling the administrative grid of its observations. Much of the statecraft of the late eighteenth and nineteenth centuries was devoted to this project. "In the period of movement from tribute to tax, from indirect rule to direct rule, from subordination to assimilation," Tilly remarks, "states generally worked to homogenize their populations and break down their segmentation by imposing common languages, religions, currencies, and legal systems, as well as promoting the construction of connected systems of trade, transportation, and communication."[67]

As the scientific forester may dream of a perfectly legible forest planted with same-aged, single-species, uniform trees growing in straight lines in a rectangular flat space cleared of all underbrush and poachers,[68] so the exacting state official may aspire to a perfectly legible population with registered, unique names and addresses keyed to grid settlements; who pursue single, identifiable occupations; and all of whose transactions are documented according to the designated formula and in the official language. This caricature of society as a military parade ground is overdrawn, but the grain of truth that it embodies may help us understand the [State's] grandiose plans....[69] The aspiration to such uniformity and order alerts us to the fact that modern statecraft is largely a project of internal colonization, often glossed, as it is in imperial rhetoric, as a "civilizing mission." The builders of the modern nation-state do not merely describe, observe, and map; they strive to shape a people and landscape that will fit their techniques of observation.[70]

[...]

State officials can often make their categories stick and impose their simplifications, because the state, of all institutions, is best equipped to insist on treating people according to its schemata. Thus categories that may have begun as the artificial inventions of cadastral surveyors, census takers, judges, or police officers can end by becoming categories that organize people's daily experience precisely because they are embedded in state-created institutions that structure that experience.[71] The economic plan, survey map, record of ownership, forest management plan, classification of ethnicity, passbook, arrest record, and map of political boundaries acquire their force from the fact that these synoptic data are the points of departure for reality as state officials apprehend and shape it. In dictatorial settings where there is no effective way to assert another reality, fictitious facts-on-paper can often be made eventually to prevail on the ground, because it is on behalf of such pieces of paper that police and army are deployed.

These paper records are the operative facts in a court of law, in an administrative dossier, and before most functionaries. In this sense, there are virtually no other facts for the state than those that are contained in documents standardized for that purpose. An error in such a document can have far more power – and for far longer – than can an unreported truth. If, for example, you want to defend your claim to real property, you are normally obliged to defend it with a document called a property deed, and to do so in the courts and tribunals created for that purpose. If you wish to have any standing in law, you must have a document that officials accept as evidence of citizenship, be that document a birth certificate, passport, or identity card. The categories used by state agents are not merely means to make their environment legible; they are an authoritative tune to which most of the population must dance.

NOTES AND REFERENCES

1 As one might expect, independent towns were likely to privilege local knowledge far more than royal towns, which were designed with administrative and military order in mind.

2 The Casbah's illegibility, however, was not insurmountable. The FLN's resistance there was eventually broken, although at great long-run political cost, by determined police work, torture, and networks of local informers.

3 The inability of many US municipal authorities to effectively govern inner cities has prompted attempts to bring back the "cop on the beat" in the form of "community policing." The purpose of community policing is to create a cadre of local police who are intimately familiar with the physical layout of the community and especially the local population, whose assistance is now judged vital to effective police work. Its aim is to turn officials who had come to be seen as outsiders into insiders.

4 I am grateful to Ron Aminzade for sending me the explanatory notes (*mémoires*) meant to accompany two of the maps the military officials had prepared as part of this *haute reconnaissance* in the city of Toulouse in 1843. They come from the *Archives de l'Armée, Paris*, dossier MR 1225. They note the streets or terrain that would be difficult to traverse, watercourses that might impede military movement, the attitude of the local population, the difficulty of their accents, the locations of markets, and so on.

5 René Descartes, *Discourse on Method*, trans. Donald A. Cress (Indianapolis: Hackett, 1980), p. 6, quoted in R. P. Harrison, *Forests: The Shadow of Civilization*, (Chicago: University of Chicago Press, 1992) pp. 111–12.

6 Lewis Mumford, *The City in History: Its Origins, Its Transformations, and Its Prospects* (New York: Harcourt Brace Jovanovich, 1961), p. 364.

7 Ibid., p. 387.

8 Quoted in ibid., p. 369.

9 Thomas More's utopian cities, for example, were to be perfectly uniform, so that "he who knows one of the cities will know them all, so exactly alike are they, except where the nature of the ground prevents" (More's *Utopia*, quoted in ibid., p. 327).

10 St Petersburg is the most striking example of the planned utopian capital, a metropolis that Dostoyevsky called the "most abstract and premeditated city in the world." See Marshall Berman, *All That Is Solid Melts into Air: The Experience of Modernity* (New York: Penguin, 1988), chap. 4. The Babylonians, Egyptians, and, of course, the Romans built "grid-settlements." Long before the Enlightenment, right angles were seen as evidence of cultural superiority. As Richard Sennett writes, "Hippodamus of Miletus is conventionally thought the first city builder to conceive of these grids as expressions of culture; the grid expressed, he believed, the rationality of civilized life. In their military conquests the Romans elaborated the contrast between the rude and formless camps of the barbarians and their own military forts, or castra" (*The Conscience of the Eye:*

The Design and Social Life of Cities [New York: Norton, 1990], p. 47).

11   Well, almost. There are a few streets – among them Lincoln, Archer, and Blue Island – that follow old Indian trails and thus deviate from the geometric logic.

12   It may have occurred to the reader that certain grid sections of upper Manhattan and Chicago are, despite their formal order, essentially ungoverned and dangerous. No amount of formal order can overcome massive countervailing factors such as poverty, crime, social disorganization, or hostility toward officials. As a sign of the illegibility of such areas, the Census Bureau acknowledges that the number of uncounted African-Americans was six times the number of uncounted whites. The undercount is politically volatile since census figures determine the number of congressional seats to which a state is entitled.

13   See the mind-opening book by the geographer Yi-Fu Tuan, *Dominance and Affection: The Making of Pets* (New Haven: Yale University Press, 1984).

14   The plan created not only a more legible fiscal space but also the fortunes of the small coterie who used their inside knowledge of the plan to profit from real-estate speculation.

15   There was an older, quasi-planned, baroque city bequeathed to Paris by her absolutist rulers, especially those prior to Louis XIV, who for his part chose to lavish his planning on a "new space," Versailles.

16   As Mark Girouard notes, the plan included public facilities and institutions such as parks (notably the huge Bois de Boulogne), hospitals, schools, colleges, barracks, prisons, and a new opera house (*Cities and People: A Social and Architectural History* [New Haven: Yale University Press, 1985], p. 289). Roughly a century later, against greater odds, Robert Moses would undertake a similar retrofit of New York City.

17   Mumford writes, "Were not the ancient medieval streets of Paris one of the last refuges of urban liberties? No wonder that Napoleon III sanctioned the breaking through of narrow streets and culs-de-sac and the razing of whole quarters to provide wide boulevards. It was the best possible protection against assault from within" (*The City in History*, pp. 369–70).

18   Quoted in Louis Girard, *Nouvelle histoire de Paris: La deuxième république et le second empire, 1848–1870* (Paris, 1981), p. 126. Cited in J. M. Merriman, *Aux marges de la ville: Faubourgs et banlieues* (Paris: Seuil, 1994), p. 15. The parallels with the later *ceinture rouge*, the leftist working-class suburbs ringing Paris, are striking. Soweto and other black townships in South Africa under apartheid, although established explicitly for the purposes of segregation, also became illegible, subversive spaces from the perspective of the authorities.

19   Since the planners lacked a reliable map of the city, the first step was to build temporary wooden towers in order to achieve the triangulation necessary for an accurate map. See David H. Pinkney, *Napoleon III and the Rebuilding of Paris* (Princeton: Princeton University Press, 1958), p. 5.

20   Quoted in Jeanne Gaillard, *Paris, la ville, 1852–1870* (Paris, 1979), p. 38, cited in Merriman, *Aux marges de la ville*, p. 10.

21   Ibid., pp. 8–9.

22   Pinkney, *Napoleon III*, p. 23. A commonplace of demographic history has been that urban populations in Western Europe, beset with epidemics and generally high mortality, did not successfully reproduce themselves until well into the nineteenth century; the growth of cities came largely from in-migration from the healthier countryside. Although this position has been challenged, the evidence for it is still convincing. See the judicious synthesis and assessment by Jan de Vries, *European Urbanization, 1500–1800* (Cambridge: Harvard University Press, 1984), pp. 175–200.

23   Merriman, *Aux marges de la ville*, pp. 7–8. See also T. J. Clark, *The Painting of*

Modern Life: Paris in the Art of Manet and His Followers (Princeton: Princeton University Press, 1984), p. 35. Louis Napoleon's and Haussmann's mania for straight lines was the butt of many jokes. A character in a play by Edmond About, for instance, dreams of the day when the Seine itself will be straightened, because, as he says, "its irregular curve is really rather shocking" (quoted in Clark, *The Painting of Modern Life*, p. 35).

24 Pinkney, *Napoleon III*, p. 93.

25 Clark, *The Painting of Modern Life*, p. 66. For a superb analysis of how tidy Orientalist expositions depicting Old Cairo, the peasant village, and so on gave Arab visitors to Paris a completely new way of seeing their society, see Timothy Mitchell, *Colonizing Egypt* (Berkeley: University of California Press, 1991), especially chaps. 1–3.

26 Gaillard, *Paris, la ville*, p. 568, quoted in Merriman, *Aux marges de la ville*, p. 20.

27 David Harvey, *Consciousness and the Urban Experience* (Baltimore: Johns Hopkins University Press, 1985), p. 165, quoted in Merriman, *Aux marges de la ville*, p. 12. See also David Harvey, *The Urban Experience* (Baltimore: Johns Hopkins University Press, 1989), which covers much of the same ground.

28 Jacques Rougerie, *Paris libre, 1871* (Paris, 1971), p. 19, quoted in Merriman, *Aux marges de la ville*, p. 27.

29 I owe this astute observation about *The Witness* to Benedict Anderson. More generally, his analysis of the census and the map as totalizing classificatory grids, particularly in colonial settings, has greatly influenced my thinking here. See Anderson, *Imagined Communities: Reflections on the Origin and Spread of Nationalism* (London: Verso, 1983), and also the remarkable book by Thongchai Winichakul, *Siam Mapped: A History of the Geo-Body of a Nation* (Honolulu: University of Hawaii Press, 1994).

30 See, for example, William E. Wormsley, "Traditional Change in Imbonggu Names and Naming Practices," *Names* 28 (1980): 183–94.

31 The adoption of permanent, inherited patronyms went far, but not the whole way. How is a state to associate a name, however unique and unambiguous, with an individual? Like identity cards, social security numbers, and pass systems, names require that the citizenry cooperate by carrying them and producing them on the demand of an official. Cooperation is secured in most modern state systems by making a clear identity a prerequisite for receiving entitlements; in more coercive systems, harsh penalties are exacted for failure to carry identification documents. If, however, there is widespread defiance, individuals will either fail to identify themselves or use false identities. The ultimate identity card, then, is an ineradicable mark on the body: a tattoo, a fingerprint, a DNA "signature."

32 To my knowledge, Iceland is the only European nation that had not adopted permanent surnames by the late twentieth century.

33 In the West, women, domestic servants, and tied laborers were typically the last to adopt surnames (and to be given the vote), because they were legally subsumed as minors in the charge of the male head of family.

34 Other surnames referring to fathers are not quite so obvious. Thus the name "Victor Hugo" would originally have meant simply "Victor, son of Hugo."

35 I am indebted to Kate Stanton, an astute research assistant, for her background research on this issue.

36 See C. M. Matthews, *English Surnames* (London: Weidenfeld and Nicolson, 1966), pp. 35–48.

37 As Matthews notes, "The humble peasant with only one virgate of land was as anxious to claim it by right of being his father's eldest son as the rich man inheriting a large estate. The land could be claimed and awarded only at the Manorial Court, being held 'by copy of the Court Roll' [that is, being a copyhold],

which meant that the life tenant's name was inscribed there on permanent record. This system provided a direct incentive to men to keep the same surname that had been put down on the roll for their father and grandfather" (ibid., p. 44). And given the vagaries of the mortality rate in fourteenth-century England, younger sons might want to keep the name as well, just in case.

38 In historical documents one can occasionally glimpse a moment when a permanent surname seems to gel. Under Henry VIII in the early sixteenth century, for example, a Welshman who appeared in court was asked for his name, and he answered, in the Welsh fashion, "Thomas Ap [son of] William, Ap Thomas, Ap Richard, Ap Hoel, Ap Evan Vaughan." He was scolded by the judge, who instructed him to "leave the old manner,... whereupon he after called himself Moston, according to the name of his principal house, and left that name to his posteritie" (William Camden, *Remains Concerning Britain*, ed. R. D. Dunn [1605; Toronto: University of Toronto Press, 1984], p. 122). This "administrative" last name almost certainly remained unknown to Thomas's neighbors.

39 See the classic study by Rodney Hilton, *Bond Men Made Free: Medieval Peasant Movements and the English Rising of 1381* (New York: Viking Press, 1977), pp. 160–64.

40 I am particularly grateful to Rosanne Ruttan, Otto van den Muijzenberg, Harold Conklin, and Charles Bryant for putting me on the track of the Philippine case. The key document is Domingo Abella, ed., *Catalogo alfabetico de Apellidos* (Manila: National Archives, 1973). See also the short account in O. D. Corpuz, *The Roots of the Filipino Nation*, vol. 1 (Quezon City: Aklahi Foundation, 1989), pp. 479–80. For a perceptive analysis of naming and identity formation among the Karo-Batak of colonial East Sumatra, see Mary Margaret Steedly, "The Importance of Proper

Names: Language and 'National' Identity in Colonial Karoland," *American Ethnologist* 23, no. 3 (1996): 447–75.

41 For nearly three hundred years, the Spanish calendar for the Philippines had been one day ahead of the Spanish calendar, because Magellan's expedition had not, of course, adjusted for their westward travel halfway around the globe.

42 Abella, *Catalogo alfabetico de Apellidos*, p. viii.

43 Ibid., p. vii.

44 As if the Filipinos did not have perfectly adequate oral and written genealogical schemes to achieve the same end.

45 Abella, *Catalogo alfabetico de Apellidos*, p. viii.

46 For the best treatment of permanent patronyms in France and their relation to state-building, see the insightful book by Anne Lefebvre-Teillard, *Le nom: Droit et histoire* (Paris: Presses Universitaires de France, 1990). She examines the process whereby state officials, both administrative and judicial, gradually authorized certain naming practices and limited the conditions under which names might be changed. The civil registers, along with the *livret de famille* (family pass book), established toward the end of the nineteenth century, became important tools for police administration, conscription, civil and criminal justice, and elections monitoring. The standard opening line of an encounter between a policeman and a civilian – "Vos papiers, Monsieur" – dates from this period. Having experienced the "blinding" of the administration caused by the destruction of civil registers in the burning of the Hôtel de Ville (city hall) and the Palais de Justice at the end of the Commune in 1871, officials took care to keep duplicate registers.

47 Robert Chazon, "Names: Medieval Period and Establishment of Surnames," *Encyclopedia Judaica* (Jerusalem and Philadelphia: Keter Publishers and Coronet Books, 1982), 12:809–13. In the

1930s the Nazis passed a series of "name decrees" whose sole purpose was to distinguish what they had determined as the Jewish population from the Gentile population. Jews who had Aryan-sounding names were required to change them (or to add "Israel" or "Sarah"), as were Aryans who had Jewish-sounding names. Lists of approved names were compiled, and contested cases were submitted to the Reich Office for Genealogical Research. Once the administrative exercise was complete, a person's name alone could single out him or her for deportation or execution. See Robert M. Rennick, "The Nazi Name Decrees of the Nineteen Thirties," *Journal of the American Name Society* 16 (1968): 65–88.

48 Turkey, for example, adopted surnames only in the 1920s as a part of Ataturk's modernization campaign. Suits, hats (rather than fezzes), permanent last names, and modern nationhood all fit together in Ataturk's scheme. Reze Shah, the father of the deposed Shah, ordered all Iranians to take the last name of their town of residence in order to rationalize the country's family names. Ali Akbar Rafsanjani thus means Ali Akbar from Rafsanjan. Although this system has the advantage of designating the homes of the generation that adopted it, it certainly doesn't clarify much locally in Rafsanjan. It may well be that the state is particularly concerned with monitoring those who are mobile or "out of place."

49 Dietary laws that all but preclude commensality are also powerful devices for social exclusion. If one were designating a set of cultural rules in order to wall off a group from surrounding groups, making sure its members cannot easily speak to or eat with others is a splendid beginning.

50 This is true despite the fact, as Benedict Anderson insightfully points out, that the "national past" is so often fitted with a bogus pedigree.

51 Eugen Weber, *Peasants into Frenchmen: The Modernization of Rural France, 1870–1914* (Stanford: Stanford University Press, 1976), chap. 6. Weber points out that in the last twenty-five years of the nineteenth century, fully half of the Frenchmen reaching adulthood had a native tongue other than French. See Peter Sahlins's remarkable book *Boundaries: The Making of France and Spain in the Pyrenees* (Berkeley: University of California Press, 1989) for a discussion of French language policy at its periphery. Although administrative official languages have a lineage that goes back to at least the sixteenth century, the imposition of a national language in other spheres comes in the mid-nineteenth century at the earliest.

52 For an illuminating analytical account of this process, see Abram de Swaan, *In Care of the State* (Oxford: Polity Press, 1988), especially chap. 3, "The Elementary Curriculum as a National Communication Code," pp. 52–117.

53 Ibid., p. 197.

54 For a careful depiction of the geography of standard market areas, see G. William Skinner, *Marketing and Social Structure in Rural China* (Tucson: Association of Asian Studies, 1975).

55 Much of the following material on the centralization of transport in France comes from the fine survey by Cecil O. Smith, Jr., "The Longest Run: Public Engineers and Planning in France," *American Historical Review* 95, no. 3 (June 1990): 657–92. See also the excellent discussion and comparison of the Corps des Ponts et des Chaussées with the US Army Corps of Engineers in Theodore Porter, *Trust in Numbers: The Pursuit of Objectivity in Science and Public Life* (Princeton: Princeton University Press, 1995), chap. 6.

56 Weber, *Peasants into Frenchmen*, p. 195.

57 Smith, "The Longest Run," pp. 685–71. Smith claims that the Legrand Star meant that many reservists being mustered for World War I had to funnel through Paris, whereas, under a more

decentralized rail plan, there would have been far more direct routes to the front: "Some reservists in Strasbourg [were] journeying via the capital to don their uniforms in Bordeaux before returning to fight in Alsace." General Von Möltke observed that he had six different rail lines for moving troops from the North German Confederation to the war zone between the Moselle and the Rhine, while French troops coming to the front had to detrain at Strasbourg or Metz, with the Vosges mountains in between. Finally, and perhaps most important, once Paris was surrounded, the Legrand Star was left headless. After the war, the high command insisted on building more transverse lines to correct the deficiency.

58   See Ian Hacking, *The Emergence of Probability: A Philosophical Study of Early Ideas About Probability, Induction, and Statistical Inference* (Cambridge: Cambridge University Press, 1975).

59   I am extraordinarily grateful to the City Museum of Amsterdam for staging the fine and unsparing exhibition "Hunger-winter and Liberation in Amsterdam" and the accompanying catalogue, *Here, back when...* (Amsterdam: City Museum, 1995).

60   *Here, back when...*, p. 10.

61   Since, as we know best from the case of Anne Frank, a good many citizens were willing to hide Jews in the city and the countryside, deportation as a systematic administrative exercise eventually failed. As the Jewish population became increasingly opaque to the authorities, they were increasingly forced to rely on Dutch collaborators who became their local trackers.

62   Even when these facts appear dynamic, they are usually the result of multiple static observations through time that, through a "connect the dots" process, give the appearance of continuous movement. In fact, what actually happened between, say, observation A and observation B remains a mystery, which

is glossed over by the convention of merely drawing a straight line between the two data points.

63   This is the way that Benedict Anderson puts it in *Imagined Communities,* p. 169.

64   I am grateful to Larry Lohmann for insisting to me that officials are not necessarily any more abstract or narrow of vision in their representation of reality than laypeople are. Rather, the facts that they need are facts that serve the interests and practices of their institutional roles. He would have preferred, I think, that I drop the term "simplification" altogether, but I have resisted.

65   There are at least three problems here. The first is the hegemony of the categories. How does one classify someone who usually works for relatives, who may sometimes feed him, let him use some of their land as his own, or pay him in crops or cash? The sometimes quite arbitrary decisions about how to classify such cases are obscured by the final result, in which only the prevailing categories appear. Theodore Porter notes that officials in France's Office of National Statistics report that even trained coders will code up to 20 percent of occupational categories differently (*Trust in Numbers,* p. 41). The goal of the statistical office is to ensure the maximum reliability among coders, even if the conventions applied to achieve it sacrifice something of the true state of affairs. The second problem, to which we shall return later, is how the categories and, more particularly, the state power behind the categories shape the data. For example, during the recession in the United States in the 1970s, there was some concern that the official unemployment rate, which had reached 13 percent, was exaggerated. A major reason, it was claimed, was that many nominally unemployed were working "off the books" in the informal economy and were not reporting their income or employment for fear of being taxed. One could say then and today that the fiscal

system had provoked an off-stage reality that was designed to stay out of the data bank. The third problem is that those who collect and assemble the information may have special interests in what the data show. During the Vietnam War the importance of body counts and pacified villages as a measure of counterinsurgency success led commanders to produce inflated figures that pleased their superiors – in the short run – but increasingly bore little relation to the facts on the ground.

66 The goal is to get rid of intersubjective variability on the part of the census takers or coders. And that requires standard, mechanical procedures that leave no room for personal judgment. See Porter, *Trust in Numbers*, p. 29.

67 Charles Tilly, *Coercion, Capital, and European States*, A.D. *990–1992* (Oxford: Blackwell, 1990), p. 100.

68 Indicative of this tendency in scientific forestry is the substantial literature on "optimum control theory," which is imported from management science. For an application and bibliography, see D. M. Donnelly and D. R. Betters, "Optimum Control for Scheduling Final Harvest in Even-Aged Forest Stands," *Forest Ecology and Management* 46 (1991): 135–49.

69 The caricature is not so far-fetched that it does not capture the lyrical utopianism of early advocates of state sciences. I quote the father of Prussian statistics, Ernst Engel: "In order to obtain an accurate representation, statistical research accompanies the individual through his entire earthly existence. It takes account of his birth, his baptism, his vaccination, his schooling and the success thereof, his diligence, his leave of school, his subsequent education and development, and, once he becomes a man, his physique and his ability to bear arms. It also accompanies the subsequent steps of his walk through life; it

takes note of his chosen occupation, where he sets up his household and his management of the same, if he saved from the abundances of his youth for his old age, if and when and at what age he marries and whom he chooses as his wife – statistics look after him when things go well for him and when they go awry. Should he suffer shipwreck in his life, undergo material, moral, or spiritual ruin, statistics take note of the same. Statistics leave a man only after his death – after it has ascertained the precise age of his death and noted the causes that brought about his end" (quoted in Ian Hacking, *The Taming of Chance* [Cambridge: Cambridge University Press, 1990], p. 34). One could hardly ask for a more complete list of early nineteenth-century state interests and the paper trail that it generated.

70 Tilly, echoing the colonial theme, describes much of this process within the European nation-state as the replacement of indirect rule with direct rule (*Coercion, Capital, and European States*, pp. 103–26).

71 This process is best described by Benedict Anderson: "Guided by its [the colonial state's] imagined map, it organized the new educational, juridical, publichealth, police and immigration bureaucracies it was building on the principle of ethno-racial hierarchies which were, however, always understood in terms of parallel series. The flow of subject populations through the mesh of differential schools, courts, clinics, police stations and immigration offices created 'traffichabits' which in time gave real social life to the state's earlier fantasies" (*Imagined Communities*, p. 169). A related argument about the cultural dimension of state-building in England can be found in Philip Corrigan and Derek Sayer, *The Great Arch: English State Formation as Cultural Revolution* (Oxford: Blackwell, 1991).

11

The Anti-Politics Machine

James Ferguson

The Effects of "Failure"

By 1979, the Thaba-Tseka Project was already beginning to be considered a failure. It was clear by then that, for all the expensive road building and construction work, the project had not come close to meeting any of its production targets. All the money put into the project, critics said, had not managed to produce any demonstrable increase in agricultural production at all – only a lot of ugly buildings. One CIDA spokesperson reportedly admitted in 1979 "that this project is now considered a very large and costly mistake."[1] At the same time, the project was becoming the subject of newspaper articles with titles like "Canadian aid gone awry?" and "CIDA in Africa: Goodby $6 million."[2] Meanwhile, in Lesotho, the project became a commonly cited example of "development" gone wrong. One local writer declared that "the people of Thaba-Tseka have now come to think in terms of the 'failure' of the project" (Sekhamane 1981); a student at the National University even called it "a monster clinging to the backs of the people." But the bad news came not only from the press and the other critics in and out of the "development" establishment. Even the local people, according to a 1979 CIDA evaluation (CIDA 1979: 22), considered "neither the households nor the area to be better off," five years after the start of the project. Instead, the report said, "the quality of village life as perceived by the people and as measured by people's perceptions of well-being has not improved and has, in fact, declined." In 1982, a dissertation by a former project employee reviewed the project history and concluded that "[t]here is little evidence that this huge investment in the mountain region has had any effect in raising agricultural production or improving the well-being of rural households" (Eberhard 1982: 299).

At the start of Phase Two of the project, there had been some talk of a "commitment" for at least ten more years of CIDA funding, and that is apparently what the original planners anticipated.... But, when the project's inability to effect the promised transformations in agriculture – particularly in the area of livestock – was compounded by the collapse of the "decentralization" scheme in

From *The Anti-Politics Machine: "Development," Depoliticization, and Bureaucratic Power in Lesotho*, pp. 251–77, 302–13. Minneapolis: University of Minnesota Press, 1994.

1980–1, CIDA elected to pull out. By 1982, CIDA's chief interest was in getting out as quickly and gracefully as possible. The 1982 revision to the Plan of Operations was tailored to do just that. Funding was gradually phased out and, by March 1984, the CIDA involvement in Thaba-Tseka was over. Moreover, I was told explicitly by officials at CIDA headquarters in Ottawa that the pullout had not been a matter of lack of funds, but that the project had been discontinued on its merits. At last report, neither CIDA nor any other donor has sought to continue the project.

But even if the project was in some sense a "failure" as an agricultural development project, it is indisputable that many of its "side effects" had a powerful and far-reaching impact on the Thaba-Tseka region. The project did not transform crop farming or livestock keeping, but it did build a road to link Thaba-Tseka more strongly with the capital; it did not bring about "decentralization" or "popular participation," but it was instrumental in establishing a new district administration and giving the Government of Lesotho a much stronger presence in the area than it had ever had before. The construction of the road and the "administrative center" may have had little effect on agricultural production, but they were powerful effects in themselves.

The general drift of things was clear to some of the project staff themselves, even as they fought it. "It is the same story over again," said one "development" worker.[3] "When the Americans and the Danes and the Canadians leave, the villagers will continue their marginal farming practices and wait for the mine wages, knowing only that now the taxman lives down the valley rather than in Maseru."

But it was not only a matter of the taxman. A host of Government services became available at Thaba-Tseka as a direct result of the construction of the project center and the decision to make that center the capital of a new district. There was a new Post Office, a police station, and an immigration control office; there were agricultural services such as extension, seed supply, and livestock marketing; there were health officials to observe and lecture on child care, and nutrition officers to promote approved methods of cooking. There was the "food for work" administration run by the Ministry of Rural Development, and the Ministry of the Interior, with its function of regulating the powers of chiefs. A vast number of minor services and functions that once would have operated, if at all, only out of one of the other distant district capitals had come to Thaba-Tseka.

But, although "development" discourse tends to see the provision of "services" as the purpose of government, it is clear that the question of power cannot be written off quite so easily. "Government services" are never simply "services"; instead of conceiving this phrase as a reference simply to a "government" whose purpose is to serve, it may be at least as appropriate to think of "services" which serve to govern. [O]ne of the central issues of the deployment of the Thaba-Tseka Project was the desire of the Government to gain political control over the opposition strongholds in the mountains. [M]any of the project's own resources and structures were turned to this purpose. But, while this was going on, a much more direct political policing function was being exercised by other sections of the district administration the project had helped to establish. The Ministries of Rural Development and of the Interior, for instance, were quite directly concerned with questions of political control, largely through their control over "food for work" and chieftainship, respectively; then, too, there were the police. Another innovation that came with the "development" center in Thaba-Tseka was the new prison. In every case, state power was expanded and strengthened by the establishment of the local governing machinery at Thaba-Tseka.

In the increasingly militarized climate of the early 1980s, the administrative center constructed by the project in Thaba-Tseka quickly took on a significance that was not only political, but military as well. The district capital that the project had helped establish was not only useful for extending the governing apparatus of government services/government controls; it also facilitated direct military control. The project-initiated district center was home not only to the various "civilian" ministries, but also to the "Para-Military Unit," Lesotho's army. The road had made access much easier; now the new town provided a good central base. Near the project's end in 1983, substantial numbers of armed troops began to be garrisoned at Thaba-Tseka. . . . Indeed, it may be that in a place like Mashai, the most visible of all the project's effects was the indirect one of increased Government military presence in the region. The project of course did not cause the militarization of Thaba-Tseka, any more than it caused the founding of the new district and the creation of a new local administration. In both cases, however, it may be said to have unintentionally played what can only be called an instrumental role.

The Anti-Politics Machine

It would be a mistake to make too much of the "failure" of the Thaba-Tseka Project. It has certainly been often enough described in such terms, but the same can be said for nearly all of the other rural development projects Lesotho has seen. One of the original planners of the project, while admitting that the project had its share of frustrations, and declaring that as a result of his experience with Thaba-Tseka, he would never again become involved in a range management project, told me that in fact of all the rural development projects that have been launched in Lesotho, only Thaba-Tseka has had any positive effects. Indeed, as the project came to an end, there seemed to be a general move in "development" circles both in Ottawa and Maseru toward a rehabilitation of the project's reputation. It may have been a failure, but not any worse than many other similar projects, I was told. Given the "constraints," the Project Coordinator declared in 1983, "I think we've got a success story

here." As one CIDA official pointed out, with what appeared to be a certain amount of pride, the project "was not an unmitigated disaster."

In a situation in which "failure" is the norm, there is no reason to think that Thaba-Tseka was an especially badly run or poorly thought out project. Since, as we have seen, Lesotho is not the "traditional," isolated, "peasant" society the "development" problematic makes it out to be, it is not surprising that all the various attempts to "transform" it and "bring it into the 20th Century" characteristically "fail," and end up as more or less mitigated "disasters." But it may be that what is most important about a "development" project is not so much what it fails to do but what it does do; it may be that its real importance in the end lies in the "side effects" such as those reviewed in the last section. Foucault, speaking of the prison, suggests that dwelling on the "failure" of the prison may be asking the wrong question. Perhaps, he suggests,

one should reverse the problem and ask oneself what is served by the failure of the prison; what is the use of these different phenomena that are continually being criticized; the maintenance of delinquency, the encouragement of recidivism, the transformation of the occasional offender into a habitual delinquent, the organization of a closed milieu of delinquency. (Foucault 1979: 272)

If it is true that "failure" is the norm for development projects in Lesotho, and that important political effects may be realized almost invisibly alongside with that "failure," then there may be some justification for beginning to speak of a kind of logic or intelligibility to what happens when the "development" apparatus is deployed – a logic that transcends the question of planners' intentions. In terms of this larger unspoken logic, "side effects" may be better seen as "instrument-effects" (Foucault 1979); effects that are at one and the same time instruments of what "turns out" to be an exercise of power.

For the planners, the question was quite clear: the primary task of the project was to boost agricultural production; the expansion of government could only be secondary to that overriding aim. In 1980, the Programme Director expressed concern about the project's failure to make headway in "what is really the only economic basis for the existence of the Thaba-Tseka District, the rangeland production of livestock." He went on to declare:

> If this economic base, now as shaky as it appears to be, is not put on a much firmer footing, it is inevitable that the Thaba-Tseka District will eventually become an agricultural wasteland where there will be no justification whatsoever for developing and maintaining a social infrastructure with its supporting services of health, education, roads, rural technology development, etc. (TTDP Quarterly Report, October-December 1980, p. 5)

If one takes the "development" problematic at its word, such an analysis makes perfect sense; in the absence of growth in agricultural output, the diversion of project energies and resources to "social infrastructure" can only be considered an unfortunate mistake. But another interpretation is possible. If one considers the expansion and entrenchment of state power to be the principal effect – indeed, what "development" projects in Lesotho are chiefly about – then the promise of agricultural transformation appears simply as a point of entry for an intervention of a very different character.

In this perspective, the "development" apparatus in Lesotho is not a machine for eliminating poverty that is incidentally involved with the state bureaucracy; it is a machine for reinforcing and expanding the exercise of bureaucratic state power, which incidentally takes "poverty" as its point of entry – launching an intervention that may have no effect on the poverty but does in fact have other concrete effects. Such a result may be no part of the planners' intentions – indeed, it almost never is – but resultant systems have an intelligibility of their own.

But the picture is even more complicated than this. For while we have seen that "development" projects in Lesotho may end up working to expand the power of the state, and while they claim to address the problems of poverty and deprivation, in neither guise does the "development" industry allow its role to be formulated as a political one. By uncompromisingly reducing poverty to a technical problem, and by promising technical solutions to the sufferings of powerless and oppressed people, the hegemonic problematic of "development" is the principal means through which the question of poverty is de-politicized in the world today. At the same time, by making the intentional blueprints for "development" so highly visible, a "development" project can end up performing extremely sensitive political operations involving the entrenchment and expansion of institutional state power almost invisibly, under cover of a neutral, technical mission to which no one can object. The "instrument-effect," then, is two-fold: alongside the institutional effect of expanding bureaucratic state power is the conceptual or ideological effect of depoliticizing both poverty and the state. The way it all works out suggests an analogy with the wondrous machine made famous in Science Fiction stories – the "anti-gravity machine," that at the flick of a switch suspends the effects of gravity. In Lesotho, at least, the "development" apparatus sometimes seems almost capable of pulling nearly as good a trick: the suspension of politics from even the most sensitive political operations. If the "instrument-effects" of a "development" project end up forming any kind of strategically coherent or intelligible whole, this is it: the anti-politics machine.

If unintended effects of a project end up having political uses, even seeming to be "instruments" of some larger political deployment, this is not any kind of conspiracy; it really does just happen to be the way things work out. But because things do work out this way, and because "failed" development projects can so successfully help to accomplish important strategic tasks behind the backs of the most sincere participants, it does become less mysterious why "failed" development projects should end up being replicated again and again. It is perhaps reasonable to suggest that it may even be because development projects turn out to have such uses, even if they are in some sense unforeseen, that they continue to attract so much interest and support.

Some Comparative Observations

So far I have extended specific conclusions about the "development" apparatus and its operation only to the case of Lesotho.... I will here provisionally suggest some possible points of commonality between Lesotho and a few other "development" contexts, after first noting a few of the particularities that make Lesotho such a special case.

First of all, any attempt to expand the conclusions presented here to the global "development" apparatus in general must take account of the peculiarities of the Lesotho case. Lesotho is a very unusual national setting, and one that makes the "developers' " task extraordinarily difficult. Many of the most common "development" assumptions are there more completely confounded by reality than almost anywhere else one could name. Where "development" often sees itself entering an aboriginal, primitive agricultural setting, Lesotho offers one of the first and most completely monetized and proletarianized contexts in Africa. Where "development" requires a bounded, coherent "national economy," responsive to the principle of "governmentality," Lesotho's extraordinary labor-reserve economy is as little defined by national boundaries, and as little responsive to national planning, as any that could be imagined. Lesotho is not a "typical" case ...

The extremity of the case of Lesotho has the effect of exaggerating many "development" phenomena. The divide between academic and "development" discourse, the gap between plans attempted and results achieved, the paucity of economic transformations next to the plenitude of political ones, all are more extreme than one might find in a more "typical" case. But the unusualness of Lesotho's situation does not in itself make it irrelevant to wider generalization. Indeed, the exaggeration it produces, if properly interpreted, may be seen not simply as a distortion of the "typical" case, but as a clarification, just as the addition by a computer of "extreme" colors to a remote scanning image does not distort but "enhances" the photograph by improving the visibility of the phenomena we are interested in.... [T]he task of denaturalizing and "making strange" the "development" intervention is facilitated by the very atypicality of Lesotho.

One of the main factors supporting the view that some degree of generalization may be possible from the case of Lesotho is that ... many aspects of "development" interventions remain remarkably uniform and standardized from place to place. One aspect of this standardization is simply of personnel. If "development" interventions look very similar from one country to the next, one reason is that they are designed and implemented by a relatively small, interlocked network of experts. Tanzania may be very different from Lesotho on the ground, but, from the point of view of a "development" agency's head office, both may be simply "the Africa desk." In the Thaba-Tseka case, at least, the original project planners knew little about Lesotho's specific history, politics, and sociology; they were experts on "livestock development in Africa," and drew largely on experience in East Africa. Small wonder, then, that they often looked on the Basotho as "pastoralists," and took the nomadic Maasai of Kenya as a favorite point of comparison. Small wonder, too, if the Thaba-Tseka Project ended up with such visible similarities to other livestock projects in very different contexts.

But it is not only that "development" interventions draw on a small and interlocking pool of personnel. More fundamental is the application in the most divergent empirical settings of a single, undifferentiated "development" expertise. In Zimbabwe, in 1981, I was struck to find local agricultural "development" officials eagerly awaiting the arrival and advice of a highly paid consultant who was to explain how agriculture in Zimbabwe was to be transformed. What, I asked, did this consultant know about Zimbabwe's agriculture that they, the local agricultural officers, did not? To my surprise, I was told that the individual in question knew virtually nothing about Zimbabwe, and worked mostly in India. "But," I was assured, "he *knows development*." It is precisely this expertise, free-floating and untied to any specific context, that is so easily generalized, and so easily inserted into any given situation....

Another aspect of standardization is to be seen in specific program elements. Because of the way "development" interventions are institutionalized, there are strong tendencies for programs to be mixed and matched out of a given set of available choices.... Plans that call for non-standard, unfamiliar elements are more difficult for a large routinized bureaucracy to implement and evaluate, and thus less likely to be approved. With standardized elements, things are much easier.... Lesotho's empirical situation may be unlike that of many other countries, but the specific "development" interventions that have been attempted there, from irrigation and erosion control schemes to grazing associations and "decentralization," are nearly all familiar elements of the standard "development" package.

Finally, there is clearly a sense in which the discourse of "development" in Lesotho, too, is part of a "standard" discursive practice associated with "development" in a broad range of contexts.... [E]ven casual observation is enough to suggest that it is not only in Lesotho that "development" discourse seems to form a world unto itself.... This is sometimes put as a matter of "jargon," but it is much more than that. Indeed, my own unsystematic inspection would suggest that "development" discourse typically involves not only

special terms, but a distinctive style of reasoning, implicitly (and perhaps unconsciously) reasoning backward from the necessary conclusions – more "development" projects are needed – to the premises required to generate those conclusions....

Moreover, the maneuvers used in constructing these chains of reasoning, if not identical from place to place, do seem at least to bear what one might call a strong family resemblance. The figures of the "aboriginal society," "national economy," and "traditional peasant society" can be easily found in other contexts, as, for instance, in the World Bank's definitive declaration (1975: 3) that "[rural development] is concerned with the modernization and monetization of rural society, and with its transition from traditional isolation to integration with the national economy." The fourth characteristic figure for Lesotho, "governmentality," is perhaps even more widespread. Indeed, the extreme state-centeredness of "development" discourse in a wide range of settings is nearly enough to justify Williams's blanket claim (1986: 7) that "Policy makers, experts, and officials cannot think how things might improve except through their own agency."

The above considerations are perhaps enough to suggest that there may be important commonalities at the level of discourse, planning, and program elements between "development" interventions in Lesotho and those in other countries. But do these standardized elements, deployed in a wide range of different settings, produce anything like standard effects? Are the "instrument-effects" identified for Lesotho part of a general, regular global pattern? Is the "anti-politics machine" peculiar to Lesotho, or is it a usual or even inevitable consequence of "development" interventions?

[...]

The first and most immediate point of comparison is with South Africa. Although "development" agencies in Lesotho resolutely refuse to see any connection between Lesotho and the South African "homelands," the South African experience of government intervention in the rural areas is in some ways continuous with that of Lesotho. In particular, the long history of South African "betterment" schemes in the "reserves" and "homelands" bears some striking similarities with "development" interventions in Lesotho....

"Betterment" schemes were first instituted in South Africa in the late 1930s as a way of "rationalizing" and improving agriculture and land use in the "reserves," with the aim of slowing out-migration to the urban areas. Responding to perceptions of inefficiency of "native agriculture" and crisis in soil erosion, the state set about reorganizing the settlement and cropping patterns in the reserves. Village settlements and family landholdings were alike "consolidated," and land carefully divided into distinct zones of residential, crop, or range usage. Model villages were laid out in straight-line grids.... Grazing lands were fenced for rotational grazing, and "improved" practices encouraged, with stock limitation and culling enforced by law. Erosion was combated through extensive contour works, and village woodlots were established (Beinart 1984, Yawitch 1981, Unterhalter 1987, Platzky and Walker 1985, de Wet 1981).

With the rise to power of the Nationalist government and its *apartheid* program in 1948, the "reserves" acquired new prominence as the intended "*bantustans*" or "homelands" for the whole of the African population. The Tomlinson Commission, set up to explore the viability of "separate development" in the "*bantustans*" -to-be, ... recommended that 50 percent of the population of the reserves should leave farming to dwell in "closer settlements" as full-time workers, leaving the other 50 percent as a "viable," productive, class of professional farmers.... The job of "betterment," in this scheme, was to bring about this transition. But, as the grim process of "separate development" proceeded, it became more and more clear that "betterment" was functioning less as a means for boosting agricultural production in the "homelands" than as a device for regulating and controlling the process

through which more and more people were being squeezed on to less and less land, and through which the dumped "surplus people" (Platzky and Walker 1985) relocated from "white areas" could be accommodated and controlled. As the *bantustans* assumed their contemporary role as dumping grounds, "betterment" schemes, as one source puts it, "lost almost entirely any aspect of improvement or rationalization of land use and became instead principally instruments of coercion" (Unterhalter 1987: 102).[4]

These "betterment" interventions have been fiercely resisted by the supposed "beneficiaries" from the very start. Indeed, attempts in the name of "betterment" to move people's homes and fields, to control and regulate their cultivation, and to restrict and cull their livestock have provoked many of the most intense and significant episodes of rural resistance in South African history (Beinart 1982, 1984; Beinart and Bundy 1981, 1987; Unterhalter 1987; Yawitch 1981).

A number of similarities between South Africa's "betterment" schemes and Lesotho's "development" will be immediately apparent. Government interventions in colonial Basutoland, from the 1930s onward, centered on consolidation and pooling of fields (e.g., the "Pilot Project" of 1952–8), and, especially, soil erosion control (Wallman 1969). They also involved tree-planting and mandatory culling, especially of sheep (Palmer and Parsons 1977: 25). Since independence, too, many elements of South African "betterment" have been replicated by various "development" projects. Fencing and rotational grazing, of course, were attempted at Thaba-Tseka, woodlots have been planted not only by the Thaba-Tseka Project, but by a nationwide "woodlot Project" funded by the Anglo-American Corporation, the giant South African conglomerate. Soil erosion control and contouring was the focus of the large Thaba-Bosiu project in the early 1970s, while in the same period, amalgamation of fields was attempted in the Senqu River Project. And finally, when I returned to Thaba-Tseka for a brief visit in 1986, I was told by the District Extension Officer that the latest plan for "development" of the mountain area involved dividing land up into residential, crop, and grazing zones, and consolidating some small, scattered settlements into larger and more accessible villages on approved sites.

But it is not only program elements that are similar. In both cases, technical, apolitical aims justified state intervention. And, in both cases, economic "failure" of these interventions ended up meeting other needs....

Moreover, in the "homelands," as in Lesotho, there is the same central tension between espoused goals of "professionalizing" farming on the one hand, and the political need to settle, stabilize, and regulate the regional economy's "redundant," "surplus people" on the other. And in both cases, the political imperative of keeping people tied to the land has generally predominated over any economic "rationalization." In both cases, too, the "anti-politics machine" has been at work, as state power has been simultaneously expanded and depoliticized. "Betterment," like "development," has provided an apparently technical point of entry for an intervention serving a variety of political uses.

In many respects, of course, the South African case is also a strong contrast with Lesotho. Most obviously, Lesotho does not share the South African government's *apartheid* agenda, and is concerned not with implementing the bad dream of "separate development," but with coping with its consequences. But more than that, the nature of the state, and thus the nature of state interventions, is very different in the two cases. In place of the institutionally and financially weak Lesotho state, the South African state has had the administrative capability to direct and enforce massive rural relocations and disruptions. It has demonstrated the capability and the willingness to routinely use staggering levels of coercion to achieve its desired results. Where in Lesotho, "development" failures are easily written off as resulting from poor administrative capacity and an inability to make "tough" political choices, in South Africa, a strong and

often brutal state is able to radically transform the countryside. In the "homelands" and rural areas, millions have been relocated (Platzky and Walker 1985), while villages have been "dressed" in rows, plots radically rearranged, and the culling and fencing of livestock enforced in a way that is difficult to imagine for Lesotho. "Betterment" was more than a plan on paper; according to one source, by 1967, 60 percent of the villages in Natal were "planned," while 77 percent of the plan for Ciskei and 76 percent and 80 percent of the plans for the Northern and Western Territories (respectively) had been implemented (Platzky and Walker 1985: 46).

But the force of state intervention has not meant economic "success." With respect to the stated goals of establishing a viable, stable population of professional farmers and improving peasant agricultural production, South Africa's experience with "betterment" must be judged to have "failed" nearly as completely as Lesotho's with "development." But in South Africa just as surely as in Lesotho, economic "failures" have produced their own political rationality. No doubt there have been important economic effects, but "betterment," in its "instrument-effects," is not ultimately about agricultural production, but about managing and controlling the labor reserves and dumping grounds.

... Elsewhere in Africa, Beinart (1984) has made a convincing case for strong parallels between the South African experience and those of colonial Zimbabwe and Malawi, where struggles over land and political control were also filtered through a range of apparently technical interventions connected with soil erosion, conservation, and "inefficient" African farming.

[...]

For Zimbabwe, Ranger (1985) has given a detailed demonstration of how government interventions ostensibly aimed at agricultural improvement and soil conservation became a central terrain in rural political struggles throughout the colonial period. As in South Africa, "conservation," "centralization," and "improvement" were closely linked to land alienation and control, while coopted African "Demonstrators," ostensibly agents of agricultural improvement, came eventually to serve as a kind of rural police. The peasants, driven off their land and policed on the deteriorating "reserves," responded with an anger rising at times to "seething hatred" (Ranger 1985: 151). This anger very logically found expression in attacks on such symbols of "conservation" and "improvement" as contour ridges and dip tanks, as well as on the African Demonstrators themselves. For failing to see the benefits of their own subordination, the peasants were of course characterized as "backward," and thus all the more in need of controlling interventions (see Ranger 1985: 99–171).

It appears, moreover, that the specifically political role of the "development" intervention in Zimbabwe has not ended with Independence. The revolution has undoubtedly brought some real gains for the peasantry insofar as land-starved occupants of "Tribal Trust Lands" were in at least some cases able to press successfully for land redistribution through squatting on land abandoned by white farmers, and to benefit from higher producer prices instituted by the new government (Ranger 1985). But it is also clear, as Ranger notes, that as the revolutionary situation fades and the ability of the peasants to apply political pressure on the government diminishes, "the unusual advantageous position of Zimbabwe's peasants *vis-à-vis* the state will give way to quite another balance of power," in which the state may well "become a predator" in relation to the peasantry. For Ranger, this "gloomy expectation" is not inevitable; but the prospects for a different outcome are "cripplingly handicapped by the lasting effects of . . . colonial agrarian history" (Ranger 1985: 319–20).

The suggestion that "development" even in liberated Zimbabwe may be principally about state control and not economic improvement or poverty amelioration is strengthened by Williams's analysis (1982) of one of independent Zimbabwe's key policy documents for "development" strategy (Rid-

dell 1981). Williams shows how government plans for the impoverished "Tribal Trust Lands," involving the consolidation of village holdings, and the division of all land into residential, grazing, and arable zones, virtually duplicate key aspects of the "betterment" schemes of South Africa. It is far from clear that such an extraordinary expenditure of governmental energies will do anything to improve farming. But there is no doubt, as Williams notes (Williams 1982: 16), that, like other "development" interventions, "it will subject farmers to more effective control and administrative supervision." The plan also calls for the regrouping of settlements into "unified village settlements" where "village leadership committees" would, so the planners anticipate, "plan the whole life of the village" (Riddell 1981: 688), including allocating land and coordinating a planned pension and social security scheme. . . . Once again, what look like technical, apolitical reforms seem to bring with them political "side-effects" that overwhelm whatever might exist of the originally intended or claimed "main effects." As Williams concludes:

> As is so often the case, "rural development" turns out to be a strategy for increasing state control of the peasantry. The policies outlined in the Riddell report bring together many of the worst aspects of the agricultural policies of Kenya (dependence on large-scale maize farming), Nigeria (settlement and irrigation schemes), Tanzania (villagization) and South Africa (betterment schemes). Thus far, Zimbabwean peasants have resisted them, both under white rule and since independence.
> (Williams 1982: 17)

[. . .]

"Development," insistently formulated as a benign and universal human project, has been the point of insertion for a bureaucratic power that has been neither benign nor universal in its application (Coulson 1975, 1981, 1982; von Freyhold 1979; Bernstein 1981; Hyden 1980; Shivji 1976, 1986; Malkki 1989; Moore 1986).

... [M]y sense is that elsewhere in Africa, and likely in Latin America and Asia as well, it might be possible to show that technical "development" interventions ostensibly organized around such things as agricultural production, livestock, soil erosion, water supply, etc., have in fact often had "instrument-effects" that would be systematically intelligible as part of a two-sided process of depoliticization and expansion of bureaucratic state control. If so, this would not of course prove that such an association is in any way inevitable or universal, but it would suggest that at least some of the mechanisms that have been explored for the case of Lesotho may be of some wider relevance.

Etatization?

A few writers have recently attempted to formulate a general model for the involvement of "development" interventions with the expansion of state power in Africa, based on the concept of "etatization" (Dutkiewicz and Shenton 1986; Dutkiewicz and Williams 1987; Williams 1985). According to this picture, ... the state-dominated economies of the late colonial period set the stage for the emergence of a distinctive post-colonial "developmental state" (Dutkiewicz and Williams 1987: 41). The "developmental state" was distinguished by the central and direct involvement of the state in the appropriation of surplus value from producers, and by the dependence of the "ruling elite" (Dutkiewicz and Shenton 1986: 110) upon this form of appropriation. Under these distinctive circumstances, the state bureaucracy expanded rapidly, while the larger economy was more and more subordinated to the needs of the state sector. The "ruling elite," meanwhile, became a "ruling group," united by its near-total dependence for its social reproduction upon its control of the state apparatus. As the state expanded, so did the power of this ruling group, which in turn required, for its reproduction, the continued expansion or "involution" (Dutkiewicz and Williams

1987: 43) of the bureaucracy. But this very process eventually led to a crisis of "diminishing reproduction" (Dutkiewicz and Shenton 1986) of the social resources (especially peasant, household-based production) on which the state depended for its own reproduction. "Etatization" ended up, as in the current crisis, threatening to kill the goose that laid the golden egg.

At every stage, in this view, whether under socialist or capitalist ideologies, this expansion of state power "is justified by the notion of 'national development' " (Dutkiewicz and Williams 1987: 43). With an infinitely expandable demand for "development" providing the charter for state expansion, whatever "problems" can be located are just so many points of insertion for new state programs and interventions for dealing with them. "Development," then, is an integral part of "etatization." And if the "development" interventions fail, as they usually do, that, too, is part of the process. As Dutkiewicz and Shenton put it:

Like corruption, inefficiency in establishing and managing state enterprises, financial institutions, import and exchange rate policies, and development projects, rather than preventing the social reproduction of this ruling group, was an absolute prerequisite for it. The ruling groups' social reproduction required an ever-expanding number of parastatals to be created and development projects to be begun. The completion, or, in a rational capitalistic sense, the efficient operation of such parastatals or development projects would have obviated the need to generate further plans and projects to achieve the ends which their predecessors failed to do. In this sense inefficiency was "efficient," efficient for the expanded reproduction of the ruling group. One result of this was the geometric expansion of a poorly skilled and corrupt lower level bureaucracy incapable of fulfilling even its few professional obligations, itself fuelled by academics and others who saw the solution to every problem in the creation of yet another position or agency to deal with it and to employ

more of their own number. By generating a
never-ending series of parastatals and development projects the ruling group provided
employment and, no matter how small, in-
advertent or fleeting, an amelioration of the
conditions of life and a share of state resources for at least some members of the
underclasses. In doing so, the conditions of
the social reproduction of the ruling group
increasingly penetrated and reshaped the
conditions for the reproduction of society
as a whole.
(Dutkiewicz and Shenton 1986: 111)

The international "development" establishment is, in this view, deeply implicated in
this process as well. "Development" agencies
have not only promoted statist policies, the
"development" bureaucracy is itself part of
the sprawling symbiotic network of experts,
offices, and salaries that benefits from "etatization." As Williams argues:

Since their origins in the colonial period, the
project of "development" itself [along with]
the "development community" which has
grown up to implement it, has instigated,
legitimated and benefitted from the process
of "Etatization". Within the "development
community", whatever disagreements there
may be about particular policies and institutions, L'Etat is internationalized and multi-
lateralized.
(Williams 1985: 11)

The argument, like my summary of it, is
extremely general, and unashamedly short on
specifics. . . . And it is far from clear that "Africa," an entire continent with a gigantic
range of different economic and political realities, is really a suitable object for such a
general model. . . . In spite of such serious reservations, it must be said that as a broad,
general characterization, the "etatization"
thesis is provoking and stimulating in a way
that the familiar, localized "case study" cannot be. . . .
The "etatization" synthesis is important
not only for its bold attempt at significant
generalization, but also as a corrective to

what has sometimes been a kind of romance
between the academic Left and the Third
World state. Perceiving the state as the chief
counter-force to the capitalist logic of the
market and the chief instrument for bringing
about progressive economic transformations,
leftists have too often been willing to take
statist interventions at their word and to interpret them uncritically as part of a process
of "self-directed development" or "socialist
construction." . . .
However, it seems to me that in seeking to
describe and explain the "instrument-effects"
of the "development" apparatus, there are
important limitations to the utility of this
notion of "etatization." . . . First of all, while
it clearly points out the way in which "development" figures in the expansion of bureaucratic state power, it does not so clearly
identify the second axis along which the
"anti-politics machine" operates – the axis
of de-politicization. Dutkiewicz and Shenton
(1986) note that state "development" interventions may in fact inhibit or squash peasant
production, leading to the "crisis of diminished reproduction." But they do not give
enough emphasis to the parallel fact that
this same "development" may also very effectively squash political challenges to the
system – not only by enhancing the powers
of administration and repression, but by insistently reposing political questions of land,
resources, jobs, or wages as technical "problems" responsive to the technical "development" intervention. In other words, the
conceptual "instrument-effects" of the "development" deployment may be as important
as the institutional ones.
A second, and more fundamental, limitation has to do with the way in which the
"etatization" thesis theorizes the state and
the relation of state power to "the ruling
group." In the picture sketched by Dutkiewicz, Shenton, and Williams, "the state" and
"the ruling group" both appear as unitary
entities. What is more, the relation between
the two is seen as one of simple instrumentality. Instead of seeing the "etatizing" results of
"development" interventions as emerging

counter-intentionally through the working out of a complex and unacknowledged structure of knowledge in interaction with equally complex and unacknowledged local social and cultural structures, as I have tried to do here, these authors explain such an outcome as the simple, rational projection of the interests of a subject (the "ruling group") that secretly wills it. "Etatization" thus appears as an almost intentional process, guided by the calculations of this ill-defined "ruling group." Indeed, for Dutkiewicz and Shenton, the expansion of state power is not simply an effect of failed state interventions, it is the *purpose* of such interventions. "Etatization" occurs, they seem to imply (in functionalist fashion), because the social reproduction of the ruling group "requires it" (Dutkiewicz and Shenton 1986: 111). And because the ruling group's position is based exclusively on its control of the state, "state power" in such a formula becomes interchangeable with the power held by the ruling group in its extractive relations with the peasantry. "Etatization" thus reduces to a straightforward attempt on the part of this unitary "ruling group" to augment its own power *vis à vis* the peasants.

This portion of the "etatization" argument is in fact unsettlingly reminiscent of Hyden's (1980) notion of a post-colonial state with a historic mission to "capture" its peasantry.... [I]n both cases, the state is seen as a tool "in the hands of" a unitary subject, and state interventions are interpreted as expressions of the project of a "ruling group" bent on controlling and appropriating peasant production. Both views agree on what the struggle is over (the control and appropriation of peasant production) and who the protagonists are ("the state" and "the peasantry"). Their difference, which is real enough, lies at another level: for Hyden, the peasantry is "uncaptured," insufficiently subordinated to the needs of a weak and ineffectual state, thus "development" is frustrated; for Dutkiewicz, Shenton, and Williams, it is precisely the heavy hand of an overgrown state (e.g., through state marketing monopolies) that suffocates peasant production.

These contrasting interpretations contain within them a puzzle: Is state power in these settings feeble and ineffectual (as Hyden would have it), or is it overgrown and crushing (as Dutkiewicz, Shenton, and Williams seem to suggest)? Does the African state have too much power, or too little?

This puzzle in fact lies at the center of much recent debate by political scientists and political economists on the nature of the post-colonial state. In the 1970s, a number of theorists argued ... that the historical legacy of coercive colonial state apparatuses had laid the foundation for "overdeveloped" post-colonial states, in which overgrown state institutions ... could dominate the rest of society (Alavi 1972; Saul 1979; cf. also Leys 1976). Against this view, in the 1980s a number of writers have suggested that notwithstanding often autocratic and despotic appearances, post-colonial states are more typically "enfeebled" (Azarya and Chazan 1987) than they are "overdeveloped" or "overcentralized." Thus Migdal (1988), for instance, argues that "fragmented" structures of social control in post-colonial societies often make effective state control impossible, while writers like Chabal (1986), Bayart (1986), and Geschiere (1988) emphasize the extent to which state plans are frustrated by a deceptively powerful "civil society." These writers differ only on the question of who is hero and who is anti-hero in this epic struggle between "state" and "civil society." ...

It is possible to move beyond this debate only by formulating the expansion of state power in a slightly different way. One can begin by saying that the state is not an entity that "has" or does not "have" power, and state power is not a substance possessed by those individuals and groups who benefit from it. The state is neither the source of power, nor simply the projection of the power of an interested subject (ruling group, etc.). Rather than an entity "holding" or "exercising" power, it may be more fruitful to think of the state as instead forming a relay or point of coordination and multiplication of power relations. Foucault has described the process through which power relations come to be "statized" in the following terms:

> It is certain that in contemporary societies the state is not simply one of the forms or specific situations of the exercise of power – even if it is the most important – but that in a certain way all other forms of power relation must refer to it. But this is not because they are derived from it; it is rather because power relations have come more and more under state control (although this state control has not taken the same form in pedagogical, judicial, economic, or family systems). In referring here to the restricted sense of the word *government*, one could say that power relations have been progressively governmentalized, that is to say, elaborated, rationalized, and centralized in the form of, or under auspices of, state institutions.
> (Foucault 1983: 224)

"The state," in this conception, is not the name of an actor, it is the name of a way of tying together, multiplying, and coordinating power relations, a kind of knotting or congealing of power. It is in this spirit that I have tried to describe the effects of the "anti-politics machine" in terms of "bureaucratic power" or "bureaucratic state power" rather than simply "state power" – in order to emphasize the adjectival over the nominative. The usage is meant to suggest not an entity possessed of power, but a characteristic mode of exercise of power, a mode of power that relies on state institutions, but exceeds them. I have argued that the "development" apparatus promotes a colonizing, expanding bureaucratic power, that it expands its reach and extends its distribution. By putting it this way, I have meant to imply not that "development" projects necessarily expand the capabilities of "the state," conceived as a unitary, instrumental entity, but that specific bureaucratic knots of power are implanted, an infestation of petty bureaucrats wielding petty powers.

On this understanding, it is clear that the spread of bureaucratic state power does not imply that "the state," conceived as a unitary entity, "has" more power – that it is, for example, able to implement more of "its" programs successfully, or to extract more surplus from the peasants.[5] Indeed, it is no paradox to say that "etatization" may leave the state even less able to carry on "its" will or "its" policies. As "state power" is expanded, "the state" as a plan-making, policy-making, rational bureaucracy may actually become "weaker," less able to achieve "its" objectives. . . .

The expansion of bureaucratic state power, then, does not necessarily mean that "the masses" can be centrally coordinated or ordered around any more efficiently; it only means that more power relations are referred through state channels – most immediately, that more people must stand in line and await rubber stamps to get what they want. What is expanded is not the magnitude of the capabilities of "the state," but the extent and reach of a particular kind of exercise of power.

In this respect, the way in which power is linked up with the state in a country like Lesotho differs from the model of a state-coordinated "bio-power" that Foucault (1980a) has described for the modern West. In Foucault's account, the development and spread of techniques for the disciplining of the body and the optimization of its capacities, followed by the emergence of the "population" as an object of knowledge and control, has made possible in the modern era a normalizing "bio-power," watching over, governing, and administering the very "life" of society. In this process, the state occupies a central, coordinating role – managing, fostering, and, according to its own calculus, "optimizing" the vital and productive forces of society. In a country like Lesotho, no doubt many planners of state interventions would like to take on such a role – to control the size of the population, for instance, or to set about making it more productive, healthy, or vital. But the empirical fact is that such interventions most commonly do not have such effects. The growth of state power in such a context does not imply any sort of efficient, centralized social engineering. It simply means that power relations must increasingly be referred through bureaucratic circuits. The state here does not have a single rationality, and it is not capable of optimally ordering the biological resources of its population in the sense of the "biopower" model.

[. . .]

Up to now, I have explored some possible lines of empirical generalizations: some issues to be explored concerning the applicability of the specific conclusions reached for Lesotho to the wider world. There remain a few suggestions to be made about possible generalizations at a more abstract or theoretical level. . . .

Discourse, Knowledge, and Structural Production

I have argued up to now that even a "failed" development project can bring about important structural changes. This means that even where new structures are not produced in accordance with discursively elaborated plans, they are all the same produced, and the role of discursive and conceptual structures in that production is by no means a small one. The investigation has demonstrated two facts about the Thaba-Tseka case: first, that the project's interventions can only be understood in the context of a distinctive discursive regime that orders the "conceptual apparatus" of official thinking and planning about "development" in Lesotho; and secondly, that the actual transformations that were brought about by the project were in no way congruent with the transformations that the conceptual apparatus planned. This pairing of facts raises an important theoretical question: if official planning is not irrelevant to the events that planned interventions give rise to, and if the relation between plan and event is not one of even approximate congruence, then what is the relation between blueprints and outcomes, between conceptual apparatuses and the results of their deployment?

I want to suggest that, in order to answer that question, it is necessary to demote inten-

tionality – in both its "planning" and its "conspiracy" incarnations – and to insist that the structured discourse of planning and its corresponding field of knowledge are important, but only as part of a larger "machine," an anonymous set of interrelations that only ends up having a kind of retrospective coherence. The use of the "machine" metaphor here is motivated not only, as above, by science-fictional analogy, but by a desire (following Foucault [1979, 1980a] and Deleuze [1988]) to capture something of the way that conceptual and discursive systems link up with social institutions and processes without even approximately determining the form or defining the logic of the outcome. As one cog in the "machine," the planning apparatus is not the "source" of whatever structural changes may come about, but only one among a number of links in the mechanism that produces them. Discourse and thought are articulated in such a "machine" with other practices, as I have tried to show; but there is no reason to regard them as "master practices," over-determining all others.

When we deal with planned interventions by powerful parties, however, it is tempting to see in the discourse and intentions of such parties the logic that defines the train of events. Such a view, however, inevitably misrepresents the complexities of the involvement of intentionality with events. Intentions, even of powerful actors or interests, are only the visible part of a much larger mechanism through which structures are actually produced, reproduced, and transformed. Plans are explicit, and easily seen and understood; conspiracies are only slightly less so. But any intentional deployment only takes effect through a convoluted route involving unacknowledged structures and unpredictable outcomes.

If this is so, then a conceptual apparatus is very far from being irrelevant to structural production. It is part of the larger system through which such production actually occurs; but it is only part of a larger mechanism. When one sees the whole process, it is clear that the conceptions are only one cog among others; they are neither mere ornament nor are they the master key to understanding what happens. The whole mechanism is, as Deleuze (1988: 38) puts it, a "mushy mixture" of the discursive and the non-discursive, of the intentional plans and the unacknowledged social world with which they are engaged. While the instrumental aims embodied in plans are highly visible,[6] and pretend to embody the logic of a process of structural production, the actual process proceeds silently and often invisibly, masked or rendered even less visible by its contrast with the intentional plans, which appear bathed in the shining light of day. The plans, then, as the visible part of a larger mechanism, can neither be dismissed nor can they be taken at their word. If the process through which structural production takes place can be thought of as a machine, it must be said that the planners' conceptions are not the blueprint for the machine; they are *parts* of the machine.

Plans constructed within a conceptual apparatus do have effects but in the process of having these effects they generally "fail" to transform the world in their own image. But "failure" here does not mean doing nothing; it means doing something else, and that something else always has its own logic. Systems of discourse and systems of thought are thus bound up in a complex causal relationship with the stream of planned and unplanned events that constitutes the social world. The challenge is to treat these systems of thought and discourse like any other kind of structured social practice, neither dismissing them as ephemeral nor seeking in their products the master plans for those elaborate, half-invisible mechanisms of structural production and reproduction in which they are engaged as component parts.

NOTES

1   Cited in Brian Murphy, "Smothered with Kindness," *New Internationalist*, No. 82, 1979.

2   "Canadian Aid Gone Awry?" *The Citizen* (Ottawa), October 6, 1979; "CIDA in Africa: Goodby $6 Million," *Sunday Star* (Toronto), July 22, 1979.

3   Quoted in Murphy, "Smothered with Kindness," p. 13.

4   More recently, "homeland" governments have taken up "development" schemes, which have involved resettling subsistence farmers to make way for large commercial farms established by Pretoria-funded "development corporations" (Unterhalter 1987, Yawitch 1981). At the same time, the bantustans have taken up the theme of "basic needs," organizing rural settlements (in familiar "betterment" style) around "rural service centers," ostensibly for the purpose of providing government services more efficiently. A recent study concludes (Dewar *et al.* 1983: 59) "that the approach is unlikely to result in significant economic development or basic needs improvement and that the strategy in its present form is primarily directed toward containing 'surplus' rural population in a politically manageable way."

5   Dutkiewicz, Shenton, and Williams seem to be aware of this, as for instance when Dutkiewicz and Williams (1987: 43) observe that "The expanded scope of state activity and regulation has the consequence of reducing the state's capacity to manage and control." But they are unable to convincingly explain it, since they see "state power" as power essentially *belonging to* "the political class" (Dutkiewicz and Shenton's "ruling group"). On this understanding, as more and more of society comes under "state control," the power of this political class ought to be augmented to the point of total domination over the rest of society. The logical consequence of this view is that the political class should become (as in the usual models of "totalitarian society") *more* able to "manage and control" the rest of society, not less. See also Williams (1986: 20), who notes that state intervention has commonly had the effect of reducing export earnings and tax revenues, but is left unable to explain why

it is that "[t]his consideration has not done much to convince African governments... to stop strangling the geese that lay the golden eggs."

6 I use "visible" here in a way that is almost exactly the reverse of the way that Deleuze (1988) uses the term. For Deleuze, the "visible" is opposed to the "articulable," as the non-discursive is to the discursive, the seeable to the sayable. The prison is "visible," criminology "articulable." I use the term "visible" in a more specific sense, to pick out the way that plans and programs explicitly present themselves for everyone to see as blueprints for bringing about change, while the social structures and processes that these plans confront (though integral parts of the "mechanism") are often "unseen" and unacknowledged by both the planners and those who view their efforts. In this sense, then, "development" planning is "visible," while the elaborate set of social process and institutions that also figures in the process is much less so.

REFERENCES

Alavi, H. 1972. "The State in Post-colonial Societies: Pakistan and Bangladesh." *New Left Review*, 74, 59–81.

Azarya, V. and N. Chazan. 1987. "Disengagement from the State in Africa: Reflections on the Experience of Ghana and Guinea." *Comparative Studies in Society and History*, 29, 106–31.

Bayart, J. F. 1986. "Civil Society in Africa," in *Political domination in Africa: Reflections on the limits of power*, P. Chabal (ed.). Cambridge University Press.

Beinart, W. 1982. *The Political Economy of Pondoland, 1860–1930*. Cambridge University Press.

1984. "Soil Erosion, Conservationism and Ideas about Development: A Southern African Exploration, 1900–1960." *Journal of Southern African Studies*, 11, 1, 52–83.

Beinart, W. and C. Bundy. 1981. "State Intervention and Rural Resistance: The Transkei, 1900–1965," in *Peasants in Africa*, M. Klein (ed.), Beverly Hills: Sage.

1987. *Hidden Struggles in Rural South Africa*. London: James Currey.

Bernstein, H. 1981. "Notes on State and Peasantry: The Tanzanian Case." *Review of African Political Economy*, 21, 44–62.

Chabal, P. 1986. "Introduction: Thinking about Politics in Africa" in *Political domination in Africa: Reflections on the limits of power*, P. Chabal (ed.). Cambridge University Press.

CIDA (Canadian International Development Agency). 1979. *Thaba Tseka Project Second Evaluation Report*. Ottawa: CIDA.

Coulson, A. 1975. "Peasants and Bureaucrats." *Review of African Political Economy*, 3.

1981. "Agricultural Policies in Mainland Tanzania, 1946–76," in *Rural Development in Tropical Africa*, J. Heyer, P. Roberts, and G. Williams (eds.). New York: St. Martin's Press.

1982. *Tanzania: A Political Economy*. Oxford: Clarendon Press.

Deleuze, G. 1988. *Foucault*. Minneapolis: University of Minnesota Press.

Dewar, D., A. Todes and V. Watson. 1983. "Development From Below? Basic Needs, Rural Service Centers, and the South African Bantustans, with Particular Reference to the Transkei." *African Urban Studies*, 15, 59–75.

de Wet, C., 1981. "Betterment and trust in a rural Ciskei Village." *Social Dynamics*, 6, 2.

Dutkiewicz, P. and R. Shenton. 1986. "Crisis in Africa: 'Etatization' and the Logic of Diminished Reproduction." *Review of African Political Economy*, 37, 108–15.

Dutkiewicz, P. and G. Williams. 1987. "All the King's Horses and All the King's Men Couldn't Put Humpty-Dumpty Together Again." *IDS Bulletin*, 18, 3, 39–44.

Eberhard, A. A. 1982. "Technological Change and Rural Development: A Case Study in Lesotho." Ph.D. Thesis, University of Edinburgh, November 1982.

Foucault, M. 1979. *Discipline and Punish: The Birth of the Prison*. New York: Vintage.

1980a. *The History of Sexuality: Volume One: An Introduction.* New York: Vintage.

1983. "Afterword: The Subject and Power," in *Michel Foucault: Beyond Structuralism and Hermeneutics* (second edition), H. Dreyfus and P. Rabinow (eds.). Chicago: University of Chicago Press.

Freyhold, M. von. 1979. *Ujamaa Villages in Tanzania: Analysis of a Social Experiment.* London.

Geschiere, P. 1988. "Sorcery and the State: Popular Modes of Action among the Maka of Southeast Cameroon." *Critique of Anthropology,* 8, 1, 35–63.

Hyden, G. 1980. *Beyond Ujamaa in Tanzania: Underdevelopment and an Uncaptured Peasantry.* Berkeley: University of California Press.

Leys, C. 1976. "The 'Overdeveloped' Postcolonial State: A Re-evaluation." *Review of African Political Economy,* 5, 39–48.

Malkki, L. 1989. "Purity and Exile: Transformations in Historical-National Consciousness among Hutu Refugees in Tanzania," Ph.D. dissertation, Department of Anthropology, Harvard University.

Migdal, J. 1988. *Strong Societies and Weak States: State-Society Relations and State Capabilities in the Third World.* Princeton: Princeton University Press.

Moore, S. F. 1986. *Social Facts and Fabrications: A Century of 'Customary Law' on Kilimanjaro.* Cambridge University Press.

Palmer, R. and N. Parsons (eds.). 1977. *The Roots of Rural Poverty in Central and Southern Africa.* Berkeley: University of California Press.

Platzky, L. and C. Walker. 1985. *The Surplus People: Forced Removals in South Africa.* Johannesburg: Ravan Press.

Ranger, T. O. 1985. *Peasant Consciousness and Guerrilla War in Zimbabwe.* Berkeley: University of California Press.

Riddell, R. 1981. "Report of the Commission of Inquiry into Incomes, Prices, and Conditions of Service" (Roger C. Riddell, chairman). Harare: Government of the Republic of Zimbabwe.

Saul, J. 1979. "The State in Postcolonial Societies: Tanzania," in *The State and Revolution in Eastern Africa,* J. Saul (ed.). New York: Monthly Review Press.

Shivji, I. 1976. *Class Struggles in Tanzania.* London: Heinemann.

Shivji, I. (ed.). 1986. *The State and the Working People in Tanzania.* Dakar: CODESRIA.

Unterhalter, E. 1987. *Forced Removal: The Division, Segregation, and Control of the People of South Africa.* London: International Defence and Aid Fund.

Wallman, S. 1969. *Take Out Hunger: Two Case Studies of Rural Development in Basutoland.* London: Athlone.

Williams, G. 1982. "Equity, Growth, and the State." *Africa,* 53, 2.

1985. "The Contradictions of the World Bank and the Crisis of the State in Africa." Mimeo.

1986. "Rural Development: Partners and Adversaries." *Rural Africana,* 25–6, 11–23.

World Bank (International Bank for Reconstruction and Development). 1975. *Lesotho: A Development Challenge.* Washington, D. C.

Yawitch, J. 1981. *Betterment: The Myth of Homeland Agriculture.* Johannesburg: Institute of Race Relations.

Section III

Violence, Law, and Citizenship

The articles included in this section examine the practices, representations, and effects of violence. The definition of violence here is quite wide, including physical violence (both military-inflicted and domestic violence), structural violence (caused by socioeconomic inequalities), and discursive violence (exclusions and hatreds created by narrowly defined legal categories of national belonging). These articles argue that violence engages with the concepts that are centrally connected with the idea of the state: sovereignty, citizenship, and nation. The distinctive feature of the three articles in this sub-section on militarization, immigration laws, migration, and citizenship, is that they trouble the usual tendency to analyze these concepts entirely within the frames of the nation-state, highlighting instead their *transnational* character. The authors set their discussion of militarization, citizenship, migration, and violence against the backdrop of transnational capital and neoliberalism, the inter-state system of sovereign nations, transnational discourses of human rights, and transnational activism.

Catherine Lutz studies US militarization as a violent social process that is not simply contained in the "classic" military apparatus, like the army or the Pentagon. She pays careful attention to how social relations and spaces are transformed through the spread of military practices and ideologies. Lutz uses the concept of "mode of warfare" to delineate the discursive and material effects of militarization. By "mode of warfare," she means the entire complex of social arrangements engendered by a particular military strategy or doctrine. Different modes of warfare, such as "mass industrial warfare," "nuclearism," or "humanitarian war," have transformed societies. For instance, they have reshaped urban landscapes and impoverished some cities; accelerated suburbanization in other regions; used different ideological constructs to "naturalize" militarization;

reshaped welfare, rights, and civil liberty regimes; altered production processes and relations by privileging some forms of labor and some groups of workers over others; remade socioeconomic relations, and entrenched social hierarchies of class, gender, sexuality, and race; and redefined citizenship, idealizing it in the white, male, heterosexual soldier/national hero. Lutz links up state agencies, social institutions, transnational capitalism, and the media in her analysis of militarization ideologies, practices, and effects. This allows her to connect physical, structural, and discursive forms of violence and to move beyond "the state" when discussing what is often considered the classic activity of sovereign states – war-making.

If defending the nation through making war is one activity intimately connected with the state, defining the national community through making immigration laws and instituting citizenship regimes is another. Coutin and Bhattacharjee approach the notions of law, citizenship, and belonging through the experiences of different immigrant communities in the USA, and demonstrate the deeply unequal (and therefore violent) and transnational nature of these notions. These two authors show how human migrations and regimes of immigration and naturalization, which are articulated with the needs of global capital, are reshaping modes of belonging based on the nation, community, and family, and altering the relationship between states and territories.

Coutin uses the example of Salvadoran migrants residing in the USA to delineate the transnationalization of citizenship and transterritorialization of states. She juxtaposes the reasons behind Salvadoran migrants' bid to naturalize as US citizens against official discourses and representations of citizenship to bring out the tensions between the exclusive affiliations presumed by naturalization (which is grounded in a theory of national sovereignty) and interdependent transnationalism. Salvadoran migrants residing in California desire to become American citizens in order to fight the inequalities they face in a context increasingly hostile to immigrants. Naturalization also allows Salvadorans the freedom to travel to El Salvador and sustain connections with their country of origin. As US citizens these Salvadorans are "claimed" by the transterritorialized nation-state of El Salvador even though they no longer reside there. The Salvadoran state incorporates members of the diaspora into the political life of the "home" nation by positioning these emigrants as a national resource with the potential to influence US foreign policy vis-à-vis El Salvador. In contrast to the migrants' desire to naturalize in order to *maintain* transnational linkages with their country of origin, the official US legal discourse on naturalization represents citizenship as a *clean break* with the place of origin. Official discourse portrays naturalization as a process of freely choosing one citizenship among several available options. By contrast to this model of citizenship as *singular*, Salvadoran migrants articulate an additive and transnational understanding of citizenship that highlights the lack of choice that drives them to naturalize. The experience of Salvadoran migrants in the USA stresses the inequalities of belonging based in "difference" (cultural, racial, and class, for instance), and therefore troubles both the presumed generic quality of citizenship and the purportedly equal membership in the national public.

Bhattacharjee illustrates the hierarchies of belonging, the violence of exclusionary definitions of nation and community, and the unequal and private character of the public sphere through her analysis of domestic violence against women and domestic workers in South Asian immigrant communities in the USA. She directly challenges the Western liberal distinction between the public and private realms, and therefore raises questions about liberal definitions of the state. Some Western feminists, taking this boundary for a given, have argued that victims of domestic violence can access justice by projecting the oppressions they suffer in their private homes into the public sphere. This strategy would work if the public (the realm of rights and equality) and the private were clearly separate. Bhattacharjee questions this by showing how immigration laws (which are raced, gendered, classed, and sexualized) render immigrant homes public. These laws stipulate what constitutes a "good faith" (heteropatriachal) marriage and therefore define the legitimate family that can reunite through immigration. The "private" quality of the home is complicated for migrant domestic workers whose workspace is someone else's home. Furthermore, immigration laws also privatize the public realm of rights by defining national belonging in exclusive terms; the public is therefore not equally accessible to those denied full membership in the national community. The physical violence experienced by immigrant women and domestic workers is compounded by the violence of restrictive legal categories. If the boundaries of the public and the private are constantly shifting, as Bhattacharjee shows, then feminists cannot uncritically advocate public intervention as a strategy for countering domestic violence.

SUGGESTED READINGS

Agamben, Giorgio
    1998   Homo Sacer: Sovereign Power and Bare Life. D. Heller-Roazen, trans. Stanford, CA: Stanford University Press.
Alexander, M. Jacqui
    1997   Erotic Autonomy as a Politics of Decolonization: An Anatomy of Feminist and State Practice in the Bahamas Tourist Economy. In Feminist Genealogies, Colonial Legacies, Democratic Futures. M. J. Alexander and C. T. Mohanty, eds. Pp. 63–100. New York: Routledge.
Aretxaga, Begona
    2000   Playing Terrorist: Ghastly Plots and the Ghostly State. Journal of Spanish Cultural Studies 1(1):43–58.
Butalia, Urvashi
    1993   Community, State and Gender: On Women's Agency during Partition. Economic and Political Weekly of India 28(17):WS12–WS34.
Das, Veena, and Deborah Poole, eds.
    2004   Anthropology in the Margins of the State. School of American Research Seminar Series. Santa Fe, NM: School of American Research Press.

Enloe, Cynthia
  2000   Maneuvers: The International Politics of Militarizing Women's Lives. Berkeley: University of California Press.
Flores, William V., and Rina Benmayor, eds.
  1997   Latino Cultural Citizenship: Claiming Identity, Space, and Rights. Boston: Beacon Press.
Glick Schiller, Nina, and George E. Fouron
  1999   Terrains of Blood and Nation: Haitian Transnational Social Fields. Ethnic and Racial Studies 22(2):340–366.
Jean-Klein, Iris
  2000   Mothercraft, Statecraft, and Subjectivity in the Palestinian Intifada. American Ethnologist 29(1):100–127.
Lutz, Catherine
  2001   Homefront: A Military City and the American Twentieth Century. Boston: Beacon Press.
Menon, Ritu, and Kamla Bhasin
  1993   Recovery, Rupture, Resistance: Indian State and Abduction of Women during Partition. Economic and Political Weekly of India 28(17):WS2–WS11.
Merry, Sally E.
  2001   Spatial Governmentality and the New Urban Social Order: Controlling Gender Violence through Law. American Anthropologist 103(1):16–29.
Nelson, Diane
  1999   A Finger in the Wound: Body Politics in Quincentennial Guatemala. Berkeley: University of California Press.
Ong, Aihwa
  1999   Flexible Citizenship: The Cultural Logics of Transnationality. Durham, NC: Duke University Press.
Rose, Nikolas
  1989   Governing the Soul: The Shaping of the Private Self. London: Free Association Books.
Sunder Rajan, Rajeswari
  2003   The Scandal of the State: Women, Law, and Citizenship in Postcolonial India. Durham, NC: Duke University Press.
Tilly, Charles
  1985   War Making and State Making as Organized Crime. In Bringing the State Back In. P. Evans, D. Rueschemeyer, and T. Skocpol, eds. Pp. 169–191. Cambridge: Cambridge University Press.
Verdery, Katherine
  1998   Transnationalism, Nationalism, Citizenship, and Property: Eastern Europe Since 1989. American Ethnologist 25(2):291–306.

12

Making War at Home in the United States: Militarization and the Current Crisis

Catherine Lutz

It takes a good deal more courage, work and knowledge to dissolve words like "war" and "peace" into their elements, recovering what has been left out of peace processes that have been determined by the powerful, and then placing that missing actuality back in the center of things.... The best corrective is, as Dr. Johnson said, to imagine the person whom you are discussing – in this case the person on whom the bombs will fall – reading you in your presence.

– Edward Said, "The Public Role of Writers and Intellectuals"

I will not begin with the story of a pair of people holding hands as they leapt to their deaths from the Towers on September 11. It has been told, and often sold, a thousand times over. I cannot begin with the story of a man holding his child in Afghanistan later that autumn, listening to the approach of distant US bombers that would soon cut him and his child down like daisies. This one has had far fewer tellings, for it has had little

exchange value in the modern economy of war, race, mass media, cultural politics, and oil. Neither story can be told to fully good purpose without first unearthing what they evoke beyond the wailing webs of mourning that ramify from each life extinguished.

That, I will argue, is the long process of militarization and empire building that has reshaped almost every element of global social life over the 20th century. By militarization, I mean "the contradictory and tense social process in which civil society organizes itself for the production of violence" (Geyer 1989:79). This process involves an intensification of the labor and resources allocated to military purposes, including the shaping of other institutions in synchrony with military goals. Militarization is simultaneously a discursive process, involving a shift in general societal beliefs and values in ways necessary to legitimate the use of force, the organization of large standing armies and their leaders, and the higher taxes or tribute used to pay for them. Militarization is intimately connected not only to the obvious increase

From *American Anthropologist*, 104(3), 2002, pp. 723–35. ©2002, American Anthropologist Association. All rights reserved. Used by permission.

in the size of armies and resurgence of militant nationalisms and militant fundamentalisms but also to the less visible deformation of human potentials into the hierarchies of race, class, gender, and sexuality, and to the shaping of national histories in ways that glorify and legitimate military action (Bernstein 1999; Linenthal and Engelhardt 1996). While it is often called by such names as "military strength," or framed as a tool to defend freedom, militarization is a process that helped spawn the violence of September 11 and the violent response of October 7: To understand militarization, so many must hope, is to put some impediment in its deadly path.

While militarization has been shaped within innumerable states, corporations, and localities, the United States is now the largest wellspring for this global process. A nation made by war, the United States was birthed not just by the Revolution of 1776 but also by wars against Native Americans and the violence required to capture and enslave many millions of African people. Twentieth-century US militarization accelerated in three major bursts: with the 1939 loosing of fascist forces in a world never recovered from the First World War,[1] again with the establishment of the national security state in 1947, and now with the events of September 11, 2001.

Bitterly watching the United States charge headlong onto the slaughter fields of Flanders and US intellectuals' enthusiastic drumbeat of acquiescence, Randolph Bourne called war "the health of the state" (1964). He meant that the state's power grows in wartime, accumulating legal powers and public wealth to pursue the battle, and that it often maintains that expanded power far into the putative peacetime that follows. Bourne was certainly proven prescient, as the last century's wars enlarged the government and enriched military corporations, shrank legal controls over both entities, and captured an empire of postconflict markets (e.g., Jensen 1991; Kaplan and Pease 1993; Sherry 1995). And, in 1947, with the institution of the National Security Act and a whole host of other anti-

democratic practices, the broad latitude of political elites in what is euphemistically called "statecraft" was to be taken for granted.

While many, particularly progressives and libertarians, see and worry about these changes, the entrenched notion that war is the health of the nation has garnered little attention and no irony. It is instead widely accepted that military spending preserves freedom and produces jobs in factories and in the army. The military is said to prepare young people for life, making men out of boys and an educated workforce out of warriors through college benefits. Virtues like discipline and teamwork are seen as nurtured by military trainers and lavishly exported to society at large. That these contentions are problematic becomes evident in the close ethnographic view of communities shaped by military spending outlined below.

It is true, however, that the capillaries of militarization have fed and molded social institutions seemingly little connected to battle. In other words, the process of militarization has been not simply a matter of weaponry wielded and bodies buried. It has also created what is taken as knowledge, particularly in the fields of physics and psychology, both significantly shaped by military funding and goals (Leslie 1993; Lutz 1997). It has redefined proper masculinity and sexuality (D'Amico 1997; Enloe 2000), further marginalizing anyone but the male heterosexual – the only category of person seen fit for the full citizenship conferred by combat. Militarization emerges from the images of soldiers in recruitment ads that blast across the popular culture landscape through both the $2 billion annual recruitment budget and Hollywood fare from *The Sands of Iwo Jima* to *Black Hawk Down*. It has rearranged US social geography through internal migrations to the South and West for military work (Markusen et al. 1991) and has accelerated the suburbanization process and the creation of black bantustans in the core of older cities. It created the bulk of both the federal deficit and the resistance to social welfare benefits in a workforce divided into those soldiers and veterans with universal health care, a living wage, and other benefits, and those without them (Hardin 1991). It has contributed to the making of race and gender in the United States through the biases of military spending toward the whiter and more male segments of the workforce.

Much of the history and the physical and symbolic costs of war on the home front and of war itself have been invisible to people both inside and outside the military. This is the outcome of secrecy laws, of an increasingly muzzled or actively complicit corporate media, and of the difficulty of assessing a highly complex and far-flung institution and the not-so-obviously related consequences of its actions. The costs have also been shrouded behind simplified histories, public relations work, or propaganda. Most recently, Tom Brokaw's *The Greatest Generation*, Stephen Spielberg's *Saving Private Ryan*, and the many best-selling paeans to soldiering by Stephen Ambrose are responsible for selling a powerful nostalgia and desire for war in a new generation. These popular culture works assert that war builds character, makes men, and grants freedom to the nation and a kind of supercitizenship to those who wage it. This militarization in the United States is not, of course, what the current crisis is supposedly about. The bookshelves of stores that have a section devoted to our current predicament burst with books on Islam and fundamentalist Islam, the Taliban, and Nostradamus. They are on "the Arab World" and the vectors of danger to the US population in the form of germs and weapons of mass destruction, weapons that are construed as dangerous only in the hands of the immature nations, something Hugh Gusterson has termed "nuclear orientalism" (1999).

September 11 has been treated in the media and by politicians as both a rupture in history and as the next "Good War." From that war, of course, come the constant references to Pearl Harbor and President Bush's imagination of the enemy as the "Axis of Evil." The same people who busily proclaimed the

end of history a few years ago now say it has just begun, with September 11 as the starting point. The US involvements in global affairs that may have precipitated these events in some way have been ignored: The people who jumped from those downtown workplace windows flew free of history. Attempts to explain the events through historical contextualization were shouted down as treasonable excuse. Those who died in Afghanistan, by contrast, were historically particularized, each implicated in a prior chain of conspiracy that sent jumbo jets crashing into buildings, each recoded as a Taliban terrorist, and so their deaths were justified.

A number of anthropologists, alongside historians, have written for years against these erasures. They have found or put themselves in the midst of violent whirlwinds: Carolyn Nordstrom (1997), Linda Green (1994), Veena Das (1990), Orin Starn (1999), Begona Aretxaga (1997), Michael Taussig (1987), Liisa Malkki (1995), Allen Feldman (1991), C. Valentine Daniel (1996), Cynthia Mahmood (1996), and a long list of others have shown us that war is about social deformation, silencing, and resilience as much as it is about the body's physical destruction.[2] The anthropologies of immiseration produced by such scholars as Brett Williams (1994), Nancy Scheper-Hughes (1992), Philippe Bourgois (1996), Katherine Newman (1999), June Nash (1979), Gerald Sider (1986), Paul Farmer (1996), Ida Susser (1996), Kim Hopper (1991), and Judith Goode and Jeff Maskovsky (2001) are also important to set alongside the more explicitly war-centered works. They reveal what the epigraph above suggests is often hidden: the indistinguishability and interdependence of physical and structural violence. This is in contrast to the notion that violence is mere tool or accident en route to the pursuit of a state's political interest, or that there are separate "forms" of power, such as military, political, and economic.[3] These works can be used to illustrate the intertwining of the violence of the 20th century with the widening international and intranational gap between the rich and poor and with the surges of old and new forms of racism. I focus here on the context of the emergence of this violence focusing on the historical and anthropological contexts of war and war preparation in, or involving, the United States.

This article is organized around two central questions: (1) What is the 20th-century history of militarization, and how is it related to the notion of militarism, to the nation-state, to changing modes of warfare, and to broader social changes? and (2) How can we connect global and national histories with specific ethnographically understood places and people involved in the militarization process? I can begin to answer these questions with reference to ethnographic and historical research in a military city, Fayetteville, North Carolina. Its 120,000 people live next to the Army's giant Fort Bragg, and its story tells about the history of US cities more generally (Lutz 2001). In closing, I suggest how this can help us understand the crisis that erupted on September 11.

Militarism, Militarization, and States

The term *militarism* has sometimes been used synonymously with the term *militarization*. It is usually much narrower in scope than the latter, however, identifying a society's emphasis on martial values. It also focuses attention on the political realm and suggests warlike values have an independent ability to drive social change, while *militarization* draws attention to the simultaneously material and discursive nature of military dominance. In addition, North American scholarship has rarely applied the term *militarism* to the United States; it more often projects responsibility onto countries it thereby "others." This makes it hard to identify growing military hegemony in the United States and in other societies in which ideological claims suggest the nation is peaceful by nature, and engages in war only when it is sorely provoked (Engelhardt 1995). Moreover, there is no universal set of "military

values" whose rise indexes a process of militarization because cultural forms have intersected with and remade society's military institutions. So, for example, faith in technology has supported a high ratio of arms to soldiers in the US military. While some might assume that this is the natural outcome of US affluence or of high-tech weaponry's superior efficacy as a modality of war, neither is necessarily the case, as the Vietnam War and September 11 both demonstrated. Such technological faith comes through the power of military industrial corporations to shape political discourse and decisions in the United States through lobbying and campaign contributions, via the revolving door between military and military industrial leadership, and military corporate advertising. The faith is also rooted deeply in advertising campaigns for better living through those sciences that brought advances in transportation, food technology, home appliances, and computers.

Military institutional growth and a glorification of war and its values, however culturally defined, have not always developed in tandem: US military spending remained low in the 19th and early 20th centuries while political culture glorified war and the martial spirit. Oliver Wendell Holmes Jr., told students at Harvard in 1895 that: "So long as man dwells upon the globe, his destiny is battle.... War's ... message is divine" (Karsten 1989:33). William James even argued against war while still assuming a love of battle: "The popular imagination fairly fattens on the thought of wars.... Militarism is the great preserver of our ideals of hardihood" (Karsten 1989:36). Contemporary American political culture does not tolerate such talk of the merits of violence. Instead, politicians, pundits, and some Fayetteville citizens speak about soldiers as those who are "placed in harm's way," reversing the image of soldiers as warrior–killers and eliding the state's role in their movements. At the same time, substantial resources are allocated to war preparation.

These elisions aside, however, the growth of a behemoth military and of military industrial corporate power have helped make what C. Wright Mills called "a military definition of reality" (1956:191) become the common sense of the nation. That is, it is deeply and widely believed that human beings are by nature aggressive and territorial, that force is the only way to get things done in the world, and that if one weapon creates security, 1,000 weapons create that much more. By this definition, as one soldier told me, "defense is the first need of every organism" (anonymous, conversation with author, June 30, 1999).

Militarization is a *tense process*, that is, it can create conflict between social sectors, and most importantly between those who might benefit from militarization (e.g., corporations interested in expanding international markets for their goods) and those who might not, but who nonetheless may bear some of its costs. This conflict happens on the local level as well. In the 640 US communities with large military bases, realtors and retail owners benefit from the military's presence, unlike lawyers, public sector workers, and retail workers who must cope with the shrunken tax base associated with the military bases' federal land. The structural violence a war economy creates is not the simple equation so often painted of subtracting the government's military spending from its social spending. An example of the more complex factors involved is found in Fayetteville, where retail labor is the main category of work created by the post, as Fort Bragg soldiers take their salary dollars there to shop. Not only do retail jobs pay less than any other type of job, but retail workers also face the reserve army of unemployed military spouses whose in-migration to Fayetteville the military funds. Fayetteville wage rates are lower than in any other North Carolina city as a result.

Militarization also sets *contradictory* processes in motion, for example, it accentuates both localism (as when Fayetteville and other cities compete for huge military contracts or bases) and federalism (as when the fate of dry cleaning businesses in Fayetteville can hinge on Pentagon regulations on putting starch in uniforms or on sudden deployments of large numbers of soldiers). Militarization might seem always to have the latter centralizing tendencies but there has been, in the United States especially, a tradition of what Lotchin (1984) calls the "entrepreneurial city" – competing for interstates, country seats, conventions, prisons, and military bases and contracts. This curbs the state, as does citizens' ability to make more claims on a government in exchange for their mobilization for war.

Charles Tilly has argued that most states are birthed by and wedded to war. He in fact names the state a kind of protection racket, raising armies that safeguard the people from violent threats they pretend to see, provoke themselves, or wreak on their own people. He also, however, leaves open the possibility for legitimate defensive armies to emerge in some contexts. "Someone who produces both the danger and, at a price, the shield against it is a racketeer. Someone who provides a needed shield but has little control over the danger's appearance qualifies as a legitimate protector, especially if his price is no higher than his competitors" (Tilly 1985:170–1). Most of the armies that emerged from the 18th century onward claimed to be the primary tool of the state – or, more grandly, the very enablement of a people. These armies could be defined as virtually the sine qua non of both state and nation.

States that formed earlier in the modern period, such as those in Europe and the United States, were better able to externalize their violence, protecting at least the middle and upper classes from the violence their global extraction of resources required. States that emerged more recently have often been shaped as clients to those earlier and more powerful ones. For this reason, the latter show a much greater disproportion of power between military and civil forces (however much those two categories problematically entail or contain each other). In these client states, the military is favored, as the state strikes bargains more with the foreign patron (who provides military assistance in exchange for commodities, labor pools, and access) than with the people within that state. This has certainly been relevant in the current crisis, as Saudi Arabia's elites, for example, struggle to be seen as defenders of the nation rather than clients of the United States, and as the United States exempted Saudi Arabia from its list of terrorist states, despite the fact that almost all the hijacker–murderers of September 11 were from that country.

Beyond this general relationship between the state and violence, many historians have noted the United States' especially intimate relationship to war, that US violence has centered on the idea of race and, moreover, has contributed to the making of races. The early US Army was defined as a kind of constabulary whose purpose was nation-building through "Indian clearance," rather than defense of national borders (Weigley 1967:27). The Army also built roads and forts to facilitate colonial settlement, an aim so intrinsic to the military that "any difference between soldiering and pioneering escaped the naked eye" (Perret 1989:137). The real and imagined threat of slave insurrection rationalized the raising of local official militias in the 19th century as well, and the military fought the Mexican–American and the Spanish–American Wars with racial rationales. European colonialism was, of course, also rooted in race violence, and the World War, which ran with brief interruption from 1914 to 1945, was fueled by contests over colonial holdings and militant expansionism based in racial supremacism (whether European, American, or Japanese).[4] US military power went global as the 20th century opened, when Filipinos, Puerto Ricans, and Hawaiians were made racial wards of the state.

This long history of race and war is encapsulated in Fayetteville's annual International Folk Festival. It begins with a parade down the city's main street led by a contingent of the Fayetteville Independent Light Infantry, a militia begun in the slave era, and still in existence, though more as social club than armed force. The soldiers in archaic dress costume are followed by a march of war refugee nations from Puerto Ricans and Okinawans to Koreans and Vietnamese who have made the city home.

20th-Century Modes of US Warfare

To understand when, why, and how the militarization process has sped up in the United States and globally in the 20th century, when and how warfare has emerged from it in the contemporary world, and how social relations are reshaped, I begin with the notion of an era's dominant "mode of warfare." While many accounts of warfare remain technocentric, that is, focused on the scientifically and technically advanced tool purportedly at its center (such as the machine gun, the atom bomb, or the computer, e.g., Ellis 1975), this phrase draws our attention beyond the central weapon or strategy of a country or era's military organization to the wider array of social features any type of war making leads to. The mode of warfare that emerged with industrial capitalism and the nation state most extensively by the 19th century was mass industrial warfare. This required raising large armies, whether standing or relatively episodic. War in this mode also centered on manufacturing labor, with many workers required to produce tens of thousands of relatively simple guns, tanks, and ships, and, eventually, airplanes. The advantage of industrial warfare over artisanal warfare was immediately evident in colonial wars in which the European powers captured vast territories. This point can be overemphasized, however; the Belgian Congo represents a case in which simple guns, chains, and severed hands did the work of creating a labor force to extract the colony's wealth (Hochschild 1998) and Maori guerilla warfare in New Zealand was effective for years against the more technically advanced weaponry of the British (Belich 1986).

As or more important than the efficacy of a mode of warfare, however, has been the form of life it has encouraged inside the nation waging it. Industrial modes of warfare, for example, pressed governments to extend civil rights and social benefits to gain the loyalty and labor of those larger segments of the population conscripted into the mass army (Skocpol 1993; Tilly 1985) as well as taxed. For, first of all, mass industrial armies confront the problem of labor, and the symbolic benefits of citizenship have often been exchanged for them. World Wars I and II were fought in this mass industrial mode and helped shape the labor geographies and gender/race/class structures of the societies that waged them. They further entrenched patriarchal authority by excluding women from armies (except as sexual aids to soldier morale) and from high-paying manufacturing jobs (even if they temporarily involved some women and racial minorities during wartime). These wars also helped absorb excess industrial capacity that increasingly threatened capital accumulation. They did so by producing massive numbers of commodities whose function it was to be destroyed. In round numbers, America produced 300,000 planes, 77,000 ships, 20 million small arms, 6 million tons of bombs, 120,000 armored vehicles, and 2.5 million trucks in World War II alone (Adams 1994:71). The wars also prevented crisis within the US economy after the war by requiring retooling of factories for domestic production and by providing new markets, commodities, and desires both overseas and domestically (Baran and Sweezy 1966).

The Cold War's beginning has been variously dated from 1917 to 1947, but after World War II, US–Soviet enmity became associated with a new mode of warfare. Termed "nuclearism," it was initiated in 1945 with the bombing of the US western desert and then Hiroshima and Nagasaki. While technocentrism suggests that the new weapon and its massive destructive power were key to the transformation that began that year, what changed, more importantly, was the perception of danger among the people purportedly protected by nuclear weapons and the new

social relations that emerged because of these weapons' manufacture. Nuclearism's economy centered on producing more and more complex forms of the bomb and what are euphemistically called "platforms," such as jet fighters, nuclear submarines, and other forms of war machinery (Kaldor 1981). This mode of warfare allowed nations to keep smaller armies since air-delivered nuclear and other weapons replaced ground forces.[5] As weapons became more elaborate and fewer in number, the number of workers needed to produce them (and the unions associated with manufacturing) declined. Scientific and engineering labor – overwhelmingly white and male both in 1945 and today – became more important than manufacturing labor.

Nuclearism and the military budget undergirding it have not been neutral in their redistributional effects, exacerbating class, gender, and racial disparities in wealth and status. Military industrial jobs migrated to areas of the country with fewer African Americans. When women found work in such industries, they encountered a gender pay gap wider than the one prevailing in the civilian sector (Hardin 1991; Markusen and Yudken 1992). These workers were often nonunionized: Indeed, the Pentagon actively advocated relocation of weapons companies to nonunion areas, sometimes even billing taxpayers for the move. While North Carolina, for example, has numerous military bases, more Department of Defense tax dollars come out of North Carolina than go back into it (Markusen et al. 1991; Markusen and Yudken 1992), and the inability of localities to tax federal property has further impoverished the several counties from which Fort Bragg land was taken. One of those, Hoke County, with a heavy African American population, has been near the top of the state's 100 counties in its poverty rate, and the jobs it has been able to attract are mainly in its numerous prisons and poultry processing plants.

This mode of warfare also spawned expanded codes of secrecy to protect the technical knowledge involved in weapons development (as well as to hide the fraud and waste, accidents, and environmental costs entailed): The homosexual, in particular, was seen as a "weak link" who could be blackmailed to give up military secrets. Such fantasies envisioned the Soviets undermining US culture from within (Dolan 1994). This secrecy also fundamentally deformed norms of democratic citizenship already under pressure from consumerist notions of self and eroded civil liberties. Nuclearism also reshaped forms of masculinity and femininity. The physical bravery and male bonding seen necessary for earlier forms of warfare were replaced by technical rationality and individual strength. Middle-class womanhood, too, was reframed: The home a woman kept for her family was newly conceived as a bomb shelterlike haven (May 1988).

While civilians died in large numbers during the first half of the century under industrial regimes of war (primarily in colonial wars but also in the European theatres of war), the nuclear mode of warfare sharply eroded the practical, if not the conceptual, distinction between soldiers and civilians, as each was equally targeted by other nuclear powers. This takes Tilly's (1985) point a step further: The power of governments with nuclear weapons is greatly strengthened, as much against its own people as others', forcing the people of nuclear nations into a more lopsided bargain with their states, trusting them with not only their own future but also with that of the human race. Nuclear empowerment also helped both the Soviet Union and the United States administer their populations by suggesting that the nation's survival depended on subsuming internal conflict to the demands of national unity. It is in this sense that Mary Kaldor (1991) called the nuclearism-based Cold War "the Imaginary War": war that was more scenario than actual battle, its cultural force came from managing internal social divisions (for example, controlling the demands of the civil rights movement in the United States) more than from its defense of the nation (see also Horne 1986). So it was in Fayetteville in the

1950s that debates about Communism and Jim Crow were wedded. Segregationists argued that the subversive aims of the Soviets would be advanced through "race mixing" or by race conflict, which Communist propaganda would exploit. A local civil rights leader had to defend the need to integrate schools within the same paradigm: "Our deeds must match our ideals and words concerning the rights of men and their equality before the law, or the two-thirds of the world's population that is not white will turn to the communists for leadership.... America [would then be] doomed to suffer attacks with atom and hydrogen bombs, leaving millions of us lying in unsegregated graves or interned in integrated prison camps" (Lutz 2001:114–15).

What some nuclear planners discovered, moreover, was that nuclear weapons were unusable, because (as one general observed of war itself) they "ruined a perfectly good army." They were also prone to kill downwinders and to accidents whose consequences were as likely to destroy lives at home or in colonial holdings like Micronesia (Alcalay 1984) as overseas. The 40 major nuclear accidents of the Cold War era contaminated US and Soviet soil and water at their own hands, not the enemy's (Rogers 2000). This recognition occurred even as other planners fully contemplated first strike use to disable enemy nuclear capacities, even though a *single* one of the tens of thousands of extant nuclear weapons in the late 1950s would totally devastate a 500-square-mile area and start fires over an additional 1,500 square miles.

The nuclear mode of warfare also spawned a twin – proxy wars against both nonviolent and violent insurgencies that threatened US and Soviet interests overseas. These movements arose especially in those societies in which class differences were gaping, but the insurgency wars were joined with US and Soviet weapons and training particularly where investment or strategic aims were at stake. In those counterinsurgency wars, 10 million people lost their lives (Rogers 2000:35). Perception is as important as the reality, and official chronologies now speak of the "bless-ings" of nuclear weapons, ignoring this deflected body count as well as the environmental damage they and their proxy wars caused. Instead, they focus on the lack of a nuclear exchange between the superpowers, and call one party the "victor."[6] Despite the dissolution of the Soviet Union, a nuclear abolitionist movement, and the perception that nuclear weapons are a thing of the past, the United States continued to have 10,500 nuclear weapons in 2000 (Center for Defense Information 2002a). Nearly $65 billion has been spent on the chimerical idea of a nuclear "missile shield," a program that both continues the deterrence dream of nuclear warfare, on the one hand, and is a radically less spectacular (and bombastically masculine) form, "distinguished by stealth, speed, and accuracy... far less arresting than the bomb and its mushroom cloud" (Lam 2001), on the other. The compression of time and space through these and other military means – the focus on seeing the enemy as tantamount to destroying his "assets" – has led some to call this another and new mode of warfare, the visual or the postmodern (Gray 1997; Virilio 1990).

During this period, the number of countries with substantial middle classes and dropping poverty rates increased, but the extent of structural violence intensified in other, especially African, states. This was the result of a steady decline in the price of raw materials, disinvestment in areas both intra- and internationally seen as "basket cases" or human refuse zones, and the increasing indebtedness of poorer states to wealthier ones and the banking enterprises within them. These factors meant an increasing rate of wealth flow from poorer to wealthier states. The promotion of neoliberalism by the elites of nations rich and poor has meant that whatever legal protections for local markets had been in place have been dismantled; the people who suffer as a result look for the source of their immiseration and find local elites rather than the foreign powers who might have once been so identified.

The post–Cold War period saw the United States emerge as human history's first truly global power. Even before the massive increases of 2002, its military spending was equal to that of the next 12 most significant national militaries combined. By way of comparison, Britain's 19th-century empire appears a weakling; the two next largest navies together equaled the British navy (Mann 2001:58). The reach of the US military that began to widen in World War II remained breathtaking and unprecedented: There are currently 672 US overseas military installations that serve as a far-flung archipelago of what is euphemistically called "forward basing" rather than imperial outposts.[7] "Platforms" such as battleships, nuclear submarines, and jets, as well as spy satellites and other listening posts, go even further toward creating a grid of operations and surveillance that comprehensively covers the globe.

The social and environmental costs of US global military operations, however, include apartheid-like conditions, prostitution, and other retrogressive effects on women in the surrounding communities, and environmental devastation around bases at home and abroad (Armstrong 1999; Enloe 2000; Shulman 1992). Overseas, these costs have been levied in the name of these societies whose people are seen as helpmates to the explicit project of US global patronage and policing. What all these military functions share is the idea of the potential necessity for the violent defense of white and male supremacism, now simply called "civilized values," against those of savagery or barbaric evil (Slotkin 1992).

While many people believe that the Cold War's end shrank the US military substantially, it did not. There was an initial 18 percent drop in military spending, but a groundswell of aggressive lobbying by defense contractors, weapons labs, and the Pentagon mended the losses.[8] Budgets had reached the original Cold War levels of $343 billion even before September 11. The military, however, did restructure in the 1990s as business had in tune with the new tenor of a neoliberal age: It downsized and temped its force (active duty troops dropping from just over 2 million to about 1.4 million, and reserves increasing), out-sourced more of its work (training the militaries of other countries to do proxy work for US interests, while retaining plausible deniability when human rights abuses occur), and it privatized some of its otherwise public workforce (as when it gave the contract for guarding Fort Bragg's huge ammunition dump to a private security firm) (Sheppard 1998). With the demise of the Soviet Union, US military industries became not just the source of the state's coercive power but also of its economic power in a more direct sense: It became the largest global merchant of arms, exporting as much as all other arms producing countries combined.[9]

New war-making doctrines were developed, their intention or outcome being to protect the military and its industries from decimation. Christened "Operations Other than War," they included Evacuation Operations, Support to Domestic Civil Authorities, and Disaster Relief, among many others. Some missions gave the military tasks once seen as civilian jobs, such as famine relief. As it took on social and policing jobs that one soldier from Fayetteville described dismissively to me as "babysitting," it could seem that the army was demilitarizing. Such contradictory effects are also evident in the response to environmental damage found on the military bases that were closed to allow reallocation of funds to military industry purchases. On the one hand, the mess, sometimes of monumental proportions, was cleaned up partially with EPA funds, which could be considered militarized when allocated to that purpose. On the other hand, military funds might be considered demilitarized when they were used to clean and convert bases to civilian uses.

It was in this flurry of new mission development that "humanitarian war" came to be seen, not as oxymoron but as an adjunct to human rights work and democratic aspirations around the world. It emerged as the newest mode of warfare and was distinguished from ordinary modern warfare primarily by its ideological force. This is a powerful and paradoxical combination of social evolutionist and human rights discourse. The reinvigoration of social evolutionism in the United States in the 1980s and 1990s was evident and promoted in books proclaiming a "clash of civilizations" between the Western and advanced, and the barbaric elsewheres, or predicting a "coming anarchy" of clashes between the rich and poor nations, but with an America triumphant because of its superior culture (Huntington 1996; Kaplan 1994). The humanitarian wars that drew on these various and seemingly antithetical discourses did little to prevent or stop such gross human rights violations as the genocide in Rwanda, the 1999 massacres in East Timor, and the rubbling of Chechnya by the Russians; this is an index of the frequent use of the term *humanitarian war* as pretext for other national purposes.

Humanitarian warfare has often been twinned (as was nuclearism with counterinsurgency) with what Mary Kaldor identifies as "the New Wars." Paramilitaries fight these wars without clear lines of command; they target civilians with torture, rape, and terror bombings. Their aim is "to sow fear and discord, to instill unbearable memories of what was once home, to desecrate whatever has social meaning" (Kaldor and Vashee 1997:16).[10] As Carolyn Nordstrom (1997) has noted, their intention to prevent dissent or even discussion is signified by their frequent maiming of eyes, ears, and tongues. These are often civil wars rather than wars between states and they have involved the use of "small" or inexpensive arms that are thereby made widely available, further raising the death toll of civilians that reached 90 percent of all war deaths by the end of the century. In some cases, US arms and training are thrown on one side or the other in line with larger strategic interests, and especially in pursuit of corporate access to resources and labor. Some forms of new warfare need no weapons or soldiers at all, such as the deadly use of sanctions in Iraq. Warfare it is, however, with its intention to coerce regime change through bodily suffering (Arnove 2000).

The United States has increasingly relied on executive order for engagement in war, an antidemocratic practice that became ensconced with the national security state in 1947 (Lens 1987). So did the rise of so-called black budgets in military agencies, which were estimated at $39 billion per year in the late 1980s; these are tax dollars exempt from public knowledge or oversight (Weiner 1990). Anti-democratic effects also accompanied the turn from a conscripted to an all-volunteer force, which came in 1973 in response to active rebellion within the military against the war and played out on Fayetteville's streets and at Fort Bragg (Lutz 2001). The volunteer army rearranged the exchanges that had taken place between the state and citizens during the era of conscription: Civilians were no longer potential involuntary soldiers or sacrificers of their children, but spectators (Mann 1987). The soldiers recruited became increasingly conservative in their politics, something that has changed the political climate in Fayetteville as well as throughout the nation. While tacitly remembering the Army's rebellion, however, explicit politically molded memories of the Vietnam era suggest a still unreciprocated bargain with veterans of that war that continues to shape both political culture and military strategy (Gibson 1994). These various forms of memory, for example, have lowered tolerance for US battlefield deaths. Together with the longstanding ascendancy of the Air Force and Navy among service branches under the regime of nuclearism in which they specialized, this has meant a sometimes nearly exclusive reliance on aerial bombardment in US-led wars. This is a devastating choice for the people of a host of countries targeted for such attention (Blum 1995), but one that ensured fewer political costs for the United States whose populace could be convinced that there was moral virtue (the bombs were labeled *smart*) and little cost to the nation from warfare so waged.

The people of the United States emerged from the Cold War $16 trillion dollars (Center for Defense Information 2002b:43)

poorer, however. If the concept of friendly fire were extended to structural violence, the impoverishment would be much greater. It would include joblessness, attendant human suffering, and premature deaths and hunger that have resulted from the inequalities the military budget exacerbates. It does this by creating fewer jobs per dollar spent than equivalent social spending (Anderson 1982) and by derailing the movement for expanded social welfare benefits, as noted above. In Fayetteville, where the contrast in benefits given soldiers and civilians is most visible (even as some of the lowest rank-enlisted soldiers with families qualify for food stamps), this division plays out rancorously. The upper hand in the debate, however, goes to those who can appeal to the idea of soldiering as a unrecompensable sacrifice for the nation (even as the likelihood of death in battle has been minuscule over the last 20 years, when a total of 563 American soldiers died from "enemy" fire).[11] With the growing transnationalism of corporate operations and the search for cheap labor overseas, that violence has increasingly been from the fist inside the glove of neoliberal trade policies and foreign loans, which together have provided the means and rationale for the flow of resources and wealth from the south to the north, the brown to the white areas of the globe. It remains an entrenched notion among the US population, however – increasingly subject to control of information flows about global realities by media beholden to corporate and state interests – that aid and wealth flows from north to south.[12]

This larger picture of militarization and its history is connected to particular communities and individual lives. The long home front and its future fate hinge on our reconnecting both sides of the fence that separates the Fort Braggs and the Fayettevilles and seeing what militarization has wrought both at home and abroad. The current crisis and the socioeconomic and legal changes that it has already prompted will take their steep toll first in those places like Fayetteville that are most enmeshed in military institutions. An

understanding of their past and present predicament can provide transferable insights to
other places and help elucidate how the national context has come to have the textures it
does. Ethnographic understanding of militarization's shaping of all US places seems an
urgent project for anthropology, as it will
allow us to see the seams, fissures, and costs
in the otherwise seemingly monolithic and
beneficent face of state-corporate-media war
making.

Militarization and the Current Crisis

How can the national, historical, and local
ethnographic understanding just outlined
help us understand the current crisis? There
are deep continuities with the past, despite
the claim that September 11 represented a
major historical rupture both because the
United States was attacked and because it
announced merely the beginning of a campaign of terrorism that fundamentally
threatens global wellbeing. The attacks on
New York and Washington are said to represent a new asymmetric warfare in which a
militarily much smaller adversary exploits
weaknesses to strike blows at a larger power
with minimal costs to itself.[13] Guerrilla warfare, however, has been similarly defined.
Forces within the state claimed to require
new monies and powers to combat this
novel risk. Regardless of the name used,
the state was to engage in much business as
usual, which is to say purchases of expensive
weapon systems such as battleships and nuclear weaponry designed for earlier modes of
warfare. While their expensive weaponry and
surveillance equipment were completely irrelevant, as we saw, to the box cutters of
September 11, military industrial corporations like General Dynamics, Raytheon,
and Lockheed Martin experienced a sharp
rise in their stock prices in the immediate
wake of the September 11 attacks. They
were to be the prime beneficiaries of the immediate increase of $48 billion dollars and

the five-year increase of $120 billion in the
military budget proposed by the Bush administration with the crisis mentality created by
September 11.[14] This war, like others of the
20th century, will differentially affect the fortunes of various social sectors in the United
States, increasing social inequality nationally
and in places like Fayetteville.

Continuities of discursive militarization
abound as well: the simple dualisms of Mani-
chean nationalism in which evil empires or
terrorist networks confront the Goodness of
US freedom; the blurring of the boundary
between policing and soldiering, and between
the civilian and the military worlds and identities, even as those boundaries have been
sharpened in other ways, and especially
through the allocation of a kind of supercitizenship to soldiers (Kraska and Kappeler
1997; Lutz 2001); the growth of secrecy and
erosion of civil liberties, although with the
recent crisis the drop seems especially pre-
cipitous; and the melding of state and media
pronouncements on the war that has been
ongoing as media mergers and corporatiza-
tion (sometimes with the very companies that
have so benefited from militarization) have
intensified since deregulation in the 1980s
(Bagdikian 2000; MacArthur 1992). In this
war, the press has militarized even more dramatically, boosting "America's New War"
(this CNN moniker itself a kind of "brand-
ing") as a new commodity. The state has used
the tools of public relations in modern warfare since early in the 20th century; this process is simply accelerating in the current
crisis. A professional firm has been hired to
manage information flow and interpretation
and the Pentagon's specialists in disinforma-
tion have received more funding, new offices,
and new names. Their work includes both a
careful whitewashing of the extent and
"look" of war deaths, particularly of civilians, and collaboration with Hollywood fiction filmmakers.[15]

Moreover, the notion that we have encountered radically new conditions of global and
national life draws attention away from the
fact that the bombing of Afghanistan (and of

other countries that may follow in the days between the writing and your reading of this article) has causes deeper in the past and broader in scope than the planning and carrying out of the terror attacks on New York and Washington. US support for the Taliban in the immediate period leading up to the bombing was fueled by the desire to "normalize" relations in the interest of securing a trans-Afghanistan pipeline to Central Asian oilfields for US corporate and strategic interests (Rashid 2000). In this, the story is similar to many instances where repressive regimes were supplied arms and money in exchange for access to resources (Klare 2001). The list includes Saudi Arabia, Israel, Iran, Iraq, Guatemala, El Salvador, Honduras, Chile, South Korea, Indonesia, South Vietnam, and so on. With their country's food poverty and relative arms wealth, the Afghans in power share characteristics with many regimes around the world, where a generation of war, much of it originally Cold War enflamed, has created the social conditions for militancy.

Sources of hope are available. Pressures for demilitarization have exerted themselves throughout global and US national history. In the United States, an antimilitarist tradition has been a vigorous force at many points from the framing of the Constitution through the anti-ROTC movement of the World War I period to the antiwar novels and films of the 1930s and the 1960s to the current mass movement to combat the democratic losses and intensified militarizations of this most recent period (Ekirch 1956).[16] That tradition has existed within the military as well. Dwight Eisenhower, an important example, expressed his unhappiness with the mushrooming military budget of the 1950s and believed it "would leave the nation a militarized husk, hardly worth defending" (Brands 1999). People around the world have made claims against impunity for repressive government and paramilitary forces from Israel to Colombia to South Africa (Feldman 1998; Gill and Green 2000; Hitchens 2001; Said 2001). The international human rights movement helped bring down Eastern European

police states, made possible a dramatic rise in international legal mechanisms to control violence, and pressed to define not only physical violence but also structural violence as a human rights violation. The Jubilee and nuclear abolitionist movements gained wide support, and conventions against the use of landmines, chemical and biological weapons, nuclear weapons testing, and state torture have been almost universally accepted.[17] In just one instance, as this article was being completed, a treaty to ban the use of children as soldiers had just come into force, a claim against the current use of an estimated half-million children in militaries and paramilitaries worldwide. Voluminous and immediate sources of information to counter official lies as well as avenues for solidarity and anti-militarization work have opened up with the internet.

Conclusion

I vividly remember a day in the early 1980s when the anthropologist Ben Colby began to speak at a small conference on culture and cognition. He had been studying the distinct beauty and richness of mathematical thinking among the Ixil people of Guatemala. He said he could not talk of mathematics and cognition in Guatemala because his friends there were dead or fleeing in panic from the aerial bombardments of the scorched earth campaign viciously perpetrated by the Guatemalan military: Their anticommunism was a front for landowners' anxiety about other Guatemalans' claims for fairness in land allocation, labor conditions, and allowable identities in their own communities. It was an ideology in some synchrony with US anticommunism, and training and arming the Guatemalan military (Schirmer 1998). He brought the war home to us, as a previous group of anthropologists brought the war in Vietnam home to the discipline. As each of these clarion calls grew fainter, with the urge to "normalcy" and to "innocence," anthropological thoughts turned on how to write less imperial ethnographies, but not ethnographies of imperialism.

Our practice of anthropology has not prevented many of the hundreds of thousands of college graduates who have taken our courses from being shocked by the violent opening of the 21st century. Students may have encountered an anthropology that deconstructed the myth of a single modernity and of progress. They may even have learned about the violence that plagues other lands and been taught to seek its sources in inequalities and ideologies. They may have heard about the vast genocide and enslavements that accompanied the encounter between "Europe and the People without History." Yet too few were shown the tortured bodies and burned landscapes visible behind a Potemkin multicultural village. Too few were confronted with the idea of the US imperium, of global militarization, and of the cultural politics that make its wars seem either required of moral persons or simply to be waited out, like bad weather. These missing pieces of anthropological knowledge have only now come home to roost with great urgency. Would that they had not, but because they have, we now are called to address the realistic and unrealistic fears of our students, neighbors and colleagues, and work tirelessly to ensure those fears are redirected to the irrationalities and hidden purposes behind the glittering face of power and its moral claims.

NOTES

1 The usual periodization of the World Wars might more aptly be World Wars Ia and Ib.

2 See Lutz 1999 for a historical account of ethnography's relationship to war.

3 For a fuller account of this relationship and review of the literature that gives it ethnographic depth, see Lutz and Nonini 1999.

4 The race hatred that fueled World War II was evident in the exterminationist aims of many Allied actions against the Japanese; in contrast, the Germans and Italians were sorted into the good and the bad among them (Dower 1986).

5 The US Army's size and budget, for example, shrank by half and the Air Force grew explosively in the early 1950s (Bacevich 1986). This also fundamentally shaped US science and engineering, as its talent went to work in military R and D, which took fully 70 percent of federal research dollars by the mid 1980s (Marullo 1993:145).

6 How this becomes possible has been traced by Gusterson in his important study of US nuclear scientists (1996). The lobbying and educational role of the transnational community of dissident nuclear scientists, however, was one key to the Soviet Union's embarking on a course of denuclearization before its demise (Evangelista 1999).

7 Including national guard, reserve, and minor installations, there were 3,660 global US military sites in 1999 (US Department of Defense 2000).

8 These are among the interests that Marullo (1993) has dubbed the "Iron Pentagon": military contractors (whose profits were double those of other corporations in the 1980s), the Defense Department, weapons laboratories, Congress (with members heavily subsidized by military corporate donations), and military industry labor.

9 The United States had 49 percent of the share of global arms exports in 1999, which totaled $53 billion (International Institute for Security Studies 2001).

10 See Sluka 2000 on the unparalleled contemporary levels of state and extrastate torture and terror.

11 The combat death total is equivalent to the number of people who die every five days on US roads (a number that could count as an indirect war death, as traffic fatalities are much lower in countries that invested in public transportation more than in armies) (National Center for Statistics and Analysis 2001).

12 See Mann 2001 for important distinctions between regions.

13 Some strategists define asymmetric warfare as an indirect approach to affect a counterbalancing of force, and see it as more likely in the world of a single overwhelming hegemony like the United States.

14 This would bring the Department of Defense total to $451 billion in 2007, a figure that excludes many additional billions of military-related costs (such as interest on the debt) found in other budget categories.

15 In October 2001, studio heads announced they would help wage war on terrorism through their products. One of them, *Black Hawk Down*, was made in close consultation with the Pentagon and the White House, which edited the final script (International ANSWER 2002).

16 On long-standing campaigns to demilitarize US public schools and offer counterrecruitment information see, for example, American Friends Service Committee 2001.

17 The United States often voted alone or with a very small set of states, often those termed "rogue" by the United States itself, against any limits on its military's prerogatives; votes, for example, were 109–1, 95–1, 98–1, and 84–1 on 1980s resolutions to ban the proliferation of chemical and biological weapons, and 116–1 and 125–1 on resolutions prohibiting the development and testing of new weapons of mass destruction (McGowan 2000).

REFERENCES

Adams, Michael C. C.
1994   The Best War Ever: America and World War II. Baltimore: Johns Hopkins University Press.

Alcalay, Glen
1984   Maelstrom in the Marshall Islands: The Social Impact of Nuclear Weapons Testing. *In* Micronesia as Strategic Colony: The Impact of U.S. Policy on Micronesian Health and Culture. Catherine Lutz, ed. Pp. 25–36. Cambridge: Cultural Survival Occasional Papers.

American Friends Service Committee
2001[1998]   National Youth and Militarism Program. Electronic document, www.afsc.org/youthmil.htm. Accessed May 21.

Anderson, Marion
1982   The Price of the Pentagon. Lansing, MI: Employment Research Associates.

Aretxaga, Begona
1997   Shattering Silence: Women, Nationalism, and Political Subjectivity in Northern Ireland. Princeton: Princeton University Press.

Armstrong, David
1999   The Nation's Dirty, Big Secret. The Boston Globe, November 14: A1.

Arnove, Anthony, ed.
2000   Iraq under Siege: The Deadly Impact of Sanctions and War. Boston: South End Press.

Bacevich, A. J.
1986   The Pentomic Era: The U.S. Army between Korea and Vietnam. Washington, DC: National Defense University Press.

Bagdikian, Ben H.
2000   The Media Monopoly. 6th edition. Boston: Beacon Press.

Baran, Paul, and Paul Sweezy
1966   Monopoly Capital: An Essay on the American Economic and Social Order. New York: Monthly Review Press.

Belich, James
1986   The Victorian Interpretation of Racial Conflict: The Maori, The British, and the New Zealand Wars. Montreal: McGill-Queen's University Press.

Bernstein, Barton J.
1999   Reconsidering "Invasion Most Costly": Popular-History Scholarship, Publishing Standards, and the Claim of High U.S. Casualty Estimates to Help Legitimize the Atomic Bombings. Peace and Change 24(2):220–48.

Blum, William
1995   Killing Hope: U.S. Military and CIA Interventions since World War II. Monroe, ME: Common Courage Press.

Bourgois, Philippe
  1996   In Search of Respect: Selling Crack in El Barrio. Cambridge: Cambridge University Press.
Bourne, Randolph
  1964   War and the Intellectuals: Essays by Randolph S. Bourne, 1915–1919. Carl Resek, ed. New York: Harper Torchbooks.
Brands, H. W.
  1999   *Review of* Destroying the Village: Eisenhower and Thermonuclear War. Journal of American History 86(2): 839–40.
Center for Defense Information
  2002a   The World's Nuclear Arsenals. Electronic document, http://www.cdi.org/issues/ nukef&f/data-base /nukearsenals.html#United States. Accessed April 1.
  2002b   2001–2002 Military Almanac. Washington, DC: Center for Defense Information.
D'Amico, Francine
  1997   Policing the U.S. Military's Race and Gender Lines. *In* Wives and Warriors: Women and the Military in the United States and Canada. Laurie Weinstein and Christie C. White, eds. Pp. 199–234. Westport, CT: Bergin and Garvey.
Daniel, E. Valentine
  1996   Charred Lullabies: Chapters in an Anthropology of Violence. Princeton: Princeton University Press.
Das, Veena
  1990   Mirrors of Violence: Communities, Riots and Survivors in South Asia. Oxford: Oxford University Press.
Dolan, Frederick M.
  1994   Allegories of America: Narratives, Metaphysics, Politics. Ithaca: Cornell University Press.
Dower, John W.
  1986   War without Mercy. New York: Pantheon Books.
Ekirch, Arthur A., Jr.
  1956   The Civilian and the Military. New York: Oxford University Press.

Ellis, John
  1975   A Social History of the Machine Gun. New York: Pantheon.
Engelhardt, Tom
  1995   The End of Victory Culture: Cold-War America and the Disillusioning of a Generation. New York: Basic Books.
Enloe, Cynthia
  2000   Maneuvers: The International Politics of Militarizing Women's Lives. Berkeley: University of California Press.
Evangelista, Matthew
  1999   Unarmed Forces: The Transnational Movement to End the Cold War. Ithaca: Cornell University Press.
Farmer, Paul
  1996   Infections and Inequalities: The Modern Plague. Berkeley: University of California Press.
Feldman, Allen
  1991   Formations of Violence: The Narrative of the Body and Political Terror in Northern Ireland. Chicago: University of Chicago Press.
  1998   Faux Documentary and the Memory of Realism. American Anthropologist 100(2):494–501.
Geyer, Michael
  1989   The militarization of Europe, 1914–1945. *In* The Militarization of the Western World. John Gillis ed. Pp. 65–102. New Brunswick, NJ: Rutgers University Press.
Gibson, James William
  1994   Warrior Dreams: Paramilitary Culture in Post-Vietnam America. New York: Hill and Wang.
Gill, Lesley, and Linda Green, eds.
  2000   Biting the Bullet: Local Perspecting on Military Reorganization, Economic Restructuring and Daily Life. Santa Fe: School of American Research Press.
Goode, Judith, and Jeff Maskovsky
  2001   The New Poverty Studies: The Ethnography of Politics, Policy and Impoverished People in the U.S. New York: New York University Press.
Gray, Chris Hables
  1997   Postmodern War: The New Politics of Conflict. New York: Guilford Press.

Green, Linda
1994   Fear as a Way of Life. Cultural Anthropology 9(2):227–56.
Gusterson, Hugh
1996   Nuclear Rites: A Weapons Laboratory at the End of the Cold War. Berkeley: University of California Press.
1999   Nuclear Weapons and the Other in the Western Imagination. Cultural Anthropology 14(1):111–43.
Hardin, Bristow
1991   The Militarized Social Democracy and Racism: The Relationship between Militarism, Racism and Social Welfare Policy in the United States. Ph.D. dissertation, Department of Sociology, University of California at Santa Cruz.
Hitchens, Christopher
2001   The Trial of Henry Kissinger. London: Verso.
Hochschild, Adam
1998   King Leopold's Ghost: A Story of Greed, Terror, and Heroism in Colonial Africa. Boston: Houghton Mifflin.
Hopper, Kim
1991   A Poor Apart: The Distancing of Homeless Men on New York's History. Social Research 58(1):107–33.
Horne, Gerald
1986   Black and Red: W. E. B. Du Bois and the Afro-American Response to the Cold War, 1944–1963. Albany: State University of New York Press.
Huntington, Samuel P.
1996   The Clash of Civilizations and the Remaking of World Order. New York: Simon and Schuster.
International ANSWER
2002   Protest "Black Hawk Down." Electronic document, www.internationalanswer.org/ news/update/011802black hawkdown.html. Accessed April 1.
International Institute for Security Studies
2001   The Military Balance 2000–2001. London: Oxford University Press.
Jensen, Joan M.
1991   Army Surveillance in America, 1775–1980. New Haven, CT: Yale University Press.

Kaldor, Mary
1981   The Baroque Arsenal. New York: Hill and Wang.
1991   The Imaginary War: Understanding the East–West Conflict. London: Blackwell.
Kaldor, Mary, and Basker Vashee, eds.
1997   Restructuring the Global Military Sector, vol. 1: New Wars. London: Pinter.
Kaplan, Amy, and Donald E. Pease, eds.
1993   Cultures of United States Imperialism. Durham, NC: Duke University Press.
Kaplan, R. D.
1994   The Coming Anarchy. Atlantic Monthly 273(2):44–76.
Karsten, Peter
1989   Militarization and Rationalization in the United States, 1870–1914. In The Militarization of the Western World. John Gillis, ed. Pp. 30–44. New Brunswick, NJ: Rutgers University Press.
Klare, Michael
2001   Resource Wars. New York: Metropolitan Books.
Kraska, Peter B., and Victor E. Kappeler
1997   Militarizing American Police: The Rise and Normalization of Paramilitary Units. Social Problems 44(1):1–18.
Lam, Ilisa
2001   Turbulent Spaces, Shifting Discourses: Gendered Dimensions of American Militarization in the Western Pacific. Paper presented at the American Ethnological Society annual meetings, Montreal, Canada, May 3–6.
Lens, Sidney
1987   Permanent War: The Militarization of America. New York: Schocken.
Leslie, Stuart W.
1993   The Cold War and American Science: The Military–Industrial–Academic Complex at MIT and Stanford. New York: Columbia University Press.
Linenthal, Edward T., and Tom Engelhardt, eds.
1996   History Wars: The Enola Gay and Other Battles for the American Past.

New York: Metropolitan Books/Henry Holt and Co.

Lotchin, Roger W., ed.
1984 The Martial Metropolis: U.S. Cities in War and Peace. New York: Praeger.

Lutz, Catherine
1997 The Psychological Ethic and the Spirit of Containment. Public Culture 9:135–59.
1999 Ethnography at the War Century's End. "Ethnography: Reflections at the Century's End," theme issue, Journal of Contemporary Ethnography 28(6): 610–19.
2001 Homefront: A Military City and the American Twentieth Century. Boston: Beacon Press.

Lutz, Catherine, and Donald Nonini
1999 The Economies of Violence and the Violence of Economies. In Anthropological Theory Today. Henrietta Moore, ed. Pp. 73–113. London: Polity Press.

MacArthur, John
1992 Second Front: Censorship and Propaganda in the Gulf War. New York: Hill and Wang.

Mahmood, Cynthia Keppley
1996 Fighting for Faith and Nation: Dialogues with Sikh Militants. Philadelphia: University of Pennsylvania Press.

Malkki, Liisa
1995 Purity and Exile: Violence, Memory, and National Cosmology among Hutu Refugees in Tanzania. Chicago: University of Chicago Press.

Mann, Michael
1987 The Roots and Contradictions of Modern Militarism. New Left Review 162:35–50.
2001 Globalization and September 11. New Left Review (n.s.) 12:51–72.

Markusen, Ann, Peter Hall, Scott Campbell, and Sabina Deitrick
1991 The Rise of the Gunbelt: The Military Remapping of Industrial America. New York: Oxford University Press.

Markusen, Ann, and Joel Yudken
1992 Dismantling the Cold War Economy. New York: Basic Books.

Marullo, Sam
1993 Ending the Cold War at Home: From Militarism to a More Peaceful World Order. New York: Lexington Books.

May, Elaine Tyler
1988 Homeward Bound: American Families in the Cold War Era. New York: Basic Books.

McGowan, David
2000 Derailing Democracy: The America the Media Don't Want You to See. Monroe, ME: Common Courage Press.

Mills, C. Wright
1956 The Power Elite. New York: Oxford University Press.

Nash, June
1979 We Eat the Mines and the Mines Eat Us: Dependency and Exploitation in Bolivian Tin Mines. New York: Columbia University Press.

National Center for Statistics and Analysis
2001 2000 Annual Assessment of Motor Vehicle Crashes. Electronic document, www-nrd.nhtsa.dot.gov/pdf/nrd-30/NCSA/Rpts/2001/Assess2K.pdf. Accessed April 1.

Newman, Katherine S.
1999 No Shame in My Game: The Working Poor in the Inner City. New York: Knopf.

Nordstrom, Carolyn
1997 A Different Kind of War Story. Philadelphia: University of Pennsylvania Press.

Perret, Geoffrey
1989 A Country Made by War: From the Revolution to Vietnam – The Story of America's Rise to Power. New York: Random House.

Rashid, Ahmed
2000 Taliban: Militant Islam, Oil and Fundamentalism. New Haven, CT: Yale University Press.

Rogers, Paul
2000 Losing Control: Global Security in the Twenty-First Century. London: Pluto Press.

Said, Edward
2001 The Public Role of Writers and Intellectuals. The Nation, September 17: 27–36.

Scheper-Hughes, Nancy
  1992 Death without Weeping: The Vio-
    lence of Everyday Life in Brazil. Berke-
    ley:University of California Press.
Schirmer, Jennifer G.
  1998 The Guatemalan Military Project: A Vio-
    lence Called Democracy. Philadelphia: Uni-
    versity of Pennsylvania Press.
Sheppard, Simon
  1998 Foot Soldiers of the New World
    Order: The Rise of the Corporate Mili-
    tary. New Left Review 228:128–38.
Sherry, Michael S.
  1995 In the Shadow of War: The United
    States since the 1930s. New Haven, CT:
    Yale University Press.
Shulman, Seth
  1992 The Threat at Home: Confronting
    the Toxic Legacy of the U.S. Military.
    Boston: Beacon Press.
Sider, Gerald M.
  1986 Culture and Class in Anthropology and
    History: A Newfoundland Illustration.
    Cambridge: Cambridge University Press.
Skocpol, Theda
  1993 Protecting Soldiers and Mothers: The
    Political Origins of Social Policy in the
    United States. Cambridge: Cambridge
    University Press.
Slotkin, Richard
  1992 Gunfighter Nation: The Myth of the
    Frontier in Twentieth-Century America.
    New York: Harper Perennial.
Sluka, Jeffrey A. ed.
  2000 Death Squad: The Anthropology of
    State Terror. Philadelphia: University of
    Pennsylvania Press.
Starn, Orin
  1999 Night Watch: The Politics of Protest in
    Peru. Durham, NC: Duke University Press.
Susser, Ida
  1996 The Construction of Poverty and
    Homelessness in U.S. Cities. Annual Re-
    view of Anthropology 25:411–35.
Taussig, Michael
  1987 Shamanism, Colonialism, and the
    Wild Man: A Study in Terror and Heal-
    ing. Chicago: University of Chicago
    Press.
Tilly, Charles
  1985 War Making and State Making as
    Organized Crime. In Bringing the
    State Back In. Peter Evans, Dietrich
    Rueschemeyer, and Theda Skocpol,
    eds. Cambridge: Cambridge University
    Press.
US Department of Defense, Office of the
  Deputy Under Secretary of Defense (Installations)
  2000 Department of Defense Base Structure
    Report, Fiscal Year 1999. Washington,
    DC: Government Printing Office.
Virilio, Paul
  1990 War and Cinema: The Logistics of
    Perception. P. Camiller, trans. London:
    Verso.
Weigley, Russell F.
  1967 History of the United States Army.
    New York: Macmillan.
Weiner, Tim
  1990 Blank Check: The Pentagon's Black
    Budget. New York: Warner Books.
Williams, Brett
  1994 Babies and Banks: The "Reproduct-
    ive Underclass" and the Raced, Gen-
    dered Masking of Debt. In Race. Steven
    Gregory and Roger Sanjek, eds. Pp. 348–
    65. New Brunswick, NJ: Rutgers Univer-
    sity Press.

13

Cultural Logics of Belonging and Movement: Transnationalism, Naturalization, and US Immigration Politics

Susan Bibler Coutin

As a nation of immigrants in which nativism flourishes (Higham 1974; Sánchez 1997), the United States has long had a complex relationship with the migrants who enter its territory. Migrants are desired as laborers but are excluded from certain public benefits (Calavita 1996; Huber and Espenshade 1997), praised for contributing to society but suspected of maintaining disparate loyalties (Calavita 2000; Chavez 2001; Starn 1986), seen as evidence that the United States is superior to other nations yet condemned as a challenge to national sovereignty (Sassen 1996), and both celebrated and denigrated for weaving diverse cultural heritages into the national fabric (Johnson et al. 1997; Perea 1997). In the mid-1990s, these tensions came to the fore in searing debates over where to place legal and other boundaries around those who would be included in the nation. In California, Proposition 187, which required educators, physicians, and other ser-

vice providers to identify and report suspected illegal aliens, was overwhelmingly approved by the California electorate (see Martin 1995). In 1996, Congress passed the Illegal Immigration Reform and Immigrant Responsibility Act (IIRIRA), which stiffened border enforcement and made it more difficult for undocumented immigrants to legalize their presence. Other restrictive immigration measures, such as denying citizenship to the US-born children of undocumented immigrants, were also considered (Chock 1999). At the same time, these more restrictive immigration policies, unprecedented numbers of naturalization applicants, changing demographics, and the 1996 presidential election coalesced to make naturalization a national priority (Baker 1997).[1] Thus, in 1996, President Clinton launched Citizenship USA, a drive to naturalize one million legal permanent residents in a single year. By the mid-1990s, the US Immigration and Naturaliza-

From *American Ethnologist*, 30(4), 2003, pp. 508–26. © 2003, American Anthropological Association. All rights reserved. Used by permission.

tion Service (INS) was holding mass naturalization ceremonies in which as many as 2,000–5,000 legal permanent residents simultaneously took the oath of citizenship. Both the adoption of restrictive measures and the celebration of naturalization shed light on the meanings of exclusion from and inclusion in the US polity.

These seemingly contrary trends – the adoption of restrictive policies and the promotion of naturalization – are linked to what scholars have described as a disjuncture between the realities of global interdependancy, on the one hand, and the official models of incorporation in countries such as the United States, on the other hand (Guarnizo 1998; Portes 1997). The adoption of restrictive policies may be a response to the increased international movements of persons, goods, and ideas that accompany globalization. As financial systems and labor markets become global, corporations move to take advantage of differentials in labor costs and workers move from capital-poor to capital-rich countries to take service-sector and other jobs (Hamilton and Chinchilla 1991; Harvey 1989; Kearney 1986; Menjívar 2000; Ong et al. 1994; Sassen 1991). Migrant workers become, in a sense, resources for their countries of origin. Not only do many send remittances to family members back home (Menjívar et al. 1998), but they also become a focus of transnational political organizing with some potential to influence policies in both their countries of residence and origin (Guarnizo 1998; Itzigsohn 2000). Naturalization drives can be key to such organizing, as naturalization confers voting rights and can further ethnicity- or nationality-based politicking. Nonetheless, in the United States, official models of naturalization presume that immigration consists of leaving one society and joining another (making a "clean break"; cf. Smith 1998; Yngvesson 1997) and that naturalization creates equivalent and generic citizen–subjects. Moreover, for migrants' decisions to naturalize to be seen as voluntary (and therefore legitimate), one has to presume a sort of free market of citizenship, in

which migrants select the nation whose social system best permits them to develop their personal talents. Such presumptions ignore the international relationships and inequities that propel migration, downplay the incommensurability of migrants' histories, and legitimize immigration systems that constitute some migrants as illegal and therefore exploitable (Jenkins 1978; but see Delgado 1993).

To examine the seeming disjuncture between transnationalism and nation-based forms of membership, I juxtapose the US immigration history of Salvadorans and the celebration of Americanization, choice, and nation-building that characterized mass naturalization ceremonies held in Los Angeles in 1996 and 1997. Many Salvadorans wanted to naturalize but, in part because of the adoption of more restrictive policies in 1996, were not eligible to do so. These two contexts are interlinked in numerous ways. Salvadorans – among whom I have been doing fieldwork since the mid-1980s – began entering the United States in large numbers following the onset of the Salvadoran civil war in 1980. A relatively recent and initially largely undocumented immigrant group, Salvadorans experienced the difficulties of living in the United States without legal status or with temporary legal status (for instance, permission to remain in the country while an asylum application was pending). These migrants' experiences of exclusion led many to desire not only legal permanent residency but also naturalization, as a means of guaranteeing their rights in the United States, securing the ability to travel internationally (particularly, to reenter the United States if they left), acquiring a greater political voice, and improving their ability to petition for the legalization or immigration of family members. During the mid-1990s, Salvadoran community organizations in the United States therefore promoted naturalization and voter registration on the part of eligible immigrants. Immigrants' anxiety over their legal rights – an anxiety that was widespread during the mid-1990s because of California Proposition

187 and IIRIRA – fueled these naturalization drives and was one factor leading to record numbers of naturalization applicants during that period. Despite the political context, the naturalization ceremonies that actually produced large numbers of new citizens during that time attributed naturalization to immigrants' desire for Americanization, their choice of the United States over their country of origin, and the need of the United States to be renewed through immigrants' enthusiasm and "new blood." Examining the rhetoric of the ceremonies therefore reveals the disconnect between the assumption that naturalization is about Americanization, choice, and nation-building and the broader context that led immigrants to naturalize in large numbers – and that also prevented some would-be citizens from naturalizing.

By juxtaposing Salvadorans' struggles for US residency with the rhetoric of mass naturalization ceremonies, this article makes three contributions to analyzing the disjuncture between transmigration (Schiller et al. 1995) and national membership. First, though they seem incommensurable, national forms of membership can be put in service of transnational goals. Thus, Salvadoran activists' promotion of naturalization and voter registration sought not only to increase Latinos' political clout in the United States but also to affect US immigration policies in ways that would aid El Salvador. Moreover, given the trends toward dollarization and dual nationality in Latin America and increasing dependency on migrant labor in the United States (Portes et al. 1999), naturalization can be a way of furthering international integration rather than merely transferring migrants' allegiance from one nation to another. Second, this juxtaposition suggests that immigrants' full legal inclusion is limited by the forms of personhood that citizen–subjects can recognizably assume. Naturalization ceremonies celebrate the creation and incorporation of new citizen–subjects, but these subjects are created by (ritually) erasing histories and rendering difference generic. Such moves may contradict both migrants' understandings of

their own identities and the ethnicity- and nationality-based organizing that promotes (and seeks to benefit from) naturalization. Third, although it presumes the sovereignty and choice-making capacity of both the naturalizing subject and the nation-state that naturalizes, naturalization can be linked to a lack of alternatives and to interdependency. Thus, individuals may naturalize not only out of a desire to become Americans but also because they feel that, as noncitizens, their rights are in jeopardy. As this article will demonstrate, although the disjuncture between nation-based forms of membership and transnational linkages is profound, there are also ways in which each of these cultural logics serves or is redefined by the other.

My analysis begins with the case of Salvadoran immigrants, focusing on how the politics of immigration reform prioritized and defined naturalization for some would-be citizens. Next, I examine the ritual and rhetoric of naturalization ceremonies, identifying disjunctures between the broader context that fueled the celebration of naturalization in the mid-1990s and the models of subjecthood, nationhood, and citizen–state relations that were ritually enacted as new citizens were produced. Finally, I reexamine these disjunctures, linking my analysis of the case of Salvadorans and the rhetoric of naturalization ceremonies to the literature on the gap between national memberships and global interconnections. This reexamination reveals that, although the logics of national membership and of global interdependencies are at odds, transnational interconnections can promote and be furthered by individuals' placement in the very national membership categories that deny these interconnections.

Migration and Exclusion: The Case of Salvadorans

Migration from El Salvador to the United States is a good example of both the ways that global forces compel movement and the ways that nation-based categories restrict membership. Migration between El Salvador and the United States is embedded in geopolitical, economic, and sociocultural ties between the two countries. Perhaps the most significant of these ties is US support for the Salvadoran government during the 1980–92 Salvadoran civil war. During the 1980s, the Reagan administration defined the conflict in El Salvador as part of a broader struggle between communism and democracy and provided over $1 million a day to assist Salvadoran forces in their fight against guerrilla insurgents. Some observers attribute the prolongation of this conflict, which soon reached a military stalemate, precisely to US support. By 1985, political violence had displaced 27 percent of the Salvadoran population (Kaye 1997), and reports published during the mid- to late 1980s estimated the Salvadoran population in the United States at 500,000 to 800,000 (Aguayo and Fagen 1988; Ruggles et al. 1985), and even as high as one million (Montes Mozo and Garcia Vasquez 1988). In addition to military support, investment and development aid from the United States to El Salvador has been extensive (Hamilton and Chinchilla 1991). As Saskia Sassen (1989) has pointed out, investment and development aid facilitate migration by displacing workers from their traditional occupations, paving the way for ties between potential migrants and potential employers (e.g., US managers who might seek nannies or other workers) and familiarizing workers with the country from which investment or development aid originates. Such ties have also forged strong social and cultural connections between the United States and El Salvador. In short, geopolitical concerns, capital flows, the transnationalization of labor markets, cultural diffusion, and social interconnections have contributed to migration from El Salvador to the United States.

Migration between El Salvador and the United States also exemplifies the gap between global forces that compel movement and nation-based categories that restrict membership. Although their movements are embedded in processes that transcend national boundaries, Salvadoran immigrants have been treated by the US government as members of a single nation – El Salvador – and therefore regarded as aliens. Because of the difficulties of obtaining visas, most Salvadorans who immigrated to the United States during the war years did so without the permission of the US government. The Reagan administration defined these migrants as deportable economic immigrants rather than as persecution victims who deserved asylum in the United States. In 1986, only 2.6 percent of the asylum applications filed by Salvadorans were approved, in contrast to higher approval rates for applicants fleeing communist countries.[2] By the early 1990s, continued human rights abuses in El Salvador and the *American Baptist Churches v. Thornburgh* (ABC) lawsuit, which charged that the US government discriminated against Salvadoran and Guatemalan asylum seekers, garnered Salvadorans the right to apply for asylum under special rules and 18 months of Temporary Protected Status (TPS), followed by several years of Deferred Enforced Departure Status (DED). These temporary statuses, however, did not permit recipients to leave and reenter the United States (without first obtaining special authorization from the INS), become legal permanent residents, naturalize, or petition for relatives to immigrate. In the mid-1990s, restrictionist sentiment in the United States grew, producing IIRIRA, which made legalization more difficult for undocumented immigrants.[3] The approximately 300,000 Salvadorans and Guatemalans who had applied for political asylum through the ABC settlement agreement found that they were not only unlikely to obtain asylum (because of peace accords that ended civil conflict in both countries) but other avenues of legalization also were closed or greatly restricted. In 1997, Congress passed the Nicaraguan Adjustment and Central American Relief Act (NACARA), which restored these migrants' eligibility for a form of legalization known as suspension of deportation.[4] Nonetheless, according to one estimate from the INS asylum division, it could take as long as 20 years to adjudicate all of the applications for US residency under NACARA. In the meantime, these applicants are still aliens who lack permanent membership in the US polity.

Their experiences of transnational migration and legal exclusion have shaped Salvadoran immigrants' senses of their actual and desired positioning within the United States. My description of their understandings is based on fieldwork conducted in Los Angeles between 1995 and 1997, a period when restrictionist sentiment peaked and immigration reform was implemented. Fieldwork entailed observing the legal services programs of three major Central American community organizations in Los Angeles, attending some 129 proceedings in US immigration courts, following Salvadoran immigrants' campaigns for legal permanent residency, and interviewing 90 legal service providers, community activists, and Central Americans with pending legalization claims. Here I draw on interviews with members of the latter two groups. The activists were predominantly Salvadorans who had supported popular struggles in El Salvador, immigrated during the civil war, and participated in solidarity work in the United States. Most activists were legal permanent residents or naturalized US citizens; a few of the younger activists were US-born Salvadoran college students. Most of the activists also were men, although I made a point of seeking interviews with Salvadoran women who had assumed leadership roles in the solidarity movement or in advocacy work on behalf of Central American immigrants. I met Central Americans with pending legalization claims through community organizations and through several immigration attorneys who worked for nonprofit organizations. Most of these interviewees had immigrated to the United States during the civil war and had applied for political asylum through the ABC settlement agreement.... My sample of individuals with pending legalization claims was fairly evenly divided between men and women; most did low-income work in construction,

child-care, housecleaning, the garment sector, and the service industry.

Regardless of their prior political affiliations, Salvadoran interviewees feared that they would never be regarded as full members of the US polity. Citing the passage of California Proposition 187 and widespread anti-immigrant sentiment, interviewees complained that Latinos were being blamed for social problems that were not of their making.... Interviewees linked immigration and racial discrimination to economic marginalization, noting that immigrants and Latinos (categories that they saw as interconnected) took the lowest paying and least desirable jobs. Interviewees who had held professional positions in El Salvador described the economic deprivation they had suffered on immigrating. Gregorio Orozco, who had been a professor in El Salvador and who, at the time of our interview, worked as a janitor in Los Angeles, saw marginalization as spatialized along class and racial lines. Describing Latinos as "second-class citizens," Gregorio criticized the overcrowding and disrepair of buses and other public services in his neighborhood of North Hollywood, as compared with Beverly Hills. Overwhelmingly, interviewees characterized restrictive immigration policies and anti-immigrant sentiment as directed against minorities in general rather than immigrants in particular.

Although they feared that it might not secure their *full* inclusion in the United States, interviewees saw naturalization as potentially strengthening their ties with their communities of origin. Thus, paradoxically, naturalization, which is accomplished by formally renouncing ties to another state, can reinforce transnational connections. Interviewees – most of whom stated that they would like to naturalize, if permitted to do so – said that they wanted US citizenship to gain the freedom to travel internationally, the ability to petition for undocumented relatives, the right to vote, and better retirement benefits. Some pointed out that, as legal residents or US citizens, they would be better connected to families and communities abroad than they were as asylum applicants who jeopardized their applications if they left the United States. One asylum applicant stated, "The day that I receive [legal permanent residency] papers, that very day, I'm catching a plane to go to El Salvador again. It's been 11 years since I've seen my parents." Few interviewees saw legalization primarily as choosing the United States over El Salvador....

Moreover...most interviewees suggested that they had had no alternative but to immigrate and then to seek permanent residency and US citizenship. Given the violence and economic devastation of the Salvadoran civil war, it is not surprising that many interviewees characterized migration as a necessity. One activist, for example, insisted, "We [Salvadorans] didn't want to be here just because we want to, [because] we love the United States, or just because you can go to Disneyland.... So you came here for a necessity. Either, you leave your country, or you're going to be one of the statistics of the deaths." Interviewees also stated that the difficulties of living without papers had made them apply for TPS and political asylum.[5] One asylum applicant, for example, explained why he had applied for TPS instead of remaining undocumented: "It was not a question of choosing or not choosing, it was something that had to be done. Because one couldn't be hidden forever." Both activists and nonactivists noted that the more restrictive immigration policies adopted in 1996 had sharpened distinctions between US citizens and legal permanent residents and had made naturalization necessary to safeguard legal rights....

Although naturalization has largely been construed legally as a transfer of allegiance, interviewees' descriptions of their relationships to the United States and to El Salvador articulated an *additive* model of citizenship. According to this model, national membership is not exclusive, individuals can acquire multiple citizenships, and these multiple ties can be both meaningful to individuals and manifested through social practices and relations. Thus, as they sought to acquire permanent residency and citizenship in the United States, many interviewees (but not all – see above and see Mahler 1998) also maintained an identification with El Salvador. One member of a Salvadoran organization that is promoting citizenship and civic participation commented, "Becoming citizens, we don't lose anything. We remain Salvadoran at heart." Such comments depicted legal citizenship as a formality that could leave other measures of membership and identity untouched. Interviewees suggested, for example, that regardless of legal citizenship, "Salvadoranness" was an immutable fact of nature, conferred by birth on Salvadoran soil, relationship to Salvadoran family members, and having Salvadoran blood.[6] One young man (who was a naturalized US citizen) told me, "A Salvadoran is born, not made. Being Salvadoran is your culture, your family, your grandmother who is still in El Salvador and who writes all the time." These comments suggest that interviewees, many of whom hoped one day to naturalize, saw US citizenship as *adding to* rather than replacing their national allegiances. In fact, El Salvador permits dual citizenship, so naturalization does not strip Salvadorans of their former allegiance – although not all interviewees were aware that this is the case. Such dual (or multiple) identities and affiliations are common among recent immigrants, who, regardless of their geographic mobility (Popkin 1999), orient their lives around multiple local and national realities (Goldring 1998; Guarnizo 1997, 1998; Schiller and Fouron 1999; Smith 1998).

To obtain permanent residency, counter restrictionist immigration policies, and promote the well-being of their families and communities in El Salvador, Salvadoran immigrant community organizations promoted naturalization, voter registration, and alliances with other ethnicity- and nationality-based groups in the United States. At numerous meetings of community organizations in 1996 and 1997, I heard activists urge Central Americans to encourage eligible relatives to apply for naturalization. At a meeting with ABC class members in 1996, a staff member of the

Association of Salvadorans of Los Angeles (ASOSAL) explained this strategy. The speaker told those present that "20,000 people became citizens here in Los Angeles last month" and that individuals from ASOSAL had gone to the swearing-in ceremonies to register the new citizens to vote. He stressed, "We can't vote because we aren't citizens yet, but this is a way for us to register our opinions and to increase our impact."[7]

[...]

Securing immigration benefits for the US Salvadoran population was, at least in part, a transnational political strategy. Claims to space, presence, and membership rights not only sought to increase Central Americans' political clout in the United States but also to affect El Salvador. During the 1980s, Salvadorans sought refugee status in the United States both as a means of preventing deportations and to obtain US recognition of human rights abuses being committed in El Salvador. Activists hoped that such recognition would make it difficult for the US government to send assistance to the Salvadoran government and that, without such assistance, the war would end with either a negotiated settlement or a guerrilla victory. After the signing of peace accords, community activists continued to seek legal residency, but as immigrants rather than as refugees. Activists argued that permanent residency would prevent potentially destabilizing mass deportations and permit Salvadorans to continue to support their family members and home communities by working in the United States. This argument was made not only by Salvadoran activists but also – and perhaps more remarkably – by Salvadoran officials. Well aware of the economic significance of the US Salvadoran population, which in 2000 sent $1.7 billion in remittances to El Salvador, Salvadoran officials have also urged US officials to grant permanent residency to Salvadoran immigrants and have encouraged Salvadorans to take advantage of legalization opportunities such as ABC and NACARA.

The immigration strategies pursued by Salvadoran immigrants, activists, and officials are far from unique.... Like that of El Salvador, the governments of other countries of emigration (such as Mexico, Haiti, and the Dominican Republic) have encouraged their citizens to legalize in the United States (Foner 1997; Guarnizo 1997) and have lobbied the US government for immigration benefits for their citizens (Popkin 1999). At the same time, these governments have redefined citizenship in ways that permit their citizens to have dual or multiple allegiances and have developed policies and programs to incorporate émigrés into national life "at home" (Goldring 1998; Guarnizo 1997, 1998; Guarnizo and Smith 1998; Landolt et al. 1999; Smith 1998). The prevalence of such strategies suggests that sending states are defining émigrés as resources that can provide much needed infusions of US dollars and can sometimes influence US policies vis-à-vis their countries of origin (Guarnizo 1998). These processes, which, according to some scholars, make states transterritorial (Goldring 1998; Guarnizo 1998; Schiller and Fouron 1999; Smith 1998), have given naturalization new meanings. Rather than signaling a clean break in allegiance from one country to another, naturalization can add a national affiliation to preexisting ones, preserve migrants' abilities to remit, and give sending countries a voting constituency through which to influence US policy makers. Why then, did naturalization become a national priority in the United States even as restrictive immigration measures were being adopted? What does naturalization mean to the receiving nation?

Naturalization as a National Priority

In the mid-1990s, a number of factors converged to make naturalization a priority in the United States. First, by mid-1995, most of the 2.7 million individuals who legalized through IRCA had completed the five-year residency requirement that made them eligible for citizenship (Paral 1995). Second, restrictive immigration measures, such as

IIRIRA and other reforms that limited noncitizens' access to public benefits may have spurred the naturalization of immigrants who otherwise would have remained legal permanent residents (Paral 1995; Sánchez 1997).[8] Third, community organizations around the United States promoted naturalization through drives that included lessons on civics, assistance in completing applications, and preparation for examinations and interviews (Immigrant Policy Project of the State and Local Coalition on Immigration 1996). Fourth, the Mexican government considered and eventually adopted constitutional changes that permitted dual nationality (Guarnizo 1998). This development encouraged Mexican immigrants, who have traditionally naturalized at lower-than-average rates, to apply for US citizenship. Fifth, in 1992, the INS instituted a green card replacement program. Some green card holders may have chosen to naturalize rather than to replace their green cards (Immigration and Naturalization Service 1999).

By 1995, the INS was facing a processing backlog of 700,000 naturalization applications (Immigrant Policy Project of the State and Local Coalition on Immigration 1996) ... (see also NatzNews 1998).... President Clinton launched Citizenship USA, an effort to naturalize one million citizens in 1996. As part of this effort, the INS streamlined its naturalization procedures.... This naturalization drive was successful, as 1,044,689 individuals were naturalized during 1996. In contrast, during the previous five years, the average number of individuals naturalized per year was 357,037 (Immigration and Naturalization Service 1999). The naturalization drive was not uncontroversial, however. Republican Party leaders accused Clinton of simply trying to create more Democratic voters before the November 1996 presidential election. Errors in the processing of applications ... led the INS to reexamine its procedures ... and revoke some new citizens' naturalization (Wilgoren 1998). Community organizations came under fire for allegedly completing and mailing in voter registration cards for individuals who had not yet naturalized. ...

This overview of naturalization trends, in conjunction with the foregoing description of migrants' legalization strategies, explains why naturalization came to be a national priority, albeit a controversial one. It does not convey, however, how the ceremonies that actually produced new citizens addressed the anxieties regarding racial and ethnic discrimination, migrants' rights, and international interdependency that, in part, fueled these ceremonies. I therefore turn now to the rhetoric of these ceremonies, noting the remarkable *absence* of explicit reference to the broader political context in which they occurred. In essence, the issues that concerned Salvadorans who desired to naturalize disappeared within the ceremonies themselves. Despite this absence, the ceremonies' attention to diversity, valorization of choice, and insistence on the sovereignty of the receiving nation suggest that, like Salvadoran immigrants' struggle against legal exclusion, these ceremonies were part of broader debates over the meanings of difference, membership, and the nation. The contrasts between the logics of belonging put forward by Salvadoran interviewees and by US officials during these ceremonies illustrate the disjuncture between transnational migration and nation-based models of membership.

Naturalization Ceremonies

I first attended a mass naturalization ceremony in February 1996, when Salvadoran community activists asked me to join them outside the Los Angeles Convention Center to help newly naturalized citizens register to vote.[9] In nine ceremonies taking place over three days, some 30,000 new citizens were naturalized. Imagine the setting. The already clogged freeways that converged near downtown Los Angeles were further congested by as many as 5,000 naturalization applicants and their family members attempting to arrive for an 8:00 a.m. ceremony. After parking in crowded parking structures, candidates raced to the proper convention hall, a huge facility usually used for conferences or trade expositions, where they lined up at a doorway labeled *New Citizens*. Security guards checked their appointment notices and directed accompanying family members to the visitor section, which was partitioned off by yellow security tape. The new citizens were ushered to their seats, where each found a little US flag and a booklet containing a copy of the citizenship oath and the US Constitution. The only decoration in the room was a giant US flag, and the only signage pointed to the restrooms. Soon, the new citizens were directed to turn in their green cards at one of the numbered tables that lined the walls of the room. Meanwhile, family members in the visitor section strained with video cameras to glimpse the applicants. This part of the process took over an hour, as the 2,000–5,000 candidates for citizenship filed up to the tables and back to their seats.

Suddenly the tedium was interrupted by the sound of a gavel. A court clerk announced, "Please rise, this court is now in session." A motion to admit the candidates to citizenship was quickly made by an INS official and granted by a judge, and the new citizens cheered, applauded, and, on cue, waved their flags. The oath of allegiance was administered, and the judge and an INS official made remarks. Any members of the armed forces who were naturalizing were singled out for commendation. The new citizens watched a video extolling the United States, and an INS official led all present in singing the national anthem. The clerk led the new citizens in the pledge of allegiance, and the ceremony concluded. The visitors were ushered out so that the new citizens could receive their naturalization certificates, after which they emerged from the convention center to face well-wishers, vendors hawking souvenirs, and volunteers carrying clipboards with voter registration forms.

During 1996 and 1997, I attended ten such naturalization ceremonies at the LA Convention Center.... [T]hese ceremonies were

fairly standardized, and I found that there were occasions when the same judge officiated and gave the same speech that he or she had given previously. Six judges presided over these ten ceremonies: a white woman, a Chinese American man, and four white men. One was the son of an immigrant, another was a naturalized US citizen, and two stated that their families had been in the United States since the signing of the US Constitution. As rituals, these ceremonies – like the term *naturalization* (Anderson 1983:145) – were remarkable. They fluctuated between the tedium of bureaucratic processing and the mysticism of a religious conversion. To examine how these rites produced citizens – and the nation – I turn now to the rhetoric of the ceremonies themselves. I focus on (1) how ceremonies tried to create similarity out of difference; (2) ways that ceremonies contrasted "birth" and "choice" as two methods of becoming American; and (3) how ceremonies configured nations as members of an international community. These three problematics emerged as central themes within the ceremonies and also are germane to broader debates over the degree to which immigrants assimilate, the bases for conferring citizenship, and the relationship between immigration and national sovereignty.

Identity and difference

One focus of naturalization ceremonies was the meaning of diversity. Diversity is linked to the disjuncture between transnationalism and the nation-state in that, if migrants are transnational beings – as Salvadoran interviewees asserted – then presumably they maintain some degree of foreignness, adding US nationality to their preexisting allegiances. On the other hand, state-based categories of membership have traditionally been assumed to be exclusive, and in the United States, "difference" has taken the form of a private ethnic affiliation rather than a public national one. According to Greenhouse, negotiating the public and private meanings of *difference* requires the mythicization of identities – for example, ethnic and racial identities – as categorical personifications of "difference." This mythic operation, which in the United States makes key differences generic, and generic in the same way, is what makes a construction such as "the melting pot" (for example) conceivable. [1996:217; see also Chock 1995]

Applying this insight to the conferral of citizenship through law rather than through birth suggests that in these ceremonies naturalization privatized, homogenized, and tamed what might otherwise be characterized as disruptive foreign differences and thus created generic public citizens (see also Asad 1990; Gilroy 1987). In other words, naturalization – in the United States, at least – is simultaneously a ritual denaturalization, a stripping away of the public, legal character of difference defined as membership in a foreign state. Such denaturalization reconstitutes difference as private and therefore as a source of commonality or something that everyone has. Naturalizing difference makes it possible for foreigners to acquire new and equivalent legal personae.

Officials at these ceremonies frequently remarked on the diversity of the new citizens. For example, scanning the crowd, one judge commented, "I see that many of you come from so many different countries around the world." This remark suggested that difference is transparent, something that can be read or seen by any observer. In contrast, an INS official who addressed those assembled described diversity through statistics, stating, "You represent 123 nations throughout the world. This is the testimony to the diversity of our nation, and especially the Los Angeles area. That's when you consider that there's approximately 188 countries throughout the world. You represent over three-fourths of the nations." This official's use of the term *represent* was significant. This term suggested both that protocitizens' public personae were linked to their citizenship and that the nations that were represented (three-fourths of the

world) were convinced of the superiority of the United States. . . .

Diversity and difference seemed to be a source of anxiety to some officials. While giving instructions about how to turn in green cards, one official commented, "The American way is to do things in order. If we wanted mob violence, we wouldn't become citizens." Through his use of the term *we*, this official seemed to be speaking for the new citizens, much as a teacher speaks for students (e.g., "We don't throw our pencils on the floor now, do we?"). Moreover, given that these ceremonies occurred only four to five years after the LA riots (see Gooding-Williams 1993), references to mob violence evoked the alleged potential disruptiveness of diversity (see Greenhouse 1996). Echoes of the Rodney King incident were also clear in the following comment from a judge: "Today, we have, right here in southern California, one of the most important challenges that this country has ever had. And that is, how do we get along?" Commenting that "southern California is so different from when I was a boy," the same judge noted that the second largest population group of many nations was found in Los Angeles rather than in the territories of those nations. By drawing attention to the diversification of Los Angeles rather than the Americanization of immigrants, this judge implied that the United States might be colonized instead of colonizer. Urging the new citizens to "love their differences," this judge depicted southern California as the experiment on which the fate of the world depended: "If we cannot live here in southern California, the world is never going to progress. It will continue in its old ways, and civilization will never raise its [standards]."

Given such anxiety about the potential disruptiveness of diversity, one task of naturalization ceremonies was to make difference a source of unity. To accomplish this task, officials told immigrants who had formerly "represented" their nations that their public allegiance was now to the United States.

Differences – which officials listed as consisting of language, culture, and foods – were
relegated to a domestic sphere, to be remembered and passed on to children. Once in the
private sphere, these differences were homogenized and made part of both familial and
national heritages. For example, one judge
told the new citizens that when a Muslim
immigrant had married his daughter, it had
added to his family's traditions. The judge
then jumped from his family to the nation,
stating, "[This is] just another extension of
what we're doing here today. We're bringing
new people, we're bringing new strengths.
We're gonna blend them together." As *heritages*, differences became a source of unity.
One judge explained that everyone has "an
American story. They're all interesting,
they're all different.... [But] each illustrates
the same principle." The unifying principle of
these stories, the judge elaborated, is "why
we came." By defining new citizens according
to their allegedly unified motive for immigrating – namely, the search for a better life
– instead of their different national origins,
naturalization ceremonies erased both difference and history. Such erasures were explicit
in judges' comments. To give but one example: "Would it make any difference
whether they [my ancestors] came from Vietnam, from Japan, or from Mexico, Canada,
Yugoslavia? I don't see why. They're all
Americans.... It doesn't matter where they
come [from], it does not matter when."

Erasing difference and history made it possible for judges to define the public sphere as
an arena of equality. Judges evoked not only
Rodney King but also Martin Luther King Jr.
One judge, for example, predicted that the
children of immigrants would "seek a world
in which nobody cares what nation you are,
nobody cares what your religion is, nobody
cares what your skin color is, nobody cares
about those things. What they care about is
what kind of person you are." Of course, the
very necessity of such a quest suggested that,
in fact, public life was not characterized by
equality.... Through... anecdotes, judges invoked the construct of the citizen who is

"equal before the law" (Collier et al. 1995)
and therefore legally identical to every other
citizen. Officials at naturalization ceremonies
depicted such public equality or sameness as a
means of overcoming divisiveness....

The emphasis of naturalization ceremonies
on public equality defined citizenship as
generic – a claim that contrasts sharply with
Salvadoran interviewees' fears that they
would never be regarded as fully American.
Judges and officials stated, for example, that
one person's citizenship was interchangeable
with that of another.... Officials... implied,
through the use of terms such as *we* and
fellow citizens, that their own citizenship
was no different from that of the new citizens.
Immediately after administering the oath, one
judge told the new citizens – who had previously been characterized by *diversity* – to
take a moment to "congratulate each other,
your neighboring citizens!" Difference had
been made alike through naturalization. The
generic nature of this likeness was made clear
by one judge's attempt to overcome the im-
personality of the mass ceremony. Stating
that he wished he could greet every new citizen individually, he told his audience that if
one of them ever met him in the street after
the ceremony, that person should walk up to
him and say, "Hello citizen!" The term *citizen*
would be sufficient to name both the judge
and the person the judge had naturalized.
Another judge ritually created generic citizenship by having all of the new citizens yell out
the names of their places of origin on the
count of three. When this produced an unintelligible shout, the judge explained, "That
little exercise illustrates a point, and that
point is that no one person was able to out-
shout the other. And when you shout out your
names in unison, it all blended in. And that's
what America is all about." As the public
voice of the new citizens is blended and rendered homogeneous, it is only in private
(where no one else is shouting) that differences can be articulated.

Officials at naturalization ceremonies
depicted the transformation of national diversity into generic citizenship as a quasi-

mystical experience. The new citizens, judges suggested, were united by a feeling, a unique sensation, almost a spirit. One judge, who was himself a naturalized citizen, described this feeling as follows: "I felt from the outset, as I believe you feel, that unique sensation of freedom upon the taking of the oath. I saw, as I believe you will see in succeeding years, that the promise of America is not empty. It is real, it is vibrant, it is challenging. It reaches out and embraces you all." The transformation from legal permanent resident to citizen, in other words, had been animated by a spirit: the promise of America. Officials' remarks emphasized the transformative nature of naturalization ceremonies. Now that the new citizens had partaken of this spirit, they were reborn and could proselytize to others. One judge recommended that the new citizens "continue this feeling, to foster it to your children and your friends."... Judges frequently referred to new citizens' presumed high emotions (e.g., "You ought to be very, very happy, very emotional now"). Officials also expected the new citizens to remember the date of their naturalization, much as one remembers a birth date. One official invited the new citizens to "imagine, if you will, how your lives will be changed by your new citizenship." The most concrete example of this change that officials could provide, however, was that with citizenship, those present could vote and serve on juries.[10] To understand officials' references to the spirit that allegedly unites new citizens, it is necessary to examine how officials contrasted citizens by choice with citizens by birth.

Blood and choice

Like diversity, choice is central both to naturalization ceremonies and to the disjuncture between transnationalism and nation-based membership categories. The literature on globalization emphasizes the structures in which migrants are situated and tends to depict migrants "as passive subjects, coerced by states and marginalized by markets" (Smith

1998:201). Although Salvadoran interviewees did not depict themselves as passive, these migrants did emphasize that, because of political and economic difficulties in their countries of origin and legal restrictions in the United States, they had no alternative but to migrate and then seek legal status. In contrast, the ability to make choices is central to naturalization as a legal process. Choices that are coerced rather than freely taken are not legal, and the citizenship oath itself concludes "I take this obligation freely, without any mental reservation or purpose of evasion, so help me God." Defining new citizens as people who can choose makes it possible to recognize them as subjects of liberal law who have the capacity to realize their human potential through the rights and protections afforded by national membership (Collier et al. 1995). Ceremonies' emphasis on choice also speaks to mid-1990s debates over measures of worthiness. Advocates of restrictive immigration measures argued that migrants exhibited illegitimate forms of agency, that migrant women, for example, sneaked across the US–Mexico border to have US-citizen children and collect welfare (see Perea 1997). Some also questioned whether the mere fact of being born on US soil made the children produced through "illegitimate" agency deserving of US citizenship (see Chock 1999). In contrast, by emphasizing the *mutuality* of choice (new citizens and the nation choose each other), naturalization ceremonies suggested that the naturalizing citizens had demonstrated their worthiness and that, far from compromising national sovereignty, incorporating the deserving reinvigorated the nation.

During ceremonies, officials emphasized that naturalized citizens were both equivalent to and different from citizens by birth. Citizens' equivalency derived from their common generic citizenship.... Their difference lay in the means by which each had acquired citizenship. One judge used the analogy of adoption to explain this distinction: "I compare this to, perhaps, a child born in a family, a child by birthright is within the family. Then there are those children who are as a matter of course outside the family, but adopted into the family.... You are the adoptees of this country, and this country has adopted you. You really have adopted this country."[11] Officials left no doubt in new citizens' minds about whether adopting or being born into US citizenship was superior. One judge, who stated that it is the naturalized citizens who were held in the "highest esteem," explained, "We [citizens by birth] do not have to do anything, we do not have to make a decision. However, you have made a choice.... You made an active choice to give up your citizenship of birth and to join us."[12] The fact that they had to make this choice, officials suggested, meant that the new citizens would not take their citizenship for granted: "You chose to come here. So when you compare myself to yourself, for all those citizens who were born here. We were given that birthright. We take everything for granted." In contrast, officials explained, new citizens were filled with "the immigrant spirit" that made them "totally different from those people who remained here for years and years and years and forgot." New citizens were therefore, according to officials, the most authentic Americans – "much more American," as one judge put it – in that their lives encapsulated the history of the nation.

In valorizing *choice*, officials also indicated that to naturalize, those who chose US citizenship had to first be judged and found deserving. In other words, naturalization gave not only immigrants but also the nation a choice in allocating citizenship. Judges ... defined citizenship as a reward that immigrants earned, in contrast to the gift that the native-born received regardless of their worthiness.[13] The example set by individuals who had earned citizenship allowed officials to reaffirm the United States as a land of opportunity in which dreams could be fulfilled. Stories of the self-made man (and at the ceremonies I attended, it was always a man) abounded during these proceedings.... One judge explained the lessons of such stories: "No one in America is going to tell you artificially what your utmost achievement can

be. We are empowered to defeat naysayers who say we can't do it. Because we can. We can, because we are Americans. In America, that old saying, 'The sky's the limit,' is truer now than ever." Amidst such celebrations of opportunity and self-sufficiency, however, appeared veiled warnings against applying for welfare. One judge, for example, admonished the new citizens to teach their children "to never ever think first of someone else taking care of them."

By demonstrating their worthiness and choosing to naturalize, immigrants reproduced the history of the nation.... [A] ... judge depicted new citizens as a renewing force: "We welcome your fresh appreciation of what citizenship in this country really means. We welcome your zeal, your eagerness, and your determination to become good loyal citizens. You are indeed a stimulating force, which cannot help but bring a new luster to the image of America." In such comments, the *we* of fellow citizens is replaced with a we–you distinction, according to which the old citizens are associated with a somewhat tarnished America that the new citizens can polish. This judge went on to equate immigration with a blood transfusion, stating, "New citizens are the new blood of America, and we need it." It is interesting that the nation needs immigrants' blood, which presumably would be foreign. Once naturalized, however, this blood is seemingly purer or stronger than native blood. From whence does this need for new blood arise?

A nation of immigrants

The apparent dependence of the United States on continual transfusions of immigrant blood is, in these ceremonies at least, connected to the complex claim that the United States is a nation of immigrants – a claim that ignores both forced immigrants, such as enslaved Africans, and Native Americans, whose "citizenship" has been "reserved." According to the "nation of immigrants" construct, the erasure of previous public difference and the choice for the United States produce a clear-cut shift in new citizens' allegiance. As R. C. Smith notes,

> In the citizenship model, membership in a nation state and in the national political community are seen to be coterminous and exclusive; one can be a member of only one state and nation at a time.... Given this definition of membership in a community, immigration necessarily involves an "uprooting" (Handlin 1951) and "clean break" with the country of origin. [1998:199]

Clean breaks make naturalization a rebirth of sorts, giving new citizens a quasi-biological connection to the United States (Bauböck 1994; Stolcke 1997). The infusion of new citizens' blood, of those who can be self-made men, affirms that the United States is a land of opportunity and therefore superior to other nations. As a "nation of immigrants," the United States is presumed to be the top choice of deserving individuals who could have chosen to stay in their country of origin or to go elsewhere. According to this logic, immigration occurs not because of global interconnections that compel movement but, rather, because the distinctiveness of the US way of life draws those who can appreciate the opportunities offered by this nation....

Judges sometimes treated both naturalization and the space of the convention center qua courtroom as metonymic with the nation (see also Coutin 2000).[14] One judge, for instance, commented, "What we have in this room is this country itself. This is the United States of America right here in this room. This is what we have from border to border, ocean to ocean." In this comment, the space and populace of the nation were equated with the room and assembly, respectively. This positive rendering of diversity can be read against another judge's comment that large numbers of people from many nations reside in southern California. Although a courtroom and naturalizing citizens could be equated with the country, such contrasts suggested that southern California might be

becoming the territory of other nations. This latter possibility, which resembles the notion of "trans-territorialization" put forward by scholars of transnationalism, was largely unremarked, however, given the celebration of Americanization that predominated in naturalization ceremonies. The spatialization of the courtroom as the nation in certain ways paralleled the spatialization of identity that permitted and forbade naturalization itself. For example, to naturalize, immigrants had to be physically present in the United States, just as, to naturalize, candidates for citizenship had to be physically present in the courtroom when the oath was administered. "Presence" was clearly a legal construct, as indicated by an official's warning that if the new citizens accidentally sat in the visitor section during the ceremony, they would not be naturalized and would have to attend another ceremony to be sworn in.

Officials conveyed the meaning of the "nation" to the new citizens in part through a music video that was shown during the ceremony. The video featured the music of the Lee Greenwood country-western song "God Bless the USA," accompanied by images of national greatness. The video began with a shot of a white man (Greenwood?) sitting on a tractor in the middle of a field and looking pensive, as Greenwood sang, "If tomorrow all the things were gone I'd worked for all my life, and I had to start again with just my children and my wife" (Greenwood and McLin 1993:244) – a situation that was probably not unusual among immigrants. The video continued with shots of national monuments, landscapes (coasts, mountains, prairies, and fields), citiscapes, fighter jets, the US flag, the moon landing, and the Olympic torch. The only people who appeared – and their appearances were brief – were astronauts on the moon and disembarking from the space shuttle, the man on the tractor, and Bruce Jenner winning the decathlon. The near absence of people in the video was striking, given judges' speeches about the meanings of ethnic and cultural diversity. The US flag was a recurring image – the one that was planted on the moon was replicated by the small flags that the new citizens waved and the giant flag that adorned the wall of the convention center. By celebrating such national achievements as placing people on the moon, winning world sports competitions, and conquering territory, the video suggested that new citizens had joined a truly great nation. Moreover, the lyrics, which celebrate the freedom that would allow a man who has lost everything to rebuild his life, reiterated the notions of opportunity and progress that were explicit in officials' speeches. The moon landing, with the planting of the US flag, evoked continued expansionism, the last frontier.[15]

By advocating patriotism, naturalization ceremonies told immigrants who to root for in the future.[16] The words of the oath of allegiance depicted naturalization as transferring new citizens' loyalties exclusively from one nation to another: "I hereby declare on oath that I absolutely and entirely renounce and abjure all allegiance and fidelity to any foreign prince, potentate, state or sovereignty, of whom or which I have heretofore been a subject or a citizen." Yet some of the loudest applause in the ceremony occurred when INS officials enumerated the top five nations represented in the ceremony. When Mexico – which was number one at all of the ceremonies that I attended – was announced, the applause grew to a crescendo of loud cheering.[17] Such public and national partisanship, much like Salvadoran interviewees' discussions of citizenship as additive and naturalization as furthering transnational ties, would seem to contradict the "generic" nature of naturalized citizenship.

Officials also used immigration itself to suggest that immigrants were "voting with their feet" for the United States over their countries of origin. . . . In words reminiscent of the American Jeremiad (Bellah 1975; Bellah et al. 1985; Bercovitch 1978), judges described the United States as "a beacon for truth," "that shining example of democracy on earth," and something that "lights up the

earth." These comments implied that the rest of the world would like to come to or even be the United States, if only it could. Judges also connected immigration to manifest destiny. One judge credited immigrants with having spread the country "from coast to coast," and another instructed citizens, "You have become a citizen of a country that is still growing to the fulfillment of its destiny." These comments linked the growth of the national populace through immigration to territorial growth and national mission. This mission, according to judges, was "to build a more perfect America. And hopefully, solutions to peace on earth." Naturalizing citizens and thus incorporating and disarming difference could be seen as part of efforts to Americanize peoples, markets, and territory abroad. One judge urged immigrants to "be infectious, like a disease" in convincing others to emulate the United States – a comment that acknowledged the possibility of resistance, however misguided, to Americanization.

Despite lofty rhetoric about equality, inclusiveness, and choice, naturalization ceremonies hinted at structures of state power that defined identity and that might be responsible for record rates of naturalization. In requiring residents to turn in their green cards, for example, officials reminded their audiences that these documents were government property rather than individual possessions. Clearly, the government that could issue or recall such documents could also confer or deny particular statuses. By celebrating the rights that new citizens would acquire on naturalization, judges emphasized that the state grants rights through social membership. After idealistic speeches, each ceremony ended with these words: "Ladies and gentlemen, please be seated and await further instructions regarding the distribution of your certificates. This court session is now adjourned." Such references to the *need* to document citizenship link these ceremonies to the broader context – including other, less celebratory court hearings that deny status and order immigrants deported – in which these rites occurred. To conclude, let me return to these disjunctures in light of such linkages.

National Disjunctures and Linkages

Naturalization ceremonies put forward logics of migration, membership, and the nation that are linked in complex ways to the models that Salvadoran immigrants and activists have developed in response to human rights violations and economic problems in El Salvador and to legal exclusion in the United States. Sameness–difference, choice–nonchoice, and sovereignty–interdependency are key to these logics. First, during naturalization ceremonies, officials ritually erased public, legal elements of difference to constitute new citizens as equivalent juridical subjects of the United States. In this multicultural formulation, difference could be celebrated as a source of commonality, a background, a presumed shared history of immigrating to the United States in search of a better life. "Difference" was also relevant to Salvadoran interviewees, who, like recent migrants from other nations, suggested that as categories, "citizen" and "American" connote whiteness and that, regardless of their legal citizenship, members of ethnic minority groups would always be seen by some as less than full citizens. Moreover, Salvadorans, including Salvadoran officials, expressed or promoted dual identities, according to which, rather than being a clean break, naturalization adds US citizenship to migrants' preexisting Salvadoran nationality.

Second, the emphasis on choice during naturalization ceremonies suggested that the United States simply attracted immigrants as a matter of course because of its superior way of life. The fact that migrants had made the choice to naturalize and that the United States had agreed that they were deserving affirmed the mutual wisdom of the relationship being formed between new citizens and the nation. "Nonchoice" (which does not mean a lack of agency) was key to Salvadoran

migrants' accounts of migration and of their subsequent quest for legal status. These accounts demonstrate an awareness of the structures and relationships that shape human action. Thus, migrants attributed their original entry into the United States to political violence, economic necessity, and the need to support family members in El Salvador. Their decisions to apply for legal status and their desire for as-yet-unobtainable US citizenship were linked at least in part to the exclusion they experienced as noncitizens. Furthermore, Salvadoran migrants' and officials' campaigns for US residency for the Salvadoran immigrant population stressed ongoing social, political, and economic ties between the United States and El Salvador, including the US need for immigrant labor. This logic links migration to interdependancy, rather than solely to individualistic quests for opportunity and self-advancement.

Third, naturalization ceremonies depicted continued immigration as demonstrating the superiority of the United States as a *sovereign* nation. If the best and the brightest sought out the opportunities that the United States offers when they could have chosen to remain in their countries of origin or to migrate elsewhere, then clearly, the United States was the best among an array of nations from which migrants could choose. Such an account of migration would seem to justify US efforts to spread its way of life to other countries through modernization and democratization. "Interdependency" was key to Salvadoran interviewees' models of movement and belonging. In fact, Salvadoran officials' and activists' immigration-related strategies characterized the dispersal of the Salvadoran citizenry in ways that resembled scholars' use of the term *transterritorialization*.[18] In other words, instead of representing a loss of Salvadoran citizens, migration made El Salvador transnational, provided it with a source of remittances, and gave Salvadorans greater potential to influence US policies vis-à-vis El Salvador. In contrast to naturalization ceremonies' emphasis on distinct citizenries and competing national systems, these strategies focused on transnational ties and multiple and overlapping allegiances.

Despite these disjunctures between naturalization officials' and Salvadoran interviewees' logics of belonging and movement, juxtaposing these logics reveals ways that nation-based categories of membership can serve transnational ends. One such connection is that although legal status officially defines an individual as a member of a particular nation, individuals may seek such status to better access resources in both their country of residence and of origin. Both US immigration law and international law pertaining to migrants presume that individuals have a single, clear-cut nationality (Bosniak 1991; Marrus 1985). Nonetheless, studies of migrant communities have noted that these groups span borders and attend to multiple national realities (Hagan 1994; Kearney 1998; Levitt 2001; Rouse 1991). *Transmigration* was coined by Schiller et al. (1995) to refer to the way that, rather than leaving one society and joining another, migrants now develop and maintain ties to multiple societies. Hometown associations (Popkin 1999; Smith 1998) have received particular attention as examples of institutions that are key to transnational identities, and border studies has emerged as a field that examines transnational zones that both supersede and are defined by national boundaries. Consistent with my argument here, some have suggested that, regardless of their transnational orientations, migrants seek legal status not only as part of the settlement process (a process that may include coming to identify with their new country of residence) but also as a form of political expediency (Hagan 1994). Migrants need legal status *both* to access those opportunities that, in the United States, at least, are restricted to citizens and to legal permanent residents *and* to obtain travel documents that permit them to further develop their connections with their countries of origin.

Recognizing that legal status can better connect migrants to their countries of origin suggests that debates over whether or not transnationalism is rendering national forms of membership obsolete are misplaced. Regarding this debate, Soysal (1994) notes that in Europe, instead of being restricted to nationals, rights are increasingly being granted to individuals on other bases, such as their humanity (see also Bauböck 1994; Bosniak 2000; Hammar 1990) or their membership in a supranational entity, the European Union. In contrast, Wilmsen and McAllister (1996) argue that far from becoming obsolete, ethnicity and nationalism have been increasingly reasserted in recent decades. Immigration policies, which, in receiving nations, have tended to become more restrictive (Freeman 1992), have been singled out as phenomena that seem to defy the trend toward globalization (Cornelius et al. 1994). Some have attempted to reconcile these competing positions by pointing out that globalization simultaneously can strengthen local identities (Kearney 1995), as communities market themselves and their products as somehow unique or different from other areas (Maurer 1997), and can break down national boundaries, as distant groups are caught up in common structures and processes (Ong 1999). Robertson (1995) used the term *glocalization* to convey the simultaneity of such seemingly incompatible events. Similarly, my analysis of US immigration politics in the 1990s suggests that even national categories of membership can be given transnational meanings (see also Maurer 1998). Thus, restrictive immigration policies can derive from nation-based models of membership and of international relations while simultaneously making the acquisition of citizenship key to transnational organizing.

Given that legal status can facilitate transnational organizing efforts, "difference," which was a focus both of Salvadoran interviewees' criticisms of discriminatory policies and naturalization ceremonies' celebrations of Americanization, can both be erased in the acquisition of legal subjecthood and used as a basis for political organizing. With the rise of the modern nation-state, the more abstract citizen–state relationship replaced what had been a more concrete (in theory at least) subject–sovereign tie.[19] Citizenship therefore has a generic quality.... In the United States, immigrants who undergo naturalization acquire this generic and equivalent quality, even as their histories distinguish them from those who are citizens by birth. Naturalization mimics citizenship by birth, and vice versa, in that citizens by birth are presumed to have accepted the authority of the Constitution (see Foucault 1977), as have naturalized citizens, and naturalization imbues new citizens with an identity or quasibiological connection to the United States, as does birth.[20] Nonetheless, as feminists and critical race theorists have pointed out, citizenship in the United States is never fully generic (see, e.g., Matsuda et al. 1993; Nelson 1984; Sapiro 1984; Williams 1991), given that legal citizenship does not guarantee equal rights to women, ethnic minorities, and other marginalized groups. In fact, both "whiteness" and "maleness" have been prerequisites for citizenship historically (Augustine-Adams 2000; Goldberg 2001; Haney López 1996; Salyer 1995), and the citizenship of economically marginalized individuals is sometimes questioned (Marshall 1950). Similarly, critical uses of the term *naturalize* draw attention to the ambiguity that is intrinsic to naturalization: That which is natural is supposed to be given or intrinsic, yet naturalization constructs as *natural* something that, originally at least, was not.[21] If naturalized citizens *appear* to be the equivalent of citizens by birth, and if naturalization *appears* to turn alienage into commonality, then what happens to the differences that naturalization erases?[22] They become remainders that lead the authenticity of naturalized identities to be questioned but that also enable migrant groups to use ethnicity and nationality as a basis for political organizing. Such groups' refusals to consign "difference" to the private sphere, where it becomes a source of commonality, challenges the requirement that public citizenship assume a generic form.

Recognizing the incommensurability of migrants' histories gives the nation multiple pasts and positionings. Creating a nation requires simultaneously creating a national history (Anderson 1983). In the United States, this history centers on immigration. National histories celebrate the idea that beginning with the Pilgrims, immigrants have come to the United States in search of freedom and opportunity, and, through capitalizing on opportunity, have recreated the nation (Bellah et al. 1985; Bercovitch 1978). Within this narrative, immigration (and naturalization) is a mutual choice – immigrants choose the nation that offers them opportunity, and the nation chooses those immigrants who are capable of maximizing these opportunities (Chock 1991). For the arrival and incorporation of new immigrants to be considered a choice, however, both the nation and the immigrant must be sovereign beings (Bauböck 1994). Yet, migrants move because of political repression, economic dislocation, and family obligations (Hamilton and Chinchilla 1991; Kearney 1986; Menjívar 2000; Sassen 1988, 1989); they legalize, in part, to protect their rights in their countries of residence. Similarly, nations admit migrants, either officially or unofficially, because of a dependence on foreign, often unskilled, labor (Bach 1978; Jenkins 1978; Sassen 1991). It is therefore possible that both immigration and naturalization are fueled by the very conditions – nonchoice, interdependency – that national narratives deny (Coutin et al. 2002).[23] Acknowledging this possibility means recognizing that alongside the nationalistic history of the United States as a nation of immigrants are other, less-celebratory histories, involving labor exploitation, racism, and foreign intervention. The "nation of immigrants" construct, for example, ignores the forcible migration–importation of African slaves, for whom naturalization consisted of being defined as natural beings outside the boundaries of civil society.[24]

In sum, because the political struggles of the excluded and the ceremonies that award citizenship to the deserving are two moments within broader processes and logics of movement and belonging in the contemporary United States, there are deep interconnections between the notions of sameness–difference, choice–nonchoice, and sovereignty–interdependency that are linked to naturalization and to transnationalism, respectively. The dual or multiple identities that make migrants publicly different can be furthered by the acquisition of generic US citizenship, which permits greater freedom of movement internationally.[25] The record numbers of naturalization applicants in the mid-1990s may have been partially due to community groups' efforts to mobilize legal permanent residents and US citizens as part of ethnicity- and nationality-based political campaigns. Naturalization is not only a choice to acquire US citizenship but also a response to a set of circumstances that, in the mid-1990s, included anti-immigrant sentiment and the adoption of more restrictive immigration policies. Nationality- and ethnicity-based organizing is significant not only to US based activists but also to foreign governments that have urged their nationals to seek legal status in the United States. Such strategies prevent potentially destabilizing deportations, create an empowered constituency that may have the ear of US policy makers, promote the transterritorialization of states, and give other nations access to sources of remittances. Furthermore, prioritizing naturalization and authorizing other forms of temporary or permanent legalization may acknowledge US obligations to and dependence on migrant labor. In short, there are ways that naturalization, which places individuals in national categories, serves transnational ends.

The complex and contradictory relationships between transnationalism and nation-based membership may be linked to the long-standing ambivalence toward immigration in the United States. Perhaps it is not surprising that restrictive immigration policies adopted in the mid-1990s were accompanied by a drive to formally include more foreign-born individuals in the nation. Prioritizing naturalization can be seen as an effort to eliminate or domesticate the foreign, but it also can be viewed as an acknowledgment of the pres-

ence and the rights of those individuals, as well as of the needs of immigrant-sending countries. The adoption of restrictive measures was followed, after all, by discussions of some form of guest worker, legalization, or amnesty program. Yet, following the attacks on the World Trade Center towers and the Pentagon on September 11, 2001, there has been a renewal of caution and a return to more restrictive measures. It may now be more difficult for immigrants to assert a right to simultaneously be fully recognized members of US society and maintain loyalties to and ties with their countries of origin. Clearly, this mix of acknowledging interdependency and mutuality, on the one hand, and of asserting national boundaries and rights, on the other hand, will play out differently at different historical moments.

NOTES

1   The high numbers of naturalization applicants were due in large part to the 1986 amnesty program, a component of the 1986 Immigration Reform and Control Act (IRCA), which permitted certain seasonal agricultural workers and individuals who had lived in the United States continuously and illegally since January 1, 1982, to apply for legal permanent residency. After five years of legal permanent residency, the individuals who legalized through IRCA became eligible to apply for naturalization.

2   The United States Committee for Refugees reported that between 1983 and 1986,

[asylum] applicants from Iran had the highest approval rate..., 60.4 percent, followed by the Soviet bloc countries, Romania (51.0), Czechoslovakia (45.4), Afghanistan (37.7), Poland (34.0), and Hungary (31.9). Among the countries with the lowest approval rates were El Salvador (2.6), Haiti (1.8), and Guatemala (0.9). [1986:8]

3 IIRIRA eliminated or restricted preexisting methods of legalization. Under the act's regulations, asylum applications had to be filed within one year of applicants' entry into the United States, individuals who petitioned for their relatives had to meet new deeming requirements, individuals who were illegally present in the United States and who left the country faced new bars to legal reentry, and the requirements for legalizing on the grounds that one has lived in the United States and established roots were heightened. See ACLU Immigrants Rights Project et al. (1996) for further details.

4 Winning a suspension case requires proving (1) seven years of continuous residency, (2) good moral character, and (3) that deportation would cause extreme hardship to the applicant or to a US citizen or legal permanent resident relative of the applicant.

5 Of course, there may be a significant population of Salvadoran immigrants who do not seek or desire legal status. Given that I met most interviewees through community organizations that provided legal services to the undocumented, my sampling methods did not enable me to reach such individuals.

6 In fact, the US-born children of Salvadoran citizens are eligible for Salvadoran citizenship, and my interviews with Salvadoran officials indicated that the Salvadoran government is eager to inculcate a sense of Salvadoran identity among US Salvadoran youth.

7 This strategy is premised on the idea that new citizens and recent immigrants share certain opinions and perspectives and that if more new citizens actually vote, there is a greater chance of promoting policies that favor immigrants.

8 Welfare reform, which made even legal immigrants ineligible for most federal benefits, was adopted in 1996. That was the same year that California voters passed Proposition 209, which eliminated affirmative action. This proposal was followed in 1998 by the Unz initiative, which dismantled bilingual education in California.

9 This voter registration drive was activists' response to anti-immigrant initiatives, such as California Proposition 187. Reasoning that immigrants would have more political clout if they could vote, numerous Central American groups, including ASOSAL, the Organization of Salvadoran-Americans (OSA), and the Central American Resource Center (CARECEN), sent volunteers – some of whom were undocumented – to help newly naturalized Spanish-speaking citizens fill out voter registration cards. These groups were not alone in seeking to register new voters. Representatives of both the Democratic and Republican Parties – including a man dressed as Uncle Sam – sought to register new citizens.

10 Tomas Hammar (1990) argues that there are three gates through which immigrants pass on the road to naturalization. The first gate regulates entry into the country, the second gate regulates presence and social participation, and the third gate regulates full political rights. Using his terminology, before naturalizing, immigrants pass through the first and second gates, thereby securing almost complete social membership before obtaining citizenship itself.

11 As described by the judge, this adoption was mutual. It occurred not only because the parent country was in search of children but also because the children actively sought out parents.

12 Despite the oath of citizenship, naturalized citizens from countries that allow dual nationality might not, in fact, give up their citizenship of birth.

13 Because citizenship was depicted as a reward that immigrants had earned, it is not surprising that naturalization ceremonies in some ways resembled both graduation ceremonies and school assemblies. One official's comments to the new citizens made this analogy explicit: "It's always a happy occasion for us to be here. It's almost like a graduation ceremony." The flag-waving of the naturalized citizens reminded me of

graduates who throw their caps during commencement. When giving instructions, officials sometimes treated the new citizens like schoolchildren. One official, for instance, announced to the new citizens, "We're going to be dismissing you by groups" and then had members of each of the designated groups rehearse this procedure by raising their hands when called. Officials also occasionally used infantilizing terminology, such as saying that they didn't want to have any "boo-boos" when the new citizens filed over to the INS tables, or asking the naturalizing immigrants to say, "Bye-bye, green cards!" Another official asked the visitors not to stand on their seats to take pictures during the ceremony. Certain elements of the naturalization ceremony, such as the pledge of allegiance, are also daily rituals in public schools.

14 As Shapiro notes, "Modern citizenship is situated primarily in the juridical network of the (imaginary) international system of state sovereignties ... The territorial state remains the dominant frame for containing the citizen body, both physically and symbolically" (2001:118).

15 In my experience, the crowd responded enthusiastically to the video. People sitting near me, for example, commented that the video gave them goose bumps.

16 Not surprisingly, naturalization ceremonies were unabashedly patriotic. Judges urged the new citizens to consider serving in the armed forces, to "stand tall" for the United States, and to practice patriotism on a daily basis. One man sitting near me was so moved by the ceremony that he resolved to bring his children the next time that someone in his family naturalized. The ceremonies were heavily publicized. Press crews filmed certain ceremonies, local papers covered these events in both English and Spanish, and at least one ceremony was transmitted to schoolchildren in the Philippines via satellite. Both officials and judges cited the

many freedoms that US citizenship provided, including freedom of movement, speech, and assembly. Officials' examples of how new citizens could demonstrate their patriotism – such as paying taxes, not littering, voting, and serving in parent–teacher associations – were surprisingly prosaic, given the lofty rhetoric about feelings, freedoms, and national missions. Nonetheless, the ceremonies inspired the crowd to cheer for the United States, on at least this one occasion.

In this sense, these rites were analogous to sporting events – particularly international ones. One judge, for instance, commented that the naturalization ceremony was "no different than my attending the opening ceremony at the Olympics in Atlanta just a couple of weeks ago, as I sat there and watched a parade of nations come by." This reference to nations reiterated the difference that naturalization could not quite overcome. Sports analogies were also clear in other aspects of the ceremonies, such as the images of the Olympic torch and Bruce Jenner in the Lee Greenwood video and the waving of national flags, which occurs during soccer matches as well as naturalization ceremonies. One official similarly instructed the new citizens to do the "immigration wave" by rising in turn when he called their sections. Of interest, journalists sometimes also use sports analogies to flesh out immigrants' allegiances. In one news story about the 1986 Immigration Reform and Control Act, a journalist asked a young man who was applying for legalization whether he would root for a Mexican soccer team or a US soccer team. See Coutin and Chock 1995 and Mathews 1986.

17 At the ceremonies that I attended, the other top nations were Vietnam, El Salvador, the Philippines, Korea, and Iran.

18 For instance, the Salvadoran vice president observed during a conference in San Salvador in August 2000, "We have become an emigrant people." An official in

the Salvadoran Ministry of Foreign Relations similarly told me that El Salvador has become "a completely transnational society now" and that to confront this situation, every ministry was being required to develop a plan for addressing the needs of Salvadorans in the exterior.

19 On the corporality of the sovereign, see Kantorowicz 1957. I am grateful to Susan Sterett for bringing the relevance of this source to my attention.

20 Bauböck explains that the term *naturalization*

> can be understood to define the receiving group as a natural one and to require that new members change their nature . . . . In France and England from the 14th to the 18th century the native-born are seen to be *natural* subjects of a sovereign and naturalization signifies a *natural* way of obtaining a similar status by residing permanently in a country, acquiring property and obeying its laws. [1994:44–5]
>
> See also Stolcke 1997.

21 Feminists and critical race theorists, for example, have used the term *naturalize* to draw attention to the processes that make socially and historically constructed categories and practices appear natural and impossible to change. Thus, Yanagisako and Delaney define naturalizing power as "ways in which differentials of power come already embedded in culture. . . . Power appears natural, inevitable, even god-given" (1995:1).

22 The possible disloyality or multiple loyalities of naturalized citizens and of other immigrants has troubled those concerned about large-scale immigration to the United States. The World War II internment of the Japanese (Salyer 1995; Starn 1986) and the post–September 11, 2001, questioning of Arab Americans' loyalties are cases in point. Diasporic peoples, who claim loyalties to deterritorialized nation-states (Basch et al. 1994; Bosniak 2000), have not always been well received by their countries of residence. Some analysts of

immigration argue that the United States already tolerates and even encourages a degree of cultural and ethnic diversity that makes governance difficult. Peter Schuck and Rainer Münz note that in the United States

> many restrictionists . . . fear that the country has lost its capacity to absorb migrants as a consequence of government multicultural policies, including bilingual classes aimed at reinforcing ethnic and cultural identities and affirmative action policies. . . . They argue that these policies, along with a cultural norm that legitimates the maintenance of group identities, is further fragmenting a society already divided along racial lines. [1998:xx]

23 I do not mean to suggest that migrants lack agency. See Coutin 1998 for a discussion of this issue.

24 I am grateful to Tom Boellstorff for reminding me of this form of naturalization.

25 Legal permanent residents also enjoy considerable freedom of movement internationally. To maintain their eligibility for naturalization, however, legal permanent residents must have been physically present in the United States for at least six months out of each year for five years. Moreover, legal permanent residents do not travel with the US passports that may afford easier entry into certain countries.

REFERENCES

ACLU Immigrants Rights Project, Catholic Legal Immigration Network, Immigrant Legal Resource Center, National Immigration Law Center, and National Immigration Project of the National Lawyers Guild
    1996 Background Materials: The 1996 Immigration Law. Los Angeles: National Immigration Law Center.
Aguayo, Sergio, and Patricia Weiss Fagen
    1988 Central Americans in Mexico and

the United States: Unilateral, Bilateral, and Regional Perspectives. Washington, DC: Center for Immigration Policy and Refugee Assistance, Georgetown University.

Anderson, Benedict
  1983 Imagined Communities: Reflections on the Origin and Spread of Nationalism. Rev. edition. London: Verso.

Asad, Talal
  1990 Multiculturalism and British Identity in the Wake of the Rushdie Affair. Politics and Society 18(4):455–480.

Augustine-Adams, Kif
  2000 Gender States: A Comparative Construction of Citizenship and Nation. Virginia Journal of International Law 41(1):93–140.

Bach, Robert L.
  1978 Mexican Immigration and the American State. International Migration Review 12(4):536–558.

Baker, Susan González
  1997 The "Amnesty" Aftermath: Current Policy Issues Stemming from the Legalization Programs of the 1986 Immigration Reform and Control Act. International Migration Review 31(1):5–27.

Basch, Linda, Nina Glick Schiller, and Cristina Szanton Blanc
  1994 Nations Unbound: Transnational Projects, Postcolonial Predicaments, and Deterritorialized Nation-States. Langhorne, PA: Gordon and Breach.

Bauböck, Rainer
  1994 Transnational Citizenship: Membership and Rights in International Migration. Aldershot, UK: Edward Elgar.

Bellah, Robert N.
  1975 The Broken Covenant: American Civil Religion in Time of Trial. New York: Seabury.

Bellah, Robert N., Richard Madsen, William M. Sullivan, Ann Swidler, and Steven M. Tipton
  1985 Habits of the Heart: Individualism and Commitment in American Life. New York: Harper and Row.

Bercovitch, Sacvan
  1978 The American Jeremiad. Madison: University of Wisconsin Press.

Bosniak, Linda S.
  1991 Human Rights, State Sovereignty and the Protection of Undocumented Migrants under the International Migrant Workers Convention. International Migration Review 25(4):737–770.
  2000 Citizenship Denationalized. Indiana Journal of Global Legal Studies 7(2):447–510.

Calavita, Kitty
  1996 The New Politics of Immigration: "Balanced-Budget Conservativism" and the Symbolism of Proposition 187. Social Problems 43(3):284–305.
  2000 The Paradoxes of Race, Class, Identity, and "Passing": Enforcing the Chinese Exclusion Acts, 1882–1910. Law and Social Inquiry 25(1):1–40.

Chavez, Leo R.
  2001 Covering Immigration: Popular Images and the Politics of the Nation. Berkeley: University of California Press.

Chock, Phyllis Pease
  1991 "Illegal Aliens" and "Opportunity": Myth-Making in Congressional Testimony. American Ethnologist 18(2):279–294.
  1995 Culturalism: Pluralism, Culture, and Race in the Harvard Encyclopedia of American Ethnic Groups. Identities 1(4):301–323.
  1999 "A Very Bright Line": Kinship and Nationality in U.S. Congressional Hearings on Immigration. PoLAR: Political and Legal Anthropology Review 22(2): 42–52.

Collier, Jane F., Bill Maurer, and Liliana Suárez-Navaz
  1995 Sanctioned Identities: Legal Constructions of Modern Personhood. Identities 2(1–2):1–27.

Cornelius, Wayne A., Philip L. Martin, and James F. Hollifield
  1994 Controlling Immigration: A Global Perspective. Stanford: Stanford University Press.

Coutin, Susan Bibler
  1998 From Refugees to Immigrants: The Legalization Strategies of Salvadoran Immigrants and Activists. International Migration Review 32(4):901–925.

2000 Legalizing Moves: Salvadoran Immigrants' Struggle for U.S. Residency. Ann Arbor: University of Michigan Press.

Coutin, Susan Bibler, and Phyllis Chock
1995 "Your Friend, the Illegal": Definition and Paradox in Newspaper Accounts of U.S. Immigration Reform. Identities 2(1–2): 123–148.

Coutin, Susan Bibler, Bill Maurer, and Barbara Yngvesson
2002 In the Mirror: The Legitimation Work of Globalization. Law and Social Inquiry 27(4):801–843.

Delgado, Hector
1993 New Immigrants, Old Unions: Organizing Undocumented Workers in Los Angeles. Philadelphia: Temple University Press.

Foner, Nancy
1997 What's New About Transnationalism? New York Immigrants Today and at the Turn of the Century. Diaspora 6(3):355–376.

Foucault, Michel
1977 Discipline and Punish: The Birth of the Prison. Alan Sheridan, trans. New York: Pantheon.

Freeman, Gary P.
1992 Migration Policy and Politics in the Receiving States. International Migration Review 26(4):1 144–1166.

Gilroy, Paul
1987 "There Ain't No Black in the Union Jack": The Cultural Politics of Race and Nation. Chicago: University of Chicago Press.

Goldberg, David Theo
2001 States of Whiteness. In Between Law and Culture: Relocating Legal Studies. David Theo Goldberg, Michael Musheno, and Lisa C. Bower, eds. Pp. 174–194. Minneapolis: University of Minnesota Press.

Goldring, Luin
1998 The Power of Status in Transnational Social Fields. In Transnationalism from Below. Michael Peter Smith and Luis Eduardo Guarnizo, eds. Pp. 165–195. New Brunswick, NJ: Transaction.

Gooding-Williams, Robert, ed.
1993 Reading Rodney King/Reading Urban Uprising. New York: Routledge.

Greenhouse, Carol J.
1996 A Moment's Notice: Time Politics across Cultures. Ithaca: Cornell University Press.

Greenwood, Lee, and Gwen McLin
1993 God Bless the U.S.A.: Biography of a Song. Gretna, LA: Pelican Publishing.

Guarnizo, Luis Eduardo
1997 The Emergence of a Transnational Social Formation and the Mirage of Return Migration among Dominican Transmigrants. Identities 4(2): 281–322.
1998 The Rise of Transnational Social Formations: Mexican and Dominican State Responses to Transnational Migration. Political Power and Social Theory 12:45–94.

Guarnizo, Luis Eduardo, and Michael Peter Smith
1998 The Locations of Transnationalism. In Transnationalism from Below. Michael Peter Smith and Luis Eduardo Guarnizo, eds. Pp. 3–34. New Brunswick, NJ: Transaction.

Hagan, Jacqueline Maria
1994 Deciding to be Legal: A Maya Community in Houston. Philadelphia: Temple University Press.

Hamilton, Nora, and Norma Stolta Chinchilla
1991 Central American Migration: A Framework for Analysis. Latin American Research Review 26(1):75–110.

Hammar, Tomas
1990 Democracy and the Nation State: Aliens, Denizens and Citizens in a World of International Migration. Aldershot, UK: Avebury.

Handlin, Oscar
1951 The Uprooted. Boston: Little, Brown.

Haney López, Ian F.
1996 White by Law: The Legal Construction of Race. New York: New York University Press.

Harvey, David
   1989 The Condition of Postmodernity. Cambridge: Blackwell.
Higham, John
   1974[1963] Strangers in the Land: Patterns of American Nativism, 1860–1925. New York: Atheneum.
Huber, Gregory A., and Thomas J. Espenshade
   1997 Neo-Isolationism, Balanced-Budget Conservatism, and the Fiscal Impacts of Immigrants. International Migration Review 31(4):1031–1054.
Immigrant Policy Project of the State and Local Coalition on Immigration
   1996 Immigrant Policy News . . . The State-Local Report 3(1). Washington, DC: Immigrant Policy Project of the State and Local Coalition on Immigration.
Immigration and Naturalization Service
   1999 Statistical Yearbook of the Immigration and Naturalization Service. Washington, DC: Immigration and Naturalization Service.
Itzigsohn, José
   2000 Immigration and the Boundaries of Citizenship: The Institutions of Immigrants' Political Transnationalism. International Migration Review 34(4): 1126–1154.
Jenkins, J. Craig
   1978 The Demand for Immigrant Workers: Labor Scarcity or Social Control? International Migration Review 12(4): 514–535.
Johnson, James H., Jr., Walter C. Farrell Jr., and Chandra Guinn
   1997 Immigration Reform and the Browning of America: Tensions, Conflicts and Community Instability in Metropolitan Los Angeles. International Migration Review 31(4):1055–1095.
Kantorowicz, Ernst H.
   1957 The King's Two Bodies: A Study in Mediaeval Political Theology. Princeton: Princeton University Press.
Kaye, Mike
   1997 The Role of Truth Commissions in the Search for Justice, Reconciliation, and Democratisation: The Salvadorean and Honduran Cases. Journal of Latin American Studies 29(3): 693–716.
Kearney, Michael
   1986 From the Invisible Hand to Visible Feet: Anthropological Studies of Migration and Development. Annual Review of Anthropology 15:331–361.
   1995 The Local and the Global: The Anthropology of Globalization and Transnationalism. Annual Review of Anthropology 24:547–565.
   1998 Transnationalism in California and Mexico at the End of Empire. In Border Identities: Nation and State at International Frontiers. Thomas M. Wilson and Hastings Donnan, eds. Pp. 117–141. Cambridge: Cambridge University Press.
Landolt, Patricia, Lilian Autler, and Sonia Baires
   1999 From Hermano Lejano to Hermano Mayor: The Dialectics of Salvadoran Transnationalism. Ethnic and Racial Studies 22(2):290–315.
Levitt, Peggy
   2001 The Transnational Villagers. Berkeley: University of California Press.
Mahler, Sarah J.
   1998 Theoretical and Empirical Contributions toward a Research Agenda for Transnationalism. In Transnationalism from Below. Michael Peter Smith and Luis Eduardo Guarnizo, eds. Pp. 64–100. New Brunswick, NJ: Transaction.
Marrus, Michael R.
   1985 The Unwanted: European Refugees in the Twentieth Century. New York: Oxford University Press.
Marshall, T. H.
   1950 Citizenship and Social Class, and Other Essays. Cambridge: Cambridge University Press.
Martin, Philip
   1995 Proposition 187 in California. International Migration Review 29(1): 255–263.
Mathews, Jay
   1986 Home Is Where the Heart Is: Mexican Immigrants Arrive Looking over Their Shoulders. Washington Post, May 2: H5.

Matsuda, Mari J., Charles R. Lawrence III, Richard Delgado, and Kimberle Williams Crenshaw
1993 Words That Wound: Critical Race Theory, Assaultive Speech and the First Amendment. Boulder: Westview Press.

Maurer, Bill
1997 Recharting the Caribbean: Land, Law, and Citizenship in the British Virgin Islands. Ann Arbor: University of Michigan Press.
1998 Cyberspatial Sovereignties: Offshore Finance, Digital Cash and the Limits of Liberalism. Indiana Journal of Global Legal Studies 5(2):493–519.

Menjívar, Cecilia
2000 Fragmented Ties: Salvadoran Immigrant Networks in America. Berkeley: University of California Press.

Menjívar, Cecilia, Julie DaVanzo, Lisa Greenwell, and R. Burciaga Valdez
1998 Remittance Behavior among Salvadoran and Filipino Immigrants in Los Angeles. International Migration Review 32(1):97–126.

Montes Mozo, Segundo, and Juan Jose Garcia Vasquez
1988 Salvadoran Migration to the United States: An Exploratory Study. Hemispheric Migration Project. Washington, DC: Center for Immigration Policy and Refugee Assistance, Georgetown University.

NatzNews
1998 NatzNews Vol. 7, April 17. Washington, DC: Immigration and Naturalization Service, Office of Naturalization Operations.

Nelson, Barbara J.
1984 Women's Poverty and Women's Citizenship: Some Political Consequences of Economic Marginality. Signs 10(2): 209–231.

Ong, Aihwa
1999 Flexible Citizenship: The Cultural Logic of Transnationality. Durham, NC: Duke University Press.

Ong, Paul, Edna Bonacich, and Lucie Cheng
1994 The New Asian Immigration in Los Angeles and Global Restructuring. Philadelphia: Temple University Press.

Paral, Rob
1995 Naturalization: New Demands and New Directions at the INS. Interpreter Releases 72(27):937–943.

Perea, Juan F., ed.
1997 Immigrants Out! The New Nativism and the Anti-Immigrant Impulse in the United States. New York: New York University Press.

Popkin, Eric
1999 Guatemalan Mayan Migration to Los Angeles: Constructing Transnational Linkages in the Context of the Settlement Process. Ethnic and Racial Studies 22(2): 267–289.

Portes, Alejandro
1997 Immigration Theory for a New Century: Some Problems and Opportunities. International Migration Review 31(4):799– 825.

Portes, Alejandro, Luis E. Guarnizo, and Patricia Landolt
1999 The Study of Transnationalism: Pitfalls and Promise of an Emergent Research Field. Ethnic and Racial Studies 22(2):217–237.

Robertson, Roland
1995 Globalization: Time-Space and Homogeneity-Heterogeneity. In Global Modernities. Mike Featherstone, Scott Lash, and Roland Robertson, eds. Pp. 25–44. London: Sage.

Rouse, Roger
1991 Mexican Migration and the Social Space of Postmodernism. Diaspora 1(1):8–23.

Ruggles, Patricia, Michael Fix, and Kathleen M. Thomas
1985 Profile of the Central American Population in the United States. Washington, DC: Urban Institute.

Salyer, Lucy E.
1995 Laws Harsh as Tigers: Chinese Immigrants and the Shaping of Modern Immigration Law. Chapel Hill: University of North Carolina Press.

Sánchez, George J.
1997 Face the Nation: Race, Immigration, and the Rise of Nativism in Late Twentieth Century America. International Migration Review 31(4):1009–1030.

Sapiro, Virginia
    1984 Women, Citizenship, and National-
    ity: Immigration and Naturalization Pol-
    icies in the United States. Politics and
    Society 13(1):1–26.
Sassen, Saskia
    1988 The Mobility of Labor and Capital: A
    Study in International Investment and
    Labor Flow. New York: Cambridge Uni-
    versity Press.
    1989 America's Immigration "Problem":
    The Real Causes. World Policy Journal
    6(4):811–831.
    1991 The Global City: New York, London,
    Tokyo. Princeton: Princeton University
    Press.
    1996 Losing Control? Sovereignty in an
    Age of Globalization. New York:
    Columbia University Press.
Schiller, Nina Glick, Linda Basch, and Cris-
tina Szanton Blanc
    1995 From Immigrant to Transmigrant:
    Theorizing Transnational Migration.
    Anthropological Quarterly 68(1):48–63.
Schiller, Nina Glick, and Georges E. Fouron
    1999 Terrains of Blood and Nation: Hai-
    tian Transnational Social Fields. Ethnic
    and Racial Studies 22(2):340–366.
Schuck, Peter H., and Rainer Münz, eds.
    1998 Paths to Inclusion: The Integration of
    Migrants in the United States and Ger-
    many. New York: Berghahn Books.
Shapiro, Michael J.
    2001 For Moral Ambiguity: National Cul-
    ture and the Politics of the Family. Min-
    neapolis: University of Minnesota Press.
Smith, Robert C.
    1998 Transnational Localities: Community,
    Technology and the Politics of Member-
    ship within the Context of Mexico and
    U.S. Migration. In Transnationalism
    from Below. Michael Peter Smith and Luis
    Eduardo Guarnizo, eds. Pp. 196–238.
    New Brunswick, NJ: Transaction.

Soysal, Yasemin Nuhoglu
    1994 Limits of Citizenship: Migrants and
    Postnational Membership in Europe.
    Chicago: University of Chicago Press.
Starn, Orin
    1986 Engineering Internment: Ant-
    hropologists and the War Relocation
    Authority. American Ethnologist 13(4):
    700–721.
Stolcke, Verena
    1997 The "Nature" of Nationality. In Citi-
    zenship and Exclusion. Veit Bader, ed.
    Pp. 61–80. New York: St. Martin's Press.
United States Committee for Refugees
    1986 Despite a Generous Spirit: Denying
    Asylum in the United States. Washing-
    ton, DC: American Council for Nation-
    alities Service.
Wilgoren, Jodi
    1998 Thousands in Crackdown Face Loss
    of Citizenship. Los Angeles Times, Feb-
    ruary 2:A1, A13.
Williams, Patricia J.
    1991 The Alchemy of Race and Rights.
    Cambridge, MA: Harvard University
    Press.
Wilmsen, Edwin N., and Patrick McAllister,
eds.
    1996 The Politics of Difference: Ethnic
    Premises in a World of Power. Chicago:
    University of Chicago Press.
Yanagisako, Sylvia, and Carol Delaney, eds.
    1995 Naturalizing Power: Essays in Femi-
    nist Cultural Analysis. New York: Rou-
    tledge.
Yngvesson, Barbara
    1997 Negotiating Motherhood: Identity
    and Difference in "Open" Adoptions.
    Law and Society Review 31(1):31–80.

14

The Public/Private Mirage: Mapping Homes and Undomesticating Violence Work in the South Asian Immigrant Community

Anannya Bhattacharjee

In my work against domestic violence in New York, I have felt increasingly dissatisfied with the fact that much of this work is focused exclusively on the family home. Such a focus is consistent with the understanding that the mainstream battered women's movement in the US has of domestic violence. Domestic violence is mainly understood within the parameters of gender inequality and the patriarchal family home. Such a formulation of domestic violence is directly linked to Western feminist theories of "private" and "public," terms that have been central to the analyses of violence against women (indeed, the general status of women).[1] "Private," in this context, has been understood as the patriarchal family home. Western feminists have established that for the collective condition of women to change, women must project their experiences of oppression in their private lives into the public. "Public," in this

analysis, has been generalized as outside-the-family-home.

However, in my experience with immigrants in the South Asian community, I have found that "home," commonly accepted as the primary site of domestic violence, represents multiple concepts for people whose consciousnesses are shaped by migration. An analysis of the entire range of meanings of "home," as experienced by a South Asian immigrant woman, changes conventional notions of "private" and "public." It is my hope that what we learn from such an investigation will help us redefine the parameters of our understanding of domestic violence work in the US.

In the following text, I begin by first examining the term "South Asian," the community within which this study is situated. Proceeding from there, I describe the conventionally understood concepts of public, private, state,

From M. J. Alexander and C. T. Mohanty, *Feminist Genealogies, Colonial Legacies, Democratic Futures*, pp. 308–29, 396–8. New York and London: Routledge, 1997.

and home in Western feminism because these are the concepts with which this essay engages. After this review, I map the multiple "homes," as experienced by South Asian immigrants and South Asian immigrant women. This mapping allows me to demonstrate the need to look at Western feminist theorizations of public, private, and state in new ways. In concluding, I point to possible opportunities for intervention from this perspective.

"South Asian" as Identity and as Community

The term "South Asia" refers most immediately to that area of the world which today contains countries such as Bangladesh, Bhutan, India, Nepal, Pakistan, and Sri Lanka. However, "South Asia" is a term that most people of South Asian origin do not automatically ascribe to themselves. Its specific use as a form of personal identity has mostly evolved recently among people who are working for social change within this community in the US. Whereas cultural or mainstream political organizations in the South Asian community in the US define themselves around particular nationalities within South Asia, the progressive groups within this community often identify themselves and organize around the term "South Asia." It is important to examine this term, which has gained such currency among those South Asians who define themselves in terms that are opposed to the mainstream hegemonic (and often nationalist) sentiments.

I am by birth a Hindu and an Indian. I work extensively with the larger South Asian community, and I define myself as South Asian. The label's attraction for South Asians such as myself lies, to a large extent, in its ability to subsume more than one nation. It is thus seen by those skeptical of oppressive conditions of nationhood as something less rigid; it has little institutional authority (such as a flag or an embassy) and less solidified cultural homogeneity. In the competing ethnic real-

ities of the United States, it is also a way to amass numbers.

However, I would like to sound a few cautionary notes here. In the United States, the term "South Asia" has been and still is used to describe a discipline of study within the university and carries Orientalist associations. Regional politics in South Asia also affect the way such an identity is received within the community. Pakistan and Bangladesh have a complicated history, and India has often been described as imperialist vis-à-vis its neighboring countries in South Asia. In this context, the phrase "South Asian," when used in reference to groups of activists composed predominantly of Indians without adequate representation from other South Asian nationalities, can convey overtones of domination and exclusion. Therefore, much as progressive groups would like to organize under an identity that goes beyond oppressive associations of nationhood, some South Asians may actually see their nationality as a positive means for distinction and identification.

I have described the Indian immigrant community in the US at length in an earlier essay, but it is useful to summarize briefly some of those ideas here.[2] In that essay, I argued that the ideological force of the nation plays a dominant role in this immigrant community's construction of its identity. I found this to be consistent with the fact that the community members, who have the resources to construct actively this identity, belong predominantly to the male bourgeoisie, the creator of nations. The bourgeoisie in the South Asian community, upon displacement from the nation of its origin, finds itself represented in the form of an immigrant community in a foreign nation. Where once it had posited itself through a hegemonic process as the universal norm in the nation of its origin, it now perceives itself to be in a position defined by difference and subordination. The immigrant bourgeoisie's desire to overcome this condition and regain its power of self-universalization manifests itself in its projection of itself as the leader of the community, guarding and propagating the essence of national culture. It aligns itself with a nationalist spirit which involves learning Western technology and participating successfully in the US economy while, at the same time, protecting the cultural and spiritual essence of the East. In the essay, I also noted that US institutions describe Asian immigrants as the "model minority," and their encouragement of this community's economic success is based on their satisfaction with a group of people who are perceived to be conciliatory and motivated to succeed according to US standards of success. A competitive relationship between different minorities, who vie with one another for "model" status, is thus set up, at the same time as they are seen to be distinct from the majority. Such a relationship impacts directly on the community's understanding of race relations in the US. This, briefly, is the kind of immigrant community in which I situate the discussion here.

In my experience, I have found the South Asian community in the US to be lacking a sharp awareness and understanding of race relations. I find this to be dangerous, particularly when unity among peoples of color has become increasingly necessary in this age of neocolonialism, when covert imperialist policies of First-World countries such as the US are difficult to see. South Asians, it seems, perceive Britain to be more clearly a colonizing power than the US. South Asian immigration to Britain (compared to the US) has a longer history and arises directly out of Britain's history of colonization. The South Asian immigrant community in Britain has also been more working-class in character than its US counterpart, although the composition of the community in the US is changing. It is not possible to do an extensive comparison between South Asian immigration to the US and to Britain in this essay, but I would like to note that the comparative histories of political activism in the two South Asian communities demonstrate that South Asians in Britain have a more radical experience and understanding of race relations than those in the US.

In response to the US state's racialization of ethnic minorities, the South Asian community resists such categorization of itself. It tries to rescue the Caucasian elements that it imagines itself to possess. In her essay "Racist Response to Racism: The Aryan Myth and South Asians in the United States," Sucheta Mazumdar describes the popularity of the Aryan myth and its use by South Asians to prove that they are white. A representative letter in *India Abroad* (a publication targeting the immigrant East Indian community in the US) illustrates well the community's ahistorical approach to race politics. In this letter, Kaleem Kawaja makes an easy comparison between US immigration history, based on policies that promote the interests of the US capitalist nation-state, and centuries of complex, pre-nation-state Indian history. He says, "From ancient times India welcomed people who came from outside, bringing their religions, their cultures and their practices, and tried to mingle them in the Indian soil. That is how today's rich multicultural Indian society has developed. In that respect there is a parallel with the US, where successive waves of immigrants have enriched America." In idealizing immigration from the Third World to the First World, Kawaja erases different histories in a single sweep in order to insist that the US and India are, deep down, one and the same. The writer of the letter does not have to face up to the uncomfortable consequences of racial and ethnic discrimination in the here and now.

On the other hand, Dilip Hiro's description of Asian activism in *Black British, White British* shows at length the radical race politics ascribed to by South Asians in Britain. One example is the United Black Youth League, formed by South Asians who "planned to attract both Asian and West Indian youths, and function as a radical, revolutionary organization" (175). Another example that Hiro provides, illustrating the alliances between Asians and other people of color, is the Southhall Youth movement in 1982, which believed that "its political colour was black, the colour of the oppressed, which represented the social position of the Asian and Afro-Caribbean peoples in Britain" (176). Similarly, the goals of the Indian Workers' Association (IWA) formed in 1938, prior to the independence and partition of India and Pakistan, demonstrate an understanding of different forms of oppression. Some of these goals were to "promote co-operation and unity with the trade union and labour movement in Great Britain; fight against all forms of discrimination based on race, colour, creed or sex" (139). These examples illustrate that Asian activism in Britain has a stronger working-class tradition and a commitment to antiracist struggles which allows for greater solidarity with oppressed peoples of color. As Mazumdar notes, in the US, "where the urban professional bourgeoisie still are numerically the larger group, it is too early to tell whether segments of the South Asians in the United States will . . . form similar alliances" (53).

This, then, is the South Asian community. I have described the term "South Asian" and the immigrant community at length because its shape and determination form the backdrop to the discussion that follows.

Conventional Mappings

Western feminism has made the separation between the private and public the focus of its debate and struggle, and the volume of Western feminist theorization about these concepts is great and varied. Catharine A. MacKinnon's *Toward a Feminist Theory of the State* is one influential and representative text in this debate on the home, the public, and the private. Since this essay deals with these same concepts, I present my argument as an engagement with MacKinnon's text.

The "private" that MacKinnon examines at length is defined by her as the patriarchal family home. She critically analyzes the privacy doctrine that maintains the separation of the private home from the public on the basis of "individual" (synonymous with "male") freedom in the private space: the "privacy

doctrine is most at home at home, the place women experience the most force, in the family" (190–1). She adds that "the core of privacy doctrine's coverage" is composed of "the very things feminism regards as central to the subjection of women – the very place, the body: the very relations, heterosexual: . . . and the very feelings, intimate" (193). This "private," MacKinnon sees to be opposed to the "public."

The "public" she describes is closely aligned with the liberal state. For example, "public," "government," and "state" are used almost synonymously in her text. She says, for instance,

> the idea of privacy embodies a tension between . . . *public* exposure or *governmental* intrusion . . . and . . . personal self-action. . . . To complain in *public* of inequality within the private contradicts the liberal definition of the private. In the liberal view no act of the *state* contributes to shaping its internal alignments or distributing its internal forces, so no act of the *state* should participate in changing it. (187–90, my italics)

Although she strongly disagrees with the separation of public from private in liberalism, she does not dispute that the public and private spaces *are* different and separate. The state as definitionally public – not private – is the underlying assumption of her argument. She continues to use "state" and "public" interchangeably in her analysis of the problem and in her suggested course of action. The consequences of these assumptions are what I want to analyze in this essay.

MacKinnon understands the power of the state to be "embodied in law, exist[ing] throughout society as male power at the same time as the power of men over women is organized as the power of the state" (170). Law is central to her exposition of state power because "[l]aw, as words in power, writes society in state form and writes the state onto society" (163). Her extensive analysis demonstrates that, contrary to the popular conception of the liberal state "as a neutral arbiter among conflicting interests," the state is a gendered entity (159). Her primary concern is contained in the questions she directs toward the state: "What in gender terms, are the state's norms of accountability, sources of power, real constituency? . . . Is the state constructed upon the subordination of women?" (161).

In light of the fact that definitions of "private" and "public" are critical to feminist theory and that feminist visions of social change involve intervening in these spaces, the importance of thoroughly understanding these spaces and their interactions and intersections cannot be overestimated. In this essay, I focus on South Asian immigrant women's experiences of domestic violence in the US. I do not do this so as to introduce yet another missing category into Western feminism's facile embrace of diversity or to include another special case in the feminist encyclopedia. Domestic violence allows me to focus on "home," and in turn map the multiple significations of "home" as experienced by immigrants and as constructed by the US nation-state. This process illuminates the now-you-see-it-now-you-don't, mirage-like quality of spaces understood as public or private.

I choose the example of South Asian immigrant women because the current historical position of the South Asian immigrant woman in the US is useful for the task of challenging conventional definitions of home, private, and public. The South Asian community in the US is a relatively recent immigrant community. Even though its history in the US goes back to the nineteenth century, it has begun to grow significantly only since the mid-twentieth century. In such a community, a South Asian immigrant woman's condition is marked by immigration, which has consequences for the purposes of this discussion. Due to the relatively recent history of immigration, "home" is not yet a solidified concept; it is in flux and still being negotiated. This provides us with an opportunity to see different spaces in formation. Through this discussion, I hope to show that the Western feminist assumptions of home, private, public, and the state are funda-

mentally questionable. This argument has implications not just for immigrant women but for all women because it calls for a rethinking of the basis of feminist formulations and activism.

Mapping Homes

Home appears to be defined at three different levels for immigrants. One definition is the (conventional) domestic sphere of the heterosexual and patriarchal family.[3] A second definition is as an extended ethnic community separate and distinct from other ethnic communities. The common application of the word "family" by particular communities to themselves is made possible by this definition. The third reference of "home" for many immigrant communities is to their nations of origin, often shaped by nationalist movements and histories of colonialism. These three definitions of "home" have to be examined in the light of migration from excolonized Third-World locations, such as South Asia, to the First World.

I want to situate my discussion of domestic violence and "home" in the context of this complex and contradictory history of Third-World immigration to the US. Domestic violence, in the heterosexual and patriarchal home, can involve physical, emotional, and sexual abuse. A woman can be denied food, money, adequate clothing, shelter, her right to see a doctor, and all that one may see as part of basic subsistence. She can be forced to live in isolation by her abuser, who can lock her up or instruct her not to answer the phone, thus denying her access to other community members. Isolation is one of the most severe forms of abuse in the home by a man against a woman, contributing to a battered woman's perception that her condition is uncommon and shameful. It is one of the primary ways in which a man makes sure that the woman's voice is never heard and that she remains dependent on him in every way.

Immigration laws are another means by which a man can control his wife in the home. Early US immigration policies allowed only men to petition for their wives to accompany them into the country; women could not do the same. However, immigration activists point out that "[w]hile immigration law has since been changed and policy references are now gender neutral, it is the women who experience continued subjugation and vulnerability under their husbands" (Family Violence Prevention Fund, et al. IV-2). In the South Asian immigrant community, it is common for single men first to come to the US on employment-based visas and later marry a woman from South Asia, or for married men to come here on employment-based visas, accompanied by their wives. In both cases, the woman is dependent on the man's sponsorship in order to obtain her legal immigration status through spouse-based visas. Her dependency on him during this process opens up opportunities for abuse because he knows that without proper status, the woman is, for all practical purposes, nonexistent in the US.

Women comprise the majority of applicants for spouse-based visas (FVPF et al. V-18). According to the laws governing spouse-based visas, the woman, when sponsored by her spouse, gets conditional residency status in the US at first. This status becomes permanent only after two years, when she proves to the immigration authorities that she entered into the marriage in "good faith."[4] "Good faith" means that the beneficiary (often a woman) entered into the marriage with the intention of building a family and not for immigration benefits. Thus, a woman's primary motivation, presumably, should be familial commitment to the man she marries, not legal status for herself. She must demonstrate her "good faith" with wedding photographs and invitations, official documents, and oral narratives proving that they have lived together as a "proper" married couple and that they did not marry for immigration benefits. In other words, she has to prove the *nonexistence* of immigration reasons.[5]

This procedure has two implications. One is that the beneficiary is under suspicion of im-

migration fraud until proven innocent, thus further propagating the image of woman as untrustworthy. This is reminiscent of immigration policies of the late 1800s, which,

> in essence, assumed that all "Oriental" females seeking to immigrate to California were doing so in order to engage in "criminal and demoralizing purposes" [such as prostitution]. This... gave the immigration commissioner the right to determine whether the incoming woman was "a person of correct habits and good character." (Sucheta Mazumdar *Making Waves* 3)

The second implication is that the absence of immigration-related motives on the beneficiary's part is enough to establish the "good faith" of the marriage. The motives of the *petitioner* (often a man), though they need not be immigration-related, are not examined. Perhaps he married her to get free domestic help or a free sex partner. Questions regarding such issues are not asked.

Furthermore, it is quite common for a man, on whom the woman is dependent for legal status, to withhold his sponsorship of her even for the conditional (temporary) residency status. In such circumstances, a woman, who perhaps initially came to the US on a different visa following her marriage, with the understanding that her husband would sponsor her once she was here, could easily become undocumented as her short-term legal status expires.

As is well-known, undocumented women are a growing population in the US. In order to provide women in these vulnerable positions with some rights and to enable them to regain their legal status, immigrants' rights groups pushed Congress to pass a crucial provision within the Violence Against Women Act that would dramatically help immigrant women.[6] This provision is meant to relieve a woman's dependency on her husband for sponsorship by allowing her to petition for herself, in the event of his refusal and abusive behavior. However, some senators expressed concern about possible misuse of the provision by women who, in "bad faith," may falsely claim to be battered in order to be able to self-petition. Their concern is ironic because other bills which provide far more dangerous opportunities for misuse (often by state agencies themselves) frequently get approved. Misuse of any legislation is always a possibility. But, when it comes to an act that will greatly benefit undocumented immigrant women, exceptions rather than the rule are cited to argue against it.

Yet, very little is said about the "bad faith" of the sponsor, often a male US resident or citizen, who is refusing to petition. When the husband does not file a petition, he is not held accountable. Such a marriage becomes unstable as the woman is undocumented and subject to deportation, which would, of course, destroy the family. The sanctity of the marriage at that point is not upheld.

At first, the "good faith" argument seems to be based on concern for the immigrants' marriage and family. However, this perception gets dispelled when one realizes that there is no real support for the immigrant woman's right to self-petition and remain legally with her family. What this demonstrates is that the sanctity of the family is selectively respected by the nation-state. Feminists such as MacKinnon see the state, organized around male power and expressed in law, as that which remains conveniently out of private homes. It appears, however, that for immigrant homes, the state can hardly be accused of inaction – if anything, it is actively involved in determining the very existence of the family.

Western feminists also stress the importance of projecting the private into the public so that women can have public recourse. MacKinnon asserts that the public is constituted by laws and judicial process and that ultimately it is possible to remake this space on the basis of feminist jurisprudence. Implicit is the assumption of the existence of available public spaces, to intervene in and transform. In this discussion, the domestic worker, as a worker (often a woman) in a family home, is significant because one sees

that the family home can actually be a public space. But its publicness is of no avail to those who are not official members of the public. The condition of the domestic worker overturns a lot of conventional ideas regarding the private and the public.

Domestic workers are primarily poor immigrant women. They may be either undocumented or, in some rare instances, sponsored by their employers for employment visas. In either case, they may face severe abuse from their employers, and their situation is often similar to that of the battered wife. The employer may deny her sponsorship or hold the power to do so over her. She is extremely vulnerable to all forms of abuse, often works around the clock, and may be denied basic subsistence. She, too, can face complete isolation as her employer can control her movements much like a husband controls those of a battered wife.

> The domestic helper is one of the most, if not the most, vulnerable and marginalized among migrant workers. The work is menial and the live-in-arrangement ensures that she is at the beck and call of the employer virtually 24 hours a day. The job demands submission and servility. As a foreigner coming from a poor country, she is in a constant state of powerlessness. (Gina Alunan, *Women on the Move* 53)

This parallel between the domestic worker and the battered wife is particularly relevant to my discussion in this essay because, in the family home, the domestic worker is a worker and the battered woman is a spouse. The former is commonly perceived to be a part of that "public" space, the workplace, and the battered wife is a part of that very "private" space, the home. The "private" home is the domestic worker's workplace (that which is considered "public"): her "public" workplace is her "home" (that which is considered "private"). Her immigration status, which is usually contingent upon an employment-based visa for unskilled workers, makes a private slave of her (almost as does a spouse-based visa), and she is usually isolated from other workers even though her kind of workplace employs many like her (employers disregard or are often ignorant of the fact that labor laws, such as they are, do actually apply to domestic workers). I think her condition illustrates the contradictory, multiple, and shifting definitions of the "private" and the "public," and reveals their construction to be largely imaginary. One sees here the innumerable ways in which what is presumably "public" becomes "private," and what is presumably "private" becomes "public."

In MacKinnon's analysis, a woman's status as a legally recognized member of the public is taken for granted. What remains for feminist jurisprudence is to assert this status better through public (synonymous with state) recourse. However, what remains unexplored is the very ideology of nationhood that forms the basis of the public in a nation-state, that body of people bound together within national boundaries.

By leaving out nationhood, it is possible for MacKinnon to talk about state machinery that is not necessarily tied to a bounded space and people. But bringing nationhood into the discussion immediately introduces the notion of a space to be defended and bounded: in fact a *private* space.

The absence of analysis of the nation-state in US mainstream feminism leads to the uncritical and automatic assumption of a public whose subject, then, is a US citizen. The process of immigration, which has played a singularly significant role in carving out the US nation-state, is erased, and we see a nation that has always been here, from time immemorial. I am reminded of Benedict Anderson's statement about how "nations to which [nation-states] give political expression always loom out of an immemorial past, and, still more important, glide into a limitless future. It is the magic of nationalism to turn chance into destiny" (11–12).

Immigration laws have *privatized* the nation; it is now a bounded space into which only some of the people can walk some of the

time. A man's control over his wife or an employer's control over the domestic worker in the home extends to controlling her recognition as a member of what constitutes the public – in this case, being a legal resident of a national community (in itself a private concept). This control is encouraged by the legal structures (such as immigration laws) of a so-called public (but, in a crucial sense, private) space, the US nation. The figure of the undocumented woman, who is an "illegal alien," however, is a reminder of the not-public – that is, private – basis of the nation-state. Family home, then, is not the only unambiguously private space, and public recourse can only be, in the final analysis, a mirage for a feminism that does not recognize the privateness of the national public.

The nation-state's control over its population comes into focus when, as we have seen, the beneficiary is singled out for the "good faith" test, which seems to suggest that in the eyes of the "nation," motives based on immigration are deemed worse than other motives on the part of the petitioner, such as a desire to acquire free labor or mail-order brides. Thus, whereas conditionally admitted individuals (the beneficiaries, who are obviously not part of the "public") must demonstrate their "good faith" in order to be worthy to reside legally on US soil, the petitioners and the "public" need not demonstrate their "good faith" as sponsors committed to abuse-free families. Again, in the case of the domestic worker, her position is defined by US immigration law as an "unskilled" worker. This categorization puts the availability of legal status almost outside her reach; she is low on the priority list for becoming part of the "public" even though her intensely exploited labor contributes significantly to the nation that will not open its actually private space to her.

Nicos Poulantzas points out that in the capitalist state, "everyone is free and equal before the law [based on bourgeois juridical axiom] on condition that he is or becomes a bourgeois. And that, of course, the law at once allows and forbids." (90) In the context of this essay, women of "bad faith" and "unskilled" workers fall outside bourgeois notions of citizenship. Immigration policies of the host country, in their power to define the (non)existence/(il)legality of individuals, can make invisible, for all practical purposes, large sections of the population. As Chandra Mohanty has noted, "Citizenship and immigration laws are fundamentally about defining insiders and outsiders." ("Cartographies" 24).

A second kind of "home" is the ethnic community. South Asian immigrants see their community as an extended "family," separate and distinct from other ethnic communities. The immigrant community sees itself, in all its specific ethnicity, as a private space, within which it must guard its own national heritage against intervention from mainstream US cultural practices. These definitions of national heritage are anchored in ideas of womanhood, as interpreted by the guardians of tradition.[7] However, the very fact that US immigration laws control the composition of the ethnic community indicates the publicness of this space (which is seen as private by the immigrant residing in it). Here, I use the term "publicness" to refer to the crafting of the community through immigration laws that follow the dictates of an appropriate public in the *private* US nation.

In the United States, immigration policy has been "the domestic reflection of United States foreign policy and the expression of industry's needs for labor to produce and compete in domestic and international markets" (FVPF et al. IV-1). Asian immigration began in the nineteenth century with the migration of Chinese laborers, only to be followed by the Chinese Exclusion Act of 1882, a result of labor fights between white Americans and Chinese immigrants. Subsequent Japanese migration then began, again leading to legislation barring Asian immigration for decades after 1917. However, as a result of a labor shortage in the US, Filipino immigration was encouraged from 1910 to 1934, after which, Filipinos were also excluded.[8] Legislation such as the National Origins Quota Acts of 1921 and 1924 were passed to "preserve

the northern- and western-European character of the population in the United States" (FVPF et al. IV-4). It is not surprising to learn that in keeping with the use of immigration policies to control labor markets, these same policies also served to "deport those who asserted their labor and political rights" (FVPF at al. IV-5).[9] This is the kind of state intervention that Nicos Poulantzas refers to as being sometimes necessary and strategic in a capitalist economy, although such intervention is still dictated by the "*general coordinates of the reproduction of capital*" (181). The state executes such functions, because if they are done directly by capital, they could heighten internal crisis and deepen contradictions, circumstances that would jeopardize capital itself. Thus, immigration laws of the US state, as they set about carving quotas for specified immigrants, fulfill the needs of the free market in the US capitalist economy.

In the Asian community, US immigration laws are mainly employment-based and they encourage professional bourgeois, conservative, and predominantly male immigration, thus leading to a homogenized idea of the community as economically successful.[10] US legislation that punishes undocumented or "illegal aliens" and sets standards for determining the appropriateness of candidates for naturalized citizenship further motivates the "model" immigrant community to dissociate itself from all those that it sees as "undesirable."[11] Those considered to be undesirable could be the undocumented, gays and lesbians, low-income people, and those on public assistance. In this context, a battered woman, who often derives her class and legal status from her husband, may potentially move to an "undesirable" status if she decides to leave her marriage. For a woman from a low-income family, leaving the marital home may plunge her into further obscurity.

At the same time that US laws actively construct immigrant communities, US institutions can *selectively* display "respect" for the privacy of an immigrant's "home" culture, in the sense of an "authentic" culture to be found in its pure form in a distant country of origin. This again demonstrates the confusion surrounding definitions of the "public" and "private." The critical role that conceptions of womanhood play in such "authentic" definitions of cultures and the dangerous implications of such conceptions for a South Asian woman can be seen in the following incidents. In my work on domestic violence, I have done workshops with counselors and teachers of public schools in South Asian neighborhoods in New York, and I have talked extensively to young South Asian women. Guidance counselors in such schools have told me about their experiences regarding young South Asian girls who are taken out of public schools by their fathers to get married early. The father, projecting himself as the protector of his daughter's sexuality, often justifies his decision on the basis of the "home" country's cultural norms. In such cases, the school personnel are hesitant to speak up because, as they have told me, they are fearful of appearing disrespectful of the immigrants' national cultures. Here, the father's judgment of cultural norms is accepted with a certain amount of "good faith" in spite of US laws regarding education and marriage. In this context, school personnel see immigrant national culture as "private," even though US laws carry clear guidelines for education of young people. Thus, as "public" officials working with the "public" (in this case, the young girl), they hesitate to cite US legislation specifically meant for the "public" in the United States that ensures the young immigrant girl's right to education.[12] In this instance, the privacy of an immigrant's national culture is privileged over a young girl's legislated right to education.

Yet, when, as it happened in a real case, a student refuses to stand up during the singing of the American national anthem (since he or she is probably bewildered by this allegiance assumed of him or her), teachers are inclined to worry about the student's inability to conform, to start making phone calls, and to call a meeting with the parents. In this instance, "public" officials in the school find it possible to uphold the public norm of showing respect

for the United States anthem, a symbol of the nation-state. But they do not appear anxious about the privateness of the immigrants' allegiance to their home country's national anthem.

Whether the ethnic community is a private or a public place appears to shift and change. In either case, the woman concerned continues to experience marginalization. The ethnic community, as a private space and a second home in which the immigrant community guards its national heritage and cultural values, is oppressive for women, who often serve as the instruments for such safekeeping. In such a community, a battered South Asian woman potentially faces denial of her abusive condition. On the other hand, the battered woman who leaves her abuser faces possible loss of "model" status and risks her standing as an appropriate member of the community, in part because this community occupies a public space policed by US federal laws. Her status often falls outside desirable categories, economically, culturally, and politically. Here again, we see the limitations of Western feminist analysis of public space as a space of recourse and as a zone automatically lying outside an easily and singularly recognized "home."

The nation of origin, the third meaning of "home" for immigrants, is viewed as containing the true principles of their essential national heritage. These are the principles which the South Asian community seeks to preserve in the foreign country. In such nationalist ideologies of the home countries, "woman" has been an instrument for the founding principles. As Sangari and Vaid point out, "The recovery of tradition throughout the proto-nationalist and nationalist period was always the recovery of the 'traditional' woman – her various shapes continuously readapt the 'eternal' past to the needs of the contingent past." (10) "Woman" has been defined in the crossfire of colonial accounts and Indian male nationalist accounts as each tried to assert its role in protecting "womanhood," a concept that is almost synonymous with the nation itself.

In the South Asian immigrant community, the leaders of the community (predominantly male and wealthy) often invite "cultural/religious experts" from South Asia to come to the US to impart their expertise and to lend authenticity to transplanted cultural activities. In the case of India, these "experts" are mainly of a Hindu, Brahmanical tradition – that is, from the dominant cultural tradition. A consequence of such an essentialized definition of "home" is a homogenization of national culture and, in fact, the provision of immense support for the most vociferous and exclusionary South Asian organizations on issues of "national heritage." Within national histories of South Asia, movements for social change – such as the women's movement or the gay and lesbian movement – are largely unacknowledged.

In the wake of communal violence in South Asia, this is an especially dangerous phenomenon. The parallels one sees among the organizing strategies of Hindu fundamentalist organizations in India and those found among dominant Hindu and Indian cultural organizations and institutions in the US are not accidental. Tanika Sarkar describes the organizing strategies of the RSS (Rashtriya Swayamsevak Sangh, or National Volunteer Corps), an organization that has supported attempts by the VHP (Vishwa Hindu Parishad, or World Hindu Council) and the BJP (Bharatiya Janata Party, or Indian People's Party) to create a monolithic Hindu nation.[13] She notes, in particular, the effectiveness of the organizing principles of the RSS, which "calls itself a family." (31) Organizations such as the VHP, which also has counterparts in the United States, see themselves as the keepers of the national culture of a Hindu India. They have been responsible for a resurgence of religious fundamentalist forces and for the politicization of religion both in South Asia and in the immigrant communities in the US. In her essay "Compu-Devata: Electronic Bulletin Boards and Political Debates," which deals with fundamentalist discourse in electronic mail (e-mail), S. Sudha objects to the fact that groups in

the US (such as student organizations) are sponsored through "financial backing and guidance by VHP members who hold camps and training sessions." The goals of these groups include "re-interpretation of Indian history from a Hindu perspective, and presentation of current events from the viewpoint of the Hindu nationalists." (6) The means "to achieve these goals include study groups and a series of widely publicized VHP-organized conferences." (7) These organizations, because of their self-appointed roles as custodians of the national heritage, have particularly strong appeal in the immigrant communities of the US. Their presence is especially ominous as their activities are legitimized under the honorable banner of preserving one's culture for one's children. In the Indian, Hindu portion of the community, one can often see the connections between priests in temples, the leaders of the most wealthy Indian (predominantly Hindu) cultural organizations in the US, and the leaders of the Hindu fundamentalist parties in India. These links are well-illustrated by the example of a "respectable" man who is a part of the leadership in a Hindu temple in New York City and conducts marriages and religious festivals for the community. He is also part of the leadership of an umbrella Indian cultural organization in the US that has held benefit dinners to honor leaders of the Hindu fundamentalist party in India. Such a figure highlights the links between the guardians of national culture (as leaders of religious institutions are often seen to be), the financial strength of such guardians (as members of well-funded cultural organizations), and the political leadership (demonstrated by political leaders whom the guardians recognize and honor). What we see here is a clear collusion between money and cultural and political leadership intricately woven into the fabric of the community.

As the above discussion about the multiple "homes" of an immigrant demonstrates, women are in danger of being made invisible in all three "homes" known to them as immigrant women in the United States. Women who are silenced in the heterosexual and patriarchal home are often afraid to leave this home as they face nonrecognition outside it, in the other homes. If they are undocumented (when their spouses refuse to file a petition), they face invisibility in the US with regard to the state, and subsequently, within the immigrant community. At the same time, they also fear rejection and nonrecognition back in their home countries as well as in the extended family of the immigrant community, where a homogeneous and essentialized definition of national culture leads to dismissal or rationalization of abuse against women.

Undomesticating Violence Work

For immigrant women, work against domestic violence has to be seen as global – not only because domestic violence affects women everywhere but also because the parameters of *each* immigrant woman's experience of domestic violence spans the patriarchal home, the community, the host nation, and the nation of origin. Attention to the global parameters of an immigrant woman's experience helps us to contextualize the conventionally accepted spaces of private and public and to show that an unnuanced belief in social change through intervention in public spaces is an illusion; there are no such unambiguous spaces to be labelled "public" or "private." By tracking the private and the public spaces through this essay, I have shown the shifting grounds of both and thus in the process problematized common perceptions of the "public" and the "private."

As shown above, the immigration ideology of the US nation-state controls the composition of immigrant communities within its boundaries. It selectively secures the status of immigrant families and intervenes in their memories as they define their "original" heritage. The immigration policy of a nation-state is more than legal language and dry quota numbers. Behind these surface details lie a whole worldview and a comprehensive approach to global politics. However, mainstream domestic violence organizations often lack a rigorous understanding of the *system* of immigration. Their leadership has primarily consisted of US citizens, for most of whom the system of immigration, *on the surface*, appears not to have immediate relevance. In situations where mainstream organizations do know about immigration laws, they still lack an understanding of the *ideology* of immigration. Mohanty refers to this sort of lack in mainstream feminism in her assertion that

> (white) feminist movements in the West have rarely engaged questions of immigration and nationality... analytically these issues are the contemporary metropolitan counterpart of women's struggles against colonial occupation in the geographical third world. In effect, the construction of immigration and nationality laws, and thus of appropriate racialized, gendered citizenship, illustrates the continuity between relationships of colonization and white, masculinist, capitalist state rule ("Cartographies" 23).

Often, the mainstream feminist understanding of immigration, while liberal and well-meaning, is grounded in confused notions about ethnic pluralism and cultural sensitivity. Mainstream domestic violence agencies acknowledge the presence of "minorities" by providing their staffs with multicultural workshops. A new term that is increasingly being used to describe immigrants is "New Americans." The term is seen to compensate for the negative connotations that the word "immigrant" signifies in the current anti-immigrant climate.[14] The term "New Americans" is supposed to evoke images of immigrants going through temporary adjustments in a transitional process, after which they will be like other Americans. Such a view, needless to say, not only homogenizes an entire nation but also leaves out people, such as those that I have described in this essay, for whom legal status is well out of reach.

Immigrant women from the Third World in the United States see difference as more complicated than "temporary" variation in food, clothing, and language. For immigrant women, Cheryl Johnson-Odim's comment in another context is appropriate. She points out that women's progress

is not just a question of ... equal opportunity between men and women, but the creation of opportunity itself; not only the position of women in society, but the position of the societies in which Third World women find themselves (320).

Immigrant women working against domestic violence must necessarily traverse all the different spaces of "home." It is not enough to fight the abuse in the family home alone. It is also necessary to fight the violence inherent in the community's use of the figure of the woman to construct its identity, and in its summoning up of essentialized and elitist national culture. It is important to fight the way definitions of the immigrant family, the immigrant community, and immigrants' national heritage conveniently work toward creating a privatized US nation-state based on oppression. Domestic violence work, by its very focus on "home," is radical in that it challenges the foundations of hegemonic and well-entrenched systems. The multiple definitions of home, as set out above, signal the potential challenge for domestic violence work to be carried out through the most rigorous and broad investigation of an intervention in hegemonic social processes. Such an understanding enriches the work against domestic violence and opens up possibilities for building alliances. However, such a status is not usually granted to domestic violence work. Work around domestic violence is often itself *domesticated* as social service.

The battered women's movement's absorption of the full implications of globalizing and undomesticating domestic violence work is constrained in practice by the historical realities of domestic violence work in the US. The domestic violence movement in the US aspired to develop on the basis of feminist analysis and "most of the early shelters were begun by feminists or women who were able to work within a feminist framework" (NiCarthy et al. 13). However, as Diane Mitsch Bush observes,

the original emphasis of the battered women's movement on empowerment of women by shifting responsibility for violence from the woman to the perpetrator and locating his actions in a patriarchal power structure was lost as many shelters and their goals became institutionalized (Bush 587–608).

At this time, the movement has settled relatively comfortably into an institutional and professional pattern that predictably replicates itself across the United States. The subordination of feminist analysis to social service has distanced the battered women's movement from giving attention to the structural or systemic aspects of domestic violence.

However, I question whether it is sufficient for the battered women's movement to align itself simply again along a Western feminist framework, given that such a framework for understanding "home," "private," and "public" leaves certain fundamental assumptions unsatisfactorily analyzed or explored. To return to the example of MacKinnon, she discusses at length the problems with a private ideology that prohibits women from collectively sharing one another's experiences by projecting their private oppression into the public, and thus cuts off their ability to seek state support to end such oppression (193). MacKinnon has argued against the misguided notions of state inaction in the private realm. She finds inaction to be an acceptance by default of the male point of view, and she calls for active feminist jurisprudence among feminists in the United States. She believes that "[t]he law of equality, statutory and constitutional, ... provides a peculiar jurisprudential opportunity, a crack in the wall between law and society"(244). Equality, according to her, will require not state abdication, but state intervention, although according to the terms of feminist

jurisprudence (249). But MacKinnon's definition of the state remains reified, primarily
legislative, and therefore uncritically "public." She envisions intervention through the
eyes of a US citizen who is a (white) woman
and definitely part of the public.

Some Western feminists, such as Zillah
Eisenstein, have, however, contributed toward establishing the complexity of the situation for people of color. For example, in
Color of Gender, Eisenstein questions the abstract figure of the individual with universal
rights and rethinks democracy by replacing
this figure with the concrete body of the pregnant woman of color. Feminists like Aida
Hurtado have also pointed out that

> ...white feminist theory has yet to integrate
> the facts that for women of Color race, class,
> and gender subordination are experienced
> simultaneously and that their oppression is
> not only by members of their own group but
> by whites of both genders." (839)

Referring back to women's struggles in the
nineteenth century in the US, Hurtado points
out the difference between white suffragists
who were married to prominent white men
and black women activists who were "at birth
owned by white men" (841, emphasis in original). She reminds the reader that white ab-
olitionists did not want to give citizenship
rights to slaves (839). The analysis here is
made with great clarity with regard to race.
But, although her point is well-taken, Hurtado's comments remain confined within an
unanalyzed nation-state. She indicates the de-
sirability of obtaining citizenship but does
not question the exclusionary basis of citizenship itself. However, the figure of the immigrant is a reminder of the oppressive system
of exclusion by which some are more citizen-
like than others in a private nation that crafts
its identity opportunistically according to the
needs of its labor market. Citizenship in
nation-states is, by definition, a privatized
and selective concept; no matter how broadly
defined, oppressions remain inscribed in
its grain.

Hurtado asserts that white women have
focused on making the personal political because they have always had a space that is
personal or private. According to her,
"Women of Color have not had the benefit
of the economic conditions that underlie the
public/private distinction." The consciousness of women of color stems from an awareness that the public is *personally* political.
Thus, while white women struggle to project
private-sphere issues into the public, feminists of color focus instead on public issues.
Hurtado describes "Women of Color" as
more concerned with public issues such as
"affirmative action...prison reform...voter
registration...issues that cultivate an awareness of the distinction between public policy
and private choice" (850). Hurtado refers to
the state as a body that women of color struggle with frequently but, again, her argument
lacks a self-conscious and critical analysis of
the public/private split and the nation-state.

MacKinnon's exhortation to project the
private into the public and Hurtado's emphasis on the public being personal both rely
on the underlying assumption that spaces can
be identified as private or public in relationship to a nation and a state. As my discussion
has shown, there are no such clearly definable
spaces. Thus, working for change in commonly perceived public spaces (which feminists like Hurtado and MacKinnon advocate)
without examining the national bases of such
definitions is ultimately short-sighted and reformist. The oppression that undergirds the
so-called public (actually private) space is left
intact. As long as that happens, change
through the public space can only remain an
illusion.

It is useful at this point to consider another
conception of state put forth by Poulantzas,
while keeping in mind that, for him, class
relations remain primary and he pays little
attention to other parallel forms of oppression. In *State, Power, Socialism*, Nicos Poulantzas moves away from unambiguously
equating the state with repression and ideology because he finds that approach to be too
simplistic. Such an approach makes the power

of the state appear as only negative, overlooking the positive power of the state in creating and making reality. There is no room, in such a case, for understanding both the repressive and the enabling functions of the state. Instead, he suggests that we look at power relations as being primarily made up of social struggles, and he notes that these relations define the state itself; it cannot be understood as autonomous and separate from them (44–45). He describes the state as the *"material condensation* of a relationship of forces among classes and class fractions" (129). Class contradiction, he notes, is the very stuff of the state.

Like Hurtado and MacKinnon, Poulantzas does not adequately describe the public space. However, his description of the private does acknowledge the active role of the state in selectively creating such spaces. He explains:

> the individual-private is not an intrinsic obstacle to state activity, but a space which the modern State constructs in the process of traversing it.... For it is not the "external" space of the modern family which shuts itself off from the State, but rather the State which, at the very time that it sets itself up as the public space, traces and assigns the site of the family through shifting, mobile partitions." (72).

This description of state activity is more attentive to the full complexity of the relationship between private, public, and state than MacKinnon's view of the state as problematically inactive in the private realm because of the dictates of the privacy doctrine.

Instead of a pyramidal structure of state power, Poulantzas sees a network of intersecting powers. Poulantzas's definition of the state has the advantage of discerning state power to be a permeating network of power relations that is not limited only to the conventionally recognized state apparatus. This has immediate significance for resistance because it marks out the opportunities for intervention to be multiple. Thus, the ultimate goal of resistance is not occupying the summit of state power from where state laws can be remade, but rather the overturning of dominance in the network of power relations.

In this essay, I have explored and extended the scope of looking at "home," not to point to larger and better spaces than the family "home," but in order to enable us to think about spaces in a new way. Understanding the historical basis for spaces being declared private or public enables us to seize those opportunities for intervention that fundamentally overturn the opportunistic and oppressive bases of such declarations. Instead of being seduced or hindered by spaces perceived as public or private, we need to be vigilant against their miragelike quality. Only by thoroughly and fundamentally understanding their constructions can we hope to change them.

Organizing through and around Home

Organizations working for social change in the South Asian community continually wrestle with questions about their own legitimacy in regard to the multiple "homes" of the immigrant. At the same time, these very same organizations, which challenge the status quo in the multiple "homes," are also in a position to redefine "home." In this position, the organizations need to be self-reflexive about the new definitions they are setting out to establish. They need to ask themselves: who comprises the organizations that create these spaces that are sometimes called "home"; who is excluded from them; and what is the price of maintaining them.

For example, in Sakhi for South Asian Women, the organization with which I have been working, questions about whether Sakhi is located inside or outside the "community" have been important – especially so in the early years of its history.[15] Discussions within the initial group of women in Sakhi would point out that, as individuals, we were not significantly active in mainstream cultural organizations and practices and, as a consequence, Sakhi's position could be easily challenged by mainstream voices in the community. This group was comprised of Indian, Hindu, professional women. But the South Asian women who have contacted Sakhi for information and assistance come from very diverse backgrounds with regard to nationality, religion, class, and educational background. One of our highest priorities and most difficult tasks has been the expansion and diversification of the organization's base and leadership through the inclusion of just the sort of women who approach Sakhi for assistance.

As Sakhi's base began to grow, we actively began to reclaim and assert what has always been true – Sakhi is a community, a "home." However, I feel it is also our responsibility to continually redefine such a home lest it solidify into an oppressive and exclusionary space. Even as Sakhi strives to bring together South Asian women, questions of diversity, political beliefs and decision-making must remain ever open. It is crucial, though difficult, to balance two forces: being united by certain issues, and recognizing that unification is an evolving process and must not become a remaking of oppressive alliances. For example, issues of class or sexual orientation, as introduced into the organization by its expanding composition of women, make it increasingly necessary for women from various class backgrounds or with different sexual orientations to understand the need for different kinds of alliances. It is easy for those who share a certain upbringing and culture to exclude – if not deliberately then unconsciously – those who do not share their backgrounds. In spaces under siege, such as a women's organization or a workers' rights' organization, it is especially tempting to fall into the trap of making alliances that exclude on grounds other than political, as exclusion always makes those within feel safer together. Only through continual self-reflection can one avoid this trap.

My reason for analyzing "home" and uncovering the public/private mirage is so that we, as feminists, can understand and think about these concepts in new and enabling ways. However, even as I show that these definitions need to be fundamentally questioned, we continually succumb to commonly perceived and pernicious notions of home. For example, in my experience of working against domestic violence, we rarely step into the home of the heterosexual, patriarchal family itself. We find ourselves working around the home but never within it. Even in our most radical moments, it is a space we cannot enter, as it is sacred and private. When a woman is at home with her abuser (her spouse), we cannot approach her. Only when she leaves her marital home can we openly approach her. It is that sense of respect for that "sacred" space we call home, and the fear that it inspires, that continues to haunt us in our work.

By demonstrating that spaces hitherto imagined as being opposite to home can display characteristics typical of home and vice versa, this essay takes a step towards rethinking spaces, imagining action in new ways, and committing itself to a thorough investigation of common perceptions of private and public. I would like to conclude by returning to the domestic worker, whose anomalous position makes it possible for us to see spaces in a different way. By including domestic workers as part of the domestic realm, one comes to see the home as a workplace bearing the resonances of publicness rather than privateness. At the same time, we are forced to realize the limitations of public spaces within which a worker, who is undocumented and "unskilled," remains invisible. Interestingly enough, US labor laws do cover undocumented workers; these laws specify only that their subject is a "worker," and say nothing about his or her immigration status. However, for all practical purposes, the undocumented domestic worker remains invisible and fearful, unprotected by other US laws, demonstrating once again the ideological power of citizenship and nationhood regardless of particular pieces of legislation.

Sakhi's attention to domestic workers in the recent past has pushed perspectives on domestic violence and workers' rights in new directions. In domestic violence work, the figure of the abused worker liberates us from conventional mappings and helps us to conceptualize the home as a place not necessarily charged with privacy and familial ties. The isolated position of the domestic worker challenges common assumptions of a laborer surrounded by coworkers and employed in a populated place that one can enter with relative ease.

It is critical for Western feminists to be continually attentive to the ways in which they have taken for granted those spaces they define as "public" and "private." By being uncritical in this regard, most Western feminists circumscribe and domesticate the radical potential of their own work. A rethinking of these constructs would require that feminist theory and practice let go of comfortable and familiar ideas in order to set out in new directions. The "theoretical" component of activism must adhere to a *continual* process of overturning oppressive definitions. At the same time, it must remain watchful for opportunities to make strategic interventions within the "given" definitions themselves.

NOTES

1   Aida Hurtado, in her reference to Western feminism, claims that "[a]cademic production requires time and financial resources. . . . Not surprisingly, therefore, most contemporary published feminist theory in the United States has been written by white, educated women" (838). I would like the reader to keep this in mind as I make references to Western feminist theory. I realize that Western feminism has many strands and is not monolithic; however, there is a dominant mainstream feminism, and this is what I refer to in this essay. I also do not mean to say that the criticisms I make of Western feminisms cannot be made of feminisms elsewhere.

2   For a longer discussion, see Bhattacharjee, "The Habit of Ex-nomination: Nation, Woman and the Indian Immigrant Bourgeoisie."

3   I choose to discuss the *heterosexual* family because immigration law defines the family as such and also because that is the conventional perception of the home in which violence occurs. We need to remember that, in reality, domestic violence can take place in other relationships as well, such as those of lesbians or gays. I would also like to note that the family home I will be discussing in this essay is based on marriage specifically, because immigration laws, as we will see, are heavily invested in marital relationships.

4   If the man is a US citizen, he can sponsor the woman for conditional residency, which she can get within a short period. After that, she can come to reside with him in the US and, after two years, he can sponsor her for permanent status. If the man is a permanent resident (that is, not a citizen), she is not eligible for conditional residency but only for permanent residency after two years or more. In the meantime, she can either stay in South Asia for the waiting period or come to the US on a different temporary visa and wait until she is called for permanent residency. In the first case, the man often tries to abandon the marriage, and in the second case, her temporary visa makes her immigration status precarious during the waiting period.

5   These laws also apply to men whose legal status is sponsored by women. However, these cases are fewer and, even when they exist, instances of a woman using her power to abuse a man are rarer.

6   The Violence Against Women Act was passed in Congress subsequently, primarily because it was included in the Crime Bill, thus pitting women against people of color. It is not possible to describe, in this essay, the act or the debates around it, as it contains numerous provisions. I have focused on the provisions that significantly help immigrant women and that were heavily contested. It is fair to say

that although there have been senators who are against it, there are some who have responded favorably to the arguments presented by the lobbying groups.

7   For a longer discussion, see Bhattacharjee, "The Habit of Ex-nomination."

8   A similar tale of opportunistic "open door" periods alternating with periods of exclusion and mass deportations characterized the history of Mexican immigration.

9   US immigration history is well-documented in "The Evolution of U.S. Immigration Policy," in Family Violence Prevention Fund, et al., *Domestic Violence in Immigrant and Refugee Communities: Asserting the Rights of Battered Women*; and in "General Introduction: A Woman-Centered Perspective on Asian American History," in *Making Waves: An Anthology of Writings By and About Asian American Women*.

10 The Center for Immigrants Rights documented in March 1991 that the number of employment-based visas have "increased from 54,000 to 140,000 with new categories instituted for: 1) 'priority workers,' including individuals with 'extraordinary ability, outstanding professors and researchers and ... executives and managers'; 2) professionals holding advanced degrees or aliens of exceptional ability in the sciences, arts or business; 3) professionals with Bachelors degrees, skilled workers and other workers."

11 The likely candidates for residency or citizenship with the US can be seen in the details of the Immigration Reform and Control Act of 1986 and US criteria for testing the eligibility of naturalization candidates. Both are favorable toward heterosexual men with an established trail of the "proper" documents in the US.

12 In one workshop, a white male counselor remarked that he wished he could take his daughter out of school just like the South Asian father did because of his anxiety about the sexually open environment in the US. Here, the counselor saw his daughter as being part of a public that had certain rights defined by the

state which he could not interfere with, whereas the South Asian young woman was supposedly part of a space *outside* that public.

13 See Sarkar, 'Women's Agency within Authoritarian Communalism: The Rashtrasevika Samiti and Ramjanmabhoomi."

14 A detailed documentation of the current anti-immigrant climate in the US is beyond the scope of this essay. I am referring to the general political mood towards stopping or drastically reducing immigration, and legislative efforts or recommendations for regressive policies towards immigrants in the US.

15 Sakhi for South Asian Women was founded in 1989 by women of South Asian origin in New York City. It addresses issues of violence against women in the South Asian community through individual advocacy and community outreach and organizing. Sakhi is committed to the view that only through empowerment can women ultimately resist violence in their lives. Sakhi also believes that community education is integral to its work because it is only through the raising of awareness that fundamental change can occur.

REFERENCES

Alunan, Gina. 1993. "Abuses Against Asian Migrant Women: A Human Rights Issue." *Women on the Move: Proceedings of the Workshop on Human Rights Abuses Against Immigrant and Refugee Women*. Vienna: Family Violence Prevention Fund.

Anderson, Benedict. 1983. *Imagined Communities: Reflections on the Origin and Spread of Nationalism*. London: Verso.

Bhattacharjee, Anannya. 1992. "The Habit of Ex-nomination: Nation, Woman and the Indian Immigrant Bourgeoisie." *Public Culture*. Vol 5, no. 1 (Fall 1992: 19–44).

Bush, Diane Mitsch. 1992. "Women's Movements and State Policy Reform Aimed at Domestic Violence Against Women: A Comparison of the Consequences of Movement Mobilization in the U.S. and India." *Gender and Society* 6: 587–608.

Center for Immigrants Rights. 1991. " 'Give Me Your Professionals, Your Experts, Your Investors': The Immigration Act of 1990."

Eisenstein, Zillah R. 1994. *The Color of Gender*. Berkeley: University of California Press.

Family Violence Prevention Fund, Coalition for Immigration Rights and Services, Immigrant Women's Task Force, and National Immigration Project of the National Lawyer's Guild, Inc. 1991. *Domestic Violence in Immigrant and Refugee Communities: Asserting the Rights of Battered Women*.

Hiro, Dilip. 1991. *Black British, White British*. London: Grafton Books.

Hurtado, Aida. 1989. "Relating to Privilege: Seduction and Rejection in the Subordination of White Women and Women of Color." *Signs: Journal of Women in Culture and Society* 14: 833–55.

Johnson-Odim, Cheryl. 1991. "Common Themes, Different Contexts: Third World Women and Feminism." In *Third World Women and the Politics of Feminism*, eds. Chandra Talpade Mohanty, Ann Russo, and Lourdes Torres. Bloomington: Indiana University Press.

Kawaja, Kaleem. 1993. "Brotherhood Needed." *India Abroad*. (November). Letter to the editor.

MacKinnon, Catharine A. 1989. *Toward A Feminist Theory of the State*. Cambridge, Mass.: Harvard University Press.

Mazumdar, Sucheta. 1989a. "General Introduction: A Woman-Centered Perspective on Asian American History." In *Making Waves: An Anthology of Writings By and About Asian American Women*, ed. Asian Women United of California. Boston: Beacon Press.

———. 1989b. "Racist Responses to Racism: The Aryan Myth and South Asians in the United States." *South Asia Bulletin* 9, no. 1.

Mohanty, Chandra Talpade. 1991. "Cartographies of Struggle: Third World Women and the Politics of Feminism." In *Third World Women and the Politics of Feminism*, eds. Chandra Talpade Mohanty, Ann Russo, and Lourdes Torres. Bloomington: Indiana University Press.

NiCarthy, Ginny, Karen Merriam, and Sandra Coffman. 1984. *Talking it Out: A Guide to Groups for Abused Women*. Seattle: The Seal Press.

Poulantzas, Nicos. 1980. *State, Power, Socialism*. London: Verso.

Sangari, Kumkum, and Sangari Vaid. 1989. "Recasting Women: An Introduction." In *Recasting Women: Essays in Colonial History*. New Delhi: Kali for Women.

Sarkar, Tanika. 1993. "Women's Agency within Authoritarian Communalism: The Rashtrasevika Samiti and Ramjanmabhoomi." In *Hindus and Others*, ed. Gyanendra Pandey. New Delhi: Viking.

Sudha, S. 1993. "Compu-Devata: Electronic Bulletin Boards and Political Debates." *South Asian Magazine For Action and Reflection*. no. 2 (Summer): 4–10.

Section IV

Popular Culture

The central question in the two influential articles in this section has to do with the relation between the state and popular culture. The ability of dominant groups that control a state to gain legitimacy depends crucially on their success in molding national culture and shaping representations of the state. At a deeper level, "the state" itself cannot be conceived outside of representation or prior to it; "the state" is a phantasm that is made into a real, tangible object in people's lives through representation. In order to be effective, such representations of the state have to be popular. Thus, we can find in popular culture one of the most important sites for the mediation of class conflicts (and other conflicts as well). Such mediation is critical in enabling dominant groups who wish to establish their hegemony to incorporate the subaltern classes.

These two articles give an inkling of a vast conceptual arena that needs much further development with a wide range of critical tools. They exemplify contrasting, but not mutually exclusive, theoretical approaches: Hall's essay derives from a Gramscian perspective (see Section I), while the critical issues in Mbembe's essay are derived from Bakhtin and Bataille. Whereas Hall focuses on epochal transitions in the relations between the state and popular culture, Mbembe studies the role of the spectacular in the routine operation of power. Hall's essay concentrates on Britain from the eighteenth to twentieth centuries; Mbembe is mainly concerned with the postcolonial situation, largely drawing his examples from Cameroon. There are thus many differences in terms of subject and location between the two articles.

Hall's article takes up Gramsci's emphasis on the productive aspects of the state and on popular culture in order to explain how hegemony is established. Hall argues that neither "the state" nor "popular culture" have remained the same over time. He finds traditional approaches that emphasize their slow historical evolution to be unsatisfactory. Hall proposes instead an approach that pays attention to the drastic shifts in each of these spheres. In such a history, long periods of settlement in the relations between these spheres are interrupted by moments of radical transformation. The key question then becomes the Gramscian one of figuring out how the new configuration between the state and popular culture brought about a new hegemonic order.

Hall considers three moments in the transformation of state–culture relations since the eighteenth century. The first example is that of the role of law in the eighteenth-century British state. The British state in this period had a small and restricted domain of activity: it had no regular police or standing army and it was based on a very restrictive male franchise. In such a state, the law functioned "to hold an unequal and tumultuous society together" (p. 365). The nineteenth century saw the rise of an urban bourgeoisie, new reading publics through the rapid growth of literacy, and the rise of a "free" press. Such a press articulated the concerns of a civil society defined against the state. In this "civil society," the urban bourgeoisie, who had the vast amounts of capital necessary to own commercial presses, and the emerging middle class incorporated the popular classes into the new medium mainly as a reading and buying public. Such a definition of freedom, Hall importantly reminds us, "is not democratic but *commercial*" (p. 370). Finally, with the twentieth century, the decline of British industrial dominance accompanied by the rise of trade union organizing, and new technologies such as photography, cinema, cable and wireless telegraphy, the telephone, radio, and television profoundly disturbed existing configurations of power. In such a context, Hall demonstrates that the state assumed a greater role in broadcasting through the BBC, all the while ensuring that it stayed "independent" of direct control. The BBC exemplified the pedagogical function played by the state in that its programming aimed to "educate" the popular classes and shape their tastes and desires to consolidate the hegemonic bloc.

Hall focuses mainly on those "unsettled" periods when the relation between the state and popular culture registered momentous shifts, either because of changed class relations or technological revolutions. What Hall's article leaves out is a consideration of those "periods of settlement" in which hegemony works routinely, that is, when the control of state power by a dominant bloc is not thrown into crisis. These periods are precisely the object of Mbembe's analysis about the "banality" of power. He asks how the reproduction of the state is effected as a routine matter. Rather than emphasize the Weberian aspects of the routinization of power through institutional processes, Mbembe focuses on excess and spectacle as the armory of the creation and institutionalization of dominant meanings. In his view, the "obscene, vulgar, and the grotesque" become an essential means by which domination is secured and resisted. He rejects the position that the use of the grotesque and obscene to caricature the state by the popular classes demonstrates their resistance to power. He argues rather that the state itself deploys the obscene and vulgar as a critical means of legitimation.

SUGGESTED READINGS

Abu Lughod, Lila
  1993 Finding a Place for Islam: Egyptian Television Serials and the National Interest. Public Culture 5(3):493–513.
Anagnost, Ann
  1997 National Past-Times: Narrative, Representation, and Power in Modern China. Durham, NC: Duke University Press.
Bakhtin, Mikhail M.
  1984 Rabelais and His World. Hélène Iswolsky, trans. Bloomington: Indiana University Press.
Bataille, Georges
  1986 Erotism: Death and Sensuality. Mary Dalwood, trans. San Francisco, CA: City Lights Books.
Everard, Jerry
  2000 The Internet and the Boundaries of the Nation-State. London: Routledge.
Hall, Stuart
  1973 Encoding and Decoding in the Television Discourse. Birmingham: Centre for Cultural Studies, University of Birmingham.
  1990 The Rediscovery of "Ideology": Return of the Repressed in Media Studies. In Culture, Society, and the Media. Michael Gurevitch et al., eds. Pp. 56–90. London: Routledge.
Hayes, Joy Elizabeth
  1993 Early Mexican radio broadcasting: media imperialism, state paternalism, or Mexican nationalism? Studies in Latin American Popular Culture 12:31–55.
Mankekar, Purnima
  1993 Television Tales and a Woman's Rage . . . Public Culture 5(3):469–492.
Ozyurek, Esra
  2004 Miniaturizing Ataturk: privatization of state imagery and ideology in Turkey. American Ethnologist 31(3):374–391.
Roy, Srirupa
  2002 Moving pictures: the postcolonial state and visual representations of India. Contributions to Indian Sociology (New Series) 36(1/2):233–263.
Schlesinger P.
  1991 Media, State and Nation: Political Violence and Collective Identities. London: Sage
Siavashi, Sussan
  1997 Cultural policies and the Islamic Republic: cinema and book publication. International Journal of Middle East Studies 29(4):509–30.
Spitulnik, Debra
  1993 Anthropology and Mass Media. Annual Review of Anthropology 22:293–315.
Tauxe, Caroline S.
  1993 The Spirit of Christmas: Television and Commodity Hunger in a Brazilian Election. Public Culture 5(3):593–604.
Taylor, Diana
  1997 Disappearing Acts: Spectacles of Gender and Nationalism in Argentina's "Dirty War." Durham, NC: Duke University Press.
Wilk, Richard R.
  1994 Colonial Time and TV Time: Television and Temporality in Belize. Visual Anthropology Review, 10(1): 94–102.
Yang, Mayfair Mei-Hui
  1994 Film discussion groups in China: state discourse or a plebian public sphere? Visual Anthropology Review, 10(1):112–125.

15

Popular Culture and the State

Stuart Hall

... every state is ethical in as much as one of its most important functions is to raise the great mass of the population to a particular cultural and moral level; a level (or type) which corresponds to the needs of the productive forces for development, and hence to the interests of the ruling classes. The school as a positive educative function, and the courts as a repressive and negative educative function, are the most important state activities in this sense; but, in reality, a multitude of other so-called private initiatives and activities tend to the same end – initiatives and activities which form the apparatuses of the political and cultural hegemony of the ruling classes.

Antonio Gramsci[1]

The difficulties associated with the theory of the state Gramsci develops in *The Prison Notebooks* are well known. The sphere of the state is so expanded, reaching so deeply into the recesses of civil society, that, in some of his formulations, the distinction between the two spheres evaporates entirely. The most notorious instance is an earlier passage in *The Prison Notebooks* where Gramsci defines the

state as 'the entire complex of practical and theoretical activities with which the ruling class not only justifies its dominance but manages to win the active consent of those over whom it rules'.[2] For all that, the decisive significance of Gramsci's work, the respects in which it constitutes a veritable Copernican revolution in Marxist approaches to the state, consists in the stress it places on the positive, productive aspects of the state rather than seeing its functions as merely negative and repressive. Additionally, and for the first time, Gramsci placed questions of culture, and especially popular culture, at the very centre of the state's sphere of activity. The modern democratic state, Gramsci argued, forms and organises society not only in economic life but on a broad front. 'Its aim is always that of ... adapting the "civilization" and morality of the broadest popular masses to the necessities of the continuous development of the economic apparatus of production.'[3] The state, according to this view, is the site of a permanent struggle to conform – that is, to bring into line or harness – the whole complex of social relations, including those of civil society, to the imperatives of development

From T. Bennett, C. Mercer, and J. Woollacott (eds.), *Popular Culture and Social Relations*, pp. 22–49.

in a social formation. It constitutes one of the principal forces which mediates between cultural formations and class relations, drawing these into particular configurations and harnessing them to particular hegemonic strategies.

In this essay, I want to use this Gramscian perspective on the state to illuminate the respects in which, in different moments, the British state has always played a crucial role in conforming popular culture to the dominant culture. A detailed analysis of the history of state interventions in the sphere of popular culture cannot be attempted here. The most that can be offered is a series of 'snapshots' of different moments in the history of relations between the state and popular culture in Britain – the role of the law in mediating class cultural relations in the eighteenth century, the relations between the state and the 'free press' in the nineteenth century and the more recent development of broadcasting institutions in a relationship of 'relative autonomy' to the state. In adopting such a long historical conspectus on the relations between the state and popular culture, it is necessary to be clear that neither the state nor popular culture exhibits a continuous, uninterrupted identity throughout this long period of capitalist development. The constitution of both the state and popular culture themselves changes just as do the relations between them; indeed, their shifting constitution is, in part, an effect of the changing relations between them and of the ways in which such transformations have contributed to and been informed by more epochal shifts in the organisation of class-cultural relationships and the associated forms and mechanisms of ruling class hegemony.

I want, therefore, to argue very strongly that there is no simple historical evolution of popular culture from one period to another. The study of popular culture has been somewhat bedevilled by this descriptive approach, tracing the internal evolution of popular pastimes, from hunting wild boar to collecting garden gnomes, strung together by an evolutionary chain of 'things' slowly 'becoming'

other things. Against this approach, I want to insist that, historically, we must attend to breaks and discontinuities: the points where a whole set of patterns and relations is drastically reshaped or transformed. We must try to identify the periods of relative 'settlement' – when not only the inventories of popular culture, but the relations between popular and dominant cultures, remain relatively settled. Then, we need to identify the turning points, when relations are qualitatively restructured and transformed – the moments of transition.

This will produce a historical periodisation which goes beyond the merely descriptive to apprehend the shifts in cultural relations which punctuate the development of popular culture. These turning points occur, not when the internal inventory (contents) of popular culture changes, but when cultural relations between the popular and the dominant cultures shift. This point can be made more concrete by contrasting its implications with those of two conventional 'historical' accounts of changes in popular culture. The first – stressing evolution and continuity – compares traditional village football with the modern 'association rules' version of the game. The second acknowledges change, but sees this in terms of a change of content only: here cock-fighting, bull-baiting and other rural blood sports are substituted for by modern football – all considered 'the same' in their function, because they were all popular with the popular classes of their time. Now, of course, traditional village football bears some resemblance to twentieth-century cup and league soccer. But historically the similarities tell us very little: it is the distinctions that are telling. Pre-industrial football was highly irregular, unformalised, without standard rules (the ball could be carried, thrown, snatched as well as kicked, the only prohibition being that it could not be given – i.e. in a polite manner – to a 'less beleaguered friend'!). It sometimes involved hundreds of participants, on unmarked fields or through the town streets, each game being governed by local traditions, and not infrequently, as

Malcolmson notes, ending in the reading of the Riot Act.[4] By contrast, the modern game is highly regulated and systematised, administered centrally and organised according to universally observed and refereed rules. Its high points are national and international rather than parochial – though ties of locality remain strong. It has been redesigned for spectatorship rather than participation, the 'tumult' occurring on the terraces rather than on the field of play.

These contrasts bring out qualitative differences: between a rural society, regulated by custom, local tradition and the particularism of small, face-to-face communities, and an urban-centralised society governed by universally applied rules and a legal and rational mode of regulation. Nor was there any smooth evolution from one to the other. The traditional game became the object of a massive assault by the governing classes and authorities – part of a general attack on popular recreations in order to moralise the poorer classes and make them more regular and industrious in their habits. The separation of the game from local community life and space flowed from this destruction of older patterns of life and their thorough reorganization under new moral and social auspices in the second half of the nineteenth century: 'let them assemble in the Siddals or some such place, so as not to interfere with the avocation of the industrious part of the community', one Derby critic wrote in 1832.[5]

As to the second example: this traces an evolution from, say, cock-fighting (popular in eighteenth century) to football (popular in twentieth century). But this only makes sense if the activity is isolated from the cultural meanings and social relations in which it is embedded. The example changes at once if we look, instead, at shifts between the whole complex of social relations, not just the activity itself:

cock-fighting	football
gentry	bourgeoisie
rural labourers	industrial workers

village	city
parish	suburb
custom	law
common rights	property rights
local sanctions	public order

Here, we are looking at the 'evolution' of popular culture across a set of major historical transformations: a shift, not just from one pastime to another, but between historical epochs. Cock-fighting was made illegal, not only because it was frowned on by the 'polite' (it always was), but because some of the 'polite' acquired the means to impose habits and standards of a more urban character on rustic life (implying changes in law and state); and because politeness had assumed a new, sober and evangelical connotation (implying changes in religious and moral attitude).

These shifts in cultural practice and ideology reflected deep changes in class relations. Blood sports, for all their sanguinary nature, were indulged in by some sections of both the major agrarian classes of society (labouring poor and the bucolic country-gentry: no 'gentle' gentry *women* cock-fighters are recorded), within the complex tissue of customary understandings – the paternalist/plebeian relations – which framed so many of the relations between the rural classes. Let us not romanticise this 'organic' relationship. Because customary standards were set and power over their practice dispensed locally, a landlord and his tenant could meet individually at a 'cocking' without either presuming for a moment that he could really bridge the immense vertical distances separating the landed and the labouring classes. A very different web of relations and understandings mediates the classes involved in modern football. Modern soccer is no longer local in this sense – even where a strong sense of local loyalty persists. It is 'realised' as much through the mass spectatorship of the modern media as it is in direct participation. In its immediate culture of support, the defining presence is that of the urban-industrial classes (and their professional fellow-travellers). The dominant classes appear to be largely absent – though they are often present in the financing, administration and chairmanship of the game.

These two activities are only 'the same' in some obvious, meaningless and general way. Both were embedded in and helped to sustain a set of class-cultural relations; but each mediated and sustained a different set. Each was 'popular'; but 'popularity' was differently articulated in each case. The paternalism-deference of the first was part of a culture which *bound* and *separated* the fundamental classes of eighteenth-century agrarian capitalist society. The second is constructed through the *separation out* of the fundamental classes of advanced industrial capitalism and their *recombination* as a 'mass'. In this example, then, what matter, for the history of popular culture, in its full sense, are breaks, discontinuities, transformations, asymmetry: the sharply differing articulations of cultural space, in the two periods.

Like 'popular culture', there is no entity called 'the state' which unfolds across the ages while remaining the same. The field of action of the state has altered almost beyond recognition over the last three centuries. The eighteenth-century state had no regular police, no standing army, and was based on a highly restrictive male franchise. The nineteenth-century state owned no industries, supervised no universal system of education, was not responsible for national economic policy or a network of welfare provisions. There is no steady, unbroken line of development from 'small beginnings' to interventionist monolith. Under the mercantilist system, which flourished from the mid-sixteenth to the mid-eighteenth century, during which the early commercial expansion of Britain occurred, the state played a direct role in the economy, regulating commerce, establishing monopolies under charter and securing favourable terms of trade. *Laissez-faire* political economy, which displaced mercantilism as economic doctrine, and achieved its zenith in the nineteenth century, when Britain became 'the workshop of the world', was founded on diametrically opposite principles: the market flourished best when left to its own devices, without the interference of the state.

Changes in the political composition of the state are almost as dramatic. In the eighteenth century, the great mass of the popular classes had no vote of any kind. The nineteenth century was dominated by the struggles of the popular classes to extend the franchise – a process long delayed by a series of 'last-ditch' resistances by the powerful. Full adult suffrage was not completed until the twentieth century (1928) – the resistance against female suffrage being one of the last (and most squalid) episodes of the whole struggle.

The twentieth century, it is often argued, has seen the growth of the all-encompassing state, from the cradle to the grave. Yet its role cannot be understood unless it is separated out from what it is not. The state is both *of* and *over* society. It arises from society; but it also reflects, in its operations, the society over which it exercises authority and rule. It is both part of society, and yet separate from it. Hence, there is always a line between 'public' matters (which the state claims a legitimate right to interfere in) and 'private' spheres (which belong to the voluntary arrangements between individuals, separate from state regulation). Exactly where this boundary line falls is sometimes difficult to establish. It certainly changes from one period to another, or one society to another. In the nineteenth century, the domestic privacy of the 'home' was an Englishman's (private) castle; *his* wife was so deeply ensnared in the 'private' that she could not own property, vote or stand for public political office. In the twentieth century, the family has progressively become the site of extended state intervention, and has thus been drawn increasingly into the 'public' sphere. Under *laissez-faire* capitalism, the economy, education and the press were privately owned, organised and managed: they belonged to 'civil society'. Today, under advanced capitalism, the economy is largely private, though there is a significant 'public' or state sector; education is substantially 'public' – though the 'public schools' are still private! And the press is privately owned (could it be 'free' otherwise?).

We can see here how the *theoretical* problem which Gramsci's work raises regarding the relations between the state and civil society is, at the same time, a historical problem. The shifting boundary line between state and civil society is one whose very shifts tell us a great deal about the changing character of the state. It is a significant moment, for example, when culture ceases to be the privilege and prerogative of the cultivation of *private* individuals and begins to be a matter for which the state takes public responsibility. In this light, it is worth recalling that Gramsci's expanded definition of the state was intended to apply specifically to the modern democratic state and the expanded range of functions it abrogated for itself, reaching so deeply into civil society as to unsettle the confident nineteenth-century distinction between state and civil society, rather than as a theory of state forms in general. This is not to suggest that the development of state forms can be viewed as one of the incessant, step-by-step encroachments on the terrain of civil society. The development of the state's role in relation to popular culture from the eighteenth to the twentieth century bears witness not merely to a quantitative increase in the state's role in cultural regulation but also to a series of qualitative transformations in state–culture relations.

Law, Class and Culture: An Eighteenth-Century Example

The class which primarily benefited from the Hanoverian settlement of 1688 was the 'landed interest'. This was composed of men of substantial landed property, whether aristocrat or gentry, who gradually established themselves as a 'superbly successful and self-confident capitalist class'.[6] They secured their annual incomes by rents and agricultural improvements, expanded their estates by judicious marriage settlements and enclosures; ventured into trade and commerce for the growing markets at home and abroad; and began to develop domestic and small-scale manufacturing. Land, trade, commerce and the market created an immense belt of agrarian capitalist wealth, property and power: the material basis of a class 'profoundly capitalist in style of thought ... zestfully acquisitive and meticulous in their attention to account-ancy'[7] – i.e. the first 'bourgeois culture' the world had ever seen.

The eighteenth-century state was, in the view of many historians, a parasitic formation: small, compact, reflecting the cohesion of and vertical ties between the small élite who constituted the 'political nation'. As Namier has shown, it was divided by factional rivalry, but solidified through nepotism, patronage, favour, advancement, the purchase of office, and the free play of bribery and corruption.[8] The independent country-genry kept themselves at home. The grandees and their networks of clients and hangers-on more strenuously involved themselves in manipulating the state to their advantage, exploiting the narrow factionalism of eighteenth-century party politics. The state was therefore homogeneous, but weak. Large tracts of social life remained largely outside its effective control. State power had devolved to the local bastions of the gentry who ruled, regulated and judged in their country seats and parishes. Central state control over a tumultuous and riotous labouring population was fitful and uncertain. Sometimes power was maintained through a complicated balancing act of negotiation between the different factions; sometimes by draconian measures, excursions into the ungovernable areas and bouts of judicial terror, supplemented by the Riot Act, the threat of militia and the gallows. Yet this unique and parasitic formation – what Cobbett called 'Old Corruption' – presided over an astonishing growth in trade, the amassing of great estates and fortunes; it successfully pursued an expansionist policy abroad and, as Anderson notes, secured for the propertied at home an astonishing social stability, without the aid of either a standing army or a regular police.[9] How was this achieved? Partly through the law – 'the strongest link of the body politic' in the eighteenth century.

Was the law, then, simply a branch of the eighteenth-century state? Yes and no. Yes, because the 'rule of law' was already established. Courts and judges derived authority from state and crown. The state enforced the 'due legal process'. No, because the law was so much at the disposal of private individuals, and so thoroughly imprinted with the class relations of eighteenth-century civil society.

Seen from above, the law was a mighty, terrible engine. It was also haphazard, irregular and uncodified: a jumble of ancient common law and hastily enacted statute. It was arbitrary, with no relation between offence and sentence, and severe. The principal punishment for serious offences was death by public hanging. Judges often exercised their wide powers of discretion – but, according to Hay, in an unpredictable manner.[10] The exercise of legal power was under the practical monopoly of the leading social classes. They used it to defend and advance their rights and properties and to enhance their authority. During and after the English Revolution, the independent gentry had used the principles of the rights of free-born Englishmen, guaranteed under law, to advance their cause against crown and court. By the 'free-born' they meant themselves – since the term did not include women, domestics or the mass of the labouring poor. To them, the 'rule of law' meant the maintenance of public order, the protection of property and the preservation of liberty – their order, property, liberties. These had to be secured through the procedure and constraints of the law, and this had contradictory consequences. On the one hand, rule 'by law' further enhanced their authority. They identified themselves with it, thereby appropriating its majesty. The awe aroused in the populace by the pomp and ceremony of the law became vested in them. They used the courts to preach secular sermons on the virtues of established authority, the need for respect and the necessity for obedience. Public trials and strict procedure, at least in the higher courts, were offered as formal proof that all men were equal before the law, despite its lack of observance in prac-

tice. On the other hand, having affirmed the rule of law as the free-born Englishman's rightful inheritance, it became increasingly difficult to refuse to extend it to poor and powerless Englishmen. And though in practice the law rarely worked in the latter's favour, they were free to put themselves 'at law', to claim justice and seek redress of grievance. And they sometimes were rewarded – not often enough ever to lose sight of the class nature of the justice they received, but often enough not to regard the 'rule of law' as an empty sham. So, as Thompson has shown in convincing detail, the law came to provide a framework in which the liberties of the landed classes and the injustices against the poor were negotiated, struggled over and fought through.[11]

The exercise of justice thus presents us with a picture of the massive social power of the dominant classes – but legalised power: power that had acquired a measure of legitimacy and consent because it was articulated through the law – but also for that very reason, subject to its constraints. The law was therefore never simply and exclusively an instrument of ruling-class oppression. A plebeian version of the 'rule of law' gradually took root in popular attitudes and culture, contesting more patrician interpretations. Not only were social struggles framed by overlapping conceptions of law and justice. Legal language and precedent could be expropriated into and reworked as part of popular conceptions of 'grievance and justice'. If the popular classes were bound to power and property, through law, they could also use it to bring pressure to bear against property and power. Paradoxically, though, the very fact that conflicts were played out within the framework of law helped to hold an unequal and tumultuous society together:

Those in authority knew that protests about specific grievances were intended to provoke a remedial response, and not to challenge authority *per se*. Such an assumption was only possible as long as the aggrieved had some faith in authority's willingness to be bound by the law and the ideals it was supposed to embody. Negotiation, of course, was not carried on between equals.[12]

The delicate balances on which this negotiation depended may be observed in the judicious mixture of legal and illegal means which the popular classes used to bend the rule of law in their favour. When the price of bread rose or the supply dropped away, the labouring poor would often seek redress from a magistrate, requiring him to 'fix a fair price'. If he did not, riot and tumult frequently followed. The century was constantly interrupted by these bread riots by the hard-pressed poor who, when 'negotiation with the law' failed, took to 'bargaining by riot'.[13] Yet these riotous occasions were subject to a high degree of popular discipline. Corn sacks were ripped open, the grain scattered, butter, cheese and bacon sold at a 'fair price' – the crowd returning the money to the miller. Bread riots were highly ceremonial and disciplined occasions. Processions were decorated with flags, emblems, ribbons and favours; the crowd, led by a woman ringing a bell, or by horns and drums; the loaves draped in black crepe or smeared with blood. This was the 'theatre' of popular justice.

These cultural practices secreted alternative moral ideas and social conceptions. Rural society was still in considerable part regulated by custom, tradition and unwritten precedent. But as property, trade and the free market in goods and labour began to impress their patterns on social life, transforming rural England into a fully-fledged agrarian capitalism, the society was gradually tutored, bludgeoned, driven and enticed along a road away from 'custom' and towards the 'law' of property and the market forces. The law became one of the principal instruments of this transformation – entailing a shift from economic self-sufficiency to marketing for profit, from custom to law, from the 'organic compulsions of the manor and guild to the atomized compulsions of the free labour market ... a comprehensive conflict and redefinition

at every level, as organic and magical views of society gave way before natural law, and as the acquisitive ethic encroached upon an authoritarian moral economy'.[14] One of the principal things at stake in this historic transformation was precisely the customs, practices and ideas – the culture – of the 'common people'.

Custom informed real economic practice: for example, the decision as to what was a 'fair price'. But it was also inscribed in ideology and belief: the notion that there could be something like a fair price; that, in times of scarcity, there was a *moral limit* to the miller's or the merchant's right to profit at the expense of the poor; the belief that there was, as Thompson calls it, a 'moral economy', larger and more compulsive than the pure laws of the market.[15] That whole customary culture had to be actively dismantled, and refashioned into one based on the 'morality' of the free market. The law was one means by which a culture of custom and paternalism was reshaped into a culture of law, property and the free market. This transformation required that the older plebeian culture be broken up and set aside, so that new patterns, attitudes and habits could be formed in its place. It involved the destruction of one culture, and the 'reformation' of society, the re-education of the people, into 'a new type of civilization': the civilization of a fully-developed agrarian capitalism. The fracturing of this older culture and the construction of the habits of regular 'free labour', of private property and the laws of political economy among the popular classes was conducted, in part, through the mediation of the law and the state.

This is, of course, no more than a 'snapshot' of the relations between the law and popular culture in the eighteenth century. None the less, we can see how the state, through the law, intervened in the relations between the classes and the cultures. It helped to define and fix relations of power, authority and consent between the dominant (i.e. landed) and the dominated (i.e. labouring) classes. It also mediated the cultures (paternalist/deferential; plebeian and patrician; the authoritative-legal conceptions of 'rights' and 'justice' versus popular conceptions). It played an educative/ideological as well as a repressive/coercive role. It transformed practices – legal (from customary regulation to the formal law) and moral ones (setting a 'fair' price; 'bargaining' by riot), as well as economic. It was part of a major historic transformation. It was also an instrument through which society was 'conformed' to certain historical imperatives – the formation of a fully-formed bourgeois society; the shift from a 'natural' to a 'market' economy; the transition into agrarian capitalism. It transformed cultural habits, ideas and practices – breaking and reorganizing popular customs. It nevertheless sustained a particular type of authority (the 'rule of law'), which mediated and contained social struggles and secured a particular type of legitimacy and consent to the authority of a particular social bloc. The 'cultures' of the dominant and the popular classes were a critical site in this whole process.

The Liberties of the Press and the Voice of the People

In this second case study, we shift our attention from the law to a cultural apparatus in the more direct sense: the press. We consider the role of the state in the formation of a national popular press. Through the organs of the press, the different classes of society are given a voice. Through these organs, the people and 'popular opinion' are represented to the state. The organs of public opinion therefore institutionalise a particular set of social and cultural relations. This configuration is underpinned by an ideological model – the model of the 'free press'. It is crucial for this model that, unlike the law (which derives from the state), the press belongs to the terrain, not of the state, but of civil society. In democratic class societies, the whole *raison d'être* of the 'free press' is that it is *not* directed by, owned by, or bound to the

state. It operates freely and voluntarily. Its only limits are the laws of libel and commercial viability. Indeed, it is *because* the press is 'free' in the market sense that it is said to be the bulwark of 'the people' against the power of the state, the defender of English liberties and the independent voice of the nation. In the nineteenth century this was a *new* cultural model, a new configuration of cultural power. It organised the elements in the state –culture–class equation into a new 'equilibrium of authority and consent' on the basis of a new articulation of the relations between state and civil society.

The reading public, the market and the Fourth Estate

The rise of an independent 'public opinion', literary production for the market and a free press were all associated with the growth of the urban bourgeoisie. The expansion of reading in the second half of the eighteenth century was very rapid. The new reading public included self-taught and pious working people, small shopkeepers, skilled journeymen, independent tradesmen, the artisan classes and clerical workers. Women of all classes constituted a significant element in this new reading public. 'General literature now pervades the nation through all its ranks', Dr Johnson observed in 1779.[16] But it was the expansion of those ranks associated with commerce and manufacture and their domestic counterpart in the home – now, increasingly for this class, separated from the masculine world of work – that 'altered the centre of gravity of the reading public sufficiently to place the middle class as a whole in a dominating position for the first time'.[17]

Not yet a politically cohesive force, the middle classes nevertheless discovered, through this expanded 'public sphere' in civil society, a significant 'voice', a source of cultural power and a means of self-definition as a class. New forms and practices – the novel, the great literary periodicals, the newspapers, writing and publishing for profit, reviewing – were created *for* this new public, *about* this new public: forming their experience, giving expression to their cultural ideas and aspirations. The famous periodicals of the time – the *Tatler*, the *Spectator*, the *Gentleman's Magazine* – helped to mould the social taste and manners of men in the image of the bourgeois 'gentleman'.

Conduct books, pamphlets of religious guidance, the polite journals and the novel served, in the same way, to help create a 'private' culture and to define a domestic ideal for the bourgeoisie as a whole, and especially for women – guardians of the hearth and homes of 'fit and proper' (male) persons. The world of the new middle ranks acquired a very particular cultural definition through the newly created institutions of voluntary association (civil society). It was divided and punctuated into the great 'separate spheres' of public and private, around which urban bourgeois culture cohered. The organs of the press were paradigm instances of these new social institutions: developed outside the state, in the voluntary world of civil society, helping to constitute the classes whom they addressed, as a public cultural force. The fortunes of this rising class depended on the application of keen *laissez-faire* principles and they extended this new political economy to the world of publishing – writing for profit rather than patronage; printing and selling books like other commodities in the marketplace; catering for the private tastes of an expanded buying and reading public; and providing a channel for the classified commercial advertiser to address his clientele.

One great, new commercial publishing form was the newspaper. The state licensing system for newspapers was abolished in 1695. Thereafter, newspapers of all types, kinds and sizes expanded phenomenally. By the 1770s, there were nine London daily papers. In 1746, 2,500 copies of each issue of the *London Daily Post* were printed. The market was also flooded by an army of unstamped dailies and thrice-weeklies, often circulating at half price. Distribution within the city was supported by a 'floating and semi-destitute population of hawkers'.[18] By 1790, 4,650 copies of London papers were passing by way of the Post Office into the country. A similar distribution system developed for the provincial papers.

This rapidly expanding cultural industry constituted the 'reading public' as a *cultural market* for the first time. It introduced the standards of sales and popularity, piracy and 'scribbling', alongside the high standards of literary canon and judgement, into culture. And it helped to fashion the independent middle classes as a political, social and cultural force.

By modern standards, this was a highly regulated 'independence', for in the early stages the state was still heavily involved. For many years, the Secretaries of State acted as the principal retailers of London newspapers. In the 1760s, the extension of MPs' privilege to send franked post through the mail was used to distribute newspapers. In one week in June 1789, 63,177 copies were distributed in this way. In 1712, the first of a series of stamp duties was introduced, designed as a means of policing the press, forcing up the price of newspapers. Newspaper proprietors undertook extraordinary dodges to circumvent stamp duties – registering as pamphlets, or switching to thrice-weekly publication. Alongside the 'stamped' press arose a mass of smaller illegal papers. But in the 1740s this 'unstamped press' was undermined by a legal assault on the hawkers, their only means of distribution, and later on the publishers themselves.

At the same time, the political establishment, curbing the press with one hand, through the state, were active, as private individuals, buying themselves into positions of influence with the other. In the earlier period, the Prime Minister, Walpole, bought up the anti-government *London Journal*, turning it into a vehicle of government propaganda, set up the *Free Briton* and the *Daily Courant*, largely written by government employees, and later, the *Daily Gazeteer* [sic]. He spent over £50,000 of Treasury funds on propaganda – largely in the London newspapers.

Yet, as the whole economy was gradually transformed by the universal application of the law of free-market profit-maximizing political economy, the independence of the press came to be even more highly prized than its dependability as a kept instrument. This independence was identified with a system whereby opinions circulated, like other commodities, in the market place outside the direct control and supervision of the state.

Indeed, in the heroic version of 'Progress', which dominates popular historical writing to this day, the formation of the *middle classes* as the leading social element in society, the creation of the *free market* as the leading principle of commercial organisation, and the growth of an *independent press* as a 'Fourth Estate' separate from the state, are the essential ingredients of a heroic narrative. This story explains how state restrictions were set aside and the middle classes, basing themselves on the free market, founded a national press; and how only in this way were the liberties of the English people maintained. In fact, between the 1790s and 1830s, and again during Chartism, the ascendancy of this cultural model was powerfully challenged by *another* kind of press, articulating a *different* culture, the voice of a *different* class. This was the press that flourished as part of the radical artisan culture of the 1790s and emerged alongside the institutions of the first industrial working class in the years up to the mid-nineteenth century: the radical press, the 'unstamped', the 'poor men's guardians'. Like the plebeian culture of the eighteenth century, this alternative set of popular institutions had to be actively dismantled before 'freedom' of a quite different kind could be left to organise the opinions of 'the people'.

The challenge: the radical press and popular culture

The existence of a wide and highly 'literate' culture among the popular classes in this period has been greatly underestimated. The radicalising of political class-consciousness in the period of industrial unrest, political agitation and revolutionary wars helped actively to expand and develop that culture. Paine's *Rights of Man* sold 50,000 copies within a few weeks in 1791. Cobbett's *Address to Journeymen and Labourers* sold 200,000 in 1826, his *Political Register* sold up to 44,000 copies at twopence weekly. Wooler's *Black Dwarf* sold 12,000 in 1820 when the circulation of *The Times* was no more than 7,000.

This radical working-class press was labelled by the authorities and established classes as a subversive force. Edmund Burke called it 'the grand instrument of the subversion of morals, religion and human society itself'.[19] Lord Ellenborough, justifying the new Stamp Act of 1819, stated quite clearly that 'it was not against the respectable press that this Bill was directed, but against the pauper press'.[20] In the turbulent period between the 1790s and the Reform Act of 1832, this 'pauper press' was subject to extensive harassment and intimidation. In 1799, all printing presses were required to be registered. The press was severely curtailed in the period of the Six Acts, and again by the 'Gagging Bills' of 1819–20, which extended the scope of the stamp duty and strengthened the seditious libel law. Despite this attack, Doherty's *Voice of the People* and *The Pioneer*, Carlile's *Gauntlet* and Hetherington's *Poor Man's Guardian* all ran to several thousand readers, the first two to above 10,000.[21] The leaders of London radicalism in the 1790s were constantly before the courts on charges of seditious libel in this period. In fact, as Thompson has remarked (and quite contrary to the myth):

> There is perhaps no country in the world in which the contest for the rights of the free press was so sharp, so emphatically victorious, and so peculiarly identified with the cause of the artisans and labourers. If Peterloo established (by a paradox of feeling) the right of public demonstration, the rights of a 'free press' were won in a campaign extending over fifteen or more years, which has no

comparison for its pig-headedness, bloody-minded and indomitable audacity.[22]

This popular agitation resulted in the repeal of the 'taxes on knowledge' – without which no free press could exist. The duty on pamphlets was abolished in 1833, on advertising in 1853. The stamp duty was reduced from 4d. to 1d. in 1836, and abolished in 1855. This victory for 'freedom of opinion' was one in which the radical popular press had been greatly instrumental. Yet it was not this, but the commercial bourgeois press that inherited its fruits. How did this occur?

Synthesis, transformation, incorporation

In fact, a new cultural model, and a new set of class-cultural relationships prevailed. In this formation, 'freedom' was redefined. It no longer meant 'free from the tyranny of established authority'. Instead, it came to mean that opinion was regulated *exclusively* by the laws of the market, free competition, private ownership and profitability. Such a market is *formally* 'free', in the sense that the state or the law prohibits no one from owning or publishing a newspaper and expressing views and opinions – provided they have the capital. The state 'interferes' with this freedom only externally and negatively – by insisting that the laws of libel, obscenity, competition and fair trading, and so on, are not infringed. Of course, this type of formal 'freedom' also has its own very real positive limits. Gigantic accumulations of capital are required to own, publish, distribute, capitalise and maintain a modern newspaper. The vast majority of people are, basically, free only *to consume* the opinions which others provide.

In fact, the new commercial press which expanded in the wake of the abolition of the 'taxes on knowledge' *did* increasingly depend on the popular classes: but as a reading and buying public, not as a popular cause which it

championed. So the 'free market' did build the popular classes into the newspaper business, but only as a necessary economic support. At the same time and by the same process, it *incorporated* them in a *subordinate* position, politically, culturally and socially within a set of relationships institutionalised by the principles of capital investment and free-market competition. Within this class-cultural relationship, 'freedom' acquired a special but restricted meaning: it meant freedom from state intervention, freedom to compete and survive: freedom for the laws of capital accumulation, private appropriation and market competition to operate unhindered. It established no positive *collective* right to express opinions and had little radical-popular content. This definition of freedom is not democratic but *commercial*.

This type of relationship gradually came to dominate the press from the mid-nineteenth century onwards. It contained the seeds of a cultural pattern which became dominant in the modern relations between the state, the classes and public opinion. It hastened the separation of the society into two, distinct and simplified 'publics': the small, 'élite' public, important not because of numbers but because of the strategic nature of its power and influence (attractive, for this reason to advertisers), and the 'mass public' who compensate for their lack of influence by their sheer numerical strength.

This pattern was then reproduced as a cultural distinction – between the 'quality' and the 'popular' press. The latter first began to discover its characteristic cultural form – or formula – in this period. This formula was, in essence, a cultural solution to the problem of the power, rights and opinions of the popular classes – that is, the problem of *democracy*. The problem was essentially this: how to contain the popular classes within the orbit and authority of the dominant culture, while allowing them the formal right to express opinions. To do this, a press was created that *reflected* popular interests, tastes, preoccupations, concerns, levels of education (sufficient, that is, to win popular identification and consent); but which *did not become* an authentic 'voice' of the popular interest, which might then be tempted to voice its opinions independently, and thus forge a unity as a social and political force (as the Chartist press had attempted to do). The new 'popular' press was a press *about* and *bought by* but not *produced by*, or *committed to the cause of*, the popular classes. The formula for this type of cultural incorporation was generated out of a synthesis between two earlier models: the Sunday press and the popular miscellanies.

The 'Sundays' had often had larger circulations than the daily press, with a wider social readership. They were fully commercial enterprises, reflecting the largely non-political concerns of urban popular culture, giving prominence to crime and violence, sex and scandal, sensation and titbits. As the century advanced, this formula provided the model for the new commercial 'popular press'. For the Sunday formula represented a synthesis between the old, non-political tradition of popular chap-book, criminal confession, life-of-the-highwayman or 'dying speech', and the more recent political radicalism of the Unstamped and Chartist press: 'It was an important half-way stage in the development of the modern popular press; but the commercial pressures inherent in its appeal to a mass audience resulted, too, in a significant dilution and manipulation of the many traditions of the earlier radical press.'[23]

This formula *synthesised* traditional and radical elements: the 'plain-spoken bluntness' of the radical tradition was diluted into a style ('The Daily... is not afraid to call a spade a bloody shovel...') and the 'vigour' of traditional popular culture appeared as a dispersed sensationalism ('Read all about it'!). These elements were, however, synthesised on the ground of capitalist commercial principle and organization. John Cleave's highly successful *Weekly Police Gazette*, for example, combined popular radicalism and police court cases. *Lloyds*, with a very similar mix, was the first to sell a million copies.

In summary, then, we can see how, in the transition of the press from state to market regulation, a new (and highly contradictory) configuration of class and cultural elements emerged. This formation was very different from that which prevailed a century before. It was achieved through a new cultural institution – the 'free' commercial press (i.e. the *withdrawal* of the state from the sphere of competition). This, in turn, institutionalised a new set of class-cultural relationships (that is, gave them a 'permanent' form, regularised, stabilised, and fixed them in a certain pattern). The heart of this relationship was the constitution of the popular classes as an economically essential but culturally and ideologically dependent and subordinate element. They were bound to, or incorporated into, the ascendancy of the dominant classes, through a *new form*: the so-called 'popular press' formula. This formula transformed and reworked old elements (radical and traditional) into a new synthesis. This is the origin and basis of the modern discourses of the popular press and popular commercial journalism. Through the operation of these discourses, the press was subdivided into two unequal parts: the 'quality' and the 'popular', each carrying a different cultural value or index. 'Quality' is serious; 'popular' is entertaining but trivial. The whole terrain of cultural practices and relationships in contemporary British society is *mapped into* these mutually exclusive, polarized binary opposites. What is 'popular' cannot be 'serious'. What is 'quality' must be powerful. What is entertaining cannot be 'quality', and so on. The readers are also constructed as two distinct kinds of public: highbrow and lowbrow. Through these processes, a new 'equilibrium of power' was established. The popular classes entered the free market in opinions under the leadership and authority (hegemony) of bourgeois opinions: the latter were secured in their place of dominance (ideologically) by the 'logic' of commercial capital (economic).

State, Culture and Public Authority: The Case of Broadcasting

The class-cultural relations institutionalised through the free press/free market principle have survived into the twentieth century. The principle that culture should be largely organised on the private choice/market competition/private profitability system, outside the state, remains a powerful one. Thus, even today, the British state plays a far less extensive role in cultural matters than in other European societies. Eastern European – and some Western – countries have their Ministries of Culture; Britain has only the Department of Education and Science. France's 'academies' define national standards in scholarship in ways to which the British Royal Society does not aspire. Britain keeps no regular cultural statistics, as other UNESCO member-states do, as indicators of the direction of 'cultural development' or 'life-long education'. We do now have an Arts Council financed through state subsidy, and other bodies to protect the national heritage. But attitudes to the Arts Council are notoriously ambiguous. Though financed by the state, its detailed policies are defined by 'independent committees' – the famous British 'mixed' system.

Of course, the British state has assumed wide responsibilities for the *conditions for culture* in a broader sense. Especially through its education systems, it assumes responsibility for the definition and transmission of cultural traditions and values, for the organization of knowledge, for the distribution of what Pierre Bourdieu calls 'cultural capital' throughout the different classes; and for the formation and qualification of intellectual strata – the guardians of cultural tradition. The state has become an active force in *cultural reproduction*.

What is more, in critical areas, the voluntary private market-dominated system of organization ceased for much of the twentieth century to be the dominant one through which class-cultural relations are arranged (though in the 1980s its dominance in culture is being vigorously restored). New sources of cultural authority and new models of cultural hegemony were developed, constituting new class-cultural relations and cementing a new 'equilibrium of authority'. And all of these were in the early and middle decades of the twentieth century, much more directly mediated by and through the state. In our third case, we look at one such development, focusing on another period of historical transition – that which occurred at the end of the nineteenth and beginning of the twentieth centuries.

The containment of democracy

This is a period of profound historical transformation. It precipitated a social crisis, the main elements of which were as follows. Firstly, Britain's industrial and commercial dominance ended with the industrialisation of the other major powers, and the intensification of economic competition and imperialist rivalry. Secondly, this was reflected in a loss of leadership in the field of economic production, as UK productivity levels were surpassed by Germany, Japan and the US. Thirdly, this break-up of past economic supremacy triggered off a fragmentation and reconstruction of political parties, formations, and philosophies. *Laissez-faire* political economy and political individualism, which had been pivotal to the parties and ideas of liberal reform (the dominant political philosophy of the middle of the century), lost their hegemony and new political formations emerged, totally transforming the political scene. The modern forms of mass-industrial labour first appeared in this period, giving rise to new types of labour organisation (the *general* trade unions for semi-skilled and unskilled labour, replacing the craft unions and skilled 'aristocracies of labour' which had dominated trade union and radical-liberal politics in the earlier period). Eventually, this social force broke its alliance with the radical tail of the Liberal party and emerged on the political stage as an independent 'party of labour' – the Labour Party. Women entered the struggle for mass political enfranchisement.

What condensed these different levels of social and economic crisis into a problem of *class authority* was the shift in the balance of social forces which came to be defined as 'the problem of democracy'. The struggle to widen the political franchise to all adult males was at last near its end. And, as the great majority of the men in the popular classes entered the 'political nation' fully enfranchised as citizens, the challenge of democracy to the old class alliances and political leaderships assumed a new thrust. This was compounded by the emergence of a vigorous and determined feminism, struggling to win the same rights of representation for adult women.

The 'rise of democracy' shook earlier models of class and cultural authority to their foundations. The state could no longer be the arena in which the established classes simply 'took note of' and accommodated the views and interests of the unrepresented parts of the nation. It had become, formally at least, fully representative (one man, and shortly thereafter, one person, one vote) and its rule had, therefore, to assume the appearance of universality – treating all its citizens, equally. This posed quite new problems of political, social and cultural management. The leading social classes and their interests had to sustain their position of dominance – yet, somehow, within a state which claimed that political power had been equalised and 'democratised'. The question, then, was how to *contain* democracy while, at the same time, maintaining popular consent, in the circumstances of economic upheaval and intensified international rivalry. This required a programme of social reconstruction – to modernise, renovate and restructure society and the state, while retaining the existing hierarchy of power and authority, and securing to this national programme the cohesion of popular consent: a problem, in short, not of 'democ-

racy' but of hegemony! The only force capable of imposing authority and leadership in these circumstances was a new type of state: the universal neutral state, representative of all the classes; the 'representative state', the state of 'the people', the common good, the 'general interest'; the state that could steer, incite and educate society along certain definite pathways, while retaining its appearance of universality and class independence – 'above the struggle', party to none.

Such a profound reconstruction of the British state did, indeed, occur: in true pragmatic British fashion, not all at one stroke; not all in the same period; with backwards and forwards movements, accreting itself, as Middlemass has put it, through the slow growth of a 'collectivist bias' rather than by the brutal imposition of a Prussian-type state solution.[24] The question of how democracy could be contained was also a cultural one: how to create, above the contending class-cultures and interests, a source of national cultural authority which could defend the leadership of the dominant class-cultural formations, but so stamp it with the 'seal of general social recognition' as to incorporate into it the respect and consent of other classes.

This period is, consequently, massively cross-cut by varieties of new doctrines about society and the state: encroaching into, borrowing from, distinguishing themselves in strident debate against one another. These proliferating discourses and ideas were united, *negatively*, by their desertion of the old ground of liberal-individualism and *laissez-faire; positively*, by their subscription to new models of social collectivism, at the centre of which stood a new conception of the 'ethical' role of the state. This new conception of the state was articulated through a range of doctrines: Social Imperialism, 'national efficiency', tariff reform, 'new' liberalism, Fabian socialism, Lloyd George coalitionism, Social Darwinism, ethical Christianity, and other philosophical schools and political tendencies which contributed to the formation of a new collectivism, based on the ideal of a universal, interventionist state.

In the cultural sphere, this had been germinating for some time. As early as 1867, in the sound of the Hyde Park railings being rattled during the reform agitations, Matthew Arnold thought he heard the approach of democracy. But, like so many of his cultivated contemporaries and successors, he interpreted it as the harbinger of 'anarchy'. In *Culture and Anarchy*, Arnold's principal theme was how to create an alternative centre of authority to democracy and the costs which the nation would have to pay for leaving the resolution of the problem to a straight struggle between the aristocratic, middle and working classes. These needed, in troubled times, he argued, something that could transcend the ding-dong, establish criteria of excellence and intelligence – a realm of the ideal, of 'sweetness and light', beyond, above and against immediate cultural-class interests. This ideal – which he called 'Culture' – could not, in his view, be constructed unless it were founded squarely on an authority which could abstract itself from each class and stand for or represent only society's 'best self'. The source of this authority must be the state.[25]

The brute force of monopoly

This ideal was set in place in the management of opinion and consent via the assertion of state regulation of the new and developing means of communication. The period from the later years of the nineteenth century to the 1920s saw the birth, in rapid succession, of the still photograph, moving photography and the cinema, cable telegraphy, wireless telegraphy, the phonograph, the telephone, radio and finally television. The technical and commercial pioneer of wireless and radio was the great international Marconi Company, founded in 1897. But 'broadcasting of speech and music', first made in 1906, seemed trivial, at first, in comparison with the commercial potential of 'telegraphy without connecting wires', quickly dominated by Marconi – an oligopoly of a quite new type.

The strategic role of wireless only became obvious during the First World War. But this introduced a new factor: the question of control. Its strategic importance made wireless a subject of great interest to the military and defence establishment. By the Wireless Telegraphy Act in 1904, 'all transmitters or receivers of wireless signals had to have a licence, the terms and conditions of which were laid down by the Post Office'. Amateur radio broadcasts were banned between 1914 and 1919. The Imperial Communications Committee complained in 1920 that the Marconi broadcasts were 'interfering with important communications'.[26] The state had already established 'an interest', even though the general shape of broadcasting remained chaotic, its full potential unperceived.

Then several factors converged to reshape this chaos into a very definite and novel formation. First, the producers wished to consolidate their commercial dominance against the competition from amateurs and smaller rivals: but to do so they first had to subordinate competition between themselves to the consolidation of their monopoly. This was done by an amalgamation of the 'big six' (Marconi, Metropolitan Vickers, General Electric, Radio Communications, Hotpoint and Western Electric), with the 'small two' companies (Burndept and Siemens), a development that the government actively encouraged. This formed the commercial-industrial base of the British Broadcasting Company. This was a powerful and restrictive amalgamation; a less polite name for it was a cartel.

To this was added a second element. The 'boom' conditions in which radio expanded in the United States in the early period (1914–20) came to serve as an awful warning. American radio was a riotous and unregulated competition, leading to problems of airwave congestion and 'jamming'. Broadcasting became an open race for the 'radio business', a field for lucrative investment and a channel for competitive advertising. On the one hand, this commercial competition precipitated 'interference and overlapping, a jumble of signals and a blasting and blanketing of rival programmes'.[27] On the other, the unregulated quality of broadcast material precipitated a 'frivolous' use of the medium – a 'toy to amuse children rather than the servant of mankind'.[28]

The Post Office and the government in Britain set their face against this 'chaos of the ether', which they attributed to the unlicensed and unregulated nature of commercial competition (indeed, the very same market that was claimed to have served the freedom of the press so well), on which no public interest or serious social purpose could be stamped. Accordingly, once the commercial interests had sorted themselves out into an amalgamation – a monopoly with which the state could deal – the state itself entered into a sort of cultural partnership with it. It was, therefore, to the amalgamated British Broadcasting Company that the Post Office granted, in January 1923, an exclusive licence to broadcast 'news, information, concerts, lectures, educational matter, speeches, weather reports, theatrical entertainment and any other matter ... within the scope or orbit of the said Licence ...'.[29] This extraordinary hybrid beast became the basis of public broadcasting in Britain: a 'broadcasting authority thinly disguised as an arm of private enterprise yet bearing a curious resemblance to an officially blessed monopoly.'[30] J.W.C. Reith was appointed as the first General Manager of the Company to guide its cultural fortunes.

The BBC was a cultural institution of a quite new type. Regulation by 'pure market forces', by open and unhindered competition – which had served to 'free' the press – was no longer adequate to sustain a new locus of cultural authority in a mass democracy based on a technical medium of such immense social and political power. What was required was a new kind of partnership between monopoly capital, the people, and the state. Such an institution also required a new 'philosophy'. And it was Reith, above all, who provided it. High-minded and public-spirited, in the Arnoldian way, though morally narrower and more self-righteous, Reith was convinced

that, in the face of the 'chaos' of rival parties, forces and doctrines in a democracy, society needed firm moral guidance, respect for the traditional values and a 'best self'. The consent and confidence of the people must be won for an authority which would not merely *reflect* public tastes and values through the medium of the free market, but educate, steer, guide and *shape* public taste and values towards 'higher things'. Reith thus imposed on broadcasting a high, austere, idealist and traditionalist ethical regime. But such a task, a vocation, could not, in his view, be achieved without the full authority of the state. Only the state could stamp broadcasting with the legitimacy of cultural leadership. Reith, in this sense, though in no way a 'collectivist', was nevertheless a new kind of intellectual guardian – an organic state intellectual. This new instrument of cultural education required, in his view, an ideal of public service, a sense of moral obligation and assured finance. None of this was possible without what he called 'the brute force of monopoly'.[31] And so the man appointed as General Manager of a licensed monopoly gave the Crawford Committee the critical evidence which convinced them to convert the 'Company' into a 'Corporation': a public authority – with Reith himself as its first Director-General! The formula for this new kind of cultural institution was, as usual, delicately but precisely formulated by Reith: 'a public service, not only in performance but in constitution – but certainly not as a department of state'.[32] This delicate positioning – *in*, drawing authority *from*, but not *of* the state – has been the basis of the BBC's cultural operations, the foundations of both its 'dependence' and its 'independence', ever since.

Like the state, whose development in a sense it has mirrored, the BBC's whole thrust has been 'centralising'. The range and variety, achieved in the press through free and unregulated competition, had to be somehow *designed* as a matter of *strategy* within the mixed programming *policies* of a corporate institution. The variety of 'publics' and interests and tastes and differences of opinion had to be orchestrated into a corporate unity. Broadcasters – its cultural guardians – had to discharge the public responsibility of reflecting the culture of the whole people as an organic *national* culture while, at the same time, defending traditional values and standards and educating popular taste towards its 'better self'. This was a conception of national cultural policy modelled on the state itself (which is supposed to balance all interests within itself, and act disinterestedly) rather than on the market.

An instrument of the national culture

Between its reconstruction as a 'public service' channel and the Second World War, the BBC became a national cultural institution. Two words which became associated with the BBC in this period provide a shorthand clue as to how this cultural ascendancy was accomplished. The BBC was regarded as an 'authority'. And it was a 'corporation'. Both words have to be understood in their literal as well as their metaphorical sense.

Literally, the BBC had been authorised – i.e. licensed – to broadcast to the nation. But figuratively it established an ascendancy (that is, an authority) over its publics. Its standards, its particular combinations of programmes, its received pronunciations, its musical tastes, literacy and entertainment judgements, its 'broadcasting manners' (for a time, all of Reith's newscasters wore evening dress and black ties, though they could not be seen!) set the authoritative criteria by which public service broadcasting itself was judged.

Again, literally, it was a 'corporation': it incorporated into one body or institution all the elements deemed necessary to provide a national broadcasting medium. But, figuratively, it incorporated – drew together into an organic, though diverse, unity – all the publics in the nation: regional, local, metropolitan; and all the tastes and interests in the nation: Home, Light, Third and World. It was also integrative in the sense that it found a place for all these classes and publics – but it

arranged and organised them within a particular hierarchy. Its centre of gravity was the educated, broad-minded, serious, cultivated, public-spirited, disinterested middle classes. Arnold's guardians. But it designed an acceptable, though subordinate, place for – and thereby incorporated into the national audience – the many regional and working-class audiences.[33] In these ways the BBC identified itself with a certain representation of the nation – a national (that is, not a sectional) medium for a national audience. Then, in its programmes and policies, it set out to address the nation it had so constructed, reconciling the many English voices into its 'Voice'. The whole gamut of 'national voices' was reflected back to the nation through the medium of the sound waves. Yet the Standard Voice – the 'received' accent, pronunciation and tonal pitch of the 'BBC voice' – circumscribed and *placed* them all. This was not, of course, 'Cockney' or 'Scouse' or even, quite, 'Oxbridge'. It was a variant synthesis of the educated, middle-class speech of the Home Counties. It was this Voice that read the news, introduced the programmes, described the symphonies, interviewed spokespersons, made the announcements, filled the gaps between programmes and provided broadcasting with its vocal cement.

In its other area of programming – its political, rather than its cultural role – much the same process unfolded. Here, too, the BBC represented itself as the Voice, not of the state, the government, or even 'the people', so much as of the nation. One key episode in this transformation into a national institution was the General Strike. During the General Strike, in 1926, the country was deeply divided along class and political lines. Baldwin's Cabinet, egged on by Churchill, seriously considered commandeering the BBC, as it had done the press. Reith, though sympathetic to the government side, fought hard to maintain the BBC's 'independence'. The BBC's relative autonomy from the state, secured through the principles and practices of 'impartiality and balance', were first powerfully enunciated and defended in this moment. Reith, in a confidential letter to senior staff once the Strike had ended, expressed the delicate balances on which this autonomy rests in memorable words. By remaining independent, Reith argued, 'we had secured and held the goodwill and even the affection of the people; ... been trusted to do the right thing at all times; ... were a national institution and even a national asset ...'. 'On the other hand', Reith continued, 'since the BBC was a national institution and since the Government in this crisis were acting for the people ... the BBC was for the Government in the crisis too ...'. Briggs comments that this intricate statement of principle clarifies the desire of the BBC to convey 'authentic, impartial news', while at the same time remaining in every sense of the word 'an organization within the constitution'.[34] The complicated balancing act through which the BBC remains both inside, and yet independent of, the state – both for the government and of the nation – are writ large in these richly ambiguous formulations.

In very brief outline, this is the story of how BBC radio forged for itself an identity as a national cultural institution: how it served, at one and the same time, to maintain the cultural standards and values of the dominant class-cultures by organizing them into a single 'voice', while incorporating the other class and regional 'voices' within its organic and corporate framework. The story of how the BBC then became not simply a 'national' but a popular institution, temporarily identified with the fate and fortunes of the whole British people, is really a story of the great ascendancy it established during the years of the Second World War, when it came positively to symbolise many of the things for which the British people believed they were fighting.

Broadcasting – the 'shadow state'

However, as soon as the spirit of 'national unity' in the face of the enemy ebbed, the model on which the BBC had been founded,

and which it had matured over three decades, began itself to be challenged. The lure of a new, and highly lucrative, alternative medium to radio first emerged in the early 1950s with the new experiments in television; and the questions about the most appropriate models of cultural leadership once more surfaced. The fact that an ITV (commercial), rather than a second BBC (public authority), television channel was chosen in 1954 suggests that the regulation and ordering of culture through the free market remains as an active alternative to state 'incorporation' for societies like Britain, even in the latter half of the twentieth century. Indeed, the preference for market rather than state regulation has become more, not less, popular since the 1950s. This, in turn, suggests that the leading social classes remain divided between at least two different and competing cultural and economic 'models': free-market and state-sponsored. It also reminds us that, though the state is the necessary point through which the many conflicting lines of policy are drawn together and shaped into a more coherent thrust of government, its 'unity' is never complete. The state remains contradictory, riven by conflicting perspectives and policy interests; and these often reflect the real divergencies among and within the different sections of the dominant class.

The Conservative Party, for example, was deeply split on the question of whether the second channel should be structured in a 'public service' or a 'market-commercial' way. Selwyn Lloyd, in opposition to the more 'paternalist' members of his own party (such as Lord Hailsham), signed a minority report to the Beveridge Committee, favouring the market principle. A Conservative backbenchers' pressure group in alliance with the same sort of commercial interests that had struggled to colonise the BBC in the early days (equipment manufacturers, advertising agencies, large investors, and so on) eventually carried the day when the Television Act 1953, which established the ITV network, was finally drafted. The second channel was financed through the sale of advertising time, not through a public licence. It had therefore to submit to the logic of the market. This meant catering more explicitly to the mass-popular audience in its consumer form, with programmes which might make an immediate appeal to existing audience tastes. Thus, for the first time in Britain since the birth of the radio and television era, two kinds of cultural institution, founded on two competing cultural models, orchestrating the relations between the classes and the cultures in two, contrasting ways – the 'paternalist' BBC, the 'populist' ITV – vied with each other for cultural leadership in a period of intense competition.

The effects of competition were, however, complex. The BBC was obliged to become more populist, more demotic, more calculatingly competitive in its struggle to secure a majority of the audience. But ITV also broadened and varied its ouput over time, producing a higher proportion of 'quality' material, in the face of public criticism. In the event, the two channels have come to resemble one another more than they differ.

On the other hand, this 'peaceful coexistence' (i.e. fierce competition) between the two elements of the duopoly which has dominated national television since can be easily misread, so far as the state's involvement in culture is concerned. For the ITV (like the new fourth channel) is not and never has been a pure instance of the commercial free-market model, as the nineteenth-century press was. Though independently organised and financed, it had imposed on it, by the terms of the Act (in principle) and by the regulation 'authority' of the Independent Broadcasting Authority (IBA) set over it, many public service standards, criteria and requirements. In its own ways, ITV is also required to 'serve the nation', to meet a public service ideal. It, too, must meet certain required programme standards; must offer to serve a broad range of public interests and tastes; that is, address itself to the nation. Its practices are monitored through the IBA. Its applications for franchise have to meet certain requirements (though the details remain private) and, in the area of news and current affairs, the requirements of 'balance, neutrality, impartiality' – the terms on which broadcasting is allowed to be both 'independent' and yet 'within the constitution' – are broadly the same as those governing BBC practice. Actually, they are more clearly and formally stated in the ITV's Act than they are in the BBC's Charter.[35]

In these different ways, then, television is linked, in a multitude of visible and invisible, direct and indirect, ways, to the state. While retaining a great deal of day-to-day independence, broadcasters and the general strategies of broadcasting are organised within the state's field of force. The definitions of political reality which are assumed as 'legitimate' within the state provide the limits within which broadcasting's versions of reality move. The broadcasters will not immediately reproduce a government's views; they are not, in that sense, the mere mouthpieces of the political party in power. But, just as the state does not favour one manufacturer against another, but does maintain the system of private enterprise *as a whole*, so broadcasting does not illegally swing its weight behind one political party or another, but it does respect and cherish the whole ideological framework, the basic structure of social relations, the existing dispositions of wealth, power, influence, prestige, on whose foundations it ultimately rests. In debating any of these questions, broadcasting's starting point, parameters and frames of references will be the same as those established for society through the state. Sensitive points for the state (Northern Ireland, picketing, trade union power, nuclear strategy, inflation, left advances in the political parties) are also, sooner or later, broadcasting's sensitive points. The broadcasting institutions constantly orientate and acclimatise themselves to the shifts and trends in the established political culture. When controversial issues have to be debated, what the established definition of a problem is, within the state, is what any broadcaster with an instinct for survival will take as the starting point. And when the nation divides, or problems drive the parties and the classes apart, the only point of rest or ultimate authority, which secures for broadcasting some element of legitimacy, and licenses it to continue to broadcast, is whatever is left of the consensus as represented through the state.

In general, it seems that in this new broadcasting model both BBC and ITV behave like, or model themselves on, and tend to reproduce the practices of, the state, though to different degrees. In periods of relative calm or national unity, it is the general consensus (which, in liberal-democratic theory, is supposed to be represented by the state) which provides broadcasting with its authority, legitimacy and practical guiding light. In periods of controversy and social or political division, the broadcasters ride out the rifts in the consensus by adopting – as state civil servants do – a position of impartiality and neutrality, 'above the struggle'.

This set of underlying parallels between broadcasting and the state (especially strong in the areas of news, current affairs and political coverage) can be traced through to the actual practices of particular programmes. Current affairs television programmes, as a form, thus signify nothing so much as the source of their coherence: the state. They are organised as if the BBC really were a sort of 'shadow state': the studio, a microcosm of Parliament; the TV compère, none other than the 'Speaker of the House' himself; and its 'expert' commentators, the equals of senior civil servants and departmental permanent secretaries with their neutral briefs – disinterested guardians of the 'public interest'.[36]

lations of force' between the classes and the cultures. They remodel and refashion the nature of cultural leadership in society. They mobilise consent and help to win popular support for, and thus secure, different types of class-cultural authority. The restructuring of these relations is central to the processes by which hegemony – a condition of social ascendancy, of cultural, moral and political leadership by a particular social bloc – is, or is not achieved, in particular historical periods. I have thus shown how, in each of the three cases considered, a different model of cultural authority was in the course of formation, how that model achieved a sort of dominance, for a time, and thus secured (again, for a time) the cultural leadership of a particular social force or alliance of social forces, positioning and fixing the dominated classes in the place of subordination. I have also outlined the pressures that led to the eventual disintegration of each of these models and its supersession by an alternative model.

Clearly, there is no simple, linear progression in the transitions between these models, in the cultural role of the state. Even in the twentieth-century model of broadcasting, the state-culture relations have been differently organised, within even clearer evidence – accumulating rapidly under Thatcherism – of acute ruling class dissension as to how they *should* be organised. None the less, the general tendency – the main point in Gramsci's expanded view of the state – for hegemony to become increasingly reliant, in mass democracies, on the enlarged cultural role of the state is undeniable.

Conclusion

I have tried, in this essay, to show how cultural institutions and practices institutionalise (settle, fix, secure, stabilise) a particular pattern of relations between the cultures and the classes in society. These configurations shift in line with much broader and more far-reaching 'epochal' shifts and historical transitions. They are not, however, simply rearrangements of an existing pattern. They establish new 're-

NOTES AND REFERENCES

1 A. Gramsci, *Selections from The Prison Notebooks*, Lawrence and Wishart, 1971, p. 258.
2 Ibid., p. 244.
3 Ibid., p. 242.
4 See R. Malcolmson, *Popular Recreations in English Society, 1700–1850*, Cambridge University Press, 1973, p. 40.

5 Ibid., p. 143.

6 E.P. Thompson, 'Peculiarities of the English', in *The Poverty of Theory and Other Essays*, Merlin Press, 1978, p. 43.

7 Ibid., p. 43.

8 See L. Namier, *The Structure of Politics*, Macmillan, 1929.

9 See P. Anderson, *Arguments within English Marxism*, Verso/New Left Books, 1980, p. 92.

10 See J. Hay, 'Property, authority and the criminal law', in D. Hay, P. Linebaugh and E.P. Thompson (eds), *Albion's Fatal Tree*, Allen Lane/The Penguin Press, 1975.

11 See E.P. Thompson, *Whigs and Hunters*, Allen Lane, 1975.

12 J. Brewer and J. Styles (eds), *An Ungovernable People*, Hutchinson, 1980, pp. 18–19.

13 See G. Rudé, *The Crowd in History*, Wiley, 1964; and E. Hobsbawm and G. Rudé, *Captain Swing*, Allen Lane/The Penguin Press, 1975.

14 Thompson, 'Peculiarities of the English'.

15 See E.P. Thompson, 'The moral economy of the English crowd', *Past and Present*, no. 50, February 1971.

16 Cited in R. Altick, *The English Common Reader*, University of Chicago Press, 1957, p. 41.

17 I. Watt, *The Rise of the Novel*, Peregrine, 1963, p. 49.

18 M. Harris, 'Structure, ownership and control of the press, 1620–1780', in J. Curran (ed), *Newspaper History: From the Seventeenth Century to the Present Day*, Constable, 1978, p. 9.

19 Cited in A. Aspinall, *Politics of the Press, 1780–1859*, Harvester, 1973, p. 1.

20 J. Curran (ed), *Newspaper History*, p. 46.

21 See E.P. Thompson, *The Making of the English Working Class*, Penguin, p. 789.

22 Ibid., p. 791.

23 V. Berridge, 'Popular Sunday papers and mid-Victorian society' in J. Curran, *Newspaper History*, p. 247.

24 See K. Middlemass, *The Politics of Industrial Society*, André Deutsch, 1980.

25 See M. Arnold, *Culture and Anarchy*, Cambridge University Press, 1963, p. 204.

26 A. Briggs, *The Golden Age of Wireless*, Oxford University Press, 1961, pp. 48–9.

27 Ibid., p. 64.

28 Ibid., p. 48.

29 Ibid., p. 127.

30 A. Boyle, *Only the Wind will Listen*, Hutchinson, 1972, p. 128.

31 A. Briggs, *Wireless*, p. 238.

32 J. Reith, *Into the Wind*, Hodder, 1949, p. 102.

33 For further details of this moment in the BBC's history see the essay by David Cardiff and Paddy Scannell in this collection and their 'Serving the Nation: Public Service Broadcasting before the War', in B. Waites, T. Bennett and G. Martin (eds), *Popular Culture: Past and Present*, Croom Helm, 1982.

34 A. Briggs, *Wireless*, pp. 365–6.

35 See K. Kumar, 'Holding the middle ground', in J. Curran, M. Gurevitch and J. Woollacott (eds), *Mass Communications and Society*, Edward Arnold, 1977.

36 See, for a fuller discussion of these aspects of current affairs television, S. Hall, I. Connell and L. Curti, 'The "Unity" of Current Affairs Television', in T. Bennett, S. Boyd-Bowman, C. Mercer and J. Woollacott, *Popular Television and Film*, British Film Institute, 1981.

16

The Banality of Power and the Aesthetics of Vulgarity in the Postcolony

Achille Mbembe

Translated by Janet Roitman

In this article, I will examine the banality of power in the "postcolony." By "banality of power," I am not simply referring to the way bureaucratic formalities or arbitrary rules, implicit or explicit, have been multiplied, nor am I simply concerned with what has become routine. To be sure, banality implies predictability precisely because it is made up of repeated daily actions and gestures. Yet, by the "banality of power" I am also evoking those elements of the obscene, vulgar, and the grotesque that Mikhail Bakhtin claimed to have located in "non-official"[1] cultures, but which, in fact, are intrinsic to all systems of domination and to the means by which those systems are confirmed or deconstructed.

The notion "postcolony" simply refers to the specific identity of a given historical trajectory: that of societies recently emerging from the experience of colonization. To be sure, the postcolony is a chaotic plurality, yet it has nonetheless an internal coherence. It is a specific system of signs, a particular way of fabricating simulacra or of stereotypes. It is not, however, just an economy of signs in which power is mirrored and *imagined* self-reflectively. The postcolony is characterized by a distinctive art of improvisation, by a tendency to excess and disproportion as well as by distinctive ways in which identities are multiplied, transformed, and put into circulation.[2] It is likewise made up of a series of corporate institutions, and apparatuses which, once they are deployed, constitute a distinctive regime of violence.[3] In this sense, the postcolony is a critical and dramatic site in which are played out the wider problems of subjection and its corollary, indiscipline.

With respect to trajectories of this type, then, I am concerned with the ways in which state power:

From *Public Culture*, 4(2), Spring 1992, pp. 1–30, trans. J. Roitman. All rights reserved. Used by permission of the publisher.

1) *creates*, through its administrative and bureaucratic practices, a world of meanings all of its own, a mastercode which, in aiming for a primary centrality, also, and perhaps paradoxically, governs the logics of the constitution of all other meanings within these societies.

2) attempts to institutionalize its world of meanings as a "socio-historical world,"[4] and to make that world fully real, turning it into a part of people's common sense not only by instilling it in the minds of its *cibles* (or "target population"),[5] but also in the imaginary of an epoque.

The basic argument of this article is that, to account for both the imagery and efficacy of postcolonial relations of power, we must go beyond the binary categories used in standard interpretations of domination (resistance/passivity, subjection/autonomy, state/civil society, hegemony/counterhegemony, totalization/detotalization). These oppositions are not helpful;[6] rather, they cloud our understanding of postcolonial relations.[7] In the postcolony, the *commandement*[8] seeks to institutionalize itself, in order to achieve legitimation and hegemony [*recherche hégémonique*], in the form of a *fetish*.[9] The signs, vocabulary, and narratives that it produces are not only destined to become objects of representation. They are officially invested with a surplus of meanings which are not negotiable, and which one is thus officially forbidden to transgress. So as to insure that such transgression does not in fact take place, the champions of state power invent entire constellations of ideas; they select a distinct set of cultural repertoires and powerfully evocative concepts;[10] but they also have resort to the systematic application of pain,[11] the basic goal being the production of an imagery. To account for postcolonial relations is thus to pay attention to the workings of power in its minute details, and to the principles of assemblage which give rise to its efficacy. That is, one must examine the orderings of the world it produces; the types of institutions, knowledges, norms, and practices that issue from it; the manner in which these institutions, knowledges, norms, and practices structure the *quotidien*; as well as the light that the use of visual imagery and discourse throws on the nature of domination and subordination.

The focus of my analysis is Cameroon. As a case study, it demonstrates how the grotesque and the obscene are two essential characteristics that identify postcolonial regimes of domination. Bakhtin claims that the grotesque and the obscene are, above all, a matter of plebeian life. He maintains that, as a means of resistance to the dominant culture and as a refuge from it, obscenity and the grotesque are parodies which undermine officialdom by exposing its arbitrary and perishable character, turning it all into a figure of fun.[12] But, while this view is not totally invalid, the answers to the questions raised at the beginning of this article, require a shift of perspective such that the grotesque and the obscene can also be located in 1) the places and times in which state power organizes the dramatization of its magnificence, 2) the displays in which it stages its majesty and prestige and, 3) the way it offers these artifacts to its "targets" [*cibles*].

It is only through such a shift in perspective that we can come to understand that the postcolonial relationship is not primarily a relationship of resistance or of collaboration, but is rather best characterized as a promiscuous relationship: a convivial tension between the *commandement* and its "targets." It is precisely this logic of familiarity and domesticity that explains the fact that acts of the dominated do not necessarily lead to resistance, accommodation, "disengagement," the refusal to be captured,[13] or to an antagonism between public facts and gestures and those *sous maquis* [of the underground]. Instead, it has resulted in the mutual "zombification" of both the dominant and those whom they apparently dominate. This "zombification" means that each robbed the other of their vitality and has left them both impotent [*impouvoir*].

Indeed, the examples in this article suggest that the postcolony is made up not of one coherent "public space," nor is it determined by any single organizing principle. It is rather a plurality of "spheres" and arenas, each having its own separate logic yet nonetheless liable to be entangled with other logics when operating in certain specific contexts: hence the postcolonial "subject" has had to learn to continuously bargain [*marchander*] and improvise. Faced with this plurality of legitimizing rubrics, institutional forms, rules, arenas, and principles of combination, the postcolonial "subject" mobilizes not just a single "identity," but several fluid identities which, by their very nature, must be constantly "revised" in order to achieve maximum instrumentality and efficacy as and when required.[14]

If there is, then, a "postcolonial subject," he or she is publicly visible only at the point where the two activities overlap – on one hand, in the common daily rituals that ratify the *commandement*'s own institutionalization (its *recherche hégémonique*) in its capacity as a fetish[15] to which the subject is bound; and, on the other, the subject's deployment of a talent for play and a sense of fun which makes him *homo ludens par excellence*. It is this practice, as *homo ludens*, that enables subjects to splinter their identities and to represent themselves as constantly changing their persona; they are constantly undergoing mitosis,[16] whether it be in "official" spaces or not. Thus, it seems that one would be mistaken to continue to interpret the postcolonial relation in terms of "resistance" or absolute "domination," or as a function of the dichotomies and binary oppositions generally adduced in conventional analyses of movements of indiscipline and insubordination[17] (counter-discourses, counter-society, counter-hegemony, second society).

Excess and the Creativity of Abuse[18]

This manner of proceeding – like the questions which are at stake – requires a few additional explanatory remarks. To begin with, there is the question of the grotesque and obscene

being used as means of erecting, ratifying, or deconstructing particular regimes of violence and domination. In a study devoted to what has been termed "political derision" in Togo, C. Toulabor shows how, under one-party rule, the people developed ways of separating words or phrases off from their conventional meanings, giving them second significances. He also illustrates how, in this manner, they created an ambiguous, or equivocal, vocabulary parallel to the official discourse.[19] Until recently, Togo was the perfect example of a postcolonial construction. The official discourse made use of all necessary means to maintain the fiction of a society devoid of conflict. Here, "postcoloniality" was glimpsed behind the façade of an entity – that is, state power – which considered itself as simultaneously indistinguishable from society and as the upholder of the law and the keeper of the truth. State power was embodied in a single person: the President. He alone controlled the law and could, on his own, grant or abolish liberties. In similar vein, in Cameroon, the Head of State can publicly declare: "I brought you to liberty.... You now have liberty. Make good use of it."[20]

In Togo, the single-party, Rassemblement du Peuple Togolais (RPT), claimed to control the totality of public and social life, subjecting it to the pursuit of what were decreed to be communal goals and proclaiming the unity of the people among whom no divisions could be allowed to exist. In this context, all dissidence was denied, if it had not already been repressed administratively or forcibly killed off. However, even though one would expect to find a society deprived of its resources, a dissociation persisted between, on the one hand, the representation that State power projected of itself and society and, on the other hand, the way in which the ordinary people played with and manipulated this representation not just well away from officialdom, out of earshot, out of sight of power,[21] but also within the actual arenas where they were gathered publicly to confirm the legitimacy of the State.

Thus there were avenues of escape from the *commandement*, and whole areas of social discourse eluded control in a discontinuous and uninterrupted manner. Verbal acts of this kind offer some good examples – and are excellent indices of what can be considered commonplace (and hence banal). For instance, when Togolese were called upon to shout the party slogans, many would travesty the metaphors meant to glorify state power. With a simple change in intonation, the same metaphor could take on several meanings. Thus, under the cover of official slogans people sang about the sudden erection of the "enormous" and "rigid" presidential phallus, of how it remains in this position, and of its contact with "vaginal fluids." "The powerful key of Eyadéma penetrates the keyhole. People, 'applaud!'" "Eat your portion, Paul Biya," echoed the Cameroonians, making allusion to the intensified prebendalization[22] of their state since 1982 when Mr Ahidjo resigned and was replaced constitutionally by his former Prime Minister. The "poaching" of meanings can go much farther. For example, the Togolese party acronym (RPT), was identified with "the sound of faecal matter dropping into a septic tank" or "the sound of a fart emitted by quivering buttocks" which "can only smell disgusting."[23] "Cut it up and dole it out!" [redépécer][24] was preferred by Cameroonians, who thus gave another meaning to the name of the former sole party, the RDPC (Rassemblement Démocratique du Peuple Camerounais) and in this way incorporated the state within the imaginary of the belly and eating, the right of capture and the redistribution of spoils – all these being metaphors common in local vernaculars of power.[25]

Ultimately, the obsession with orifices and genital organs came to dominate Togolese popular laughter. But the same is also to be found in writings and speech in other Sub-Saharan countries. For example, the Congolese author, Sony Labou Tansi, repeatedly describes the "strong, delivering, thick thighs" and "the essential and bewitching ass" of girls not only in the context of his reflections on "the tropicalities of his Excellency" and on the ability of the latter to bring about a "digital orgasm," but also in his insistence on the irony involved in the momentary impotence of the autocrat's "natural member":

The Providential Guide went to the toilet for a final verification of his weapons. There, he undressed.... For this woman... he intended to proceed with long and deep penetrations, interrupted by foamy come, like he did when he was young. But, because of the disorder in his loins, he could no longer turn inside them to make them wet. He could no longer produce that special sensation of air being pumped by the pistons of a motor [pétaradants], or of spurts of flowing liquid [cataractes], or the effect of a stopper, or a plug [bouchons]. Old age had dealt him a nasty blow from below, so to speak. But he was still a dignified male, still even a male who could perform, able to rise and fall – achieving undulation [les ondulants], among other things.[26]

The emphasis on orifices and protuberances has to be understood in relation to two factors especially. The first derives from the fact that the commandement in the postcolony has a marked taste for lecherous living. In this respect, ceremonies and festivities are the two key vehicles for indulging the taste. But the language of its forms and symbols is above all the mouth, the penis, and the belly.[27] One must, moreover, understand this language from the point of view of postcolonial gouvernementalité:[28] it is not enough to bring into play the mouth, the penis, or the belly, or merely to refer to them in order to automatically produce obscenity. The mouth, the penis, and the belly – as structuring principles as well as objects of verbal acts and popular laughter – are in fact given multiple and ambivalent meanings. They are called upon to comment on various aspects of social life – a relationship to time, to play, and pleasure. In short, they are mobilized by those who want to make a statement about human existence and the ordering of society, death, inequality, or "witchcraft." In this sense, they serve as primary referents or critical metaphors in the production of the political in the postcolony.

But beyond the particular sites represented by the mouth, the belly, and the penis, the principal locus of both the self-narration of power and the places in which it imagines itself is the body. And yet, if, as we have just indicated, ceremonies and festivities constitute the pre-eminent means by which the *commandement* speaks and the way in which it dramatizes its magnificence and prodigality, then the body to which we are referring is, foremost, the body that eats and drinks, and which (in both cases) is thus open. Hence the significance of orifices – and the central part they play in popular laughter.

Togolese references to the "loud fart" or "faecal material," the Cameroonians reiteration of *redépeçage*, or the oft-cited "goat that grazes where it is tethered" are all recalling the mouth and the belly at the same time as they are also celebrating the great feasts of food and drink that set the pattern not only of official banquets but also of the more banal yet still major occasions of daily life – such as the purchase of traditional titles, weddings, promotions and appointments, the awarding of medals. The obesity of men in power, their impressive physique and, more prosaically, the flow of shit which results from such a physique – these appeal to a people who can enjoy themselves with mockery and laughter, and, sometimes, even join in the feast. They thus become themselves part of a system of signs that the *commandement* leaves, like tracks, as it passes on its way, and so make it possible to reconstruct the times and places in which it attempts to colonize the common people's imaginary. And, because of this, one can find those signs reproduced, recurring even in the remotest, tiniest corners of everyday life – in relations between parents and children, between husbands and wives, between police and their victims, teachers and pupils.

Is the ultimate question for the postcolonial *homo ludens*, then, one of "parodying," or "deriding," the *commandement*, as the interpretive categories put forth by Bakhtin would have it? To a large extent, popular bursts of hilarity are actually taking the official world seriously; that is to say, at face value or at least the value officialdom itself gives it.[29] In the end, whether the encounter is "masked" or not is of little consequence. What is important is that, as a specific trajectory of domination, the postcolony strikes precisely in its earthiness and its verbosity. In fact, the *commandement* derives its "aesthetics" from its immoderate appetite and the immense pleasure that it encounters in plunging in ordure. The sodomite gesture readily goes hand in hand with the orgy and buffoonery. The body of the despot, his frowns and smiles, his decrees and edicts, the redundancy of his public notices and communiqués repeated over and again: these are the primary signifiers. It is these that have force, that get interpreted and re-interpreted, and feed back further significance into the system.

The question of knowing whether comic performance in the postcolony is an expression of "resistance" or not – or if it is, *a priori*, an "opposition" or the manifestation of hostility toward state power – is, then, a secondary question for the time being. For the most part, people who laugh are only reading the signs left like rubbish in the wake of the *commandement*. Thus, the president's anus of which they speak is not a solar anus. What the people see and experience is a concrete anus, capable of defecating like any commoner's. And what amuses the populace is the fact that, in its glorious foolishness and indifference to all veracity, the official monologism claims the contrary.

Confrontation occurs the moment that the rulers compel obedience and define, in a constraining manner, what they prefer the ruled to simulate. The problem here is not that they do not obey (nor even pretend to obey). Conflict arises from the fact that the postcolony is a chaotic plurality. And, as such, it leaves an enormous space open to improvisation. In other words, it is practically impossible to enclose its system of signs, images, and traces in fixity and inertia. That is why they are constantly recaptured and reshaped – as much by the rulers as by the ruled – in the refabulization of power.[30]

This is why, too, the postcolony is the simulacral regime *par excellence*. Indeed, by freeing up the potential for play, improvisation, and amusement, within the very limits set by officialdom, the simulacrum allows ordinary people to a) simulate adherence to the innumerable official rituals that life in the postcolony requires (such as the wearing of uniforms or the carrying of the party card, performing public gestures of support for the autocrat, posting portraits of the despot in one's home); and b) thus avoid the annoyances which necessarily arise from frontal opposition to the orders of power and its decrees.

And yet, having interpreted the prevalence of orifices and protuberances in popular laughter in function of the fact that the postcolonial *commandement* is of a luxurious temperament, I must quickly add that the essential point would be lost if one reduced these gestures, and the manner in which they are recharged with sense in popular hilarity, to an ensemble of primitive customs. Rather, I would argue that defecation, copulation, pomp and sumptuousness are all classical ingredients in the production of power, and that there is nothing specifically African about it. That is why I must now insist on another aspect of my argument. I would go further: the obsession with orifices has to be seen as due to the fact that in the postcolony the *commandement* is constantly engaged in projecting an image both of itself and of the world – a fantasy that it presents to its subjects as a truth that is beyond dispute, a truth that has to be instilled into them in order that they acquire a habit of discipline and obedience.[31] The *commandement* itself aspires to be a cosmogony. Yet owing to its very oddity, it is this "order of the world," in its eccentricity, that popular laughter causes to capsize, often quite unintentionally.

What gives rise to conflict is not the frequent references to the genital organs of the men of power; but rather the way in which the people who laugh kidnap power and force it, as if by accident, to contemplate its own vulgarity. In other words, in the postcolony, the very display of grandeur and prestige always entails an aspect of vulgarity and the baroque that the official order tries hard to hide,[32] but which ordinary people bring to its attention – sometimes intentionally, often unwittingly. The following incident from Kenya shows how, in practice, the baroque can go well beyond the limits of fun:

> A woman from Busia was recently exposed to an agonizing experience as she helplessly watched the police beat her husband with their batons. As she wept and pleaded with the police to spare her husband, the police ordered the couple to take off their shoes. According to the police, the man was punished for failing to stand to attention while the national flag was being lowered. The incident took place last Tuesday, 6 February 1990 at a roadblock on the Kisumu-Busia road. The woman and her husband were sitting on the side of the road, waiting for transport to take them back to Busia.[33]

It is with the conscious aim of avoiding such trouble that people locate the fetish of state power in the realm of the ridicule; there, they can tame it, or shut it up and render it powerless. Once having symbolically bridled its capacity to annoy [*capacité de nuisance*], they can then enclose it in the status of an idol. But we are then dealing with a congenial idol that is familiar and intimate and which is, henceforth, part of the domesticity of the dominant as much as the dominated.[34]

This double act of both distancing and domesticating is not necessarily the expression of a fundamental conflict between worlds of meaning which are in principle antagonistic. In fact, officialdom and the people share many references in common, not the least of which is a certain conception of the aesthetics and stylistics of power, the way it operates and the modalities of its expansion. Hence, for example, the *commandement* has to be extravagant since, apart from feeding itself, it also has to feed its clientele. Likewise, it must furnish public proof of its prestige and glory by a sumptuous (yet burdensome) presentation of its status, displaying the heights of luxury in matters of dress and lifestyle, thereby turning prodigal acts of generosity into grand theatre.[35] Similarly, it must proceed by extraction – through taxes and different levies, rents of various kinds, forcible confiscation and other ways of siphoning off wealth. As S. Labou Tansi notes, special teams

> come to collect taxes twice a year, they demand a head tax, a land tax, a levy on children, a levy to show faith in the Guide, a contribution for economic recovery, a travel tax, the patriotism levy, the militants' contribution, the levy for the War against Ignorance, the levy for soil conservation, the hunting tax.[36]

The actions that signal sovereignty have to be carried through with an adequately harsh firmness, otherwise the splendor of those exercising the trappings of authority is dimmed. To exercise authority is above all to tire out the bodies of those under it, to "disempower" them not so much in an effort to make them economically productive as to render them docile. To command is, moreover, to publicly demonstrate a certain delight in eating and drinking well and, as S. Labou Tansi shows, to pass most of one's time in "pissing grease and rust into the backsides of young girls."[37] Pride in possessing an active penis has to be dramatized, with sexual rights over subordinates [droit de cuissage], the keeping of concubines, and so forth. And the unconditional subordination of women to the principle of male pleasure remains one of the pillars of the phallocratic cycle.

It seems, then, that one can reasonably conclude from these preliminary remarks that the postcolony is a world of anxious virility – hostile to continence, frugality, and sobriety. Furthermore, the set of images, idioms, and legitimizing rubrics evoked above is shared and used as much by those we designate as dominant as by the dominated. Those who laugh, whether they do so in the public arena or under cloak in the "pri-

vate sphere," are not necessarily "bringing power down" or even "resisting" it. Confronted with the state's eagerness to cover up its vulgar origins, people are simply bearing witness, often unconsciously, to the fact that the grotesque is no more foreign to officialdom than the common (wo)man is impervious to the charms of majesty.

Indeed, in its own longing for grandeur the popular world borrows the whole ideological repertoires of officialdom, along with its idioms and forms. Conversely, the official world mimics popular vulgarity, inserting it at the very core of the procedures by which it claims to rise to grandeur. It is unnecessary, then, to do as Bakhtin does and insist on oppositions [dédoublements][38] or, as conventional analysis has it, on the purported logic of resistance, disengagement, or disjunction.[39] Instead the emphasis should be upon the logics of conviviality, on the dynamics of domesticity and familiarity, which inscribe the dominant and the dominated in the same epistemological field.

What distinguishes the postcolony from other regimes of violence and domination, then, is not only the luxuriousness of style and the down-to-earth realism that characterizes its power or even the fact that it is exercised "in the raw" [à l' état brut]. Peculiar also to the postcolony is the fact that the forging of relations between those who command and their subjects operates, fundamentally, through a specific pragmatic: the simulacrum. This explains why dictators can go to sleep at night lulled by roars of adulation and support [motions de soutien] only to wake up the next morning to find their golden calves smashed and their tablets of law overturned. The applauding crowds of yesterday have become today a cursing, abusive mob. That is to say, people whose identities have been partly confiscated have been able, precisely because there was this pretense [simulacre], to glue back together the bits of and pieces of their fragmented identities. And by annexing official signs and languages, they make use of them to refabulate their own universe of sense while "zombifying," or preying on, the *commandement*. Strictly speaking, this process does not increase either the depth of people's subordination or their levels of resistance; it simply produces a situation of disempowerment [*impouvoir*] for both the ruled and the rulers.[40] This process is, fundamentally, of a magical nature. Though it may demystify the *commandement* or even erode its supposed legitimacy, it does not do violence to the *commandement*'s material base. At best, it creates pockets of indiscipline on which the *commandement* may stub its toe, though otherwise it glides unperturbed over them.

As I noted above, the *commandement* defines itself as a cosmogony or, more simply, a fetish. A fetish is, among other things, an object which aspires to sacralization; it demands power and seeks to maintain an intimate and proximate relationship with those who carry it.[41] Fetish can also take the form of a talisman which one can call upon, honour, or dread. In the postcolony, the power of the fetish is invested not only in the figure of the autocrat, but also in all figures of the *commandement* and its agents (the Party, policemen, soldiers, administrators and officials, courtiers and traffickers, militiamen). It turns the postcolonial autocrat into an object of representation that feeds upon applause, flattery, and lies. By virtue of its exercising power in the raw [*à l' état brut*], the fetish – as embodied in the autocrat and his agents – takes on itself an autonomous existence. It becomes unaccountable or, in the words of Hegel, capriciousness that has reached the contemplation of itself.[42] If so, we should not underestimate the violence that can be set in motion to protect the vocabulary used to denote the *commandement* or to speak to it, and to safeguard the official fictions that underwrite the apparatus of domination[43] – since these are essential to keeping the people under the spell of the *commandement*, within an enchanted forest of adulation[44] that at the same time makes people laugh.

For, if it is a matter of playing and amusement for the ruled, the rulers are consumed, rather, by the question of fabricating and imposing an imaginary. What for the ruled may seem funny is nonetheless treated by the powerful as sacrilege (as in the case of the Kenyan couple who failed to honour the flag). In this context laughter or mere indifference is blasphemous, not because people intend it so but because those in power consider it blasphemous. Categories, however, like blasphemy or sacrilege are inadequate to convey the sense of eating [*dévoration*] that is clearly involved here. This is so, because, if we follow Bakhtin and thus accept (even provisionally) that carnivalesque praxis attacks a cosmology and creates a myth whose central subject is the body, we have to conclude that what we have in the postcolony is a case of theophagy[45] where the god himself is devoured by his worshippers.

In those operations, the totem that acts as a double to power is no longer protected by taboo.[46] There is a breach in the wall of prohibitions. In transgressing taboos and interdictions, people are stressing their preference for conviviality. They unpack the officialese and its protective taboos and, often unwittingly, tear apart the gods that African autocrats aspire to be. In this way an image such as that of the presidential anus is brought down to earth; it becomes nothing more than a common-or-garden arse [*un anus bien du terroir*] that defecates like anyone else's. So too the penis of His Excellency turns out to be no more than a peasant's [*un pénis bien du pays*], unable to resist, amidst the aromas of everyday life, the scent of women.

However, if ordinary people can – even inadvertently – dismember and devour the gods the autocrats aspire to be, the converse is also true. This is shown by the following account of the public execution of two malefactors in Cameroon:

> At dawn on August 28th ... they were taken to the "Carrefour des Billes" along the main Douala to Yaounde road (where) they saw the crowd. Apart from the local population – totalling several hundred people – there were the authorities: the Governor of the Littoral

province, the Prefect of Wouri, the Public Prosecutor, the Deputy Prefect, the officer in command of the G.M.I. squadron, the Governor of Douala central prison, a priest, a doctor, one of their lawyers..., several militiamen and policemen, soldiers impeccably dressed in combat gear, firemen.

In the military bus that drove them to the place of execution, they were brought food. They refused to take their last meal, preferring to drink instead. They were given whisky and red wine which they rapidly drained.... At seven o'clock..., they were taken to the stakes, which were set about ten metres apart. While Oumbé let himself be tied up, Njomzeu continued to struggle ... He was forced to his knees. When it came to his turn, he broke down and started to cry.... The priest and the pastor who were there came up and called on them to pray. To no avail.

The soldiers who were to carry out the execution – there were twenty-four of them, twelve for each man – advanced in line, marching in step under the command of a captain and came to a halt at thirty metres range: twelve kneeling, twelve standing. At the command of the captain: "Ready!" the soldiers cocked their rifles and took aim. "Fire!": a short, terrible burst drowned the cries of the condemned. Twelve bullets moving at 800 metres per second. Then the *coup de grâce*. And, incredible but true, the crowd broke into frenzied applause, as if it was the end of a good show.[47]

We could use here, since the situation is not dissimilar, the narrative structure that Michel Foucault employed in his account of the punishment of Damiens.[48] But we must not forget that the case above occurred in a postcolony. That does not imply that the postcolonial rationale bears no relationship to the "colonial rationale."[49] Indeed, the colony had its own arsenal of punishments and devices for disciplining the "natives." At its most vicious, the native's body was fastened by an iron collar, as was the practice with convicts in the Cour de Bicêtre, with the neck bent back over an anvil.[50] The colony also had its convicts.[51] "Coloniality," as a

power relation based on violence, was meant to cure Africans of their supposed laziness, protecting them from need whether or not they wanted such protection. Given the degeneracy and vice which from the colonial viewpoint characterized the indigenous world, colonialism found it necessary to rein in the abundant sexuality of the "negro," to tame his/her spirit, police his/her body – and ensure that the productivity of his/her labour increased.[52]

To a large extent, coloniality was a way of disciplining bodies with the aim of making better use of them – docility and productivity going hand in hand. How brilliant power could become, how magnificent its display, depended on that increase in productivity. So if, as on several occasions, atrocities against Africans were found to be excessive, the right to punish in this way was nonetheless generally justified in terms of an overriding concern for profits and productivity.[53] Yet it would be wrong to reduce the meaning of colonial violence to mere economics. The whip and the cane also served to force upon the African an identity concocted for him/her, an identity that allowed him/her to move in the kind of spaces where he/she was always being ordered around, and where he/she had unconditionally to put on show his/her submissiveness – in forced labour, public works, local corvée labour, military conscription.

In the postcolony, the primary objective of the right to punish (represented here by the execution of the condemned) is however not to create useful individuals or to increase their productive efficiency. This is well illustrated by the misadventures of a teacher, Mr Joseph Mwaura, as reported by a Kenyan newspaper. On 21 January 1990, the District Commissioner, Mr Mwanga went to Gitothua, an Independent Pentecostal Church, to address the trouble-torn congregation. Here is an account given by Enock Anjili in *The Standard* of April 7:

On this occasion, the District Commissioner had asked all those present to give their views on how the problems facing the

Church could be solved. As the teacher got up to air his views, Mr Mwanga, fuming with anger, spotted him and called him out to the front, asking him his name and occupation. After realizing that Mr Mwaura was a teacher and, therefore, a civil servant, Mr Mwanga asked him why he was sporting a goatee. "As a civil servant, you are supposed to be knowledgeable about the civil service book of Ethics and Conduct. Why do you have a beard? You look like a he-goat with that beard," Mr Mwanga was quoted to have said amid laughter from the crowd. "You will shave that beard now."

Smiling nervously, Mr Mwaura fingered through his beard and went to sit down. However, Mr Mwanga summoned a policeman and told him to take Mr Mwaura aside. Another policeman was sent to buy a razor blade for Mr Mwaura's use. The teacher was taken behind an outhouse where he started shaving the offending beard under the supervision of another policeman.

Realizing that he could not get any water or soap to ease the task, Mr Mwaura ended up using his own spittle to wet his fuzzy chin. Inevitably, Mr Mwaura, without a mirror to guide his now shaking fingers, nicked himself several times, producing spots of blood.

The task took him less than 15 minutes, after which he stealthily went out of the meeting.[54]

The story does not end there. In March, the teacher who had had his goatee forcibly shaved off on orders of the District Commissioner, was facing further disciplinary action from the Teachers' Service Commission. He was ordered to trim his now re-grown beard and have copies of photographs of the trimmed beard sent to the *Kenya Times* and the Teachers' Service Commission. The Teachers' Service Commission also ordered Mr Mwaura to inform the newspaper that after further advice, he had decided to trim his beard because it was not in keeping with the ethics of the teaching profession.

Postcolonial convicts are, then, of a different kind. Authorities can requisition their bodies and make them join in the displays and ceremonies of the *commandement*, requiring them to sing or dance or wriggle their bodies about in the sun.[55] We can watch these dancers, "these hungover rounds of meat reeking of wine and tobacco, the heavy mouths, dead eyes, the laughter and the faces"[56] carried away by the staccato rhythm of the drums as a presidential procession goes by on a day set aside to celebrate the party or the "Shining Guide of the Nation" [*Guide éclairé de la nation*].

These bodies could just as easily be in a state of abandon, caught, as the novelist says, "by the beer, the wine, the dancing, the tobacco, the love pumped out like spit, strange drinks, the sects, the palaver – everything that might stop them being the bad conscience of their Excellencies." These same bodies can be neutered – whenever they are thought to be "disfiguring" a public place, or are considered a threat to public order (just as demonstrations are crushed in bloodshed)[57] – or whenever the *commandement*, wishing to leave imprinted on the minds of its subjects a mark of its enjoyment, sacrifices them to the firing squad.

But even in this case, punishment does not involve the same degree of physical pain as Damiens endured. First, the status of the condemned is not the same. Damiens had made an attempt on the king's life; the two who died at Douala had been charged with minor crimes. Passing over here the instruments of torture and the dramatic cases where the scalpel takes over (as in the crude display of pieces of flesh cut off; the parade of the handicapped, maimed and armless; the burials in mass graves), the death penalty here seems to have no other purpose than death. The bodies of the victims are shattered but once, though with such overwhelming force the *coup de grâce* is used simply to mark the formal end of their existence. However, as in the staged rituals examined by Foucault, the execution is definitely a public, highly visible act. The power of the state seeks to dramatize its importance and to define itself in the very act of appropriating the lives of two people and ending them.

Whereas the two lives are in principle private, the appropriation of them by the state is organised as a public performance, to be impressed upon the minds of the people and to be remembered. Yet the public performance has to appear spontaneous, and its setting intimate.

Thus, the crowd is summoned because, without it, the execution lacks its glamour; it is the crowd that bestows on the event its purely lavish form.

In this way, the public execution not only reveals the almighty power of the State, but it also becomes a social transaction. The public face of domination can make use of the execution's threatening implications. Does one of the condemned men refuse to be bound to the stake? He is made to kneel down. Does he refuse the food offered to him? He has the choice of whisky or wine. The ranking that operates at such ceremonies (first the Governor, then the Prefect, the representatives of justice, the police, the militia, the clergy, the medical profession) is evidence that power is not an empty space. It has its hierarchies, institutions, and techniques. But above all, in the postcolony it is an *economy of death*. Or more precisely, it opens up a space for enjoyment at the very moment it is making room for death; hence the wild applause which, like the bullets, stifled the cries of the condemned.[58]

This also accounts for the *baroque* character of the postcolony: its eccentric and grotesque art of representation, its taste for the theatrical and its violent pursuit of wrongdoing to the point of shamelessness. Obscenity here resides in a mode of expression that might seem macabre were it not that it is an integral part of the stylistics of power. In this sense, the notion of obscenity has no moralizing connotation. Rather, it harks back to the "radiance" things can emit, to the dizzying nature of social formalities, including the suppression of life (since, through such an important act of authority, as an execution, a hermeneutics of madness, pleasure, and drunkenness is laid out).[59]

In the remaining remarks, I will seek to identify some particular sites in which the obscene and the grotesque are laid out in the postcolony. I will draw most of my examples from Cameroon, and will privilege the discourses and actions in which power, or those that speak for it, put themselves on show.

The Intimacy of Tyranny[60]

Without underestimating the efficacy of these micro-regulations, it is important not to lose sight of the way in which what Foucault calls "the politics of coercion" is thwarted but also reproduced and amplified by the populace in the very structures of everyday life. Precisely because the postcolonial mode of domination is as much a regime of constraints as *a practice of conviviality and a stylistic of connivance* – marked by innate caution, constant compromises, small tokens of fealty, and a precipitance to denunciate those who are labelled "subversive" – the analyst must be attentive to the myriad ways in which ordinary people bridle, trick, and actually *toy* with power instead of confronting it directly.

These evasions (as endless as Sisyphus') can be explained only because people are always being trapped in a net of rituals that reaffirm tyranny; and secondly, these rituals, however minor are intimate in nature. Recent Africanist scholarship has not studied in detail the logic of this ensnarement and that of avoidance, nor the point where they are *knotted* so that they become part of one and the same dynamic. And yet, an understanding of this intermingling depends on our knowledge of the logics of "disorder,"[61] conviviality and improvisation that are inherent in the postcolonial form of authority.

For now, it is sufficient to observe that, at any given moment in the postcolonial historical trajectory, the authoritarian mode can no longer be interpreted strictly in terms of "surveillance," and "the politics of coercion." The practices of ordinary people cannot always be read in terms of "opposition to the state," "deconstructing power," and "disengagement." In the postcolony, an *intimate tyranny* links the rulers with the ruled, just as obscenity is only another aspect of munificence and vulgarity the very condition of state power. If subjection appears more intense than it might be, it is also because the subjects of the *commandement* have internalized the authoritarian epistemology to the point where they reproduce it themselves in all the minor circumstances of daily life, such as social networks, cults and secret societies, culinary practices, leisure activities, modes of consumption, dress styles, rhetorical devices, and the political economy of the body. It is also because, were they to detach themselves from these ludic resources, they would lose the possibility of multiplying their identities.

Yet it is precisely this possibility of assuming multiple identities which accounts for the fact that the body which dances, eats, drinks, dresses in the party uniform, "encumbers" the roads, "assembles *en masse*" along the main avenues, and applauds the passing of the presidential procession in a ritual of confirmation, is nonetheless, willing to dramatize its subordination through these small tokens of fealty. At the same time, instead of keeping silent in the face of obvious official lies and the truculence of elites, this body breaks into laughter. And by laughing, it drains the official universe of meaning and sometimes obliges it to function in emptiness, or powerlessness [*impouvoir*]. This is what allows us to assert that, by dancing publicly for the benefit of power, the "postcolonized subject" is proving his or her loyalty and by compromising with the corrupting control that state power tends to exercise at all levels of everyday life (over benefits, services, pleasures, . . .) the subject is confirming, in passing, the existence of an undoubtable institution; all this, precisely in order to better "play" with it and modify it whenever possible.

Thus, the public affirmation of the postcolonized subject is not necessarily found in acts of opposition, or resistance, to the *commandement*. What defines the postcolonized subject is his/her ability to engage in baroque practices which are fundamentally ambiguous, mobile, and "revisable," even in instances where there are clear, written, and precise rules. These simultaneous yet apparently contradictory practices ratify, *de facto*, the status of the *fetish* that state power so violently claims as its right. And, by the same token, they maintain, even while drawing upon officialese (its vocabulary, signs, and symbols), the possibility of altering the place and time of this ratification. Concretely, this means that the recognition of state power as a *fetish* is significant only at the very heart of the *ludic relationship*. It is here that the official sign or sense is most easily unfurled, disenchanted, and recharged, and the simulacrum becomes the dominant modality of transactions between the state and society, or between rulers and those who are supposed to obey. This is what makes postcolonial relations *relations of conviviality, but also of powerlessness par excellence* – from the point of view either of the masters of power or of those whom they crush. But, because these processes are essentially *magical*, they in no way disinscribe [*désinscrire*] the dominated from the epistemological field of power.[62]

Consider, for example, ceremonies for the so-called "transfer of office" [*passation de service*] which punctuate postcolonial bureaucratic time and profoundly affect the imaginary of individuals, elites and masses alike. One such ceremony took place in October 1987 in the small town of Mbankomo in the Central Province. Mr Essomba Ntonga Godfroy, the "newly elected" municipal administrator was to be "installed in his post," along with his two assistants, Mr André Effa Owona and Jean Paul Otu. The ceremony was presided over by the prefect of Mefou, Mr Tabou Pierre, who was assisted by the sub-prefect of Mbankomo district, Mr Bekonde Belinga Henoc-Pierre. Among the main personalities on the "official" stand were the president of the party's departmental section, representatives of the elites from inside and outside the district, "traditional" authorities, and cult priests. The dancers were accompanied by drums and xylophones. A church choir also made its contribution. According to a witness:

Elation reached a feverish climax when the tricolour scarves were presented to the municipal administrator and his two assistants, and their badges were handed to the three elected of October 25. Well before this outburst of joy, the Prefect, Mr Tabou, gave a brilliant and well received brief speech explaining the meaning of the day's ceremony to those elected and to the people – celebration of recovered democracy.[63]

He did not forget also to rattle off the list of positions held by the recently promoted official. The Prefect not only mentioned his age, but also reminded the audience of his sporting successes.[64] But it was at the installation of Mr Pokossy Ndoumbe as head of the borough of Douala that the most detailed presentation was given:

Mr Pokossy Ndoumbe first saw the light of day on August 21, 1932 at Bonamikengue, Akwa. He attended the main school in Akwa, obtaining his certificate in 1947. Then he left for France. He passed his first courses without difficulty at the Jules Ferry school in Coulonniers. He passed the baccalaureate in experimental science in 1954 at the Michelet high school in Vanves. He was drawn to pharmaceutical studies in Paris, and he diligently attended the faculty of pharmacy in Paris, where he obtained his diploma in 1959. During his final years at the University, he worked as an intern at the Emile Roux Hospital in Brevannes before returning to his native country in January 1960.[65]

Such attention to detail should not come as a surprise; it is part of the art of distinction.[66] The enumeration of the slightest educational achievement is one of the postcolonial codes of prestige, with special attention being given to distinctions attained in Europe. Thus, for example, people cite the number of diplomas with great care, they exhibit their titles (doctor, chief, president,...) with great affectation as a way of claiming honour, glory, and consideration. In such paradoxical ostentation and deference, the delineation of scholarly achievements (the enumeration of

the number of diplomas and titles one has amassed, the names of the schools and universities that have been attended...) also constitutes a marker of rank and status.[67]

Another obvious example is the ceremony where decorations and medals are awarded. During the 20 May 1989 ceremonies alone, more than 3,000 people were decorated with 481 gold medals, 1,000 vermeil medals, and 1,682 silver medals. The medals, which were obtained from the Ministry of Labor and Social Welfare, cost CFA 11,500 each for the gold ones, CFA 10,500 for the vermeil, and CFA 8,500 for the silver ones. Apart from this, "contributions" were given by businesses to the recipients of the medals to help with family festivities.[68] Here, family festivities included "libations, feasting, and diverse orgies (which) are the norm in such circumstances."[69] To be sure, one could be troubled by the purely lavish form of these expenditures, since it is rare to find a recipient of a medal who is not heavily indebted the day after the festivities. But, that would overlook the point that, in this context, the granting of a medal is a political act through which bureaucratic relations are transformed into clientelistic networks where pleasures, privileges, and resources are distributed in exchange for political compliance.[70] The lavish distribution of food and other marks of prodigality are of interest only to the extent that they make manifest relations of superiority; what circulates are not gifts but tokens creating networks of indebtedness and subordination.[71]

The day they told me that I was to be decorated, my wife and I were so excited that we stayed up all night talking about the event. Until then, we had only taken part in celebrations when others had been decorated. This time, we would be celebrating our own medal....On the day I received the medal, my wife had prepared a pretty bouquet of flowers which she presented to me on the ceremonial stand to the sound of public applause.[72]

In the postcolony, magnificence and the desire to shine are not the prerogative of only those who command. The people also want to be honoured, to shine, and to take part in celebrations.

> Last Saturday, the Muslim community of Cameroon celebrated the end of Ramadan. For thirty days, members of the community had been deprived of many things from dawn till dusk. They refrained from drinking, eating, smoking, sexual relations, and saying anything that goes against the Muslim faith and law. Last Saturday marked the end of these privations for the whole Muslim community of Cameroon.[73]

From this, one can say that the obscenity of power in the postcolony is also fed by a desire for majesty on the part of the people [la plèbe]. Because the postcolony is characterized, above all, by scarcity the metaphor of food "lends itself to the wide angle lens of both imagery and efficacy."[74] Food and tips [pourboire] are a constitutive aspect of what politics or resistance mean.[75] But the question of eating, like that of scarcity, is indissociable from particular regimes of death, specific economies of pleasure, and specific therapeutic quests.[76] This is why "the night"[77] and "witchcraft,"[78] the "invisible,"[79] the "belly," and the "mouth"[80] or the "penis" are all historical phenomena in their own right. They are institutions and sites of power in the same way that pleasure or fashion are said to be:

> Cameroonians love slick gaberdine suits, Christian Dior outfits, Yamamoto blouses, shoes of crocodile skin. . . .[81]
> The label is the true sign of class . . . . There are certain names that stand out. They are the ones that should be worn on a jacket, a shirt, a skirt, a scarf, or a pair of shoes if you want to win respect.[82]
> Don't be surprised if one day, when you enter an office unannounced you discover piles of clothing on the desks. The hallways of ministries and other public or private offices have become the market place par excellence. Market conditions are so flexible that everyone – from the director to the mes-

senger [planton] – finds what they want. Indeed, owing to the current crisis, sellers give big reductions and offer long-term credit. . . .
> Business is so good that many people throw themselves into it head down. A veritable waterhole, where sophisticated ladies rub shoulders with all kinds of ruffians and layabouts. The basis of the entire "network" is travel. It is no secret that most of the clothes on the market come from the West. Those who have the "chance" to go there regularly are quick to notice that they can reap great benefits from frequent trips. A few "agreements" with customs officials, and the deal is on.[83]

Even death does not escape this desire to shine and to be honoured. The rulers and the ruled want more than ceremonies and celebrations to show off their splendour. Those who have accumulated goods, prestige and influence are not only tied to the constraint of giving.[84] They are also taken by the desire to "die well," and to be buried with pomp.[85] Funerals constitute one of the occasions where those who command gaze at themselves, in the manner of Narcissis.[86] Thus, when Joseph Awunti, the Presidential Minister in charge of relations with parliament, died on 4 November 1987, his body was received at Bamenda airport by the then Governor of the North-western province, Mr Wabon Ntuba Mboe, who was himself accompanied by the Grand Chancellor, the then first Vice-President of the party, plus a variety of administrative, political, and "traditional" authorities. Several personalities and members of the government were also present, including the "personal" representative of the head of state, Mr Joseph Charles Dumba, Minister to the Presidency. The Economic and Social Council was represented by its president, Mr Ayang Luc, the National Assembly by the president of the parliamentary group, and the Central Committee of the Party by its Treasurer.[87] Here, the approbation of power penetrated the very manner in which the dead was to be buried. It thus appears that those who command seek to familiarize themselves with death, thereby paving the way for their own burial to take on a certain quality of pleasure and expenditure.

During the funeral of Mr Thomas Ebonga-lame, the former Secretary of the National Assembly, member of the Upper Council of the Magistracy, Administrative Secretary of the Central Committee of the Party, board member of many different parastatals, and "an initiated member of the secret society of his tribe," the procession left Yaoundé by road. Huge crowds had come from various parts of the Southwestern province to pay its last respects to the deceased:

> At Muyuka, Ebonji, Tombel, and Nyasos, primary and secondary school students formed human hedges several hundred meters long. When the body arrived in Kumba, the main town of Meme, the place turned itself into a procession. At the head was the ENI-ENIA fanfare playing a mournful tune. People wept profusely. ... In this town, with a population of 12,000, all socio-economic activity had been put on ice since 30 April, when the tragic news was heard. People awaited instructions from Yaoundé. No fewer than ten meetings were held to organize the funeral program.[88]

As we have seen, obscenity and vulgarity – when regarded as more than a moral category – constitute one of the modalities of power in the postcolony. But it is also one of the arenas of its deconstruction or its ratification by subalterns. Bakhtin's error was to attribute these practices to the dominated. The production of burlesque is not specific to them. The real inversion takes place when, in their desire for splendour, the masses join in madness and clothe themselves in the flashy rags of power so as to reproduce its epistemology; and when, too, power, in its own violent quest for grandeur and prestige, makes vulgarity and wrongdoing [délinquance] its main mode of existence. It is here, within the confines of this intimacy, that the forces of tyranny in Sub-Saharan Africa have to be studied. Such research must go beyond institutions, beyond formal positions of power

and the written rules, and examine the way the implicit and the explicit are interwoven, and how the practices of those who command and of those who are assumed to obey are so entangled as to render them powerless. For it is precisely the situations of powerlessness [impouvoir] that are the situations of violence par excellence.

NOTES AND REFERENCES

1 I have in mind his understanding of the way in which "non-official" cultures invert and desecrate "official" values in carnavalesque activities. Cf. M. Bakhtin, L'oeuvre de Rabelais et la culture populaire du Moyen-Age et sous la Renaissance (Paris: Gallimard, 1970). For a recent critique, see R. Lachmann, "Bakhtin and Carnival: Culture as Counter-Culture," Cultural Critique (Winter 1987–89), 115–52.

2 This is well attested in the contemporary African novel. In the words of S. Labou Tansi, the postcolony is the place where "l'indépendance, ça n'est pas costaud costaud." La vie et demie (Paris: Seuil, 1979), 41. Other examples of this insight into the postcolony are found in the same author's Les yeux du volcan (Paris: Seuil, 1988). Also, Ibrahima Ly, Toiles d'araignées (Paris: L'Harmattan, 1982).

3 See Achille Mbembe, "Pouvoir, violence et accumulation," Politique Africaine 39 (1990). See also the special issues of Politique Africaine devoted to "the power to kill," 2, no. 7 (1982) and "violence and power," 42 (June 1991). Otherwise, consult C. Geffray, La cause des armes au Mozambique. Anthropologie d'une guerre civile (Paris: Karthala, 1990).

4 I owe this manner of problematization to C. Castoriadis, L'Institution imaginaire de la sociéte (Paris: Seuil, 1975), 475.

5 I use the notion of cible in the sense indicated by Michel Foucault when, in response to the question of "what

constitutes the art of governing," he delineated objects of power as, on the one hand, a territory and, on the other hand, the people who live in the territory, or the population. *Cible* is thus used to designate "the people who live" the postcolony. For details, see M. Foucault, "La gouvernementalité," *Magazine Littéraire* 269 (1989). [The overly literal translation, "target population," will be hereafter indicated by the shorthand "subjects." Translator's note.]

6 On these complex questions, cf. J.-F. Bayart, "L'énonciation du politique," *Revue française de science politique* 35 (1985), 343–73.

7 The poverty of the hypotheses which guide a number of studies is, in this regard, telling in that the question posed by such research is limited to the problem of knowing whether the acts they describe and interpret are inscribed or not in a process of either resistance or accommodation to the established order; of "engagement" or "disengagement" with respect to the field of domination; or, more crudely, if such movements are "conservative" or "progressive." For some examples of recent efforts to overcome these impasses, read V. Azarya and N. Chazan, "Disengagement from the State in Africa: Reflections on the Experience of Ghana and Guinea," *Comparative Studies in Society and History* 29, no. 1 (1987), 106–31; the pieces presented in D. Rothchild and N. Chazan (eds.), *The Precarious Balance: State and Society in Africa* (Boulder, CO: Westview Press, 1987). Some of the limitations to these works are made evident by J.L. Roitman, "The Politics of Informal Markets in Sub-Saharan Africa," *Journal of Modern African Studies* 28, no. 4 (1990), 671–96. Otherwise, refer to J. Scott, *Weapons of the Weak* (New Haven, CT: Yale University Press, 1985).

8 I am using the term *commandement* in the way it was used to denote colonial authority. That is, insofar as it embraces the images and structures of power and coercion, the instruments and agents of their enactment, and a degree of rapport between those who give orders and those who are supposed to obey them without, of course, discussing them. Hence, the notion of "commandement" is used here to refer to the authoritarian modality *par excellence*. On the colonial theorization of this mode, read, for example, R. Delavignette, *Freedom and Authority in French West Africa* (London: Frank Cass, 1968); or, more generally, W.B. Cohen, *Rulers of Empire* (Stanford, CA: Hoover Institution Press, 1971). [The French term will be retained in the text. Translator's note.]

9 On the notion of the "fetish" as applied in the African context, cf. the special issue of the *Nouvelle Revue de Psychanalyse* 2 (1970), entitled "Objets du fétichisme." Of particular interest are the contributions of J. Pouillon, A. Adler, and P. Bonnafé, 131–94.

10 See, in respect to Zaïre, T.M. Callaghy, "Culture and Politics in Zaïre," unpub. m.s., October 1986.

11 See the examples documented by M.G. Schatzberg, *The Dialectics of Oppression in Zaïre* (Bloomington: Indiana University Press, 1988).

12 This point is demonstrated in M. Bristol's recent study of the carnival in England during the Renaissance. Cf. *Carnival and Theater: Plebeian Culture and the Structure of Authority in Renaissance England* (New York: Methuen, 1985). For other commentaries, refer to A. Falassi (ed.), *Time Out of Time: Essays on the Festival* (Albuquerque, NM: University of New Mexico Press, 1987); and D.A. Poole, "Accommodation and Resistance in Andean Ritual Dance," *The Drama Review* 34, no. 2 (1990), 98–126.

13 Here, I have in mind G. Hyden's *Beyond Ujamaa in Tanzania: Underdevelopment and an Uncaptured Peasantry* (London: Heinemann, 1980).

14 This is amply demonstrated in the works of S. Berry. Cf., for example, "The Significance of Investment: Farmers, Strategies and Agrarian Change in Africa."

Paper presented to the conference on "Identity, Rationality and the Post-colonial Subject: African Perspectives on Contemporary Social Theory," Columbia University, New York, 28 February 1991.

15 Understood as the institutionalized forms adopted by a regime of domination in seeking to legitimize violent practices.

16 I am indebted to Susan Roitman for this apt metaphor, Personal communication, 24 August 1991.

17 This simplistic dichotomy is taken up by J. Scott in his *Domination and the Arts of Resistance: The Hidden Transcript* (New Haven, CT: Yale University Press, 1990). It also strongly marks recent East European sociological work. See, for example, E. Hankiss, "The 'Second Society': Is There an Alternative Social Model Emerging in Contemporary Hungary?" *Social Research* 55, nos. 1–2 (1988). Binary categories are likewise to be found in J. Comaroff, *Body of Power, Spirit of Resistance: The Culture and History of a South African People* (Chicago: University of Chicago Press, 1985).

18 The subtitle derives partly from D. Parkin, "The Creativity of Abuse," *Man (N.S.)* 15 (1980), 45. The author uses the term in the context of ritualized verbal exchanges, whereas I am taking it to interpret more strictly defined political situations.

19 C. Toulabor, "Jeu de mots, jeux de vilain. Lexique de la dérision politique au Togo," *Politique Africaine* 3 (1981), 55–71. And see also his *Togo sous Eyadéma* (Paris: Karthala, 1986), notably 302–9.

20 *Cameroon Tribune*, no. 4778, 4 décembre 1990, 11, translator's translation. [All excerpts from French news sources will hereafter be understood to be the translator's renderings. Translator's note.]

21 Read, in this respect, M. Schatzberg's analysis of the State as "eye" and "ear" in *The Dialectics of Oppression in Zaire*

(Bloomington: Indiana University Press, 1988).

22 For a case study of the specificity of this notion, cf. R. Joseph, *Democracy and Prebendal Politics in Nigeria* (Cambridge: Cambridge University Press, 1988).

23 For another instance of poaching on the rhetorical territories of a pseudo-revolutionary regime – this time Burkina Faso under Sankara – consult C. Dubuch, "Langage du pouvoir, pouvoir du langage," *Politique Africaine* 20 (1985), 44–53.

24 The sense of dismemberment is the essence of this verb. Translator's note.

25 See J.-F. Bayart, *L'Etat en Afrique. La Politique du ventre* (Paris: Fayard, 1989).

26 S. Labou Tansi, *La vie et demie*, 42. Read also 55–6 and 68.

27 On the anthropological significance of "the belly" in Southern Cameroon, see L. Maillart Guimera, *Ni dos ni ventre* (Paris: Société d'Ethnologie, 1981). For a political interpretation of the same metaphor, cf. J.-F. Bayart, *L'Etat en Afrique* (Paris: Fayard, 1989); or, op. cit.

28 On this notion, cf. M. Foucault, "La gouvernementalité," *Magazine Littéraire* 269 (1989).

29 This is starkly evident in the colonial African novel. Read, for example, the classic F. Oyono, *Le vieux nègre et la médaille* (Paris, 1957).

30 See, for example, the accounts of the use of familial and parental metaphors in Zaïre, and in Cameroon under the regime of M. Ahmadou Ahidjo, in M. Schatzberg, *The Dialectics of Oppression in Zaïre* (Bloomington: Indiana University Press, 1988). Or, more recently, his "Power, Language and Legitimacy in Africa," Paper presented at the conference on "Identity, Rationality and the Post-colonial Subject: African Perspectives on Contemporary Social Theory," Columbia University, New York, 28 February 1991.

31 See D. Bigo, *Pouvoir et obéissance en Centrafrique* (Paris: Karthala, 1989).

32 I am extrapolating, for my own purposes, from an argument developed in another context by E. Tonkin, "Masks and Powers," *Man (N.S.)* 14 (1979), 237–48.

33 See the full account in "Police beat up man over flag," *The Standard*, no. 23547, 8 February 1990, 1–2.

34 On this intimacy and domesticity (the way in which the "fetish" adheres to the corporality of the citizens, decorates their houses, invades the stadiums, marks clothing, is flattered and nourished in songs; in short, colonizes all the paths of everyday life), read the comments of J.M. Ela, *Quand l'Etat pénètre en brousse* (Paris: Karthala, 1990), 52–8.

35 Compare this ostentatious consumption to the ethos of prestige and the system of courtly expenditure in the society of Europe as revealed by N. Elias in *La société de cour*, tr. P. Kamnitzer et J. Etoré (Paris: Flammarion, 1985), 47–61. See also the following chapter on the etiquette and logic of prestige, 63–114.

36 S. Labou Tansi, *La vie et demie*, 122.

37 S. Labou Tansi, *Les yeux du volcan* (Paris: Seuil, 1988), 98.

38 A point well argued by P. Stallybrass and A. White, *The Politics and Poetics of Transgression* (Ithaca, NY: Cornell University Press, 1989), especially 26.

39 As does, for example, J. Scott, "Prestige as the Public Discourse of Domination," *Cultural Critique* 12 (1989), 145–66.

40 See, from this perspective, J.D. Gandalou's description of the "sapeurs" of Congo Brazzaville in, *Dandies à Bacongo. Le culte de l' élégance dans la société congolaise contemporaine* (Paris: L'Harmattan, 1989).

41 See M. Coquet, "Une esthétique du fétiche," *Systèmes de pensée en Afrique noire, Cahier* 8 (1985), 111–38.

42 Cf. F. Hegel, *La raison dans l' histoire* (Paris: Plon, 1965).

43 An example is the case against M. Célestin Monga and the newspaper, *Le Messager*, for having allegedly "insulted the Head of State" in January–February 1991.

44 Refer to what M. Bakhtin calls the "official monologism," or the naïve pretention to possess "a whole truth," in *La poétique de Dostoïesvski* (Paris: Gallimard, 1970), 155.

45 I reappropriate, at my own risk, an interpretive rubric taken from Greek mythology: the case of the dismemberment of Dionysius by his mother and other women, which was undertaken according to a specific ritual. For more details, cf. J. Kott, *The Eating of the Gods: An Interpretation of Greek Tragedy*, tr. B. Taborski and E. Czerwinski (New York: Random House, 1970). For a similar dramatization, see also G. Bataille, *Death and Sensuality. A Study of Eroticism and the Taboo* (New York: Ballantine Books, 1962).

46 S. Freud, *Totem and Taboo* (London: Routledge and Kegan Paul, 1983).

47 This account is from *La Gazette* (Douala), no. 589, September 1987.

48 M. Foucault, *Surveiller et punir. Naissance de la prison* (Paris: Gallimard, 1975), 9–11.

49 On this question, cf. Achille Mbembe, *Afriques indociles* (Paris: Karthala, 1988), 207–12.

50 See the case of Kayembe Beleji of Zaïre. In 1953 he was taken on as a lumberjack by a Belgian saw-mill at Cisamba. He refused to take his wife there because of rumors that white bachelors courted young women not for sexual relations, "but to make them live with their dogs." "For not wanting to comply, I was whipped, lying naked on my bust; I received twenty-five strokes on my left buttock, twenty-five on my right. A black policeman hit me, and Bwana Citoko counted. I got up, my backside covered in blood. And the next day, we were taken in a jeep to Cisamba – my wife, my two children and I." From, B. Jewsiewicki, "Questions d'histoires intellectuelles de l'Afrique: la construction du soi dans l'autre au Zaïre," unpub. ms., 1990.

51 Read H.R. Manga Mado, *Complaintes d'un forçat* (Yaoundé: Clé, 1969).

52 R.L. Buell, *The Native Problem in Africa* (New York, 1928).

53 Cf. C. Coquery-Vidrovitch, *Le Congo au temps des compagnies concessionaires* (Paris: Mouton, 1971).

54 E. Anjili, "You must also shave your goatee. TSC orders bearded teacher to drop case," *The Standard*, no. 23597, 7 April 1990.

55 See, for example, A. Marenya, "Kenyans mark Moi day with pomp," *The Standard*, no. 23757, 11 October 1990.

56 Cf. S. Labou Tansi, *La vie et demie*, 114–15.

57 On Kenya, see the newspapers during the riots that followed the government's refusal to take steps toward a multiparty system, and note the way in which those who contested power were defined: "Drug addicts are bent on breaking law"; "Chaos in Nairobi and Kisumu. Police battle with crowds"; "Police use force in dealing with hooligans."

58 Cf. J. Miller, "Carnivals of Atrocity. Foucault, Nietzsche, Cruelty," *Political Theory* 18, no. 3 (1990), 470–91.

59 I am borrowing an insight found in the title of G. Bataille's *Death and Sensuality: A Study of Eroticism and the Taboo* (New York: Ballantine Books, 1962).

60 Here, I am reversing the title of a book by R. Sennet, *Les tyrannies de l'intimité*, tr. A. Berman and R. Folkman (Paris: Seuil, 1979).

61 Understood here in the sense used by R. Boudon in *La place du désordre* (Paris: Presses Universitaires de France, 1981).

62 Cf. the metaphor of the cat and the mouse used by E. Canetti, *Crowds and Power*, tr. C. Stewart (New York: Farrer Straus, Giroux, 1988), 281–2.

63 P. Essono, "Installation de l'administrateur municipal de Mbankomo. La fête de la démocratie retrouvée," *Cameroon Tribune*, no. 4027, 4 December 1987, 11.

64 One is also told, among other things, that he was an ex-champion and record holder of the 400 metre in Cameroon (50 1/10 sec.), having received a gold medal in the Francophone school and in a university competition in May 1957.

65 Mouelle Bissi, "Communauté urbaine de Douala. Place à M. Pokossy Ndoumbe," *Cameroon Tribune*, no. 4372, 19 April 1989, 3.

66 Refer to P. Bourdieu, *La distinction: Critique sociale du jugement*, Paris: Editions de Minuit, 1979, with special attention to the section on struggles over symbols.

67 On the government of rites and of private conduct, as well as the notion of the "code of circulation/distinction," cf. E. Goffman, *La mise en scène de la vie quotidienne. Les relations en public*, tr. Alain Kihm (Paris: Editions de Minuit, 1973), 19–72.

68 Figures are taken from R. Owona, "Un prix fort," *Cameroon Tribune*, no. 4391, 18 May 1989.

69 P. Ntete Ntete, "Un privilège qu'il faut mériter," *Cameroon Tribune*, no. cité, 15.

70 E. Leach's, *Political Systems in Highland Burma* (Cambridge: Harvard University Press, 1954) has already indicated how the rules of a system can be manipulated in order to maximize prestige and social honorability, 155–6 and 183–90.

71 On these questions, cf. M. Mauss, *Essai sur le don*, 269.

72 See *Cameroon Tribune*, no. 4391, 18 May 1989, 14. For a similar case, see the report of the ceremonies for the decoration of army officers, *Cameroon Tribune*, no. 4371, 18 April 1989. And for a theoretical perspective, refer to E. Hatch, "Theories of Social Honor," *American Anthropologist* 91 (1989), 341–53, even though the author confines himself to a dichotomy between materialist and non-materialist approaches.

73 J.B. Simgba, "La communauté musulmane du Cameroun en fête," *Cameroon Tribune*, no. 4383, 7 and 8 May 1989, 7.

74 J.I. Guyer, "British Colonial and Postcolonial Food Regulation, with reference to Nigeria: An Essay in Formal Sector Anthropology," m.s., 7.

75 Understood here in the sense intended by J.-F. Bayart in his *L'Etat en Afrique. La politique du ventre* (Paris: Fayard, 1989), where he uses the Foucaultian notion of "gouvernementalité" to speak of the "gouvernementalité du ventre" [belly politics] in black Africa.

76 Cf. M. Taussig, *Shamanism, Colonialism and the Wild Man. A Study of Terror and Healing* (Chicago: University of Chicago Press, 1988).

77 Cf. E. de Rosny, *Les yeux de ma chèvre* (Paris: Plon, 1977).

78 Cf. P. Geschiere, "Sorcery and the State: Popular Modes of Political Action among the Maka of Southeast Cameroon," *Critique of Anthropology* 8 (1988).

79 See P. Bonnafé, *Nzo Lipfu, le lignage de la mort. La sorcellerie, idéologie de la lutte sociale sur le plateau kukuya* (Paris: Labethno, 1978).

80 Read E.P. Brown, *Nourrir les gens, nourrir les haines* (Paris: Société d'ethnographie, 1983).

81 Read R. Owona, "Branché sur les cinq continents," *Cameroon Tribune*, no. 4378, 27 April, 1989.

82 D. Ndachi Tagne, "Le venin hypnotique de la griffe," *Cameroon Tribune*, numéro cité.

83 C. Mien Zok, "Le prêt-à-porter fait du porte-à-porte," *Cameroon Tribune*, no. 4378, 27 April 1989.

84 P. Veyne, *Le pain et le cirque. Sociologie historique d'un pluralisme politique*, (Paris: Seuil, 1976), 230.

85 See the remarks by J. Omoruyi, "Nigerian Funeral Programmes: An Unexplored Source of Information," *Africa* 58, no. 4 (1988), 466–9.

86 But they are also one of the sites where the innumerable conflicts linked to inequalities and the distribution of inheritance are played out. On this point, read C. Vidal, "Funérailles et conflit social en Côte d'Ivoire," *Politique Africaine* 24 (1987); and M. Gilbert, "The Sudden Death of a Millionaire: Conversion and Consensus in a Ghanaian Kingdom," *Africa* 58, no. 3 (1988), 291–313.

87 Nzeke Mbonwoh, "Le corps de Joseph Awunti repose désormais à Kedju Ketinguh," *Cameroon Tribune*, no. 4010, 12 November 1987, 3.

88 Monda Bakoa, "Heures de tristesse dans le Sud-Ouest," *Cameroon Tribune*, 14 and 15 May 1989, 3.

Index

warrior leagues, 198–200
welfare of population, 140
welfare state
  and liberalism, 146–7, 151–3, 154, 155
  postcolonial, 22
  and women, 190–1, 196
wireless telegraphy, 374–7
Wireless Telegraphy Act 1904, 374
women

domestic violence work and South Asian
  immigrants, 337–55
empowerment programs, 13–16, 17
and masculinist state power, 187–210
and private sphere, 194–6, 199, 337–55
written word, state emphasis on, 13–14

Zimbabwe, 274–5, 277–8
"zombification," and postcolony, 382, 387–8

Lightning Source UK Ltd.
Milton Keynes UK
UKOW05f1849040917
308573UK00003B/9/P